READER'S DIGEST

Microwave
Cookbook

READER'S DIGEST

Microwave
Cookbook

READER'S DIGEST · SYDNEY

READER'S DIGEST MICROWAVE COOKBOOK
was conceived and designed by Dorling Kindersley Limited
in conjunction with The Reader's Digest Association Limited

Copyright © 1990 Dorling Kindersley Limited and The Hearst Corporation

First published in Australia in 1991 by
Reader's Digest (Australia) Pty Limited (Inc. in NSW)
26-32 Waterloo Street, Surry Hills, NSW 2010

National Library of Australia cataloguing-in-publication data

Readers Digest microwave cookbook.

Includes index.
ISBN 0 86438 206 5.

1. Microwave cookery. I. Title: Microwave cookbook.

641.5882

Typesetting by Typecellars, 263 Liverpool Street, Darlinghurst, NSW 2010

Colour separations by Bright Arts (HK) Limited

Printed and bound by Everbest Printing Co. Ltd., Hong Kong

Foreword

A new kind of cooking has taken us by storm. In busy households all across the country, and in many other parts of the world as well, the microwave oven is becoming the cooking appliance of choice. That's what this book is all about. Whether you are a novice microwave cook or an experienced one, the Reader's Digest Microwave Cookbook is the book you can turn to for everything you'll need to know. It's full of delicious step-by-step recipes, cooking tips, techniques and useful charts, plus easy-to-understand information about microwave ovens and cooking methods ... all you need to guarantee perfect food every time you cook.

A beautiful full-colour 'picture book' index of all the recipes is found at the beginning of the book, organised in menu order according to the time required for preparation and cooking. This makes recipe selection and meal planning easy, because you can see exactly how the food will look and how long it will take to make the dish you select.

Next, we tell you step-by-step how to prepare the recipes. We illustrate the cooking techniques you will use, list the equipment needed and tell you exactly how long the recipe will take from start to finish. And, to help you ensure good nutrition and healthy eating, each recipe includes not only the kilojoule count per serving but beneficial nutritional information as well.

Menus are included throughout the book to show how to combine recipes for everyday and special occasion meals, and a timetable is included with each menu so you will know what to prepare and when.

All the recipes were developed and thoroughly tested in a wide variety of 600-, 650- and 700-watt microwave ovens. Because time is of the essence, they have been made as simple as possible and cookware has been kept to a minimum. We hope, through the pages of this new cookbook, that you will discover what fun microwave cooking is ... and that it is possible to produce almost everything a conventional oven does - only faster and better.

— The Editors

Contents

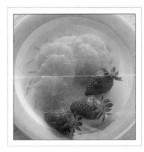

How to use the book

The Reader's Digest Microwave Cookbook contains everything today's cook needs to know to make delicious meals in the microwave. The book is divided into three major sections - Microwave Know-How, The Colour Index and the Recipes - with problem-solving Questions and Answers and a comprehensive Index at the back. The recipe section also contains tips on preparing ingredients and ideas for serving and presentation, plus full-colour menus for entertaining.

Even if you are an experienced microwave cook, it is a good idea to read through Microwave Know-How first, as the information in this section clearly illustrates many tried-and-tested microwave cooking techniques. Then you can browse through The Colour Index to choose those dishes that suit your schedule and meal plans. Finally turn to the listed page in the appropriate chapter of recipes and follow the simple step-by-step instructions for culinary success.

MICROWAVE KNOW-HOW
This introductory chapter illustrates the cookware and cooking techniques you need to serve attractive and well-prepared food. Also included are tips for using the microwave oven in conjunction with conventional cooking appliances, and for entertaining, as well as advice on taking care of your microwave.

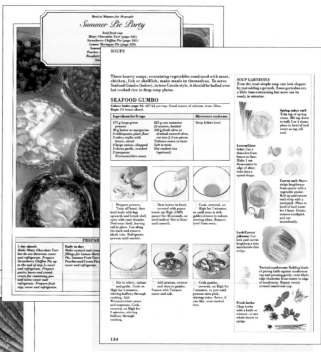

THE COLOUR INDEX
In this section you will find photographs of over 500 specially created recipes in menu order, organised according to the time required for preparation and cooking – under 30 minutes, 30–60 minutes, over 1 hour. Captions describe the dishes in detail, inform you how many servings they make, suggest appropriate garnishes, and direct you to the pages where the recipes appear in the main section of the book.

THE RECIPES
Among over 600 triple-tested recipes are more than 170 key recipes and over 1000 step-by-step photographs. Where applicable, key recipes are written for 4, 2 and 1 servings. Every recipe is accompanied by a kilojoule count and other nutritional information. You will also find explanations and illustrations throughout for preparation and serving techniques, including handling ingredients, types of equipment, and making garnishes. There is also a wide selection of menus for lunches, dinners, parties and picnics, each photographed in colour and accompanied by a preparation timetable.

Microwave Know-How

All about microwave ovens

Microwave ovens offer many choices, so you will be certain to find one just right for you. *Free standing ovens* that sit on a firm work surface are the most popular. To save space, some models can be installed under a wall cupboard or built into a base unit. An *above-the-stove microwave oven* with built-in ventilation and light takes the place of a range hood. Another option, a built-in double oven, is an all-in-one unit that features an eye-level microwave oven above a gas or electric oven. A *combination microwave oven* can be used as a convection oven, a microwave oven or with the two methods together. It's like having three ovens in one, and some even have a griller as well. A convection oven is a thermal oven like a conventional electric oven, but it has a fan to circulate the hot air so it cooks more quickly than a conventional oven. Fan-assisted ovens also brown and crisp foods more quickly.

Microwave ovens are available in a variety of sizes. *Full-size ovens* (41–45.8 litres) are ideal for families or anyone who entertains a lot because they are roomy enough for large cookware and bulky foods. *Mid-size ovens* (25–30.8 litres) are a good compromise when you need a fair amount of cooking space but do not have the room for a full-size model. *Compact ovens* (17–21 litres) are perfect for cooking for one or two, or to use as a second or back-up oven.

MICROWAVE WATTAGE AND POWER
It is essential to know the wattage output of your oven – it tells you the amount of microwave power available for cooking. Oven wattages range from 500–800 watts. Higher-wattage ovens (600–800 watts) cook faster than lower-wattage ovens (500–550 watts). The most popular oven wattage is 700, and all the microwave recipes in this book have been developed for cooking in 600- to 700-watt ovens. With a lower wattage, food takes longer to cook and you need to increase cooking time.

Variable power levels let you adjust the cooking power to get better, more even results. This is accomplished by cycling the microwave power on and off at various intervals to achieve different percentages of full power. Most models provide five preset microwave power levels.

All microwave ovens have an automatic defrost facility, but a manual Defrost setting is useful for some types of food.

MICROWAVE FEATURES
Microwaves are distributed in the oven in a variety of ways. An oven may have a stirrer fan, rotating antenna or turntable, all designed for even cooking of food. Some ovens have both a stirrer fan and a turntable, which makes it possible to remove the turntable and then cook food in large or awkwardly shaped containers that would not normally rotate.

Electronic touch controls are more accurate than mechanical dial-type controls. They are easy to use and greatly expand the oven's functions.

Automatic programmes eliminate guesswork and are particularly helpful to people new to microwave cooking. All that is necessary is to enter the food category, desired result and weight or amount. The oven then automatically selects the correct time and power levels to cook, defrost or reheat. Some models have sensors to monitor humidity, vapour or heat given off by food, and the oven uses this information to calculate precise cooking times.

Convenient one-touch functions can include pads marked with standard food items, a double-quantity key that automatically increases the cooking time for twice the amount of food, and reheat sensors, labelled 'refrigerator', 'freezer' or 'room temperature' for no-guess warming up (although it is still advisable to test food before being served).

A temperature probe is another feature on some ovens; it works like a thermometer. The probe is inserted into the food and the desired temperature is set. When that temperature is reached, the oven turns off automatically.

COOKING WITH A TURNTABLE OVEN
Instructions given in the recipes in this book for rotating or otherwise rearranging dishes all apply to ovens that are equipped only with a stirrer fan or antenna to distribute microwaves. If your oven features a turntable as well as, or instead of, a stirrer fan or antenna, you do not need to manually rotate the dish – this function is automatically carried out by the turntable. However, it is still essential to carry out all other instructions for moving food – stirring, turning, elevating, etc – to ensure thorough and even cooking.

MICROWAVE FOOD SAFETY
All microwave ovens are manufactured to the highest possible standards, and all food cooked or heated in them will be safe if manufacturers' instructions are followed. Food in a microwave can reach a temperature of up to 100°C and hold that temperature long enough to destroy food contaminant.

Microwave ovens have 'hot' and 'cold' spots; when instructions are given for stirring, turning, rotating, rearranging or otherwise moving food, and for standing, it is important to follow these instructions to ensure that food is cooked. When reheating ready-prepared foods, these techniques should also be applied.

It is also essential to know the wattage output of your oven. If your oven has a low wattage output, food will take longer to reach its required temperature than in one with a higher wattage.

A temperature probe turns the oven off when desired temperature is reached.

HOW MICROWAVE OVENS WORK

C **Stirrer fan or rotating antenna:** distributes microwaves throughout oven cavity

B **Wave guide:** tunnel-like path microwaves take to oven cavity

D **Metal walls:** provide surface for microwaves to bounce off

A **Magnetron tube:** converts electricity into microwaves

E **Door:** when opened, microwaves cannot be generated

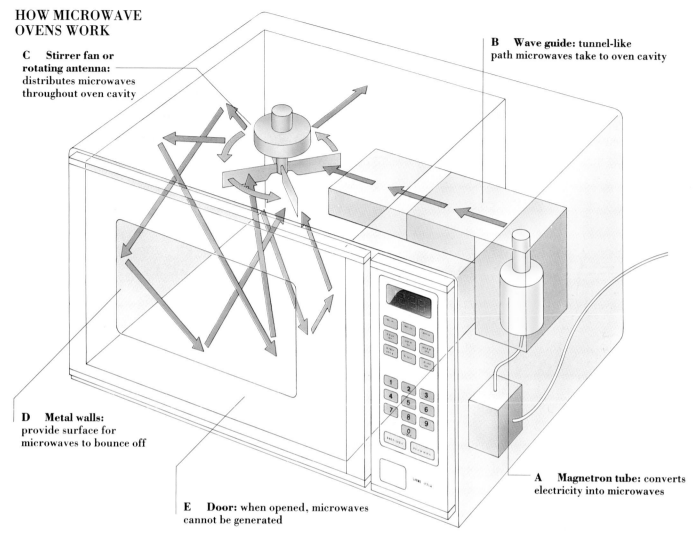

Microwaves are high-frequency, electro-magnetic waves, similar to radio waves. When a microwave oven is turned on, microwaves are generated by the magnetron tube (A), which converts household electricity into microwaves. It's a little like having a miniature broadcasting station in your oven.

Microwaves travel from the magnetron through a tunnel-like wave guide (B) and enter the oven cavity through one or two openings at the top, bottom or sides. A stirrer fan or rotating antenna (C) distributes microwaves throughout the oven's cavity. Never operate an empty microwave; if food isn't present to absorb the microwaves, the oven may be damaged.

Because microwaves cannot penetrate metal, they bounce off the oven's metal walls (D) and penetrate the food from all directions to a depth of up to 4 cm. They don't cause any structural or chemical change in food molecules; they simply cause water, fat and sugar molecules in food to vibrate about 2½ billion times per second, producing heat from friction. The centre of the food is cooked by transference of heat (conduction), as in conventional cooking.

When the oven is turned off, or the door (E) is opened, microwaves cannot be generated and none remain inside, just as when you turn off your radio the sound stops.

MICROWAVE TIMINGS

Most of the recipes in this book give a range of microwave-cooking times, for instance, '3–4 minutes', because of the variations in microwave wattage, cookware and density of food. To avoid overcooking, choose the shorter time, then check to see if food is done (page 26). Continue cooking for the longer cooking time, if necessary, then check again. Food should be thoroughly cooked through and piping hot right to the centre.

POWER LEVELS

High	100% power
Medium-High	70% power
Medium	50% power
Medium-Low	30% power
Low	10% power

Among manufacturers there is no standard language for power levels. The recipes in this book, however, all use the scale on the left.

If your microwave has different power settings, i.e. 100%, 80%, 60%, 40%, 20%, you will have to experiment.

Cookware and utensils

Cookware and utensils specifically designed for use in the microwave are widely available; a selection is featured below. For the most part this special equipment is made from materials that allow microwave energy to pass through their surfaces to heat the food within. However, they can still become hot to the touch if the food gives off a lot of heat. Remember, too, that the density of cookware affects cooking time so that plastic, for example, cooks faster than glass and porcelain.

Browning dishes are designed to make the finished appearance of microwaved food resemble conventionally cooked food. They are only for use in the microwave oven.

Many everyday kitchen items can also be used, including casseroles, bowls and dishes made of heatproof glass, glass-ceramic, china and pottery free of metal. Plastic containers marked 'microwave-safe' or 'suitable for the microwave' are extremely useful. Paper goods can be used for short-term heating. Do not use recycled paper towels as they may contain metal fragments.

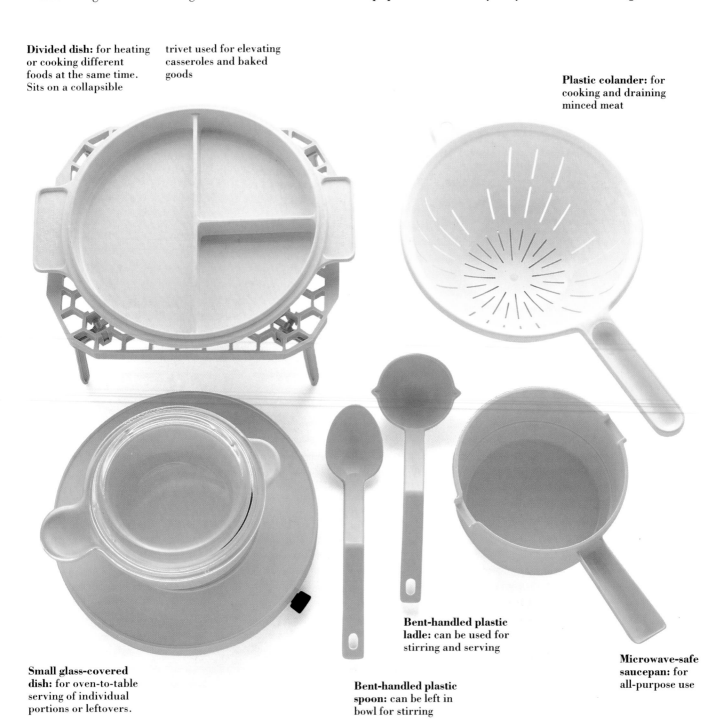

Divided dish: for heating or cooking different foods at the same time. Sits on a collapsible trivet used for elevating casseroles and baked goods

Plastic colander: for cooking and draining minced meat

Small glass-covered dish: for oven-to-table serving of individual portions or leftovers.

Bent-handled plastic spoon: can be left in bowl for stirring

Bent-handled plastic ladle: can be used for stirring and serving

Microwave-safe saucepan: for all-purpose use

Loaf dish: for cakes, meat loaves and pâtés

Individual ramekins: can be used for poached eggs, muffins and small cakes

Egg and cake pan: can also be used for muffins

Plastic ring mould: for cakes, casseroles and meat loaves

Plastic ridged ring mould: for cakes and custards

Roasting dish with nonstick finish: can also be used for casseroles and vegetables

Browning dish with nonstick insert: for searing and colouring

Roasting dish with rack for roasts: can also be used for whole chicken and chicken pieces

Browning dish: to brown and crisp meats, fish and poultry

Roast and grill rack with ridges: for fat to run off

13

Suitable kitchenware

Testing for microwave safety: To determine the suitability of a piece of cookware, pour cold water into a 1-cup glass jug and place it in the microwave oven alongside the dish or utensil to be tested. Heat on High (100% power) for 1 minute. The water should be warm, the dish or utensil still cool. If the dish is warm, do not use it in the microwave – it is possible it may overheat and break.

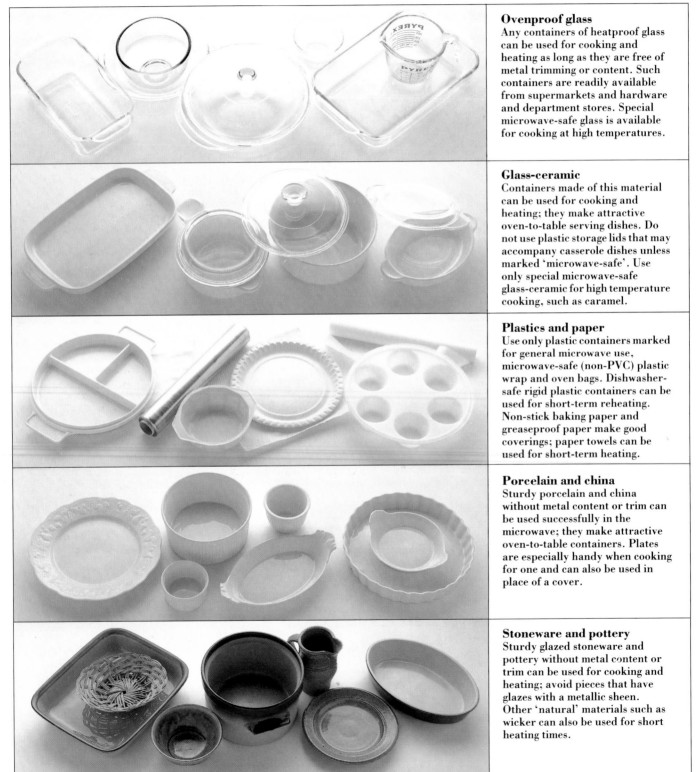

Ovenproof glass
Any containers of heatproof glass can be used for cooking and heating as long as they are free of metal trimming or content. Such containers are readily available from supermarkets and hardware and department stores. Special microwave-safe glass is available for cooking at high temperatures.

Glass-ceramic
Containers made of this material can be used for cooking and heating; they make attractive oven-to-table serving dishes. Do not use plastic storage lids that may accompany casserole dishes unless marked 'microwave-safe'. Use only special microwave-safe glass-ceramic for high temperature cooking, such as caramel.

Plastics and paper
Use only plastic containers marked for general microwave use, microwave-safe (non-PVC) plastic wrap and oven bags. Dishwasher-safe rigid plastic containers can be used for short-term reheating. Non-stick baking paper and greaseproof paper make good coverings; paper towels can be used for short-term heating.

Porcelain and china
Sturdy porcelain and china without metal content or trim can be used successfully in the microwave; they make attractive oven-to-table containers. Plates are especially handy when cooking for one and can also be used in place of a cover.

Stoneware and pottery
Sturdy glazed stoneware and pottery without metal content or trim can be used for cooking and heating; avoid pieces that have glazes with a metallic sheen. Other 'natural' materials such as wicker can also be used for short heating times.

Unsuitable equipment

While much equipment normally found in the kitchen can be used in your microwave oven, certain items should definitely be avoided; not only will they interfere with the normal microwave cooking processes, but they may also cause damage to your oven. The main materials to avoid are metal – it can cause arcing (blue sparks), which can pit oven walls or cause fires – unglazed pottery, certain plastics (see below) and recycled paper. If in doubt, carry out the simple suitability test shown on the opposite page.

Metals and foils
Do not use any metal item unless it is marked 'microwave-safe' or your microwave instruction booklet gives guidelines for its use. Avoid metal or part-metal pots, pans, thermometers, skewers, baking trays and utensils. Make sure containers do not have metal in their handles or around their rims, or any metal screws. Do not use paper bags and boxes, large sheets of foil, or metal ties for oven bags. Small, smooth pieces of foil used for shielding food should not come into contact with the oven's walls; keep at least 2.5 cm away. Carefully follow recipe instructions and any other guidelines on using foil in the microwave.

Melamine and polystyrene
Some hard and soft plastics, like Melamine dinnerware and polystyrene cups and boxes, may overheat and break or melt if used in the microwave. Foods high in fat or sugar can also cause plastic containers to distort or melt.

Decorated china and glass
Many dinner sets contain gold or silver decorative trims. These pieces are not suitable for the microwave – they can cause arcing and a broken dish or damaged oven can result. Do not use lead crystal or any glass and china that has been repaired with glue.

Unglazed pottery
Do not use pottery or earthenware, either handmade or commercially produced, if it is not covered with glaze on the outside as well as inside; it may absorb moisture and become hot. Pottery with a metallic glaze is also unacceptable for use in the microwave.

Food facts

Microwave energy cooks food quickly but not always evenly. Microwaves penetrate food up to a depth of about 4 cm and heat is conducted from the outer edges towards the centre (much as it is in conventional cooking); it is therefore possible to overcook or burn the outside edges of foods while the centres remain underdone. Special techniques have been developed to enable microwaves to reach every part of the food to ensure that food is cooked evenly throughout; these are shown on the following pages. But the composition of the foods themselves can also affect the way they react to microwaves. Size, shape, density, temperature,

thickness, fat and bone content of food together with the presence of a membrane, casing, or hard skin, all affect the cooking process and the final result.

Knowing how and why food reacts the way it does will mean there will be fewer surprises for you when it is cooked, and will make clear why the recipes recommend that you cook food in a particular way. Moreover, the 'starting' temperature of foods can make a big difference in cooking results. Recipes in this book assume that meat, fish, poultry, eggs and most vegetables will be at refrigerator temperature and canned and dry goods at room temperature.

THE COMPOSITION OF FOOD

Water attracts microwaves, so food high in water like tomatoes as well as food low in moisture like popcorn, can be cooked without added liquid or fat.

Fat attracts microwaves, too. Cheese cooks quickly but does not brown. Bacon cooks and browns quickly. Large joints of meat brown only with prolonged cooking.

Sugar also attracts microwaves. The sugary fillings of foods such as pastries and turnovers reach a high temperature faster than the outsides.

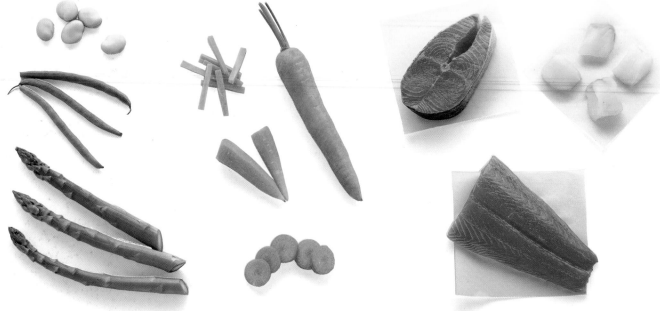

Moisture content of food
Foods that have a high moisture content cook better and more quickly in the microwave oven than those with a low moisture content.

Size of food
Large, bulky pieces take longer to cook than smaller or thinner pieces. The more exposed the surface area, the faster the item will cook. Here, the slices and thin strips will cook more quickly than the larger pieces and the whole carrot.

Shape of food
The thinner parts of unevenly shaped food will cook more quickly than the thicker parts. Here, the salmon cutlet and gemfish pieces will cook more evenly than the fillet; thinner edges must be placed in the centre of the dish or folded under.

Bone content
Bones conduct heat, so cuts that contain bone, or the part of the meat that does, cook more quickly than boneless parts.

Fat content
Since fat attracts microwaves, meat high in fat will cook more quickly than lean meat. Lean, boneless meat cuts cook more slowly but more evenly than those with a higher fat and bone content. Both bone and fat attract microwaves, resulting in quicker, less even cooking.

Membranes
Egg yolks, oysters and chicken livers have membranes that need piercing to stop steam from building up and causing bursting.

Casings
Frankfurters, sausages and other foods with casings should also be pierced to prevent steam buildup and bursting.

Outer skins
Vegetables such as potatoes, sweet potatoes, capsicums and tomatoes should be pierced to prevent steam build-up.

Density of food
Dense, heavy foods like potatoes take longer to cook than porous, airy ones like breads and cakes.

Temperature of food
Recipe timings are influenced by the 'starting' temperature of foods used; microwave cooking is so fast that this can make a big difference. Room-temperature foods, whether fresh, packaged or canned, normally cook faster than chilled or frozen foods.

Height of food in the oven
Areas closer to the source of energy cook fastest. The breast of a whole chicken, which is closer to the top of the oven and receives more energy in some microwave ovens, is therefore likely to be cooked before the centre part. Chicken pieces in a casserole, however, are more likely to cook evenly.

Arranging food for better cooking

For an even result throughout, food should be cooked in dishes of the appropriate shape and size. Ring-shaped dishes are best as microwave energy penetrates the food from the centre, sides and bottom. Round dishes also permit fairly even cooking. With square and oblong dishes, corners cook faster than the centres. When cooking more than two dishes at a time, arrange them in a circle if possible.

The centre of a dish heats more slowly than its edges, so place foods that take longer to cook towards the outer edges of dish, quicker-cooking ones towards the centre. If possible, arrange pieces of food in a circle, and leave space between the pieces. This allows microwave energy to penetrate the food quickly and evenly. Smaller amounts of food cook more quickly than larger ones, and so do the thin ends of meat, fish and poultry, and meat near the bone. These must be shielded – covered with smooth strips of foil to prevent overcooking. If the strips of foil are applied at the beginning of cooking time, be sure to remove them in time to allow the shielded portions of food to cook thoroughly.

Always be sure to use the exact size and shape of dish specified in the recipe, or the timing and the finished results may be different from those expected.

Unequal food composition
Delicate, quicker-cooking parts should be placed towards the centre and more fibrous, less tender parts closer to the edges.

Unevenly shaped foods
Alternate ends of food such as corn-on-the-cob, then rearrange halfway through cooking to produce an overall uniformity in the finished dish.

Foods of uniform size
Place food in a circle with space between pieces. This enables microwave energy to reach all sides of food so it cooks evenly.

Foods of different densities
Place denser, slower cooking ingredients near edge of dish, more delicate, quicker cooking ones in centre to ensure even cooking.

Pieces, slices and whole items
Pieces and slices cook more quickly than whole items. Thinner parts should be placed towards the centre of a dish while the thicker ends should face outwards.

Large or small quantities
Small amounts cook faster than large ones. Cooking time in the microwave is always directly related to the amount of food and increases with the quantity; the more food, the longer the cooking time. Individual portions cook faster than large casseroles or roasts.

Individual portions
Placing small dishes or ramekins in a circle with space in between the dishes will result in more even cooking, particularly in ovens without turntables. However, individual dishes may need to be rearranged during cooking due to uneven heat patterns in the oven.

Shielding vulnerable parts of food
Shield thin ends of meat, bone tips, meat near the bone and the cut edges of roasts and poultry with smooth strips of foil to prevent them from overcooking.

ARRANGING FOOD FOR REHEATING

Make certain all the food is of the same temperature, either chilled or at room temperature. Arrange thick and dense pieces of food such as chicken pieces on the outside of the plate, with quicker-to-heat foods such as rice on the inside. If possible, arrange foods in a ring shape and spread them so they are low and even in the dish. You can do this with mashed potato, for instance, by making a depression in the centre. Delicate foods like stuffing should be placed underneath denser meat slices to prevent overcooking. Cover plates with plastic wrap and cook in the microwave until all the food is piping hot, rotating plate as often as possible.

Covering techniques

By covering food to be cooked in the microwave, moisture is retained and steam is produced. Steam heat, added to the molecule-vibrating action of microwaves, results in a faster cooking time and more even cooking of certain foods. Steam also tenderises foods. Those that especially benefit from covering are vegetables, casseroles, less tender cuts of meat, thicker pieces of fish and soups.

Microwave-safe casserole lids, oven bags and plastic wrap are all equally effective in retaining heat and moisture. However, when cooking foods that require frequent stirring, rearranging and/or checking such as custards, sauces, stews and casseroles, it is easiest to use a lid. Use greaseproof paper to hold in some steam and to prevent spatters with food that does not need much steam to tenderise, such as a roast. Greaseproof paper is often blown off the food by the action of the microwave's fan; crumpling the paper slightly helps to keep it in place.

Microwave-safe paper towels are good for short-term heating and reheating and for foods that can be cooked uncovered but tend to spatter, such as bacon and butter or margarine. They are also useful in absorbing extra fat or moisture and for keeping bread surfaces dry. For more information on the type of paper towel to use in the microwave, see pages 14 and 231.

Lids and covers
Casserole and dish lids made of microwave-safe material are perfectly adequate, if the recipe does not specify any other.

Plastic wrap
Use microwave-safe plastic wrap (non-PVC) to cover dishes without lids. Steam can cause splitting, so vent when using (see opposite).

Greaseproof paper
This forms a looser covering than plastic wrap and is particularly good for preventing spatters. Use it with foods that might become soggy if tightly covered.

Paper towels
When used as a covering, white microwave-safe paper towels allow steam to escape and prevent spatters. They can also be used on the oven floor, to help absorb moisture.

Plates as covers
If no other suitable cover is available, a plain, untrimmed and undecorated plate can be used. Select one large enough to completely cover the cooking bowl.

Venting plastic wrap
Cover casserole or dish with plastic wrap, then turn back a corner to form a narrow vent; this allows excess steam to escape.

Removing plastic wrap
Carefully peel back the plastic away from you to avoid any escaping steam, which can cause burns.

Removing lids
Use a pot holder to lift the cover as it will be hot from rising steam; open it away from you to avoid escaping steam.

Paper towels
Wrap them around food or place them underneath to soak up excess moisture and prevent certain foods from becoming soggy.

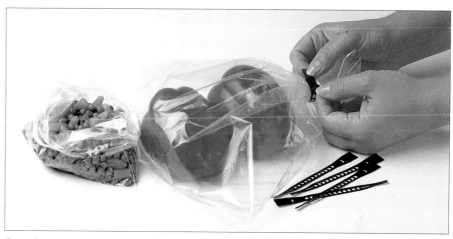

Oven bags
These can be used to reheat leftovers or to steam food. If cooking large items, which take longer and reach a high temperature, use an oven bag loosely fastened with string or plastic ties. Pierce if instructed in recipe, or according to manufacturer's instructions.

LINING DISHES

Microwave-safe plastic wrap
This can be used under meat loaves, pâtés and terrines to prevent sticking and in order to remove them easily.

Paper towels, greaseproof paper and non-stick baking paper
Cut to fit, these can be used to line cake moulds and dishes for baking; they will prevent contents from sticking when removed. The paper is not affected by microwaves and can easily be peeled off the bottom of the cake after standing time.

Browning techniques

Most food cooked in the microwave is done so quickly that fat rarely has a chance to rise to the surface and brown. This is why meat, for instance, usually looks different from meat that has been cooked conventionally. Some foods, such as roasts with a good fat covering, bacon, whole chickens and turkey breasts, will brown because they have a high fat content. Except for bacon, however, they will not crisp.

Specially designed cookware, called browning dishes or grills, sear and brown foods the way a conventional frying pan does. They are made from, or coated with, a special material that absorbs microwave energy and

reaches temperatures of 220°C–280°C. They have feet or ridges to keep work surfaces safe from scorching. (Even so, be careful not to place them directly on surfaces that are not heat-resistant.) Before placing any food on a browning dish, it should be preheated in the microwave according to the manufacturer's instructions.

For foods that cannot be cooked on a browning dish, there is also a wide variety of readily available sauces and coatings that are brushed or sprinkled on, or rubbed into the food to produce a more attractive finished appearance. Some even add extra flavour and texture to the meat.

Browning dish or grill
Both contain a special substance that causes them to become extremely hot. Often there is a well to catch drippings, and feet to protect work surfaces.

Using a browning dish or grill
Preheat the dish or grill according to the manufacturer's instructions. Add meat, pressing down so that it is seared on the hot surface, then return to oven. Do not cover dish. Turn meat over to brown the other side – if possible, on an unused part of the dish. If food is cooked in batches, the dish may need to be reheated. Always follow the manufacturer's instructions.

Using a browning agent
Chicken cooked in the microwave without a browning agent is pale, such as the leg above. However, if it is coated with a browning sauce, as on the whole bird (right), it looks brown and crisp.

BROWNING AGENTS

Soy and teriyaki sauces and diluted browning sauces are highly seasoned coatings for meat and poultry.

Barbecue sauce can be brushed on meat and poultry occasionally during cooking to add flavour and colour.

Fruity brown or Worcestershire sauces can be brushed on to beef, pork or lamb cuts, or hamburgers.

Paprika is a delicious coating for poultry. Brush on melted butter first, then sprinkle paprika on the surface.

Breadcrumbs, seasoned or unseasoned, can be used on top of uncovered foods or casseroles before cooking.

Herb and spice mixes, if added to poultry pieces and hamburgers before cooking, enhance appearance and taste.

Microwave browning should be sprinkled on meats and poultry before cooking as an appearance enhancer.

Dry onion soup or gravy powder can be sprinkled on hamburgers and other beef and lamb cuts before cooking.

Brown sugar can be sprinkled on cakes and fruit loaves before, during or after cooking.

Marmalade or jam can be brushed on ham after cooking and on poultry halfway through cooking.

Cinnamon sugar or toasted coconut can be sprinkled on muffins, fruit loaves and cakes before, during or after cooking.

Toasted chopped nuts make an attractive topping for cakes and fruit loaves. Sprinkle on before cooking.

Brushing on browning and seasoning sauces gives meat and poultry a darker, richer colour.

Rubbing soy or barbecue sauce on poultry skin before cooking can improve its normally light appearance.

Glazing with marmalade or specially prepared fruit glaze improves both appearance and flavour of ham slices.

Sprinkling on microwave browning or other seasoning can make hamburgers look more tempting.

Cooking techniques

Because microwaves penetrate food only to a certain depth, it is often necessary to stir, turn over, rearrange or rotate the food to guarantee thorough and even cooking. Various techniques have evolved to enable microwaves to reach every part of the food.

Some microwave ovens have areas with a concentration of microwaves ('hot spots'), where food cooks more quickly. To identify these spots, place some water-filled microwave-safe dishes in the oven and heat on High (100% power); check to see which one or ones start to bubble first. Food in these areas will cook most quickly.

As a reminder to stir or rotate foods according to recipe instructions, set the oven to that time, rather than the total cooking time given in the recipe, then reset as necessary.

Identifying 'hot spots'
Place water-filled dishes on oven floor and heat on High (100% power). Food will cook faster in areas where water bubbles first.

Stirring foods
Casseroles, soups and stews should be stirred from the outer edges (where the food cooks first) towards the centre; the cooler food at the centre should be pushed towards the edge of the dish.

Whisking sauces
During the cooking process, whisking keeps sauces smooth and ensures more even cooking. A microwave-safe whisk has a bent handle so that it can be left in the bowl while the microwave is in operation.

Turning foods
Dense pieces such as fish cakes should be turned over, as should food cooked in liquid. Hot liquid in the bottom of a dish can transfer additional heat to one side of food and result in uneven cooking.

ROTATING A DISH IN THE MICROWAVE

Casseroles or baked dishes may need to be rotated for even cooking. Make certain to rotate a dish in one direction only.

For a quarter turn, rotate the casserole or dish so that the side that faced the back of the oven faces the side of the oven.

For a half turn, rotate the casserole or dish until the side facing the back of the oven is to the front.

ELEVATING FOODS

Raise foods like crumbles, cakes and quiches off the oven floor to allow microwave energy to cook the centre bottom. Special microwave-safe racks or trivets can be used underneath dishes; meat racks in roasting dishes keep poultry and joints from stewing in their own juices.

Elevate loaf dish, bowl or casserole on an inverted microwave-safe plate or ramekin, if you do not have a special microwave-safe rack or trivet.

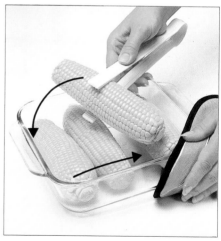

Rearranging dishes
For individual portions to cook evenly, it may be necessary to rearrange them at least once during cooking. Turn each dish so that outside edges move to the inside.

Rearranging delicate foods
With delicate foods that can be damaged through handling, such as baked apples, you can rearrange food by turning the entire dish.

Rearranging pieces of food
Pieces of food such as corn-on-the-cob have to be turned over or rotated during cooking. Take food from the centre and move to the outside, and vice versa.

25

Testing for readiness

When removed from the oven, microwave-cooked food may look different from conventionally cooked food, so there are tests to tell whether it is ready to eat.

In assessing the readiness of food, you must take into account the standing time if this is indicated in the recipe. Standing time is part of the cooking process and allows uneven heat to equalise itself. The food is removed from the oven and allowed to stand, covered, for several minutes while it finishes cooking. This is why it can look underdone when it is first removed from the oven, but will be ready after standing for the time given in the recipe. For this reason, many tests for readiness are carried out after standing time. Most of the recipes in this book give a range of cooking times for 600- to 700-watt microwave ovens. But it is also important to recognise that your microwave may have a 'personality' and cooking pattern of its own, which you should get to know, that can also influence cooking time. To avoid overcooking, choose the lesser amount of time, check to see if food is ready, then cook longer if necessary. Always undercook rather than overcook and allow the food to stand exactly as instructed in the recipe; if it is underdone, it can be cooked further. When cooking individual portions, test each one separately.

THERMOMETERS

Microwave-safe thermometer: for meats such as lamb and pork, the most reliable test is a thermometer. This can be used inside a microwave oven.

Probe: certain ovens contain probes that monitor food temperatures throughout the cooking process and turn off the oven when the preset temperature is reached.

Instant-read thermometer: this is used to test food outside the microwave. It should be inserted in food immediately after it is taken out of the oven.

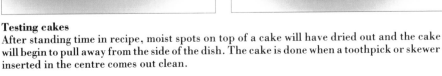

Testing reheated food
Feel underneath the dish with your hand; if the centre is hot, the food is heated through; if it is cool, so is the food.

Testing cakes
After standing time in recipe, moist spots on top of a cake will have dried out and the cake will begin to pull away from the side of the dish. The cake is done when a toothpick or skewer inserted in the centre comes out clean.

Testing custards
These are done when a knife inserted halfway between the centre and edge comes out clean. The centre will look soft but will set during standing time.

Testing fish
Fish is cooked when flesh is opaque; it should flake easily when tested with a fork.

Testing meat
Meat reaches its final desired temperature outside the oven. Small pieces or cubes are done when a fork easily penetrates the surface through to the bottom.

Testing a whole chicken
Chicken is done when the thickest part of the leg feels soft when pressed with fingers and juices run clear if this part is pierced.

Standing time
Foods continue to cook by internal heat after they are removed from the microwave. For instance, eggs should be just past the runny stage when removed from the oven. After standing for 1–2 minutes, they will be set and will look similar to conventionally cooked eggs.

TENTING
Standing time is important for roasts. The internal temperature of the meat rises significantly during standing time, and this extra time is necessary for it to reach the final, desired temperature. Letting roasts stand also allows their juices to settle and the meat to firm up for easier carving. Most roasts should be left to stand, covered with a loose tent of foil, and checked with a thermometer to see if they have reached the final temperature specified in the recipe.

Cook's tips

Use your microwave oven for a variety of cooking techniques. Soften cream cheese or butter for cakes and biscuits, melt chocolate without fuss, toast seeds or nuts for many dishes. You can even make caramel in the microwave: follow recipe instructions, watching carefully since caramel continues to cook and darken when removed from the oven. Do not stir unless instructed in the recipe.

Melt chocolate
Place 30 g cooking chocolate in a small bowl. Heat on High (100% power) for 1–2 minutes, just until shiny. Stir until melted and smooth.

Soften butter
Place butter in non-foil wrapper on a plate. Heat on Medium-Low (30% power) for 30–40 seconds for 125 g, until spreadable.

Soften cream cheese
Place 250 g cream cheese on a plate. Heat on Medium-Low (30% power) for 1½ (1:30)–2 minutes, until spreadable.

Toast coconut
Place 250 g dessicated coconut on a plate. Heat on High (100% power) for 5–6 minutes, until toasted, stirring occasionally.

Toast sesame seeds
Place ½ cup sesame seeds in a shallow pie plate. Heat on High (100% power) for 3–5 minutes, until golden, stirring occasionally.

Toast nuts
Place ½ cup shelled nuts in a shallow pie plate. Heat on High (100% power) for 2½ (2:30)–4 minutes, until lightly browned, stirring occasionally.

Scald milk
Pour 1 cup milk into a 2-cup glass jug. Heat on High (100% power) for 2–2¾ (2:45) minutes, until small bubbles form around edge.

Caramelise sugar
Place 1 cup sugar in a 4-cup glass jug; add 2 tablespoons water. Cook on High (100% power) for 5–7 minutes, without stirring, until mixture is golden.

Clarify butter
Place 125 g butter, cubed, in a 2-cup glass jug; Heat on High (100% power) for 1½ (1:30)–2 minutes, until melted. Skim foam from top.

Soften peanut butter
Remove lid from jar of peanut butter. Heat on High (100% power) for 1½ (1:30) minutes per 250 g. If softening more than 250 g, stir halfway through.

Soften crystallised honey
Remove lid from jar of hardened and crystallised honey. Heat on High (100% power) for 30 seconds; stir until honey loses its granular texture and is smooth. Repeat if necessary.

Soften brown sugar
Place sugar in a glass dish. Add 1 apple wedge or 1 slice bread. Heat, covered, on High (100% power) for 30–40 seconds. Allow to stand for 30 seconds; remove apple and stir sugar once.

Prove yeast bread dough
Place dough in a bowl alongside a 4-cup glass jug containing 3 cups very hot tap water. Heat, covered with paper towel, on Low (10% power) for 20–25 minutes.

Flavour mixed peel and glacé fruit
Pour ¼ cup liqueur into a small bowl. Heat on High (100% power) for 30 seconds. Add 1 cup mixed peel or chopped fruit; stir to mix. Heat on High for 2 minutes. Allow fruit to stand until liquid is absorbed.

Blanch almonds
Heat 1 cup water in a small bowl on High (100% power) for 3–4 minutes, until boiling. Add 1 cup whole shelled almonds. Heat on High for 1 minute; drain. Cool, slip off skins; dry on paper towels.

Dissolve gelatine
Sprinkle gelatine over measured liquid in a small bowl. Heat on High (100% power) for 1–2 minutes, stirring until dissolved.

Soften dried fruit
Place 1 cup dried fruit and ¼ cup water in a 4-cup glass jug. Heat, covered, on High (100% power) for 45 seconds. Allow to stand for 1 minute.

Shell nuts
Place 2 cups nuts and ¼ cup water in a medium bowl. Heat, covered, on High (100% power) for 2–3 minutes until boiling. Allow to stand for 1 minute. Drain; shell.

Cook's tips

The microwave oven can also be used to prepare fruit and vegetables. It can ripen avocados, take the chill off refrigerated fruit and have crisp- or soft-skinned baked potatoes ready for filling or eating plain in a matter of minutes. It can also make it easier to squeeze lemons, limes and oranges, and will substantially reduce the time involved in peeling tomatoes and garlic cloves – and onions without tears!

Take chill off refrigerated foods
To bring out the flavour of fruit that has been stored in the refrigerator, place it on a plate and heat on High (100% power) for 1–2 minutes.

Soften underripe avocado
Place unpeeled avocado on oven floor. Heat on High (100% power) for 1 minute, or until slightly softened. Cool completely, peel, then slice or mash.

Tear-free onions
Trim ends of large onion; place on paper towel on oven floor. Heat on High (100% power) for 1 minute. Remove skin, then chop or slice as desired.

Squeeze citrus fruit more easily
Place 1 orange, lemon or lime on oven floor. Heat on High (100% power) for 30 seconds, or just until warm. Cut in half and squeeze to get fresh juice.

Bake potatoes
With fork, pierce skin of one 250 g potato in several places; place on paper towel. Cook on High (100% power) for 4–6 minutes, until tender, turning over halfway through.

Crisp- or soft-skinned potatoes
After removal from oven, wrap baked potato in paper towel for crisp skin; for soft skin, wrap in foil. Allow to stand for 5 minutes.

Peel tomatoes
Add 2 tomatoes to 2 cups boiling water in a 4-cup glass jug. Heat on High (100% power) for 45–60 seconds, until skins split. Place in cold water; peel.

Peel small onions
Place ½ cup small trimmed onions in a small glass bowl. Heat on High (100% power) for 45 seconds. Squeeze stalk end until onions pop out of skins.

Peel garlic
Place 3 garlic cloves on oven floor. Heat on High (100% power) for 15–30 seconds, just until warm. Squeeze at one end until clove pops out of skin.

Use the microwave oven to get foods ready just before you bring them to the table. It's easier to spread jams, spoon ice creams and pour syrups if they are heated for a short time. Savoury biscuits and crisps can be refreshed; pies and muffins can be warmed for a freshly baked taste. Cheese can be brought to room temperature; uncooked poppadoms can be heated until beautifully crisp.

Soften jams
Remove lid from jar of jam that has become difficult to spread. Heat on High (100% power) for 1½ (1:30)–2 minutes per 250 g.

Heat maple or golden syrup
Remove lid from syrup bottle or transfer to a serving jug. Heat on High (100% power) for 1½ (1:30)–2 minutes per 1–2 cups syrup, until warm.

Refresh potato crisps
Place 2–3 cups potato crisps in thin layer on paper towel on a plate. Heat on High (100% power) for 15–60 seconds. Allow to stand for 5 minutes.

Soften ice cream
Place 1-litre carton ice cream on oven floor. Heat on Medium-Low (30% power) for 30–40 seconds, until softened enough for easy serving.

Heat tacos
Place 8–10 precooked, crisp taco shells on paper towel. Heat on High (100% power) for 1–3 minutes, until warm. Spoon in filling of your choice.

Warm biscuits
Wrap 2–4 biscuits in paper towel. Heat on High (100% power) for 30–40 seconds, until biscuits are warm and slightly softened.

Bring cheese to room temperature
Place 250 g unwrapped cheese on a plate. Just before serving, heat on Medium (50% power) for 45 seconds–1 minute.

Warm individual serving of pie
Place 1 serving of pie on a plate. Heat on High (100% power) for 30–45 seconds, until warm.

Crisp poppadoms
Brush poppadoms lightly with oil. Place on paper towel on oven floor. Heat on High (100% power) for 1 minute, or until crisp, turning once.

How to convert your favourite recipes

You may not always find your favourite recipe in this or any other microwave cookbook, so it helps to know how to take a recipe normally cooked on the stove or in a conventional oven and convert it to microwave cooking – it will save time and energy!

As examples, on this and the opposite page we've taken three different recipes and shown you how simple it is to change them for microwave cooking.

GUIDELINES FOR CONVERTING CONVENTIONAL RECIPES TO MICROWAVE COOKING

1 Look for a microwave recipe that is similar to the conventional one you're trying to convert and use it as a guide. Recipes that serve up to eight people – no more – work best.

2 Reduce or omit fats, liquids and seasonings (see Ⓐ, Ⓒ, Ⓓ, Ⓔ).

3 Use microwave-safe cookware and utensils (see Ⓕ).

4 Cut back cooking time to between one quarter and one half of the conventional recipe time depending on size, shape, density and composition of food (see Food facts, page 16).

5 Remember, food cooked in the microwave may need several minutes standing time to complete the cooking process.

To microwave:

Ⓐ Reduce to 1 tablespoon

Ⓑ Reduce to 1 clove

Ⓒ Omit

Ⓓ Reduce slightly

Ⓔ Reduce slightly

Ⓕ Place oil and vegetables in a 4-litre, microwave-safe baking dish. Cook, covered, on High (100% power) for 6 minutes, or until soft, stirring twice; put aside.

Ⓖ In microwave-safe colander set over microwave-safe pie plate, cook beef mince on High for 4 minutes, or until no longer pink, stirring twice; discard drippings. Add meat to vegetables in baking dish.

Ⓗ Stir in tomato paste, tomatoes, wine, oregano and salt.

Ⓘ Cook sauce, covered, on High for 10 minutes, or until thickened, stirring twice.

Example 1: MEAT SAUCE FOR PASTA

8 servings

2 tablespoons olive oil Ⓐ
1 carrot, finely chopped
1 celery stalk, finely chopped
1 onion, finely chopped
2 cloves garlic, finely chopped Ⓑ
500 g beef mince

¾ cup tomato paste
825 g can tomatoes
⅓ cup water Ⓒ
¼ cup dry red wine
1½ teaspoons dried oregano Ⓓ
1 teaspoon salt Ⓔ

1. Heat oil in a 4-litre saucepan. Add carrot, celery, onion and garlic. Cook over medium-high heat for about 15 minutes, until tender. Ⓕ
2. Add beef mince. Cook until well browned, stirring frequently. Ⓖ Add tomato paste, tomatoes, water, wine, oregano and salt; heat to boiling. Ⓗ
3. Reduce heat to low; cover and simmer for 30 minutes or until sauce thickens. Ⓘ

If all vegetables are chopped to equal size, they will cook quickly and evenly.

Replace saucepan with microwave-safe cookware that can be used for serving; this saves on washing-up.

Stir from the outer edge towards the centre, pushing cooler food to the edge.

Cooking minced meat in a microwave-safe colander greatly reduces fat content of finished dish.

COOKING FAVOURITE RECIPES IN THE MICROWAVE

Here are two more recipes ideal for converting to microwave cooking: the potatoes cook faster and cakes take less time and are moist and light when cooked in the microwave. Underneath the conventional recipes, instructions are given for successful adaption to the microwave.

Example 2: TWICE-BAKED POTATOES

6 servings

6 medium potatoes, scrubbed and unpeeled	Toppings: Finely chopped onion, chopped chives, diced
45 g butter or margarine	Cheddar cheese, crumbled
1 teaspoon salt	crisp bacon
¼ teaspoon white pepper	
⅓ cup milk	

1. Preheat conventional oven to 230°C. Pierce potatoes in several places then place in oven and bake for 45 minutes or until fork-tender.
2. Holding each potato with clean oven glove, slice lengthways with a sharp knife to remove top quarter.
3. Carefully scoop out potatoes with a spoon to form 6 shells. Scrape potato from top quarters; discard tops.
4. In a large bowl with mixer at low speed, beat scooped-out potato, butter, salt and pepper until well combined and fluffy.
5. Slowly add milk, beating constantly until smooth. Pile mashed potato mixture back into reserved potato shells.
6. Sprinkle generously with topping of your choice (above). Place filled potatoes on baking tray; return to oven and bake for 10 minutes or until tops are golden.

To microwave: Pierce potatoes in several places; place on paper towels on oven floor. Cook on High (100% power) for 16–20 minutes, turning potatoes over and rearranging halfway through cooking. Prepare potato mixture as above. After filling, reheat for 5–7 minutes, until hot. *Saves about 30 minutes.*

Example 3: BANANA AND PECAN LOAF

Makes 1 loaf

1¾ cups plain flour	125 g butter or margarine
⅔ cup caster sugar	2 very ripe medium bananas, mashed
1 teaspoon ground cinnamon	1 teaspoon grated lemon rind
1 teaspoon baking power	
¼ teaspoon bicarbonate of soda	2 eggs, beaten
½ teaspoon salt	½ cup shelled pecans, chopped

1. Preheat conventional oven to 180°C. Grease a 23-cm x 12.5-cm loaf tin.
2. Combine flour, sugar, cinnamon, baking powder, bicarbonate of soda and salt in a bowl. Cut in butter with fingertips or 2 knives until mixture resembles coarse crumbs. Stir in bananas, lemon rind, eggs and pecans, reserving 1½ tablespoons pecans for garnish, just until flour is moistened. Spoon into prepared loaf tin, smoothing surface. Sprinkle over reserved pecans.
3. Bake for 55 minutes or until a toothpick or skewer inserted in the centre of the loaf comes out clean. Cool loaf in tin on a rack for 10 minutes; remove from tin and finish cooling on rack.

To microwave: Line a 23-cm x 12.5-cm microwave-safe loaf dish with paper towel. Omit salt. Spoon mixture into prepared loaf dish and sprinkle with reserved nuts. Cook, covered loosely with greaseproof paper, on Medium (50% power) for 15 minutes, or until top of loaf is moist and springs back when lightly touched, rotating a quarter turn every 2 minutes. Allow to stand in dish for 10 minutes. Invert on to rack; remove paper towel; cool. *Saves about 40 minutes.*

Caring for your microwave

Microwave ovens are simple to care for and easy to clean. Because they stay cool, spills do not cook on. It is best to wipe spills off while they are still warm, however, because if they are left in the oven they can absorb microwave energy during cooking. Do not worry if some moisture forms on oven walls or door; it is normal for foods to give off moisture and steam during cooking. Just wipe away after cooking.

CLEANING THE OVEN

It is easy to wipe the inside of a microwave after every use, so cleaning is not hard work at all. To clean the touch-control panel, be sure to open the door first to prevent the oven from starting accidentally. For combination ovens, follow the manufacturer's recommended cleaning methods in the instruction booklet. If your oven has a removable turntable, check the instructions to see if it can be put in the dishwasher.

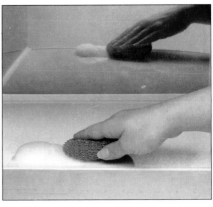

1. Use a clean cloth or sponge dipped in a mild all-purpose cleaner or a solution of liquid dishwashing detergent dissolved in warm water. Rinse well with clear, warm water and dry with a soft cloth or sheets of paper towel.

2. Pay special attention to thoroughly cleaning the area around the door seal; this is where small pieces of food or spatters often get trapped.

3. If there are areas of cooked-on food, clean them by rubbing gently with a plastic scrubbing pad. An alternative method of removing stubborn food is to soften it with steam by boiling some water in the oven. Do not use steel-wool scrubbing pads.

CLEANING MICROWAVE DISHES

To clean plastic microwave-safe dishes stained by tomatoes, berries or other foods, make a solution of 1 tablespoon household bleach per 1 cup water. Soak dishes for about 1 hour, then wash, rinse and dry. For everyday cleaning, use a mild dishwashing liquid. Rub gently with a plastic scrubbing pad to remove stuck-on food.

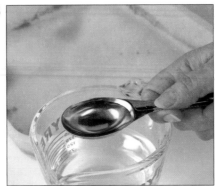

DEODORISING THE OVEN

The microwave oven may pick up odours from cooking. Air the oven occasionally by leaving the door ajar, and wipe the inside with bicarbonate of soda dissolved in warm water. From time to time, use this highly effective deodorising formula: Combine *1 cup warm water* and *a few thyme sprigs* or *2 lemon slices* or *2 teaspoons mixed spice* in a 4-cup glass jug. Heat on High (100% power) for 3 minutes, or until boiling. As a bonus, your whole kitchen as well as the inside of your oven will smell fresh.

BEFORE YOU RING FOR SERVICE

Are you using your microwave oven correctly? Before you ring for service, make the following checks:

Oven not turning on?
Make sure the oven door is securely closed. The oven will not switch on if it is not closed properly; this is a safety measure built into microwave ovens. Check that the oven is properly plugged in, that no circuit breakers are open and that the fuses are not blown. Also check that the oven's master switch is in the operation position.

Food isn't cooking?
Check that the oven is not set on 'timer' or 'hold'.

In recipes where food is cooked in its own packaging, such as shop-bought frozen vegetables, be sure the packaging is not foil, through which microwaves cannot pass. Check that your cookware is microwave-safe (page 12); some materials block microwave energy.

Food cooking too slowly?
The oven may not be operating at full power if it is sharing a circuit with another appliance. Also your oven may be a lower wattage than that used in the recipe you are following; all recipes in this book have been developed for cooking in 600- to 700-watt ovens but if your oven has a lower wattage, cooking is slower.

Check to see if the required power level is set correctly.

Also, make sure food is at the correct temperature. Meat, fish, poultry and most vegetables should be at refrigerator temperature and canned and dry goods at room temperature.

If standing time is included in the recipe, make sure you allow the dish to stand for the full time specified. The standing time is needed to equalise the temperature through the food and to complete the cooking process; it should not be ignored. Also, be sure the food is left covered or tented during standing, if instructed in the recipe. You should always check that the food has been cut to the size specified in the recipe; you may have cut it too large.

Food cooking too quickly?
The starting temperature of food going into the microwave affects cooking time. Microwave recipes assume that foods used in the recipe have been stored correctly. Refrigerated food should be cold, not brought to room temperature before use, or it will cook too quickly.

You may have a single-setting oven which cooks certain foods like eggs and cheese too quickly. If this is the case, pour 2 cups water into a glass jug and place in the oven while cooking these foods. The water attracts microwave energy and 'slows' down the oven.

Check that the power level is set correctly and that food is cut to the specified size and not smaller.

Check the wattage of your oven. The higher the wattage, the faster food will cook.

Food cooking unevenly?
Make sure the air vent in your microwave is not blocked. There are also several techniques to prevent uneven cooking in the microwave, such as elevating the dish on a trivet, rack or inverted ramekins; this exposes areas at the bottom of the dish to the microwaves. Other techniques include arranging food with thicker parts towards the edges of the dish and stirring and rotating during cooking.

In recipes calling for food to be cut into pieces, check that the pieces are of a uniform size to prevent uneven cooking.

Some microwave ovens have 'hot spots' where there is a concentration of microwaves. Fans and turntables inside the oven help to distribute the microwaves more evenly, but it is still necessary to use the techniques described on pages 24–25 to ensure even and thorough cooking.

Blue sparks (arcing)?
Be sure any foil you use to shield food, or to cover food you do not want cooked, is smooth and at least 2.5 cm away from oven walls. Check that the cookware is microwave-safe (even metal rims on dishes can cause arcing) and that any ties used to seal oven bags are made of nylon or string, not metal.

MICROWAVE SAFETY

Microwave ovens are made in compliance with strict safety standards; a seal around the oven door keeps the microwaves inside, and a special system stops the generation of microwaves the instant the door is opened. You should, however, examine a new oven for any signs of damage.

Never operate the oven if the door does not close properly, or if the door, its latch, hinge or sealing surfaces have been damaged in any way. Never block the vents of your oven because they keep the microwave-producing magnetron tube cool and cut down on moisture build-up, enabling you to get the best results from your oven.

Microwave ovens are cooking appliances, designed to defrost, heat and cook food. You may have heard of other uses for the oven – do not try them; they can be dangerous, possibly lead to a fire and, at the very least, damage your oven. Use the microwave oven only as intended. Always use microwave-safe cookware and utensils (page 12) and do not turn the oven on when the cavity is empty. If you have young children, it is a good idea to leave a bowl of water in your microwave when the oven is not in use. This way, if the oven is accidentally turned on, the water attracts the microwaves and prevents damage to the oven.

If you are concerned about the safety of your oven, have it tested by a qualified service person – do not try using 'leakage detectors' which are inaccurate and unreliable.

Meal planning with a microwave

The microwave oven can be a great boon when planning meals for yourself or the whole family and when entertaining. It can help save on preparation and cleaning time and it preserves the nutrients in the food as well. To plan meals to be cooked in the microwave, there are certain points to keep in mind.

BASIC PRINCIPLES

1. The more food in the oven, the longer it takes to cook. It is best to keep the number of servings down to eight to take advantage of the oven's ability to cook quickly. If serving meat and potatoes to feed 12, for example, cook the roast in the microwave but plan to bake the potatoes in the conventional oven.

2. You can switch power settings in the time it takes to push a button. This means that after you have cooked the roast on a lower power setting you can cook the vegetables on High (100% power) without waiting for the oven to warm up, as you would when cooking conventionally. There is no need to cool the microwave either when going from a higher to a lower power setting.

3. Dense foods such as roasts, whole poultry and casseroles usually require standing time to complete the cooking process; they retain heat well after being removed from the oven. While they finish cooking outside the oven, you have time to cook the vegetables and reheat soups and sauces, rolls, bread and so on.

4. Use microwave-safe dishes, serving platters and casseroles so you can heat up food between courses and bring it to the table piping hot. Pretty china and cooking and serving pieces for use in the microwave are widely available.

COMBINATION COOKING

A microwave used in combination with one or more other appliances is often the most efficient way to prepare a meal. For example, you can prepare pasta just as quickly on top of the stove, leaving the microwave oven free for ensuring your favourite sauce is ready at the same time.

After cooking a casserole in the microwave, you can place it under the grill to brown the top while using the microwave to cook accompanying vegetables. Or you can brown meat on top of the stove before you begin cooking it in the microwave. Look for cookware that can be used on top of the stove and in the microwave as well as in a conventional oven.

FREEZER-TO-TABLE COOKING

It is easy to cook food in advance, freeze it, then pop it in the microwave oven when guests arrive so that it is ready in a matter of minutes. For example, the Sausage Parcels and Crab-filled Mushrooms in the Starters chapter can be frozen for up to 1 month ahead, then cooked in the microwave just before you are ready to serve. For a piping hot, homemade snack, muffins can be cooked ahead and frozen, then quickly defrosted and reheated in the microwave as and when you need them (see the Chart on page 349 for timings).

Celebration cakes, pies and tarts can be made ahead of time; favourites such as mince pies defrost well in the microwave. A 23-cm flan or tart takes only 6–8 minutes on High (100% power) to defrost completely and evenly.

COOKING FOR THE BARBECUE

Use the microwave to precook vegetables before you finish them on the barbecue: the time can be reduced to 2–5 minutes if you cook your vegetables first in a small amount of water until almost tender (see vegetable charts on pages 239–253). Meats and poultry can be partially cooked so the barbecuing time is cut in half. Avoid spoilage by barbecuing immediately after precooking in the microwave – never leave precooked food out at room temperature. Barbecue sauces can also be prepared in double-quick time using the microwave.

ENTERTAINING MADE EASY

Throughout the *Reader's Digest Microwave Cookbook* there are suggestions on serving and garnishing the food to make it perfect for special occasions. Also included are special Meal in Minutes menus, complete with preparation timetables and serving suggestions to cover most of your entertaining needs. Not all the dishes and ingredients in these menus are prepared in the microwave; many can be bought commercially prepared and some are conventionally cooked. In each menu however, the microwave is used as much as possible to make entertaining easier. The preparation timetables also give advice for advance preparation so there should be no last-minute panics and you can enjoy the meal as much as your guests.

SUMMARY OF MICROWAVE COOKING ESSENTIALS

1. Check wattage output of your oven. Remember, the recipes in this book have been developed for cooking in 600- to 700-watt ovens. Add approximately 15–20 seconds per minute cooking time for a 500 watt oven.

2. Always follow recipe instructions for stirring, turning, elevating, rotating, rearranging or otherwise moving food; if your oven has a turntable it is not necessary to manually rotate dishes, however it is still essential to carry out any other instructions for moving and arranging food.

3. Use only microwave-safe cookware.

4. Be sure to use the exact size and shape of dish specified in the recipe or the timing and finished results may be different from those expected.

5. Remember – the 'starting' temperature of foods can make a big difference in cooking results: recipes in this book assume that meat, fish, poultry, eggs and most vegetables will be at refrigerator temperature, and canned and dry goods at room temperature.

6. Always allow food to stand, covered, exactly as instructed in the recipe; standing time is essential to complete the cooking process.

The
Colour Index

HOT PRAWN DIP WITH DILL
*Prawns, garlic, spring onion and celery
blended with a peppery sauce. Served with
tortellini on skewers; garnished with dill.
Makes 2 cups. Page 112*

BACON DIP
*Cream-cheese-based dip in a capsicum
bowl. Served with celery, breadsticks and
bagel chips; garnished here with chives.
Makes 2 cups. Page 111*

CURRIED CRAB DIP
*Crab meat combined with pimientos, curry
powder and cream cheese. Served with a
selection of fresh vegetables.
Makes 2 cups. Page 111*

BAKED STUFFED TOMATOES
*Scooped-out tomatoes filled with
Parmesan cheese, breadcrumbs and
garlic; garnished with sprigs of parsley.
4 tomatoes. Page 121*

SAVOURY BREADSTICKS
*Bacon rashers wrapped around
breadsticks and cooked until browned;
garnished with tomato slices and chives.
Makes 12. Page 118*

ANGELS ON HORSEBACK
*Oysters flavoured with Worcestershire
sauce and mustard then wrapped in
bacon; garnished with lemon and parsley.
24, 12, 6 oysters. Page 117*

MEDITERRANEAN EGGPLANT DIP
*Cooked eggplant mixed with onion, garlic,
capsicum, tomato and herbs. Served with
pita bread; garnished with parsley.
Makes 3 cups. Page 111*

BOMBAY MIXED NUTS (left) *Assorted
nuts cooked in spices. Makes 2 cups.
Page 296.* **MEXICAN DIP** *Cream cheese
with taco sauce; garnished with chopped
spring onion. Makes 1 cup. Page 112*

SCALLOPED OYSTERS
*Oysters in a lightly seasoned cream sauce
with Melba-toast crumb topping;
garnished here with lemon and parsley.
4 servings. Page 124*

SPICY CHICKEN WINGS
Chicken wings cooked in a tomato and orange sauce. Served with celery and a yoghurt dip; garnished with parsley.
12 pieces. Page 116

NACHO BAKE
Alternate layers of corn chips and a spicy mixture of melted cheese, chillies, onion, coriander and sliced black olives.
6 servings. Page 116

CHEESE STICKS
Breadsticks spread with a cheese mixture, rolled in poppy seeds, sesame seeds, chives and paprika; garnished with chives.
16 sticks. Page 117

OYSTERS ROCKEFELLER
Oysters topped with a spinach mixture and diced bacon then cooked on the half-shells; garnished here with lemon.
12 oysters. Page 124

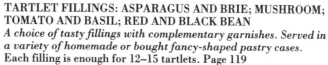

CREAMED MUSHROOMS
Quartered mushrooms cooked in a sherried cream sauce. Served with toast; garnished with finely sliced spring onion.
4 servings. Page 122

TARTLET FILLINGS: ASPARAGUS AND BRIE; MUSHROOM; TOMATO AND BASIL; RED AND BLACK BEAN
A choice of tasty fillings with complementary garnishes. Served in a variety of homemade or bought fancy-shaped pastry cases.
Each filling is enough for 12–15 tartlets. Page 119

30–60 MINUTES

POTATO SKINS WITH TASTY CHEESE
Wedges of scooped-out baked potatoes topped with a cheese mixture. Served with sour cream; garnished with spring onion.
16, 8, 4 pieces. Page 116

CHEESE AND CHILLI CHAPATIS
Tortilla 'sandwiches' with a tasty filling. Served here with chutney, yoghurt, radish, lettuce and a chilli flower.
16 wedges. Page 115

STUFFED ARTICHOKE BOTTOMS
Bacon mixed with sultanas, onion and breadcrumbs in cooked artichoke cases. Served with salad; garnished with lemon.
4, 2, 1 servings. Page 120

MIDDLE-EASTERN MEATBALLS
Spicy beef mince mixture shaped into bite-sized meatballs. Served on skewers; garnished with lemon and mint leaves.
About 26 meatballs. Page 117

POACHED APPLES WITH PROSCIUTTO *Apples cooked in spiced wine then filled with sour cream and blue cheese. Served with prosciutto and salad.*
6 servings. Page 121

NUTTY GOAT CHEESE TOASTS
Walnut-coated goat cheese on toasted French bread with sun-dried tomatoes and olive oil; garnished with salad greens.
Makes 24. Page 118

ARTICHOKES WITH LEMON AND GARLIC *Artichokes cooked with lemon, garlic and wine. Served with clarified butter; garnished with lemon and parsley.*
4, 2, 1 servings. Page 122

PIZZA TARTLETS
Warmed pastry cases filled with pizza sauce, mozzarella cheese, anchovies and black olives; garnished with basil.
Makes 16. Page 118

ELEGANT SEAFOOD SALAD
Chilled cooked prawns, scallops and mussels. Served on salad greens with a lemon and basil sauce and cocktail sauce.
6 servings. Page 124

CRAB-FILLED MUSHROOMS
*Mushroom caps filled with a tangy crab
and mayonnaise mixture; garnished here
with parsley sprigs and lemon twists.*
12 mushrooms. Page 120

SEAFOOD PÂTÉ
*Prawns and scallops with tarragon,
tomato and cream. Served chilled;
garnished with tarragon and tomato.*
16 servings. Page 114

COUNTRY-STYLE PORK PÂTÉ
*Minced beef and pork combined with diced ham, chicken livers, herbs
and spices and cooked in a bacon-lined dish. Served chilled and sliced;
garnished with gherkins, salad greens and stuffed olives.*
16 servings. Page 114

CHICKEN LIVER PÂTÉ
*Chicken livers, brandy and herbs. Served
on radish flowers, pear slices and savoury
biscuits with assorted garnishes.*
Makes 1 cup. Page 115

SAUSAGE PARCELS
*Spicy sausage and cheese mixture rolled in
vine leaves, 'tied' with pimiento strips;
garnished here with lemon and basil.*
12 parcels. Page 120

CHEESY STUFFED PRAWNS
*King prawns filled with a savoury cheese
and capsicum mixture; garnished here
with salad greens and peach slices.*
4, 2, 1 servings. Page 121

SOUPS

FRESH TOMATO SOUP
Tomatoes and vegetables blended until smooth then cooked in a seasoned stock; garnished with sour cream and chives.
Makes 6 cups. Page 129

LIGHT AND CREAMY ASPARAGUS SOUP *Asparagus, onion and vegetable stock with cream. Served hot or chilled; garnished with yoghurt and chervil.*
Makes 4 cups. Page 130

VEGETABLE STOCK
Leek, onion, celery, carrots, tomatoes and mushrooms cooked with tomato juice, seasonings and water, then strained.
Makes 3 cups. Page 127

CARROT SOUP WITH ORANGE
Thinly sliced carrots cooked with onion and grated orange rind in chicken stock then blended until smooth and reheated; garnished with feathered cream and a sprig of parsley.
Makes 4 cups. Page 130

CHICKEN STOCK
Chicken bones cooked in water with herbs, peppercorns, leek, carrot, celery and parsley, then strained.
Makes 3 cups. Page 127

FISH STOCK
Fish bones cooked in dry white wine and water with leek, carrot, celery, thyme and peppercorns, then strained.
Makes 3 cups. Page 127

FRENCH ONION SOUP
Sliced onions simmered in beef consommé flavoured with sherry and tomato paste. Served piping hot with the classic topping of toasted French bread slices covered with melted cheese.
Makes 6 cups. Page 133

HEARTY BEAN SOUP
Black, bortolli, red kidney and haricot beans cooked with vegetables and bacon in stock; garnished with celery leaves.
Makes 7 cups. Page 131

CURRIED PARSNIP SOUP
Parsnips blended with onion, apple, curry powder, vegetable stock and milk; garnished with almonds and coriander.
Makes 6 cups. Page 131

WINTER VEGETABLE SOUP
Carrot, parsnip, celery, cabbage, turnip and onion cut into delicate pieces and cooked in a seasoned vegetable stock.
Makes 6 cups. Page 130

CORN CHOWDER
Frozen corn kernels cooked in a creamy potato, celery and onion mixture; garnished with chopped parsley.
Makes 6 cups. Page 135

CREAM OF OYSTER SOUP
Bottled oysters lightly cooked in a rich mixture of seasoned milk and cream. Served piping hot, accompanied here by slices of French bread; garnished with a sprinkling of paprika.
4 servings. Page 135

VEGETABLE CHOWDER
Carrots, onions, celery, parsnip, potato and herbs cooked with tomatoes, beans and stock; garnished with parsley.
Makes 6 cups. Page 135

SOUPS

CREAM OF SPINACH SOUP (left) *Blended spinach, potatoes and chicken or vegetable stock enriched with cream; garnished with a swirl of yoghurt. Makes 4 cups. Page 129.* **VICHYSSOISE** *Classic creamy leek and potato soup blended until smooth. Served chilled; garnished with apple slices and a sprig of parsley. Makes 8 cups. Page 129*

CHICKEN NOODLE SOUP
Tender pieces of chicken and vegetables in chicken stock with fine egg noodles added. Served here with savoury cracker biscuits. Makes 4 cups. Page 133

MINESTRONE
Fresh vegetables cooked with prosciutto, green beans, haricot beans, pasta and tomatoes, topped with Parmesan cheese. Makes 8 cups. Page 132

BEEF STOCK
Beef bones, onion and tomato roasted conventionally; cooked with water, leek, herbs and peppercorns, then strained. Makes 3 cups. Page 127

SPLIT PEA AND HAM SOUP
Ham bone cooked in chicken stock with split peas and vegetables. Served here with French bread; garnished with parsley. Makes 8 cups. Page 131

SEAFOOD GUMBO
Prawns, oysters and okra in a thick, spicy tomato base with celery, onions and garlic. Served here with Hot Cooked Rice. Makes 8 cups. Page 134

PEACH SOUP (left) *Fresh peaches cooked with dry white wine, sugar and green ginger, then puréed. Served chilled; garnished with yoghurt and mint leaves. Makes 3 cups. Page 136.* **RED PLUM SOUP** *Plums cooked in spiced red wine, then puréed. Served chilled; garnished with sour cream or yoghurt and slivers of fresh plum. Makes 3 cups. Page 136*

EGGS BAKED IN HAM NESTS
Shredded ham, chopped spring onions and an egg baked in individual dishes. Served here with toast triangles.
4, 2, 1 servings. Page 139

POACHED EGGS
Eggs simply cooked in water and vinegar. Served here on toast with herb-flavoured sausage patties; garnished with parsley.
4, 2, 1 servings. Page 140

SCRAMBLED EGGS
Seasoned eggs cooked until fluffy. Served here with toast triangles and cherry tomatoes; garnished with a parsley sprig.
4, 2, 1 servings. Page 141

PIPÉRADE
Capsicums and chopped onion, cooked then scrambled with eggs. Served here with French bread; garnished with basil.
6 servings. Page 141

BACON AND EGGS
Crisply 'fried' bacon rashers and an egg. Served with a warm roll and a tomato half sprinkled with chopped chives.
4 servings. Page 142

EGGS IN BRIOCHES
Hollowed-out individual brioches lined with Gruyère or Swiss cheese are used as cases for baked eggs. Served with smoked salmon and fresh asparagus with Hollandaise Sauce; garnished with chives.
6 servings. Page 139

EGGS AND CHEESE

WELSH RAREBIT
*Well-seasoned thickened cheese topping.
Served on toast; garnished with gherkins,
olives, pickled onions and parsley.*
6 servings. Page 144

SWISS CHEESE FONDUE
*A variation of the traditional cheese and
wine mixture. Served hot with bread
cubes, tomatoes and capsicum for dipping.*
4 servings. Page 144

MACARONI CHEESE
*Elbow macaroni covered in a thick, onion-
flavoured cheese sauce with breadcrumb
topping; garnished with parsley.*
4 servings. Page 144

TOMATO AND CAPSICUM OMELETTE *(left) Sliced onion and
chopped green capsicum and tomato fill this savoury omelette; garnished
with parsley.* 2 servings. Page 143. **FRENCH DESSERT OMELETTE**
*Moist omelette with a filling of sliced strawberries; decorated with a
dusting of icing sugar and a whole strawberry.* 2 servings. Page 143

EGGS FLORENTINE
*Eggs and spinach on muffin halves. Served
with asparagus and Hollandaise Sauce;
garnished with chives and bacon.*
4 servings. Page 140

CAMEMBERT IN VINE LEAVES
*Camembert layered with apple slices
and wrapped in vine leaves. Served with
apple wedges; garnished with parsley.*
2 servings. Page 146

SOUFFLÉED CHEESE OMELETTE
*Egg yolks folded into beaten whites give a
light, fluffy omelette; garnished with
cucumber slices, tomato and parsley.*
2 servings. Page 143

**MEXICAN CHEESE AND TOMATO
BAKE** *Creamy onion and tomato mixture
flavoured with herbs and Tabasco sauce,
layered with corn chips and melted cheese.*
6 servings. Page 145

TOMATOES WITH GOAT CHEESE AND BASIL SOUFFLÉ *Hollowed-out tomatoes filled with goat cheese soufflé. Served here with salad; garnished with basil.* 8 servings. Page 147

CHEESE SOUFFLÉ
Grated Swiss and Parmesan cheeses in a white sauce form the basis of this microwave version of an old favourite. 6 servings. Page 147

SMOKED SALMON AND CHIVE ROULADE *(top) A light soufflé roll with a filling of smoked salmon slices and herbed cream cheese; garnished with chives. 4 servings. Page 148.* **MUSHROOM AND CHEESE ROULADE** *Rolled soufflé filled with onion, tomatoes and mushrooms cooked in wine, with cheese added; garnished with basil. 4 servings. Page 148*

ASPARAGUS TIMBALES
Asparagus, onion, eggs and cheese cooked in ramekins. Served with smoked salmon; garnished with asparagus and lemon. 4 servings. Page 145

CRUSTLESS BROCCOLI AND CHEESE QUICHE *(left) Lightly steamed broccoli and onion cooked in a creamy egg and cheese mixture. Served warm. 6 servings. Page 146.* **BACON AND POTATO QUICHE** *Potato cubes, fresh peas, sliced spring onions and crisp bacon in a mixture of Cheddar cheese and eggs. 8 servings. Page 146*

UNDER 30 MINUTES

SAVOURY FISH CUTLETS
Ocean trout topped with spring onion and mayonnaise; garnished with radish flowers, spring onions and cucumber. 2 servings. Page 157

FLOUNDER FILLETS WITH SAVOURY SAUCE *(left) Flounder fillets in crumb coating. Served here with salad and two sauces. 4 servings. Page 162.* **WHITING ROLLS WITH CUCUMBER, TOMATO AND BASIL SAUCE** *Whiting fillets with cucumber stuffing, with a cucumber, tomato, basil and wine sauce; garnished with basil. 4 servings. Page 163*

FLOUNDER VÉRONIQUE
Flounder or sole fillets, seasoned with tarragon, in a creamy wine sauce with grapes; garnished with lemon and parsley. 4, 2, 1 servings. Page 162

SKATE AMANDINE
Tender skate or swordfish with a buttery toasted almond and chopped parsley sauce; garnished with a sprig of parsley. 4 servings. Page 161

SNAPPER CUTLETS WITH SALSA
Snapper, jewfish or kingfish cutlets with a sauce of tomatoes, green capsicum, onion and olives; garnished with coriander. 2 servings. Page 156

MULLET WITH RIBBON VEGETABLES
Whole mullet brushed with butter, sherry and lime juice. Served with a colourful assortment of carrot and yellow and green zucchini ribbons; garnished with salad greens, orange and lemon slices. 6 servings. Page 155

FISH FILLETS FLORENTINE
Fish fillets rolled with spinach, mushrooms and bread cubes, topped with grated cheese. Served with tomato wedges. 4 servings. Page 162

TUNA STIR-FRY *(left) Tuna strips cooked with oriental flavourings. Served on snow peas, mushrooms, spring onions, tomatoes and corn.* 4 servings. Page 161. **GEMFISH SATAY WITH CHUNKY PEANUT SAUCE** *Gemfish, capsicum and spring onions. Served with a satay sauce; garnished with lemon and spring onions.* 4 servings. Page 159

BREAM AND ASPARAGUS WITH CHEESE SAUCE *Tender bream fillets rolled with asparagus spears in a creamy cheese sauce; garnished with lemon twists.* 4 servings. Page 161

CHINESE SNAPPER
Whole fish cooked with julienned capsicum, carrots, celery and spring onions in a sauce of sherry, soy sauce, garlic and ginger; garnished here with kiwifruit and toasted almonds.
4 servings. Page 153

SCALLOPS IN CHIVE CREAM
Scallops cooked in stock, cream and white wine flavoured with chives. Served here in scallop shells; garnished with chives.
4 servings. Page 170

SALMON WITH LETTUCE AND CAPSICUM *Salmon cutlets cooked on a bed of lettuce and thinly sliced red capsicum, seasoned with soy sauce.* 2 servings. Page 157

SPICY PRAWN SAUCE *(left) Tomato-based sauce served here with tagliatelle.* 4 servings. Page 175. **SMOKED OYSTER SAUCE** *(centre) Bacon and smoked oysters in a sauce served here with linguine.* 4 servings. Page 175. **TUNA AND TOMATO SAUCE** *Rich tuna sauce served here with farfelle (bow tie pasta).* 4 servings. Page 175

PIQUANT PRAWNS *(left) Prawns tossed in herbs and cooked in beer with a dash of Worcestershire sauce; garnished here with lime. 4, 2, 1 servings. Page 166.* **CREOLE PRAWNS** *Fiery mixture of prawns with green capsicum, onions, Worcestershire sauce, tomatoes and Tabasco sauce. Served with rice; garnished with thyme. 4 servings. Page 167*

SCALLOPS WITH BACON AND BASIL *Scallops, bacon and mushrooms in a cream sauce flavoured with shredded fresh basil; garnished with basil leaves. 2 servings. Page 171*

CURRIED SCALLOPS *Scallops cooked in a curry and butter mixture with onion, celery and carrots; garnished with coriander leaves. 4 servings. Page 171*

MUSSELS IN CREAM AND GARLIC *Fresh mussels steamed open with wine in the microwave. Served in the half shells with a slightly thickened sauce of finely chopped onion, garlic, cream, mussel liquid and chopped parsley. 4 servings. Page 170*

CREAMED OYSTERS IN PUFF PASTRY *Oysters cooked in a creamy mixture. Served in vol-au-vent cases with chopped bacon; garnished with lemon and parsley. 4 servings. Page 171*

CRAB CAKES *(top) Tasty patties; garnished with lemon and coriander. 12 crab cakes. Page 172.* **DEVILLED CRAB** *Crab in a piquant creamy sauce; garnished with lemon. 4 servings. Page 172*

CHILLI CRAB *Fresh crab cooked in a spicy sauce; garnished with spring onion curls. Accompanied here by rice and cucumber. 2 servings. Page 172*

30–60 MINUTES

TUNA AND SPINACH LOAF
Satisfying dish of chopped spinach and flaked tuna mixed with bread, sour cream and eggs, seasoned with lemon juice and Tabasco sauce, then cooked in a loaf pan; garnished with lemon slices and parsley.
6 servings. Page 164

MEDITERRANEAN JEWFISH
Jewfish or snapper cutlets seasoned with oregano. Served with a rich tomato and vegetable sauce; garnished with oregano.
2 servings. Page 158

PEPPERY KINGFISH CUTLETS
Chilli-flavoured capsicum sauce spooned over kingfish cutlets. Served here with green beans; garnished with basil.
6 servings. Page 158

TUNA PATTIES FLORENTINE
Tuna and spinach patties. Served here with tomato, cucumber and salad greens; garnished with lemon wedges and parsley.
6 servings. Page 165

STUFFED TROUT *(top) Trout stuffed with a well-seasoned mixture of onion, carrot, celery and chopped walnuts; garnished with lemon slices and walnut halves. 4, 2, 1 servings. Page 154.* **CAJUN TROUT** *Whole trout coated in seasoned cornmeal. Served with a herbed sauce of onion, capsicum and tomatoes; garnished with lime. 2 servings. Page 154.*

30–60 MINUTES

STUFFED DORY FILLETS
Dory fillets with a prawn, vegetable and breadcrumb stuffing. Served here with Hollandaise Sauce; garnished with dill.
4, 2, 1 servings. Page 164

SNAPPER WITH OYSTER STUFFING
Whole snapper with a rich stuffing of coarsely chopped oysters, onion, celery, garlic, white wine, cream and breadcrumbs, seasoned with tarragon; garnished with slices of lemon and lime.
4 servings. Page 153

PERCH IN PAPER PARCELS
Perch fillets cooked in baking paper with orange-flavoured vegetables; garnished with orange slices and basil leaves.
4, 2, 1 servings. Page 163

MUSSELS IN WHITE WINE
Mussels cooked in a tomato and white-wine sauce seasoned with garlic and basil. Traditionally served with French bread.
4, 2, 1 servings. Page 170

SEAFOOD AND CHICKEN BAKE
Tasty stew of lobster, prawns and chicken with corn kernels, onion and tomatoes. Served here with chive-topped potatoes.
4 servings. Page 175

COUNTRY-STYLE TAILOR
Hearty dish of whole tailor brushed with pan drippings and cooked on a bed of browned, chopped bacon, thickly sliced onions and chunks of potato; garnished here with a sprig of thyme.
6 servings. Page 153

CIOPPINO
A traditional dish of tomatoes and red wine with a selection of prawns, pipis, scallops and crab. Served here with French bread.
8 servings. Page 175

STIR-FRIED PRAWNS AND BROCCOLI
Prawns with sherry and ginger, tossed with broccoli, capsicum and mushrooms. Accompanied by Hot Cooked Rice.
4, 2, 1 servings. Page 168

STUFFED PRAWNS SUPREME
King prawns with zucchini and capsicum stuffing, cooked in a sherry and lemon sauce. Served with walnut-coated cheese.
4 servings. Page 167

LOBSTER THERMIDOR *(top) Chunks of lobster meat in a creamy mushroom sauce. Served in the half-shell; garnished with a sprig of parsley. 4, 2, 1 servings. Page 169.* **SZECHUAN LOBSTER** *Lobster and green vegetables cooked in a blend of garlic, cashews, chilli, soy sauce and sesame oil. 4 servings. Page 169*

PRAWN AND CAPSICUM RISOTTO
Prawns, snow peas and red capsicum pieces mixed into Italian arborio rice that has been cooked in fish stock and white wine with chopped vegetables and garlic; garnished with fresh basil leaves.
6 servings. Page 168

PRAWNS IN SAFFRON CREAM
Prawns tossed in a creamy saffron-flavoured sauce. Served with tender-crisp snow peas and cooked julienned carrots.
6 servings. Page 166

FISH AND SHELLFISH

SAVOURY FISH KEBABS
Swordfish, capsicum, mushrooms and tomatoes marinated in a mixture of spring onions, curry powder and Worcestershire sauce then cooked on skewers. Served on herbed rice; garnished with lemon and parsley.
4, 2, 1 servings. Page 159

ORIENTAL FISH IN LETTUCE LEAVES
Fish fillets wrapped in lettuce leaves. Served with vegetables cooked in chicken stock; garnished with coriander.
4, 2, 1 servings. Page 160

CHILLI SNAPPER
Snapper cutlets marinated in chilli, lime juice, oil and honey before cooking; garnished with lime and parsley.
4, 2, 1 servings. Page 156

DELUXE SEAFOOD PIE
Scallops, prawns, mussels and crab sticks in a thyme-flavoured onion sauce with mushrooms and peas; cooked in a gratin dish with a mashed potato topping. Served here browned under a conventional griller.
4 servings. Page 174

SALMON CUTLETS WITH MARINATED CUCUMBER *Salmon with cucumber slices. Served with Green Mayonnaise Dressing; garnished with salad and lemon.*
4, 2, 1 servings. Page 157

PAELLA
Classic party dish of shellfish, spicy sausage, chicken, capsicum and tomatoes cooked with rice; garnished with parsley.
8 servings. Page 173

BOUILLABAISSE
Well-seasoned Mediterranean stew of mussels, lobster and fresh fish. Served here with crusty French bread.
8 servings. Page 174

SPICY CRUMBED CHICKEN
*Chicken coated with mustard, honey,
breadcrumbs and spices. Served with
salad greens, cucumber, tomato and lime.
4 servings. Page 185*

CREAMY CHICKEN BREASTS
*Chicken in a mildly curried asparagus and
spring onion sauce. Served here with rice;
garnished with chopped spring onion.
4 servings. Page 190*

CHICKEN À LA KING
*Vol-au-vents filled with cooked chicken,
onion, mushrooms, capsicum and pimiento
in a rich sauce; garnished with dill sprigs.
4 servings. Page 193*

DEVILLED CHICKEN
*Chicken pieces coated in a mustard
mayonnaise and breadcrumb mixture;
garnished with lemon wedges and parsley.
4 servings. Page 188*

CHICKEN LIVERS WITH TOMATO
SAUCE *Livers in a tomato-based sauce
seasoned with oregano and thyme. Served
here with rice; garnished with parsley.
4 servings. Page 189*

BARBECUED CHICKEN *(left) Chicken thighs cooked until tender in a
piquant onion and capsicum sauce; garnished with parsley. 4 servings.
Page 188.* **HONEY-SOY CHICKEN** *Chicken pieces with an oriental glaze.
Served with a medley of snow peas, carrot and mushrooms.
Accompanied here by rice with spring onion garnish. 4 servings. Page 187*

COQ AU VIN
Microwave version of the classic French dish of chicken pieces cooked in a red wine sauce with pickled pork or bacon, carrots, mushrooms, tomatoes and tiny onions; garnished with chopped parsley.
4, 2, 1 servings. Page 186

CHICKEN PAPRIKASH
Chicken pieces cooked in a tomato sauce flavoured with paprika. Served here with sour cream; garnished with chives.
4 servings. Page 186

LEMON CHICKEN
Chicken pieces in a piquant lemon and pimiento sauce and topped with crumbs; garnished with lemon and parsley.
4 servings. Page 186

CHICKEN CACCIATORE
Chicken pieces in a tomato sauce with olives, capsicum, herbs and onions. Served with spaghetti; garnished with basil.
4 servings. Page 185

CHICKEN MARENGO
Classic dish of chicken, prawns, onions and mushrooms in a tomato sauce with wine and rosemary; garnished with parsley.
4 servings. Page 185

QUICK BRAISED CHICKEN
A hearty stew of chicken pieces, potatoes, carrots, green beans and onion cooked in stock; garnished with chopped thyme.
4 servings. Page 187

CHICKEN KIEV
Boned, skinned chicken breasts rolled around a chilled butter filling, dipped in egg yolk mixture then coated with seasoned breadcrumbs. Served here with a green salad; garnished with lemon and parsley.
4 servings. Page 192

CHICKEN FRICASSÉE
Chunks of boneless chicken breasts with peas, carrots and green beans in a rich sauce. Served here with tagliatelle.
4 servings. Page 191

BROCCOLI-STUFFED CHICKEN BREASTS *Breadcrumbed chicken stuffed with ham, broccoli and cheese. Served with cheese sauce; garnished with parsley.*
6 servings. Page 192

POACHED CHICKEN WITH VEGETABLES *Chicken breasts with leeks, mushrooms and artichoke hearts; garnished here with basil leaves.*
4, 2, 1 servings. Page 191

CHICKEN BREASTS PARMESAN
Cheesy breadcrumb-coated chicken with an olive, basil and tomato sauce. Served here with tagliatelle; garnished with basil.
4 servings. Page 190

MEXICAN PANCAKES
Cooked chicken, onion, capsicum, tomato and corn in crêpes, with taco sauce and cheese; garnished with coriander and lime.
4 servings. Page 195

WHOLE STUFFED SPATCHCOCK *(left) Crumbed poussins with a savoury stuffing of mushrooms, zucchini, cheese and rice. Served with julienned vegetables.* 2 servings. Page 184. **SEASONED SPATCHCOCK** *Poussin halves with a garlic and herb stuffing. Served here with cherry tomatoes; garnished with basil.* 4, 2, 1 servings. Page 184

CHICKEN CRÊPES FLORENTINE
*Crêpes with spinach and cooked chicken,
topped with Parmesan-flavoured Basic
White Sauce; garnished here with chives.
4, 2, 1 servings. Page 194*

CHICKEN RATATOUILLE
*Cooked chicken, capsicum, zucchini,
tomatoes and herbs topped with melted
mozzarella cheese; garnished with parsley.
4 servings. Page 194*

CHEESY CHICKEN BREASTS
*Breadcrumbed chicken breasts with a
herbed cheese filling. Served with curly
endive, asparagus and cherry tomatoes.
8 servings. Page 191*

**CHICKEN ROLLS WITH CHEESE
FILLING** *Crumbed chicken fillets with
cheese, herbs and sun-dried tomatoes;
garnished here with basil and green salad.
4, 2, 1 servings. Page 189*

CHICKEN AND PASTA BAKE
*Chunks of chicken breast with peas and
noodles in a creamy sauce, topped with
crumbs; garnished here with parsley.
4 servings. Page 193*

DUCK BREASTS WITH APPLE AND GREEN PEPPERCORNS *(top)*
*Sliced duck breasts and apple. Served with a green peppercorn sauce;
garnished with parsley. 4 servings. Page 197.* **WALNUT CHICKEN**
*Chicken breasts with a honey and walnut coating. Served sliced with a
redcurrant sauce; garnished with parsley. 6 servings. Page 190*

TURKEY BREAST WITH CHESTNUT STUFFING *Turkey breast with a delicious stuffing of chestnuts, celery and sultanas; garnished with parsley.*
16 servings. Page 198

CURRIED CHICKEN THIGHS
Marinated chicken coated in breadcrumbs. Served with a curried yoghurt sauce; garnished with lime and mint.
4 servings. Page 189

APRICOT GLAZED DUCKLING
Duck glazed with mustard, apricot jam, soy sauce and ginger. Served here with vegetables; garnished with parsley.
4 servings. Page 196

DUCKLING WITH ORANGE SAUCE
Tender quarters of duck in a rich orange sauce flavoured with brandy and julienned orange rind; garnished with orange slices and a sprig of parsley. Accompanied here by tender-crisp snow peas.
4 servings. Page 196

DUCKLING WITH CHERRY SAUCE
Quarters of duck in a rich sauce of stock, red wine, garlic and canned cherries; garnished with sprigs of watercress.
4 servings. Page 197

DUCKLING WITH OLIVES AND ALMONDS *Duck quarters in a sauce of almond-stuffed olives, onions and sherry; garnished with lemon and coriander.*
4 servings. Page 197

UNDER 30 MINUTES

STEAK AU POIVRE
Succulent beef fillet steaks with a coating of crushed peppercorns and topped with a flavoursome brandy, red wine and cream sauce. Served here with sautéed julienned leeks.
4, 2, 1 servings. Page 207

BEEF STROGANOFF
Tender beef and mushrooms in a sour cream sauce. Served here with buttered noodles; garnished with chopped parsley.
6 servings. Page 209

STEAK FORESTIÈRE
Juicy beef fillet steaks with a mushroom, tomato and port sauce. Served here with green beans; garnished with watercress.
4 servings. Page 207

STEAK WITH MUSHROOMS AND ARTICHOKES *Beef fillet steaks well seasoned with marjoram. Served with vegetables cooked in a red wine sauce.*
4 servings. Page 207

DINNER BURGERS
Beef burgers topped with onion rings cooked in a red wine sauce. Served here with carrot and zucchini ribbons.
2 servings. Page 214

SURPRISE BURGERS
Pimiento, olive, and chilli sauce-filled burgers. Served here in buns with baby corn, salad greens and sliced tomato.
4, 2, 1 servings. Page 213

CHEESEBURGERS
Beef mince and grated cheese patties in a seasoned coating, topped with a lightly spiced mixture of onion rings and sliced mushrooms. Served here with toast triangles; garnished with parsley.
4 servings. Page 213.

KEEMA CURRY
*Beef mince, tomatoes, peas and capsicum
with garlic, ginger and spices. Served here
on rice; garnished with coriander.*
4 servings. Page 214

MEXICAN BEEF CASSEROLE
*Beef mince mixed with olives, corn kernels and a spicy sauce, then
layered with chopped tomatoes, corn chips and grated tasty cheese;
garnished with sliced black olives and sprigs of coriander.*
6 servings. Page 215

INDIVIDUAL MEAT LOAVES
*Seasoned beef, cheese and cucumber
shaped into loaves and topped with cheese;
garnished with salad and parsley sprigs.*
4, 2, 1 servings. Page 212

CHILLI CON CARNE
*A spicy chilli topped with sour cream,
grated cheese and coriander. Served
here with corn chips and taco sauce.*
6 servings. Page 215

STIR-FRIED PORK FILLET
*A traditional dish of pork fillet slices soaked in an oriental-style marinade
before cooking. Served with a selection of tender-crisp vegetables
in a butter and lemon sauce; garnished with spinach leaves.*
4 servings. Page 229

61

PORK WITH VEGETABLES
*Juicy pork schnitzels cooked until tender in stock and arranged with
lightly cooked asparagus, baby carrots and chicory. Served with a cream
sauce flavoured with spring onion, mustard and, if you like, brandy.*
4 servings. Page 229

HAM AND BEAN CASSEROLE
*A substantial casserole with smoked
ham cubes, haricot beans and vegetables
cooked in a herby chicken stock.*
6 servings. Page 233

VEAL MARSALA
*Veal steaks dipped in Marsala butter and
coated with breadcrumbs. Served here
with asparagus; garnished with parsley.*
4, 2, 1 servings. Page 226

VEAL WITH SPINACH
*Thin slices of veal steak in a seasoned
breadcrumb coating. Served with lemon-
flavoured spinach and cherry tomatoes.*
4 servings. Page 226

HASH BROWN PORK AND POTATOES
*Cubes of cooked roast pork combined with
onion, potatoes, eggs and cream. Served
here with carrots; garnished with parsley.*
4 servings. Page 228

LAMB NOISETTES WITH ORANGE
*Boneless loin chops on parsleyed toast with
an orange Béarnaise Sauce. Served here
with snow peas; garnished with rosemary.*
8 servings. Page 221

BACON-WRAPPED LAMB CHOPS
*Juicy boneless lamb loin chops with a fruity bread filling, wrapped in
bacon and cooked. Served here with green beans, new potatoes
sprinkled with chopped chives and Redcurrant and Orange Sauce.*
4 servings. Page 220

FRANKFURTER CASSEROLE
A ratatouille-style casserole of eggplant,
zucchini and capsicum, with added sliced
frankfurters and chick peas.
6 servings. Page 236

MEAT LOAF MILANESE
Seasoned beef mince mixed with red wine, breadcrumbs and fresh basil.
Served with new potatoes and green vegetables, and a tomato, wine and
basil sauce; garnished here with chopped parsley and lemon julienne.
6 servings. Page 212

FRANKFURTERS AND RED CABBAGE
Frankfurters, apples and shredded red
cabbage cooked with apple juice, sugar
and vinegar; garnished with watercress.
4 servings. Page 236

SAUSAGES WITH GLAZED ONIONS
Sausages and seasoned onions cooked with
soy sauce, sugar and herbs. Served here
with mashed potatoes and sliced zucchini.
4 servings. Page 235

ROAST FILLET OF BEEF WITH HERBS
Tender beef coated with a herbed mustard, black pepper and
breadcrumb mixture before being cooked to medium-rare. Served cut
into thin slices; garnished with whole radishes and basil leaves.
10 servings. Page 204

63

30–60 MINUTES

BEEF AND SNOW PEAS IN BLACK BEAN SAUCE *(left) Beef strips and snow peas with black bean and chilli; garnished with a spring onion curl.* 4 servings. Page 208. **STIR-FRIED BEEF IN OYSTER SAUCE** *Strips of rump steak with capsicum and spring onions with ginger, soy and oyster sauces; garnished here with coriander.* 4 servings. Page 208

SWEDISH MEATBALLS
Balls of minced meat, onion, cream and dill in a sour cream sauce. Served here with rice and carrots; garnished with dill. 6 servings. Page 231

SAVOURY RIBS
Pork spareribs cooked in a tangy tomato sauce with caraway seeds, sauerkraut and capsicum. Served here with salad greens. 4 servings. Page 232

PORK LOIN WITH GARLIC SAUCE
Boneless loin of pork cooked in seasoned stock with whole garlic; garnished with sprigs of watercress. 10 servings. Page 228

HAM STEAKS WITH ORANGE AND HONEY GLAZE *Ham with a tangy sauce. Served here with new potatoes; garnished with orange segments and parsley.* 2 servings. Page 233

SHEPHERD'S PIE
Traditional dish of minced lamb, tomatoes and mushrooms topped with potato; garnished here with a sprig of parsley. 6 servings. Page 223

ZESTY LEG OF LAMB
Leg of lamb brushed with a flavoursome glaze of chutney, mustard, garlic, vinegar and Worcestershire sauce during cooking. Served here with new potatoes and peas; garnished with a sprig of mint. 8 servings. Page 219

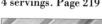

APRICOT-GLAZED RACK OF LAMB
A delicious glaze of apricot jam, lemon juice and tangy mustard gives this tender lamb roast its beautiful colour. Served with carrots glazed in the same mixture; garnished with watercress sprigs.
4 servings. Page 219

SAVOURY SAUSAGES
Chunks of spicy sausages with onions and green, yellow and red capsicums in a fennel-flavoured tomato sauce.
6 servings. Page 235

KNACKWURST AND POTATOES
Wurst and potatoes in a piquant onion sauce on a bed of curly endive with bacon; garnished with sliced baby beetroot.
4 servings. Page 235

OVER 1 HOUR

STUFFED CABBAGE
Cabbage leaves with a beef, rice and raisin filling. Served with a delicately spiced tomato sauce; garnished with parsley.
4 servings. Page 217

CORNED BEEF AND CABBAGE
A traditional, hearty dish of spiced corned beef with cabbage wedges and a mixture of sliced carrot, onions and celery.
6 servings. Page 206

SAVOURY TOPSIDE
Lean topside cooked in a tangy barbecue sauce. Served here with dill-topped potatoes and salad.
6 servings. Page 206

PASTA BOLOGNESE
Pasta shells and chopped vegetables in a hearty meat sauce, sprinkled here with Parmesan; garnished with parsley.
6 servings. Page 217

STEAK AND MUSHROOM PIE
Beef, mushrooms and onions cooked in a wine sauce with a conventionally cooked pastry crust. Served here with carrots.
8 servings. Page 210

OLD-FASHIONED POT ROAST
A classic combination of beef and chunky vegetables cooked in a rich wine stock until tender; garnished with parsley.
6 servings. Page 205

BEEF BOURGUIGNON
Cubes of beef with mushrooms, tiny onions, carrots and celery in a red wine sauce; garnished with a sprig of parsley.
4 servings. Page 209

STANDING RIB ROAST
A traditional succulent beef roast on the bone, seasoned with spices and herbs and cooked to medium-rare. Served here with steamed broccoli, carrot sticks and roast potatoes.
6 servings. Page 204

STEAK AND KIDNEY PUDDING
Fillet or rump steak, lamb kidneys and mushrooms in a rich gravy, cooked in a traditional suet pastry case.
4 servings. Page 210

BEEF CARBONNADE
A casserole of beef, bacon and onions cooked in beer. Served here with potatoes sprinkled with chopped parsley.
8 servings. Page 211

TRADITIONAL BEEF STEW
An old-fashioned dish of vegetables and beef cooked in tomato-flavoured beef stock with thyme and a bay leaf.
6 servings. Page 211

BEEF GOULASH
A hearty blend of beef, onions and capsicum in a tomato and paprika sauce. Delicious alone or with buttered noodles.
6 servings. Page 209

PARTY BURGERS
Well-seasoned sirloin steak burgers arranged on herb-dipped toast rounds with a selection of decorative toppings.
12 servings. Page 214

GLAZED HAM
Ham coated with an apple and mustard glaze. Served here with carrot strips and baby corn; garnished with watercress.
8 servings. Page 233

FREEZER-TO-TABLE POT ROAST
A convenient pot roast cooked with carrots and sliced swede in a seasoned orange sauce; garnished with a sprig of parsley.
12 servings. Page 205

PORK LOIN WITH APRICOT STUFFING *Boneless loin of pork surrounded by fruity stuffing. Served cut into thin slices; garnished with parsley.*
12 servings. Page 228

PORK STEW WITH LEEKS
A wholesome dish of boneless pork cubes, leeks, carrots and new potatoes, seasoned and cooked in its own juices.
6 servings. Page 232

PORK JAMBALAYA
A hearty casserole of pork cubes, rice, celery, spring onion and capsicums cooked in beef stock with Creole flavourings.
6 servings. Page 231

67

SPICY PORK TURNOVERS
Pork mince wrapped in cheesy cornmeal pastry. Served here with taco sauce and sour cream; garnished with coriander.
4 servings. Page 230

ROAST LOIN OF VEAL WITH PURÉE OF SWEDE *A tender veal roast with a garlicky swede purée. Served here with zucchini; garnished with watercress.*
8 servings. Page 225

PARTY VEAL ROAST *(top) Lean veal breast stuffed with spinach, cheese and canned pimientos. Served here with Capsicum Medley. 12 servings. Page 224.* **STUFFED SHOULDER OF VEAL** *Boned veal roast with a stuffing of spinach-filled ravioli, diced ham and cheese, cooked in dry white wine and stock; garnished with parsley. 10 servings. Page 225*

HERBED VEAL AND RICE
Shin of veal, vegetables and rice in a tomato and wine sauce with fresh herbs; garnished with a sprig of parsley.
4 servings. Page 226

VEAL PROVENÇALE
Seasoned veal cubes, onions, capsicums and olives in a herbed sauce. Served here with pasta tossed with chopped parsley.
4 servings. Page 227

VEAL RAGOÛT
Veal cubes, onions, mushrooms, celery and carrot in a cream sauce. Served here with herbed rice; garnished with parsley.
4 servings. Page 227

LAMB CURRY
Indian-style dish of tender lamb cubes cooked in a spicy fruit and vegetable sauce with toasted almonds and coriander leaves. Served here with rice; garnished with parsley. Accompanied by mango chutney.
4 servings. Page 222

MOROCCAN LAMB WITH COUSCOUS
Savoury couscous topped with a mixture of lamb cubes, chick peas and vegetables cooked in a richly spiced tomato sauce.
6 servings. Page 222

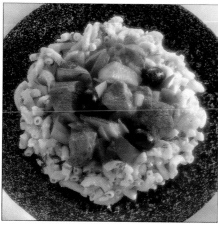

LAMB STEW WITH FETA
Traditional mixture of lamb, zucchini and olives cooked in tomatoes and wine. Served over cheesy macaroni with chopped dill.
6 servings. Page 223

MARINATED CUTLETS WITH MINTED PEAS *Lamb cutlets marinated in mustard, garlic, mint and apple jelly. Served with peas; garnished with mint.*
4, 2, 1 servings. Page 220

LAMB PILAF
Vegetables, rice and cubes of cooked roast lamb in a curried stock. Served with a yoghurt sauce; garnished with mint.
8 servings. Page 219

MOUSSAKA
Layered eggplant slices, herbed minced lamb, tomato and feta cheese topped with a cheese sauce; garnished with coriander.
6 servings. Page 223

CITRUS THAI KEBABS
Cubes of lamb soaked in a spicy minted lemon and lime juice marinade and cooked with chunks of fresh pawpaw and green capsicum on wooden skewers. Served on a bed of Hot Cooked Rice.
4 servings. Page 221

UNDER 30 MINUTES

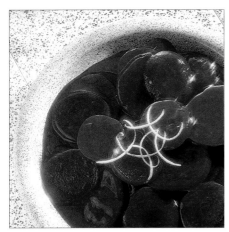

PICKLED BEETROOT
*An easy dish of canned beetroot cooked in
a tangy sweet and sour sauce. Served
hot; garnished with orange julienne.*
4, 2, 1 servings. Page 256

NEAPOLITAN BROCCOLI
*Broccoli flowerets cooked with olives,
capers, capsicums, garlic and spring
onions; garnished with flaked almonds.*
4 servings. Page 257

ASPARAGUS WITH CELERY AND WALNUTS *(top) Asparagus
spears and celery sticks cooked with garlic until tender-crisp then
tossed with lightly toasted walnuts.* 4 servings. Page 254. **ASPARAGUS
BUNDLES** *Asparagus spears with spring onion tie in a buttery
pimiento, lemon and spring onion sauce.* 4, 2, 1 servings. Page 254

CREAMED CORN WITH CAPSICUM
*Fresh or canned corn kernels with slices of
green capsicum, onion and tomato in a
creamy sauce flavoured with oregano.*
4 servings. Page 263.

**BROAD BEANS WITH BUTTERED
BREADCRUMBS** *Frozen broad beans
with Parmesan cheese added; sprinkled
with crisply browned breadcrumbs.*
4, 2, 1 servings. Page 255

PETIT POIS À LA FRANÇAISE
*Frozen peas cooked with diced bacon,
shredded lettuce and chopped onion;
garnished with finely chopped parsley.*
6 servings. Page 269

BRUSSELS SPROUTS WITH ONIONS
Tiny onions and Brussels sprouts cooked in bacon drippings and stock then tossed with crisply cooked diced bacon.
6 servings. Page 258

GREEN BEANS WITH PEANUT SAUCE
Cooked beans tossed in a spicy sauce with ginger, peanut butter and red capsicum; garnished with coriander and capsicum.
4, 2, 1 servings. Page 255

SUCCOTASH
A favourite American combination of corn kernels, broad beans, diced potatoes and diced bacon with tomatoes and capsicum.
4 servings. Page 263

GINGERED CARROTS
Fine strips of carrot cooked with orange juice, soy sauce, ginger and spring onions; garnished with orange julienne.
4 servings. Page 259

GLAZED CARROTS
Sliced carrots cooked in stock and sugar until tender-crisp then glazed with butter; garnished with a sprig of parsley.
4 servings. Page 260

CAPSICUM BUTTER *(top) Finely chopped green capsicum, crushed black peppercorns and cayenne pepper in melted butter.* **FRESH HERB BUTTER** *(centre) Chopped fresh herbs in melted butter and lemon juice.* **GOLDEN SPICED BUTTER** *Curry powder and French mustard in melted butter. Each serving enough for 4 cobs of corn.* Page 263

CAULIFLOWER WITH MINTED SPINACH *(left) Cauliflower flowerets cooked in a spiced spinach mixture with yoghurt added; garnished with mint. 6 servings. Page 261.* **CAULIFLOWER WITH LEMON AND DILL SAUCE** *Whole cauliflower served with a creamy sauce flavoured with lemon and dill; garnished with extra lemon and dill. 8 servings. Page 260*

SZECHUAN EGGPLANT
Strips of eggplant in a spicy-hot oriental sauce with sliced spring onion added; garnished with a spring onion curl. 4 servings. Page 264

OKRA, HAM AND TOMATOES
Diced ham and onion with whole okra cooked in a spicy tomato sauce. Served here over rice; garnished with lemon slices. 4 main-course servings. Page 267

STEWED FRESH TOMATOES
Peeled tomato wedges and sliced spring onions flavoured with garlic salt; garnished here with spring onion curls. 6 servings. Page 274

GREEN TOMATO CURRY
Wedges of green tomato with apple slices and finely chopped onion cooked with a mixture of curry and chilli powders. 4 servings. Page 274

MUSHROOMS À LA GRECQUE
Whole button mushrooms with herbed vinegar, garlic, and chunks of tomato and onion; garnished with chopped parsley. 6 servings. Page 266

CREAMED ONIONS
Pearl onions cooked in a sauce flavoured with nutmeg; sprinkled here with paprika and garnished with chopped chives. 8 servings. Page 268

PEAS WITH ONIONS AND BACON
Pearl onions and frozen peas cooked in bacon drippings for extra flavour then sprinkled with crisply cooked diced bacon. 4 servings. Page 269

LEMON PEAS
*A simple dish of tender peas lightly cooked
with grated lemon rind and butter;
garnished with lemon slices and mint.*
4, 2, 1 servings. Page 269

MASHED POTATOES
*Cooked potatoes seasoned and beaten with
butter and cream then cooked again before
serving; garnished with chopped chives.*
4 servings. Page 271

SPRING VEGETABLES WITH LEMON AND CHIVE BUTTER
*(left) Zesty butter is spooned over this seasonal selection of tender-
crisp vegetables.* 6 servings. Page 277. **NEW POTATOES WITH
BUTTER AND CHIVES** *An elegant dish of small new potatoes with
chive butter; garnished here with chives.* 4, 2, 1 servings. Page 270

BROCCOLI WITH SESAME SAUCE
*Broccoli cooked until tender-crisp. Served
cold with a sauce of toasted sesame seeds,
spring onions, garlic and soy sauce.*
4 servings. Page 257

COUNTRY-STYLE POTATOES
*Diced potatoes cooked with sliced onion in
bacon drippings, with cooked diced bacon
added; garnished with chopped parsley.*
4 servings. Page 271

CURRIED POTATOES WITH PEAS
*Potato chunks and peas cooked in a
tomato sauce spiced with ginger, chilli and
coriander; garnished with a chilli flower.*
6 servings. Page 272

30–60 MINUTES

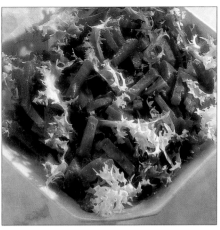

**EGGPLANT BROCHETTES WITH
SATAY SAUCE** *Baby eggplant cooked on
skewers. Served with a peanut sauce;
garnished with tomatoes and parsley.*
4 servings. Page 265

FRESH BEETROOT WITH ENDIVE
*Curly endive with tender strips of beetroot
coated in a tangy dressing of olive oil, red
wine vinegar, mustard and oregano.*
6 servings. Page 256

BROCCOLI MORNAY
*Tender-crisp broccoli coated in a cheese
sauce with a hint of mustard and sprinkled
with an onion and breadcrumb topping.*
4 servings. Page 257

SCALLOPED CABBAGE
*Shredded cabbage and sliced onions
with cream added, then topped with
breadcrumbs; garnished here with dill.*
8 servings. Page 258

CHICORY WITH CHEESE SAUCE *(top) Chicory with a rich sauce; garnished
here with parsley.* 4 servings. Page 262. **BRAISED CHICORY** *(bottom)
Chicory cooked in herbed stock.* 4, 2, 1 servings. Page 262. **CARROT AND
POTATO PANCAKES** *Grated carrot and potato cakes. Served here with
Apple Purée and sour cream; garnished with dill.* 4 servings. Page 260

PIQUANT RED CABBAGE
*Brown sugar and red wine vinegar give
red cabbage a distinctive flavour;
garnished with apple slices and parsley.*
8 servings. Page 259

CELERIAC PURÉE
Celeriac and potato cooked in stock then puréed with butter, cream and seasonings; garnished with a sprig of parsley.
6 servings. Page 261

STUFFED ONIONS
Cooked whole onions filled with celery, red capsicum, onion and breadcrumbs; garnished here with parsley.
4, 2, 1 servings. Page 268

SWEET AND SOUR ONIONS
Sliced onions cooked in stock, red wine and vinegar until glazed; garnished here with a scattering of parsley.
8 servings. Page 268

LEEKS WITH HAM IN CHEESE SAUCE
Leeks cooked in stock then wrapped with ham. Served in a creamy sauce; garnished here with parsley and curly endive.
4, 2, 1 servings. Page 265

BRUSSELS SPROUTS WITH CHESTNUTS *A hearty side dish of tender Brussels sprouts cooked in stock with butter and whole chestnuts.*
4, 2, 1 servings. Page 258

POTATOES AU GRATIN
Classic dish of sliced potatoes topped with cheese, onion and seasoned breadcrumbs; garnished here with parsley.
8 servings. Page 270

STUFFED POTATOES ORIENTALE *(left) Baked potatoes with a Chinese-style vegetable filling; garnished here with spring onion curls.*
4, 2, 1 servings. Page 271. **ORIENTAL MUSHROOMS** *Marinated pork with mushrooms, snow peas and tomato strips in ginger and soy sauce; garnished with parsley.* 4 main-course servings. Page 266

CREAMED SPINACH
Cooked spinach in a lightly seasoned white sauce. Served here drizzled with sauce; garnished with slices of lemon.
8 servings. Page 273

30–60 MINUTES

GOLDEN MASHED VEGETABLES
Mashed pumpkin and swede with orange liqueur, orange rind and cinnamon; garnished with orange julienne and parsley.
8 servings. Page 276

RATATOUILLE
A traditional Mediterranean vegetable mixture of capsicum, eggplant, zucchini and tomatoes; garnished with basil.
8 servings. Page 277

COMBINATION VEGETABLES
An attractive selection of sliced carrots, broccoli flowerets and whole button mushrooms cooked until tender then combined with strips of red capsicum and a soy sauce and spring onion sauce.
8 servings. Page 276

GARDEN MEDLEY
A colourful combination of zucchini, red capsicum, eggplant, potatoes, onions and tomato; garnished with a basil sprig.
6 servings. Page 276

SPAGHETTI SQUASH WITH MEAT SAUCE *Sausage meat in a herb-seasoned capsicum and tomato sauce tops tender strands of cooked spaghetti squash.*
4 servings. Page 274

BRAISED BEANS WITH TOMATOES AND ONIONS *A flavourful mixture of whole green beans and tomato and onion slices; sprinkled with Parmesan cheese.*
4 servings. Page 254

TWICE-BAKED SWEET POTATOES
A mixture of cooked sweet potato, yoghurt and chilli powder in sweet potato shells; garnished here with chopped parsley.
4, 2, 1 servings. Page 272

PUMPKIN BAKE
Pumpkin mashed with cream, butter and spice then cooked with a crumb and walnut topping; garnished here with parsley.
10 servings. Page 272

MARINATED OKRA
Lightly cooked okra marinated in oil, vinegar, mustard, sugar, thyme and crushed chillies; garnished with parsley.
4 servings. Page 267

ZUCCHINI WITH SUN-DRIED TOMATOES AND PINE NUTS *Zucchini strips cooked with pine nuts, basil and sun-dried tomatoes; garnished with basil.*
4 servings. Page 275

STUFFED ZUCCHINI
Zucchini halves filled with capsicum, tomato, breadcrumbs and Parmesan; garnished with basil and lemon.
2 servings. Page 275

EGGPLANT WITH TABOULEH (top) *Eggplant halves filled with a minted burghul mixture; garnished with lemon and mint.* 4 main-course servings. Page 264. **SPINACH GNOCCHI WITH BUTTER AND PARMESAN** *Italian dish of spinach and ricotta ovals with melted butter and Parmesan cheese; garnished here with parsley.* 8 servings. Page 273

UNDER 30 MINUTES

30–60 MINUTES

SPINACH SALAD WITH HOT BACON DRESSING *English spinach leaves and red onion slices tossed in a tangy mustard dressing and sprinkled with diced bacon.* 4, 2, 1 servings. Page 278

WARM SALAD OF ROCKET AND CORN *Shredded rocket with corn kernels and sliced onion; garnished with avocado slices and crisply cooked diced bacon.* 8 servings. Page 279

OLD-FASHIONED CHICKEN SALAD *Tender chicken breast chunks in a mayonnaise dressing with celery, onion and pimiento; garnished here with lettuce.* 4, 2, 1 main-course servings. Page 282

CHICKEN CLUB SALAD *Thyme-flavoured chicken breasts sliced and served with crisp bacon, tomato slices, lettuce and toast triangles.* 2 main-course servings. Page 282

ANTIPASTO SALAD *(top) Vegetables, salami and cheese in Vinaigrette Dressing.* 6 main-course servings. Page 283. **CAPSICUM SALAD** *(bottom) Capsicums, onion and olives with feta cheese and dressing.* 6 servings. Page 279. **CLASSIC POTATO SALAD** *Potatoes, celery and egg in mayonnaise; garnished here with parsley.* 6 servings. Page 281

DELICATESSEN SALAD *Potatoes, bacon, celery and onion in a tangy dressing. Served with salad greens, sliced cold meats and strips of cheese.* 6 main-course servings. Page 283

**WARM SALAD OF ARTICHOKE
HEARTS AND CHERRY TOMATOES**
*Artichoke hearts and tomatoes in tarragon
and wine sauce; garnished here with dill.*
6 servings. Page 279

THAI-STYLE BEEF AND NOODLE SALAD *(left) An imaginative dish
of beef with red capsicum, noodles and cashews in an oriental dressing.
4 main-course servings. Page 283.* **PRAWN AND SNOW PEA SALAD**
*Prawns, snow peas, spring onions, red capsicum and baby corn cooked
in wine then seasoned with lemon and dill. 4 servings. Page 284*

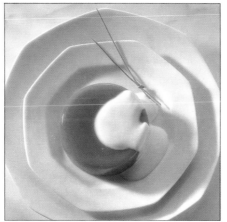

VEGETABLE AND PASTA SALAD
*A hearty combination of fresh vegetables,
cubes of cheese and farfelle (bow tie pasta)
in a well-seasoned dressing.*
6 main-course servings. Page 280

TOMATO ASPIC
*A simple, chilled tomato mould spiced with
Tabasco sauce; garnished with natural
low-fat yoghurt and a sheaf of chives.*
4, 2, 1 servings. Page 281

CHICKEN AND POTATO SALAD
*Chicken with potatoes, red onion, yellow
capsicum and black olives in a creamy
dressing; garnished here with basil.*
6 main-course servings. Page 282

PRAWN SALAD SUPREME
*Prawns, quartered new potatoes, green
beans, chick peas, sliced capsicum and
olives tossed with Zesty Mayonnaise.*
6 servings. Page 284

HIGH-FIBRE SALAD *(left) Colourful dish of beans and chick peas in
a seasoned dressing. 8 servings. Page 280.* **LENTILS VINAIGRETTE**
*(centre) Lentils and vegetables in a fresh herb dressing. 8 servings.
Page 280.* **WILD RICE SALAD** *Wild rice and long-grain rice with
spring onions, apple, celery, pine nuts and raisins. 8 servings. Page 281*

SPAGHETTI WITH SPICY MEAT SAUCE *A tomato-based beef mince sauce with herbs, red wine and vegetables served over cooked spaghetti.*
4, 2, 1 servings. Page 288

PENNE WITH DOUBLE-CHEESE SAUCE *Sliced onions, capsicums and olives tossed with mozzarella and Cheddar cheeses, parsley and pasta.*
4 servings. Page 288

CHEESE TORTELLINI WITH BROCCOLI AND PINE NUTS
A hearty dish of cheese-filled tortellini and broccoli cooked with crushed dried chillies, garlic and pine nuts for added flavour, then tossed with grated Parmesan cheese.
8 servings. Page 289

TAGLIATELLE WITH BACON, MUSHROOMS AND PEAS *Pasta tossed with a creamy spring onion, mushroom and pea sauce, with bacon and Parmesan.*
4 servings. Page 288

MADE-IN-MINUTES SPAGHETTI SAUCE *(left) A mixture of minced beef, mushrooms in a tomato sauce seasoned with basil and thyme; garnished here with a sprig of basil.* 6 cups. Page 290. **CREAMY TOMATO SAUCE** *A tomato-based sauce with herbs, crushed garlic and a touch of cream; garnished here with parsley.* 2 cups. Page 291

CHEESE-FILLED SHELLS
Large pasta shells filled with a mixture of ricotta, mozzarella and Parmesan cheeses, egg and parsley, then cooked in a tomato sauce; garnished with chopped parsley and grated Parmesan cheese.
4 servings. Page 290

CHICKEN AND VEGETABLE PASTA
Farfelle (bow tie pasta) combined with strips of chicken breast and vegetables cooked in an oriental-style sauce.
4 servings. Page 289

SAVOURY RICE
Rice cooked in chicken stock with onion and capsicum then combined with cheese and sour cream; garnished with parsley.
4, 2, 1 servings. Page 293

MILANESE-STYLE RISOTTO
Rice, garlic and onion cooked in saffron-flavoured stock then mixed with peas and Parmesan cheese; garnished with basil.
4 servings. Page 293

FETTUCCINE PRIMAVERA
A colourful combination of vegetables – leeks, broccoli, mushrooms, zucchini, capsicums, carrots and tomatoes – mixed with a creamy white sauce, grated cheese and conventionally cooked fettuccine.
4 servings. Page 289

30—60 MINUTES

RED BEANS AND RICE
*Rice topped with red kidney beans, celery
and onion in a spicy sauce, sprinkled with
crisp diced bacon; garnished with parsley.*
4 servings. Page 293

ORIENTAL RICE WITH PORK
*Cubes of tender boneless pork loin cooked with onion, celery, red
capsicum and rice, then flavoured with a soy sauce and ginger sauce;
accompanied here with a bowl of soy sauce.*
4 servings. Page 292

INDIAN PILAF
*Spiced rice, chopped coriander and raisins
topped with golden-brown slivered
almonds; garnished with coriander.*
4 servings. Page 294

ARROZ CON POLLO
*Chicken pieces coated in flour and browned in oil, then cooked with
turmeric-flavoured rice, smoked ham, onion, celery and capsicum;
garnished with strips of canned pimiento and parsley leaves.*
4, 2, 1 servings. Page 292

BURGHUL PILAF
*Cracked wheat softened in stock then
mixed with capsicums, mushrooms, garlic
and basil; garnished here with basil leaves.*
8 servings. Page 295

BARLEY WITH DRIED MUSHROOMS
A savoury combination of pearl barley and mushroom pieces cooked until tender in beef stock; garnished with a parsley sprig.
4 servings. Page 295

SAUSAGE, RICE AND BEANS
Pork sausages, cooked rice, kidney beans, onions and tomatoes with oregano and garlic; garnished with basil leaves.
4 servings. Page 292

CANNELLONI MILANESE *(top) Meat with herbs, currants and pine nuts in cannelloni tubes. Served here with Basic White Sauce and Parmesan; garnished with basil.* 4 servings. Page 291. **WILD RICE AND MUSHROOM PILAF** *Wild rice cooked in stock then combined with onion, mushrooms and seasoning; garnished with coriander.* 4 servings. Page 294

POLENTA WITH MEAT SAUCE
Seasoned cornmeal and mozzarella cheese shaped and cooked with Made-in-Minutes Spaghetti Sauce; garnished with basil.
4 servings. Page 295

LASAGNA
Layers of meat sauce, pasta and cheese, topped with mozzarella and Parmesan cheeses. Served here with salad greens.
10 servings. Page 290

CANNELLONI WITH SPINACH AND MUSHROOMS *Cannelloni with vegetable filling. Served here with Creamy Tomato Sauce; garnished with parsley.*
4 servings. Page 291

CHILLI BUNS
Beef mince, onion, capsicum and celery in a chilli and tomato sauce on hamburger buns; garnished here with celery leaves.
4 servings. Page 305

EASY BEEF TORTILLAS
Savoury beef mince in a spicy tomato sauce heaped on tortillas. Served here with grated cheese, sour cream and taco sauce.
4 servings. Page 304

PORK SCHNITZEL ROLLS
Breadcrumbed pork topped with barbecue sauce and coleslaw in a hamburger bun; garnished here with sprigs of watercress.
4 servings. Page 303

SMOKED CHICKEN AND CHEESE ON CROISSANTS *Croissants with mustard, smoked chicken, tomato and Swiss cheese; garnished here with salad greens.*
4 servings. Page 299

BEEF AND BRIE SIZZLER
Tarragon and flavoured butter on bread with hot roast beef and Brie. Served here with cherry tomatoes and tarragon.
4 servings. Page 303

WARM VEGETABLE SALAD IN PITA *(top) Crisp onion, celery, carrot, capsicum and mushrooms with melted cheese in pita breads; garnished here with parsley.* 4, 2, 1 servings. Page 301. **PITA POCKETS WITH SOUVLAKI** *Sliced lamb with piquant vegetables and feta cheese in toasted pita breads.* 4 servings. Page 302

DESIGNER BAGELS
Warmed bagel halves topped with a choice of: orange julienne with Orange Butter; black olives, sun-dried tomatoes and basil with ricotta cheese; capsicum strips with Smoked Salmon and Chive Spread. Makes 12 bagel halves. Page 301

MOZZARELLA BREAD
French bread filled with cheese, pimiento-stuffed olives, prosciutto and spring onions; garnished here with salad greens. 8 servings. Page 306

CHEESY GARLIC BREAD
This popular accompaniment to Italian food has oregano and mozzarella cheese added. Served here with salad greens. 6 pieces. Page 306

HOT TUNA MUFFINS
Tuna in a piquant cream-cheese mixture topped with melted cheese on toasted muffins. Served here with salad greens. 4 servings. Page 301

CHICKEN CLUB SANDWICHES
A filling double sandwich of chicken coated with stuffing mix, with bacon, lettuce and tomatoes in wholemeal toast. 4 servings. Page 300

REUBEN SANDWICHES
Corned beef, sauerkraut and Swiss cheese on rye with Thousand Island dressing; garnished with dill pickles and parsley. 4, 2, 1 servings. Page 302

OPEN TURKEY SANDWICHES WITH GRAVY *Thinly sliced cooked turkey on wholemeal toast with piping hot gravy; garnished here with a parsley sprig. 2 servings. Page 299*

CALZONE
Italian-style folded pizzas with a choice of hearty, tasty fillings; garnished here with radicchio leaves and parsley. 2 servings. Page 308

30–60 MINUTES

CHICKEN FAJITAS
*Chicken and capsicum in pita bread with
Guacamole, sour cream, cheese and Pico
de Gallo; garnished with parsley.*
4 servings. Page 300

SLICED STEAK SANDWICHES
*Slices of rump steak topped with capsicum,
onion and melted cheese in toasted French
bread; garnished here with parsley.*
4, 2, 1 servings. Page 303

TOASTED SANDWICHES WITH CAMEMBERT AND PEARS *(top) Unusual
combination of Camembert cheese and fresh pear in white bread, browned
and cut into quarters; garnished with pear slices and mint.* 4 servings. Page 306.
CROQUE MONSIEUR *A classic ham and Swiss cheese toasted sandwich.
Served here with salad greens.* 4, 2, 1 servings. Page 305

MEATBALL ROLLS
*Garlic and mushroom flavoured meatballs
in a tasty tomato sauce. Served on toasted
crusty rolls; garnished with parsley.*
4 servings. Page 305

FOUR SEASONS PIZZA
*Artichoke hearts, prosciutto, tomatoes
and canned pimientos top pesto sauce or a
layer of dried basil on a pizza base.*
4 servings. Page 308

MEDITERRANEAN PIZZA
*Sliced onion and dried herbs with tangy
crumbled goat cheese or feta cheese create
an original topping on a pizza dough base.*
4 servings. Page 308

CHERRIES IN RED WINE
Fresh stoned cherries or canned cherries cooked in a wine sauce flavoured with redcurrant jelly and cinnamon, then thickened. Served here with ice cream; decorated with a sprig of mint.
6 servings. Page 317

POACHED PEARS WITH CHOCOLATE SAUCE *Poached pear 'fans'. Served with a rich chocolate sauce; decorated here with mint and a feathering of cream.*
4 servings. Page 319

GLAZED APPLE RINGS
Fluted apple rings gently poached in apple juice with brown sugar, spices and lemon rind; decorated here with a sprig of mint.
4 servings. Page 315

GLAZED BANANAS
Banana pieces and orange segments in a cinnamon-flavoured sugar and butter glaze with pecan nuts and orange julienne.
4 servings. Page 317

DRIED FRUIT COMPOTE
Dried apricots, prunes and figs cooked with glacé cherries in a spiced sauce; decorated with orange julienne.
8 servings. Page 324

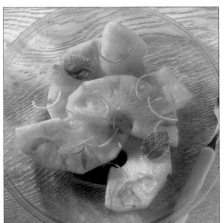

SPICED PINEAPPLE
Ground ginger or cinnamon flavour these sugar-glazed pineapple slices; decorated with lime julienne and mint leaves.
4 servings. Page 320

RED FRUIT COMPOTE
A colourful dish of mixed fresh berries and canned cherries in a sauce flavoured with orange liqueur; decorated with kiwifruit.
8 servings. Page 321

APPLE AND WALNUT CRUMBLE
A spiced walnut, flour and sugar topping over apples. Served here with whipped cream; decorated with apple and mint.
8 servings. Page 316

APPLE CARAMEL DESSERT
Lightly spiced pastry base topped with decoratively arranged apple slices cooked in a rich caramel sauce.
6 servings. Page 316

DELUXE BAKED APPLES
Seedless raisins, chopped walnuts and ground cinnamon mixed with butter or margarine fill hollowed-out cooking apples that are then cooked and basted with apple juice and golden syrup.
4, 2, 1 servings. Page 315

SPICED APPLE BETTY
Wholemeal breadcrumbs and apple sauce in a sweetly spiced pudding. Served here with cream; decorated with orange slices.
6 servings. Page 315

CHOCOLATE AND WALNUT PUDDING
A warm dessert made from a chocolate mixture topped with cocoa, brown sugar and walnuts; lightly dusted with icing sugar.
8 servings. Page 328

SYRUP SPONGE PUDDING
A classic sponge pudding flavoured with vanilla essence and lemon rind. Served here with extra warmed golden syrup.
4 servings. Page 330

CARAMEL PEARS IN STRAWBERRY SAUCE
Poached whole pears with a smooth strawberry purée. Served on individual dessert plates accompanied by a bowl of creamy caramel sauce; decorated here with mint sprigs.
4, 2, 1 servings. Page 319

RICH NOODLE PUDDING
Conventionally cooked noodles with cottage cheese, sour cream, dried apricots and sultanas topped with breadcrumbs.
8 servings. Page 328

ZABAGLIONE WITH CHERRIES
A rich Italian-style dessert of egg yolks beaten with sugar and kirsch or Marsala. Served over fresh or canned cherries.
4 servings. Page 317

PLUM KUCHEN
Fresh plum quarters arranged in a baking dish on a pizza-base dough and topped with a crumble mixture of brown sugar, butter and melba toast crumbs. Served here browned under a conventional griller.
6 servings. Page 320

WHITE CHOCOLATE MOUSSE
A chilled dessert made with melted white chocolate, eggs, vanilla essence and cream; decorated with raspberries and mint.
8 servings. Page 325

CHOCOLATE-DIPPED FRUIT
A selection of fresh ripe strawberries, grapes and orange segments dipped in melted milk or white chocolate.
14–30 pieces. Page 324

COCONUT CHOCOLATE CUPS
Ice cream served in chocolate and coconut cases. Served with Chocolate-dipped Fruit; decorated here with a mint sprig.
6 servings. Page 326

CREAMY RICE PUDDING
A favourite mix of milk, vanilla essence, spices and raisins. Served warm or chilled; garnished here with orange julienne.
6 servings. Page 329

OLD-FASHIONED BREAD AND BUTTER PUDDING *Cinnamon, nutmeg, cloves and vanilla essence add spice to this variation of a classic nursery dessert.*
10 servings. Page 329

ORANGE BREAD PUDDING
A new version of an old-fashioned idea with French bread, cream, orange juice and ground nutmeg for extra flavour.
10 servings. Page 329

OVER 1 HOUR

CHOCOLATE MOUSSE TORTE
A creamy chocolate mousse with a crunchy chocolate and nut base; decorated here with cream, nuts and Chocolate Rounds.
16 servings. Page 326

STRAWBERRIES 'NOUVELLES'
Halved strawberries arranged on a duo of chilled orange and chocolate custard sauces; decorated with mint.
6 servings. Page 322

PEARS WITH CHOCOLATE AND RASPBERRY SAUCE *An elegant dessert with a sumptuous sauce; decorated here with mint and a feathering of cream.*
6 servings. Page 318

CRÈME CARAMEL
A velvety smooth set custard flavoured with vanilla essence; served chilled with its own golden-brown caramel sauce.
4 servings. Page 331

LIGHT CHEESE RING WITH FRUIT (top) *A moulded sweetened cottage cheese and cream cheese mixture. Served with a selection of sliced fruit; decorated with strawberries and mint.* 8 servings. Page 324. **STRAWBERRY CHARLOTTE** *A rich mousse encased in savoiardi; decorated with cream and strawberries and tied with ribbon.* 12 servings. Page 323

CRÈME BRÛLÉE
Melted brown sugar forms a crisp topping over a chilled, rich custard base; decorated here with a strawberry fan.
4 servings. Page 331

VANILLA ICE CREAM
Classic ice cream. Served here with sliced oranges, strawberries and peeled kiwifruit; decorated with mint.
8 servings. Page 332

MANGO SORBET
Mango, lime juice and rum puréed then frozen with a sugar syrup; decorated with lime julienne.
4 servings. Page 332

KIWIFRUIT SORBET
A frozen purée of kiwifruit and lemon juice. Served here with kiwifruit slices; decorated with mint leaves.
4 servings. Page 332

ELEGANT POACHED PEACHES
Halved fresh peaches filled with amaretti crumbs. Served on a raspberry sauce; decorated with raspberries and mint.
4 servings. Page 318

INDIVIDUAL RASPBERRY CHEESECAKES *Puréed raspberries in a cream cheese mixture on a biscuit base; decorated with raspberry, purée and mint.*
8 servings. Page 321

RASPBERRY PARFAITS *(left) Layers of luscious raspberry mousse and whipped cream; decorated here with Chocolate Curls.* 6 servings. Page 321. **ICED LEMON SOUFFLÉS** *Delicately flavoured lemon custard whipped with cream and egg whites. Served frozen; decorated with lemon slices and mint leaves.* 8 servings. Page 323

RHUBARB RICE CREAM
A favourite rice pudding combined with rhubarb and made richer with a topping of whipped cream; decorated here with mint.
8 servings. Page 322

CHOCOLATE CHESTNUT CREAM
Chestnut purée and chocolate set with gelatine; decorated with piped whipped cream and Chocolate Curls.
12 servings. Page 328

NUTTY CHOCOLATE DELIGHT
Chopped nuts add crunch to this smooth rich dessert topped with whipped cream; decorated with ground cinnamon.
6 servings. Page 327

RICH CHOCOLATE MOUSSE
A simple mousse of dark chocolate and eggs flavoured with vanilla essence; decorated here with whipped cream.
4 servings. Page 326

TINY CHOCOLATE CONES
A chocolate and cream mixture piped into colourful foil cones and sprinkled with finely chopped macadamia nuts.
Makes 25 cones. Page 325

TIRAMISU
Layers of almond-flavoured cake, mascarpone, coffee and liqueur. Served chilled; decorated with a dusting of cocoa.
16 servings. Page 330

CHOCOLATE CREAM LOAF
Finely chopped pistachio nuts top this chilled dessert of cooking chocolate, egg yolks and whipped cream. Served sliced with a purée of raspberries; decorated here with Chocolate Leaves.
16 servings. Page 327

CHOCOLATE ALMOND DESSERT
Raisins plumped in almond liqueur with amaretti biscuits in a chocolate-covered dessert; decorated with almonds.
8 servings. Page 325

ORANGE CHIFFON PIE
Orange rind and orange and lemon juice are added to this classic pie; decorated with cream and orange julienne.
10 servings. Page 340

BANANA COCONUT TART
Sliced banana covered with a creamy vanilla filling in a Shortcrust Pastry Base; decorated with toasted coconut.
10 servings. Page 340

CRÈME PÂTISSIÈRE
A variety of plain and flavoured classic cream fillings served in pastry cases with complementary garnishes: Almond Filling and Mocha Filling (left); plain Crème Pâtissière (top); Orange Filling (right).
Makes 3 cups. Page 337

BISCUIT CRUMB CRUST
This versatile pie shell is shown here with a creamy chiffon filling decorated with whipped cream and mandarin segments.
Makes one 23-cm crumb crust. Page 335

PASTRY FLAN SHELL
A conventionally baked, classic shell for pies and tarts of all types; filled here with glazed fresh strawberries.
Makes one 23-cm–25-cm shell. Page 335

SHORTCRUST PASTRY BASE
A traditionally baked pastry shell shown with a Scalloped Edge; filled here with custard and gooseberries.
Makes one 23-cm base. Page 335

LEMON MERINGUE PIE
A classic all-time favourite of lemon-flavoured custard in a Shortcrust Pastry Base with an attractively swirled meringue topping; baked in a conventional oven until golden. Served warm or cooled slightly.
10 servings. Page 339

DELUXE APPLE PIE
An open pie filled with lightly spiced apples topped with a crumble mixture of brown sugar and rolled oats.
10 servings. Page 337

LIGHT LEMON AND ALMOND TART
A creamy lemon and almond filling in a Shortcrust Pastry Base, topped with cream, almonds and lemon julienne.
10 servings. Page 344

PEACHES AND CREAM PIE
Crème Pâtissière combined with peach jam in a Biscuit Crumb Crust, topped with fresh peach slices lightly poached in syrup.
10 servings. Page 339

SUMMER FRUIT TART
Creamy custard in a sweet biscuit crust topped with glazed strawberries, raspberries, blueberries and kiwifruit.
10 servings. Page 338

STICKY WALNUT TART
Syrup and walnuts combined with eggs and butter in a Shortcrust Pastry Base. Served chilled; decorated here with cream.
10 servings. Page 345

BLACK BOTTOM PIE
A Ginger Crumb Crust filled first with a layer of rich chocolate custard then topped with another layer of delicate rum-flavoured custard; decorated with piped whipped cream.
10 servings. Page 342

FRUIT AND NUT TARTLETS
A commercially made or home-made fruit mince filling with added diced apple, chopped walnuts, brown sugar and lemon juice in conventionally baked pastry cases topped with pastry holly leaves, hearts and stars.
10 servings. Page 345

AMARETTO PIE
Amaretto-flavoured filling in an amaretti crumb crust; decorated with whipped cream and toasted flaked almonds.
10 servings. Page 344

CHOCOLATE WALNUT PIE
A chocolate and walnut filling in a Shortcrust Pastry Base; decorated with whipped cream and walnut halves.
10 servings. Page 344

PECAN PIE
Butter, brown sugar and golden syrup in a pecan-topped pie shown in a Shortcrust Pastry Base with a Plaited Edge.
10 servings. Page 345

MINTY CHOCOLATE TART
The filling in this Chocolate Crumb Crust is a luscious whipped combination of creamy custard, coffee, crème de menthe liqueur and cream; decorated with Chocolate Curls.
10 servings. Page 342

COCONUT CREAM PIE
A toasted coconut crust holds a chiffon filling flavoured with coconut and almond; decorated with cream and coconut.
10 servings. Page 343

STRAWBERRY CHIFFON PIE
Strawberry slices top a light and creamy filling in a Biscuit Crumb Crust; decorated with a whole strawberry and glazed.
10 servings. Page 341

HIGHLAND CREAM PIE
A rich vanilla filling with whisky, whipped cream and egg whites in a Shortcrust Pastry Base shown with Leaf Edge.
10 servings. Page 341

RASPBERRY CUSTARD TART
Fresh raspberries top raspberry jam and Crème Pâtissière in a Shortcrust Pastry Base shown with Plaited Edge.
10 servings. Page 338

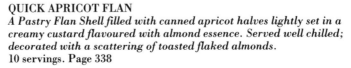

CHOCOLATE CREAM PIE
A generous layer of whipped cream tops a luscious chocolate filling in a Vanilla Crumb Crust; decorated with cream.
10 servings. Page 343

QUICK APRICOT FLAN
A Pastry Flan Shell filled with canned apricot halves lightly set in a creamy custard flavoured with almond essence. Served well chilled; decorated with a scattering of toasted flaked almonds.
10 servings. Page 338

UNDER 30 MINUTES

BANANA MUFFINS
A sugar, cinnamon and nutmeg topping complements these muffins flavoured with banana and grated orange rind.
Makes 12. Page 349

CARROT AND PINEAPPLE LOAF
Moist and munchy, this loaf combines crushed pineapple and grated carrot. Served here sliced with butter curls.
12 servings. Page 351

GINGER MUFFINS
Spicy muffins made with ground ginger, cinnamon, cloves, nutmeg, sour cream and golden syrup. Served here with butter.
Makes 12. Page 349

30–60 MINUTES

BERRY AND WALNUT LOAF
Plain sweet biscuit crumbs add flavour and extra texture to this fruit loaf made with blueberries, walnuts, orange rind and orange juice. Served here sliced with pats of butter.
12 servings. Page 350

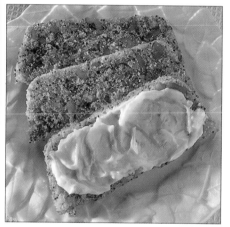

ZUCCHINI LOAF
Walnuts, poppy seeds and lemon rind are combined with grated zucchini for extra flavour. Served here with Orange Butter.
12 servings. Page 350

DATE AND NUT LOAF
A traditional snacktime favourite made simply in the microwave. Served here sliced with dainty butter curls.
12 servings. Page 350

GINGERBREAD
Sour cream and treacle make this traditional loaf deliciously moist. Served here sliced and spread with softened cream cheese; decorated with apple slices and a sprig of parsley.
12 servings. Page 351

OVER 1 HOUR

CREAMY CHEESECAKE
A classic cheesecake on a crumb crust;
topped here with sour cream decorated
with strawberries, raspberries and mint.
12 servings. Page 361

VICTORIA SPONGE
Basic sponge mixture baked in layers.
Served sandwiched with cream and jam;
decorated with a dusting of icing sugar.
12 servings. Page 352

CHOCOLATE AND AMARETTI CHEESECAKE *(top) Chocolate*
mousse-like cake with amaretti crust; decorated with piped whipped cream
and Chocolate Curls. 12 servings. Page 361. **CHOCOLATE PROFITEROLES**
Choux pastry puffs filled with Crème Pâtissière, drizzled with Chocolate
Glaze; decorated here with icing sugar. 12 profiteroles. Page 360

PINEAPPLE UPSIDE-DOWN CAKE
Popular and easy-to-make, this treat has canned pineapple rings and
maraschino cherries in a sugar and butter glaze topping a simple vanilla-
flavoured sponge cake. Served warm or chilled to serve later.
8 servings. Page 351

TWO-TONED LAYER CAKE
Chocolate mousse spread between four
cake layers, the whole cake then lavishly
covered with Chocolate Cream.
12 servings. Page 353

APRICOT CREAM ROULADE
Elaborate to look at yet deceptively simple to make, this light-as-a-feather sponge cake is rolled and filled with apricot jam then covered with decorative pipings of almond-flavoured whipped cream.
14 servings. Page 359

BLACK FOREST CAKE
Kirsch flavours this rich cake made from devil's food cake mix; decorated with whipped cream, cherries and chocolate.
12 servings. Page 356

CHOCOLATE CREAM SPONGE
Crème Pâtissière sandwiched between layers of sponge, topped with Chocolate Glaze and feathered Glacé Icing.
12 servings. Page 355

STRAWBERRY CREAM LAYER CAKE
Whipped cream flavoured with vanilla essence is combined with strawberries to fill and top a luscious three-layer cake.
8 servings. Page 354

BÛCHE DE NOËL
A traditional French Christmas 'log' of chocolate cake rolled with chilled chocolate mousse, covered with Chocolate Cream and marked to resemble bark; decorated here with icing sugar and a holly sprig.
14 servings. Page 357

CAKES

MARBLED CHOCOLATE RING
Devil's food cake mix encases a surprise filling of sweetened vanilla-flavoured cream cheese; cooked in a fluted ring mould and drizzled when cooled with Chocolate Glaze.
16 servings. Page 359

APPLE SPICE CAKE
A packet cake mix well spiced then topped with apple slices, a walnut crumble mixture and a drizzle of Glacé Icing.
6 servings. Page 354

WHITE CHOCOLATE AND STRAWBERRY GÂTEAU *Sponge layered with strawberries and White Chocolate Mousse; decorated with strawberries.*
12 servings. Page 358

SUNNY ORANGE LAYER CAKE
Canned mandarin segments top this orange cake filled with Lemon Butter and covered with Orange Whipped Cream.
10 servings. Page 353

CARROT CAKE
Ground cinnamon, allspice, nutmeg and ginger combine with sultanas, walnuts and grated carrots in this ever-popular cake; topped traditionally with Cream Cheese Frosting and extra walnuts.
10 servings. Page 352

BUTTERSCOTCH SQUARES
*Walnuts, desiccated coconut and dark
chocolate bits are added to the basic mix in
these flavour-packed slices.*
24 biscuits. Page 363

MINT CHOCOLATE SQUARES
*Plain sweet biscuit crumbs combine with
mint-flavoured chocolate and chopped
walnuts in these no-bake slices.*
24 biscuits. Page 362

CHOCOLATE MOUSSE BOMBE
*A rich, chocolate fudge packet cake mix, cooked and hollowed out
then lavishly filled with creamy chocolate mousse; beautifully decorated
with piped whipped cream rosettes and a fine dusting of cocoa.*
10 servings. Page 360

FUDGE BROWNIES
*Moist brownies enriched with eggs and
topped with chocolate and chopped
walnuts; chilled, after cooking, until firm.*
24 brownies. Page 362

CREAM CHEESE BROWNIES *(left) Softened cream cheese sweetened
and flavoured with almond essence creates a marbled design in a fudge
brownie mixture.* 16 brownies. Page 362. **ROCKY ROAD BROWNIES**
*Miniature marshmallows, dark chocolate bits and chopped walnuts top
a rich traditional brownie mixture.* 16 brownies. Page 363

BISCUITS

COCONUT ROUNDS
Delicate toasted coconut biscuits flavoured with orange rind; attractively decorated when cool with melted chocolate.
30 biscuits. Page 364

LEMON TUILES
Light-as-a feather biscuits flavoured with lemon rind and almond essence, and sprinkled liberally with flaked almonds.
30 biscuits. Page 364

FRUIT AND NUT BARS
Dried apricots, raisins, prunes, almonds and walnuts covered with melted dark chocolate then chilled until firm.
16 biscuits. Page 368

MEXICAN WEDDING BISCUITS
Light and delicate crescent-shaped walnut biscuits dusted when cool with a thick layer of icing sugar until covered.
24 biscuits. Page 365

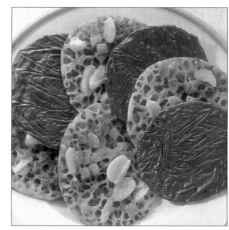

ALMOND SHORTBREAD
Vanilla and almond essences flavour this classic, beautifully light shortbread which is simplicity itself to bake in the microwave; attractively topped with toasted flaked almonds before cooking.
8 wedges. Page 363

FLORENTINES
Thin chewy wafers with flaked almonds and glacé fruit or mixed peel; cooled then coated on one side with melted chocolate.
24 biscuits. Page 365

MAPLE SNAPS
Buttery walnut biscuits flavoured with a combination of maple and golden syrups and cooked until lightly browned.
24 biscuits. Page 365

CHOCOLATE NUT CRISPS
Sweetened and lightly spiced biscuits flavoured with walnuts and topped with extra walnuts and dark chocolate bits.
30 biscuits. Page 368

VIENNESE MELTAWAYS *(top) Melt-in-the-mouth biscuits made with ground almonds; some dusted here with icing sugar, others with cocoa. 36 biscuits. Page 364.* **CARAMEL PECAN BARS** *Vanilla-flavoured biscuit base topped with pecan halves and creamy caramel then drizzled with melted chocolate when cool. 24 biscuits. Page 368*

CHOCOLATE MARSHMALLOW FUDGE
Squares of rich fudge with added dark and milk chocolate, chopped walnuts and melted marshmallows.
36 pieces. Page 371

MINT IMPERIALS
White, green and pink peppermint fondant; shown here half-dipped into melted chocolate for added interest.
36 pieces. Page 369

PEANUT BRITTLE
A classic combination of roasted peanuts and crunchy toffee made from golden syrup, water, sugar and butter.
Makes 500 g. Page 370

SWEETS

GOLDEN WALNUT DROPS
Confectionery based on the delicious combination of walnuts and vanilla essence, sweetened with brown sugar.
42 pieces. Page 369

PISTACHIO BITES
Vanilla essence and chopped pistachios flavour layers of creamy white chocolate in this melt-in-the-mouth confectionery.
32 pieces. Page 372

CHOCOLATE AND CHERRY FUDGE SLICES *Plump maraschino cherries in a chocolate fudge roll, coated with melted caramel and chopped walnuts.*
36 pieces. Page 371

BUTTER CARAMELS
Individually wrapped chewy caramels made simply from cream, caster sugar, golden syrup, butter and vanilla essence.
64 pieces. Page 370

COCONUT HAYSTACKS
Lightly toasted desiccated coconut mixed with melted dark cooking chocolate then shaped to resemble haystacks.
20 pieces. Page 372

CHOCOLATE CHERRY CUPS *(top) Tiny chocolate cups filled with a cream and orange liqueur mixture, each topped with a maraschino cherry on a stalk.* 36 cups. Page 370. **CHOCOLATE TRUFFLES** *Melted dark cooking chocolate with added butter, cream and almond essence; attractively piped into gold foil cases.* 30 truffles. Page 371

PEACH SAUCE
Simple purée of peaches flavoured with almond essence and nutmeg. Served here with raspberries; decorated with mint.
Makes 1 cup. Page 383

BRANDIED STRAWBERRY SAUCE
Strawberries and brandy added to melted redcurrant jelly. Served here chilled over ice cream; decorated with mint.
Makes 2½ cups. Page 382

FUDGE SAUCE
Luscious sauce of cocoa, sugar, butter and cream. Served here over sautéed bananas; decorated with flaked almonds.
Makes 1¼ cups. Page 383

CUSTARD SAUCE
A popular dessert sauce of cream, milk, sugar, egg yolks and vanilla. Served here over a variety of sliced fruits.
Makes about 1¼ cups. Page 382

ORANGE SAUCE
Orange-flavoured liqueur and grated orange rind in a sugar syrup. Served here with orange slices and whole strawberries.
Makes 2½ cups. Page 382

MELBA SAUCE
A sieved, thickened sauce of raspberries and redcurrant jelly. Served here with poached pear halves; decorated with mint.
Makes about 1 cup. Page 383

CHOCOLATE SAUCE
Chocolate melted with sugar, cream and butter, and flavoured with vanilla essence. Served here over a banana split.
Makes about 3 cups. Page 382

HOT FRUIT SAUCE
Chopped nectarines and plums cooked with sugar and orange juice. Served here with ice cream; decorated with mint.
Makes 4 cups. Page 382

MULBERRY SAUCE
Delicately spiced mulberries with sugar and lemon. Served here with a poached whole peach; decorated with a mint sprig.
Makes about 1 cup. Page 383

105

UNDER 30 MINUTES

BUTTERSCOTCH SAUCE
A traditional sauce of brown sugar, cream, golden syrup and butter. Served warm; here poured over slices of ice cream.
Makes 1 cup. Page 382

CHERRY SAUCE
Cherries cooked with sugar and water, flavoured with almond essence. Served warm; here poured over folded crêpes.
Makes 2 cups. Page 383

HARD SAUCE
A butter-based sauce with icing sugar and vanilla essence. Served here with warm Fruit and Nut Tartlets.
Makes about ⅔ cup. Page 383

BÉARNAISE SAUCE
White-wine vinegar, spring onion, tarragon and parsley in a classic French sauce. Served here with a steak and salad.
Makes about 1 cup. Page 381

HOLLANDAISE SAUCE
A seasoned sauce of egg yolks, lemon juice and melted butter. Served here with asparagus spears; garnished with herbs.
Makes about 1 cup. Page 381

BARBECUE SAUCE
An onion, garlic, chilli and bottled tomato sauce mixture. Served here with barbecued chicken, parsleyed potatoes and salad.
Makes about 1 cup. Page 379

BROWN GRAVY
A traditional gravy made from vegetables and stock. Served here with lamb cutlets and vegetables; garnished with parsley.
Makes about 2 cups. Page 380

SATAY SAUCE
A peanut butter sauce with garlic, diced red capsicum, green ginger, vinegar and soy sauce. Served here with chicken kebabs; garnished with lemon slices, a radish flower and coriander leaves.
Makes about 1⅓ cups. Page 379

CORN RELISH
A mixture of corn kernels, capsicums, tomato, onion and vinegar. Served here with chicken; garnished with parsley. Makes about 4 cups. Page 376

GIBLET GRAVY
A strained, thickened stock and vegetable sauce, with added chicken or turkey giblet meat. Served here with roast turkey slices, parsleyed potatoes, baby carrots and cranberry sauce; garnished with chives. Makes 4 cups. Page 380.

MINT JELLY
Mint, apple juice and vinegar in a set jelly. Served here with lamb chops, new potatoes and beans; garnished with mint. Makes 4 cups. Page 378

TOMATO AND BASIL SAUCE
A thickened sauce flavoured with spring onion, garlic, parsley and basil. Served here with prawns; garnished with dill. Makes about 2½ cups. Page 380

APRICOT AND PINEAPPLE SPREAD
A delicious preserve of dried apricots and crushed pineapple. Served here on a toasted muffin with butter curls. Makes about 2 cups. Page 375

TOMATO SAUCE
A piquant relish flavoured with vinegar and mixed spices. Served here with a hamburger on a bun and French fries. Makes 3 cups. Page 379

107

OVER 1 HOUR

ROCKMELON CHUTNEY
Lightly curried melon, tomatoes, onions and sultanas. Served here with samoosas; garnished with lime and coriander.
Makes about 4 cups. Page 377

CAPSICUM JELLY
A sweetened mixture of capsicum juice and white vinegar. Served here with rolled ham slices, tomato and mixed salad greens.
Makes 2 cups. Page 378

CRANBERRY RELISH
A spicy mixture of cranberries, marrons, sultanas and onions. Served here with cold sliced roast turkey and a mixed salad.
Makes 4 cups. Page 376

APPLE AND ONION CHUTNEY
Apples, onions, capsicum and prunes spiced with ginger, mustard and chilli. Served here with cheese and crusty bread.
Makes about 4 cups. Page 377

GREEN TOMATO CHUTNEY
Spiced tomatoes, capsicums and onion. Served here with cheese and biscuits; garnished with chicory and a radish.
Makes 4 cups. Page 377

BLACKBERRY SPREAD *(left) A zesty blackberry and apple mixture.*
Makes 4 cups. Page 375. **STRAWBERRY JAM** *(centre) Crushed fresh strawberries, sugar and lemon juice.* **Makes about 4 cups. Page 375.**
PEACH PRESERVES *Sliced peaches in a sugar and lemon syrup.* **Makes 4 cups. Page 376.** *All served here with croissants, bread rolls and butter.*

Starters

DIPS · SPREADS · PÂTÉS · CANAPÉS · TARTLETS · ENTRÉES

Starters

A microwave makes short work of preparing entrées and appetisers, thus making entertaining easier. Some of the dishes in this chapter can be frozen up to a month before serving; instructions are given in individual recipes. They can then be popped into the microwave oven to be ready in moments. If you arrange canapés on microwave-safe trays when cooking, they can be served straight from the oven, saving on extra dishwashing. Also, they can be quickly popped back into the microwave for reheating during the course of the occasion. You can even add toothpicks before cooking; plain wooden or plastic picks, including those with frills, may be used, as can bamboo skewers. Do not use coloured toothpicks, however; these may leave dye on your food.

When unexpected guests drop in, you can have something hot and delicious to welcome them with in only a few minutes. Variously shaped pastry cases can be kept in the freezer and, when needed, defrosted in the microwave oven and quickly filled.

In addition to the delicious assortment of starters included here, many of the recipes in the Snacks and Sandwiches chapter (pages 297–308) can be adapted for casual entertaining, buffet arrangements and other occasions. The microwave oven can also be used for preparing a wide variety of commercially available packaged and frozen entrées; just follow the microwave instructions provided with the product.

The microwave can be used to soften cheeses for use in dips or for making into cheese balls, and it is wonderful for bringing cheese from the refrigerator to perfect eating temperature. Place 250 g unwrapped cheese in the microwave and heat on Medium (50% power) for 30–45 seconds, until the chill has gone. To bring refrigerated dips to room temperature, heat 2 cups of dip on Medium for 1–2 minutes just before serving. You can also use the microwave to refresh stale snacks such as pretzels, popcorn and potato crisps. Heat them in 2- or 3-cup batches on High (100% power) for 30–60 seconds.

QUICK AND EASY FIRST COURSES

When unexpected guests drop in, use the microwave as an extra helper in the kitchen to create quick and easy starters from ingredients on hand. In a matter of minutes, you'll have an attractive dish that looks like it took a great deal of time and effort to prepare.

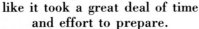

Sliced tomato and avocado (left), drizzled with Italian salad dressing and sprinkled with microwave-crisp bacon. Garnished with basil leaves.

Well-drained canned pineapple rings (right) topped with cream cheese and chives, sprinkled with paprika. Garnished with celery leaves, chives and lime twists (page 134).

Dips

CURRIED CRAB DIP

Colour Index page 38. Makes 2 cups. 206 kJ per tablespoon. Low in sodium.
Begin 15 minutes ahead.

15 g butter or margarine	*250 g cream cheese*
2 teaspoons curry powder	*3 teaspoons milk*
1 small onion, finely chopped	*1 teaspoon lemon juice*
1 celery stalk, finely chopped	*250 g crab meat*
30 g canned pimientos, drained and diced	*2 tablespoons chopped fresh parsley*
	Crudités

1. Combine butter, curry powder, onion, celery and pimientos in a medium bowl. Cook on High (100% power) for 2½ (2:30) minutes, or until vegetables are softened, stirring twice.
2. Add cream cheese. Cook on High for 1 minute, or until softened. Stir until well mixed.
3. Stir in milk, lemon juice, crab and parsley.
4. Spoon dip into a bowl. Serve with crudités.

BACON DIP

Colour Index page 38. Makes 2 cups. 212 kJ per tablespoon. Good source of calcium, riboflavin.
Begin 25 minutes ahead.

4 rashers rindless bacon, diced	*¼ teaspoon pepper*
250 g cream cheese	*Capsicum bowl (below, optional)*
½ cup sour cream	*Celery stalks, potato crisps, breadsticks and bagel chips*
2 tablespoons horseradish cream	

1. Cook bacon in a 30-cm x 20-cm baking dish on High (100% power) for 4 minutes, or until browned, stirring occasionally. Transfer bacon to paper towel to drain.
2. Discard all but 1 teaspoon bacon drippings. Add cheese to drippings in dish. Soften on High for 1 minute.
3. Stir in sour cream, horseradish and pepper. Crumble bacon; add to dip. Cover and refrigerate for at least 20 minutes.
4. Spoon dip into a small serving dish or capsicum bowl. Serve with celery, potato crisps, breadsticks and bagel chips.

Making the capsicum bowl

Cut top off capsicum and cut a thin slice from the bottom so that capsicum sits flat.

Scrape out seeds and white membrane from top (stalk end) of capsicum; discard.

Dips are always popular because they are easy to prepare and can be served at any time. Freshly cut raw vegetables, or crudités, are low-kilojoule accompaniments, while potato crisps, corn chips and bagel chips (available at larger supermarkets) are more substantial.

MEDITERRANEAN EGGPLANT DIP

Colour Index page 38. 88 kJ per tablespoon. Low in cholesterol, fat.
Begin 25 minutes ahead.

Ingredients for 3 cups		Microwave cookware
1 medium eggplant (about 750 g)	*2 teaspoons chopped fresh thyme or*	30-cm x 20-cm baking dish
1 small red onion	*½ teaspoon dried thyme*	Medium bowl
1 green capsicum	*½ teaspoon salt*	
4 cloves garlic	*6 green olives, chopped*	
2 celery stalks	*1 tablespoon capers, drained*	
¼ cup olive or vegetable oil	*Pepper to taste*	
1 tomato, chopped	*Parsley sprigs to garnish*	
1½ tablespoons red wine vinegar	*Pita bread, toasted and cut into triangles*	
3 teaspoons sugar		
1 tablespoon chopped fresh oregano or 1 teaspoon dried oregano		

1 Line baking dish with paper towel. Pierce skin of eggplant in several places; place in baking dish. Cook on High (100% power) for 7 minutes, or until softened, turning over halfway through cooking.

2 Meanwhile, chop onion, capsicum, garlic and celery.

3 Mix chopped vegetables, oil, tomato, vinegar, sugar, oregano, thyme and salt in bowl. Cook, covered, on High for 3 minutes; put aside.

4 Cut eggplant in half lengthways; scoop out flesh. In food processor with knife blade attached or in blender, process flesh until smooth. Spoon into bowl with vegetables.

5 Stir vegetable mixture and puréed eggplant together. Add olives, capers and pepper. Chill.

6 Spoon dip on to individual plates or into a serving bowl; garnish with parsley. Serve with toasted pita triangles.

Light Summer Lunch

Artichokes with Lemon and Garlic (page 122)
Pipérade (page 141) with
Heart-shaped Croûtons (below)
Fresh fruit platter

PREPARATION TIMETABLE

1½ hours ahead:	*Prepare a selection of fresh seasonal fruit. Sprinkle cut fruit with lemon juice to prevent discoloration; cover and refrigerate.*
1 hour ahead:	*Prepare and cook Artichokes with Lemon and Garlic; do not garnish. Arrange on serving plates and keep warm. Make Croûtons. Prepare Pipérade up to the end of step 2.*
Just before serving:	*For artichokes, reheat butter in microwave; garnish. Finish cooking Pipérade from start of step 3; garnish with Croûtons and basil.*

HEART-SHAPED CROÛTONS

1 Remove crusts from **4 slices bread.** Cut bread diagonally into quarters.

2 Round off top 2 corners of each triangle; cut a 'V' from top centre to form a heart shape. Bake conventionally as for Croûtons (page 129).

3 Dip tops of croûtons into **2 tablespoons melted butter,** then into **4 tablespoons chopped fresh parsley.**

MEXICAN DIP

Colour Index page 38. Makes 1 cup. 251 kJ per tablespoon. Low in sodium.
Begin 15 minutes ahead.

1 spring onion, finely chopped	*1–2 tablespoons milk*
15 g butter or margarine	*Chopped spring onion to garnish*
185 g cream cheese	
¼ cup bottled taco sauce (or to taste)	

1. Place finely chopped spring onion and butter in a medium bowl. Cook on High (100% power) for 1 minute, or until softened.
2. Add cream cheese. Heat on Medium (50% power) for 1–1½ (1:30) minutes, until softened. Stir until smooth.
3. Stir taco sauce into mixture; add enough milk to thin dip to desired consistency.
4. Spoon dip into a small serving bowl; garnish with spring onion.

HOT PRAWN DIP WITH DILL

Colour Index page 38. Makes 2 cups. 139 kJ per tablespoon. Low in fat.
Begin 20 minutes ahead.

1 tablespoon olive or vegetable oil	*2 tablespoons plain flour*
3 cloves garlic	*1¼ cups milk*
1 spring onion, thinly sliced	*1½ teaspoons tomato paste*
1 celery stalk, cut into 5-cm lengths	*¼ teaspoon salt*
250 g green prawns, shelled and deveined (page 166)	*⅛ teaspoon cayenne pepper (or to taste)*
	2 teaspoons lemon juice
	Fresh dill to garnish
	Cooked tortellini

1. Combine oil, garlic, spring onion, celery and prawns in a medium bowl. Cook, covered, on High (100% power) for 3 minutes, or just until prawns turn pink, stirring halfway through cooking.
2. Remove prawn mixture from bowl with a slotted spoon, reserving the liquid. In food processor with knife blade attached or on a chopping board, finely chop prawn mixture; put aside.
3. Add flour to liquid remaining in bowl; stir until blended and smooth. Cook on High for 1 minute. Remove from microwave.
4. Gradually stir milk and tomato paste into flour mixture. Add salt and cayenne pepper. Cook on High for 4 minutes, or until thickened, stirring twice.
5. Stir in lemon juice and reserved prawn mixture. Cook on High for 2 minutes, or until hot.
6. Spoon dip into a serving bowl; garnish with dill. Serve immediately with tortellini.

Simple Cheese Spreads

These delicious spreads, made with a variety of cheeses, can be served on your favourite bread, rolls or biscuits. After making, use immediately or refrigerate for serving later. To soften refrigerated spreads, place a small quantity in a microwave-safe container. Heat on High (100% power) for 5 seconds at a time, until just spreadable.

BASIC YOGHURT CHEESE

Makes about 1 cup. 51 kJ per tablespoon. Good source of riboflavin, calcium.
Begin 1 day ahead.

1 cup natural yoghurt
Salt and white pepper to taste

1. Line a strainer with a double thickness of muslin or a coffee filter and place over a bowl. Spoon yoghurt into the strainer; allow to drain overnight in the refrigerator.
2. Discard liquid. Spoon yoghurt cheese into a serving bowl. Season with salt and pepper. Serve immediately or cover and refrigerate.

APRICOT AND CHEESE SPREAD: Prepare Basic Yoghurt Cheese (above); stir in **2 tablespoons apricot jam** and **½ teaspoon ground ginger.**
Makes 1 cup. 79 kJ per tablespoon.

BLUE CHEESE SPREAD

Makes about 1½ cups. 168 kJ per tablespoon. Good source of calcium, riboflavin.
Begin 5 minutes ahead.

125 g blue cheese, crumbled
90 g cream cheese
2 tablespoons finely chopped spring onion
3 teaspoons milk

1. Place cheeses and spring onion in a 4-cup bowl. Heat on Medium (50% power) for 1–2 minutes, until cheeses are softened.
2. Add milk to cheese mixture; stir until smooth. Serve immediately or cover and refrigerate.

BLUE CHEESE AND WALNUT SPREAD: Prepare Blue Cheese Spread (above); stir in **¼ cup finely chopped walnuts.** Makes about 1¾ cups. 179 kJ per tablespoon.

CREAM CHEESE AND CHIVE SPREAD

Makes about 1¼ cups. 128 kJ per tablespoon. Good source of calcium, riboflavin.
Begin 5 minutes ahead.

90 g cream cheese
90 g cottage cheese
3 teaspoons milk
2 tablespoons chopped fresh chives
White pepper to taste

1. Heat cheeses in a 2-cup bowl on Medium (50% power) for 1–2 minutes, until softened.
2. Add milk and chives to cheese mixture, stirring until blended. Season with pepper. Serve immediately or cover and refrigerate.

SMOKED SALMON AND CHIVE SPREAD: Prepare Cream Cheese and Chive Spread (above); stir in **60 g chopped smoked salmon** and **1 teaspoon lemon juice.**
Makes about 1½ cups. 123 kJ per tablespoon.

CHEDDAR CHEESE SPREAD

Makes about 2¼ cups. 273 kJ per tablespoon. Good source of calcium.
Begin 5 minutes ahead.

125 g butter or margarine
250 g Cheddar cheese, grated (2 cups)
3 tablespoons milk
2 spring onions, finely chopped
¼ teaspoon Tabasco sauce

1. Heat butter in a 4-cup bowl on Medium (50% power) for 30 seconds–1 minute, until softened.
2. Beat cheese into butter; add milk, stirring until well blended. Stir in spring onions and Tabasco sauce. Serve immediately or cover and refrigerate.

MEXICAN CHEESE SPREAD: Prepare Cheddar Cheese Spread (above); stir in **1 chopped green chilli, ¼ cup bottled taco sauce** and **1 tablespoon chopped fresh coriander.** Makes 2½ cups. 307 kJ per tablespoon.

Pâtés

Pâtés make elegant starters that cook quickly in the microwave but need to be well chilled to be at their best. In Seafood Pâté (below) plastic wrap is used to line the loaf dish for easier removal, and the dish is elevated to ensure even cooking.

SEAFOOD PÂTÉ

Colour Index page 41. 538 kJ per serving. Good source of iodine, niacin, zinc. Begin early in day.

Ingredients for 16 servings		Microwave cookware
250 g green prawns, shelled and deveined (page 166)	500 g scallops	23-cm x 13-cm loaf dish
1 shallot, finely chopped	1½ cups chilled cream	Small bowl
15 g butter or margarine	1 egg	Trivet, rack or ramekin
1 small tomato, seeded and chopped	¼ teaspoon salt	
2 tablespoons chopped fresh tarragon leaves	⅛ teaspoon white pepper	
	Tarragon leaves and chopped tomato to garnish	
	Mayonnaise (optional)	

1 Line loaf dish with plastic wrap, extending it 5 cm beyond the edges of the dish.

2 Chop prawns; mix with shallot and butter in bowl. Cook on High (100% power) for 1 minute, stirring once. Add tomato and tarragon; stir and put aside.

3 In food processor with knife blade attached or in blender, process scallops until smooth. Gradually pour in cream until well mixed; blend in egg, salt and pepper. Transfer mixture to a mixing bowl; fold in reserved prawn mixture.

4 Gently spoon pâté into loaf dish; smooth top with back of spoon. On a level surface, tap corner of dish several times to disperse any air bubbles. Fold edges of plastic wrap over pâté mixture.

5 Elevate dish on trivet or rack, or on ramekin turned upside down. Cook on Medium (50% power) for 10 minutes, or until pâté is set. Cover dish with a baking tray to flatten surface of pâté. Allow to stand for 20 minutes. Refrigerate for at least 3 hours.

6 Unfold edges of plastic wrap. Place a chilled serving platter upside down on dish and invert to unmould; remove plastic wrap. Garnish pâté with tarragon and tomato. Serve, if you like, with mayonnaise.

COUNTRY-STYLE PORK PÂTÉ

Colour Index page 41. 16 servings. 829 kJ per serving. Good source of vitamin A, iron. Begin 1 day ahead.

12 rashers rindless bacon	1 tablespoon finely chopped fresh oregano or 1 teaspoon dried oregano
375 g beef mince	
375 g pork mince	
250 g cooked ham, diced	½ teaspoon ground cloves
250 g chicken livers, finely minced	½ teaspoon ground nutmeg
1 medium onion, grated	
4 cloves garlic, crushed	½ teaspoon pepper
¼ cup brandy	¼ teaspoon salt
1 tablespoon chopped fresh thyme or 1 teaspoon dried thyme	Sliced gherkins, salad greens and stuffed olives to garnish

1. Line a 23-cm x 13-cm loaf dish with 8 bacon rashers, allowing bacon to hang over edges of dish; put aside.
2. Finely chop remaining 4 bacon rashers. Mix with beef mince, pork mince, ham, chicken livers, onion, garlic, brandy, thyme, oregano, cloves, nutmeg, pepper and salt in a large bowl; stir until well combined.
3. Spoon pâté into bacon-lined dish; smooth top with back of spoon. On a level surface, tap corner of dish several times to disperse any air bubbles. Fold bacon over top of pâté mixture.
4. Elevate dish on a trivet or rack, or on a ramekin turned upside down. Cook, covered loosely with greaseproof paper, on High (100% power) for 20 minutes. Pour off excess fat.
5. Allow pâté to stand for 30 minutes to cool. Cover dish with greaseproof paper or plastic wrap, then foil-wrapped cardboard and foil-wrapped weight (below). Refrigerate overnight.
6. Remove weight, cardboard and greaseproof paper. Place plate or chopping board upside down on dish and invert to unmould. Scrape off any coagulated cooking juices and excess fat.
7. Transfer pâté to serving platter; garnish with gherkins, salad greens and olives. Serve cut into thin slices.

Wrapping and weighting the pâté

Cut piece of cardboard to size of top of loaf dish and wrap completely in foil. Place on top of greaseproof paper covering pâté mixture.

Wrap a brick in foil or use several cans to weight pâté. Place weight on foil-wrapped cardboard.

Canapés

CHICKEN LIVER PÂTÉ

Colour Index page 41. Makes 1 cup. 257 kJ per tablespoon. Low in sodium. Good source of vitamin A. Begin early in day.

60 g butter or margarine	½ teaspoon dried thyme
1 spring onion, chopped	½ teaspoon pepper
1 clove garlic, crushed	Savoury biscuits
250 g chicken livers	Radish flowers and pear
2 teaspoons brandy	slices (below)

1. Place butter, spring onion and garlic in a 1-litre casserole. Cook on High (100% power) for 1 minute, or until softened, stirring halfway through cooking.
2. Pierce chicken livers with a fork; add to butter mixture. Cook, covered loosely with greaseproof paper, on High for 3–5 minutes, just until livers are no longer pink, stirring halfway through cooking. Allow to stand for 2 minutes.
3. In food processor with knife blade attached or in blender, process chicken liver mixture, brandy, thyme and pepper until well blended and smooth, stopping occasionally and scraping sides with a rubber spatula.
4. Spoon mixture into a freezer-to-microwave container; cover and freeze.
5. About 15 minutes before serving, take pâté from freezer; remove container cover. Cook pâté, covered loosely with greaseproof paper, on Medium (50% power) for 4–6 minutes, just until thawed but not warm, stirring twice.
6. Spoon pâté into a small dish. Serve with biscuits, radish flowers and pear slices.

Making the radish flowers

Cut zig-zag pattern through radish about 5 mm from stalk end.

Twist top from bottom of radish, leaving flower-shaped cup.

Making the pear slices

Cut pear into quarters lengthways. Core centres, then cut quarters into thin slices.

Rub each pear slice with cut lemon to prevent flesh discolouring.

CHEESE AND CHILLI CHAPATIS

Colour Index page 40. 352 kJ per wedge. Good source of calcium. Begin 35 minutes ahead.

Ingredients for 16 wedges		Microwave cookware
6 fresh green chillies	8 chapatis (bought)	Browning dish
185 g Cheddar cheese	Salad greens and	
½ cup chopped fresh	radishes to garnish	
coriander leaves	Chutney or relish	
2 spring onions, sliced	(optional)	
130 g can whole-kernel	Natural yoghurt	
corn, drained	(optional)	

1 Make chilli flowers: With sharp knife, slit 4 chillies several times, about 1.25 cm from stem. (If you like, wear rubber gloves for protection.)

2 Place cut chillies in iced water to separate petals; put aside. Meanwhile, preheat browning dish according to the manufacturer's instructions.

3 Grate cheese on to a flat dish. Finely chop remaining chillis; add to cheese with coriander, spring onions and corn.

4 Spoon an equal amount of mixture on to each of 4 chapatis.

5 Cover each chapati with remaining chapatis to make a sandwich.

6 Place 1 sandwich on preheated browning dish. Cook on High (100% power) for 1½ (1:30) minutes, or until hot, turning over after 1 minute.

7 Remove sandwich from dish; allow to stand for 2 minutes. Meanwhile, cook remaining chapatis. Reheat browning dish as necessary and keep cooked chapati sandwiches warm.

8 Cut each sandwich into 4 wedges. Arrange on plates.

9 Garnish each plate with salad greens and radishes. Serve chapatis, if you like, with chutney and yoghurt.

POTATO SKINS with TASTY CHEESE

Colour Index page 40. 301 kJ per piece (without dip). Low in sodium.
Begin 40 minutes ahead.

Ingredients	For 16 pieces	For 8 pieces	For 4 pieces
Baking potatoes, washed and dried	*4 medium*	*2 medium*	*1 medium*
Cheddar cheese, grated	*185 g (1½ cups)*	*90 g (¾ cup)*	*30 g (¼ cup)*
Spring onions, chopped	*2*	*1*	*½*
Salt	*½ teaspoon*	*¼ teaspoon*	*to taste*
Pepper	*to taste*	*to taste*	*to taste*
Spring onions	*garnish*	*garnish*	*garnish*
Sour cream or yoghurt	*dip*	*dip*	*dip*
Microwave cookware	30-cm platter	30-cm platter	30-cm platter
Time on High (100% power)			
Potatoes	16–18 minutes	10–12 minutes	6–7 minutes
With cheese topping	4–5 minutes	2–3 minutes	1 minute
Standing time			
Potatoes	5 minutes	5 minutes	5 minutes
With cheese topping	2 minutes	1–2 minutes	1 minute

1 Pierce each potato 3 times. Place on paper towel.

2 Cook potatoes on High for time in Chart, turning over once.

3 Wrap potatoes in tea towel. Allow to stand for time in Chart.

4 Meanwhile, combine cheese and chopped spring onions in a bowl.

5 Cut each potato into quarters lengthways.

6 Scoop out potatoes, leaving 6 mm flesh on skins.

9 Cook potato skins on High for time in Chart. Allow to stand for time in Chart. Garnish with spring onions. Serve with sour cream or yoghurt as a dip.

7 Arrange skins in a circle on platter (see Chart).

8 Sprinkle with salt and pepper and top with cheese mixture.

NACHO BAKE

Colour Index page 39. 6 servings. 1365 kJ per serving. Good source of vitamin A, calcium.
Begin 15 minutes ahead.

250 g Cheddar cheese, grated (2 cups)
60 g canned green chillies, finely chopped
½ small red onion, diced
⅓ cup stoned black olives, sliced
⅓ cup chopped fresh coriander leaves
200 g packet corn chips
Sour cream and bottled taco sauce

1. Combine cheese, chillies, onion, olives and coriander in a bowl; put aside.
2. Arrange one-third of the corn chips in a single layer on a 30-cm round platter. Top with one-third cheese mixture. Continue alternating corn chips and cheese mixture, making 2 more layers and finishing with cheese.
3. Cook on High (100% power) for 2–3 minutes, until cheese is melted and bubbling.
4. Serve immediately, with bowls of sour cream and taco sauce on the side.

SPICY CHICKEN WINGS

Colour Index page 39. Makes 12. 795 kJ each. Good source of potassium.
Begin 25 minutes ahead.

6 chicken wings
1 small onion, finely chopped
⅓ cup tomato sauce
30 g butter or margarine
1½ tablespoons brown sugar
1½ tablespoons orange juice
1 teaspoon Worcestershire sauce
¼ teaspoon Tabasco sauce
3 celery stalks, cut into 10-cm lengths
1 cup natural yoghurt (optional)

1. Remove small tips from each chicken wing. Cut wings in half at joint, making 12 pieces.
2. Combine onion, tomato sauce, butter, brown sugar, orange juice, Worcestershire sauce and Tabasco sauce in a medium bowl. Cook on High (100% power) for 4 minutes, or until onion is softened and flavours blend, stirring halfway through cooking.
3. Arrange chicken pieces in a single layer in a 30-cm x 20-cm baking dish; spoon over half the sauce. Cook chicken on High for 6 minutes.
4. Turn pieces over and coat with remaining sauce. Cook on High for 6 minutes, or until chicken is tender and juices run clear.
5. Transfer chicken pieces to a warmed serving dish; garnish with celery. Serve, if you like, with yoghurt as a dip.

MIDDLE-EASTERN MEATBALLS

Colour Index page 40. Makes about 26. 128 kJ each. Low in cholesterol.
Begin 35 minutes ahead.

1 egg	½ teaspoon ground
375 g beef mince	cinnamon
1 onion, grated	¼ teaspoon ground
3 cloves garlic, crushed	cloves
2 tablespoons seedless	¼ teaspoon ground
raisins, finely chopped	nutmeg
2 tablespoons chopped	¼ teaspoon salt
fresh mint	¼ teaspoon pepper
3 teaspoons lemon juice	Lemon slices and mint
2 teaspoons ground	leaves to garnish
cumin	

1. Beat egg; combine with beef mince, onion, garlic, raisins, mint, lemon juice, cumin, cinnamon, cloves, nutmeg, salt and pepper in a bowl.
2. Shape mixture into 2.5-cm meatballs. Place on a rack set in a 30-cm x 20-cm baking dish.
3. Cook meatballs on High (100% power) for 4–5 minutes, rearranging halfway through cooking. Allow to stand, covered with paper towel, for 3 minutes before serving.
4. Thread each meatball on to a long wooden skewer and arrange on individual plates; garnish with lemon and mint.

CHEESE STICKS

Colour Index page 39. Makes 16. 377 kJ each. Low in sodium. Good source of vitamin A.
Begin 20 minutes ahead.

125 g cream cheese	¼ cup poppy seeds
30 g butter or margarine	¼ cup chopped chives
2 tablespoons grated	¼ cup sesame seeds
Parmesan cheese	¼ cup paprika
½ teaspoon French	16 breadsticks (grissini)
mustard	Chives to garnish
4 drops Tabasco sauce	

1. Place cream cheese and butter in a medium bowl. Heat on High (100% power) for 1½ (1:30) minutes; stir until smooth.
2. Add Parmesan cheese, mustard and Tabasco sauce; combine well.
3. Place poppy seeds, chives, sesame seeds and paprika on separate sheets of greaseproof paper.
4. Spread an equal amount of cheese mixture on to half of each breadstick. Lightly roll 4 breadsticks in each coating.
5. Arrange on a serving plate; garnish with chives. Serve immediately.

All of the canapés on these pages can be prepared in advance. For an alternative to Angels on Horseback (below), make Devils on Horseback by substituting stoned prunes for the oysters.

ANGELS ON HORSEBACK

Colour Index page 38. 121 kJ per oyster. Low in fat.
Begin 25 minutes ahead.

Ingredients	For 24 oysters	For 12 oysters	For 6 oysters
Bacon	12 rashers	6 rashers	3 rashers
Worcestershire sauce	1 tablespoon	2 teaspoons	1 teaspoon
French mustard	1 teaspoon	½ teaspoon	¼ teaspoon
Fresh oysters	24	12	6
Lemon slices and parsley sprigs	garnish	garnish	garnish
Microwave cookware	33-cm x 23-cm baking dish	30-cm x 20-cm baking dish	20-cm x 20-cm baking dish
Time on High (100% power) Bacon	4 minutes	2 minutes	1½ (1:30) minutes
Oysters	3 minutes	1½ (1:30) minutes	1 minute
Standing time	2 minutes	1–2 minutes	1 minute

1. Remove rind from bacon; cut each rasher in half crossways.

2. Line baking dish with double thickness of paper towel. Arrange bacon on paper, in batches if necessary; cover with paper towel. Cook on High for time in Chart. Transfer to clean paper towel to drain.

3. Meanwhile, combine Worcestershire sauce, mustard and oysters in a bowl; stir until oysters are coated in sauce mixture.

4. Wrap each oyster in a half-rasher of bacon, securing it with a wooden toothpick.

5. Arrange bacon-wrapped oysters in baking dish. Cook, covered with paper towel, on High for time in Chart, turning once. Allow to stand for time in Chart.

6. Transfer oysters to a serving platter; garnish with lemon and parsley. Serve hot.

Canapés for spur-of-the-moment entertaining can be made in minutes in the microwave, yet your guests will think you've spent hours preparing them! The recipes on this page all have an Italian flavour, and would be ideal served with an Italian aperitif such as vermouth, or an Italian dry white wine like Frascati or Soave. All the ingredients for the canapés are widely available in supermarkets and specialty food shops, and most keep well in the store cupboard – making these recipes ideal for impromptu dining.

NUTTY GOAT CHEESE TOASTS

Colour Index page 40. Makes 24. 343 kJ each. Good source of vitamin A, riboflavin, thiamine, niacin, calcium, iron.
Begin 35 minutes ahead.

Ingredients for 24		Microwave cookware
3 tablespoons crushed walnuts or pecans	1 French bread stick, about 30 cm long	Serving platter
185 g goat cheese roll	Olive oil	
60 g sun-dried tomatoes, drained if packed in oil	Salad greens to garnish	

1 Place walnuts in a shallow dish. Carefully roll goat cheese in walnuts until evenly coated all round. Wrap cheese in plastic wrap; chill in refrigerator for 20 minutes, or until firm.

2 Meanwhile, cut sun-dried tomatoes into 48 matchstick-thin strips; put aside.

3 Cut French bread into 24 x 1-cm slices, discarding rounded ends. Preheat griller to hot.

4 Toast bread slices under preheated griller until golden brown on both sides.

5 Remove chilled cheese roll from refrigerator and unwrap; cut into 24 slices. Place 1 cheese slice on top of each slice of toast. Arrange 2 strips of tomato in a lattice pattern on top of each cheese slice.

6 Arrange toasts on serving platter. Heat on Medium (50% power) for 1–2 minutes, until cheese softens slightly. Cook in batches if necessary. Drizzle each toast with a little olive oil. Garnish with salad greens. Serve hot.

PIZZA TARTLETS

Colour Index page 40. Makes 16. 607 kJ each. Low in cholesterol.
Begin 35 minutes ahead.

50 g can anchovy fillets, well drained	1 cup bottled Italian tomato sauce
90 g stoned black olives, drained	125 g mozzarella cheese, grated (1 cup)
16 x 5-cm cooked pastry cases	Basil leaves to garnish

1. Rinse anchovies under cold running water; pat dry with paper towel. Cut each fillet in half crossways, then lengthways, to make 4 strips; put aside. Slice olives into thin rings; put aside.
2. Preheat conventional oven to 180°C. Arrange pastry cases on a baking tray and place in oven for 5 minutes, or until heated through.
3. Pour tomato sauce into a small bowl. Heat on High (100% power) for 3–5 minutes, until hot, stirring twice.
4. Arrange warmed pastry cases on a serving platter. Spoon an equal amount of sauce into each case and sprinkle with grated cheese. Arrange anchovy strips on top of each tartlet in a lattice pattern and decorate with 2 olive rings.
5. Heat tartlets on Medium (50% power) for 1–2 minutes, just until cheese begins to melt, rotating platter and rearranging tartlets once.
6. Garnish with basil. Serve warm.

SAVOURY BREADSTICKS

Colour Index page 38. Makes 12. 155 kJ each. Low in cholesterol, fat.
Begin 15 minutes ahead.

6 rashers rindless lean bacon	Tomato slices and chives to garnish
12 breadsticks (grissini)	

1. Line a 33-cm x 23-cm baking dish with paper towel; put aside.
2. Cut bacon rashers in half lengthways and wrap 1 piece, spiral-fashion, around each breadstick.
3. Arrange breadsticks in prepared baking dish. Cook, covered with paper towel, on High (100% power) for 4½ (4:30)–6 minutes, until bacon is browned, rotating dish and rearranging breadsticks halfway through cooking.
4. Transfer breadsticks to a serving platter; garnish with tomato and chives. Serve hot.

Tartlets

Filled pastry cases make attractive starters. Buy the cases or make them yourself and keep in the freezer. They can be quickly heated in the microwave then filled with delicious savoury mixtures. Each filling is enough to make twelve to fifteen 5-cm tartlets.

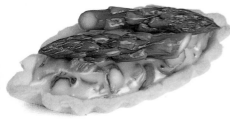

ASPARAGUS AND BRIE FILLING

Colour Index page 39. Makes 12 tablespoons (to fill 12 tartlets). 156 kJ per tablespoon. Low in cholesterol, fat, sodium.
Begin 15 minutes ahead.

500 g thin
  asparagus spears
125 g Brie cheese
2 spring onions,
  thinly sliced
1 tablespoon finely
  chopped fresh
  tarragon or
1 teaspoon dried
  tarragon
1 tablespoon water

1. Hold base of each asparagus spear firmly and bend; the end will break off where the spear becomes too tough to eat. Discard tough ends.
2. Trim asparagus tips to 5-cm pieces; put aside for garnish. Thinly slice remaining asparagus.
3. Cut Brie into 12-mm cubes. Combine sliced asparagus, Brie, spring onions and tarragon in a medium bowl. Cook, covered, on High (100% power) for 2½ (2:30) minutes. Stir until cheese is melted. Spoon filling into heated pastry cases.
4. Place reserved asparagus tips and water on a small plate. Cook, covered, on High for 1 minute. Use to garnish filled tartlets.

MUSHROOM FILLING

Colour Index page 39. Makes 15 tablespoons (to fill 15 tartlets). 117 kJ per tablespoon. Low in cholesterol, fat.
Begin 25 minutes ahead.

250 g mushrooms
4 spring onions,
  finely chopped
3 cloves garlic,
  crushed
45 g butter or
  margarine
¼ cup chopped fresh
  parsley
2 tablespoons dry
  sherry
¼ teaspoon salt
Pepper to taste
Parsley to garnish

1. In food processor with knife blade attached or on a chopping board, finely chop mushrooms.
2. Place mushrooms, spring onions, garlic and butter in a medium bowl. Cook on High (100% power) for 6 minutes, stirring occasionally.
3. Stir in chopped parsley, sherry, salt and pepper. Cook on High for 6 minutes, or until liquid evaporates, stirring halfway through cooking. Spoon filling into heated pastry cases; garnish with parsley.

TOMATO AND BASIL FILLING

Colour Index page 39. Makes 12 tablespoons (to fill 12 tartlets). 45 kJ per tablespoon. Low in cholesterol, fat.
Begin 10 minutes ahead.

2 medium
  tomatoes
2 cloves garlic,
  crushed
1 celery stalk,
  finely chopped
1 tablespoon grated
  Parmesan cheese
2 teaspoons prepared
  pesto (bottled or
  homemade)
¼ teaspoon salt
Cayenne pepper to
  taste
Small basil leaves to
  garnish

1. Seed and chop tomatoes. Combine tomatoes, garlic and celery in a medium bowl. Cook on High (100% power) for 4 minutes, or until softened, stirring halfway through cooking.
2. Stir in Parmesan cheese, pesto, salt and cayenne pepper. Spoon filling into heated pastry cases; garnish with basil leaves.

RED AND BLACK BEAN FILLING

Colour Index page 39. Makes 15 tablespoons (to fill 15 tartlets). 140 kJ per tablespoon. Low in cholesterol, fat.
Begin 15 minutes ahead.

½ small red
  onion, grated
½ red capsicum,
  finely chopped
3 cloves garlic,
  crushed
1 tablespoon
  vegetable oil
1 teaspoon dried
  oregano
2 teaspoons chilli
  powder
1 cup canned red
  kidney beans,
  drained and rinsed
2 tablespoons bottled
  black bean sauce
1½ teaspoons cider
  vinegar
⅛ teaspoon pepper
Sour cream to
  garnish

1. Combine onion, capsicum, garlic, oil, oregano and chilli powder in a medium bowl. Cook on High (100% power) for 3 minutes, or until softened, stirring halfway through cooking.
2. Stir in kidney beans, black bean sauce, vinegar and pepper. Cook on High for 3 minutes, stirring halfway through cooking. Spoon filling into heated pastry cases; garnish with sour cream.

Entrées

STUFFED ARTICHOKE BOTTOMS

Colour Index page 40. 523 kJ per artichoke. Low in cholesterol.
Begin 55 minutes ahead.

Ingredients	For 4	For 2	For 1
Artichokes, rinsed	4 medium	2 medium	1 medium
Water	½ cup	¼ cup	2 tablespoons
Rindless bacon, diced	4 rashers	2 rashers	1 rasher
White onion, chopped	1 small	½ small	¼ small
Dried breadcrumbs	½ cup	¼ cup	2 tablespoons
Sultanas	1½ tablespoons	3 teaspoons	1½ teaspoons
Dried rosemary	1½ teaspoons	¾ teaspoon	to taste
Pepper	to taste	to taste	to taste
Lemon slices, salad greens and onion rings	garnish	garnish	garnish
Microwave cookware	3-litre casserole 23-cm pie plate	2-litre casserole 23-cm pie plate	23-cm pie plate 20-cm pie plate
Time on High (100% power) Artichokes Bacon	22–24 minutes 4–5 minutes	14–16 minutes 2–3 minutes	7–9 minutes 1½ (1:30)–2 minutes
Stuffed artichokes	2 minutes	1 minute	45 seconds

1 With serrated knife, cut off stem and 2.5 cm straight across top of each artichoke. Pull off any small, loose or discoloured leaves.

2 With kitchen shears, carefully trim off thorny tips of leaves. Place artichokes, base down, in casserole or pie plate (see Chart).

3 Pour water over artichokes. Cook, covered, on High for time in Chart, until a leaf can be pulled out easily, rearranging once.

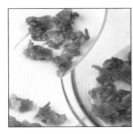

4 Place bacon in pie plate (see Chart). Cook, covered with paper towel, on High for time in Chart, stirring twice. Transfer bacon to clean paper towel to drain. Combine with onion, breadcrumbs, sultanas, rosemary and pepper in a bowl.

5 With fingers, pull off all artichoke leaves. (If you like, serve leaves with a dip.) Place artichoke bottoms on pie plate used to cook bacon. With spoon, scrape out and discard fuzzy centres (the chokes). Trim base and edges of each artichoke bottom.

6 Fill each artichoke bottom with about 2 tablespoons stuffing. Cook on High for time in Chart. Transfer artichokes to individual plates; garnish with lemon slices, salad greens and onion rings. Serve immediately.

SAUSAGE PARCELS

Colour Index page 41. Makes 12. 251 kJ each. Low in cholesterol, sodium.
Begin early in day.

2 cups water
2 tablespoons lemon juice
12 vine leaves, fresh or in brine (rinsed and drained)
125 g spicy sausages
2 tablespoons finely chopped onion
1 clove garlic, crushed
125 g canned pimientos
30 g mozzarella cheese, grated (¼ cup)
2 tablespoons dried breadcrumbs
Vegetable oil

1. Place water and lemon juice in a medium bowl. Heat on High (100% power) for 5–6 minutes, until boiling; add vine leaves. Cook, covered, on High for 10 minutes. Drain; cover with cold water.
2. Remove casings from sausages. Crumble meat into a 1-litre casserole; stir in onion and garlic. Cook on High for 2–3 minutes, stirring twice to break up large pieces. Drain well.
3. Cut 24 matchstick-thin 5-cm strips from pimientos; put aside. Chop remaining pimientos; add to meat with cheese and breadcrumbs.
4. Pat vine leaves dry. Place 1 tablespoon meat in centre of each leaf; fold sides over mixture, then roll up. Place each parcel, seam side down, on a baking tray lined with greaseproof paper and decorate each with pimiento strips; freeze until firm. Transfer to a freezer container; cover and keep frozen until ready to use.
5. About 5 minutes before serving, place parcels, seam side down, on a rack set in a 30-cm x 20-cm baking dish; brush lightly with oil. Cook, covered, on High for 2 minutes, or until hot.

CRAB-FILLED MUSHROOMS

Colour Index page 41. Makes 12. 377 kJ each. Good source of niacin.
Begin early in day.

¾ cup crab meat
⅓ cup mayonnaise
2 tablespoons dried breadcrumbs
1 tablespoon finely chopped celery
1 tablespoon finely chopped onion
3 teaspoons lemon juice
3 teaspoons dry sherry
4 drops Tabasco sauce
12 large mushrooms
1 tablespoon vegetable oil

1. Mix crab, mayonnaise, breadcrumbs, celery, onion, lemon juice, sherry and Tabasco sauce in a bowl.
2. Brush mushrooms with oil. Spoon an equal amount of crab into each. Place on a baking tray; freeze until firm. Transfer to a freezer container; cover and keep frozen until ready to use.
3. About 10 minutes before serving, place mushrooms on a rack set in a 30-cm x 20-cm baking dish. Cook on High (100% power) for 5–6 minutes, until hot.

POACHED APPLES WITH PROSCIUTTO

Colour Index page 40. Makes 6. 599 kJ per serving. Good source of fibre.
Begin 40 minutes ahead.

6 small red-skinned apples	185 g thinly sliced prosciutto or smoked salmon
1 cup dry white wine	⅓ cup sour cream
1 teaspoon whole allspice	2 tablespoons coarsely crumbled blue cheese
Salad greens	
Capers	

1. Cut off top quarter of each apple; put aside. Core apples without cutting through base.
2. Arrange apples in a 2-litre casserole; replace tops. Add wine and allspice. Cook, covered, on High (100% power) for 5 minutes, or until softened, rearranging halfway through cooking. Drain apples and tops on paper towel.
3. Arrange salad greens on individual plates and sprinkle with capers; place apples and prosciutto alongside.
4. Combine sour cream and blue cheese in a bowl. Spoon mixture into apples; replace tops.

BAKED STUFFED TOMATOES

Colour Index page 38. Makes 4. 507 kJ each. Low in cholesterol. Good source of vitamin A.
Begin 20 minutes ahead.

4 tomatoes	1 tablespoon finely chopped fresh oregano or 1 teaspoon dried oregano
¼ teaspoon salt	
¼ cup grated Parmesan cheese	
2 tablespoons dried breadcrumbs	Pepper to taste
2 cloves garlic, crushed	1 tablespoon olive or vegetable oil
1 tablespoon chopped fresh parsley	Parsley sprigs to garnish

1. Cut a thin slice from bottom of each tomato so tomatoes sit flat. Cut slice from top of each tomato and reserve.
2. Scoop out flesh and seeds from tomatoes; discard. Sprinkle the inside of each tomato with salt.
3. Combine Parmesan cheese, breadcrumbs, garlic, parsley, oregano and pepper in a bowl.
4. Arrange tomatoes about 2.5 cm apart in a 30-cm x 20-cm baking dish. Spoon stuffing into tomatoes; pack in firmly. Drizzle oil over tomatoes. Cook on High (100% power) for 6 minutes, rearranging halfway through cooking. Allow to stand for 2 minutes.
5. Transfer tomatoes to a serving platter; place reserved tomato slices on top of stuffing. Garnish with parsley. Serve immediately.

CHEESY STUFFED PRAWNS

Colour Index page 41. 473 kJ per prawn. Good source of calcium.
Begin early in day.

Ingredients	For 4	For 2	For 1
Green prawns, shelled and deveined (page 166)	12 large	6 large	3 large
Lemon juice	3 teaspoons	2 teaspoons	1 teaspoon
Dry sherry	1½ tablespoons	3 teaspoons	1½ teaspoons
Dried breadcrumbs	¼ cup	2 tablespoons	1 tablespoon
Gruyère or Edam cheese, grated	2 tablespoons	1 tablespoon	2 teaspoons
Parmesan cheese, grated	2 tablespoons	1 tablespoon	2 teaspoons
Capsicum, finely chopped	1½ tablespoons	3 teaspoons	1½ teaspoons
Tabasco sauce	to taste	to taste	to taste
Peach slices and salad greens	garnish	garnish	garnish
Microwave cookware	30-cm flan dish	25-cm flan dish	20-cm or 23-cm pie plate
Time on Medium-Low (30% power)	6–8 minutes	4–6 minutes	2–3 minutes

1 Combine prawns, lemon juice and half the sherry in a bowl. Toss to coat; put aside. In another bowl, combine breadcrumbs, cheeses, capsicum, Tabasco sauce and remaining sherry.

2 Cut each prawn three-quarters of the way through along centre back; spread open. Pound lightly to flatten.

3 Divide cheese mixture into same number of balls as prawns; roll into log shapes. Place 1 log along centre back of each prawn. Reshape prawns firmly around filling.

4 Place prawns on a baking tray lined with greaseproof paper; freeze until firm. Transfer to a freezer container; cover and keep frozen until ready to use.

5 About 15 minutes before serving, arrange prawns in a circle in flan dish or pie plate (see Chart) with tails pointing towards the centre of the dish.

6 Cook prawns, covered loosely with greaseproof paper, on Medium-Low for time in Chart, just until prawns turn pink. Turn each one over and rotate dish halfway through cooking. Garnish with peach slices and salad greens. Serve hot.

ARTICHOKES WITH LEMON AND GARLIC

Colour Index page 40. 1088 kJ per artichoke. Good source of vitamin C, iron. Begin 55 minutes ahead.

Ingredients	For 4	For 2	For 1
Artichokes, rinsed	*4 medium*	*2 medium*	*1 medium*
Lemon, thinly sliced and cut into quarters	*1 small*	*½ small*	*¼ small*
Garlic, thinly sliced	*4 cloves*	*2 cloves*	*1 clove*
Dry white wine	*½ cup*	*¼ cup*	*1½ tablespoons*
Butter	*125 g*	*60 g*	*30 g*
Lemon slices and parsley sprigs	*garnish*	*garnish*	*garnish*
Microwave cookware	3-litre casserole Medium bowl	2-litre casserole Medium bowl	23-cm pie plate Small bowl
Time on High (100% power) Artichokes Butter	22–24 minutes 1½ (1:30)–2 minutes	14–16 minutes 45 seconds–1 minute	7–9 minutes 45 seconds

1 With serrated knife, cut off stem and 2.5 cm straight across top of each artichoke. Pull off any small, loose or discoloured leaves from the bases. With kitchen shears, carefully trim off thorny tips of artichoke leaves.

2 Push lemon quarters and garlic slices between artichoke leaves. Place artichokes, base down, in casserole or pie plate (see Chart). Drizzle with wine.

3 Cook artichokes, covered, on High for time in Chart, until a leaf can be pulled out easily; rearrange artichokes halfway through cooking.

4 Place butter in bowl (see Chart). Heat, covered with paper towel, on High for time in Chart. Skim off white foam; discard. Pour clarified butter into small serving bowl.

5 Gently push artichoke leaves out from centre; remove centre leaves to expose fuzzy centres (the chokes). With spoon, scrape out and discard the chokes.

6 Place artichokes on individual plates; drizzle with cooking liquid. Garnish with lemon slices and parsley sprigs. Serve with clarified butter for dipping.

CREAMED MUSHROOMS

Colour Index page 39. 4 servings. 1026 kJ per serving. Good source of riboflavin, niacin, iron. Begin 25 minutes ahead.

500 g mushrooms
30 g butter or margarine
4 spring onions, sliced
3 cloves garlic, crushed
¾ cup chicken stock
1½ tablespoons dry sherry
1½ tablespoons cream
¼ teaspoon salt
Pepper to taste
1 tablespoon cornflour dissolved in
2 tablespoons cold water
8 slices crusty white bread, toasted and cut in half
Spring onion, finely sliced (optional)

1. Trim mushrooms and cut into quarters.
2. Place mushrooms, butter, spring onions and garlic in a 30-cm x 20-cm baking dish. Cook on High (100% power) for 5 minutes, stirring twice.
3. Stir in stock, sherry, cream, salt and pepper. Cook on High for 3 minutes. Stir in dissolved cornflour. Cook on High for 3 minutes longer, or until slightly thickened, stirring halfway through cooking.
4. Arrange 4 halves of toast on individual plates. Spoon mushroom mixture over toast; garnish, if you like, with extra spring onion. Serve immediately.

MUSHROOMS
There are many kinds of mushrooms available — fresh, dried and canned — both homegrown and imported. They are a delicious and low-kilojoule ingredient. Try mixing two or three types together in dishes like Creamed Mushrooms (above).

Shiitake mushrooms

Oyster mushrooms

Cultivated mushrooms

Button mushrooms

Meal in Minutes *for 20 people*

Cocktails For A Crowd

Cocktails with Bombay Mixed Nuts (page 296), olives and breadsticks
Bacon Dip (page 111) with crudités and bagel chips
Spicy Chicken Wings (page 116)
Cheesy Stuffed Prawns (page 121)
Country-style Pork Pâté (page 114) with dill pickles and biscuits
Cheese and fresh fruit

PREPARATION TIMETABLE

Up to 1 week ahead:	**Up to 2 days ahead:**	**1 day ahead:**	**2 hours ahead:**	**About 15 minutes ahead:**
Prepare Cheesy Stuffed Prawns up to the end of step 4. Prepare Bombay Mixed Nuts and store in an airtight container.	*Prepare Country-style Pork Pâté; wrap well and refrigerate without unmoulding. Check all bar supplies: spirits, wines, mixers and soft drinks; if necessary, buy ice or make extra ice and keep in plastic bags in the freezer.*	*Prepare double quantity of Spicy Chicken Wings; cover and refrigerate. Select cheeses and fruit; keep chilled. Make double quantity of Bacon Dip; cover and refrigerate. Prepare vegetables for crudités; keep in plastic bags in the refrigerator.*	*Arrange crudités and bagel chips on a platter. Spoon Bacon Dip into a serving bowl. Unmould pâté and accompany with pickles and biscuits. Arrange cheese and fruit on a board; keep covered until guests arrive. Arrange seasonal fresh fruit in a bowl.*	*Fill serving bowls with olives and Bombay Mixed Nuts. Arrange breadsticks for serving. Place glasses, cocktail ingredients and ice bucket on trays. Reheat chicken wings and cook prawns in microwave just before you are ready to serve.*

123

ELEGANT SEAFOOD SALAD

Colour Index page 40. 896 kJ per serving. Good source of iron.
Begin 2¼ hours ahead or early in day.

Ingredients for 6 servings		Microwave cookware
250 g green prawns, shelled and deveined (page 166)	1 cup loosely packed fresh basil leaves	30-cm x 20-cm baking dish
250 g scallops	1 clove garlic	23-cm flan dish
3 spring onions, sliced or cut into very thin strips	¼ teaspoon white pepper	
	Salad greens	
3 tablespoons lemon juice	½ cup seafood cocktail sauce (bottled or homemade)	
4 tablespoons olive oil	Green grapes, pear slices (page 115) and red currants or other fruit to garnish	
½ teaspoon salt		
12 mussels, cleaned		

1 Place prawns, scallops, spring onions, half the lemon juice, 1 tablespoon oil and half the salt in baking dish. Cook, covered, on High (100% power) for 3–5 minutes, just until prawns turn pink and scallops are opaque.

2 Stir seafood mixture. Cover and refrigerate until chilled. Meanwhile, arrange mussels in flan dish; discard any that are open.

3 Cook mussels, covered, on High for 2–2½ (2:30) minutes, just until shells open; discard any that remain closed. Remove mussels from shells; reserve 12 half-shells.

4 Make sauce: In food processor with knife blade attached or in blender, place basil, remaining oil, lemon juice, remaining garlic, 1 tablespoon water, pepper and remaining salt; process until well blended.

5 Line individual plates with salad greens; arrange prawns, scallops and mussels on top. Fill 6 reserved mussel half-shells with basil sauce and 6 with seafood cocktail sauce; arrange 1 of each on each plate.

6 Garnish each plate with grapes, pear slices and red currants.

OYSTERS ROCKEFELLER

Colour Index page 39. Makes 12. 213 kJ each. Good source of vitamin A, iron.
Begin 25 minutes ahead.

2 rashers rindless bacon, diced	2 tablespoons grated Parmesan cheese
125 g chopped cooked spinach	⅛ teaspoon cayenne pepper
2 spring onions, sliced	2 tablespoons Pernod (anise-flavoured liqueur)
1 clove garlic, chopped	
2 tablespoons chopped fresh parsley	12 large oysters on the half-shell
30 g butter or margarine	

1. Cook bacon in a 23-cm pie plate, covered with paper towel, on High (100% power) for 2–3 minutes, until browned, stirring halfway through cooking. Transfer to clean paper towel to drain.
2. Combine spinach, spring onions, garlic, parsley and butter in a medium bowl. Cook on High for 4 minutes, stirring occasionally.
3. In food processor with knife blade attached or in blender, process spinach mixture until smooth. Mix spinach with Parmesan cheese, cayenne pepper and Pernod; put aside.
4. Arrange oysters on a 30-cm platter. (If you like, steady shells by pressing them into a 6-mm-deep layer of rock salt.) Spoon spinach mixture on to oysters; sprinkle with bacon.
5. Cook oysters on High for 3–4 minutes, until hot. Serve immediately.

SCALLOPED OYSTERS

Colour Index page 38. 6 servings. 860 kJ per serving. Good source of vitamin A, iron.
Begin 20 minutes ahead.

125 g butter or margarine	½ teaspoon Worcestershire sauce
2 cups melba toast crumbs (page 193)	2 tablespoons chopped fresh parsley
48 bottled oysters, drained	Lemon slices and parsley sprigs to garnish
½ cup cream	

1. Heat butter in a 30-cm x 20-cm baking dish, covered with paper towel, on High (100% power) for 1½ (1:30)–2 minutes, until melted. Stir in melba toast crumbs. Transfer half the crumb mixture to a small bowl; put aside.
2. Spread remaining crumb mixture in a thin layer in the baking dish. Top with oysters.
3. In another small bowl, combine cream and Worcestershire sauce. Pour mixture over oysters. Top with reserved crumbs; sprinkle with chopped parsley.
4. Cook oysters on High for 4–5 minutes, until hot.
5. Spoon on to individual plates; garnish with lemon and parsley. Serve immediately.

Soups

**STOCKS · QUICK AND EASY SOUPS · VEGETABLE SOUPS
HEARTY SOUPS · FRUIT SOUPS**

Soups

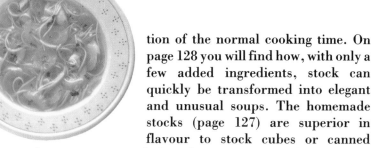

Recipes in this chapter range from simple basic stocks that can be used as soup bases, to the more substantial soups such as Split Pea and Ham Soup (page 131) and Minestone (page 132) that can be main courses. Some are warm and welcoming on a cold day; others, such as chilled Vichyssoise and Cream of Spinach Soup (page 129) and the fruit soups on page 136, are a refreshing treat on a warm day.

The microwave oven can be used to cook soups made from fresh ingredients that would take much longer if cooked conventionally. Other time-saving uses for the microwave include reconstituting dried soups, cooking ingredients from frozen, and heating canned soups (always remove soup from the can first). Soups should be stirred during cooking in the microwave and especially just before serving in order to equalise the temperature – you'll find the edges of the soup may start to bubble long before the centre is hot.

A microwave can also make stock – an essential base for soups and many other recipes – in a fraction of the normal cooking time. On page 128 you will find how, with only a few added ingredients, stock can quickly be transformed into elegant and unusual soups. The homemade stocks (page 127) are superior in flavour to stock cubes or canned consommé, and they do not contain salt, but commercial products can be used in the recipes.

Most stocks and soups can be frozen and then defrosted and reheated in the microwave. Soups are best frozen in 1- or 2-cup quantities, but make sure containers are only two-thirds full, otherwise they may overflow when reheating. If you freeze soup in a non-microwave-safe container, remove it as a block by placing the container under hot running water, then place the block in a microwave-safe bowl or casserole to defrost in the microwave. Using a fork, break the block apart as it thaws to speed up the process. (For more information on reheating frozen soup, see Chart, page 132.) If you are planning to freeze soup, season it lightly when making, then adjust the seasoning after reheating.

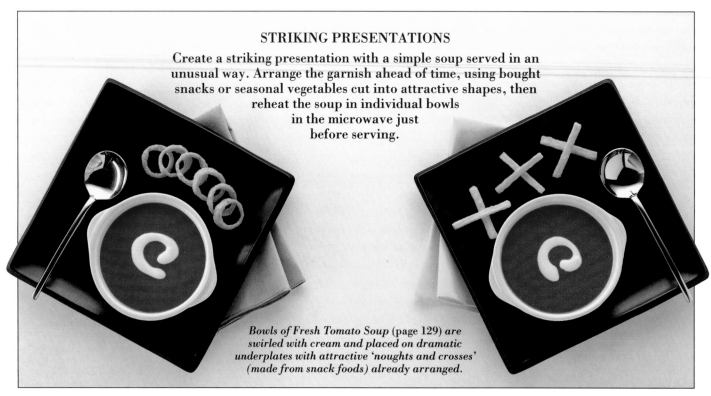

STRIKING PRESENTATIONS

Create a striking presentation with a simple soup served in an unusual way. Arrange the garnish ahead of time, using bought snacks or seasonal vegetables cut into attractive shapes, then reheat the soup in individual bowls in the microwave just before serving.

Bowls of Fresh Tomato Soup (page 129) are swirled with cream and placed on dramatic underplates with attractive 'noughts and crosses' (made from snack foods) already arranged.

A microwave oven shortens the time needed to make stock at home, and an added advantage is that you can make a small quantity quickly, as you need it. Alternatively, you can make a larger quantity and freeze it in containers.

VEGETABLE STOCK

Colour Index page 42. Makes 3 cups. 155 kJ per cup. Low in cholesterol, fat, sodium. Good source of vitamin A. Begin 40 minutes ahead.

1 leek
1 onion with skin
3 carrots
2 tomatoes
1 clove garlic
6 mushrooms, cut in half
4 celery stalks, cut into thirds
1 sprig parsley
1 bay leaf
6 whole peppercorns
½ cup tomato juice
3½ cups cold water

1. Cut leek in half lengthways; carefully wash under cold running water until all grit is removed.
2. Cut onion, carrots, tomatoes and garlic into quarters.
3. Combine all ingredients in a deep 2-litre bowl. Cook, covered, on High (100% power) for 20 minutes, stirring occasionally. Allow to stand for 5 minutes.
4. Line a strainer with a double layer of muslin. Strain liquid into a bowl; discard vegetables.

FISH STOCK

Colour Index page 42. Makes 3 cups. 172 kJ per cup. Low in cholesterol, fat. Begin 40 minutes ahead.

750 g fish bones (not from oily fish)
½ leek
½ carrot
½ celery stalk
6 whole peppercorns
1 sprig fresh thyme or ½ teaspoon dried thyme
1 cup dry white wine
3 cups cold water

1. Wash fish bones under cold running water to remove any blood or scales. Chop bones into 10-cm pieces.
2. Cut leek in half lengthways; carefully wash under cold running water until all grit is removed.
3. Combine all ingredients in a deep 2-litre bowl. Cook, covered, on High (100% power) for 15 minutes, stirring occasionally. Allow to stand for 5 minutes.
4. Line a strainer with a double layer of muslin. Strain liquid into a bowl; discard bones and vegetables.

BEEF STOCK

Colour Index page 44. Makes 3 cups. 130 kJ per cup. Low in cholesterol, fat, sodium. Begin 1½ hours ahead.

1.5 kg beef or veal bones
1 onion with skin, cut into quarters
1 tomato, cut into quarters
1 leek
2 cloves garlic, cut into quarters
1 bay leaf
1 sprig parsley
6 whole peppercorns
4 cups cold water

1. Preheat conventional oven to 230°C. Brown bones with onion and tomato in a foil-lined baking dish for about 1 hour.
2. Cut leek in half lengthways; carefully wash under cold running water until all grit is removed.
3. Combine all ingredients in a deep 2-litre bowl. Cook, covered, on High (100% power) for 20 minutes, stirring occasionally. Allow to stand for 5 minutes. Skim off any fat.
4. Line a strainer with a double layer of muslin. Strain liquid into a bowl; discard bones and vegetables.

CHICKEN STOCK

Colour Index page 42. Makes 3 cups. 197 kJ per cup. Low in cholesterol, fat, sodium. Begin 40 minutes ahead.

750 g chicken bones
1 leek
1 carrot
1 celery stalk
1 sprig parsley
1 sprig fresh thyme or ½ teaspoon dried thyme
1 bay leaf
6 whole peppercorns
4 cups cold water

1. Chop chicken bones into 10-cm pieces.
2. Cut leek in half lengthways; carefully wash under cold running water until all grit is removed.
3. Combine all ingredients in a deep 2-litre bowl. Cook, covered, on High (100% power) for 20 minutes, stirring occasionally. Allow to stand for 5 minutes. Skim off any fat.
4. Line a strainer with a double layer of muslin. Strain liquid into a bowl; discard bones and vegetables.

Use the homemade stocks (page 127) as a base for these instant soups that are suitable for a first course, a light meal, or even an after-school snack. Or create your own recipes by adding different ingredients according to taste.

Oriental-style Soup *(right)*: To *2 cups Fish Stock*, add *¼ cup chopped, cooked shelled prawns, 3 sliced spring onions* and *½ teaspoon slivered green ginger*. Cook, covered, on High (100% power) for 5 minutes, or until boiling. Garnish with *coriander leaves*.

Double Vegetable Soup *(below)*: To *2 cups Vegetable Stock*, add *¼ cup thinly sliced celery, ¼ cup thinly sliced carrot, ¼ cup thinly sliced leek* and *¼ cup chopped asparagus tips*. Cook, covered, on High (100% power) for 3 minutes. Add *¼ cup shredded spinach*. Cook, covered, on High for 2 minutes.

Beefy Italian Broth *(above)*: To *2 cups Beef Stock*, add *¼ cup sliced mushrooms, ¼ cup sliced fennel, ¼ cup diced carrots* and *1 tablespoon shredded fresh basil*. Cook, covered, on High (100% power) for 5 minutes, or until boiling. Add *¼ cup Gruyère cheese cubes*. Garnish with *fresh rosemary* and *basil leaves*.

Chicken and Pasta Soup *(left)*: To *2 cups Chicken Stock*, add *¼ cup small pasta shapes* (such as animals, alphabets or bow ties) and *¼ cup diced carrots*. Cook, covered, on High (100% power) for 5 minutes, or until boiling. Add *¼ cup cooked, shredded chicken*. Cook on High for 2–3 minutes, until boiling.

Vegetable soups

VICHYSSOISE

Colour Index page 44. Makes 8 cups. 557 kJ per cup.
Good source of vitamin C, fibre.
Begin early in day.

375 g leeks	1 small cooking apple,
500 g potatoes, sliced	peeled, cored and
30 g butter or margarine	sliced
¼ teaspoon salt	1 cup cream
¼ teaspoon white pepper	Unpeeled red-skinned
1 cup water	apple slices and
1 cup chicken or	parsley sprigs to
vegetable stock	garnish

1. Cut off roots and green tops from leeks; discard. Cut the white part of leeks into 2.5-cm pieces; carefully wash under cold running water until all grit is removed.
2. Place leeks, potatoes, butter, salt and pepper in a deep 3-litre bowl. Cook, covered, on High (100% power) for 7 minutes, stirring halfway through cooking.
3. Add water, stock and apple slices to vegetables. Cook, covered, on High for 6–8 minutes, until potatoes are tender, stirring halfway through cooking.
4. In food processor with knife blade attached or in blender, process soup until smooth (in batches if necessary). Return to bowl and stir in cream; cover and refrigerate.
5. Just before serving, garnish with apple slices and parsley sprigs. Serve chilled.

CREAM OF SPINACH SOUP

Colour Index page 44. Makes 4 cups. 728 kJ per cup.
Good source of vitamin A, vitamin C, calcium, iron, fibre.
Begin early in day.

30 g butter or margarine	1 tablespoon cornflour
1 onion, chopped	dissolved in
2 small potatoes, diced	2 tablespoons
(about 1 cup)	cold water
1¼ cups chicken or	¼ teaspoon salt
vegetable stock	¼ teaspoon white pepper
375 g spinach or	Ground nutmeg to taste
silverbeet leaves, torn	Natural yoghurt to
½ cup cream or milk	garnish

1. Combine butter, onion, potatoes and ¼ cup stock in a deep 3-litre bowl. Cook, covered, on High (100% power) for 8 minutes, or until potatoes are tender, stirring twice.
2. Add spinach. Cook, covered, on High for 5 minutes. In food processor with knife blade attached or in blender, process vegetable mixture until smooth; return to bowl.
3. Add remaining stock, cream, dissolved cornflour, salt, pepper and nutmeg; stir until smooth. Cook on High for 5 minutes, or until hot, stirring halfway through cooking.
4. Serve hot, or cover and refrigerate to serve chilled. Just before serving, garnish with a swirl of yoghurt.

FRESH TOMATO SOUP

Colour Index page 42. 230 kJ per cup. Low in cholesterol, fat. Good source of vitamin A, vitamin C, fibre.
Begin 25 minutes ahead.

Ingredients for 6 cups		Microwave cookware
1.25 kg ripe tomatoes	1 tablespoon tomato	Deep 3-litre bowl
1 onion, chopped	paste	
1 celery stalk, chopped	½ teaspoon salt	
2 cloves garlic, crushed	¼ teaspoon pepper	
½ bay leaf	Tabasco sauce to taste	
¼ teaspoon ground	Sour cream and chopped	
cloves	chives to garnish	
1 cup chicken or		
vegetable stock		

1 Remove stem ends from tomatoes; cut tomatoes into small chunks.

2 Combine tomatoes, onion, celery, garlic, bay leaf and cloves in bowl. Cook, covered, on High (100% power) for 15 minutes, or until softened, stirring often.

3 Discard bay leaf. In food processor with knife blade attached or in blender, process tomato mixture until smooth.

4 Combine with stock, tomato paste, salt, pepper and Tabasco sauce. Cook, covered, on High for 5 minutes, stirring once.

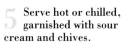

5 Serve hot or chilled, garnished with sour cream and chives.

CROÛTONS
Combine *1 tablespoon melted butter or margarine* and *2 tablespoons vegetable oil* in a baking dish. Add *4 slices bread* cut into small shapes; turn to coat. Bake in a conventional oven at 230°C for 8–10 minutes, until golden, turning once.

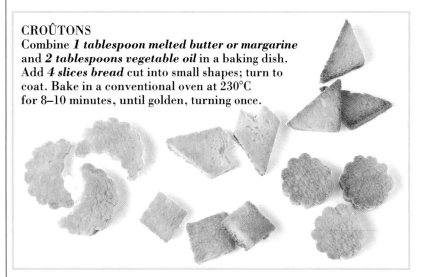

WINTER VEGETABLE SOUP

Colour Index page 43. 452 kJ per cup. Good source of vitamin A, vitamin C, fibre. Begin 35 minutes ahead.

Traditionally, vegetable soups are thick, substantial dishes. This Winter Vegetable Soup is a lighter version which can be made in much less time than if cooked conventionally. The recipe can be varied by using other seasonal vegetables.

Ingredients for 6 cups		Microwave cookware
1 large carrot	1 teaspoon finely	Deep 3-litre bowl
1 large parsnip	chopped fresh	
1 celery stalk	rosemary or	
375 g cabbage	¼ teaspoon dried	
1 medium onion	rosemary	
1 large turnip	1 bay leaf	
30 g butter or margarine	3 cups vegetable stock	
2 teaspoons finely	½ teaspoon salt	
chopped fresh thyme	Pepper to taste	
or ½ teaspoon		
dried thyme		

1 Cut carrot, parsnip and celery into matchstick-thin strips.

2 Thinly slice cabbage and onion. Peel and dice turnip.

3 Heat butter in bowl, covered with paper towel, on High (100% power) for 45 seconds, or until melted.

4 Add carrot, parsnip, celery, cabbage, onion, turnip, thyme, rosemary and bay leaf to butter. Stir in ½ cup stock; mix well.

5 Cook, covered, on High for 12 minutes, or until vegetables are tender, stirring occasionally.

6 Add remaining stock, salt and pepper to soup. Cook, covered, on High for 3 minutes, or until hot, stirring halfway through cooking. Discard bay leaf. Serve immediately.

CARROT SOUP WITH ORANGE

Colour Index page 42. Makes 4 cups. 573 kJ per cup. Good source of vitamin A, fibre. Begin 25 minutes ahead.

30 g butter or margarine
500 g carrots, thinly sliced
1 onion, finely chopped
1 teaspoon grated orange rind

2½ cups chicken stock
½ teaspoon salt
⅛ teaspoon pepper
Thickened cream and parsley sprigs to garnish

1. Heat butter in a deep 2-litre bowl on High (100% power) for 45 seconds, or until melted.
2. Add carrots, onion, orange rind and ½ cup stock. Cook, covered, on High for 12 minutes, or until carrots are tender, stirring twice.
3. In food processor with knife blade attached or in blender, process carrot mixture until smooth.
4. Return mixture to bowl. Stir in remaining stock, salt and pepper. Cook, covered, on High for 4 minutes, or until hot, stirring halfway through cooking.
5. Serve hot, or cover and refrigerate to serve chilled. Just before serving, garnish with cream and parsley.

LIGHT AND CREAMY ASPARAGUS SOUP

Colour Index page 42. Makes 4 cups. 657 kJ per cup. Good source of vitamin C, fibre. Begin 25 minutes ahead.

30 g butter or margarine
1 onion, sliced
500 g asparagus, trimmed and cut into 5-cm pieces
1 cup vegetable stock

1 cup cream
Natural yoghurt or thickened cream and chervil sprigs to garnish

1. Place butter and onion in a deep 2-litre bowl. Cook, covered, on High (100% power) for 45 seconds, or until butter is melted.
2. Add asparagus and stock to onion mixture. Cook, covered, on High for 10–12 minutes, until asparagus is tender, stirring twice.
3. In food processor with knife blade attached or in blender, process asparagus mixture until smooth. Return to bowl. Stir in cream. Cook on High for 2–3 minutes, until hot, stirring halfway through cooking.
4. Serve hot, or cover and refrigerate to serve chilled. Just before serving, garnish with a swirl of yoghurt and a sprig of chervil.

Hearty soups

CURRIED PARSNIP SOUP

Colour Index page 43. Makes 6 cups. 733 kJ per cup.
Low in sodium. Good source of vitamin A, vitamin C,
calcium, iron, fibre.
Begin 35 minutes ahead.

60 g butter or margarine	*750 g parsnips*
1 onion, chopped	*3 cups vegetable stock*
1 cooking apple, peeled, cored and sliced	*1 cup milk*
1 tablespoon curry powder	*Toasted, flaked almonds and chopped fresh coriander leaves to garnish*
½ teaspoon turmeric (optional)	

1. Combine butter, onion, apple, curry powder
and turmeric in a deep 3-litre bowl. Cook,
covered, on High (100% power) for 5 minutes, or
until softened, stirring twice.
2. Meanwhile, peel parsnips. Cut each in half
lengthways and slice thinly. Add parsnips and
stock to onion and apple mixture. Cook, covered, on High for 18–20 minutes, until parsnips
are very soft, stirring twice.
3. In food processor with knife blade attached
or in blender, process soup until smooth. Return to bowl and add milk. Cook on High for
2 minutes, or until hot, stirring halfway through
cooking.
4. Garnish with almonds and coriander. Serve
immediately.

HEARTY BEAN SOUP

**Colour Index page 43. Makes 7 cups. 1260 kJ per
cup.** Low in cholesterol. Good source of iron, fibre.
Begin 35 minutes ahead.

4 rashers rindless bacon, diced	*1 teaspoon chilli powder*
1 onion, chopped	*500 g cooked red kidney beans, drained*
1 celery stalk, chopped	*500 g cooked borlotti beans, drained*
2 cloves garlic, crushed	*500 g cooked haricot beans, drained*
1 tablespoon finely chopped fresh oregano or 1 teaspoon dried oregano	*500 g cooked black beans, drained*
1½ teaspoons ground cumin	*2 cups chicken stock*
	Celery leaves to garnish

1. Cook bacon in a deep 3-litre bowl, covered
with paper towel, on High (100% power) for
4–5 minutes, until browned, stirring halfway
through cooking.
2. Add onion, celery, garlic, oregano, cumin
and chilli powder; mix well. Cook on High for
5 minutes, or until vegetables are softened,
stirring halfway through cooking.
3. Add all beans and stock. Cook on High for
10 minutes, stirring twice.
4. In food processor with knife blade attached
or in blender, process 2 cups of soup. Return to
unblended soup; stir.
5. Ladle into soup bowls; garnish with celery
leaves. Serve immediately.

Small portions of these hearty soups can be served as entrées before
light main courses. Larger bowls of soup can make a filling, casual
lunch or dinner, especially when accompanied with bread or rolls
warmed briefly in the microwave oven.

SPLIT PEA AND HAM SOUP

Colour Index page 44. 1180 kJ per cup. Low in cholesterol. Good source of vitamin
A, thiamine, iron, fibre.
Begin 1½ hours ahead.

Ingredients for 8 cups		Microwave cookware
500 g split peas *½ smoked ham hock, or ham bone with about 500 g meat left on* *1 onion, chopped* *1 carrot, thinly sliced* *1 celery stalk, thinly sliced* *1 tablespoon chopped fresh thyme or 1 teaspoon dried thyme*	*2 teaspoons chopped fresh rosemary or ½ teaspoon dried rosemary* *1 bay leaf* *3 cups water* *3 cups chicken stock* *Pepper to taste* *Chopped parsley to garnish*	Deep 3-litre bowl

1 Rinse split peas in a
strainer under cold
running water.

2 Combine peas, ham
hock, onion, carrot,
celery, thyme, rosemary
and bay leaf in bowl. Add
water.

3 Cook, covered, on
High (100% power)
for 20 minutes, stirring
halfway through cooking.
Add stock. Cook,
covered, on High for
20 minutes longer, or
until peas are soft,
stirring halfway through
cooking. Allow to stand
on a heatproof surface,
covered, for 30 minutes.

4 Remove ham hock
and cut off meat;
discard bone. Cut meat
into bite-sized pieces and
return to soup, reserving
some for garnish; discard
bay leaf.

5 In food processor
with knife blade
attached or in blender,
process soup until
smooth (in several
batches if necessary).
Return to bowl; adjust
consistency, if you like,
by adding more water.

6 Stir reserved ham
into soup. Cook,
covered, on High for
6 minutes, or until hot.
Add pepper to taste;
garnish with parsley.
Serve hot.

Easy Italian Dinner

Antipasto with breadsticks
Minestrone (right)
Creamy Cheesecake (page 361) or bought cheesecake
Espresso (below) with amaretti biscuits

PREPARATION TIMETABLE

1 day ahead:	*If making cheesecake, prepare, cover and refrigerate overnight.*
2 hours ahead:	*Prepare antipasto: Arrange a selection of Italian salami, ham and mortadella on a platter; add prosciutto-wrapped melon chunks, black olives, sliced fennel and strips of red and yellow capsicum. Cover until ready to serve.*
1½ hours ahead:	*Prepare Minestrone. Remove cheesecake from refrigerator; place on serving plate.*
Just before serving:	*If necessary, reheat soup on High (100% power) until bubbling. Prepare espresso.*

ESPRESSO

Espresso is the perfect coffee to round off an Italian-style meal. Use a dark roast coffee, from Italian delicatessens, specialty shops and some supermarkets.

Brew **9 tablespoons Italian-roast coffee** with **2¼ cups water** in an espresso pot. Serve in demitasse cups with a *twist of lemon rind*. Add *sugar* if you like. *Amaretti biscuits* (commercially made) are a traditional accompaniment.

MINESTRONE

Colour Index page 44. Makes 8 cups. 632 kJ per cup. Low in cholesterol. Good source of vitamin A, vitamin C, calcium, iron, fibre. Begin 1¼ hours ahead.

1 tablespoon olive or vegetable oil	*2 cups water*
30 g prosciutto, thinly sliced, or cooked ham, diced	*½ cup elbow macaroni*
1 onion, diced	*½ small head cabbage, cut into 5-cm pieces*
1 celery stalk, diced	*125 g green beans, cut into 2.5-cm pieces*
1 carrot, diced	*825 g can tomatoes*
2 cloves garlic, crushed	*1 cup cooked haricot beans or 310 g can butter beans, drained*
2 teaspoons finely chopped fresh oregano or ½ teaspoon dried oregano	*½ cup shredded fresh basil leaves*
	Grated Parmesan cheese

1. Heat oil in a deep 3-litre bowl on High (100% power) for 3 minutes. Stir in prosciutto, onion, celery, carrot, garlic and oregano. Cook on High for 4 minutes, stirring twice.
2. Add water, macaroni, cabbage, green beans and tomatoes with their liquid. Cook, covered, on High for 10 minutes, stirring twice.
3. Add haricot beans. Cook, covered, on High for 10 minutes, or until vegetables and macaroni are tender, stirring twice. Add basil and allow soup to stand, covered, for 5 minutes.
4. Ladle soup into warmed bowls; sprinkle with Parmesan cheese. Serve hot.

REHEATING FROZEN SOUP

For 4	For 2	For 1
4 cups	*2 cups*	*1 cup*
Microwave cookware		
2-litre bowl	1-litre bowl	Deep bowl
Time on Medium-Low (30% power)		
12–15 minutes	6–8 minutes	3–4 minutes
Time on Medium-High (70% power)		
10–12 minutes	9–11 minutes	6–8 minutes

1. Defrost soup in microwave-safe bowl (see Chart) on Medium-Low for time in Chart, breaking soup apart with a fork as it thaws.
2. Increase power level to Medium-High and heat soup for time in Chart, until bubbling, stirring twice.

FRENCH ONION SOUP

Colour Index page 43. Makes 6 cups. 925 kJ per cup.
Good source of calcium.
Begin 45 minutes ahead.

45 g butter or margarine	6 thick slices French
3 large onions, sliced	bread, toasted
(about 4 cups)	185 g Gruyère or Swiss
300 g can beef consommé	cheese, grated
2 tablespoons dry sherry	(1½ cups)
2 cups water	
1 tablespoon tomato	
paste	

1. Heat butter in a deep 3-litre bowl, covered with paper towel, on High (100% power) for 45 seconds–1 minute, until melted.
2. Add onions; stir to coat. Cook, covered, on High for 15 minutes, or until softened, stirring twice.
3. Add undiluted beef consommé, sherry, water and tomato paste; stir until blended. Cook, covered, on High for 8 minutes, or until hot, stirring twice.
4. Ladle soup into bowls or mugs. Float 1 slice toast in each bowl and sprinkle generously with cheese.
5. Arrange soup bowls in a circle on a 30-cm round platter (in batches if necessary). Cook on High for 3 minutes, or until cheese melts. Serve immediately.

Serving the soup

Top each serving with 1 slice of toasted French bread. Sprinkle toast generously with grated Gruyère cheese.

Heat soup in microwave as in step 5 above, until the cheese melts and begins to bubble.

Freezing the soup

This soup can also be frozen. At the end of step 3, cover soup and refrigerate until cold, then ladle into freezer containers in 1- or 2-cup quantities. Seal, label and freeze. Thaw and reheat until hot before proceeding with step 4.

For a complete meal, serve one of these hearty soups with a vegetable side dish or a tossed salad and hot crusty bread. Quick and easy to prepare, they also make substantial first courses.

CHICKEN NOODLE SOUP

Colour Index page 44. 846 kJ per cup. Low in sodium. Good source of vitamin A, niacin, iron.
Begin 1¼ hours ahead.

Ingredients for 4 cups		Microwave cookware
30 g butter or margarine 1 onion, thinly sliced 1 celery stalk, thinly sliced 1 large carrot, thinly sliced 3 cups chicken stock	500 g chicken pieces, skinned 1 cup fine egg noodles Pepper to taste Chopped parsley to garnish	Deep 2-litre bowl

1 Heat butter in bowl, covered with paper towel, on High (100% power) for 45 seconds, or until melted.

2 Stir in onion, celery and carrot. Cook on High for 3 minutes, stirring halfway through cooking.

3 Add 1 cup stock to vegetables. Place chicken pieces on top. Cook, covered, on High for 10 minutes, or until chicken juices run clear, turning pieces over halfway through cooking. Transfer chicken to a board.

4 Add remaining stock and noodles to vegetable mixture. Cook, covered, on High for 7 minutes, or until noodles are al dente, stirring halfway through cooking.

5 Meanwhile, remove chicken meat from bones; discard bones. Coarsely chop chicken, then stir into soup.

6 Allow soup to stand for 3–5 minutes. Before serving, skim any fat from surface. Add pepper. Ladle soup into warmed bowls; garnish with chopped parsley. Serve hot.

These hearty soups, containing vegetables combined with meat, chicken, fish or shellfish, make meals in themselves. To serve Seafood Gumbo (below), in true Creole style, it should be ladled over hot cooked rice in deep soup plates.

SEAFOOD GUMBO

Colour Index page 44. 657 kJ per cup. Good source of calcium, iron, fibre. Begin 1¼ hours ahead.

Ingredients for 8 cups		Microwave cookware
375 g large green prawns	825 g can tomatoes	Deep 3-litre bowl
30 g butter or margarine	24 oysters, bottled	
2 tablespoons plain flour	310 g fresh okra or drained canned okra, cut into 2.5-cm pieces	
3 celery stalks with leaves, sliced	Tabasco sauce to taste	
2 large onions, chopped	Salt to taste	
2 cloves garlic, crushed	Hot cooked rice (optional)	
2 teaspoons Worcestershire sauce		

1 Prepare prawns: Twist off head, then hold body with legs upwards and break shell open with your thumbs. Peel away shell, leaving tail in place. Cut along the back and remove black vein. Refrigerate prawns until needed.

2 Heat butter in bowl, covered with paper towel, on High (100% power) for 45 seconds, or until melted. Stir in flour until smooth.

3 Cook, covered, on High for 7 minutes, or until roux is rich golden-brown in colour, stirring often. Remove bowl from oven.

4 Stir in celery, onions and garlic. Cook on High for 4 minutes, stirring halfway through cooking. Add Worcestershire sauce and tomatoes. Cook, covered, on High for 5 minutes, stirring halfway through cooking.

5 Add prawns, oysters and okra to gumbo. Season with Tabasco sauce and salt.

6 Cook gumbo, covered, on High for 7 minutes, or just until prawns turn pink, stirring twice. Serve, if you like, over cooked rice.

SOUP GARNISHES

Even the most simple soup can look elegant by just adding a garnish. Some garnishes are a little time-consuming but most can be ready in minutes.

Spring onion curl: Trim top of spring onion. Slit top down to bulb 3 or 4 times; place in bowl of iced water so top will curl.

Lemon/Lime twist: Cut a thin slice from lemon or lime. Make 1 cut from centre to edge of slice; twist into a spiral shape.

Carrot curl: Shave strips lengthways from carrot with a vegetable peeler. Roll up and secure each strip with a toothpick. Place in bowl of iced water for 1 hour. Drain; remove toothpick and use immediately.

Leek/Carrot julienne: Cut leek and carrot lengthways into matchstick-thin strips.

Turned mushroom: Holding blade of paring knife against mushroom cap and pressing gently, twist blade edge clockwise from centre to edge of mushroom. Repeat evenly around mushroom cap.

Fresh herbs: Chop herbs with a knife or scissors, or use whole leaves or sprigs.

VEGETABLE CHOWDER

Colour Index page 43. Makes 6 cups. 678 kJ per cup.
Low in sodium. Good source of vitamin A, vitamin C, fibre.
Begin 35 minutes ahead.

60 g butter or margarine	1 teaspoon finely
2 large carrots, peeled and chopped	chopped fresh thyme or ¼ teaspoon
2 large celery stalks, chopped	dried thyme
1 large onion, chopped	2 cups vegetable stock
1 large potato, peeled and chopped	425 g can tomatoes
1 medium parsnip, peeled and chopped	310 g can butter beans, drained and rinsed
1 bay leaf	½ teaspoon pepper
	Chopped parsley to garnish

1. Cook butter in a deep 3-litre bowl, covered with paper towel, on High (100% power) for 2 minutes, or until melted.
2. Add carrots, celery, onion, potato, parsnip, bay leaf and thyme; stir to combine. Cook, covered, on High for 7–9 minutes, until vegetables are tender, stirring twice.
3. Add stock, tomatoes with their liquid, beans and pepper; mix well to break up the tomatoes. Cook, covered, on High for 5 minutes, or until hot; discard bay leaf.
4. Ladle soup into warmed bowls; garnish with parsley. Serve hot.

CORN CHOWDER

Colour Index page 43. Makes 6 cups. 921 kJ per cup.
Good source of vitamin A, fibre.
Begin 35 minutes ahead.

30 g butter or margarine	½ teaspoon salt
3 teaspoons plain flour	1 cup chicken stock
2 teaspoons paprika	1 cup milk
250 g potatoes, peeled and chopped	½ cup cream
1 celery stalk, finely chopped	375 g packet frozen whole-kernel corn
½ onion, chopped	Chopped parsley to garnish

1. Heat butter in a deep 3-litre bowl, covered with paper towel, on High (100% power) for 45 seconds, or until melted.
2. Stir in flour and paprika; mix well. Add potatoes, celery, onion, salt and stock. Cook, covered, on High for 10–12 minutes, until vegetables are tender, stirring twice.
3. Add milk, cream and corn to vegetable mixture. Cook, covered, on High for 6–8 minutes, until corn is tender (do not boil), stirring twice.
4. Ladle soup into warmed bowls; garnish with parsley. Serve hot.

Chowders and thick creamy seafood soups are substantial enough to make complete meals in themselves. Cooked in the microwave oven, they can be ready for the table in less than half an hour; for hearty appetites, ideal accompaniments are French bread, crusty rolls, bagel chips or wholemeal pita bread.

CREAM OF OYSTER SOUP

Colour Index page 43. 1260 kJ per serving. Good source of calcium, iron.
Begin 30 minutes ahead.

Ingredients for 4 cups		Microwave cookware
30 g butter or margarine	1 tablespoon plain flour	Deep 3-litre bowl
48 bottled oysters, with their liquid	2 cups milk Salt and white pepper to taste	
2 spring onions, finely chopped	1 cup cream	
1 small celery stalk, finely chopped	Paprika to garnish French bread (optional)	

1 Heat butter in bowl, covered with paper towel, on High (100% power) for 45 seconds, or until melted.

2 Drain oysters in a strainer over a small bowl, reserving liquid. Add oysters to melted butter. Cook on High for 1 minute, or just until edges begin to curl. With a slotted spoon, transfer oysters to another bowl.

3 Add spring onions and celery to butter mixture. Cook on High for 3–4 minutes, until celery has softened.

4 Gradually add flour to vegetable mixture; stir until blended. Slowly stir in milk and strained oyster liquid. Add salt and pepper. Cook on High for 4–5 minutes, until slightly thickened, stirring twice.

5 In food processor with knife blade attached or in blender, process soup mixture until smooth (in batches if necessary). Return to bowl.

6 Add reserved oysters and cream to soup. Cook on High for 2–2½ (2:30) minutes, just until oysters are hot (do not boil). Garnish with a sprinkling of paprika. Serve hot, with French bread alongside.

Fruit soups

Fruit soups make an unusual, refreshing first course, especially for a summer meal. They look particularly attractive served in white china bowls or glass dessert dishes. Most fruit soups are sweetened purées diluted with wine, fruit juice or water; they take only a few minutes to cook in the microwave oven, but need time to chill in the refrigerator. Once you have tried Red Plum Soup and Peach Soup, experiment with other fruits such as cherries, raspberries, strawberries and tropical fruits.

PEACH SOUP

Colour Index page 44. 322 kJ per cup. Low in cholesterol, fat, sodium. Good source of fibre if soup is not strained.
Begin early in day.

Ingredients for 3 cups		Microwave cookware
750 g ripe, slipstone peaches	1 teaspoon grated green ginger	Deep 3-litre bowl
1 cup dry white wine	¼ cup natural yoghurt	
½ cup water	Natural yoghurt and	
¼ cup sugar	mint leaves to garnish	

1 Cut peaches in half; twist apart. Remove stones and cut peach halves into halves or quarters lengthways.

2 Combine peaches, wine, water and sugar in bowl. Cook, covered, on High (100% power) for 10 minutes, or until softened, stirring twice.

3 In food processor with knife blade attached or in blender, process peach mixture until smooth.

4 Position a strainer over bowl. Strain mixture to remove skin.

5 Stir grated ginger into peach mixture. Cook, covered with paper towel, on High for 5 minutes, or until flavours blend, stirring twice. Cover and refrigerate until chilled; stir in yoghurt until evenly blended.

6 Ladle soup into chilled bowls; garnish with yoghurt and mint leaves.

RED PLUM SOUP

Colour Index page 44. Makes 3 cups. 414 kJ per cup. Low in cholesterol, fat, sodium. Good source of fibre if soup is not strained.
Begin early in day.

750 g red plums
1½ cups light red wine
1 teaspoon vanilla essence
1 cinnamon stick

¼ cup sugar
Sour cream or natural yoghurt and plum slivers to garnish

1. Stone plums and cut into quarters. Combine plums, wine, vanilla essence, cinnamon stick and sugar in a deep 3-litre bowl. Cook, covered, on High (100% power) for 8–10 minutes, until tender, stirring twice; discard cinnamon stick.
2. In food processor with knife blade attached or in blender, process mixture until smooth. At this stage, strain to remove plum skins.
3. Cover soup and refrigerate until chilled. Garnish with sour cream and slivers of fresh plum.

GARNISHES FOR FRUIT SOUPS

A pretty garnish can add greatly to the decorative appeal of a refreshing summer soup. Edible flowers make a particularly attractive garnish, as do any of the other garnishes suggested here.

Nasturtiums

Rose petals

Toasted slivered almonds

Chopped hazelnuts

Star fruit (Carambola)

Pomegranate seeds

Sliced kiwifruit

Passionfruit pulp

Eggs and Cheese

BAKED EGGS · POACHED EGGS · SCRAMBLED EGGS
FRIED EGGS · OMELETTES · MELTED CHEESE
BAKED CHEESE · SOUFFLÉS · ROULADES

Eggs and Cheese

Eggs and cheese are delicate ingredients that need careful handling when cooked in the microwave. Cooked conventionally, the white of an egg sets before the yolk, but the opposite is true in microwave cooking. Because egg yolks contain a high proportion of fat, they attract more microwave energy; the recipes for eggs in this book, therefore, include standing times, in which the white sets without the yolk overcooking. Even when yolks and whites are mixed, as in scrambled eggs, they still require standing time. Expect scrambled eggs to look very soft when removed from the microwave. Mixing in a little cream or milk before standing slows the cooking process, making eggs creamier.

Most importantly, never put an egg in its shell into the microwave, whether to cook or reheat it; steam builds up in the shell and the egg will burst. Even out of the shell, you should always pierce the yolk with a toothpick before it is fried, baked or poached. The yolk has an outer membrane and an unpierced egg yolk can burst.

Melted cheese is a quick and easy topping for hamburgers and a popular filling for sandwiches. Because of their high fat content, most grated cheeses melt very quickly when added to a hot mixture, but not all soften at the same rate. In general, the drier cheeses such as Cheddar, Parmesan and Gruyère take more time to soften than moist ones such as cream cheese, Camembert and Bel Paese. However, cheese can quickly overcook and become stringy, so that processed cheese often produces more acceptable results. Warming unwrapped chilled cheese on Medium (50% power) for 45 seconds–1 minute in the microwave oven will make it easier to slice.

Soufflés can be cooked in the microwave oven but be sure to follow the instructions in individual recipes. Soufflés cook very rapidly; they rise very high but fall quickly when removed from the microwave, and they do not form a crust.

Egg- and cheese-based quiches and casseroles reheat successfully in the microwave, but most other egg and cheese dishes tend to toughen.

CREATIVE CHEESE TOPPINGS
Decorate soft cheese – either slices of Brie or smaller whole cheeses – by marking patterns on them with the edge of a sharp knife, then adding your choice of flavourings.

Press nuts, seeds, spices or herbs on to surface of cheese. Refrigerate, then bring to room temperature on Medium (50% power) for 5 seconds at a time when ready to serve.

COOKING EGGS

There are a few simple guidelines to follow when cooking eggs and egg-based dishes in the microwave:

- Eggs should be at room temperature.
- Most egg recipes are cooked on Medium-High (70% power) to avoid overcooking; scrambled eggs and omelettes can be cooked on High (100% power), however, because yolks and whites are mixed.
- Cover the dish for best results.
- Don't boil eggs in the microwave; there is no time saving and pressure build-up can cause the egg to explode.
- Eggs continue cooking after removal from oven, so always cook for minimum recommended time, then allow to stand for 1–2 minutes. If not done to your liking, return to oven for 15 seconds at a time.
- Sauces thickened with egg are best cooked on Low to prevent curdling.

EGGS IN BRIOCHES

Colour Index page 45. 6 servings. 1302 kJ per serving. Good source of calcium, iron. Begin 25 minutes ahead.

6 individual brioches	Smoked salmon
6 slices Gruyère or Swiss cheese	Fresh chives to garnish
6 eggs	Asparagus (page 239)
Salt and pepper to taste	Hollandaise Sauce (page 381)

1. Cut top from each brioche; put aside. Hollow out brioches, leaving 6-mm shells.
2. Line each brioche with a slice of cheese; arrange in a circle, 2.5 cm apart, on a 30-cm round plate.
3. Break 1 egg into each brioche; pierce yolk with a toothpick. Cook, covered, on High (100% power) for 4–5 minutes, until almost set.
4. Allow brioches to stand, covered loosely with greaseproof paper, for 2–3 minutes, until egg whites are opaque. If eggs are not done to your liking, cook on High for 15 seconds at a time, until done. Season with salt and pepper.
5. Arrange each brioche with its top on individual serving plates. Serve with smoked salmon garnished with chives, and Asparagus topped with Hollandaise Sauce.

Preparing the brioches

Using a spoon or small, serrated knife, hollow out each brioche.

Line the brioche with a cheese slice, pushing cheese into the hollow.

Baked eggs

Timing is crucial when cooking eggs in the microwave. Do not return eggs to the oven without letting them stand for the time specified; this allows the whites to continue cooking without overcooking the yolks. Eggs Baked in Ham Nests (below) makes an interesting change from baking eggs in ramekins.

EGGS BAKED IN HAM NESTS

Colour Index page 45. 837 kJ per serving. Good source of thiamine. Begin 15 minutes ahead.

Ingredients	For 4	For 2	For 1
Cooked ham	8 slices	4 slices	2 slices
Spring onions	2	1	½
Butter or margarine, softened	2 teaspoons	1 teaspoon	½ teaspoon
Eggs	4	2	1
Salt and pepper	to taste	to taste	to taste
Microwave cookware	4 x 13-cm baking dishes	2 x 13-cm baking dishes	13-cm baking dish
Time on Medium-High (70% power)	5–6½ (6:30) minutes	2½ (2:30)–3 minutes	1–1½ (1:30) minutes
Standing time	2 minutes	2 minutes	1 minute

1 Stack ham slices. Roll up or fold, then thinly slice.

2 Thinly slice spring onions. Place in bowl with ham; toss.

3 Brush baking dishes (see Chart) with softened butter. Arrange equal amounts of ham and spring onion mixture around the edge of each dish.

4 Break each egg on to a saucer and gently slide into the middle of ham nests; pierce the yolk of each egg with a toothpick.

5 Cook eggs, covered, on Medium-High for time in Chart, until whites are opaque but not set.

6 Allow eggs to stand, covered loosely, for time in Chart. If eggs are not done to your liking after standing time, cook on Medium-High for 15 seconds at a time, until done. Season with salt and pepper. Serve, if you like, with hot toast.

Poached eggs

POACHED EGGS

Colour Index page 45. 335 kJ per serving. Good source of vitamin A.
Begin 15 minutes ahead.

Ingredients	For 4	For 2	For 1
Water	½ cup	¼ cup	2 tablespoons
White vinegar	2 teaspoons	1 teaspoon	½ teaspoon
Eggs	4	2	1
Salt and pepper	to taste	to taste	to taste
Parsley sprigs	garnish	garnish	garnish
Microwave cookware	1-cup glass jug 4 ramekins	1-cup glass jug 2 ramekins	1-cup glass jug 1 ramekin
Time on High (100% power) Water and vinegar	3 minutes	1½ (1:30) minutes	45 seconds
Time on Medium (50% power) Eggs	3–3½ (3:30) minutes	1½ (1:30)–2 minutes	45 seconds–1 minute
Standing time	2–3 minutes	2 minutes	1 minute

1 Heat water and vinegar in jug (see Chart) on High for time in Chart, or until boiling. Meanwhile, break 1 egg into each ramekin (see Chart).

2 Pierce the yolk of each egg with a toothpick to prevent bursting during cooking.

3 Carefully pour water and vinegar over eggs. Cover each ramekin with plastic wrap; place on floor of oven.

4 Cook eggs, covered, on Medium for time in Chart, until whites are opaque but not set.

5 Allow eggs to stand, loosely covered, for time in Chart. If eggs are not done to your liking after standing time, cook on High for 15 seconds at a time, until done.

6 With slotted spoon, remove each egg from ramekin and drain over paper towel. Transfer to a serving dish and sprinkle with salt and pepper; garnish with parsley sprigs. Serve, if you like, with toast and sausage patties.

EGGS FLORENTINE

Colour Index page 46. 4 servings. 1662 kJ per serving. Good source of vitamin A, calcium, iron, fibre.
Begin 40 minutes ahead.

Hollandaise Sauce (page 381)
½ cup water
2 teaspoons white vinegar
4 eggs
Ground nutmeg to taste
Salt and pepper to taste
375 g packet frozen spinach, thawed

2 English muffins, split and toasted
250 g asparagus, cooked and drained (optional)
Fresh chives and chopped cooked bacon to garnish

1. Prepare Hollandaise Sauce; cover and keep warm, stirring occasionally.
2. Heat water and vinegar in a 1-cup glass jug on High (100% power) for 3 minutes, or until boiling. Meanwhile, break eggs into 4 ramekins; pierce each yolk with a toothpick.
3. Carefully pour water and vinegar over eggs. Arrange ramekins on a 30-cm platter. Cook, covered, on Medium (50% power) for 3–3½ minutes, until whites are opaque but not set. Allow to stand, loosely covered, for 2–3 minutes. Season with nutmeg, salt and pepper.
4. Meanwhile, place thawed spinach in a 23-cm pie plate. Cook on High for 3 minutes, or until hot, stirring halfway through cooking.
5. Place 1 toasted muffin half on each plate; top with equal amounts of hot spinach. With a slotted spoon, drain each egg over paper towel; place on spinach. If you like, accompany with cooked asparagus. Top with Hollandaise Sauce; sprinkle with chives and bacon. Serve immediately.

Assembling the Eggs Florentine

Using a slotted spoon, carefully place each egg on a spinach-topped toasted muffin half.

Spoon warm Hollandaise Sauce over each egg; garnish with chives and chopped bacon.

Scrambled eggs

PIPÉRADE

Colour Index page 45. 6 servings. 816 kJ per serving.
Good source of vitamin A, vitamin C, iron.
Begin 20 minutes ahead.

2 tablespoons olive or vegetable oil	¼ teaspoon salt
2 red or green capsicums, cut into thin strips	¼ teaspoon pepper
1 onion, chopped	Basil leaves to garnish
6 eggs	French bread (optional)
1 teaspoon shredded fresh basil or ¼ teaspoon dried basil	

1. Heat oil in a 23-cm round flan dish on High (100% power) for 3 minutes. Stir in capsicum and onion. Cook on High for 4 minutes, or until softened, stirring twice.
2. Beat eggs, basil, salt and pepper in a bowl.
3. Pour beaten egg mixture over vegetable mixture. Cook on High for 2½ (2:30) minutes, or until eggs are softly set but still very moist, stirring with a fork several times during cooking. Allow to stand, loosely covered, on a heatproof surface for 2–3 minutes.
4. If eggs are not done to your liking after standing, uncover and cook on High for 15 seconds at a time, until done.
5. Garnish with basil leaves. Serve, if you like, with slices of crusty French bread.

SCRAMBLED EGGS AND BACON BREAKFAST

It is easy to cook delicious scrambled eggs and bacon for 4 people in a matter of minutes. Begin with steps 1 and 2 of the recipe for Scrambled Eggs (right), then arrange **8 rashers bacon** on a microwave-safe platter lined with paper towel. Cover with another sheet of paper towel and place platter on the microwave-oven shelf. Cook on High (100% power) for 2–3 minutes. Turn bacon rashers over and return to microwave. Continue with steps 3, 4 and 5 of the recipe for Scrambled Eggs, cooking eggs and bacon together on High for time in Chart, until eggs are softly set but still very moist, and bacon is browned. Transfer bacon to another paper towel to drain. Remove eggs from microwave and allow to stand, loosely covered with plastic wrap, on a heatproof surface for time in Chart. If eggs are not done to your liking after standing, remove plastic and cook on High for 15 seconds at a time, until done.

To prevent overcooking, scrambled eggs should be removed from the microwave before they are completely cooked; they will set during the standing time. You can mix a little milk or cream into the eggs after they have been removed from the oven; this will slow down the cooking process and also make the eggs creamier.

SCRAMBLED EGGS

Colour Index page 45. 435 kJ per serving. Good source of vitamin A.
Begin 10 minutes ahead.

Ingredients	For 4	For 2	For 1
Butter or margarine	3 teaspoons	1½ teaspoons	1 teaspoon
Eggs	4	2	1
Water	2 tablespoons	1 tablespoon	2 teaspoons
Salt	to taste	to taste	to taste
Pepper	to taste	to taste	to taste
Microwave cookware	Medium bowl	Medium bowl	Small bowl
Time on High (100% power)			
Butter	30 seconds	15 seconds	10 seconds
Eggs	1½ (1:30)–2½ (2:30) minutes	1–1½ (1:30) minutes	45 seconds–1 minute
Standing time	2–3 minutes	2 minutes	1 minute

1 Heat butter in bowl (see Chart), covered with paper towel, on High for time in Chart, or until melted.

2 Beat eggs, water, salt and pepper in a bowl. Pour into melted butter.

3 Cook eggs on High for time in Chart, until softly set, stirring with fork several times during cooking.

4 Remove eggs from oven; they will be softly set and very moist.

5 Loosely cover bowl with plastic wrap. Allow eggs to stand on a heatproof surface for time in Chart; they will finish cooking during the standing time.

6 If eggs are not done to your liking after standing, remove plastic wrap and cook on High for 15 seconds at a time, until done.

<table>

Meal in Minutes *for 6 people*

Sunday Brunch

Champagne and orange juice
Citrus fruit compote
Eggs in Brioches (page 139) with extra smoked salmon
Asparagus (page 239) with Hollandaise Sauce (page 381)
Chocolate-dipped Fruit (page 324)
Muffins and Danish pastries
Coffee

</table>

PREPARATION TIMETABLE

1 day ahead:	*Prepare a fruit compote of grapefruit, orange and mandarin segments; cover and refrigerate. Make Chocolate-dipped Fruit; arrange on a serving plate, cover loosely, and store in a cool, dry place; do not refrigerate. Chill orange juice and Champagne.*
2 hours ahead:	*Make Hollandaise Sauce; keep warm, stirring occasionally. Prepare asparagus, but do not cook.*
30 minutes before serving:	*Prepare Eggs in Brioches up to the end of step 2. Cook asparagus according to the instructions in the Chart on page 239; arrange on a warmed serving platter with Hollandaise Sauce.*
Just before serving:	*Complete Eggs in Brioches; arrange on a platter with smoked salmon. Arrange muffins and pastries on a serving plate; if you like, heat briefly in microwave. Make coffee.*

Fried eggs

BACON AND EGGS

Colour Index page 45. 4 servings. 1130 kJ per serving. Good source of vitamin A.
Begin 15 minutes ahead.

8 rashers bacon	Chopped chives to
4 eggs	garnish
Salt and pepper to taste	Bread rolls (optional)
2 tomatoes, cut in half	

1. Preheat browning dish according to the manufacturer's instructions. Arrange bacon in a single layer in dish. Cook, covered, on High (100% power) for 2 minutes. Turn bacon over; cook on High for 2–3 minutes, until done to your liking. Transfer to paper towels to drain; put aside and keep warm. Discard half the bacon drippings.
2. Break eggs, one at a time, into a saucer. Gently slide each egg on to the browning dish, placing them evenly around dish; pierce the yolks with a toothpick.
3. Cook eggs on High for 1½ (1:30)–2 minutes, until done to your liking. Season with salt and pepper.
4. Arrange eggs and bacon on warmed individual plates; garnish with tomato halves sprinkled with chopped chives. Serve, if you like, with warm bread rolls.

FRYING EGGS
Fried eggs are quick and easy to make in the microwave. Preheat browning dish according to the manufacturer's instructions. For each *egg*, melt *15 g butter or margarine* in browning dish. Break each egg, one at a time, into a saucer, then gently slide egg on to browning dish. If frying only 1 egg, place in centre of dish; if frying more, space them evenly. Pierce each yolk with a toothpick.

Cook on High (100% power) for 1½ (1:30)–2 minutes for 4 eggs; 45 seconds–1¼ (1:15) minutes for 2 eggs; 30 seconds–1 minute for 1 egg.

If you like egg yolks cooked more than this, turn eggs over with a spatula after 1¼ (1:15) minutes for 4 eggs; 45 seconds for 2 eggs; 30 seconds for 1 egg.

Quick bacon and eggs for one:
Preheat browning dish according to the manufacturer's instructions. Cut *2 bacon rashers* in half crossways and arrange against edge of dish. Cook on High (100% power) for 45 seconds–1 minute, then turn bacon over. Break *1 egg* into a saucer, gently slide on to browning dish; pierce yolk with a toothpick. Baste egg with bacon drippings; cook on High for 45 seconds–1 minute. Allow to stand, covered, for 1 minute.

Omelettes

SOUFFLÉED CHEESE OMELETTE

Colour Index page 46. 2 servings. 1093 kJ per serving. Good source of vitamin A, calcium. Begin 15 minutes ahead.

30 g butter or margarine	¼ teaspoon salt
3 eggs, separated	⅛ teaspoon pepper
1 teaspoon milk	60 g Cheddar cheese,
2 teaspoons finely	grated (½ cup)
chopped fresh tarragon	Cucumber slices, tomato
or ½ teaspoon dried	wedges and parsley
tarragon	sprigs to garnish

1. Heat butter in a 23-cm pie plate, covered with paper towel, on High (100% power) for 45 seconds, or until melted.
2. Beat egg yolks in a small bowl with milk, tarragon, salt and pepper until well mixed.
3. Beat egg whites at high speed in a large bowl until stiff peaks form. Gently fold egg-yolk mixture into beaten egg whites.
4. Spoon egg mixture into the pie plate; smooth top. Cook on High for 1½ (1:30)–2½ (2:30) minutes, until top is almost dry.
5. Sprinkle cheese over half the omelette. With a spatula, gently fold other half of omelette over cheese.
6. Slide omelette on to a warmed serving plate; garnish with cucumber, tomato and parsley. Serve immediately.

USING LEFTOVER CHEESE: Small pieces of one or more hard cheeses can be grated and used as an alternative filling.

FRENCH DESSERT OMELETTE

Colour Index page 46. 2 servings. 875 kJ per serving. Good source of vitamin A, iron. Begin 15 minutes ahead.

½ cup strawberries,	4 eggs
sliced	1 teaspoon milk
½ teaspoon sugar	Icing sugar
30 g butter or margarine	Strawberry to garnish

1. Combine strawberries and sugar in a bowl.
2. Heat butter in a 23-cm pie plate on High (100% power) for 30 seconds, or until melted.
3. Beat eggs and milk in a bowl until well mixed; pour into pie plate. Cook on High for 1 minute. With a spoon or spatula, move cooked edge to centre of plate. Cook, covered with paper towel, on High for 1–1½ (1:30) minutes, until omelette is set but still moist in the centre.
4. Spoon reserved strawberries over half the omelette. With a spatula, fold other half of omelette over strawberries.
5. Slide omelette on to a warmed serving plate. Sift icing sugar over the top; garnish with whole strawberry. Serve immediately.

Omelettes should be cooked in shallow pie plates in order to have smooth, neat edges. To ensure a flat surface, carefully move the cooked edge to the centre with a spoon or spatula so that the uncooked egg mixture flows under the omelette. A properly cooked omelette will be set throughout but the centre top will appear moist. If the omelette is too moist when checked with a knife, return to oven and cook on High for 15 seconds at a time until done.

TOMATO AND CAPSICUM OMELETTE

Colour Index page 46. 1059 kJ per serving. Good source of vitamin A, vitamin C, iron.
Begin 15 minutes ahead.

Ingredients for 2 servings		Microwave cookware
3 teaspoons olive or vegetable oil	4 eggs 1 tablespoon milk	23-cm glass pie plate
1 onion, thinly sliced	Tabasco sauce to taste	
1 green capsicum, coarsely chopped	Salt and pepper to taste Parsley sprig to garnish	
1 tomato, chopped		

1 Combine oil, onion, capsicum and tomato in pie plate. Cook, covered, on High (100% power) for 4 minutes, or until softened, stirring twice.

2 Meanwhile, beat eggs, milk, Tabasco sauce, salt and pepper in a bowl.

3 Transfer cooked vegetable mixture to another bowl; season with salt and pepper. Slowly pour egg mixture into pie plate used for cooking vegetables. Cook on High for 1 minute.

4 With spoon or spatula, move cooked edge to centre of plate. Cook, covered with paper towel, on High for 1–1½ (1:30) minutes, until omelette is set but still moist in the centre.

5 Spoon vegetable mixture over half the omelette. With a spatula, gently fold other half of omelette over vegetables.

6 Slide omelette on to a warmed serving plate; garnish with parsley sprig. Serve immediately.

Melted cheese

Cheese is a delicate ingredient that needs careful handling in the microwave to avoid becoming tough and stringy. Most recipes call for grated cheese because in this form it melts rapidly in a hot mixture. It is important to stir grated cheese after it has been added to any hot mixture, to make sure that it melts completely and blends evenly.

MACARONI CHEESE

Colour Index page 46. 2432 kJ per serving. Good source of thiamine, riboflavin, calcium, iron.
Begin 35 minutes ahead.

Ingredients for 4 servings		Microwave cookware
250 g elbow macaroni 45 g butter or margarine 1 small onion, finely chopped 3 teaspoons plain flour 1/4 teaspoon salt 1/4 teaspoon mustard powder 1/8 teaspoon pepper	1 1/2 cups milk 250 g Cheddar cheese, grated (2 cups) 1/4 cup dried wholemeal or seasoned breadcrumbs Extra grated cheese (optional) Parsley sprig to garnish	8-cup soufflé dish or deep casserole

1 Cook macaroni conventionally; drain in colander.

2 Meanwhile, heat butter in soufflé dish or casserole, covered with paper towel, on High (100% power) for 45 seconds, or until melted. Add onion; stir well to coat. Cook on High for 2 minutes, or until softened.

3 Stir flour, salt, mustard and pepper into onion mixture until well blended. Cook on High for 1 minute, stirring halfway through cooking.

4 Gradually stir in milk. Cook on High for 3–4 minutes, until mixture thickens and is smooth, stirring twice. Remove dish from oven and add cheese. Stir sauce until cheese melts.

5 Stir drained macaroni into cheese sauce. Cook on High for 5–7 minutes, until hot, rotating dish twice during cooking. Allow to stand on a heatproof surface for 5 minutes.

6 Sprinkle breadcrumbs on top of mixture and, if you like, extra grated cheese. Cook on High for 30 seconds or, if dish is suitable, brown top under a preheated griller. Garnish with parsley. Serve hot.

WELSH RAREBIT

Colour Index page 46. 6 servings. 1453 kJ per serving. Good source of vitamin A.
Begin 15 minutes ahead.

60 g butter or margarine
1/4 cup plain flour
1/4 teaspoon mustard powder
1/8 teaspoon cayenne pepper
1/2 cup beer
1 1/2 cups milk
1 teaspoon Worcestershire sauce

250 g Cheddar cheese, grated (2 cups)
6 slices white or rye bread, toasted, or 6 English muffin halves
Gherkins, stuffed olives, pickled onions and parsley to garnish

1. Heat butter in a 2-litre casserole, covered with paper towel, on High (100% power) for 45 seconds–1 minute, until melted.
2. Stir flour, mustard and cayenne pepper into butter until smooth and blended. Cook on High for 1 minute, stirring halfway through cooking.
3. Gradually add beer, milk and Worcestershire sauce; stir until smooth. Cook on High for 5 minutes, or until mixture thickens and is smooth, stirring twice. Add grated cheese; stir until melted.
4. Spoon hot cheese mixture over toast or muffin halves; garnish with gherkins, olives, pickled onions and parsley. Serve immediately.

SWISS CHEESE FONDUE

Colour Index page 46. 4 servings. 3453 kJ per serving. Good source of vitamin A, thiamine, iron.
Begin 10 minutes ahead.

1 clove garlic, cut in half
1 1/2 cups dry white wine
500 g Gruyère cheese, grated (4 cups)
2 tablespoons plain flour
1/8 teaspoon pepper
1/8 teaspoon ground nutmeg

Paprika (optional)
1 loaf French bread, about 45 cm long, cut into 2.5-cm cubes
16 cherry tomatoes
1 green capsicum, cut into cubes

1. Place garlic and wine in a 2-litre casserole or ceramic fondue dish. Cook on High (100% power) for 4 minutes, or until wine is boiling.
2. Meanwhile, toss grated cheese with flour in a bowl until well combined.
3. Remove garlic from wine; discard. Add cheese to wine, a handful at a time, stirring constantly until cheese melts. Season with pepper and nutmeg; sprinkle, if you like, with paprika.
4. Place dish of fondue in centre of table, together with long-handled fondue forks or skewers. Serve with dishes of bread chunks, cherry tomatoes and capsicum cubes to dip into hot fondue.

ASPARAGUS TIMBALES

Colour Index page 47. Makes 4 timbales. 1314 kJ each. Good source of vitamin A, thiamine, vitamin C, iron.
Begin 40 minutes ahead.

45 g butter or margarine	¼ teaspoon ground
2 tablespoons dried	nutmeg
breadcrumbs	Pepper to taste
250 g asparagus	½ cup cream
1 small onion, finely	Lemon slices to garnish
chopped	185 g thinly sliced
4 egg yolks	smoked salmon or
¼ cup grated Parmesan	prosciutto
cheese	

1. Heat butter in a medium bowl, covered with paper towel, on High (100% power) for 45 seconds–1 minute, until melted. Brush inside of 4 x ½-cup ramekins with some of the melted butter. Sprinkle breadcrumbs around the inside of each ramekin to coat; put aside.
2. Hold base of each asparagus spear firmly and bend; the end will break off where the spear becomes too tough to eat. Discard tough ends.
3. Trim 4 asparagus tips to 5 cm long; put aside. Coarsely chop remaining asparagus. Combine chopped asparagus and onion with remaining melted butter. Cook, covered, on High for 4–5 minutes, until tender, stirring halfway through cooking.
4. Finely chop asparagus mixture; return to bowl. Beat in egg yolks, Parmesan cheese, nutmeg and pepper.
5. Heat cream in a 2-cup glass jug on Medium (50% power) for 1½ (1:30)–2 minutes, until small bubbles form around edge.
6. Gradually stir cream into asparagus mixture. Spoon one-quarter of mixture into each ramekin. Arrange in a circle on a 30-cm platter. Elevate platter on a trivet or rack, or on ramekins turned upside down. Cook on Medium for 5–7 minutes, until knife inserted 1 cm from centre comes out clean, rotating platter twice. Allow timbales to stand, covered, on a heatproof surface for 5 minutes.
7. Unmould timbales on to individual plates; garnish with reserved asparagus and lemon slices. Serve with slices of smoked salmon.

Preparing the ramekins

Using a pastry brush, brush ramekins with some melted butter.

Coat each ramekin with breadcrumbs; tilt to cover bottom and sides.

When cooking cheese casseroles or quiches, elevate the dish on a microwave-safe trivet or rack, or on ramekins turned upside down, to ensure even cooking on the underside. Filled ramekins arranged in a circle should be rotated during cooking.

MEXICAN CHEESE AND TOMATO BAKE

Colour Index page 46. 1633 kJ per serving. Good source of vitamin A.
Begin 45 minutes ahead.

Ingredients for 6 servings		Microwave cookware
3 teaspoons vegetable oil	1 cup cream	30-cm x 20-cm
1 onion, chopped	¼ teaspoon salt	baking dish
2 spring onions, sliced	Tabasco sauce to taste	Trivet, rack or
1 clove garlic, crushed	125 g Cheddar cheese,	ramekins
2 teaspoons finely	grated (1 cup)	
chopped fresh oregano	¼ cup fresh coriander	
or ½ teaspoon dried	leaves, chopped	
oregano	200 g packet corn chips	
½ teaspoon ground	Coriander leaves to	
cumin	garnish	
425 g can tomatoes,		
chopped with their		
juice		

1 Place oil, onion, spring onions, garlic, oregano and cumin in baking dish. Elevate dish on trivet or rack, or on ramekins turned upside down.

2 Cook onion mixture, covered, on High (100% power) for 3 minutes, or until softened slightly, stirring halfway through cooking.

3 Add tomatoes and cream. Cook on High for 7–8 minutes, until sauce thickens, stirring twice. Add salt and Tabasco sauce to taste.

4 Transfer half the tomato sauce to a small bowl; put aside. In another bowl, toss grated cheese with coriander until well mixed.

5 Cover remaining tomato sauce in baking dish with half the corn chips, half the cheese mixture, and the reserved sauce. Add another layer of corn chips, then cheese mixture. Cook on High for 4–5 minutes, until cheese melts and tomato sauce is bubbling, rotating dish halfway through cooking.

6 Allow dish to stand for 5 minutes on a heatproof surface. Garnish with coriander leaves. Serve hot.

Baked cheese

Traditional quiches cannot be cooked successfully in the microwave, but crustless varieties are delicious and have less kilojoules. Medium power is necessary to prevent the cheese from becoming tough and rubbery. For a perfect result – a quiche that is light and tender – preheat the liquid ingredients first, then combine with eggs. This way the eggs will not overcook, as they might if heated with a cold liquid.

CRUSTLESS BROCCOLI AND CHEESE QUICHE

Colour Index page 47. 1021 kJ per serving. Good source of vitamin A, vitamin C, calcium, fibre.
Begin 45 minutes ahead.

Ingredients for 6 servings		Microwave cookware
500 g broccoli, chopped	¼ teaspoon cayenne pepper	23-cm flan dish
1 small onion, finely chopped	Tomato rose (page 238) and basil leaves to garnish	2-cup glass jug
½ cup cream		Trivet, rack or ramekin
4 eggs		
250 g Gruyère or Swiss cheese, grated (2 cups)		

1 Place broccoli and onion in flan dish. Cook, covered, on High (100% power) for 5 minutes, stirring halfway through cooking. Put aside, covered.

2 Heat cream in jug on Medium (50% power) for 1½ (1:30)–2 minutes, until small bubbles form around edge.

3 Beat cream and eggs in a bowl until blended. Stir in cheese and cayenne pepper.

4 Pour mixture slowly over broccoli and onion; stir gently to distribute vegetables evenly. Elevate dish on trivet or rack, or on ramekin turned upside down.

5 Cook quiche on Medium for 12–14 minutes, until a knife inserted in centre comes out clean, rotating dish a quarter turn twice during cooking.

6 Allow quiche to stand, covered, on a heatproof surface for 10 minutes. Garnish with tomato rose and basil leaves. Serve warm, or refrigerate to serve chilled later.

BACON AND POTATO QUICHE

Colour Index page 47. 8 servings. 1009 kJ per serving. Good source of vitamin A.
Begin 45 minutes ahead.

6 rashers rindless bacon, cut into 5-cm pieces	6 eggs
250 g potatoes, cut into 2-cm cubes	185 g Cheddar cheese, cut into 1-cm cubes
250 g fresh peas, shelled	2 spring onions, thinly sliced
¾ cup milk	Pepper to taste

1. Cook bacon in a 25-cm flan dish, covered with paper towel, on High (100% power) for 5–6 minutes, until browned, stirring halfway through cooking. Transfer to paper towels to drain. Discard all but 2 tablespoons bacon drippings.
2. Stir potatoes and peas into bacon drippings in dish. Cook, covered, on High for 4–6 minutes, until tender, stirring halfway through cooking.
3. Heat milk in a medium bowl on High for 2–2½ (2:30) minutes, until small bubbles form around edge. Add eggs; beat until blended.
4. Add cheese, spring onion, pepper and reserved bacon; mix well. Carefully pour mixture over vegetables in dish.
5. Elevate dish on a trivet or rack, or on a ramekin turned upside down. Cook on Medium (50% power) for 10–12 minutes, until egg mixture is slightly set but still moist, stirring cooked edge towards centre twice.
6. Allow quiche to stand, covered, on a heatproof surface for 5 minutes. Serve hot.

CAMEMBERT IN VINE LEAVES

Colour Index page 46. 2 servings. 1047 kJ per serving. Good source of vitamin A.
Begin 20 minutes ahead.

1 red-skinned eating apple	2 vine leaves, fresh or in brine (rinsed and drained), or fresh lettuce leaves
2 teaspoons brandy	
125 g packet Camembert cheese	Parsley sprigs to garnish

1. Core apple. Thinly slice one-quarter of apple; cut remainder into wedges. Toss apple slices and wedges in brandy in a bowl; put aside.
2. Cut Camembert in half horizontally. Arrange apple slices on cut side of one-half of cheese; cover with remaining cheese, cut side down.
3. Place cheese in centre of 1 vine leaf. Cover with remaining leaf. Fold edges of leaves around cheese to completely enclose it; secure with string. Place wrapped cheese on a small plate. Cook on Medium (50% power) for 2 minutes. Remove string.
4. Cut wrapped cheese in half; place on individual plates with apple wedges. Garnish with parsley. Serve immediately.

Soufflés

TOMATOES WITH GOAT CHEESE AND BASIL SOUFFLÉ

Colour Index page 47. 8 servings. 444 kJ per serving. Low in sodium. Good source of vitamin A. Begin 35 minutes ahead.

8 medium tomatoes	60 g soft goat cheese
Salt and pepper to taste	1 tablespoon shredded
30 g butter or margarine	fresh basil leaves
1½ tablespoons plain	2 eggs, separated
flour	Basil leaves to garnish
½ cup milk	

1. Cut a thin slice from base of each tomato so that tomatoes sit flat. Cut another slice from top of each tomato; discard. Scoop out pulp to leave a 1-cm thick shell. Arrange tomatoes in a circle on a 30-cm round platter. Season with salt and pepper; put aside.

2. Heat butter in a medium bowl, covered with paper towel, on High (100% power) for 45 seconds, or until melted. Add flour and stir until smooth and blended. Cook on High for 1 minute, stirring halfway through cooking. Gradually stir in milk. Cook on High for 2–3 minutes, until mixture is thick and smooth, stirring twice.

3. Add cheese to sauce; stir until cheese melts. Add chopped basil, salt and pepper.

4. Blend egg yolks into cheese sauce. Beat egg whites on high speed in a large bowl until stiff peaks form. Gently fold cheese mixture, one-third at a time, into beaten egg whites, just until blended.

5. Spoon an equal amount of mixture into each tomato shell. Cook on Medium-Low (30% power) for 6 minutes. Increase power level to Medium (50% power) and cook for 5 minutes longer. Increase power level to High and cook for 2 minutes more, or just until soufflé is set.

6. Place each tomato on a warmed dinner plate; garnish with basil leaves. Serve hot.

COOKING WITH CHEESE

The quality of the cheese used in recipes cooked in the microwave makes a great difference to the finished result. Always add cheese towards the end of the cooking time so that it does not overcook and become stringy or tough. For melted cheese dishes, a well-aged, high-quality cheese will result in smooth, tasty dishes. If a sauce separates or curdles, pour sauce into a blender or food processor and blend for 1–2 minutes. To reheat cheese sauces, heat on Medium (50% power) and stir frequently.

CHEESE SOUFFLÉ

Colour Index page 47. 1402 kJ per serving. Good source of calcium. Begin 35 minutes ahead.

Ingredients for 6 servings		Microwave cookware
60 g butter or margarine	⅛ teaspoon ground	4-cup glass jug
½ cup plain flour	nutmeg	8-cup soufflé dish
1 cup milk	¼ teaspoon salt	
5 eggs, separated	Tomato Sauce (page 380,	
¼ cup grated Parmesan	optional)	
cheese		
250 g Swiss or Gruyère		
cheese, grated (2 cups)		

1 Heat butter in glass jug, covered with paper towel, on High (100% power) for 45 seconds–1 minute, until melted. Add flour and stir until well blended. Cook on High for 1 minute, stirring halfway through cooking.

2 Gradually stir milk into flour and butter until smooth. Cook on High for 2–3 minutes, until sauce is very thick, stirring twice.

3 Lightly beat egg yolks in a bowl. Stir a small amount of hot sauce into egg yolks. Slowly pour egg yolk mixture into remaining hot sauce, beating rapidly to prevent lumps forming. When well combined, stir in Parmesan cheese and ¼ cup Swiss cheese. Add nutmeg and salt.

4 Beat egg whites at high speed in a large bowl until stiff peaks form.

5 Gently fold cheese mixture and remaining cheese alternately, one third at a time, into beaten egg whites, just until blended. Pour mixture into ungreased soufflé dish; gently smooth top.

6 Cook on Medium-Low (30% power) for 8 minutes. Increase power level to Medium (50% power) and cook for 7–9 minutes longer, until top is dry but soufflé still moves when dish is shaken gently (soufflé will rise and fall several times during cooking in microwave). Serve, if you like, with Tomato Sauce.

Roulades

Soufflé-based dishes like Smoked Salmon and Chive Roulade or Mushroom and Cheese Roulade are very attractive for a buffet party. If you follow the instructions for rolling the roulades from a long end rather than a narrow end, you will find they are easier to cut into neat, thin slices – just perfect for dainty presentation on a large serving platter or tray.

SMOKED SALMON AND CHIVE ROULADE

Colour Index page 47. 975 kJ per serving. Good source of vitamin A. Begin 45 minutes ahead.

Ingredients for 4 servings		Microwave cookware
6 eggs Pepper to taste 90 g thinly sliced smoked salmon 125 g cream cheese with chives, softened	1/3 cup chopped fresh chives Chives to garnish	33-cm x 23-cm baking tray Trivet, rack or ramekins

1 Line baking tray with greaseproof paper or baking paper; put aside. Separate 4 eggs. Lightly beat egg yolks and 2 remaining whole eggs in a small bowl. Season with pepper.

2 Beat egg whites at high speed in a large bowl until stiff peaks form. Gently fold egg-yolk mixture into egg whites, just until blended.

3 Pour soufflé mixture into paper-lined tray; smooth top. Elevate tray on trivet or rack, or on ramekins turned upside down. Cook on High (100% power) for 3–4 minutes, until a knife inserted in the centre comes out clean.

4 Invert roulade on to a tea towel lined with greaseproof paper. Peel paper off top of roulade. Starting at a long end, roll roulade with greaseproof paper, Swiss-roll fashion. Allow to stand, seam side down, for 5 minutes.

5 Carefully unroll roulade. Arrange smoked salmon to within 5 cm of long edges. Spread cream cheese over salmon; sprinkle with chopped chives. Starting from same long end, roll up roulade without paper.

6 Lift roulade with a long spatula on to a serving platter. Refrigerate for 15 minutes. Cut into slices; garnish with chives.

MUSHROOM AND CHEESE ROULADE

Colour Index page 47. 4 servings. 1013 kJ per serving. Good source of vitamin A, riboflavin, iron. Begin 45 minutes ahead.

30 g butter or margarine
1 small onion, chopped
2 tomatoes, chopped
250 g mushrooms, coarsely chopped
1/4 cup dry white wine
1 tablespoon shredded fresh basil leaves
60 g Swiss cheese, grated (1/2 cup)
6 eggs
Salt and pepper to taste
Basil leaves to garnish

1. Line a 33-cm x 23-cm baking tray with greaseproof paper or baking paper; put aside.
2. Heat butter in a 20-cm x 20-cm baking dish, covered with paper towel, on High (100% power) for 45 seconds, or until melted. Add onion, tomatoes and mushrooms. Cook on High for 5 minutes, or until softened, stirring twice.
3. Add wine to vegetable mixture. Cook on High for 5 minutes, or until most of the wine has evaporated; add shredded basil. Strain liquid from vegetable mixture and discard. Stir in cheese.
4. Separate 4 eggs. Lightly beat egg yolks and 2 remaining whole eggs in a small bowl. Season with salt and pepper.
5. Beat egg whites at high speed in a large bowl until stiff peaks form. Gently fold egg-yolk mixture into egg whites, just until blended.
6. Pour soufflé mixture into paper-lined tray; smooth top. Elevate tray on a trivet or rack, or on ramekins turned upside down. Cook on High for 3–4 minutes, until a knife inserted in the centre comes out clean.
7. Invert roulade on to a tea towel lined with greaseproof paper. Peel paper off top of roulade. Starting at a long end, roll roulade with greaseproof paper, Swiss-roll fashion. Allow to stand, seam side down, for 5 minutes.
8. Carefully unroll roulade. Spread mushroom mixture to within 5 cm of long edges. Starting from same long end, roll up roulade without paper.
9. Lift roulade with a long spatula on to a serving platter. Refrigerate for 15 minutes. Cut into slices; garnish with basil leaves.

SPINACH AND RICOTTA ROULADE: Prepare as for Mushroom and Cheese Roulade (above), substituting *375 g packet frozen chopped spinach, thawed and squeezed dry*, for the mushrooms. Cook with tomatoes for 3 minutes only. Omit wine and Swiss cheese. Stir in *3/4 cup ricotta cheese* with the basil. Serve, if you like, with Tomato and Basil Sauce (page 380).

Fish and Shellfish

**WHOLE FISH · FISH CUTLETS · FISH FILLETS
CANNED FISH · PRAWNS · LOBSTER · MUSSELS · SCALLOPS
OYSTERS · CRAB · MIXED SHELLFISH**

Fish and Shellfish

The microwave is ideal for cooking both fish and shellfish, as they are naturally delicate foods and require minimal cooking to preserve their flavours and textures. Seafood cooked conventionally can dry out, toughen or break apart, so the quick, moist cooking of the microwave, combined with careful handling, can produce excellent results. Fish can be made to look grilled by cooking it in a browning dish or by brushing it with browning, teriyaki or soy sauces. Breadcrumbed fish, such as frozen fish fillets and fish fingers, can be cooked successfully in a browning dish. Fish, as a general rule, takes 1 minute per 100g to cook in the microwave.

If fish is done, the outer edge of the flesh should be opaque; it should also flake easily when tested with a fork. Fish that turns dark and dry when removed from the microwave has been overcooked. To prevent this, place thicker areas towards the edge of the dish and overlap thin ends of fillets (or tuck the thin ends under). Cook the fish in the microwave for the minimum suggested time only, then test to see if fish is done. Shielding will prevent delicate or thin areas from overcooking. Recipes for large whole fish usually call for standing time; test to see if fish is done after standing, as the fish continues to cook during that time. Shellfish cooks quickly in the microwave – about the same time as fish without a shell — so be careful not to let it overcook or it will become tough and rubbery. Prawns should be just pink; oysters should just curl at the edges; scallops should be opaque. Mussels and pipis cooked in the shell should be removed from the microwave when shells have opened; any that remain closed should be discarded.

Thick fish cutlets or pieces cooked in liquid should be carefully turned over once, halfway through cooking. To avoid uneven cooking, the dishes in which whole fish and fillets are cooked should be rotated in the microwave; this prevents heat buildup in any one part of the fish. To avoid unwanted cooking juices in the bottom of the dish, line it with paper towel or elevate the fish on a microwave-safe trivet or rack in the baking dish.

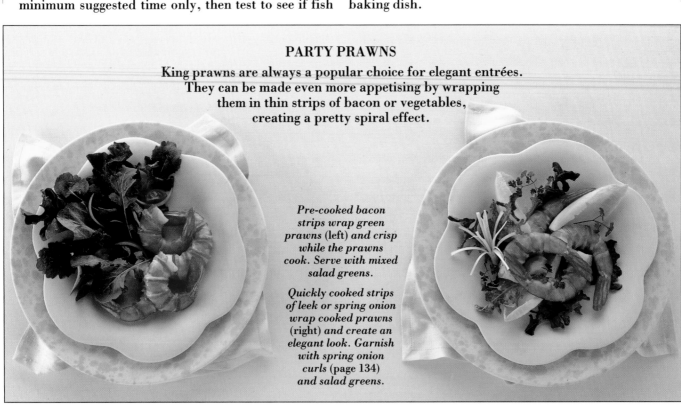

PARTY PRAWNS

King prawns are always a popular choice for elegant entrées.
They can be made even more appetising by wrapping
them in thin strips of bacon or vegetables,
creating a pretty spiral effect.

Pre-cooked bacon strips wrap green prawns (left) and crisp while the prawns cook. Serve with mixed salad greens.

Quickly cooked strips of leek or spring onion wrap cooked prawns (right) and create an elegant look. Garnish with spring onion curls (page 134) and salad greens.

Defrosting

Frozen fish and shellfish defrost rapidly in the microwave but care must be taken not to let them start cooking during the defrosting process.

Most fish fillets – and blocks of shellfish such as crab and scallops – can be defrosted in their original wrappings. If you carefully separate the pieces as soon as possible during defrosting and spread them in a single layer, they will defrost more quickly.

During defrosting, some thin areas of whole fish may become warm and start to cook; protect these spots by shielding them with smooth pieces of foil.

Whole fish and large shellfish should be left to stand, covered, after defrosting in the microwave to let the temperature equalise throughout the food. Whole fish must be completely defrosted before cooking. There must be no ice crystals in the cavity, so rinse whole fish under cold running water if cavity is still icy.

As with all frozen foods, it is best to cook fish and shellfish as soon as possible after defrosting, to prevent the growth of harmful bacteria as well as for maximum freshness and flavour. Many ovens have a special defrosting facility, in which case follow the manufacturer's instructions.

DEFROSTING A PACKET OF FISH FILLETS

Heat 500 g fish in packet on Medium (50% power) for 1½ (1:30) minutes. Turn packet over, then shield ends of packet with smooth pieces of foil.

Heat on Medium-Low (30% power) for 1½ (1:30) minutes. Turn packet over and rotate a half turn. Heat on Medium-Low for 1½ (1:30) minutes.

Allow to stand on a heatproof surface for 10 minutes. Carefully separate fillets; rinse under cold running water if some areas are still icy or stiff.

DEFROSTING WHOLE FISH AND CUTLETS
Place fish in microwave-safe dish and turn over halfway through defrosting time. Shield vulnerable areas with smooth pieces of foil after turning.

DEFROSTING SHELLFISH
Shellfish can be defrosted in a packet but large quantities are best defrosted in a shallow, microwave-safe dish. Separate pieces halfway through defrosting.

151

Cooking

Quick-cooking method
To 'steam' fish portions, place in centre of lightly moistened paper towels. Bring all corners to the centre and twist to close; place on a microwave-safe plate. Cook 1 x 250 g fish cutlet on High (100% power) for 2½ (2:30)–3 minutes; 2 x 250 g fish cutlets on High for 4½ (4:30)–5 minutes, rotating once.

Improving appearance
Fish cooked in the microwave can be made to look grilled by cooking in a browning dish (right) or by coating with browning, teriyaki or soy sauce.

Absorbing excess moisture
Absorb unwanted juices in bottom of dish by using sheets of paper towel as liners; separate ends of fish with plastic wrap. Alternatively, elevate fish on a microwave-safe rack in the dish.

Even cooking
Roll up fillets (with or without a filling); secure with wooden toothpicks and arrange around edge of round dish. Leave space between each portion and leave centre open for more even cooking.

Shielding
Cover delicate parts of a whole fish, like the tail, with smooth strips of foil.

ROTATING AND TURNING FISH AND SHELLFISH

Whole fish, lobster tails and fillets should be rotated to avoid the buildup of heat in any one spot during cooking.

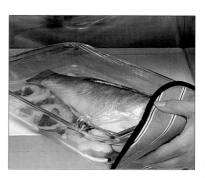

Prawns arranged in a circle with tails pointing towards the centre should be turned over with tongs and the dish rotated halfway through cooking.

Thick fish pieces or cutlets cooked in liquid should be turned over halfway through cooking to ensure even distribution of heat.

Stir-frying prawns
Because prawns cook rapidly, stir-frying in a browning dish is an ideal way to prepare them. The frequent turning and stirring ensures even distribution of heat.

Whole fish

COUNTRY-STYLE TAILOR

Colour Index page 52. 6 servings. 1402 kJ per serving. Good source of vitamin A, fibre. Begin 45 minutes ahead.

6 rashers rindless
  bacon, chopped
2 large onions, sliced
750 g small new potatoes,
  scrubbed and cut into
  quarters
Salt and pepper to taste

1.5 kg tailor or other
  oily-fleshed fish,
  cleaned and scaled,
  head removed
Rosemary sprigs to
  garnish

1. Cook bacon in a 33-cm x 23-cm baking dish, covered with paper towel, on High (100% power) for 5–7 minutes, until browned, stirring halfway through cooking. Discard all but 2 tablespoons bacon drippings.
2. Add onions and potatoes to dish. Cook, covered, on High for 8–10 minutes, until potatoes are almost tender, stirring twice. Season.
3. Brush tailor inside and out with cooking liquid from vegetables; shield tail with foil.
4. Place fish on top of potatoes. Cook, covered, on High for 6–8 minutes, just until outer edges of fish are opaque, removing foil and rotating dish halfway through cooking. Allow to stand, covered, on a heatproof surface for 5 minutes.
5. Place fish on a warmed serving platter. Spoon onion and potato mixture around fish; garnish with rosemary.

CHINESE SNAPPER

Colour Index page 49. 4 servings. 1030 kJ per serving. Good source of vitamin A, vitamin C, iron, fibre. Begin 25 minutes ahead.

1.25 kg snapper,
  cleaned and scaled,
  head removed
30 g butter or margarine,
  melted
6 spring onions, sliced
2 large red capsicums,
  cut into matchstick-
  thin strips
4 large carrots, cut into
  matchstick-thin strips

2 celery stalks, sliced
1 clove garlic, sliced
3 teaspoons vegetable oil
1½ tablespoons dry
  sherry
1½ tablespoons soy sauce
½ teaspoon ground
  ginger
Kiwifruit slices and
  toasted flaked almonds
  to garnish (optional)

1. Shield tail of snapper with a smooth strip of foil. Place fish in a 33-cm x 23-cm baking dish; brush with melted butter. Arrange spring onions, capsicum, carrot and celery around fish.
2. Place garlic and oil in a medium bowl. Cook on High (100% power) for 1½ (1:30)–2 minutes, until garlic is golden; discard garlic. Stir sherry, soy sauce and ginger into oil; pour over fish.
3. Cook, covered, on High for 12–14 minutes, just until outer edges of fish are opaque, removing foil, rotating dish and stirring vegetables halfway through cooking.
4. Allow to stand, covered, on a heatproof surface for 5 minutes. Garnish, if you like, with sliced kiwifruit and flaked almonds.

SNAPPER with OYSTER STUFFING

Colour Index page 52. 950 kJ per serving. Good source of vitamin A, iron. Begin 35 minutes ahead.

Ingredients for 4 servings		Microwave cookware

30 g butter or margarine
1 small onion, finely
  chopped
1 medium celery stalk,
  finely chopped
1 clove garlic, crushed
6 oysters with their
  liquid
2 tablespoons dry white
  wine
¼ cup thickened cream
	1 teaspoon finely
	  chopped fresh
	  tarragon leaves
	2 tablespoons dried
	  breadcrumbs
	Salt and pepper to taste
	1.25 kg snapper, cleaned
	  and scaled, head
	  removed
	Lemon and lime slices to
	  garnish
		23-cm pie plate
		33-cm x 23-cm
		  baking dish

1 Heat butter in pie plate, covered with paper towel, on High (100% power) for 45 seconds, or until melted.

2 Stir in onion, celery and garlic. Cook on High for 2–2½ (2:30) minutes, until vegetables are softened.

3 Drain oysters, reserving liquid. Strain oyster liquid through muslin or filter paper; reserve 2 tablespoons. Coarsely chop oysters.

4 Stir reserved oyster liquid, white wine, cream and tarragon into onion mixture. Cook on High for 4–5 minutes, until sauce is thickened, stirring occasionally. Stir in oysters and breadcrumbs; season.

5 Shield tail of snapper with a smooth strip of foil. Place fish in baking dish; fill cavity with stuffing, spreading any extra stuffing around fish. Cook, covered, on High for 10–12 minutes, just until outer edges of fish are opaque, removing foil and rotating dish halfway through cooking. Carefully transfer fish to a warmed serving platter; allow to stand, covered, for 5 minutes.

6 Garnish fish with lemon and lime slices. Cut top side of fish into serving-sized portions just down to bone. Remove with a narrow-bladed spatula. Serve each portion with some of the oyster stuffing. Remove backbone and repeat with other side of fish.

STUFFED TROUT

Colour Index page 51. 1444 kJ per serving. Good source of vitamin A, thiamine, iron. Begin 35 minutes ahead.

Ingredients	For 4	For 2	For 1
Butter or margarine	*60 g*	*30 g*	*15 g*
Onion, chopped	*1 medium*	*1 small*	*½ small*
Carrot, chopped	*1 small*	*½ small*	*2 tablespoons*
Celery, chopped	*2 small stalks*	*1 small stalk*	*½ small stalk*
Garlic, crushed	*2 cloves*	*1 clove*	*½ clove*
Walnuts, chopped	*¼ cup*	*2 tablespoons*	*1 tablespoon*
Fresh thyme, chopped	*1½ teaspoons*	*¾ teaspoon*	*½ teaspoon*
Dry sherry or white wine	*2 tablespoons*	*1 tablespoon*	*2 teaspoons*
Dried breadcrumbs	*¼ cup*	*2 tablespoons*	*1 tablespoon*
Trout (250 g–310 g each), cleaned and scaled, head removed	*4 whole fish*	*2 whole fish*	*1 whole fish*
Lemon slices and walnut halves	*garnish*	*garnish*	*garnish*
Microwave cookware	Large bowl 33-cm x 23-cm baking dish	Medium bowl 33-cm x 23-cm baking dish	Small bowl 30-cm x 20-cm baking dish
Time on High (100% power)			
Butter	45 seconds–1 minute	45 seconds	30 seconds
With vegetables	5 minutes	3 minutes	2 minutes
With seasonings	2 minutes	1½ (1:30) minutes	1 minute
Stuffed trout	4–5 minutes each batch	4–5 minutes	2½ (2:30)–3 minutes
Standing time	5 minutes	3 minutes	2 minutes

1 Heat butter in bowl (see Chart), covered with paper towel, on High for time in Chart.

2 Stir in onion, carrot, celery, garlic and walnuts. Cook on High for time in Chart, stirring twice.

3 Add thyme and one-third of sherry. Cook on High for time in Chart, stirring halfway through cooking. Add breadcrumbs.

4 Place an equal amount of stuffing in each fish.

5 Arrange fish in baking dish (see Chart); sprinkle with remaining sherry. Cook, covered, on High for time in Chart, until flesh is opaque, rotating dish halfway through cooking. If cooking for 4, cook fish in 2 batches. Allow to stand, covered, on a heatproof surface for time in Chart.

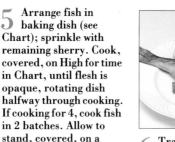

6 Transfer fish to warmed dinner plates; garnish with lemon and walnuts.

CAJUN TROUT

Colour Index page 51. 2 servings. 1913 kJ per serving. Good source of vitamin A, vitamin C, iron. Begin 35 minutes ahead.

45 g butter or margarine
1 large onion, chopped
1 green capsicum, chopped
1 clove garlic, crushed
215 g can tomatoes, chopped
Salt to taste
½ teaspoon dried thyme
½ teaspoon dried oregano
¼ teaspoon cayenne pepper

¼ cup cornmeal
¼ teaspoon caster sugar
2 trout (250 g–310 g each), cleaned and scaled, heads removed
3 teaspoons vegetable oil
Lime twists (page 134) to garnish
Hot Cooked Rice (page 295, optional)

1. Heat 30 g butter in a 2-litre casserole, covered with paper towel, on High (100% power) for 45 seconds, or until melted.

2. Stir in onion, capsicum and garlic. Cook on High for 5 minutes, or until softened, stirring twice.

3. Add tomatoes, salt and half each of thyme, oregano and cayenne pepper. Cook on High for 5 minutes, or until flavours blend; put aside.

4. Mix cornmeal, sugar, remaining thyme, oregano and cayenne pepper on a sheet of grease-proof paper. Season each trout lightly with salt. Dip in cornmeal mixture, patting cornmeal on to fish to coat well.

5. Meanwhile, preheat browning dish according to the manufacturer's instructions. Place remaining butter and oil on browning dish; add fish. Cook on High for 4–5 minutes, until flesh flakes easily when tested with a fork, carefully turning fish over once.

6. Transfer fish to warmed dinner plates. Spoon sauce around fish; garnish with lime twists. Serve, if you like, with rice.

SERVING A WHOLE FISH

Carefully slit skin along backbone; remove skin and discard. Divide top of fish into serving portions, cutting down to the bone.

Ease fish from bone with a server or spatula. Lift each portion of fish and place on a warmed plate.

Slide the server under backbone and lift to separate it from the lower section. Continue portioning fish in the same way.

SAUCES FOR FISH

Because fish and shellfish are usually delicate in flavour, they can be enhanced if served with a sauce. If making ahead, cover and refrigerate until ready to use.

Zesty Cucumber Sauce: Finely shred *1 small cucumber*; pat dry with paper towel. Combine cucumber with *¼ cup mayonnaise, 1 teaspoon chopped fresh parsley, 1 teaspoon cider vinegar* and *1 teaspoon seeded mustard*.
Makes ½ cup. 295 kJ per tablespoon.

Spicy Cocktail Sauce: Combine *¼ cup sweet chilli sauce, 3 tablespoons tomato sauce* and *1 teaspoon prepared horseradish*.
Makes ½ cup. 105 kJ per tablespoon.

Green Mayonnaise Dressing: Process *2 cups mayonnaise, ⅓ cup chopped fresh parsley, 1 tablespoon tarragon vinegar, ½ teaspoon dried tarragon* and *2 chopped spring onions* in a blender until smooth.
Makes 2 cups. 519 kJ per tablespoon.

The microwave is ideal for cooking whole fish such as bream, snapper, salmon, trout, tailor and mullet; it seals in moisture and flavour. Use smooth strips of foil to shield the tail of any whole fish that would otherwise overcook but be sure to keep foil at least 2.5 cm away from oven walls.

MULLET WITH RIBBON VEGETABLES

Colour Index page 48. 578 kJ per serving. Good source of vitamin A.
Begin 25 minutes ahead.

Ingredients for 6 servings		Microwave cookware
1.5 kg mullet, cleaned and scaled, head removed 30 g butter or margarine 2 tablespoons dry sherry 1 tablespoon lime or lemon juice ¼ teaspoon salt	¼ teaspoon pepper 1 clove garlic, crushed 1 large carrot 1 golden zucchini 1 green zucchini Salad greens, orange slices and lemon slices to garnish	33-cm x 23-cm baking dish Small bowl Large bowl

1 Wrap tail of mullet with a smooth strip of foil to prevent it from overcooking. Place fish in baking dish; put aside.

2 Place butter, sherry, lime juice, salt, pepper and garlic in small bowl. Cook on High (100% power) for 1 minute, or until melted. Lightly brush fish and fish cavity with some butter mixture; reserve remainder.

3 Cook fish, covered, on High for 6–8 minutes, just until outer edges are opaque, removing foil and rotating dish halfway through cooking. Carefully transfer fish to a warmed serving platter; allow to stand, covered, for 5 minutes.

4 Meanwhile, with vegetable peeler, shred carrot and zucchini into long ribbons about 2.5 cm wide, pressing lightly with peeler so ribbons will be very thin.

5 Gently toss vegetable ribbons and reserved butter mixture in large bowl. Cook, covered, on High for 30 seconds.

6 Arrange vegetables around fish; garnish with salad leaves and orange and lemon slices. Serve immediately.

Fish cutlets

For best results when cooking in a microwave oven, fish should be arranged in the dish so that the thickest parts are at the edges. With delicate fish, it is best to rotate the dish halfway through cooking rather than to turn fish over. Thicker fish cutlets can be turned carefully, however, to help prevent juices in the bottom of the dish transferring heat to only one side.

CHILLI SNAPPER

Colour Index page 54. 1222 kJ per serving. Good source of vitamin A, riboflavin. Begin 2¼ hours ahead.

Ingredients	For 4	For 2	For 1
Canned whole green chillies, drained	2 medium	1 medium	1 small
Lime juice	⅓ cup	2 tablespoons	1 tablespoon
Vegetable oil	2 tablespoons	1 tablespoon	2 teaspoons
Salt	½ teaspoon	¼ teaspoon	⅛ teaspoon
Honey	1 teaspoon	½ teaspoon	¼ teaspoon
Fresh oregano, chopped, or dried oregano	2 teaspoons or ½ teaspoon	1 teaspoon or ¼ teaspoon	½ teaspoon or ⅛ teaspoon
Cayenne pepper	⅛ teaspoon	pinch	pinch
Snapper cutlets (185 g each)	4 cutlets	2 cutlets	1 cutlet
Lime wedges and parsley sprigs	garnish	garnish	garnish
Microwave cookware	Browning dish	Browning dish	Browning dish
Time on High (100% power)	3–4 minutes each batch	3–4 minutes	2–2½ (2:30) minutes

1 Wearing a rubber glove for protection, slit chillies lengthways. Remove seeds and discard. Finely chop chillies.

2 Combine lime juice, oil, salt, honey, oregano, cayenne pepper and chillies in a dish.

3 Add snapper cutlets. Cover and refrigerate for 2 hours, until flavours blend, turning cutlets often.

4 Just before serving, preheat browning dish according to the manufacturer's instructions. Place cutlets on dish; press with spatula to sear.

5 Cook on High for time in Chart, just until outer edges of fish are opaque, turning once. If cooking for 4, cook in 2 batches, reheating browning dish.

6 Arrange fish on warmed plates; garnish with lime wedges and parsley. Serve immediately.

SNAPPER CUTLETS WITH SALSA

Colour Index page 48. 2 servings. 1555 kJ per serving. Good source of vitamin A, vitamin C, iron. Begin 20 minutes ahead.

215 g can tomatoes
1 green capsicum, thinly sliced
1 onion, chopped
30 g stoned black olives, cut in half
2 tablespoons coarsely chopped fresh coriander or parsley
1 tablespoon vegetable oil
1 clove garlic, crushed

2 tablespoons lime or lemon juice
2 snapper, jewfish or kingfish cutlets (185 g each)
1 tablespoon dry sherry
2 tablespoons mayonnaise
½ teaspoon cider vinegar
¼ teaspoon chilli powder
Coriander sprigs to garnish

1. Prepare salsa: Drain tomatoes, reserving 2 tablespoons tomato liquid. Combine tomatoes and reserved liquid, capsicum, onion, olives, coriander, oil, garlic and 1 tablespoon lime juice in a medium bowl; stir to break up tomatoes. Cook on High (100% power) for 5–6 minutes, until capsicum is tender-crisp, stirring halfway through cooking. Cover and put aside.
2. Lightly moisten 2 sheets paper towel; place 1 snapper cutlet on each. Combine sherry and remaining lime juice in a bowl; pour half the mixture over each cutlet.
3. Bring all corners of each paper towel to centre and twist to close. Cook fish parcels on a platter on High for 2–2½ (2:30) minutes, just until outer edges of fish are opaque, rotating parcels halfway through cooking.
4. Meanwhile, combine mayonnaise, vinegar and chilli powder in a bowl.
5. Unwrap fish; place on warmed dinner plates. Spoon mayonnaise mixture over fish and accompany with salsa; garnish with coriander. Serve immediately.

Preparing the salsa

Drain canned tomatoes in a colander placed over a bowl. Reserve 2 tablespoons tomato liquid. Cook drained tomatoes with reserved liquid, thinly sliced green capsicum, chopped onion, halved black olives, chopped coriander, oil, garlic and lime juice. The salsa can be made in advance and kept, covered, for several hours in the refrigerator.

SAVOURY FISH CUTLETS

Colour Index page 48. 2 servings. 1323 kJ per serving. Good source of vitamin A, riboflavin, niacin, omega-3 fatty acids.
Begin 10 minutes ahead.

2 ocean trout or salmon cutlets (185 g each)	*1 teaspoon finely chopped spring onion*
2½ teaspoons lemon juice	*Radish flowers (page 115), spring onions and cucumber slices to garnish*
1 teaspoon mild mustard	
2 tablespoons mayonnaise	

1. Arrange ocean trout cutlets in a 30-cm x 20-cm baking dish; sprinkle with 1 teaspoon lemon juice. Cook, covered, on High (100% power) for 2 minutes.

2. Meanwhile, combine mustard, mayonnaise, chopped spring onion and remaining lemon juice in a small bowl.

3. Turn cutlets over in baking dish; spoon the mayonnaise mixture on to each. Cook on High for 30 seconds, or just until outer edges of fish are opaque.

4. Place fish on warmed serving platter; garnish with radish flowers, spring onions and cucumber slices. Serve immediately.

SALMON WITH LETTUCE AND CAPSICUM

Colour Index page 49. 2 servings. 1511 kJ per serving. Good source of vitamin A, thiamine, riboflavin, niacin, vitamin C, iron, omega-3 fatty acids.
Begin 15 minutes ahead.

1 large red capsicum, thinly sliced	*2 salmon, jewfish or kingfish cutlets (185 g each)*
30 g butter or margarine	*2 teaspoons lemon or lime juice*
1 small head cos lettuce, cut into 7.5-cm pieces	
3 teaspoons soy sauce	
¼ teaspoon coarsely ground pepper	

1. Place capsicum, butter and lettuce in a 30-cm x 20-cm baking dish. Cook, covered, on High (100% power) for 2–3 minutes, until lettuce is slighted wilted. Add soy sauce and pepper; stir.

2. Arrange salmon cutlets on vegetables; sprinkle with lemon juice. Cook, covered, on High for 2–3 minutes, just until outer edges of fish are opaque, rotating dish halfway through cooking.

3. Place wilted lettuce and capsicum on warmed dinner plates; arrange fish on top. Serve immediately.

SALMON CUTLETS WITH MARINATED CUCUMBER

Colour Index page 54. 1340 kJ per serving (without dressing). Low in fat (without dressing). Good source of vitamin A, thiamine, riboflavin, niacin, iron, omega-3 fatty acids.
Begin early in day.

Ingredients	For 4	For 2	For 1
Salmon cutlets (250 g each)	4 cutlets	2 cutlets	1 cutlet
Lemon juice	1 tablespoon	2 teaspoons	1 teaspoon
Cucumber, thinly sliced	375 g	185 g	90 g
Salt	1 teaspoon	½ teaspoon	¼ teaspoon
White vinegar	⅓ cup	2 tablespoons	1 tablespoon
Sugar	1 tablespoon	2 teaspoons	1 teaspoon
Pepper	¼ teaspoon	⅛ teaspoon	to taste
Onion, thinly sliced	1 small	½ small	¼ small
Salad greens and lemon wedges	garnish	garnish	garnish
Green Mayonnaise Dressing (page 155)	4 tablespoons	2 tablespoons	1 tablespoon
Microwave cookware	20-cm x 20-cm baking dish	20-cm x 20-cm baking dish	20-cm x 20-cm baking dish
Time on High (100% power)	4–5 minutes	3–4 minutes	2–3 minutes

1 Arrange salmon cutlets in baking dish (see Chart); sprinkle with lemon juice.

2 Cook, covered, on High for time in Chart, just until outer edges of fish are opaque, rotating dish halfway through cooking.

3 Drain cutlets on paper towel. Return to cleaned baking dish; cover and refrigerate. Meanwhile, toss cucumber and salt in a bowl. Allow to stand for 30 minutes.

4 Pour cucumber into a strainer placed over a small bowl. Press to extract excess liquid; discard liquid.

5 Return cucumber to bowl. Add vinegar, sugar, pepper and onion; mix well. Cover and refrigerate for 3 hours, or until well chilled.

6 Place fish on individual plates with marinated cucumber; garnish with salad greens and lemon wedges. Serve with Green Mayonnaise Dressing separately.

Elegant Summer Dinner

Hot Peanut Dip (below) with crudités
Salmon Cutlets with Marinated Cucumber (page 157)
Fresh mangoes with strawberry purée
feathered with cream

PREPARATION TIMETABLE

Early in day:	*Cook salmon; cover and refrigerate. Prepare marinated cucumber and dressing; cover and refrigerate.*
30 minutes ahead:	*Prepare crudités and arrange on small plates; cover. Prepare dip; spoon into small bowls. Slice mangoes; cover and refrigerate.*
10 minutes ahead:	*Arrange salmon cutlets on plates with marinated cucumber and salad. Purée strawberries for sauce. Assemble mangoes and sauce on individual plates. Heat dip in small bowls; place on plates with crudités.*
Just before serving:	*Feather strawberry purée with cream and decorate plate with whole strawberries.*

HOT PEANUT DIP
Served with crisp vegetables, this dip makes a tasty starter.

Combine *½ cup water, ¼ cup soy sauce, ⅓ cup sugar, 3 teaspoons chilli powder* and *1 crushed garlic clove* in a 4-cup glass jug. Cook, covered, on High (100% power) for 3 minutes. Allow to stand for 5 minutes.

Whisk *⅓ cup smooth peanut butter* and *2 tablespoons lime juice* into mixture. Spoon into 4 small bowls. Heat on High for 1 minute, or until dip is hot.

MEDITERRANEAN JEWFISH

Colour Index page 51. 2 servings. 1331 kJ per serving. Good source of vitamin A, riboflavin, niacin, vitamin C, iron, fibre.
Begin 35 minutes ahead.

1 small onion, chopped	*½ cup stoned black*
1 clove garlic, crushed	*olives, cut in half*
2 teaspoons vegetable oil	*2 jewfish or snapper*
1 medium zucchini	*cutlets (185 g each)*
215 g can tomatoes	*¼ teaspoon dried*
125 g mushrooms, sliced	*oregano*
2 tablespoons tomato	*Oregano or parsley*
paste	*sprigs to garnish*

1. Place onion, garlic and oil in a 1.5-litre casserole. Cook, covered, on High (100% power) for 4–4½ (4:30) minutes, until onion is softened, stirring halfway through cooking.
2. Cut zucchini into 12-mm slices. Add zucchini, tomatoes, mushrooms and tomato paste to casserole. Cook, covered, on High for 10 minutes, stirring halfway through cooking.
3. Add olives. Cook, covered, on High for 5–7 minutes, until flavours blend, stirring halfway through cooking; put aside.
4. Lightly moisten 2 sheets paper towel; place 1 jewfish cutlet on each. Sprinkle with oregano. Bring all corners of each paper towel to centre and twist to close. Cook fish parcels on a platter on High for 2–2½ (2:30) minutes, just until outer edges of fish are opaque, rotating parcels halfway through cooking.
5. Unwrap fish; place on warmed plates. Spoon vegetable mixture around fish; garnish with oregano. Serve immediately.

PEPPERY KINGFISH CUTLETS

Colour Index page 51. 6 servings. 682 kJ per serving. Good source of riboflavin, niacin.
Begin 35 minutes ahead.

1 small onion, chopped	*¼ teaspoon cayenne*
1 small red capsicum,	*pepper*
chopped	*¼ teaspoon garlic salt*
1 celery stalk, chopped	*6 small kingfish or*
½ cup chilli sauce	*jewfish cutlets, each*
1 tablespoon vegetable	*12-mm thick*
oil	*Basil leaves to garnish*

1. Combine onion, capsicum, celery, chilli sauce, oil, cayenne pepper and garlic salt in a 1-litre casserole. Cook, covered, on High (100% power) for 6–8 minutes, stirring occasionally. Reduce power level to Medium (50% power) and cook for 3 minutes longer, or until tender.
2. Arrange kingfish cutlets in a 33-cm x 23-cm baking dish. Cook, covered, on Medium-High (70% power) for 9–10 minutes, until edges are opaque, rotating dish halfway through cooking.
3. Place fish on warmed plates. Spoon sauce over and around fish; garnish with basil leaves. Serve immediately.

GEMFISH SATAY WITH CHUNKY PEANUT SAUCE

Colour Index page 49. 4 servings. 1277 kJ per serving. Low in cholesterol. Good source of vitamin A, vitamin C.
Begin 25 minutes ahead.

1 red capsicum
4 spring onions
2 tablespoons peanut or vegetable oil
1 clove garlic, crushed
2 tablespoons soy sauce
3 teaspoons rice-wine vinegar or cider vinegar
½ teaspoon ground ginger

⅓ cup crunchy peanut butter
2 tablespoons lemon juice
1 tablespoon hot water
1 teaspoon brown sugar
¼ teaspoon crushed dried chillies
500 g thick gemfish
Lemon slices and spring onion curls (page 134) to garnish

1. Finely dice one-quarter of the capsicum; reserve. Cut remaining capsicum into 4-cm chunks; put aside. Thinly slice 1 spring onion.
2. Combine diced capsicum, sliced spring onion, 1 tablespoon oil, garlic, 1½ tablespoons soy sauce, vinegar and ginger in a 1.5-litre casserole. Cook on High (100% power) for 2 minutes, or until vegetables are softened.
3. Stir peanut butter, 1 tablespoon lemon juice, water, brown sugar and chillies until blended; stir into vegetables. Put sauce aside.
4. Combine remaining oil, soy sauce and lemon juice in a 2-cup glass jug. Cook on High for 1 minute.
5. Cut gemfish into 4-cm cubes. Cut remaining 3 spring onions into 5-cm lengths. Thread capsicum, fish and spring onion on to 25-cm wooden skewers. Brush with lemon and soy mixture. Arrange skewers on a 30-cm round platter. Cook on High for 2½ (2:30)–3½ (3:30) minutes, just until fish is opaque, turning skewers over half-way through cooking.
6. Place kebabs on individual plates with small bowls of peanut sauce; garnish with lemon slices and spring onion curls.

PREPARING KEBABS

Kebab recipes can be prepared quickly and easily in the microwave with little washing-up afterwards. For easier handling, food can be marinated, skewered and arranged for cooking all in the same baking dish, tray or platter. When cooking kebabs in the microwave, be sure to use wooden or other microwave-safe skewers, and leave a small space between each piece of food on the skewer for even cooking, as shown above.

SAVOURY FISH KEBABS

Colour Index page 54. 783 kJ per serving. Low in cholesterol, fat, sodium. Good source of vitamin A, niacin, vitamin C.
Begin 1¼ hours ahead.

Ingredients	For 4	For 2	For 1
Vegetable oil	3 teaspoons	1½ teaspoons	¾ teaspoon
Spring onions, sliced	6	4	2
Mild curry powder	1 teaspoon	½ teaspoon	¼ teaspoon
Marmalade	3 teaspoons	1½ teaspoons	¾ teaspoon
Worcestershire sauce	2 teaspoons	1 teaspoon	½ teaspoon
Swordfish or tuna, 3 cm thick	500 g	250 g	125 g
Green capsicum	1	½	¼
Mushrooms	4	2	1
Cherry tomatoes	8	4	2
Hot Cooked Rice (page 295)	2 cups	1 cup	½ cup
Fresh herbs, chopped	to taste	to taste	to taste
Lemon slices and parsley	garnish	garnish	garnish
Microwave cookware	30-cm x 20-cm baking dish	30-cm x 20-cm baking dish	30-cm x 20-cm baking dish
Time on High (100% power)			
Onion mixture	2½ (2:30) minutes	2 minutes	1½ (1:30) minutes
Kebabs	2½ (2:30)–3 minutes	1½ (1:30)–2 minutes	1–1½ (1:30) minutes

1 Combine oil, spring onions and curry powder in baking dish (see Chart). Cook, covered, on High for time in Chart. Stir in marmalade and Worcestershire sauce.

2 With sharp knife, cut swordfish into 4-cm chunks. Cut capsicum into 4-cm pieces. Cut each mushroom in half.

3 Stir fish, capsicum, mushrooms and tomatoes into spring onion mixture. Cover and allow to stand for 45 minutes.

4 Thread fish and vegetables on to 25-cm wooden skewers, alternating fish and different vegetables.

5 Arrange skewers in baking dish. Cook on High for time in Chart, just until fish is opaque, turning skewers over halfway through cooking.

6 Fork hot rice and herbs together; spoon into serving dish. Arrange kebabs on top; garnish with lemon slices and parsley sprigs.

Fish fillets

ORIENTAL FISH in LETTUCE LEAVES

Colour Index page 54. 699 kJ per serving. Low in fat. Good source of vitamin A. Begin 1¼ hours ahead.

Ingredients	For 4	For 2	For 1
Firm white fish fillets, cut into 5-cm pieces	750 g	375 g	185 g
Soy sauce	3 teaspoons	1½ teaspoons	¾ teaspoon
Rice-wine vinegar or cider vinegar	3 teaspoons	1½ teaspoons	¾ teaspoon
Garlic, crushed	2 cloves	1 clove	½ clove
Fresh ginger, grated	½ teaspoon	¼ teaspoon	to taste
Fresh coriander leaves, chopped	3 teaspoons	1½ teaspoons	¾ teaspoon
Butterhead lettuce	4 leaves	2 leaves	1 leaf
Carrots, cut into matchstick-thin strips	2 medium	1 medium	½ medium
Spring onions, thinly sliced	2	1	½
Celery, cut into matchstick-thin strips	1 stalk	½ stalk	5-cm piece
Chicken stock	1 cup	½ cup	¼ cup
Coriander leaves	garnish	garnish	garnish
Microwave cookware	33-cm x 23-cm baking dish 4-cup soufflé dish	33-cm x 23-cm baking dish Medium bowl	20-cm shallow bowl Small bowl
Time on High (100% power)			
Lettuce leaves	1–1½ (1:30) minutes	1 minute	30–45 seconds
Vegetables in stock	4–5 minutes	3–4 minutes	2–2½ (2:30) minutes
Fish bundles	3–5 minutes	2–3 minutes	1–2 minutes
Standing time	3 minutes	2 minutes	2 minutes

USING LEAVES TO MAKE PARCELS

Lettuce, cabbage, spinach and vine leaves make ideal wrappers. Stuffed Cabbage (page 217) and Camembert in Vine Leaves (page 146) also use leaves to seal in flavour.

Arrange leaves on a board, vein side up. Remove tough ribs or stalks from leaves.

After cooking leaves, fold sides over fillings making sure fillings are enclosed.

1 Combine fish, soy sauce, vinegar, garlic, ginger and coriander in a bowl; cover and leave to marinate for 45 minutes.

2 Meanwhile, cook lettuce leaves in baking dish or bowl (see Chart), covered, on High for time in Chart, just until wilted.

3 While lettuce leaves are cooling, combine carrots, spring onions, celery and stock in soufflé dish or bowl (see Chart). Cook, covered, on High for time in Chart, until vegetables are tender-crisp.

4 Place lettuce leaves, vein side up, on a flat surface. Place an equal amount of marinated fish in centre of each leaf; fold to enclose fish completely (see above right).

5 Carefully place fish bundles, seam side down, in baking dish or bowl used for lettuce; leave 2.5 cm space between each bundle.

6 Ladle hot vegetable stock mixture over fish bundles. Cook, covered, on High for time in Chart, until bundles feel soft inside when pierced with a skewer. Allow to stand on a heatproof surface for time in Chart.

7 Transfer fish to warmed soup plates. Ladle equal amounts of vegetables and stock over each bundle; garnish with coriander leaves. Serve immediately.

TUNA STIR-FRY

Colour Index page 49. 4 servings. 1226 kJ per serving. Good source of potassium, iron. Begin 25 minutes ahead.

500 g tuna, cut into 12-mm strips	125 g canned champignons or
2 tablespoons soy sauce	6 dried Chinese
2 tablespoons rice wine or sherry	mushrooms, soaked for 20 minutes
1 tablespoon honey	2 spring onions, thinly
2 tablespoons vegetable oil	sliced
½ teaspoon Chinese five-spice powder	½ punnet cherry tomatoes
125 g snow peas	425 g can baby corn cobs, drained and rinsed

1. Combine tuna, soy sauce, rice wine, honey, 1 tablespoon oil and five-spice powder in a bowl.
2. Preheat browning dish according to the manufacturer's instructions. Place tuna strips on the dish in a single layer. Cook on High (100% power) for 1 minute. Turn tuna strips over. Cook on High for 30 seconds longer; put aside.
3. Place snow peas and a little water in a 33-cm x 23-cm baking dish. Cook on High for 3–3½ (3:30) minutes, until almost tender. Rinse under cold running water; drain.
4. Combine remaining oil, mushrooms and spring onions in same dish. Cook on High for 2 minutes, or until softened, stirring halfway through cooking.
5. Add snow peas, tomatoes, corn and 1 tablespoon marinade from tuna. Cook, covered, on High for 3–4 minutes, until vegetables are tender-crisp, stirring halfway through cooking.
6. Place vegetables on a serving platter; arrange fish on top. Reheat on High for 1 minute. Serve immediately.

SKATE AMANDINE

Colour Index page 48. 4 servings. 921 kJ per serving. Good source of vitamin A. Begin 20 minutes ahead.

⅓ cup flaked almonds	1 tablespoon dry white
30 g butter or margarine	wine
¼ teaspoon paprika	1 tablespoon chopped
500 g skate or swordfish, 12 mm thick	fresh parsley
	Parsley sprig to garnish

1. Combine almonds, butter and paprika in a small bowl. Cook on High (100% power) for 4–5 minutes, until almonds are golden brown, stirring after 2 minutes, then at 1-minute intervals; put aside.
2. Cut skate into serving-size pieces and remove any skin. Place in a 20-cm x 20-cm baking dish; sprinkle with wine. Cook, covered, on High for 4½ (4:30)–6½ (6:30) minutes, just until fish is opaque, rotating dish twice.
3. Place fish on warmed plates. Stir parsley into almond mixture. Spoon sauce over fish; garnish with parsley.

BREAM AND ASPARAGUS WITH CHEESE SAUCE

Colour Index page 49. 1042 kJ per serving. Good source of calcium. Begin 30 minutes ahead.

Few things are tastier than the classic combination of cheese and wine sauce poured over delicate white fish, as in Bream and Asparagus with Cheese Sauce. Try the recipe with other varieties of fine white fish fillets available on the market, such as perch, whiting, flounder and sole. All species of dory make a superb alternative – and the asparagus gives that extra special touch.

Ingredients for 4 servings		Microwave cookware
375 g asparagus spears	3 teaspoons plain flour	20-cm x 20-cm baking dish
2 tablespoons water	¼ teaspoon salt	
4 bream fillets (185 g each)	¼ teaspoon cayenne pepper	
15 g butter or margarine	60 g Cheddar cheese grated (½ cup)	
½ cup cream	Lemon twists (page 134) to garnish	
2 tablespoons dry white wine		

1 Hold base of each asparagus spear firmly and bend; the end will break off at the spot where the spear becomes too tough to eat. Discard the tough ends. Place asparagus and water in baking dish. Cook on High (100% power) for 3 minutes, or until asparagus is crisp-tender.

2 Place bream fillets, boned side down, on a flat surface. Place an equal number of asparagus spears on the narrow end of each fillet.

3 Starting at narrow end, roll up fillets around asparagus spears.

4 Arrange fillets, seam side down, in baking dish; dot with butter. Cook, covered, on High (100% power) for 4–6 minutes, just until flesh flakes easily when tested with a fork, rotating dish halfway through cooking. Transfer fillets to a serving platter; keep warm.

5 Beat cream, wine, flour, salt and pepper into cooking liquid in baking dish. Cook on High for 3–4 minutes, until sauce thickens slightly, stirring twice. Stir cheese into sauce. Cook on High for 1 minute; stir until smooth.

6 Spoon cheese sauce over fish on serving dish; garnish with lemon twists. Serve immediately.

FLOUNDER VÉRONIQUE

Colour Index page 48. 1180 kJ per serving. Good source of vitamin A.
Begin 25 minutes ahead.

Ingredients	For 4	For 2	For 1
Flounder or sole fillets (185 g each)	4 fillets	2 fillets	1 fillet
Lemon juice	2 teaspoons	1 teaspoon	½ teaspoon
Fresh tarragon, chopped, or dried tarragon	2 teaspoons or ½ teaspoon	1 teaspoon or ¼ teaspoon	½ teaspoon or ⅛ teaspoon
Salt and white pepper	to taste	to taste	to taste
Seedless grapes	1 cup	½ cup	¼ cup
Dry white wine	2 tablespoons	1 tablespoon	2 teaspoons
Butter or margarine	30 g	15 g	1½ teaspoons
Plain flour	3 teaspoons	1½ teaspoons	¾ teaspoon
Cream	½ cup	¼ cup	2 tablespoons
Lemon slices, parsley sprigs and grapes	garnish	garnish	garnish
Microwave cookware	20-cm x 20-cm baking dish Small bowl	20-cm x 20-cm baking dish 2-cup glass jug	23-cm pie plate 1-cup glass jug
Time on High (100% power) Butter mixture With cream Fish	1 minute 3 minutes 5–6 minutes	1 minute 2 minutes 3–3½ (3:30) minutes	45 seconds 1 minute 1½ (1:30)–2 minutes

1 Brush flounder fillets with lemon juice. Combine tarragon, salt and pepper in a bowl; sprinkle evenly over fillets.

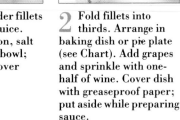

2 Fold fillets into thirds. Arrange in baking dish or pie plate (see Chart). Add grapes and sprinkle with one-half of wine. Cover dish with greaseproof paper; put aside while preparing sauce.

3 Place butter, flour, salt and pepper in bowl or jug (see Chart). Cook, covered, on High for time in Chart, or until butter has melted. Stir until smooth. Gradually stir in cream until blended. Cook on High for time in Chart, or until mixture has thickened. Stir remaining wine into sauce; cover and keep warm.

4 Cook fillets, covered, on High for time in Chart, just until flesh flakes easily. If cooking for 4, rotate dish after 4 minutes.

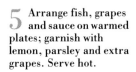

5 Arrange fish, grapes and sauce on warmed plates; garnish with lemon, parsley and extra grapes. Serve hot.

FLOUNDER FILLETS WITH SAVOURY SAUCE

Colour Index page 48. 4 servings. 984 kJ per serving (without sauce). Good source of vitamin A, thiamine, riboflavin, iron.
Begin 20 minutes ahead.

Spicy Cocktail Sauce or Zesty Cucumber Sauce (page 155)
1 cup dried breadcrumbs
2 tablespoons chopped fresh parsley
1 teaspoon grated lemon rind
¾ teaspoon paprika
4 flounder or sole fillets (185 g each)
1 egg, slightly beaten
Lettuce leaves, radish slices and cucumber slices to garnish

1. Prepare sauce of your choice.
2. Combine crumbs, parsley, lemon rind and paprika on greaseproof paper. Dip flounder fillets in egg, then coat with crumb mixture.
3. Place fillets on a rack set in a 33-cm x 23-cm baking dish. Cook on High (100% power) for 5–6 minutes, just until flesh flakes easily, rotating dish halfway through cooking.
4. Arrange fish with sauce on warmed dinner plates; garnish with lettuce, cucumber and radish. Serve immediately.

FISH FILLETS FLORENTINE

Colour Index page 48. 4 servings. 1658 kJ per serving. Good source of vitamin A, riboflavin, niacin, vitamin C, calcium, iron, fibre.
Begin 25 minutes ahead.

2 tomatoes, each cut into 8 wedges
¼ teaspoon salt
2 tablespoons vegetable oil
2 teaspoons chopped fresh oregano
250 g mushrooms, sliced
1 onion, chopped
1 cup fresh bread cubes
¼ teaspoon pepper
375 g packet frozen chopped spinach, thawed and drained
125 g Swiss cheese, grated (1 cup)
4 firm white fish fillets (185 g each)

1. Place tomatoes, salt, half the oil and half the oregano in a 1.5-litre casserole. Cook, covered, on High (100% power) for 2–3 minutes, until tomatoes are softened; put aside.
2. Place mushrooms, onion and remaining oil in a 30-cm x 20-cm baking dish. Cook, covered, on High for 5–6 minutes, stirring halfway through cooking. With a slotted spoon, transfer half the mushroom mixture to a small bowl; put aside. Stir bread cubes, pepper, spinach, remaining oregano and ¾ cup cheese into baking dish.
3. Spoon one-quarter of the spinach mixture on to one end of each fillet; fold over other end to cover mixture. Arrange fillets in baking dish; top with remaining cheese and reserved mushroom mixture. Cook on High for 5–6 minutes, just until flesh flakes easily, rotating dish once. Reheat tomatoes on High for 30 seconds.
4. Place fish on a warmed serving dish. Serve with cooked tomato wedges.

WHITING ROLLS WITH CUCUMBER, TOMATO AND BASIL SAUCE

Colour Index page 48. 4 servings. 603 kJ per serving. Good source of vitamin A.
Begin 25 minutes ahead.

15 g butter or margarine	*½ teaspoon salt*
2 spring onions, cut into matchstick-thin strips	*½ cup dry white wine*
2 teaspoons shredded fresh basil	*2 tomatoes, seeded and diced*
185 g cucumber, cut into matchstick-thin strips	*1 teaspoon cornflour dissolved in 1 tablespoon cold water*
500 g whiting fillets	*Basil leaves to garnish*

1. Heat butter in a 23-cm pie plate on High (100% power) for 30–45 seconds, until melted.
2. Stir in spring onions, half the basil and half the cucumber. Cook on High for 2–2½ (2:30) minutes, until cucumber is slightly softened.
3. Place whiting fillets, boned side down, on a flat surface; sprinkle with half the salt. Arrange one-quarter of the cooked cucumber pieces at the wide end of each fillet. Starting at wide end, roll up and secure with a wooden toothpick.
4. Arrange fish rolls in a circle in the pie plate; pour in white wine. Cook, covered, on High for 3–4 minutes, just until flesh flakes easily when tested with a fork, rotating dish halfway through cooking. Meanwhile, finely chop remaining cucumber.
5. With a slotted spatula, transfer fish rolls to a platter; put aside. Stir tomatoes, dissolved cornflour and remaining cucumber, basil and salt into wine mixture. Cook on High for 2–3 minutes, until sauce thickens, stirring twice. Add fish rolls. Cook on High for 1 minute longer.
6. Place fish rolls on warmed plates. Spoon sauce around fish; garnish with basil leaves. Serve immediately.

Rolling and arranging the fish fillets

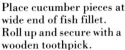

Place cucumber pieces at wide end of fish fillet. Roll up and secure with a wooden toothpick.

Stand fish rolls upright in pie plate, leaving space between each one.

PERCH IN PAPER PARCELS

Colour Index page 52. 213 kJ per serving. Low in cholesterol, sodium. Good source of vitamin A, vitamin C.
Begin 35 minutes ahead.

Ingredients	For 4	For 2	For 1
Green capsicum, cut into thin strips	*2 small*	*1 small*	*½ small*
Cherry tomatoes, cut into quarters	*8*	*4*	*2*
Spring onions, sliced	*2*	*1*	*½*
Mushrooms, sliced	*4*	*2*	*1*
Fresh basil	*8 leaves*	*4 leaves*	*2 leaves*
Orange rind, grated	*3 teaspoons*	*1½ teaspoons*	*¾ teaspoon*
Perch fillets (185 g each)	*4 fillets*	*2 fillets*	*1 fillet*
Salt	*to taste*	*to taste*	*to taste*
Butter or margarine	*1 tablespoon*	*2 teaspoons*	*1 teaspoon*
Orange slices and basil leaves	*garnish*	*garnish*	*garnish*
Microwave cookware	30-cm plate	30-cm plate	23-cm plate
Time on High (100% power)	3–3½ (3:30) minutes each batch	3–3½ (3:30) minutes	1½ (1:30)–2 minutes

1 Place capsicum, cherry tomatoes, spring onions, mushrooms, basil leaves and orange rind in a small bowl; toss to mix.

2 For each serve, fold a 35-cm x 20-cm sheet of baking paper in half lengthways. Cut a large heart shape. Place open sheets on work surface. Using half the capsicum mixture, place an equal amount on right-hand side of each heart.

3 Place 1 perch fillet, with thin end folded under, on top of each layer of capsicum mixture. Season with salt. Place remaining mixture evenly over fillets. Dot with butter.

4 Fold left side of paper over fish. Double-fold edges to seal.

5 Place parcels on plate (see Chart) with edges facing outwards. Cook on High for time in Chart, until parcels puff up, rotating plate once. If cooking for 4, cook in 2 batches.

6 Place parcels on warmed plates. With a small, sharp knife, cut a cross in the centre of each parcel to allow steam to escape. Fold back edges; garnish with orange slices and basil. Serve hot.

Canned fish

STUFFED DORY FILLETS

Colour Index page 52. 1440 kJ per serving. Good source of iron.
Begin 45 minutes ahead.

Ingredients	For 4	For 2	For 1
Hollandaise Sauce (page 381)	½ cup	¼ cup	2 tablespoons
Vegetable oil	1½ tablespoons	3 teaspoons	1½ teaspoons
Onion, finely chopped	1 small	½ small	¼ small
Garlic, crushed	1 clove	½ clove	to taste
Green capsicum, diced	¼ cup	2 tablespoons	1 tablespoon
Green prawns, shelled, deveined and chopped	500 g	250 g	125 g
Dried breadcrumbs	¼ cup	2 tablespoons	1 tablespoon
Fresh dill, chopped	1 tablespoon	2 teaspoons	1 teaspoon
Salt and pepper	to taste	to taste	to taste
John dory or silver dory fillets (185 g each)	4 fillets	2 fillets	1 fillet
Dill sprigs	garnish	garnish	garnish
Microwave cookware	2-litre casserole 30-cm x 20-cm baking dish	1-litre casserole 20-cm x 20-cm baking dish	Medium bowl 23-cm pie plate
Time on High (100% power)			
Vegetables	2–2½ (2:30) minutes	1½ (1:30) minutes	1 minute
With prawns	3 minutes	2 minutes	1½ (1:30) minutes
Stuffed dory	5–6 minutes	3–3½ (3:30) minutes	1½ (1:30)–2 minutes

1 Make Hollandaise Sauce; keep warm. Place oil, onion, garlic and capsicum in casserole or bowl (see Chart). Cook on High for time in Chart.

2 Add prawns; stir to coat with oil. Cook on High for time in Chart, or just until prawns are pink, stirring halfway through cooking.

3 Stir breadcrumbs and chopped dill into prawn mixture; mix well. Season with salt and pepper.

4 Place dory fillets, boned side down, on a flat surface. Spoon an equal amount of stuffing on to the centre of each.

5 Starting at narrow end, roll up each fillet; place, seam side down, in baking dish or pie plate (see Chart).

6 Cook stuffed fillets on High for time in Chart, just until flesh flakes easily when tested with a fork and stuffing is hot. If making for 4, rotate dish after 4 minutes. Arrange fish on warmed plates. Pour Hollandaise Sauce over fish; garnish with dill sprigs. Serve immediately.

TUNA AND SPINACH LOAF

Colour Index page 51. 6 servings. 1013 kJ per serving. Good source of vitamin A, calcium, iron, fibre.
Begin 40 minutes ahead.

1 tablespoon vegetable oil
1 onion, finely chopped
1 lemon
375 g packet frozen chopped spinach
425 g can tuna, drained

4 slices white bread
½ cup sour cream
2 eggs
¼ teaspoon salt
¼ teaspoon Tabasco sauce
Parsley to garnish

1. Lightly grease a 23-cm x 13-cm loaf dish.
2. Combine oil and onion in a medium bowl. Cook, covered, on High (100% power) for 2–3 minutes, until onion is softened; put aside.
3. Thinly slice half the lemon for garnish; cover and reserve. Squeeze juice from remaining lemon half.
4. Remove frozen spinach from packet and place on a plate. Heat on Medium-Low (30% power) for 5–6 minutes, until thawed, turning spinach over once. Drain well, squeezing spinach to remove as much liquid as possible.
5. Finely flake tuna in a large bowl. With hands, finely tear bread; add to tuna. Add onion mixture, lemon juice, spinach, sour cream, eggs, salt and Tabasco sauce; mix well. Spoon tuna mixture into prepared loaf dish.
6. Cook, covered with greaseproof paper, on Medium-High (70% power) for 11–13 minutes, until knife inserted 2.5 cm from centre comes out clean, rotating dish halfway through cooking. (If ends of loaf begin to overcook, shield with 7.5-cm-wide smooth strips of foil.) Allow loaf to stand, covered, on a heatproof surface for 5 minutes.
7. Unmould loaf on to a warmed serving platter (below); garnish with reserved lemon slices and parsley sprigs. Serve loaf cut into slices.

Unmoulding the loaf

Loosen loaf from side of dish with a knife. Place a serving platter upside down on dish and invert. Carefully remove dish to unmould loaf.

TUNA PATTIES FLORENTINE

Colour Index page 51. 6 servings. 795 kJ per serving.
Good source of vitamin A, iron.
Begin 35 minutes ahead.

30 g butter or margarine	1 tablespoon chopped
375 g packet frozen	capers
chopped spinach	1 tablespoon grated
425 g can tuna, drained	onion
and flaked	1 tablespoon lemon juice
½ cup fresh breadcrumbs	¼ teaspoon salt
(1 slice)	Lemon wedges and
2 eggs	parsley to garnish

1. Heat butter in a large bowl, covered with paper towel, on High (100% power) for 45 seconds, or until melted; put aside.
2. Remove frozen spinach from packet and place on a plate. Heat on Medium-Low (30% power) for 5–6 minutes, until thawed, turning spinach over once. Drain well, squeezing spinach to remove as much liquid as possible.
3. Add spinach, tuna, breadcrumbs, eggs, capers, grated onion, lemon juice and salt to melted butter; mix well.
4. Shape tuna mixture into six 7.5-cm patties. Place patties on a 30-cm round plate. Cook, covered with greaseproof paper, on Medium (50% power) for 12 minutes, or until firm, re-arranging patties halfway through cooking.
5. Allow to stand, covered, on a heatproof surface for 5 minutes. Garnish with lemon wedges and parsley.

SMOKED FISH

Smoked fish fillets poach or steam superbly in the microwave; use your favourite recipe, allowing 5 minutes for 500 g, covered, on High (100% power) and 5 minutes standing time. Or try the tasty recipe below.

For hot smoked whole fish, such as kippers, mackerel and tailor, place in oven bag and cook on Medium-High (70% power), allowing 6 minutes for 750 g and turning halfway through cooking; stand for 2 minutes.

Smoked blue cod with mustard butter:
Beat *75 g butter* until soft and fluffy; slowly add *1 tablespoon French Mustard* and *2 teaspoons vinegar*. Form butter into a cylinder, wrap in foil and refrigerate. Place *750 g blue cod*, skin side down, in a 33-cm x 23-cm baking dish; pour in *½ cup milk* then add enough *water* to almost cover fish. Cook on Medium-High for 6 minutes. Allow to stand for 2 minutes; drain fish. Cut in half lengthways and serve on warmed plates with slices of mustard butter. Serves 2.

Meal in Minutes *for 8 people*
Spanish Dinner Party
Olives and corn chips
Paella (page 173)
Crème Caramel (page 331) with strawberries
Sangria (below)

PREPARATION TIMETABLE

Early in day:	*Prepare double quantity of Crème Caramel in 2 batches up to the end of step 5.*
1½ hours ahead:	*Make Paella.*
Just before serving:	*Fill serving bowls with olives and corn chips. Unmould Crème Caramel and decorate. Make Sangria.*

SANGRIA

Sangria makes a delightful accompaniment to a Spanish-style meal. Use a good cask red wine and a jug large enough to hold the cut-up fruit. Be sure to serve the Sangria in large glasses so that each guest receives some wine-soaked fruit.

Pour *1 cup lemon juice, 1 cup orange juice* and *1 cup sugar* into jug; stir to dissolve sugar. Stir in *1.5 litres red wine, ½ cup brandy, 2 x 285 ml bottles chilled soda water, 2 cups sliced fresh fruit (orange, lemon, apple, peach, banana, strawberry)* and *2 trays ice cubes.*

Prawns

PIQUANT PRAWNS

Colour Index page 50. 929 kJ per serving. Good source of niacin, calcium, iron. Begin 25 minutes ahead.

Ingredients	For 4	For 2	For 1
Medium green prawns in their shells, heads removed	1 kg	500 g	250 g
Dried basil	1½ teaspoons	¾ teaspoon	½ teaspoon
Celery salt	1½ teaspoons	¾ teaspoon	½ teaspoon
Dried rosemary	1½ teaspoons	¾ teaspoon	½ teaspoon
Dried thyme	1½ teaspoons	¾ teaspoon	½ teaspoon
Mustard powder	1 teaspoon	½ teaspoon	¼ teaspoon
Fennel seed	1 teaspoon	½ teaspoon	¼ teaspoon
Cayenne pepper	to taste	to taste	to taste
Worcestershire sauce	1 teaspoon	½ teaspoon	¼ teaspoon
Beer	½ cup	¼ cup	2 tablespoons
Lemon (optional)	4 slices	2 slices	1 slice
Hot Cooked Rice (page 295)	2 cups	1 cup	½ cup
Fresh herbs, chopped	to taste	to taste	to taste
Parsley or lime	garnish	garnish	garnish
Microwave cookware	8-cup soufflé dish	8-cup soufflé dish	4-cup soufflé dish
Time on High (100% power)	8–10 minutes	4–6 minutes	2–3½ (3:30) minutes
Standing time	3–4 minutes	3 minutes	2 minutes

1 Place prawns in a colander. Rinse under cold running water to clean; drain well.

2 Combine basil, celery salt, rosemary, thyme, mustard, fennel seed and cayenne pepper in soufflé dish (see Chart) until well mixed.

3 Add prawns; toss to coat in seasonings. Add Worcestershire sauce and beer; mix well.

4 Cook prawns, covered, on High for time in Chart, just until prawns turn pink, stirring twice. Allow to stand, covered, on a heatproof surface for time in Chart.

5 Meanwhile, if you like, prepare a finger bowl for each serving by filling small bowls with warm water and floating a lemon slice in each.

6 Arrange prawns in warmed soup plates. Fork hot rice and fresh herbs together; spoon next to prawns. Garnish with parsley sprigs or lime wedges. Serve immediately.

PRAWNS IN SAFFRON CREAM

Colour Index page 53. 6 servings. 858 kJ per serving. Good source of vitamin A, vitamin C, iron. Begin 35 minutes ahead.

⅛ teaspoon saffron strands
Water
4 carrots, cut into matchstick-thin strips
750 g medium green prawns, shelled and deveined (below)
¼ cup lemon juice
¼ cup dry vermouth
2 tablespoons finely chopped spring onion
½ teaspoon salt
1 cup cream
2 teaspoons cornflour
375 g snow peas

1. Soak saffron strands in 1 tablespoon boiling water in a 4-cup glass jug.
2. Place carrots and ¼ cup water in a 30-cm x 20-cm baking dish. Cook, covered, on High (100% power) for 4–6 minutes, until tender. Transfer to a plate; cover and keep warm. Reserve cooking liquid in baking dish.
3. Place prawns, 2 tablespoons lemon juice, 2 tablespoons vermouth, half the spring onion and half the salt in a 33-cm x 23-cm baking dish. Cook, covered, on High for 5–6 minutes, just until prawns turn pink, stirring halfway through cooking. Drain prawns over a bowl; keep warm.
4. Add cream, cornflour and remaining lemon juice, vermouth, spring onion and salt to saffron mixture; stir until well blended. Cook, covered, on High for 4–6 minutes, until cream boils and thickens slightly, stirring halfway through cooking. Put aside; keep warm.
5. Add snow peas to reserved carrot liquid in baking dish. Cook, covered, on High for 4–5 minutes, until tender-crisp, stirring halfway through cooking. Add carrots to one side of dish, keeping vegetables separate. Cook, covered, on High for 1 minute.
6. Gently toss prawns in saffron cream. Spoon equal amounts on to warmed plates; arrange vegetables around prawn mixture. Serve hot.

SHELLING AND DEVEINING PRAWNS
Prawns may be shelled and deveined before or after cooking in the microwave, depending on the recipe.

Twist off head of each prawn; pull off the tail shell; peel off the legs and body shell in one piece.

Scrape away black or green vein; rinse prawn under cold running water.

CREOLE PRAWNS

Colour Index page 50. 4 servings. 1938 kJ per serving. Good source of vitamin A, niacin, vitamin C, calcium, iron.
Begin 20 minutes ahead.

60 g butter or margarine	*2 teaspoons*
3 small onions, cut into	*Worcestershire sauce*
12-mm wedges	*1 teaspoon prepared*
1 small green capsicum,	*horseradish*
cut into 12-mm pieces	*810 g can tomatoes,*
3 cloves garlic, crushed	*puréed with their juice*
750 g large green	*Salt and pepper to taste*
prawns, shelled and	*Tabasco sauce to taste*
deveined (page 166)	*2 cups Hot Cooked Rice*
¼ teaspoon ground	*(page 295)*
cloves	*Thyme sprigs to garnish*
1 tablespoon chopped	
fresh thyme	

1. Heat butter in a 2.5-litre casserole, covered with paper towel, on High (100% power) for 45 seconds–1 minute, until melted.
2. Stir in onions, capsicum, garlic, prawns, cloves and thyme. Cook, covered, on High for 6 minutes, or just until prawns turn pink, stirring twice.
3. Stir Worcestershire sauce, horseradish and puréed tomatoes into prawn mixture. Cook on High for 4 minutes, or until flavours blend, stirring halfway through cooking. Season with salt, pepper and Tabasco sauce.
4. Spoon prawns over hot rice; garnish with thyme sprigs. Serve hot.

LEMON AND LIME GARNISHES
Lemon is the traditional garnish for fish; lime adds an extra touch of colour. The acidity of these fruits balances the oil content of tailor, salmon and tuna, and brings out the flavour of more delicate white fish.

Lemon or lime loops: Cut *1 lemon* or *lime* in half lengthways, then cut each half into 6-mm slices. Cut rind from fruit, leaving 2 cm attached. Curl rind under to form loop.

Lemon or lime bundles: Place *lemon* or *lime half,* cut side down, in the centre of a small piece of muslin. Gather edges of cloth together; place *1 parsley sprig* at gathered edge and tie tightly with string.

Filled prawn dishes such as Stuffed Prawns Supreme (below) make an impressive addition to any dinner or buffet table. To assure a neat and attractive finished result, it is essential to use large prawns and to grate or very finely chop the stuffing ingredients.

STUFFED PRAWNS SUPREME

Colour Index page 53. 1461 kJ per serving. Good source of iron.
Begin 45 minutes ahead.

Ingredients for 4 servings		Microwave cookware
500 g large prawns,	*1 egg, beaten*	33-cm x 23-cm
shelled and deveined	*30 g butter or margarine,*	baking dish
(page 166)	*melted*	30-cm plate
1 cup grated zucchini	*2 tablespoons sherry*	
⅓ cup finely chopped	*1 tablespoon lemon juice*	
red capsicum	*2 tablespoons crushed*	
¼ cup dried breadcrumbs	*walnuts or pecans*	
¼ teaspoon salt	*185 g goat cheese roll*	
Cayenne pepper to taste	*Lettuce leaves to garnish*	

1 Cut each prawn along the back, three-quarters of the way through. Spread open and pound lightly to flatten.

2 Place zucchini in a colander over a bowl; press to remove excess moisture; discard liquid. Combine zucchini, capsicum, breadcrumbs, salt, cayenne pepper and beaten egg in a bowl.

3 Spoon an equal amount of zucchini mixture along the centre of each prawn; fold prawn over filling. Arrange stuffed prawns in a single layer in baking dish.

4 Combine melted butter, sherry and lemon juice in a bowl; pour over stuffed prawns. Cook, covered with greaseproof paper, on Medium-High (70% power) for 6–8 minutes, until prawns turn pink, rotating dish halfway through cooking. Put aside, covered.

5 Place crushed walnuts in a shallow dish. With a small, sharp knife, cut goat cheese into 8 slices. Press cheese slices into walnuts to coat. Place on plate. Heat on Medium (50% power) for 1–2 minutes, until cheese is softened slightly.

6 Garnish a serving platter with lettuce leaves. Arrange stuffed prawns and cheese slices in the centre of the platter; pour any remaining butter mixture over prawns. Serve immediately.

STIR-FRIED PRAWNS AND BROCCOLI

Colour Index page 53. 929 kJ per serving. Good source of vitamin A, vitamin C. Begin 40 minutes ahead.

Ingredients	For 4	For 2	For 1
Medium green prawns, shelled and deveined (page 166)	500 g	250 g	125 g
Cornflour	2 teaspoons	1 teaspoon	½ teaspoon
Dry sherry	2 tablespoons	1 tablespoon	2 teaspoons
Grated fresh ginger	½ teaspoon	¼ teaspoon	to taste
Broccoli flowerets and stalks, sliced	500 g	250 g	125 g
Water	¼ cup	2 tablespoons	1 tablespoon
Red capsicum, sliced	1 large	1 medium	1 small
425 g can straw mushrooms, drained	1 can	½ can	¼ can
Butter or margarine	3 teaspoons	1½ teaspoons	¾ teaspoon
Vegetable oil	3 teaspoons	1½ teaspoons	¾ teaspoon
Garlic, crushed	2 cloves	1 clove	½ clove
Hot Cooked Rice (page 295, optional)	2 cups	1 cup	½ cup
Soy sauce (optional)	to taste	to taste	to taste
Microwave cookware	2-litre casserole Browning dish	1-litre casserole Browning dish	Small bowl Browning dish
Time on High (100% power)			
Broccoli	4–5 minutes	3–3½ (3:30) minutes	2½ (2:30) minutes
Butter mixture	1 minute	45 seconds	30 seconds
Prawns	2–3 minutes	1½ (1:30)–2 minutes	1 minute
Vegetables	2–3 minutes	1½ (1:30)–1¾ (1:45) minutes	1 minute

1 Combine prawns, cornflour, sherry and ginger in a bowl; stir until blended. Cover and refrigerate for 15 minutes, stirring twice.

2 Place broccoli and water in casserole or bowl (see Chart). Cook, covered, on High for time in Chart; drain. Stir in capsicum and mushrooms; put aside.

3 Preheat browning dish according to the manufacturer's instructions. Place butter, oil and garlic on dish. Cook on High for time in Chart, stirring halfway through cooking. Add prawns in a single layer. Cook on High for time in Chart, just until prawns turn pink, stirring halfway through cooking. Transfer prawns to bowl; cover. Reheat browning dish.

4 Place vegetables on dish. Cook on High for time in Chart, stirring once.

5 Add prawns to vegetables; toss to mix. Serve, if you like, with rice and soy sauce.

PRAWN AND CAPSICUM RISOTTO

Colour Index page 53. 6 servings. 1829 kJ per serving. Low in fat, sodium. Good source of calcium, fibre.
Begin 40 minutes ahead.

2 tablespoons olive oil
125 g button mushrooms, cut into quarters or eighths
1 onion, finely chopped
1 celery stalk, finely chopped
1 clove garlic, crushed
1½ cups arborio rice or short-grain rice
3 cups fish stock
¾ cup dry white wine
500 g medium green prawns, shelled and deveined (page 166)

125 g snow peas, cut in half crossways
2 red capsicums, cut into 2.5-cm pieces
¼ teaspoon salt
½ teaspoon pepper
4 spring onions, finely chopped
2 tablespoons shredded fresh basil
Basil leaves to garnish

1. Place oil, mushrooms, onion, celery and garlic in a deep 3-litre casserole. Cook, covered, on High (100% power) for 3–4 minutes, until softened, stirring halfway through cooking.
2. Add rice; stir to combine. Add stock and white wine; stir again. Cook, loosely covered, on High for 15 minutes.
3. Add prawns, snow peas, capsicum, salt and pepper to rice mixture; stir gently. Cook, loosely covered, on High for 10 minutes.
4. Stir in spring onions and shredded basil until combined. Allow mixture to stand, covered, on a heatproof surface for 7–10 minutes, until most of liquid is absorbed. Risotto should be creamy, not dry; rice should be al dente (tender yet firm to the bite). Garnish with basil leaves. Serve hot.

CRAB AND FENNEL RISOTTO: Make as for Prawn and Capsicum Risotto (above), substituting 2 thinly sliced fennel bulbs for the capsicum in step 3, and 500 g cooked crab meat for the prawns. Add the crab with the spring onions in step 4, just to heat through. If you like, stir in 1 tablespoon Pernod with the spring onions, and substitute dill for basil.
1980 kJ per serving. Good source of vitamin A, vitamin C, calcium, iron, fibre.

Lobster

SZECHUAN LOBSTER

Colour Index page 53. 4 servings. 1222 kJ per serving. Good source of vitamin A, vitamin C, calcium, iron.
Begin 50 minutes ahead.

2 cooked lobsters (about 1 kg each), cut in half
3 teaspoons peanut or vegetable oil
2 teaspoons rice-wine vinegar or cider vinegar
3 cloves garlic, crushed
½ cup dry-roasted cashews

1 teaspoon chilli powder
2 teaspoons soy sauce
1 teaspoon sesame oil
250 g green beans
3 spring onions, cut into 5-cm pieces
1 green capsicum, cut into matchstick-thin strips

1. Remove meat from lobsters; cut into 5-cm pieces.
2. Combine oil, vinegar, garlic, cashews, chilli powder, soy sauce and sesame oil in a 30-cm x 20-cm baking dish. Cook, covered, on High (100% power) for 2 minutes, or until flavours blend.
3. Add beans, spring onions and capsicum; stir to coat with cashew mixture. Cook, covered, on High for 6–8 minutes, until beans are tender.
4. Add lobster to vegetables. Cook, covered, on High for 2–3 minutes, until lobster is hot.
5. Spoon on to warmed plates. Serve hot.

COOKING MUSSELS

Cooking mussels in the microwave is quick, simple and clean. All mussels should be thoroughly scrubbed with a stiff brush under cold running water to remove any sand and surface dirt; barnacles and beards should be scraped off with a small, sharp knife. Discard any mussels that are open or partially open. Arrange mussels in a soufflé dish or casserole. Cook, covered tightly with plastic wrap, on High (100% power) for time in recipe. If some mussels do not open, remove those that are opened and reserve; cover dish again and cook on High for 1–2 minutes longer. Remove opened mussels and place with others. Discard any that are still not open.

LOBSTER THERMIDOR

Colour Index page 53. 1348 kJ per serving. Good source of calcium.
Begin 45 minutes ahead.

Ingredients	For 4	For 2	For 1
Cooked lobsters (about 1–1.25 kg each)	2	1	½
Butter or margarine	60 g	30 g	15 g
Mushrooms, cut into quarters	125 g	60 g	30 g
300 g can cream of mushroom soup	1 can	½ can	¼ can
Milk	¼ cup	2 tablespoons	1 tablespoon
Medium-dry sherry	1½ tablespoons	3 teaspoons	1½ teaspoons
Parsley	garnish	garnish	garnish
Microwave cookware	Large bowl	Medium bowl	Medium bowl
Time on High (100% power)			
Butter and mushrooms	4 minutes	3 minutes	2 minutes
With soup and milk	4 minutes	2 minutes	1½ (1:30) minutes
With lobster	4 minutes	2½ (2:30) minutes	1½ (1:30) minutes

1 **Prepare lobsters:** Place each lobster, back down, on a board. With a sharp knife, pierce chest and cut down through shell to tail. Turn the lobster around and cut through shell to head.

2 **Pull the two halves of** the lobster apart. Remove spongy grey gills from the head; with the tip of a sharp knife, remove the intestinal vein running down the tail.

3 **Lift out meat from** both halves of lobster; cut into chunks and place in a large bowl. Rinse halved lobster shells; put aside.

4 **Place butter and** mushrooms in bowl (see Chart). Cook on High for time in Chart. Stir in soup and milk. Cook on High for time in Chart, stirring halfway through cooking.

5 **Stir sherry and** lobster meat into mushroom mixture. Cook on High for time in Chart, or until lobster is hot, stirring halfway through cooking.

6 **Place halved lobster** shells on each warmed plate. Spoon an equal amount of lobster mixture into each shell; garnish with parsley. Serve immediately.

Mussels

MUSSELS IN WHITE WINE

Colour Index page 52. 904 kJ per serving (without bread). Good source of iron.
Begin 35 minutes ahead.

Ingredients	For 4	For 2	For 1
Mussels	4 dozen	2 dozen	1 dozen
Olive or vegetable oil	¼ cup	2 tablespoons	1 tablespoon
Onion, finely chopped	1	½	¼
Garlic, sliced	4 cloves	2 cloves	1 clove
Tomatoes, diced	4	2	1
Dry white wine	1 cup	½ cup	¼ cup
Fresh basil, shredded, or dried basil	2 teaspoons or ½ teaspoon	1 teaspoon or ¼ teaspoon	½ teaspoon or ⅛ teaspoon
French bread	8 slices	4 slices	2 slices
Microwave cookware	8-cup soufflé dish or bowl	8-cup soufflé dish or bowl	6-cup soufflé dish or bowl
Time on High (100% power)	5–7 minutes each batch	5–7 minutes	4–5 minutes

1 Scrub mussels with a stiff brush under cold running water.

2 With a small, sharp knife, scrape away any barnacles and remove beards. Rinse.

3 Place mussels in soufflé dish (see Chart). If cooking for 4, prepare in 2 batches.

4 Add oil, onion, garlic, tomatoes, wine and basil.

5 Cook mussels, tightly covered with plastic wrap, on High for time in Chart, just until open.

6 Spoon mussels and cooking liquid into warmed soup bowls. Serve hot with French bread.

MUSSELS IN CREAM AND GARLIC

Colour Index page 50. 4 servings. 1716 kJ per serving. Low in sodium. Good source of vitamin A, calcium, iron, zinc.
Begin 25 minutes ahead.

2 kg mussels
¼ cup dry white wine
15 g butter or margarine
1 small onion, finely chopped

2 cloves garlic, crushed
1 cup cream
3 tablespoons chopped fresh parsley
½ teaspoon pepper

1. Scrub mussels with a stiff brush under cold running water. With a small sharp knife, scrape away any barnacles and remove beards. Rinse.
2. Place mussels in a deep 3-litre bowl; add wine. Cook, covered tightly with plastic wrap, on High (100% power) for 6–8 minutes, just until open. Remove mussels; put aside.
3. Strain cooking liquid through muslin into a jug; rinse out bowl.
4. Place butter, onion and garlic in cleaned bowl. Cook on High for 3 minutes, or until vegetables are softened, stirring halfway through cooking.
5. Add strained cooking liquid and cream. Cook on High for 2 minutes, or until sauce thickens and reduces slightly, stirring once; stir in parsley and pepper.
6. Discard top shell of each mussel. Arrange mussels on a large serving platter; pour over sauce. Cook on High for 1–2 minutes, until hot and bubbling. Serve immediately.

SCALLOPS IN CHIVE CREAM

Colour Index page 49. 4 servings. 921 kJ per serving. Good source of niacin, iron.
Begin 25 minutes ahead.

30 g butter or margarine
1 onion, finely chopped
500 g scallops
¼ cup cream
¼ cup chicken stock
¼ cup dry white wine
¼ cup finely chopped fresh chives

1 tablespoon cornflour dissolved in 2 tablespoons cold water
Salt and pepper to taste
Fresh chives to garnish

1. Place butter and onion in a 30-cm x 20-cm baking dish. Cook, covered with paper towel, on High (100% power) for 3–4 minutes, until onion is translucent and softened, stirring halfway through cooking.
2. Add scallops, cream, stock and wine to baking dish. Cook, covered, on High for 4–6 minutes, just until scallops are opaque.
3. Stir in chives and dissolved cornflour. Cook on High for 2–3 minutes, until thickened. Season with salt and pepper.
4. Spoon scallop mixture into 4 small dishes or into scallop shells; garnish with chives. Serve immediately.

Scallops

CURRIED SCALLOPS

Colour Index page 50. 4 servings. 774 kJ per serving.
Good source of vitamin A.
Begin 25 minutes ahead.

30 g butter or margarine	500 g scallops
1–1½ teaspoons curry powder	2 tablespoons dry white wine
1 onion, thinly sliced	Salt to taste
2 medium celery stalks, cut into matchstick-thin strips	Coriander or parsley sprigs to garnish
2 large carrots, cut into matchstick-thin strips	

1. Heat butter in a 30-cm x 20-cm baking dish, covered with paper towel, on High (100% power) for 45 seconds, or until melted.
2. Add curry powder according to taste; stir until well blended. Add onion, celery and carrots; stir to coat with curry butter. Cook on High for 2–3 minutes, until carrots are tender-crisp.
3. Add scallops; drizzle with white wine. Cook, covered, on High for 3–4 minutes, just until scallops are opaque, stirring twice. Season with salt.
4. Arrange scallops on warmed dinner plates; garnish with coriander or parsley. Serve hot.

SCALLOPS WITH BACON AND BASIL

Colour Index page 50. 2 servings. 2511 kJ per serving. Good source of vitamin A, calcium, iron. Begin 25 minutes ahead.

2 rashers rindless bacon, chopped	2 tablespoons dry white wine
250 g scallops	¾ cup cream
2 mushrooms, thinly sliced	¼ teaspoon pepper
1 small onion, thinly sliced	1 tablespoon shredded fresh basil
1 clove garlic, crushed	Basil leaves to garnish

1. Cook bacon in a deep 23-cm pie plate, covered with paper towel, on High (100% power) for 2 minutes, or until just lightly browned. With slotted spoon, transfer bacon to paper towel to drain; put aside.
2. Stir scallops into bacon drippings in dish. Cook, covered, on High for 2–2½ minutes, just until scallops are opaque. Remove and keep warm.
3. Add mushrooms, onion, garlic and wine to dish; stir to combine. Cook, covered, on High for 3 minutes, or until softened, stirring halfway through cooking.
4. Add cream and pepper to vegetable mixture; stir. Cook on High for 3–5 minutes, until sauce thickens and reduces slightly, stirring twice. Stir in reserved bacon and scallops. Cook, covered, on High for 1 minute. Stir in shredded basil.
5. Place on warmed plates; garnish with basil leaves. Serve immediately.

Oysters

Oysters are sold fresh in the shell, on the half-shell, bottled or canned. Australian oysters are generally small in size and highly prized for their flavour when eaten 'natural'. New Zealand Bluff oysters and Pacific oysters are both larger, and are also good in soups and casseroles.

CREAMED OYSTERS IN PUFF PASTRY

Colour Index page 50. 1528 kJ per serving. Good source of calcium, iron. Begin 25 minutes ahead.

Ingredients for 4 servings		Microwave cookware
4 rashers rindless bacon, chopped	4 dozen bottled oysters, with their liquid	30-cm x 20-cm baking dish
1 small onion, chopped	½ cup cream	
1 celery stalk, chopped	Salt and pepper to taste	
1 clove garlic, crushed	4 large or 8 medium vol-au-vent cases	
2 teaspoons finely chopped fresh thyme or ½ teaspoon dried thyme	Lemon twists (page 134) and parsley sprigs to garnish	
3 teaspoons plain flour		

1 Cook bacon in baking dish, covered with paper towel, on High (100% power) for 4–5 minutes, until browned, stirring twice. With slotted spoon, transfer bacon to paper towel to drain; put aside.

2 Add onion, celery, garlic and thyme to drippings in dish. Cook on High for 3–4 minutes, until onion is softened. Stir in flour until blended.

3 Drain oysters over a small bowl; reserve ¼ cup liquid. Put oysters aside. Stir oyster liquid and cream into onion mixture. Cook on High for 3–4 minutes, until mixture thickens, stirring twice.

4 Add oysters; season with salt and pepper. Cook on High for 1–2 minutes, just until edges of oysters begin to curl and sauce is hot. Allow to stand, covered, on a heatproof surface for 5 minutes.

5 Meanwhile, warm vol-au-vent cases in a conventional oven at 180°C for about 5 minutes, or until heated through.

6 Cut out centres of vol-au-vents. Place pastry cases on warmed plates. Spoon in oyster mixture; garnish with parsley and sprinkle with reserved bacon. Serve hot.

Crab

CRAB CAKES

Colour Index page 50. 498 kJ each. Good source of vitamin A, calcium, iron. Begin 25 minutes ahead.

These Crab Cakes can be made with fresh, frozen or canned crab meat or with other shellfish or fish. Popular alternatives, for example, are salmon cakes made with canned pink or red salmon. Served with a side salad or vegetables, Crab Cakes make a nourishing meal; shaped into smaller patties, they can be served as an attractive cocktail tidbit.

Ingredients for 12 crab cakes		Microwave cookware
500 g crab meat, drained if canned	1/4 teaspoon Tabasco sauce	25-cm round baking dish
1 1/2 cups fresh breadcrumbs	1/2 cup dried wholemeal breadcrumbs	
1/4 cup finely chopped red or green capsicum	2 teaspoons paprika	
1/4 cup sherry	60 g butter or margarine	
2 tablespoons finely chopped onion	Lemon wedges and coriander leaves to garnish	
1 egg, beaten	Spicy Cocktail Sauce (page 155, optional)	
1/4 teaspoon salt		

1 Pick over crab meat to remove any pieces of shell or cartilage. Add fresh breadcrumbs, capsicum, sherry, onion, egg, salt and Tabasco sauce; toss well.

2 Combine dried breadcrumbs and paprika on a sheet of greaseproof paper.

3 Shape crab mixture into 12 round patties. For Cocktail Crab Cakes, shape into 24 small patties.

4 Heat butter in baking dish, covered with paper towel, on High (100% power) for 45 seconds–1 minute, until melted. Dip patties into melted butter, then coat with crumb mixture.

5 Place 6 large or 12 miniature patties in same baking dish. Cook each batch, covered with greaseproof paper, on High for 3–5 minutes, until set, turning halfway through cooking.

6 Transfer crab cakes to warmed serving plates; garnish with lemon and fresh coriander. Serve, if you like, with Spicy Cocktail Sauce.

DEVILLED CRAB

Colour Index page 50. 4 servings. 1289 kJ per serving. Good source of calcium. Begin 20 minutes ahead.

500 g crab meat
60 g butter or margarine
1/4 cup cream
1 egg, beaten
2 tablespoons chopped fresh parsley
3 teaspoons French mustard
3 teaspoons lemon juice
1 teaspoon Worcestershire sauce
2 tablespoons dried breadcrumbs
Lemon slices to garnish

1. Pick over crab meat to remove any pieces of shell or cartilage.
2. Heat butter in a 4-cup glass jug, covered with paper towel, on High (100% power) for 45 seconds–1 minute, until melted.
3. Add cream, egg, parsley, mustard, lemon juice, Worcestershire sauce and breadcrumbs; stir until blended.
4. Gently stir crab into cream mixture until just mixed, taking care not to break up the meat.
5. Spoon one-quarter of the crab mixture into each of 4 ceramic ramekins or large scallop shells. Cook on High for 4–5 minutes, until hot.
6. Garnish with quartered lemon slices. Serve immediately.

CHILLI CRAB

Colour Index page 50. 2 servings. 959 kJ per serving. Low in fat. Good source of vitamin A, iron, zinc. Begin 25 minutes ahead.

1 large cooked crab (about 1.5 kg)
1/2 cup tomato sauce
2 tablespoons soy sauce
2 tablespoons water
1–2 tablespoons sweet chilli sauce (to taste)
1 tablespoon sugar
1 tablespoon rice-wine vinegar
1 tablespoon finely chopped green ginger
1 clove garlic, crushed
2 spring onions, sliced
Spring onion curls (page 134) to garnish

1. Prepare crab: Place crab on board, shell side down. Twist off large claws and legs from body; put aside. With thumbs, prise up tail flap on underside; twist off and discard. Remove and discard dead man's fingers and soft substance from centre of body.
2. With cleaver or large heavy knife, crack claws and legs, discarding any bits of shell and cartilage. Chop body of crab into 4–6 pieces.
3. Combine tomato sauce, soy sauce, water, chilli sauce, sugar, vinegar, ginger and garlic in a 2-cup glass jug. Cook, covered, on High (100% power) for 4–5 minutes, until sauce boils and flavours blend, stirring twice. Stir in spring onions.
4. Place crab pieces, claws and legs in a deep 2-litre bowl; pour over sauce. Cook, covered, on High for 3–4 minutes, until sauce boils and crab is hot, stirring halfway through cooking.
5. Garnish with spring onion curls. Serve hot.

Mixed shellfish

PAELLA

Colour Index page 54. 1243 kJ per serving. Good source of niacin, iron. Begin 1¼ hours ahead.

The paella of Spain has become a classic party dish all over the world. The ingredients vary from one region in Spain to another, but usually include large amounts of shellfish with chicken, sausages and rice, giving the paella its contrast of textures, colours and flavours. This microwave Paella uses a combination of different shellfish, but it is not essential to use them all; if pipis are difficult to obtain, for example, they can be omitted and the quantity of mussels increased.

Ingredients for 8 servings		Microwave cookware
2 dozen pipis 1 dozen mussels ¼ cup dry white wine 250 g spicy-hot Italian sausages 4 chicken breast halves, skinned and boned (about 500 g) 2 cloves garlic, crushed ½ teaspoon salt 1 teaspoon finely chopped fresh thyme or ¼ teaspoon dried thyme	500 g medium green prawns, shelled and deveined (page 166) 1 onion, chopped 1 green capsicum, chopped ½ teaspoon crushed saffron strands 1 cup long-grain rice 1 cup chicken stock 215 g can tomatoes, chopped Parsley sprigs to garnish	12-cup soufflé dish

1 Soak pipis in fresh water for 30 minutes to remove any sand. Meanwhile, scrub mussels with a stiff brush under cold running water; scrape away any barnacles and remove beards. Rinse.

2 Arrange pipis in a circle around edge of soufflé dish; arrange mussels in centre.

3 Add white wine. Cook, covered, on High (100% power) for 3–5 minutes, until shellfish are open.

4 Discard any pipis or mussels that have remained closed. Remove top shells of pipis and mussels; rinse shellfish in cooking liquid. Transfer to a plate; cover with plastic wrap or foil and refrigerate until needed.

5 Pour cooking liquid into a jug. Allow to stand until any sand settles. Spoon off clear stock, cover and refrigerate; discard remaining liquid.

6 Cut sausages into 2.5-cm lengths; place in soufflé dish used for shellfish. Cook, covered with paper towel, on High for 5 minutes, or until browned. Transfer to paper towel to drain. Reserve drippings.

7 Cut chicken into 5-cm strips. Combine chicken, garlic, salt and thyme in a bowl; mix well.

8 Add seasoned chicken to sausage drippings in soufflé dish. Cook, covered with paper towel, on High for 4–5 minutes, until chicken is tender, stirring halfway through cooking. Remove chicken; put aside with sausage in a bowl.

9 Add prawns, onion and capsicum to soufflé dish. Cook, covered, on High for 2–3 minutes, just until prawns turn pink, stirring halfway through cooking. Remove prawns and put aside with sausage and chicken.

10 Add saffron and rice to vegetables in dish. Stir to coat. Cook on High for 2 minutes, stirring halfway through cooking.

11 Stir in reserved cooking stock, chicken stock and tomatoes. Cook on High for 15 minutes, stirring halfway through cooking.

12 Carefully stir in reserved sausage, chicken and shellfish.

13 Cook paella, covered, on High for 2–3 minutes, until hot. Be careful not to overcook.

14 Carefully spoon paella on to a serving dish, arranging pipis and mussels on top; garnish with parsley. Serve immediately.

BOUILLABAISSE

Colour Index page 54. 858 kJ per serving. Good source of niacin, iron, zinc. Begin 1¼ hours ahead.

Ingredients for 8 servings		Microwave cookware
1 dozen mussels 2 tablespoons olive or vegetable oil 1 onion, finely chopped 3 cloves garlic, crushed 3 large tomatoes, chopped 1 bay leaf 1 cup dry white wine ¼ cup tomato paste ½ teaspoon salt 2 teaspoons finely chopped fresh thyme or ½ teaspoon dried thyme	½ teaspoon crushed saffron strands 2 cups chicken stock 1 green lobster (about 625 g) 500 g bream fillets, cut into 5-cm pieces 500 g jewfish cutlets, cut into 5-cm pieces 1 tablespoon Pernod (anise-flavoured liqueur) Tabasco sauce to taste Chopped parsley to garnish	Large bowl

1 Scrub mussels with a stiff brush under cold running water. With a small sharp knife, scrape away any barnacles and remove beards. Rinse. Place mussels in large bowl. Cook, covered, on High (100% power) for 2–3 minutes, just until open. Transfer to another bowl, rinsing each mussel in own liquid from shell to remove any sand. Strain and reserve any cooking liquid.

2 Combine oil, onion, garlic, tomatoes and bay leaf in bowl. Cook on High for 3–4 minutes, until onion is softened, stirring twice. Add wine, tomato paste, salt, thyme, saffron, chicken stock and reserved cooking liquid made up to 1 cup with water. Cook on High for 12 minutes, stirring every 3 minutes.

3 Place lobster, back down, on a board. Cut through with a sharp knife where the tail and body meet. Separate head and tail.

4 Cut through the softer tail shell with kitchen shears; split shell in half. Remove tail meat in one piece.

5 Cut tail meat into chunks. Break off claws from head section; put aside. Discard shell. Add lobster tail meat to tomato mixture. Cook on High for 4 minutes, stirring once. Add fish. Cook on High for 2 minutes.

6 Add Pernod, Tabasco sauce, mussels and reserved lobster claws; stir to blend. Allow to stand, covered, for 5 minutes. Discard bay leaf. Ladle Bouillabaise into soup bowls; garnish with chopped parsley.

DELUXE SEAFOOD PIE

Colour Index page 54. 4 servings. 2721 kJ per serving. Good source of vitamin A, vitamin C, calcium, potassium, iron, fibre. Begin 1¼ hours ahead.

1 onion, finely chopped 60 g butter or margarine 1½ tablespoons plain flour 1 cup milk 4 button mushrooms, cut into quarters 1 teaspoon finely chopped fresh thyme or ¼ teaspoon dried thyme ½ teaspoon pepper 250 g bottled mussels, drained, with liquid reserved 125 g scallops	125 g medium green prawns, shelled and deveined (page 166) 125 g crab sticks, cut into 2.5-cm pieces, or 170 g can crab meat, drained 125 g frozen peas, thawed 1 tablespoon chopped fresh parsley 750 g old potatoes, peeled 2 tablespoons water 1 cup cream ¼ teaspoon salt

1. Place onion and half the butter in a 3-litre bowl. Cook, covered, on High (100% power) for 3 minutes, or until softened, stirring halfway through cooking.
2. Stir flour into onion until smooth and blended. Cook on High for 3 minutes, stirring halfway through cooking. Gradually stir in milk; cook on High for 3–4 minutes, until sauce has thickened, stirring twice.
3. Add mushrooms, thyme, ¼ teaspoon pepper and reserved mussel liquid to sauce. Cook, covered, on High for 3–4 minutes, until mushrooms are tender, stirring halfway through cooking.
4. Add scallops and prawns to mushroom sauce. Cook, covered, on High for 3–4 minutes, just until scallops are opaque and prawns turn pink, stirring twice. Gently stir in crab, mussels, peas and parsley. Transfer to an oval 33-cm gratin dish or deep 25-cm round baking dish; put aside.
5. Cut potatoes in half lengthways; cut halves into 2.5-cm slices. Place potato slices in cleaned bowl; add water. Cook, covered, on High for 10 minutes, or until tender; drain off liquid.
6. Add remaining butter and pepper, cream and salt to potatoes; beat until smooth. Spoon potato into a large piping bag fitted with a star nozzle. Pipe potato over shellfish mixture in dish, taking care to pipe right to edges. (Alternatively, carefully spread potato over seafood and mark with a fork.)
7. Cook pie on High for 6–7 minutes, until piping hot, rotating dish a half turn every 2 minutes. Serve hot.

CIOPPINO

Colour Index page 52. 8 servings. 774 kJ per serving.
Low in fat. Good source of vitamin A, vitamin C, iron.
Begin 1¼ hours ahead.

1 dozen pipis	*1 cup dry red wine*
2 tablespoons olive or	*1 cup bottled Italian*
* vegetable oil*	* tomato sauce*
1 large onion, chopped	*250 g medium green*
1 medium green	* prawns, shelled and*
* capsicum, chopped*	* deveined (page 166)*
2 celery stalks, chopped	*250 g scallops*
2 cloves garlic, crushed	*375 g crab meat*

1. Soak pipis in fresh cold water for 30 minutes
to remove any sand. Place pipis in a deep 3-litre
casserole. Cook, covered, on High (100% power)
for 3–5 minutes, just until pipis open.
2. Discard top shells; rinse pipis in own liquid
from shell to remove any sand; place on large
plate. Strain and reserve any cooking liquid.
3. Combine oil, onion, capsicum, celery and
garlic in same casserole. Cook on High for
3–4 minutes, until vegetables have softened. Add
red wine and tomato sauce, together with any
reserved cooking liquid made up to ¾ cup with
water. Cook on High for 10 minutes, stirring
twice.
4. Add prawns and scallops. Cook, covered, on
High for 3–5 minutes, until prawns turn pink and
scallops are opaque, stirring halfway through
cooking. Add reserved pipis and crab. Cook,
covered, on High for 1–2 minutes, until hot.
Serve immediately.

SEAFOOD AND CHICKEN BAKE

Colour Index page 52. 4 servings. 1005 kJ per
serving. Good source of vitamin A, niacin.
Begin 40 minutes ahead.

2 cooked lobsters	*½ cup frozen corn*
* (about 625 g each)*	* kernels, thawed, or*
30 g butter or margarine	* canned corn, drained*
1 onion, chopped	*1 tablespoon cornflour*
2 tomatoes, chopped	* dissolved in ½ cup*
1 teaspoon shredded	* chicken stock*
* fresh basil*	*250 g cooked prawns,*
250 g chicken breasts,	* shelled and deveined*
* skinned, boned and cut*	* (page 166)*
* into 5-cm pieces*	*Salt and pepper to taste*

1. Remove meat from lobsters (page 169). Cut
meat into 5-cm pieces.
2. Place butter, onion, tomatoes and basil in a
33-cm x 23-cm baking dish. Cook on High (100%
power) for 3–4 minutes. Add chicken and corn.
Cook on High for 4–6 minutes, until chicken is
opaque, stirring twice.
3. Add stock mixture and lobster; stir. Cook on
High for 2 minutes. Add prawns. Cook on High
for 1–2 minutes, until sauce has thickened and
lobster is hot, stirring twice. Season with salt and
pepper. Serve immediately.

TUNA AND TOMATO SAUCE

Colour Index page 49. 4 servings. 1783 kJ per serving (with pasta). Low in
cholesterol. Good source of thiamine, niacin, iron.
Begin 15 minutes ahead.

250 g pasta	
3 teaspoons olive or	
* vegetable oil*	
1 small onion, chopped	
2 cloves garlic, crushed	
10 stoned black olives,	
* chopped*	
2 teaspoons capers,	
* drained*	
185 g can tuna in oil	
¼ teaspoon cayenne	
* pepper*	
425 g can tomatoes,	
* chopped with their*	
* juice*	
¼ cup chopped fresh	
* parsley*	

1. Cook pasta conventionally.
2. Meanwhile, place oil, onion, garlic, olives
and capers in a 30-cm x 20-cm casserole.
Cook, covered with paper towel, on High
(100% power) for 3–4 minutes, until onion
is translucent, stirring halfway through
cooking.
3. Add tuna and its oil and cayenne pepper,
breaking tuna into bite-sized pieces. Cook,
loosely covered, on High for 2–3 minutes,
until hot. Stir in tomatoes and parsley.
Cook, loosely covered, on High for 4–5 minutes, until bubbling, stirring twice.
4. Drain pasta and place on warmed plates;
spoon over sauce.

SMOKED OYSTER SAUCE

Colour Index page 49. 4 servings. 1863 kJ per serving (with pasta). Good
source of thiamine, niacin, iron, zinc.
Begin 15 minutes ahead.

250 g pasta	
3 rashers bacon,	
* chopped*	
1 small onion, chopped	
2 cups bottled Italian	
* tomato sauce*	
2 teaspoons finely	
* chopped fresh*	
* oregano or*	
½ teaspoon dried	
* oregano*	
105 g can chopped	
* smoked oysters,*	
* drained*	

1. Cook pasta conventionally.
2. Meanwhile, cook bacon in a 2-litre casserole, covered with paper towel, on High
(100% power) for 2–3 minutes, until
browned.
3. Add onion. Cook, covered with paper
towel, on High for 3 minutes, stirring twice.
4. Stir tomato sauce and oregano into casserole. Cook, loosely covered, on High for
3–4 minutes, until hot. Add smoked oysters.
Cook, loosely covered, on High for
2 minutes, or until hot.
5. Drain pasta and place on warmed plates;
spoon over sauce.

SPICY PRAWN SAUCE

Colour Index page 49. 4 servings. 1633 kJ per serving. Low in fat.
Begin 20 minutes ahead.

250 g pasta	
290 g can whole baby	
* clams*	
1 tablespoon olive or	
* vegetable oil*	
2 cloves garlic	
825 g can tomatoes	
3 teaspoons sherry	
½ teaspoon crushed	
* dried chillies*	
250 g medium green	
* prawns, shelled and*	
* deveined (page 166)*	
¼ cup chopped fresh	
* parsley to garnish*	
* (optional)*	

1. Cook pasta conventionally.
2. Meanwhile, drain clams, reserving the
liquid.
3. Place oil and garlic in a 2.5-litre casserole. Cook on High (100% power) for
2 minutes, stirring once. Discard garlic. Add
tomatoes with their liquid, sherry, chillies
and reserved clam liquid. Cook on High for
10 minutes, stirring twice.
4. Add clams and prawns. Cook on High for
2–3 minutes, until prawns turn pink and
clams are hot.
5. Drain pasta and place on warmed plates;
spoon over sauce. If you like, garnish with
parsley.

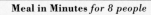

Seafood Pasta Party

Mixed melon and prosciutto platter
Breadsticks
Trio of pasta with Seafood Sauces (page 175)
Tossed green salad
Ice cream or sorbet
Espresso (page 132) with Florentines (page 365)

PREPARATION TIMETABLE

1 day ahead:	**Early in day:**	**1 hour ahead:**	**30 minutes ahead:**	**Just before serving:**
Make Florentines; store in airtight container.	*Prepare salad ingredients; store in refrigerator. Prepare Tuna and Tomato, Smoked Oyster and Spicy Prawn Sauces; cover and refrigerate. Peel and slice honeydew and rockmelon; cover and refrigerate.*	*Arrange melon slices on large serving platter with prosciutto; if you like, wrap melon with prosciutto. Garnish platter with black olives and basil leaves; cover.*	*Cook 3 kinds of pasta conventionally; keep warm. Meanwhile, reheat sauces in microwave. Place an assortment of salad greens in a bowl and toss with dressing of your choice.*	*Transfer pasta and seafood sauces to warmed serving bowls; garnish with fresh basil or parsley. Prepare Espresso.*

Poultry

WHOLE CHICKEN · CHICKEN PIECES · CHICKEN BREASTS
COOKED CHICKEN · GAME · DUCK · TURKEY

Poultry

Poultry, a naturally tender food, is ideal for the fast, moist cooking of a microwave oven. Chicken, duckling and turkey all turn out successfully, although pieces rather than whole birds are easiest to cook. A whole chicken requires shielding and turning halfway through cooking, but poussins are easy to cook whole or split. A whole turkey must be cooked conventionally if it is over 5 kg, but turkey breasts and pieces are delicious cooked in the microwave. Duckling is better cooked in the microwave, as excess fat is more easily removed. Cooked chicken should be very juicy; if the chicken is dry or tough, it has been overcooked.

Because poultry skin is high in kilojoules and cholesterol and rarely browns in the microwave, it should be removed when fat is not necessary for the recipe. To look as appetising as possible, poultry should be glazed, simmered in a sauce, or coated with crumbs or other coating mix. Plain cooked chicken, however, is ideal for use in main-course salads and other cold dishes.

If you are using a temperature probe when cooking whole chickens, make sure the weight of the bird is at least 1.5 kg. If the chicken is too small, the probe may touch a bone and cause an inaccurate reading. When cooking a whole bird, cover the wing and leg tips and the breastbone with smooth pieces of foil to prevent overcooking.

Poultry pieces have to be arranged carefully for even cooking: place meatier pieces towards edges of dish and bonier parts towards centre, then rearrange pieces halfway through cooking. Prevent uneven cooking of boneless chicken breasts by tucking thin ends under. Because the microwave sometimes renders more fat from foods than conventional methods, use a rack to cook duck pieces and cover loosely with greaseproof paper.

Poultry is done if flesh is opaque and fork-tender; juices should run clear when the flesh is pierced with a fork. Standing time is given in those individual poultry recipes where it is necessary to complete cooking before serving.

DINNER PARTY PRESENTATIONS

Transform a plain, boneless chicken breast that has been cooked in the microwave (page 180) into impressive fare by slicing it evenly, then fanning out the slices on a pool of sauce. This quick presentation works with both hot and chilled chicken.

A hot chicken breast (left) sliced and fanned on a pool of Tomato and Basil Sauce (page 380), then garnished with fresh herb sprigs.

A sliced cold chicken breast (right), arranged on Creamy Avocado Sauce (page 230). Garnished with orange julienne (page 316), avocado slices and parsley.

Defrosting

It is quick and easy to defrost poultry in the microwave – an absolute boon if you have forgotten to take something out of the freezer in time to defrost it conventionally. If possible, remove or loosen any wrappings before defrosting, taking care not to tear poultry skin. If wrapping is left on, it will retain heat and the poultry may begin to cook. After defrosting, rinse poultry under cold running water, then pat dry with paper towels. Before cooking, ensure that no ice crystals remain.

Defrosting a whole bird An average chicken weighing about 1.5 kg will take only about 20 minutes; a whole turkey breast, weighing about 4 kg, will take about 40 minutes (allowing 3–6 minutes per 500 g on Medium) or about 70 minutes (allowing 7–9½ minutes per 500 g on Medium-Low). At the end of defrosting time, remove bird from microwave and allow to stand in cold water for up to 30 minutes, to allow any ice crystals to dissolve.

Defrosting pieces Legs, breasts, wings, thighs and marylands can all be defrosted in 6–7 minutes per 500 g. Do not defrost for longer than this or poultry will lose its natural flavour and juiciness; if any areas seem to be starting to cook, shield them with smooth pieces of foil. At the end of defrosting time, there should still be some ice crystals around bony areas; allow pieces to stand for 5 minutes, then rinse under cold water and pat dry.

Place bird on a rack in baking dish. Defrost on Medium-Low (30% power) for 5–9 minutes per 500 g. Elevating on a rack prevents the bird from beginning to cook in the juices that collect in the bottom of the dish. Pour off juices twice during defrosting time.

If poultry pieces have been frozen in a polystyrene tray, remove this and any paper liner provided to absorb juices as soon as they can be separated from the poultry. If left in place, defrosting time will be prolonged.

Halfway through defrosting time, turn bird breast side down; cover with greaseproof paper to hold heat around the bird as it defrosts.

If not in a solid block, arrange boned breasts with thicker portions towards edge of dish. Break apart partially frozen pieces after half the defrosting time.

Towards end of defrosting time, uncover bird and turn breast side up. Shield any warm spots with smooth pieces of foil. The legs, wing tips and highest portion of breastbone normally defrost soonest.

Rearrange pieces so that the icier ones are towards edge of dish; defrost for remaining time.

Cooking

EXTRA-QUICK CHICKEN BREASTS

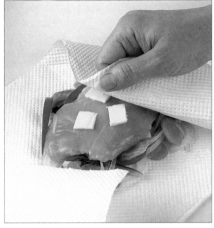

Barbecued
Place **250 g chicken breast**, skinned and boned, in a shallow casserole. Cook, covered, on High (100% power) for 2 minutes, rotating once. Brush with **2 tablespoons barbecue sauce**. Cook, covered, for 2–3 minutes, until juices run clear. Stand for 2 minutes.

Poached
Pound **1 chicken breast, boned and skinned (about 185 g)** to 12-mm thickness. Place ½ cup **mixed thinly sliced capsicums, carrots, celery** and **onion** on 2 connected sheets of paper towel; top with chicken. If you like, dot with **butter or margarine**; season. Fold sides of paper towels over chicken; tuck ends under. Place parcel on a plate; sprinkle with a little water. Cook 1 parcel on High (100% power) for 3½ (3:30)–4 minutes; 2 parcels for 5½ (5:30)–6 minutes. Allow to stand on a heatproof surface for 3 minutes before unwrapping and serving.

COOKING TIMETABLE FOR CHICKEN

Amount	Time	Power level
185 g chicken breast (skinned and boned)	3½ (3:30)–4 minutes	High (100% power)
2 x 185 g chicken breasts (skinned and boned)	5½ (5:30)–6 minutes	High
250 g chicken maryland	5–5½ (5:30) minutes	High
2 x 250 g chicken marylands	8–8½ (8:30) minutes	High
Chicken pieces	6–7 minutes per 500 g	High
Whole chicken	7–9 minutes per 500 g	Medium (50% power)

COOKING SMALL TURKEYS

Use a probe or a microwave thermometer while the bird is cooking, or check the temperature with a meat thermometer once it is out of the microwave. Turkey breast meat should register 76°C; thigh or dark meat 79°C–82°C. Choose a breadcrumb-based stuffing and pack it lightly. Heavy stuffings take too long to cook, so turkey will overcook before the stuffing is ready; cooking stuffing in a separate casserole is recommended.

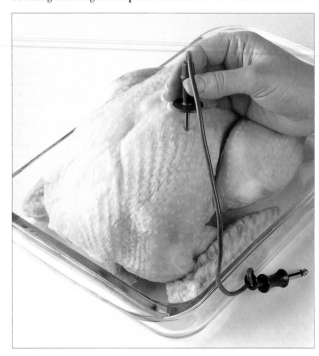

COOKING WHOLE BIRDS

Choose plump birds weighing at least 1.5 kg but no more than 5 kg. Cover wing and leg tips and breastbone with smooth pieces of foil to prevent these areas from overcooking.

Larger birds may brown due to the longer cooking times, otherwise brush bird with bottled barbecue sauce or a browning agent (see Browning, pages 182 and 183). Chicken is done if juices run clear when thickest part of thigh is pierced with a fork.

As a rule of thumb, cook whole chicken on Medium (50% power) for 7–9 minutes per 500 g. Place bird breast side down, covered with greaseproof paper for half the cooking time; turn breast side up for remaining time.

If using a thermometer, remove chicken when it reads 82°C–85°C; on standing, temperature will rise to 85°C–87°C. Always tent bird with foil to help hold in the heat.

COOKING POULTRY PIECES

Poultry skin is high in kilojoules and cholesterol. Replacing it with a crumb coating is healthier, helps keep poultry moist and improves appearance. If you like, use a rack to keep the pieces free of pan juices.

COOKING DUCKLINGS

The microwave is ideal for producing delicious results with duck. Before cooking, pierce the skin of the duck portions in several places to allow the fat to drain and to prevent the skin from splitting during cooking.

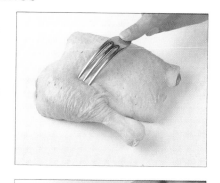

Loosely cover crumbed poultry with greaseproof paper, otherwise the crumbs will become soggy. For best results, cook poultry pieces of about the same size – pieces of different densities cook unevenly.

Place pieces on a rack in baking dish to allow excess fat to drain off; turn duck frequently during cooking.

Arrange meatier portions towards edges of dish and bonier parts towards the centre, rearranging halfway through cooking. Overcooking of chicken breasts can be prevented by tucking the thin ends under so that breasts cook evenly.

Leg portions take longer to cook than breast portions. Baste with a coating or glaze during cooking or serve with a sauce when finished.

Browning

Small poultry pieces do not look the same cooked in the microwave as when cooked conventionally. One reason is that the bird's fat does not get hot enough, in the short microwave cooking time, to caramelise – which is the way conventionally cooked poultry becomes crisp and brown.

Another reason poultry pieces do not brown is because all the fat is just below the skin's surface, unlike with some meat which is marbled with fat throughout. Larger birds, however, do brown because of their prolonged cooking time.

Great-tasting poultry from the microwave sometimes needs help to make it look its best. Commercial products such as browning agents, bottled sauces and dry coatings can be used to add colour, or the poultry pieces can be finished off under a conventional griller. Alternatively, a microwave browning dish can be used.

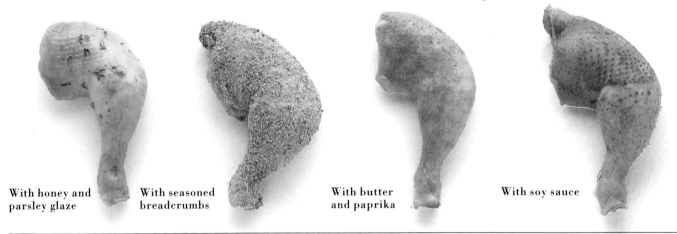

With honey and parsley glaze

With seasoned breadcrumbs

With butter and paprika

With soy sauce

BROWNING CONVENTIONALLY AND WITH BROWNING DISH

Poultry pieces cooked in the microwave can be finished in a conventional oven or under a griller for a few minutes.

Using a microwave browning dish to cook small poultry pieces is another way to brown and crisp the surface. The dish is preheated to a high temperature and oil or butter heated on it. Uncooked poultry pieces are then placed on the dish and the high temperature and hot fat gives a crisp, brown finish.

Using a griller

These chicken pieces have been cooked in the microwave. Although completely cooked, they still look pale because there was insufficient time for the surfaces to brown.

After cooking in the microwave, place chicken pieces on griller rack and brown under a preheated griller until skin is crisp and coloured. Turn pieces over halfway through grilling.

Using a browning dish

Preheat browning dish according to the manufacturer's instructions; this heats up a concealed metal plate. When hot, add butter, margarine or oil according to recipe. Do not touch dish.

When butter is melted or oil is hot, add chicken piece, skin side down, pressing lightly with tongs or spatula. Cook according to recipe, until underneath surface is browned.

With tongs, carefully turn chicken piece over. Continue cooking according to recipe, until other side is browned and juices run clear. If cooking in batches, it may be necessary to reheat dish.

SAUCES

Adding extra colour to poultry is easy to do by coating the skin with a sauce. Thin liquid preparations such as soy, teriyaki and browning sauces are best diluted with a little water, oil or melted butter, then lightly rubbed into the skin of the poultry with your fingers. Thicker, stickier sauces, such as barbecue sauce and honey-based glazes are best applied with a brush.

Barbecue sauce   Browning sauce   Redcurrant jelly   Honey

Rubbing in sauce

Dilute soy or browning sauce with a little water, oil or melted butter; this makes coating easier and softens the flavour.

Before cooking, place chicken on plate or board, dip fingers into diluted sauce and gently rub into skin, covering surface completely.

Brushing with honey and lemon

Stir chopped herbs into honey; squeeze in lemon juice. Heat on High (100% power) for 30 seconds, to make glaze easier to apply.

Begin cooking chicken according to recipe. Towards end of cooking, brush with glaze; if applied too early, the honey in the glaze may burn.

DRY PREPARATIONS

Adding dry preparations before cooking enhances chicken pieces with extra colour and texture. The pieces can be brushed with melted butter, or oil, then sprinkled with powders or with dry browning mixtures. Prepared coating mixes or breadcrumbs are applied after first dipping chicken pieces into beaten egg or milk. If you like, drizzle with melted butter.

Seasoned breadcrumbs   Prepared coating mix   Paprika   Microwave browning

Coating with crumbs

With tongs, dip chicken into lightly beaten egg or milk, coating evenly; shake off any excess.

In another dish, place seasoned breadcrumbs or prepared coating mix. Pat evenly on to chicken.

Sprinkling on powders

Lightly brush chicken with melted butter or margarine, or oil, to help powder adhere to poultry skin.

With chicken portion on plate, lightly sprinkle with powder. Paprika gives a colourful result.

Whole chicken

SEASONED SPATCHCOCK

Colour Index page 57. 2964 kJ per serving. Good source of niacin, iron. Begin 55 minutes ahead.

Ingredients	For 4	For 2	For 1
Poussins (500 g each)	4	2	1
Butter or margarine, softened	60 g	30 g	15 g
Garlic, crushed	2 cloves	1 clove	1 small clove
Shredded fresh basil or dried basil	1 tablespoon or 1 teaspoon	2 teaspoons or ½ teaspoon	1 teaspoon or ¼ teaspoon
Chopped fresh thyme or dried thyme	1 tablespoon or 1 teaspoon	2 teaspoons or ½ teaspoon	1 teaspoon or ¼ teaspoon
Chopped fresh oregano or dried oregano	1 tablespoon or 1 teaspoon	2 teaspoons or ½ teaspoon	1 teaspoon or ¼ teaspoon
Worcestershire sauce	3 teaspoons	1½ teaspoons	¾ teaspoon
Salt and pepper	to taste	to taste	to taste
Basil leaves	garnish	garnish	garnish
Sautéed cherry tomatoes (optional)	1 punnet	½ punnet	¼ punnet
Microwave cookware	33-cm x 23-cm baking dish with rack	33-cm x 23-cm baking dish with rack	20-cm x 20-cm baking dish with rack
Time on High (100% power)	12–14 minutes each batch	12–14 minutes	7–10 minutes
Standing time	3–4 minutes	3–4 minutes	2–3 minutes

1 Remove giblets and neck from inside of each poussin. Rinse birds under cold running water; pat dry with paper towel. Cut each bird in half lengthways.

2 Combine butter, garlic, basil, thyme and oregano in a bowl; mix well.

3 One at a time, place half a bird on a flat surface with breast bone facing towards you. Work fingers under skin at top of breast to make a pocket, taking care not to tear skin.

4 Stuff an equal amount of seasoning into each pocket.

5 Arrange poussins on rack in baking dish (see Chart), with breasts towards centre. If cooking for 4, cook in 2 batches.

6 Brush birds with Worcestershire sauce. Cook, covered loosely with greaseproof paper, on High for time in Chart, until juices run clear when birds are pierced with a fork, rotating dish once. Season with salt and pepper. Allow to stand for time in Chart. Arrange poussin halves on a warmed platter; garnish with basil leaves. Serve, if you like, with sautéed cherry tomatoes.

WHOLE STUFFED SPATCHCOCK

Colour Index page 57. 2 servings. 4257 kJ per serving. Good source of vitamin A, thiamine, riboflavin, niacin, calcium, iron, fibre. Begin 45 minutes ahead.

125 g small mushrooms, sliced
30 g butter or margarine
1 small zucchini, grated
60 g Swiss cheese, grated (½ cup)
1 spring onion, chopped
¼ teaspoon salt
⅛ teaspoon pepper
1 cup cooked rice
2 poussins (500 g each)
¾ cup herb-seasoned stuffing mix
1½ teaspoons paprika
Parsley sprigs and matchstick-thin strips of carrot and celery to garnish

1. Place mushrooms and half the butter in a 1.5-litre casserole. Cook on High (100% power) for 2–2½ (2:30) minutes, stirring halfway through cooking. Stir in zucchini, cheese, spring onion, salt, pepper and rice; allow to cool completely.
2. Remove giblets and neck from inside each poussin. Rinse birds under cold running water; pat dry with paper towels. Fill each cavity with half the stuffing; tie legs together with string. Heat remaining butter in a small bowl on High for 30–45 seconds, until melted. Brush over poussins.
3. Combine stuffing mix and paprika on a sheet of greaseproof paper; use to coat birds. Place on a rack set in a 30-cm x 20-cm baking dish. Cook, covered loosely with greaseproof paper, on High for 14–16 minutes, until juices run clear when birds are pierced with a fork, rotating dish halfway through cooking. Allow to stand, covered, for 5 minutes.
4. Remove string from poussins. Arrange birds on warmed plates; garnish with parsley and vegetable julienne.

Tying and brushing the poussins

Using white cotton string, tie legs of each bird together. This prevents stuffing from falling out and gives the birds a plump, attractive shape.

Heat butter or margarine in a small bowl until melted. Use a pastry brush to apply butter all over surface of poussins. This helps coating to adhere to skin of birds.

Chicken pieces

CHICKEN CACCIATORE

Colour Index page 56. 4 servings. 2344 kJ per serving. Good source of thiamine, niacin, vitamin C, calcium, iron, fibre.
Begin 45 minutes ahead.

1½ tablespoons olive oil	½ cup stoned green
2 onions, chopped	olives, sliced
1 green capsicum,	1 cup bottled Italian
chopped	tomato sauce
2 cloves garlic, crushed	½ cup chicken stock
1 tablespoon prepared	1 kg chicken pieces,
pesto or 2 tablespoons	skinned
shredded fresh basil	250 g spaghetti
2 teaspoons chopped	Salt and pepper to taste
fresh oregano or	Basil leaves to garnish
½ teaspoon dried	
oregano	

1. Combine oil, onions, capsicum, garlic, pesto and oregano in a 2.5-litre casserole. Cook on High (100% power) for 3–5 minutes, until vegetables are lightly softened, stirring twice. Stir in olives, tomato sauce and stock.
2. Add chicken to casserole, arranging thicker, meatier pieces towards edges. Cook, covered, on High for 18–20 minutes, until juices run clear, rearranging pieces halfway through cooking.
3. Meanwhile, cook spaghetti conventionally. Drain and keep warm.
4. Skim fat from chicken. Season with salt and pepper; allow to stand for 5 minutes.
5. Arrange spaghetti and chicken on warmed plates. Spoon over sauce; garnish with basil.

SPICY CRUMBED CHICKEN

Colour Index page 55. 4 servings. 1160 kJ per serving. Good source of niacin, iron.
Begin 25 minutes ahead.

2 tablespoons French	½ teaspoon paprika
mustard	½ teaspoon celery salt
1 tablespoon honey	Cayenne pepper to taste
1 tablespoon tomato	1 kg chicken pieces,
paste	skinned
½ cup dried	Cucumber slices, lime
breadcrumbs	wedges and salad to
½ teaspoon poultry	garnish
seasoning	

1. Combine mustard, honey and tomato paste in a small bowl. Combine breadcrumbs, poultry seasoning, paprika, celery salt and cayenne pepper on a sheet of greaseproof paper.
2. Coat chicken pieces, one at a time, in mustard mixture, then roll in seasoned crumbs.
3. Arrange chicken in a 33-cm x 23-cm baking dish so that thicker, meatier pieces are towards edges. Cook, covered loosely with greaseproof paper, on High (100% power) for 11–13 minutes, until chicken juices run clear, rearranging pieces once. Allow to stand on a heatproof surface for 5 minutes before serving.
4. Place chicken on warmed plates; garnish with cucumber slices, lime wedges and salad.

CHICKEN MARENGO

Colour Index page 56. 2193 kJ per serving. Good source of riboflavin, niacin, iron, fibre.
Begin 45 minutes ahead.

Ingredients for 4 servings		Microwave cookware
2 tablespoons olive or	1 kg chicken pieces	33-cm x 23-cm
vegetable oil	1 cup dry white wine	baking dish
2 onions, chopped	215 g can tomatoes,	
250 g mushrooms, sliced	chopped	
2 teaspoons chopped	¼ cup chopped fresh	
fresh rosemary or	parsley	
½ teaspoon dried	185 g shelled cooked	
rosemary	school prawns	
½ cup plain flour	Parsley sprigs to garnish	
¼ teaspoon salt	Hot Cooked Rice (page	
Pepper to taste	295, optional)	

1 Heat 3 teaspoons oil in a 30-cm frying pan over medium-high heat. Add onions, mushrooms and rosemary. Cook until onions are golden, stirring occasionally. With a slotted spoon, transfer vegetables to baking dish.

2 Combine flour, salt and pepper on a sheet of greaseproof paper. Coat chicken pieces in seasoned flour. Heat remaining oil in same frying pan. Add chicken and cook for 5 minutes, or until browned on all sides.

3 Arrange chicken pieces on top of vegetables in baking dish so that thicker, meatier pieces are towards edges.

4 Discard oil from frying pan; pour in white wine. Stir over medium heat to loosen any browned pieces. Add tomatoes and parsley. Cook until mixture boils, stirring occasionally. Pour mixture over chicken pieces.

5 Cook chicken, covered, on High (100% power) for 10–12 minutes, until juices run clear, rearranging pieces halfway through cooking. Add prawns; spoon over cooking liquid. Cook on High for 1–2 minutes, just until prawns are hot.

6 Arrange chicken and prawns on a warmed serving dish or platter. Spoon over sauce; garnish with parsley. Serve, if you like, with rice.

COQ AU VIN

Colour Index page 56. 1691 kJ per serving. Good source of vitamin A, riboflavin, niacin, iron, fibre.
Begin 55 minutes ahead.

Ingredients	For 4	For 2	For 1
Pickled pork or thick bacon, diced	125 g	60 g	30 g
Carrots, diced	2	1	½
Mushrooms, cut into quarters	250 g	125 g	60 g
Chicken pieces, skinned	1 kg	500 g	250 g
Frozen pearl onions, thawed	12	6	3
Canned tomatoes, chopped	½ cup	¼ cup	2 tablespoons
Dry red wine	1 cup	½ cup	¼ cup
Fresh thyme, chopped, or dried thyme	3 teaspoons or ¾ teaspoon	2 teaspoons or ½ teaspoon	1 teaspoon or ¼ teaspoon
Pepper	to taste	to taste	to taste
Cold butter, diced	45 g	30 g	15 g
Chopped fresh parsley	garnish	garnish	garnish
Microwave cookware	33-cm x 23-cm baking dish	30-cm x 20-cm baking dish	20-cm x 20-cm baking dish
Time on High (100% power)			
Pickled pork	4 minutes	3 minutes	2 minutes
With vegetables	3 minutes	2 minutes	2 minutes
With chicken	15–20 minutes	10–12 minutes	8 minutes

1 Cook pork in baking dish (see Chart), covered with paper towel, on High for time in Chart, stirring twice.

2 With spoon, discard excess fat from baking dish.

3 Add carrots and mushrooms to pork. Cook on High for time in Chart, stirring halfway through cooking.

4 Add chicken to baking dish, arranging in a single layer over pork and vegetables.

5 Add onions, tomatoes, wine and thyme. Cook, covered, on High for time in Chart, until chicken juices run clear, rearranging pieces halfway through cooking.

6 Transfer chicken to a warmed serving dish. Allow to stand, covered. Add pepper to sauce, then gradually beat in cold butter until well blended. Spoon over chicken; garnish with chopped parsley.

CHICKEN PAPRIKASH

Colour Index page 56. 4 servings. 1959 kJ per serving. Good source of vitamin A, niacin, vitamin C, iron, fibre.
Begin 35 minutes ahead.

60 g butter or margarine
2 onions, sliced
1 red capsicum, thinly sliced
1½ tablespoons plain flour
425 g can tomatoes
3 teaspoons paprika
2 tablespoons tomato paste
¼ cup chicken stock
1 kg chicken pieces
Chives to garnish

1. Place butter, onions and capsicum in a shallow 2.5-litre casserole. Cook, covered, on High (100% power) for 6–7 minutes, until tender-crisp, stirring twice.
2. Stir in flour. Add tomatoes with their liquid, paprika, tomato paste and chicken stock; stir well. Add chicken, arranging thicker, meatier pieces towards edges. Spoon sauce over chicken. Cook on High for 18–20 minutes, until juices run clear, rearranging pieces halfway through cooking. Skim fat.
3. Allow chicken to stand for 5 minutes; garnish with chives.

LEMON CHICKEN

Colour Index page 56. 4 servings. 1486 kJ per serving. Good source of niacin, iron.
Begin 45 minutes ahead.

¼ cup lemon juice
2 tablespoons olive or vegetable oil
1 clove garlic, crushed
30 g canned pimientos, thinly sliced
1 tablespoon shredded fresh basil or 1 teaspoon dried basil
¼ teaspoon pepper
1.5 kg chicken pieces, skinned
½ cup chicken stock
1 tablespoon cornflour dissolved in 2 tablespoons water
Salt to taste
½ cup melba toast crumbs (page 193) or dried breadcrumbs
1 teaspoon finely chopped lemon rind
Lemon twists (page 134) and parsley sprigs to garnish

1. Combine lemon juice, 1½ tablespoons oil, garlic, pimientos, basil and pepper in a 2.5-litre casserole. Add chicken; stir to coat. Arrange chicken so that thicker, meatier pieces are towards edges of casserole. Add stock.
2. Cook, covered, on High (100% power) for 15–18 minutes, until juices run clear, rearranging pieces occasionally. Stir in dissolved cornflour. Cook on High for 3 minutes, or until slightly thickened. Season with salt.
3. Combine remaining oil, crumbs and lemon rind in a bowl; sprinkle over chicken. Cook on High for 2 minutes.
4. Allow to stand for 5 minutes; garnish with lemon twists and parsley. Serve hot.

HONEY-SOY CHICKEN

Colour Index page 55. 4 servings. 2219 kJ per serving. Good source of vitamin A, niacin, vitamin C, iron.
Begin 25 minutes ahead.

1.5 kg chicken pieces	*2 tablespoons water*
¼ cup honey	*425 g can straw*
¼ teaspoon ground	*mushrooms, drained*
ginger	*3 teaspoons sesame or*
1 clove garlic, crushed	*vegetable oil*
2 tablespoons soy sauce	*1 tablespoon sesame*
250 g snow peas	*seeds*
1 carrot, thinly sliced	*Coriander to garnish*

1. Arrange chicken in a 30-cm x 20-cm baking dish so that thicker, meatier pieces are towards edges. Combine honey, ginger, garlic and 1 tablespoon soy sauce; brush half over chicken. Cook, covered loosely with greaseproof paper, on High (100% power) for 13–15 minutes, until juices run clear, rearranging pieces once. Brush chicken with remaining mixture. Allow to stand, covered, while preparing vegetables.
2. Place snow peas, carrot and water in a large bowl. Cook, covered, on High for 4 minutes; drain. Stir in straw mushrooms, oil, sesame seeds and remaining soy sauce. Cook on High for 1–1½ (1:30) minutes, until hot.
3. Arrange chicken and vegetable mixture on a warmed serving platter; garnish with coriander sprigs. Serve immediately.

QUICK BRAISED CHICKEN

Colour Index page 56. 4 servings. 2499 kJ per serving. Good source of vitamin A, niacin, vitamin C, iron, fibre.
Begin 45 minutes ahead.

500 g potatoes	*¼ teaspoon salt*
3 carrots	*¼ teaspoon pepper*
1 onion, chopped	*2 tablespoons plain flour*
1¼ cups chicken stock	*250 g frozen sliced green*
1 kg chicken pieces	*beans*
2 teaspoons chopped	*Chopped thyme or dill*
fresh thyme or	*sprigs to garnish*
½ teaspoon dried	
thyme	

1. Cut potatoes into 2.5-cm chunks; cut carrots into quarters lengthways, then across into 5-cm pieces. Combine potatoes, carrots, onion and 1 cup stock in a 4-litre casserole. Place chicken on top so that thicker, meatier pieces are towards edges; sprinkle with thyme, salt and pepper. Cook, covered, on High (100% power) for 18 minutes, stirring occasionally.
2. Stir flour into remaining stock until well blended. Add to chicken mixture with frozen beans; stir well. Cook, covered, on High for 8–10 minutes, until chicken and vegetables are tender, stirring once. Allow to stand on a heat-proof surface for 5 minutes.
3. Spoon chicken into a warmed serving dish; garnish with thyme sprigs.

Meal in Minutes *for 6 people*

French Bistro Dinner

French Onion Soup (page 133)
Coq au Vin (page 186)
Tossed mixed salad
French bread
French apple tart (bought) with whipped cream
Coffee or Espresso (page 132)

PREPARATION TIMETABLE

Early in day or 2 hours ahead:	*Prepare soup up to the end of step 2; cover and refrigerate. Prepare salad ingredients; store in plastic bags in refrigerator. Prepare salad dressing of your choice.*
1 hour ahead:	*Make Coq au Vin for 6 people; transfer to a warmed casserole dish with cover.*
15 minutes ahead:	*Ladle soup into bowls. Heat on High (100% power) until bubbling; top with bread and cheese and complete recipe. Toss salad ingredients in a bowl with dressing.*
Just before serving:	*If you like, heat French bread on High for 1 minute. Whip cream to serve with apple tart. Prepare coffee or Espresso to serve with or after the tart.*

Autumn Family Picnic

Potato crisps and pretzels
Corn Chowder (page 135) with bread rolls
Devilled Chicken (right)
Vegetable and Pasta Salad (page 280)
Pecan Pie (page 345)
Apples and pears

PREPARATION TIMETABLE

1 day ahead:	*Make a double quantity of Devilled Chicken in batches; cool. Pack in a portable container lined with paper towels; refrigerate. Make Corn Chowder; cover and refrigerate. Make Pecan Pie; cool. Pack in airtight container. Cook vegetables for salad; cover and refrigerate. Pack plates, napkins, cutlery and cups. Wrap fruit; pack potato crisps and pretzels.*
Early in day:	*For salad, cook pasta conventionally; toss with vegetables and dressing and pack in a portable container; refrigerate. Pack bread rolls in an airtight container.*
Just before leaving home:	*Reheat Corn Chowder in microwave on Medium-High (70% power) for 5 minutes, or until piping hot. Immediately pour into a wide-mouthed vacuum flask and seal tightly.*

DEVILLED CHICKEN

Colour Index page 55. 4 servings. 1226 kJ per serving. Good source of riboflavin, niacin, iron. Begin 25 minutes ahead.

1½ tablespoons mayonnaise	½ teaspoon cayenne pepper
1½ tablespoons mild mustard	½ teaspoon garlic salt
½ cup dried breadcrumbs	1.25 kg chicken drumsticks and/or thighs, skinned
1 tablespoon finely chopped fresh parsley	Lemon wedges and parsley to garnish

1. Combine mayonnaise and mustard in a bowl. Combine breadcrumbs, parsley, cayenne pepper and garlic salt on a sheet of greaseproof paper.
2. Brush chicken pieces with mayonnaise mixture, then coat with seasoned crumbs.
3. Arrange chicken in a 33-cm x 23-cm baking dish so that thicker, meatier pieces are towards edges. Cook, covered with greaseproof paper, on High (100% power) for 11–13 minutes, until chicken juices run clear, rearranging halfway through cooking. Allow to stand on a heatproof surface for 3 minutes.
4. Arrange chicken pieces on a warmed serving platter; garnish with lemon wedges and parsley sprigs.

BARBECUED CHICKEN

Colour Index page 55. 4 servings. 1616 kJ per serving. Good source of niacin, vitamin C, iron. Begin 25 minutes ahead.

2 onions, thinly sliced	2 teaspoons Worcestershire sauce
1 green capsicum, cut into matchstick-thin strips	1 teaspoon chilli powder
1 clove garlic, crushed	8 chicken thighs (about 1 kg)
⅔ cup tomato sauce	Parsley sprigs to garnish
1½ tablespoons brown sugar	

1. Prepare barbecue sauce: Place onions, capsicum, garlic, tomato sauce, brown sugar, Worcestershire sauce and chilli powder in a medium bowl. Cook, covered, on High (100% power) for 8–10 minutes, until vegetables are tender, stirring twice; cover and put aside.
2. Arrange chicken thighs in a single layer in a 30-cm x 20-cm baking dish so that thicker, meatier pieces are towards edges. Cook, covered, on High for 10 minutes, rearranging halfway through cooking; discard drippings.
3. Spoon barbecue sauce over chicken. Cook on High for 6–8 minutes, until chicken juices run clear, rearranging halfway through cooking.
4. Place chicken thighs on warmed plates; garnish with parsley.

CURRIED CHICKEN THIGHS

Colour Index page 59. 4 servings. 975 kJ per serving.
Good source of niacin, calcium.
Begin 1 day ahead.

4 chicken thighs, skinned	½ cup dried breadcrumbs
1 cup natural yoghurt	¼ teaspoon salt
2 teaspoons curry powder	2 tablespoons vegetable oil
2 cloves garlic, crushed	Lime wedges and mint sprigs to garnish
1 tablespoon finely chopped fresh coriander or parsley	

1. Combine chicken thighs, yoghurt, curry powder, garlic and coriander in a large bowl. Cover and refrigerate for 12–24 hours.
2. Thirty minutes before serving, remove thighs from marinade; put marinade aside. Combine breadcrumbs and salt on a sheet of greaseproof paper. Coat chicken with crumbs.
3. Preheat browning dish according to the manufacturer's instructions; brush with oil. Arrange thighs, spoke-fashion, on dish. Cook on High (100% power) for 5 minutes; turn chicken over. Cook on High for 5–7 minutes longer, until juices run clear. Allow to stand on a heatproof surface while preparing sauce.
4. Cook reserved marinade on Medium (50% power) for 3–4 minutes, until hot, stirring once.
5. Spoon sauce on to warmed plates; arrange chicken on top; garnish with lime and mint.

CHICKEN LIVERS WITH TOMATO SAUCE

Colour Index page 55. 4 servings. 917 kJ per serving.
Good source of vitamin A, riboflavin, niacin, iron.
Begin 25 minutes ahead.

30 g butter or margarine	2 teaspoons chopped fresh oregano or ½ teaspoon dried oregano
500 g chicken livers, cut in half	
½ cup canned tomatoes, chopped	2 teaspoons chopped fresh thyme or ½ teaspoon dried thyme
¼ cup beef stock	
1 onion, finely chopped	
1 tablespoon bottled steak sauce	Parsley to garnish

1. Heat butter in a 30-cm x 20-cm baking dish, covered with paper towel, on High (100% power) for 45 seconds, or until melted. Pierce chicken livers. Add to dish; stir. Cook, covered with paper towel, on High for 2–4 minutes, until livers lose raw appearance, stirring once. Remove livers; put aside.
2. Add tomatoes, stock, onion, steak sauce, oregano and thyme to drippings in baking dish. Cook on High for 10 minutes, or until thickened, stirring twice. Return chicken livers to dish. Cook on High for 1–2 minutes, until hot.
3. Spoon chicken livers on to warmed plates; garnish with parsley. Serve immediately.

CHICKEN ROLLS WITH CHEESE FILLING

Colour Index page 58. 1967 kJ per serving. Good source of vitamin A, niacin, calcium, iron.
Begin 35 minutes ahead.

Ingredients	For 4	For 2	For 1
Sun-dried tomatoes, drained if packed in oil	4	2	1
Boursin or other soft cheese with garlic and herbs	125 g	60 g	30 g
Mozzarella cheese, grated	¼ cup	2 tablespoons	1 tablespoon
Fresh basil, shredded	4 leaves	2 leaves	1 leaf
Chicken fillets (90 g–125 g each)	4	2	1
Butter or margarine	30 g	15 g	1½ teaspoons
Dried breadcrumbs	½ cup	¼ cup	2 tablespoons
Salt	¼ teaspoon	⅛ teaspoon	pinch
Microwave cookware	Small bowl 30-cm x 20-cm baking dish	Small bowl 30-cm x 20-cm baking dish	Small bowl 20-cm x 20-cm baking dish
Time on High (100% power) Butter Chicken	45 seconds 6–9 minutes	30–45 seconds 4–6 minutes	15–30 seconds 2½ (2:30)–3½ (3:30) minutes
Standing time	4 minutes	3 minutes	2 minutes

1 Chop tomatoes. Combine cheeses, basil and tomatoes in a bowl; stir until blended.

2 Spoon an equal amount of filling on to one end of each chicken fillet. Roll up fillets to enclose filling; secure with wooden toothpicks.

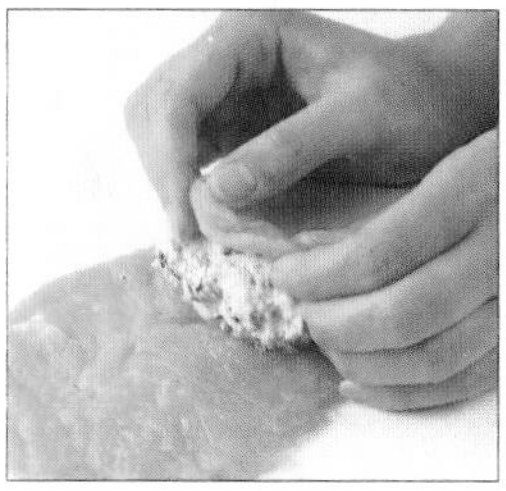

3 Heat butter in bowl (see Chart), covered with paper towel, on High for time in Chart, or until melted.

4 Mix breadcrumbs and salt in a pie plate or on a sheet of greaseproof paper. Dip chicken rolls in melted butter, then coat in crumbs.

5 Arrange rolls, 2.5 cm apart, in baking dish. Cook, covered loosely with greaseproof paper, on High for time in Chart, until fork-tender. Allow to stand for time in Chart. Slice on to warmed plates.

Chicken breasts

A crumbed coating helps keep skinned chicken moist and tender during cooking as well as making it more attractive. Because chicken breasts vary in density, they should be flattened uniformly so that they cook more evenly in the microwave. To help prevent chicken from sticking to the knife or meat mallet when pounding, place it between 2 sheets of greaseproof paper.

CHICKEN BREASTS PARMESAN

Colour Index page 57. 1595 kJ per serving. Good source of vitamin A, niacin, calcium, iron, fibre.
Begin 35 minutes ahead.

Ingredients for 4 servings		Microwave cookware
4 chicken breasts, skinned and boned	1 large onion, chopped	Medium bowl
45 g butter or margarine	1 clove garlic, crushed	33-cm x 23-cm baking dish
1 egg	425 g can tomatoes, chopped with their juice	
1/3 cup dried breadcrumbs	1/2 cup stoned black olives, sliced	
1/2 cup grated Parmesan cheese	1/3 cup packed basil leaves, shredded	
2 teaspoons chopped fresh oregano or 1/2 teaspoon dried oregano	1/4 teaspoon salt	
	Pepper to taste	
1/2 teaspoon paprika	Basil leaves to garnish	

1 Cut each chicken breast in half crossways; pound to 6-mm thickness with the dull edge of a heavy knife or the smooth edge of a meat mallet.

2 Heat two-thirds of butter in medium bowl, covered with paper towel, on High (100% power) for 45 seconds, or until melted. Allow to cool slightly; beat in egg.

3 Combine breadcrumbs, cheese, oregano and paprika on a sheet of greaseproof paper. Dip chicken pieces in butter mixture, then coat in seasoned crumbs.

4 Place chicken in baking dish. Cook, covered loosely with greaseproof paper, on High for 6–8 minutes, until fork-tender, rearranging once. Allow to stand, covered, while preparing sauce.

5 Place onion, garlic and remaining butter in bowl used to melt butter. Cook on High for 4 minutes, stirring halfway though cooking. Add tomatoes, olives, basil, salt and pepper.

6 Cook sauce on High for 2–3 minutes, until hot, stirring to combine. Arrange chicken and sauce on warmed plates; garnish with basil leaves. Serve hot.

WALNUT CHICKEN

Colour Index page 58. 6 servings. 1402 kJ per serving. Good source of niacin, fibre.
Begin 35 minutes ahead.

1 1/4 cups red currants
1/2 cup orange juice
2 tablespoons sugar
2 tablespoons port
3/4 cup walnuts or pecans, finely chopped
1/4 cup dried breadcrumbs
2 tablespoons grated orange rind
1/4 teaspoon salt
6 chicken breasts, skinned and boned
1/3 cup honey
1 tablespoon orange julienne (page 316)
Parsley sprigs to garnish

1. Place 1 cup red currants, orange juice, sugar and port in a 4-cup glass jug. Cook on High (100% power) for 4–6 minutes, until currants begin to pop, stirring twice. In food processor with knife blade attached or in blender, process mixture until smooth. Press mixture through a fine mesh strainer into a medium bowl; put aside.
2. Mix walnuts, breadcrumbs, orange rind and salt on a sheet of greaseproof paper. Brush chicken with honey; coat with walnut mixture. Arrange in a 33-cm x 23-cm baking dish. Cook, covered loosely with greaseproof paper, on High for 10 minutes, or until fork-tender, rotating dish halfway through cooking.
3. Add orange julienne and remaining red currants to reserved sauce. Cook on High for 2–3 minutes.
4. Place chicken on warmed plates with sauce alongside; garnish with parsley.

CREAMY CHICKEN BREASTS

Colour Index page 55. 4 servings. 1850 kJ per serving. Good source of vitamin A, niacin.
Begin 25 minutes ahead.

30 g butter or margarine
3 spring onions, sliced
250 g asparagus, trimmed and cut into 2.5-cm pieces
4 chicken breasts, skinned and boned
1 1/2 tablespoons plain flour
1 teaspoon mild curry powder
1 cup cream

1. Heat butter in a 30-cm x 20-cm baking dish, covered with paper towel, on High (100% power) for 45 seconds, or until melted.
2. Stir in spring onions and asparagus. Place chicken breasts on top, with thicker, meatier parts towards edges of dish. Cook on High for 5–7 minutes, just until chicken turns opaque. Transfer to a plate; cover and keep warm.
3. Combine flour and curry powder in a bowl. Add to vegetables; stir until blended. Cook on High for 1 minute. Gradually stir in cream. Cook on High for 4–5 minutes, until thickened.
4. Return chicken to baking dish; spoon over sauce. Cook on High for 1–2 minutes, until juices run clear. Serve, if you like, with rice.

CHICKEN FRICASSÉE

Colour Index page 57. 4 servings. 1905 kJ per serving. Good source of vitamin A, riboflavin, niacin, calcium, iron, fibre.
Begin 55 minutes ahead.

60 g butter or margarine	155 g shelled peas
1 onion, chopped	155 g sliced green beans
½ teaspoon poultry seasoning	155 g frozen baby carrots, thawed
¼ cup plain flour	2 egg yolks
3 cups milk	Salt and pepper to taste
500 g chicken breasts, skinned and boned	

1. Heat butter in a 2-litre casserole, covered with paper towel, on High (100% power) for 45 seconds–1 minute, until melted. Add onion and poultry seasoning. Cook on High for 2–3 minutes, until softened.
2. Stir in flour. Cook on High for 1 minute. Gradually stir in milk. Cook on High for 10–12 minutes, until thickened, stirring often.
3. Cut chicken into 4-cm chunks. Add to sauce with vegetables. Cook on High for 10–12 minutes, until juices run clear, stirring twice.
4. Lightly beat egg yolks in a small bowl. Stir in ½ cup cooking liquid until smooth. Return to chicken; stir. Cook on Medium (50% power) for 3 minutes, or until thickened, stirring twice; season. Allow to stand, covered, for 5 minutes.
5. Spoon chicken and vegetables on to warmed plates. Serve hot.

CHEESY CHICKEN BREASTS

Colour Index page 58. 8 servings. 2294 kJ per serving. Good source of vitamin A, niacin, vitamin C, iron, fibre.
Begin 35 minutes ahead.

250 g cream cheese, softened	1 clove garlic, crushed
1½ tablespoons milk	8 chicken breasts, boned
2 spring onions, finely chopped	⅓ cup dried breadcrumbs
2 tablespoons finely chopped fresh parsley	1 teaspoon paprika
2 teaspoons chopped fresh thyme	30 g butter or margarine, melted
Salt and pepper to taste	1 head chicory
	500 g asparagus, cooked
	1 punnet cherry tomatoes

1. Combine cheese, milk, spring onions, parsley, thyme, salt, pepper and garlic in a bowl.
2. Push fingers between skin and flesh of each chicken breast to form a pocket. Spread an equal amount of cream cheese mixture in each pocket.
3. Combine breadcrumbs and paprika on a sheet of greaseproof paper. Dip chicken breasts into melted butter; coat in seasoned crumbs.
4. Place chicken in a 33-cm x 23-cm baking dish. Cook, covered loosely with greaseproof paper, on High (100% power) for 15 minutes, or until tender, rotating dish halfway through cooking.
5. Arrange chicken, chicory, asparagus and tomatoes on a serving platter.

POACHED CHICKEN WITH VEGETABLES

Colour Index page 57. 1356 kJ per serving. Good source of niacin, iron, fibre.
Begin 40 minutes ahead.

Ingredients	For 4	For 2	For 1
Butter or margarine	30 g	15 g	1½ teaspoons
Vinaigrette dressing	¼ cup	2 tablespoons	1 tablespoon
Leeks, sliced	4 small	2 small	1 small
Mushrooms, cut in half	125 g	60 g	30 g
400 g can artichoke hearts, drained	1 can	½ can	¼ can
Chicken stock	1 cup	½ cup	¼ cup
Chicken breasts, skinned and boned	4	2	1
Cornflour	1 tablespoon	2 teaspoons	1 teaspoon
Cold water	2 tablespoons	1 tablespoon	2 teaspoons
Salt and pepper	to taste	to taste	to taste
Microwave cookware	33-cm x 23-cm baking dish	30-cm x 20-cm baking dish	20-cm x 20-cm baking dish
Time on High (100% power)			
Vegetable mixture	4–5 minutes	3 minutes	2 minutes
With chicken	8–10 minutes	5–6 minutes	3–4 minutes
With cornflour	3 minutes	2–3 minutes	1–2 minutes

1 Place butter, vinaigrette, leeks, mushrooms and artichoke hearts in baking dish (see Chart). Cook on High for time in Chart, or until vegetables are softened, stirring twice.

2 Stir stock into vegetable mixture. Arrange chicken breasts on top, with thicker, meatier pieces towards edges of dish.

3 Cook chicken, covered, on High for time in Chart, turning pieces over halfway through cooking.

4 Pierce chicken with a fork; chicken is done when juices run clear.

5 With a slotted spatula, carefully transfer chicken breasts to a warmed serving platter. Allow to stand, covered, while finishing sauce. Dissolve cornflour in water. Pour into baking dish; stir until well blended. Cook on High for time in Chart, until thickened. Season with salt and pepper.

6 Spoon vegetables and sauce over chicken breasts. Serve immediately.

Stuffed chicken breasts are extremely versatile, and any number of different fillings are suitable. They can be prepared well in advance and kept refrigerated until ready for cooking. The breasts should be pounded until thin, then folded over the filling with the thinner ends tucked under. Use wooden toothpicks to hold in the filling if necessary.

BROCCOLI-STUFFED CHICKEN BREASTS

Colour Index page 57. 1427 kJ per serving. Good source of vitamin A, niacin, vitamin C, calcium, iron, fibre.
Begin 45 minutes ahead.

Ingredients for 6 servings		Microwave cookware
310 g broccoli, cooked and chopped	1 tablespoon chopped fresh parsley	33-cm x 23-cm baking dish
2 spring onions, finely chopped	½ teaspoon paprika	Medium bowl
125 g tasty cheese, grated (1 cup)	45 g butter or margarine, melted	
6 chicken breasts, skinned and boned	3 teaspoons plain flour	
3 slices cooked ham, cut in half (about 90 g)	¼ teaspoon salt	
	⅛ teaspoon pepper	
1 cup fresh breadcrumbs	1 cup milk	
	Parsley sprigs to garnish	

1 Drain broccoli well; place in a large bowl. Mix in spring onions and half the cheese.

2 Pound chicken breasts to 6-mm thickness. Top each with 1 piece ham and equal amounts of broccoli mixture.

3 Carefully fold chicken in half over filling; neatly tuck ends under.

4 Combine breadcrumbs, parsley and paprika in a pie plate or on a sheet of greaseproof paper. Brush chicken with melted butter, using about one-third. Coat chicken with seasoned crumbs.

5 Place chicken in baking dish. Cook, covered loosely with greaseproof paper, on High (100% power) for 10–12 minutes, until fork-tender, rotating dish once. Arrange chicken on warmed dinner plates or serving platter. Allow to stand, covered, while preparing sauce.

6 Place remaining melted butter in bowl. Add flour, salt and pepper; mix well. Gradually stir in milk. Cook on High for 3½ (3:30) minutes, or until boiling, stirring twice. Add remaining cheese; stir until melted. Spoon sauce around chicken; garnish with parsley sprigs.

CHICKEN KIEV

Colour Index page 56. 4 servings. 1503 kJ per serving. Good source of niacin.
Begin 55 minutes ahead.

4 chicken breasts, skinned and boned	½ cup dried breadcrumbs
Salt and pepper to taste	2 cloves garlic, crushed
60 g chilled butter, shaped or cut into 4 sticks (about 5 cm x 1 cm)	2 tablespoons chopped fresh parsley
	½ teaspoon paprika
30 g butter or margarine	Lemon slices and parsley sprigs to garnish
1 egg yolk	

1. Pound each chicken breast to 6-mm thickness with the dull edge of a heavy knife or the smooth edge of a meat mallet. Season with salt and pepper. Place 1 stick of butter lengthways in the centre of each chicken breast. Fold ends over butter; roll up to enclose butter completely. Secure with toothpicks if necessary. Freeze the chicken rolls for 30 minutes; remove toothpicks.
2. Heat 30 g butter in a small bowl, covered with paper towel, on High (100% power) for 45 seconds, or until melted. Stir in egg yolk.
3. Combine breadcrumbs, garlic, parsley and paprika on a sheet of greaseproof paper. Dip chicken pieces into egg mixture, then coat with seasoned crumbs.
4. Place chicken rolls at least 2.5 cm apart in a 30-cm x 20-cm baking dish. Cook, covered loosely with greaseproof paper, on High for 8–9 minutes, until fork-tender, rotating dish halfway through cooking. Allow to stand for 4 minutes before serving.
5. Arrange chicken on individual warmed plates; garnish with lemon slices and sprigs of parsley. Serve hot.

TO MAKE CHICKEN KIEV FOR TWO:
Use **2 chicken breasts, 30 g chilled butter, 15 g butter or margarine, 1 egg yolk, ¼ cup breadcrumbs, 1 crushed garlic clove, 1 tablespoon chopped parsley** and **¼ teaspoon paprika**. Prepare as above, melting butter or margarine on High for 30–45 seconds and cooking chicken, covered loosely with greaseproof paper, in a 20-cm x 20-cm baking dish on High for 6–7 minutes. Allow chicken to stand for 3 minutes.

PREPARING CHICKEN BREASTS

With the dull edge of a heavy knife or the smooth edge of a meat mallet, pound chicken breasts to 6-mm thickness.

Cooked chicken

CHICKEN AND PASTA BAKE

Colour Index page 58. 4 servings. 2930 kJ per serving. Good source of vitamin A, thiamine, riboflavin, niacin, calcium, iron, fibre. Begin 55 minutes ahead.

250 g tagliatelle	3 medium celery stalks,
45 g butter or margarine	chopped
2 tablespoons plain flour	3 spring onions, sliced
2 cups milk	375 g packet frozen peas,
1 cup chicken stock	thawed
1 teaspoon poultry	500 g chicken breast
seasoning	fillets, cut into
1/4 teaspoon salt	4-cm chunks
4 slices melba toast	1/2 cup sour cream

1. Cook tagliatelle conventionally. Drain and keep warm.
2. Heat butter in a 33-cm x 23-cm baking dish, covered with paper towel, on High (100% power) for 45 seconds–1 minute, until melted. Stir in flour until blended. Gradually stir in milk and stock; add poultry seasoning and salt. Cook on High for 8–10 minutes, until thickened, stirring twice.
3. Meanwhile, make melba toast crumbs: Place toast in a strong plastic bag. Roll with a rolling pin until finely crushed.
4. Stir celery, spring onions, peas, chicken and tagliatelle into sauce. Cook, covered, on High for 8 minutes, stirring twice. Add sour cream; stir well. Cook, covered, on Medium (50% power) for 5–8 minutes, rotating dish halfway through cooking.
5. Sprinkle with melba toast crumbs. Cook on High for 2 minutes. Serve immediately.

Making the melba toast crumbs

Place melba toast in a strong plastic bag. Roll with a rolling pin until melba toasts are finely crushed. Alternatively, process toasts in a food processor with knife blade attached, or in blender, until crushed.

Cooked chicken can be combined with other ingredients and ready to serve in a matter of minutes. For Chicken à la King (below), you can use leftovers from any cooked whole chicken or pieces. Or, if you like, you can use the simple cooking method on page 180 for fresh chicken that adds only a few additional minutes to the cooking time.

CHICKEN À LA KING

Colour Index page 55. 2378 kJ per serving. Good source of niacin, calcium, iron. Begin 25 minutes ahead.

Ingredients for 4 servings		Microwave cookware
60 g butter or margarine	2 cups cubed cooked	4-cup glass jug
1 onion, finely chopped	chicken	
1 small green capsicum,	1 pimiento, diced	
finely chopped	2 egg yolks	
8 small mushrooms, cut	1 tablespoon dry sherry	
into quarters	Salt and pepper to taste	
1/2 cup plain flour	8 medium or 4 large vol-	
1 cup chicken stock	au-vent cases, warmed	
1 cup milk	Dill sprigs to garnish	

1 Heat butter in jug, covered with paper towel, on High (100% power) for 45 seconds–1 minute, until melted.

2 Add onion, capsicum and mushrooms; stir to coat. Cook on High for 3–4 minutes, until onion has softened slightly.

3 Stir flour into vegetable mixture until blended. Cook on High for 1 minute, stirring once. Gradually stir in stock and milk until smooth.

4 Cook sauce on High for 4–6 minutes, until thickened, stirring twice. Add chicken and pimiento. Cook on High for 3 minutes, or until chicken is hot.

5 Beat egg yolks in a small bowl. Stir 1/4 cup sauce from chicken into egg yolks. Pour egg-yolk mixture back into remaining chicken mixture, beating rapidly to prevent lumping. Stir in sherry; season with salt and pepper.

6 Place vol-au-vents on warmed plates; spoon in chicken and sauce; garnish with dill.

CHICKEN CRÊPES FLORENTINE

Colour Index page 58. 1716 kJ per serving. Good source of vitamin A, riboflavin, niacin, calcium, iron, fibre.
Begin 55 minutes ahead.

Ingredients	For 4	For 2	For 1
Basic White Sauce (page 381)	*2 cups*	*1 cup*	*½ cup*
Grated Parmesan cheese	*⅓ cup*	*2 tablespoons*	*1 tablespoon*
375 g packet frozen chopped spinach, thawed	*1 packet*	*½ packet*	*¼ packet*
Garlic, crushed	*1 clove*	*½ clove*	*¼ clove*
Butter or margarine	*15 g*	*1½ teaspoons*	*1 teaspoon*
Salt and pepper	*to taste*	*to taste*	*to taste*
Cooked chicken, cubed	*2 cups*	*1 cup*	*½ cup*
Crêpes (below right)	*8*	*4*	*2*
Microwave cookware	33-cm x 23-cm baking dish	30-cm x 20-cm baking dish	20-cm x 20-cm baking dish
Time on High (100% power)			
Spinach mixture	3–5 minutes	3 minutes	2 minutes
Filled crêpes with sauce	5–7 minutes	5–6 minutes	3–4 minutes

1 Prepare Basic White Sauce. (If making for 2 or 1, refrigerate leftover sauce to use another day.) Stir Parmesan cheese into sauce. Lightly press plastic wrap over surface to prevent skin forming; put aside and keep warm.

2 Place spinach, garlic and butter in baking dish (see Chart). Cook, covered with paper towel, on High for time in Chart, or until flavours are blended, stirring twice. Season with salt and pepper.

3 Transfer spinach mixture to a bowl. Add chicken; stir to combine. Clean baking dish with paper towels.

4 Place 1 crêpe at a time on a flat surface. Spoon an equal amount of filling on to each.

5 Roll up to enclose filling. Place crêpes at least 6 mm apart in cleaned baking dish, seam side down.

6 Pour sauce over filled crêpes. Cook on High for time in Chart, until bubbling. If suitable, place dish under preheated griller to brown top.

CHICKEN RATATOUILLE

Colour Index page 58. 4 servings. 1448 kJ per serving. Good source of vitamin A, niacin, vitamin C, calcium, iron, fibre.
Begin 40 minutes ahead.

1½ tablespoons olive or vegetable oil
2 cloves garlic, crushed
1 large onion, chopped
1 medium green capsicum, chopped
2 golden zucchini, cut into 4-cm chunks
2 green zucchini, cut into 4-cm chunks
1 tablespoon shredded fresh basil or 1 teaspoon dried basil

1 tablespoon finely chopped fresh oregano or 1 teaspoon dried oregano
2 cups cubed cooked chicken
215 g can tomatoes, chopped
Salt and pepper to taste
125 g mozzarella cheese, grated (1 cup)
Parsley sprigs to garnish

1. Place oil, garlic, onion, capsicum, zucchini, basil and oregano in a 33-cm x 23-cm baking dish; stir to combine. Cook, covered, on High (100% power) for 5 minutes. Uncover; stir. Cook on High for 5–10 minutes longer, until vegetables are tender, stirring twice.

2. Add chicken and tomatoes to vegetables; stir to combine. Season with salt and pepper. Sprinkle with cheese. Cook on High for 5–7 minutes, until cheese is melted and chicken is hot, rotating dish halfway through cooking.

3. If dish is suitable, place under a preheated griller until cheese is bubbling and golden; garnish with parsley sprigs. Serve hot on warmed plates, or cover and refrigerate to serve chilled later.

MAKING AND FREEZING CRÊPES
Beat *⅔ cup plain flour, ¼ teaspoon salt* and *3 eggs* in a bowl until smooth. Slowly beat in *1½ cups milk* and *1 tablespoon melted butter or margarine.* Cover and refrigerate batter for 2 hours.

Brush bottom and sides of an 18-cm frying pan with *melted butter.* Heat pan; pour in scant ¼ cup batter. Tip pan to coat bottom. Cook for 3 minutes over low heat, or until crêpe is set and underside browned. Turn crêpe over with a spatula and cook for 1 minute, or until golden. Slip crêpe on to greaseproof paper. Repeat with remaining batter to make 12 crêpes altogether, stacking with greaseproof paper between each crêpe.

To freeze crêpes: Wrap stack in foil; label and store in the freezer for up to 2 months. To use, preheat conventional oven to 170°C. Place wrapped, frozen crêpes on a baking tray; heat for about 30 minutes, or until hot.

Game

MEXICAN PANCAKES

Colour Index page 57. 4 servings. 2290 kJ per serving. Good source of vitamin A, riboflavin, niacin, vitamin C, calcium, iron, fibre.
Begin 45 minutes ahead.

2 cups cubed cooked chicken	8 crêpes (page 194)
1 teaspoon ground cumin	1 cup bottled taco sauce
¼ teaspoon ground cloves	215 g can tomatoes, chopped
3 teaspoons lime juice	1 tablespoon cream
1½ tablespoons peanut or vegetable oil	125 g tasty cheese, grated (1 cup)
1 onion, chopped	Lime wedges and coriander sprigs to garnish
1 medium green capsicum, chopped	Sour cream and Guacamole (page 218, optional)
2 tomatoes, chopped	
2 tablespoons chopped fresh coriander	
155 g frozen whole-kernel corn, slightly thawed	

1. Combine chicken, cumin, cloves and lime juice in a bowl. Allow to stand for 5 minutes, to blend flavours.
2. Meanwhile, combine oil, onion, capsicum and tomatoes in a 30-cm quiche dish or pie plate. Cook on High (100% power) for 3 minutes, or until softened, stirring twice.
3. Add chicken, coriander and corn; stir well.
4. Place 1 crêpe at a time on a flat surface. Spoon an equal amount of filling on to each one; roll up to enclose filling. Place, seam side down, in a 33-cm x 23-cm baking dish.
5. Combine taco sauce, chopped tomatoes and cream in a 4-cup glass jug. Cook on High for 4 minutes, or until hot and slightly reduced, stirring twice.
6. Pour sauce over filled crêpes. Cook on High for 8–10 minutes, rotating dish halfway through cooking.
7. Transfer crêpes to warmed plates. Sprinkle cheese on top; garnish with lime wedges and coriander. Serve, if you like, with sour cream and Guacamole.

ITALIAN-STYLE PANCAKES:
Make as for Mexican Pancakes (above), using *1 crushed garlic clove, 2 teaspoons chopped fresh oregano or ½ teaspoon dried oregano, 1 tablespoon lemon juice* and *1 tablespoon prepared pesto sauce* in step 1 instead of the cumin, cloves and lime juice, and substituting *shredded basil or chopped parsley* for the coriander in step 3. Omit the corn in step 3 and use *310 g can red kidney beans*, drained and rinsed, together with *60 g diced mozzarella cheese*. In step 7, sprinkle over *2 tablespoons grated Parmesan cheese* and *2 tablespoons pine nuts* instead of tasty cheese; garnish with *basil leaves* instead of lime wedges and coriander sprigs.

PHEASANT WITH MUSHROOM SAUCE

4 servings. 2297 kJ per serving. Good source of niacin, iron.
Begin 40 minutes ahead.

80 g butter
250 g mushrooms, sliced
1 kg pheasant
Chicken stock
1 tablespoon plain flour
2 teaspoons Worcestershire sauce
¼ cup port
Salt and pepper to taste
Celery salt

1. Heat 40 g butter in a 2-litre casserole, covered with paper towel, on High (100% power) for 30–45 seconds, until melted.
2. Add mushrooms. Cook on High for 3 minutes, stirring halfway through cooking.
3. Stuff pheasant with half the mushrooms and secure with wooden toothpicks; reserve remaining mushrooms. Rub bird with 20 g butter, truss with string and place in an oven bag; tie and pierce bag according to the manufacturer's instructions. Place bag in a 33-cm x 23-cm shallow baking dish, breast side down. Cook on High for 10 minutes; turn bag. Cook on High for 15 minutes longer. Drain off any liquid from bag into a measuring jug; make up to 1¼ cups with stock. Wrap pheasant in bag; keep warm while preparing sauce.
4. Heat remaining butter in a 4-cup glass jug, covered with paper towel, on High for 45 seconds. Stir in flour until smooth. Cook on High for 1 minute, stirring once.
5. Gradually stir in stock. Cook on High for 2 minutes, or until sauce is smooth and thick. Add Worcestershire sauce, port and reserved mushrooms. Cook on High for 2 minutes; season with salt, pepper and a pinch of celery salt.
6. Carve pheasant on to warmed plates. Serve with mushroom sauce. If pheasant is not done to your liking when you start carving, cook on High for 5 minutes longer.

RABBIT CASSEROLE

4 servings. 1461 kJ per serving. Good source of niacin. Low in cholesterol, sodium.
Begin 30 minutes ahead.

1 onion, finely chopped
1 stick celery, sliced
1 carrot, diced
1 clove garlic, crushed
1 tablespoon olive oil
2 tablespoons tomato paste
¼ teaspoon dried sage or 1 teaspoon chopped fresh sage
2 teaspoons chopped fresh parsley
8 rabbit joints (about 750 g)
1 tablespoon plain flour mixed with a little water
1 cup hot chicken stock
Salt and pepper to taste

1. Place onion, celery, carrot, garlic and oil in a 2-litre casserole. Cook, covered, on High (100% power) for 4 minutes, stirring halfway through cooking.
2. Add tomato paste, sage and parsley; stir well. Add rabbit joints. Cook, covered, on High for 5 minutes, stirring several times. Reduce power level to Medium-High (70% power) and cook for 15 minutes longer, stirring several times.
3. Remove rabbit; put aside. Add blended flour and hot stock to casserole; stir well. Cook on High for 2 minutes.
4. Return rabbit to casserole and season with salt and pepper. Cook, covered, on High for 4 minutes. Allow to stand for 10 minutes before serving.

Duck

DUCKLING WITH ORANGE SAUCE

Colour Index page 59. 3391 kJ per serving. Good source of thiamine, riboflavin, niacin, iron.
Begin 1½ hours ahead.

Ingredients for 4 servings		Microwave cookware
2.5 kg duckling, cut into quarters 1 orange 2 tablespoons cider vinegar 1½ tablespoons sugar 1½ cups chicken stock 2 teaspoons cornflour dissolved in 1 tablespoon cold water	2 tablespoons lemon juice 2 tablespoons brandy Salt and pepper to taste Parsley and orange slices to garnish	33-cm x 23-cm baking dish with rack 4-cup glass jug

1 Trim excess skin and fat from duck pieces. Rinse under cold running water; pat dry with paper towels. With fork, pierce skin of each piece about 10 times; this allows fat to drain off and prevents skin from splitting during cooking.

2 Arrange leg quarters, skin side down, in opposite corners of baking dish, with bones towards centre. Cook, covered, on Medium (50% power) for 20 minutes, turning pieces over once. Prick skin with fork; turn pieces over again, placing skin side down.

3 Add breast quarters, skin side down. Cook, covered loosely with greaseproof paper, on Medium-High (70% power) for 20 minutes, turning pieces over and pricking skin once. Uncover and cook on High (100% power) for 5 minutes or until juices run clear. Cover and allow to stand while preparing sauce.

4 With vegetable peeler, remove rind from orange, leaving bitter white pith behind. Stack rind and cut into fine strips. Squeeze juice from orange into a bowl.

5 Combine vinegar and sugar in jug. Cook, covered, on High for 3–5 minutes, just until mixture turns light golden, watching carefully since mixture burns easily. Stir in orange rind, orange juice and stock. Cook, covered, on High for 5 minutes. Add cornflour. Cook on High for 2–4 minutes longer, until thickened.

6 Stir lemon juice and brandy into sauce; season with salt and pepper. Arrange duck pieces on warmed plates; top with sauce. Garnish with parsley and orange slices. Serve immediately.

APRICOT GLAZED DUCKLING

Colour Index page 59. 4 servings. 3546 kJ per serving. Good source of thiamine, riboflavin, niacin, iron.
Begin 1¼ hours ahead.

2 tablespoons French mustard ½ cup apricot jam 2 tablespoons soy sauce 1 clove garlic, crushed	½ teaspoon ground ginger 2.5 kg duckling, cut into quarters Parsley sprigs to garnish

1. Combine mustard, apricot jam, soy sauce, garlic and ginger in a 4-cup glass jug. Cook on High (100% power) for 2 minutes, stirring twice; put aside.
2. Prepare and cook duck as for Duckling with Orange Sauce (left) up to end of step 3, brushing quarters with apricot glaze before cooking and every time oven is opened. Allow to stand for 5 minutes.
3. If dish is suitable, brown duck under a preheated griller until skin is crisp; garnish with parsley. Serve immediately.

Glazing the duckling

Combine mustard, apricot jam, soy sauce, garlic and ginger in a 4-cup glass jug. Cook on High (100% power) for 2 minutes.

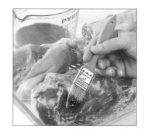

With a small pastry brush, brush the apricot glaze over duck quarters every time oven is opened.

POULTRY GLAZES
Brushing whole birds or pieces with a glaze will give poultry an attractive appearance. Similarly, brush with melted butter mixed with herbs or spices. Allow about ½ cup glaze for 2 kg–3 kg birds, 1 cup for larger birds. For information on Browning, see pages 182 and 183.

Honey Barbecue Glaze: Mix *½ cup honey, 3 teaspoons soy sauce* and *½ teaspoon ground ginger* in a 2-cup glass jug. Heat on Medium-High (70% power) for 1 minute, stirring once. Makes ½ cup.

Redcurrant Glaze: Mix *½ cup redcurrant jelly* with *2 teaspoons water*. Heat on Medium-High (70% power) for 1 minute, stirring once. Makes ½ cup.

DUCKLING WITH OLIVES AND ALMONDS

Colour Index page 59. 4 servings. 3424 kJ per serving. Good source of thiamine, riboflavin, niacin, iron.
Begin 1¼ hours ahead.

2.5 kg duckling, cut into quarters	1½ cups beef stock
3 onions, cut into 12-mm wedges	2 tablespoons dry sherry
185 g green olives stuffed with almonds, or 125 g green olives, stoned, and ¼ cup blanched almonds	2 teaspoons cornflour dissolved in 1 tablespoon cold water
	Salt and pepper to taste
	Lemon slices and coriander to garnish

1. Prepare and cook duck as for Duckling with Orange Sauce (page 196) up to the end of step 3. Transfer duck to a warmed serving dish and allow to stand, covered, while preparing sauce.
2. Remove rack from baking dish and pour off all but 2 tablespoons drippings. Add onion wedges and stir. Cook on High (100% power) for 3–5 minutes, just until softened, stirring twice. Add almond-stuffed olives or olives and almonds; stir to coat. Cook on High for 1 minute.
3. Stir stock into mixture. Cook on High for 3–4 minutes, until boiling, stirring twice. Add sherry and dissolved cornflour. Cook on High for 2–4 minutes, until thickened, stirring occasionally. Season with salt and pepper.
4. Pour sauce over duck quarters on serving dish; garnish with lemon slices and coriander.

DUCKLING WITH CHERRY SAUCE

Colour Index page 59. 4 servings. 3257 kJ per serving. Low in sodium. Good source of thiamine, riboflavin, niacin, iron.
Begin 1¼ hours ahead.

2.5 kg duckling, cut in quarters	½ clove garlic, crushed
1 tablespoon plain flour	3 teaspoons lemon juice
¼ cup chicken stock	Black pepper to taste
¼ cup dry red wine	Watercress sprigs to garnish
1 cup canned pitted dark cherries in syrup	

1. Prepare and cook duck as for Duckling with Orange Sauce (page 196) up to the end of step 3. Transfer duck to a warmed serving dish and allow to stand, covered, while preparing sauce.
2. Pour 2 tablespoons duck drippings into a 4-cup glass jug; add flour and stir until blended. Cook on High (100% power) for 30 seconds.
3. Stir in stock, wine, cherries with their syrup and garlic. Cook on High for 3–5 minutes, until thickened, stirring twice.
4. Add lemon juice to sauce; stir well. Season with freshly ground black pepper.
5. Spoon cherry sauce over duck quarters on serving dish; garnish with watercress sprigs.

When preparing duck dishes that call for breasts only, it is important to remove skin and fat first. Because of the shortness of microwave cooking time, the fat does not have enough time to melt out and drain off, therefore the skin will not crisp. A browning dish will give the meat a more attractive appearance.

DUCK BREASTS WITH APPLE AND GREEN PEPPERCORNS

Colour Index page 58. 946 kJ per serving. Low in cholesterol, sodium. Good source of thiamine, niacin, iron.
Begin 40 minutes ahead.

Ingredients for 4 servings		Microwave cookware
4 boneless duck breasts	½ cup chicken stock	Browning dish
1 cooking apple	½ teaspoon cornflour dissolved in 1 teaspoon cold water	
1 tablespoon sugar	Salt and pepper to taste	
3 teaspoons vegetable oil	Parsley sprigs to garnish	
1 tablespoon green peppercorns in brine, drained		

1 Remove skin and fat from duck breasts; discard. Preheat browning dish according to the manufacturer's instructions.

2 Meanwhile, core apple and cut into about 20 slices. Combine apple slices and sugar in a bowl; put aside. Brush browning dish with oil; arrange duck breasts on dish.

3 Cook duck breasts on High (100% power) for 2–3 minutes, until rare, turning halfway through cooking. Transfer to a warmed plate. Allow to stand, covered, while preparing sauce.

4 Reheat browning dish. Arrange apple slices in a single layer on dish. Cook on High for 2 minutes. Transfer apple slices to a warmed plate; put aside.

5 Reheat browning dish; add green peppercorns and stock. Cook on High for 3 minutes, or until bubbling. Add dissolved cornflour; stir. Cook on High for 2 minutes, or until sauce thickens. Season with salt and pepper.

6 Cut each duck breast into slices and arrange on warmed dinner plates with apple slices. Spoon sauce over each serving; garnish with parsley sprigs. Serve immediately.

Turkey

Turkey breast, available frozen as a roast in larger supermarkets and specialty poultry shops, is ideal for cooking in the microwave and, because cooking time is long enough, the skin will brown if brushed with butter or margarine and browning sauce. If you like, add another stuffing (right), cooking it separately in a casserole until a thermometer registers 73°C.

TURKEY BREAST WITH CHESTNUT STUFFING

Colour Index page 59. 1649 kJ per serving. Good source of niacin, iron, fibre. Begin 1¾ hours ahead.

Ingredients for 16 servings		Microwave cookware
3 kg turkey breast on the bone, thawed	*2 tablespoons chopped fresh parsley*	33-cm x 23-cm baking dish
125 g butter or margarine	*2 cups shelled and roasted chestnuts*	
½ teaspoon browning sauce	*1½ teaspoons poultry seasoning*	
1 onion, chopped	*¼ teaspoon salt*	
2 celery stalks, chopped	*Pepper to taste*	
6 cups fresh bread cubes	*Parsley sprigs to garnish*	
½ cup sultanas		

1 Rinse turkey breast; pat dry. Heat half the butter in baking dish, covered with paper towel, on High (100% power) for 45 seconds–1 minute, until melted. Add browning sauce; stir.

2 Place turkey breast, skin side down, in baking dish. With pastry brush, coat skin of turkey with browning sauce mixture. Cook, covered, on Medium (50% power) for 12–15 minutes per 500 g (about 1¼ to 1½ hours).

3 Meanwhile, melt remaining butter in a 30-cm frying pan over medium heat. Add onion and celery. Cook until softened, stirring occasionally.

4 Remove pan from heat; stir in bread cubes, sultanas, parsley, chestnuts, poultry seasoning, salt and pepper. Toss to mix well.

5 About 20–30 minutes before end of cooking time, carefully transfer turkey breast to a plate. Add chestnut stuffing to drippings in baking dish. Stir well to combine.

6 Place turkey breast, skin side up, on top of chestnut stuffing. Continue cooking, covered, on Medium for 20–30 minutes, until a thermometer inserted in the centre of turkey breast reaches 70°C, rotating dish twice.

7 Allow turkey and stuffing to stand in dish, tented with foil, on a heatproof surface for 10 minutes. Turkey will continue to cook and will reach 76°C on thermometer.

8 Place turkey breast on a large warmed platter. Spoon stuffing around turkey; garnish with parsley sprigs.

STUFFINGS FOR POULTRY

Shorten preparation time for stuffings by cooking some of the ingredients in the microwave, then cook stuffed large birds conventionally, or cook the stuffing separately in the microwave on High (100% power) in a 30-cm x 20-cm baking dish until a thermometer inserted in centre reaches 73°C. Spinach and Ricotta Stuffing takes 10 minutes; Bacon and Rice Stuffing takes 3 minutes.

Spinach and Ricotta Stuffing:
Place *125 g diced butter or margarine* in a deep, large bowl. Heat, covered with paper towel, on High (100% power) for 1½ (1:30)– 2 minutes, until melted. Stir in *125 g thinly sliced mushroooms, 2 diced celery stalks* and *1 small chopped onion.* Cook, covered, on High for 3–4 minutes, until vegetables are softened, stirring twice. Stir in *3 cups fresh breadcrumbs, 250 g ricotta cheese (1 cup), 1 egg, 1 tablespoon chopped fresh parsley, ½ teaspoon poultry seasoning, ¼ teaspoon pepper* and *250 g packet frozen chopped spinach,* thawed, drained and squeezed dry. Mix well.
Makes 3½ cups. 167 kJ per tablespoon.

Bacon and Rice Stuffing:
Cook *1 cup long-grain rice* conventionally. Meanwhile, place *12 diced bacon rashers* in a 33-cm x 23-cm baking dish. Cook, covered with paper towel, on High (100% power) for 4–5 minutes, until browned, stirring twice. Transfer to paper towel to drain. Discard all but 3 tablespoons bacon drippings; add *1 diced onion.* Cook, covered, on High for 2 minutes, or until softened. Stir in cooked rice and bacon.
Makes 3½ cups. 155 kJ per tablespoon.

Meat

BEEF · LAMB · VEAL · PORK · OFFAL · HAM · BACON
SAUSAGES · FRANKFURTERS

Meat

Meat cooked in the microwave is generally tastier and juicier than if cooked by other methods and, of course, it is ready much sooner. Shrinkage is minimised, especially on large roasts, by shielding ends with foil for part of the cooking time, which also ensures that the roast cooks evenly. Thinner ends of meat should always be shielded as should any bony portions.

Small cuts cook successfully on High (100% power) but larger cuts, especially roasts, are more tender when cooked at a lower power level.

Meat that is well marbled with fat and contains even layers of fat on the outside will cook more evenly and will be more tender. The drippings, which attract microwave energy away from the meat, should be removed at intervals – both to prevent spatters and to speed cooking.

Large joints of roasting meat with a good, even fat covering will brown due to their longer cooking times. Steaks and chops, which are cooked for a shorter time, are best cooked on a browning dish to sear them attractively while retaining their tenderness. Preparing hamburgers with a coating mixture and then cooking on a browning dish makes them as tasty as grilled or barbecued burgers. Standing time to complete the cooking process is important for larger cuts as it allows the internal temperature of the meat to rise to its final desired temperature. The temperature guidelines given in the recipes in this chapter should be followed when testing to see if meat is done; the appearance is not enough, as meat cooked in a microwave can often look underdone although it is fully cooked.

Choose evenly shaped cuts to cook in a microwave: roasts should have a regular diameter; meat for stews and casseroles should be cut to uniform size; steaks, chops and cutlets should be of the same density throughout. For even cooking, turn roasts and stir or rotate casseroles. Arrange irregular pieces of meat with thicker ends towards edges of dish. Use a rack, if directed, to prevent meat from cooking unevenly in its own juices.

NEW WAYS WITH HAMBURGERS

A simple hamburger quickly cooked in the microwave can be dressed up with a variety of popular accompaniments to create tasty variations.

Plain burger served in a bagel, topped with raw onion rings (left). Served with coleslaw, potato salad, dill pickle and stuffed olives.

Cheeseburger (page 213) on rounds of wholemeal toast, topped with thin slices of goat cheese (right). Served with a radish and salad greens.

Defrosting

Defrosting frozen foods is one of the great uses of a microwave oven. It must be done carefully, however, if quality is to be retained. It is important to defrost meat evenly to prevent some parts starting to cook before others have defrosted. Use a Medium-Low (30% power) or Defrost power level, or manually turn your oven on and off, allowing heat to even out during 'rest' periods.

DEFROSTING A LARGE ROAST

Remove all wrappings quickly from frozen meat. This speeds defrosting because wrapping insulates the bottom of roast.

Place roast on a rack in baking dish, so that meat does not sit in juices which could cause the surface to start cooking.

Check for warm areas as meat defrosts and shield these with smooth pieces of foil during defrosting; remove foil before starting to cook.

Using containers to fit
If transferring meat from freezer packing to dish, choose one which fits food as closely as possible; this prevents defrosted edges from spreading out and starting to cook.

Separating pieces
As soon as possible, separate frozen hamburgers, steaks or other pieces which have been stacked; place in a single layer on a rack to continue defrosting.

Breaking up beef mince
Break up mince with a fork as it defrosts; scrape off defrosted parts and put aside.

Covering with greaseproof paper
Covering meat loosely with greaseproof paper helps retain heat, thus speeding defrosting.

Separating cubes/ strips
As soon as sufficiently defrosted, separate cubes and strips of meat and arrange separately in dish, removing pieces as they defrost.

Testing with skewer
Thick meat cuts are defrosted when a skewer can go through the thickest part to centre.

Cooking

Careful choice and preparation of meat is essential for successful cooking in the microwave and an understanding of how microwave ovens work helps explain most of the techniques. Microwave energy cooks food quickly but not evenly. Therefore, choose evenly sized pieces of meat, or trim to make it more uniform in size; at the same time, trim fat so it is evenly distributed over the meat.

Arrange unevenly shaped pieces with thicker parts towards the edges of dish where they will cook faster. Thin ends of meat, bone, and cut edges tend to overcook, so shield them with strips of foil.

PREPARING MEAT FOR MICROWAVE COOKING

Removing excess fat from minced meat
Before proceeding with a recipe, place mince in a colander set over a bowl. Cook on High (100% power); discard drippings from bowl. For 500 g mince, cook for 4 minutes, stirring twice.

Even fat covering
While a certain amount of fat is desirable to tenderise and add flavour to meat, it should be evenly distributed as well as of uniform thickness; this helps the meat to cook evenly.

Trimming meat to size
Uniformity of size is important for even cooking in the microwave oven. If meat cubes are required, cut them all the same size.

Slashing sausages
To keep sausages, frankfurters and other foods with skins or casings from bursting due to steam build-up, slash or pierce them before cooking in the microwave.

Even diameter
Meat that is to be rolled should be trimmed and pounded to uniform thickness. Rolled roasts should be unrolled, pounded uniformly, then rolled up again.

Tenderising roasts
Roasts cook quickly in a microwave; if cheaper cuts of meat are used, they may need to be tenderised. Sprinkle meat with water, rub on meat tenderiser, then pierce with a fork so that tenderiser penetrates the surface.

SHIELDING

Ends of meat
To prevent cut ends of roasts from overcooking, shield with smooth, 5-cm strips of foil. Remove or retain these during cooking as necessary. Shield 'hot spots' in the same way.

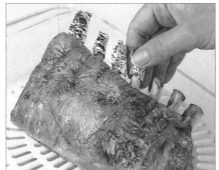

Exposed bones
To prevent overcooking, shield bony areas or ends of bones such as those on a rack of lamb cutlets, with smooth strips of foil.

Long, thin sides of steaks
If steaks are irregular in size, shield longer sides with smooth, narrow strips of foil to prevent them from overcooking. Remove foil halfway through cooking.

BROWNING

Browning conventionally
Meats that will not brown in a microwave – for example, a pot roast cooked in an oven bag – can be first browned conventionally in a frying pan.

Browning agents and coatings
Brush meat before and during cooking with a browning agent or glaze, or coat with beaten egg and a dry topping such as breadcrumbs or herbs.

Browning dish
Browning dishes are used to sear and brown meat such as cutlets, chops, steaks and hamburgers while they are cooking in the microwave oven.

COOKING TECHNIQUES FOR MEAT

Racks and trivets
Placing meat on a rack prevents it from steaming in its own juices and fats. Racks and trivets should also be used to elevate denser meat so that microwaves reach the bottom of food and it cooks more uniformly.

Standing time
It is important to let meats stand to complete the cooking process after removal from the microwave; internal temperatures will rise 5°–8° during standing.

Oven bags
Less tender meat cuts are best cooked in liquid and oven bags are ideal for this. Use plastic, nylon or cotton ties and vent to allow steam to escape; do not use metal ties.

Tenting
Keep meat warm during standing by tenting with foil, shiny side in, or greaseproof paper.

Using a mould
A ring mould allows microwaves to penetrate the food from all sides, ensuring even cooking. This is especially important in dishes that cannot be stirred, such as meat loaves.

Freezer-to-table casseroles
Fit smooth foil on to frozen surface. Place on a rack; cook on High (100% power), rotating a quarter turn every 5 minutes until defrosted. Discard foil and continue cooking until hot and bubbling.

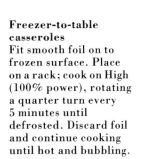

Beef

When choosing beef to cook in the microwave oven, make sure there is an even marbling of fat throughout; this will ensure even cooking and moist, tender results.

ROAST FILLET OF BEEF WITH HERBS

Colour Index page 63. 712 kJ per serving. Low in sodium. Good source of vitamin B₁₂, niacin, zinc, iron.
Begin 45 minutes ahead.

Ingredients for 10 servings		Microwave cookware
1.25 kg beef eye fillet ¼ cup dried breadcrumbs 2 tablespoons chopped fresh thyme or 2 teaspoons dried thyme 2 tablespoons chopped fresh oregano or 2 teaspoons dried oregano	2 tablespoons shredded fresh basil or 2 teaspoons dried basil 1 teaspoon freshly ground black pepper 2 tablespoons French mustard 1 clove garlic, crushed Radishes and basil leaves to garnish	30-cm x 20-cm baking dish with rack

1 Place beef fillet on rack in baking dish; shield ends of meat with smooth 5-cm strips of foil. Cook, covered loosely with greaseproof paper, on Medium (50% power) for 25 minutes, turning meat and removing foil halfway through cooking.

2 Meanwhile, combine breadcrumbs, thyme, oregano, basil and pepper in a bowl. Combine mustard and garlic in another bowl.

3 Remove greaseproof paper from meat; turn roast over. Spread mustard mixture evenly over meat and sprinkle with herb mixture; press with your fingers so that herbs adhere to mustard.

4 Insert 3 toothpicks, evenly spaced and about 2.5 cm deep, along top of meat. Cover with greaseproof paper, tenting paper over toothpicks. Cook on Medium for 7–10 minutes, until a thermometer inserted in the centre reaches 50°C for medium-rare.

5 Allow meat to stand, covered, on a heatproof surface for 5–8 minutes; temperature will reach 57°C.

6 Thinly slice beef across grain. Arrange slices on a warmed serving platter; garnish with radishes and basil leaves. Skim fat from meat juices; serve juices separately in a gravy boat.

STANDING RIB ROAST

Colour Index page 66. 6 servings. 1147 kJ per serving. Low in sodium. Good source of niacin, iron. Begin 1¼ hours ahead.

1.75 kg standing rib roast, with chine bone removed
1 teaspoon black pepper
1 tablespoon chopped fresh thyme or 1 teaspoon dried thyme

1 teaspoon onion powder
½ teaspoon paprika
3 teaspoons vegetable oil
Salt and pepper to taste
Thyme leaves to garnish

1. Trim any large areas of fat from rib roast.
2. Combine pepper, thyme, onion powder and paprika in a bowl. Rub seasonings evenly over meat.
3. Heat oil until very hot in a 30-cm frying pan over high heat. Add meat and brown on all sides. Transfer to a rack in a 33-cm x 23-cm baking dish.
4. Shield ends of bone with smooth strips of foil. Cook on Medium (50% power) for 30–40 minutes, until a meat thermometer inserted in the centre reaches 50°C for medium-rare, removing foil halfway through cooking.
5. Transfer meat to a warmed serving platter; tent with foil and allow to stand for 15–20 minutes; temperature will reach 54°C–57°C. Season with salt and pepper.
6. Sprinkle beef with thyme leaves. Serve with meat juices and vegetables of your choice.

CARVING A RIB ROAST
After cooking, a beef rib roast needs to stand for 15–20 minutes to complete cooking and allow juices to settle. Transfer meat to a warmed serving platter and tent with foil. Allow meat to stand while preparing gravy or last-minute vegetables. With practice, and good carving utensils, any roast can be carved on a garnished serving platter.

For easy carving of a rib roast on a platter at the table, it is essential to remove the chine bone before cooking – your butcher will do this for you. After standing time, cut meat into 6-mm-thick slices with a sharp carving knife, using a long-tined fork to prevent roast from slipping on platter while carving. Transfer slices to warmed individual plates; continue carving until all the guests are served.

FREEZER-TO-TABLE POT ROAST

Colour Index page 67. 12 servings. 1423 kJ per serving. Good source of vitamin A, niacin, iron. Begin 2½ hours ahead.

1 cup orange juice	2 kg topside or fresh
2 teaspoons salt	silverside, frozen
¼ teaspoon pepper	500 g carrots
1 teaspoon chopped fresh	500 g swede
thyme or ¼ teaspoon	2 tablespoons plain flour
dried thyme	2 tablespoons water
2 x 12-mm-wide strips	Parsley sprigs to garnish
orange rind	

1. Combine orange juice, salt, pepper, thyme and orange rind in a 5-litre casserole. Add topside, turning to coat with orange-juice mixture. Place smooth 5-cm strip of foil over each end of meat to prevent overcooking. Cook, covered, on Medium (50% power) for 1 hour, turning meat over and replacing foil strips halfway through cooking.
2. Meanwhile, cut carrots into 4-cm pieces. Peel swede and cut into 6-mm wedges.
3. Turn meat over again and replace foil strips; add vegetables. Cook, covered, on Medium for 1–1¼ hours longer, until meat and vegetables are tender, turning meat over and removing foil halfway through cooking.
4. Carefully transfer meat to a warmed serving platter. Arrange vegetables around meat; allow to stand, covered, while preparing sauce.
5. Skim fat from cooking liquid in casserole. Combine flour and water in a bowl until smooth. Gradually stir flour mixture into cooking liquid. Cook on High (100% power) for 2–3 minutes, until sauce thickens, stirring often.
6. Cut beef into slices; garnish with parsley. Pour sauce into gravy boat and serve separately.

OVEN GRAVY
Place *1 tablespoon butter or margarine*, or *meat drippings*, in a 4-cup glass jug. Heat, covered with paper towel, on High (100% power) for 30–45 seconds, until hot. Add *1 tablespoon plain flour*; stir until smooth. Gradually blend in *1 cup beef stock*. Cook on High for 3–5 minutes, until gravy boils and thickens, stirring twice. Season with *salt and pepper to taste*. If you like, add *¼ teaspoon browning sauce* for colour. Makes 1 cup. 62 kJ per tablespoon.

OLD-FASHIONED POT ROAST

Colour Index page 66. 1997 kJ per serving. Good source of vitamin A, niacin, vitamin C, iron.
Begin 2½ hours ahead.

Ingredients for 6 servings		Microwave cookware
3 teaspoons vegetable oil	1 teaspoon sugar	Oven bag with
1.5 kg rolled chuck roast	½ cup beef stock	plastic or nylon tie
2 large onions, cut into	1 bay leaf	33-cm x 23-cm
12-mm wedges	1 tablespoon chopped	baking dish
4 carrots, cut into 5-cm	fresh thyme or	
pieces	1 teaspoon dried thyme	
500 g small potatoes,	¼ teaspoon black pepper	
peeled and cut into	30 g butter or margarine,	
quarters	softened	
2 cloves garlic, crushed	2 tablespoons plain flour	
1 cup tomato purée	Salt and pepper to taste	
½ cup dry white wine	Parsley sprigs to garnish	

1 Heat oil in a 30-cm frying pan over high heat. Add rolled chuck and brown on all sides. Transfer meat to oven bag and place in baking dish.

2 Add onions, carrots, potatoes, garlic, tomato purée, wine, sugar, stock, bay leaf, thyme and pepper to meat. Close bag loosely with plastic or nylon tie (do not use metal tie), leaving small opening for venting.

3 Cook meat on High (100% power) for 5 minutes. Reduce power level to Medium-Low (30% power) and cook for 1½–2 hours longer, until meat is fork-tender, turning bag over every 20 minutes during cooking.

4 Carefully open oven bag and transfer meat to a board. Tent with foil and allow to stand for 15–20 minutes.

5 Meanwhile, empty contents of bag into baking dish; discard bay leaf. Skim fat from surface. Combine butter and flour in a bowl to form a soft paste. Stir small pieces into vegetable mixture, a little at a time, until blended. Cook on High for 6–8 minutes, until thickened, stirring twice. Season with salt and pepper.

6 Thinly slice beef across grain. Arrange on warmed plates and spoon sauce and vegetables over meat; garnish with parsley sprigs.

Quick Outdoor Cooking

Use the microwave to make outdoor cooking quick and easy: some foods can be partially cooked in the microwave and, while meat is cooking on the barbecue, the vegetable accompaniment can be cooked in the microwave.

BARBECUED BEEF WITH VEGETABLES

6 servings. 1155 kJ per serving. Good source of vitamin B$_{12}$, niacin, iron.
Begin 45 minutes ahead.

5-cm-thick slice rump
  steak (about 750 g),
  trimmed of fat
Vegetable oil
1 celery stalk,
  chopped
1 small green
  capsicum, sliced
1 small onion, thinly
  sliced
2 tablespoons water
½ cup chilli sauce
3 teaspoons plain
  flour
1½ tablespoons
  brown sugar
¼ teaspoon garlic salt
⅛ teaspoon cayenne
  pepper

1. Preheat barbecue. Score both sides of rump steak with a sharp knife; brush with oil. Place meat on greased grill of barbecue; cook for 7–10 minutes each side, until done to your liking, brushing occasionally with oil.
2. Meanwhile, place celery, capsicum and onion in a 30-cm x 20-cm baking dish. Cook, covered, on High (100% power) for 4 minutes, stirring twice.
3. Stir in water, chilli sauce, flour, brown sugar, garlic salt and cayenne pepper. Cook, covered, on Medium (50% power) for 10 minutes, rotating dish halfway through cooking.
4. Transfer steak to a carving board; with knife held at an angle almost parallel to board, cut thin slices across the width of the meat. Arrange slices on a warmed serving platter and surround with vegetable mixture. Serve immediately.

QUICK BARBECUE SAUCES

Each one of these easy sauces makes enough for barbecued steak to serve 6 people, or 6 beef ribs or hamburgers. They taste great on grilled foods as well.

Chilli Sauce: Place *½ cup bottled chilli sauce, 2 tablespoons cider vinegar, 2 tablespoons brown sugar, 2 finely chopped mild green chillies, ½ teaspoon salt* and *¼ teaspoon ground cumin* in a 2-cup glass jug. Cook on High (100% power) for 3 minutes, until bubbling, stirring twice. Makes 1 cup.

Soy and Apricot Sauce: Place *½ cup apricot jam, 2 thinly sliced spring onions, 2 tablespoons soy sauce, 1 teaspoon cider vinegar, 1 teaspoon mustard powder* and *¼ teaspoon ground ginger* in a 2-cup glass jug. Cook on High (100% power) for 2 minutes, until bubbling, stirring twice. Makes ⅔ cup.

Herb Butter Sauce: Place *60 g butter, 3 teaspoons vegetable oil, 3 teaspoons lemon juice, 2 teaspoons chopped fresh herbs, ¼ teaspoon salt* and *pinch of pepper* in a 2-cup glass jug. Cook on High (100% power) for 1 minute, stirring twice. Makes ⅓ cup.

CORNED BEEF AND CABBAGE

Colour Index page 65. 6 servings. 2177 kJ per serving. Good source of vitamin A, niacin, vitamin C, iron, fibre.
Begin 2 hours ahead.

1.75 kg corned brisket   6 black peppercorns
  or silverside   2 bay leaves
2 onions, sliced   375 ml bottle ginger ale
2 celery stalks, sliced   2½ cups water
1 carrot, sliced   1 small cabbage, cut into
8 whole allspice   8–10 wedges
10 whole cloves   Salt and pepper to taste

1. Place corned brisket, onion, celery, carrot, allspice, cloves, peppercorns, bay leaves, ginger ale and 1 cup water in a large oven bag. Close bag loosely with plastic or nylon tie (do not use metal tie), leaving vent. Place the bag in a 33-cm x 23-cm baking dish.
2. Cook on High (100% power) for 5 minutes. Reduce power level to Medium-Low (30% power) and cook for 1–1½ hours, until meat is fork-tender, turning bag over every 20 minutes.
3. Carefully open oven bag and transfer meat to a board. Tent with foil and allow to stand for 15–20 minutes. Reserve bag with vegetables and cooking liquid.
4. Meanwhile, pour remaining water into same baking dish. Add cabbage wedges. Cook, covered, on High for 11–14 minutes, until tender-crisp, stirring halfway through cooking. Add vegetables from bag and ¼ cup cooking liquid to cabbage. Cook, covered, on High for 2 minutes, or until cabbage is tender. Discard bay leaves; season with salt and pepper.
5. Thinly slice corned brisket across grain. Arrange on a warmed serving platter with vegetable mixture.

SAVOURY TOPSIDE

Colour Index page 65. 6 servings. 1168 kJ per serving. Good source of niacin, iron.
Begin 1¾ hours ahead.

1.5 kg corner topside   1 teaspoon
2 onions, sliced   Worcestershire sauce
½ cup bottled barbecue   3 teaspoons prepared
  sauce   horseradish
½ cup apple juice   ¼ teaspoon ground
3 teaspoons brown sugar   cloves

1. Place topside and all other ingredients in a large oven bag. Close bag with plastic or nylon tie (do not use metal tie). Place the bag in a 33-cm x 23-cm baking dish.
2. Cook on High (100% power) for 5 minutes. Reduce power level to Medium-Low (30% power) and cook for 1–1¼ hours, until meat is fork-tender, turning bag over every 20 minutes. Allow meat to stand in bag for 15 minutes.
3. Thinly slice topside across grain. Serve with cooking sauce spooned over meat.

STEAK FORESTIÈRE

Colour Index page 60. 4 servings. 1377 kJ per serving. Good source of niacin, iron.
Begin 25 minutes ahead.

2 rashers rindless bacon, chopped	¼ cup port
4 fillet steaks, cut 2.5 cm thick	½ cup beef stock
1 small onion, chopped	½ teaspoon cornflour dissolved in 1 teaspoon water
4 mushrooms, cut into quarters	Salt and pepper to taste
2 tomatoes, chopped	Watercress to garnish

1. Preheat browning dish according to the manufacturer's instructions. Add bacon. Cook on High (100% power) for 2–3 minutes, until browned, stirring halfway through cooking. Transfer bacon to paper towel to drain.
2. Reheat dish with bacon drippings. Place fillet steaks on dish, pressing lightly with a spatula. Cook on High for 3–4½ (4:30) minutes, turning over halfway through cooking. Transfer to a platter; loosely cover and keep warm while preparing sauce.
3. Discard all but 1 teaspoon drippings. Add onion, mushrooms and tomatoes and stir to coat. Cook on High for 3–4 minutes, until softened, stirring twice. Add port, stock and dissolved cornflour. Cook on High for 3–3½ (3:30) minutes, until thickened, stirring halfway through cooking. Season with salt and pepper.
4. Add reserved bacon to sauce; spoon over steaks. Garnish with watercress. Serve hot.

STEAK WITH MUSHROOMS AND ARTICHOKES

Colour Index page 60. 4 servings. 1566 kJ per serving. Good source of riboflavin, niacin, iron.
Begin 15 minutes ahead.

375 g mushrooms	½ teaspoon browning sauce
425 g can artichoke hearts, drained and cut in half	2 teaspoons finely chopped fresh marjoram or
2 spring onions, chopped	½ teaspoon dried marjoram
30 g butter or margarine	¼ teaspoon salt
1 tablespoon dry red wine	¼ teaspoon pepper
4 fillet steaks, cut 2.5 cm thick	Parsley sprigs to garnish

1. Place mushrooms, artichokes, spring onions, butter and red wine in a 1-litre casserole. Cook, covered, on High for 3 minutes, stirring twice. Put aside; keep warm.
2. Arrange fillet steaks on a rack set in a baking dish. Mix browning sauce with 1 teaspoon water; brush on to both sides of meat. Season with marjoram, salt and pepper. Cook on Medium-High (70% power) for 6–8 minutes for medium-rare, rotating dish halfway through cooking.
3. Place steaks on warmed plates. Spoon vegetables around meat; garnish with parsley.

Try using a browning dish to cook steak in the microwave. It will give the meat a seared look without sacrificing tenderness. Make sure you press the steak lightly with a spatula for even browning, as in the recipe for Steak au Poivre (below). Don't forget to reheat the browning dish if cooking steaks in batches.

STEAK AU POIVRE

Colour Index page 60. 1310 kJ per serving. Good source of niacin, iron.
Begin 25 minutes ahead.

Ingredients	For 4	For 2	For 1
Whole black peppercorns	2 tablespoons	1 tablespoon	2 teaspoons
Fillet steaks, cut at least 2.5 cm thick (185 g each)	4	2	1
Dry red wine	3 tablespoons	1½ tablespoons	3 teaspoons
Brandy	1 tablespoon	2 teaspoons	1 teaspoon
Worcestershire sauce	2 teaspoons	1 teaspoon	½ teaspoon
Cream	½ cup	¼ cup	2 tablespoons
Microwave cookware	Browning dish	Browning dish	Browning dish
Time on High (100% power) Steak	4½ (4:30)–6 minutes	3–4½ (4:30) minutes	2–3 minutes
Wine mixture	4 minutes	3–3½ (3:30) minutes	2–2½ (2:30) minutes

1 Place peppercorns in plastic bag; crush with a mallet or rolling pin. Evenly spread crushed peppercorns on a sheet of greaseproof paper.

2 Press both sides of each fillet steak in crushed peppercorns to coat.

3 Preheat browning dish according to the manufacturer's instructions. Arrange steaks on dish, pressing lightly with a spatula to brown evenly.

4 Cook steaks on High for time in Chart, turning over halfway through cooking. Transfer to a platter; loosely cover and keep warm while preparing sauce.

5 Add wine, brandy and Worcestershire sauce to browning dish. Cook on High for time in Chart, stirring twice. Gradually stir in cream.

6 Arrange steaks on warmed plates. Spoon sauce over meat; serve immediately.

BEEF AND SNOW PEAS IN BLACK BEAN SAUCE

Colour Index page 64. 1314 kJ per serving. Good source of vitamin B$_{12}$, niacin, iron, zinc.
Begin 35 minutes ahead.

Ingredients for 4 servings		Microwave cookware
500 g rump or fillet steak *2 tablespoons soy sauce* *2 tablespoons rice wine or dry sherry* *1 teaspoon sugar* *2 teaspoons cornflour dissolved in* *2 teaspoons cold water*	*125 g snow peas* *2 spring onions* *1 fresh green chilli* *2-cm piece green ginger* *3 teaspoons vegetable oil* *⅓ cup bottled black bean sauce* *Spring onion curls (page 134) to garnish*	Large bowl

1 Cut rump steak across grain into thin strips; place in bowl. Add soy sauce, rice wine and sugar; stir well to mix. Stir in dissolved cornflour; cover and leave to marinate for 10–15 minutes.

2 Meanwhile, cut snow peas in half crossways if large. Trim spring onions; slice thinly on the diagonal.

3 Wearing rubber gloves for protection, cut fresh chilli in half lengthways. Hold chilli under cold running water and rub to remove seeds. Slice chilli thinly; peel and finely chop ginger.

4 Heat oil in a large bowl on High (100% power) for 1 minute. Add snow peas, spring onions, chilli, ginger and black bean sauce; stir well to mix. Cook on High for 1–2 minutes, until vegetables are softened, stirring halfway through cooking.

5 Add beef and marinade. Cook on High for 2–3 minutes, until beef is fork-tender, stirring twice.

6 Spoon beef and vegetables on to a warmed serving platter or individual plates; garnish with spring onion curls. Serve immediately.

STIR-FRIED BEEF IN OYSTER SAUCE

Colour Index page 64. 4 servings. 950 kJ per serving. Good source of vitamin B$_{12}$, niacin, iron, zinc.
Begin 35 minutes ahead.

500 g rump or fillet steak
3 teaspoons soy sauce
3 teaspoons rice wine or dry sherry
3 teaspoons vegetable oil
1 red capsicum, cut into 2.5-cm pieces
2.5-cm piece green ginger, peeled and cut into matchstick-thin strips

¼ cup beef stock
2 tablespoons bottled oyster sauce
1 teaspoon cornflour dissolved in 2 teaspoons cold water
2 spring onions, thinly sliced

1. Cut rump steak across grain into thin strips; place in bowl. Add soy sauce and rice wine; stir well to mix. Cover the meat and leave to marinate in a cool place for 10–15 minutes.
2. Preheat browning dish according to the manufacturer's instructions. Coat surface of browning dish with oil.
3. With a slotted spoon, drain meat strips from marinade; place meat in browning dish. Press lightly with a spatula and stir quickly to brown meat. Cook on High (100% power) for 1–2 minutes, until beef is fork-tender. Transfer to a plate; put meat aside and keep warm while preparing sauce.
4. Add capsicum, ginger, stock, oyster sauce, marinade from beef and dissolved cornflour to drippings in browning dish. Cook on High for 1–2 minutes, until mixture boils, stirring twice. Add spring onion slices and beef strips; cook on High for 1 minute, or until beef is hot. Serve immediately.

TIMETABLE FOR COOKING BEEF
Beef may look underdone when removed from the microwave, so allow it to stand on a heatproof surface, tented with foil, to achieve its final temperature. As a general rule, remove beef from the microwave when the temperature is 5°–8° lower than temperature required.

Desired result	Remove at	Will rise to
Medium-rare	46°C–51°C	51°C–60°C
Medium	54°C–60°C	60°C–68°C
Well done	65°C–71°C	71°C–77°C

BEEF STROGANOFF

Colour Index page 60. 4 servings. 1440 kJ per serving. Good source of vitamin A, vitamin B$_{12}$, riboflavin, iron, zinc, fibre.
Begin 25 minutes ahead.

1 tablespoon vegetable oil	1 teaspoon Worcestershire sauce
500 g fillet steak, cut into thin strips	1 cup sour cream
15 g butter or margarine	Salt and pepper to taste
1 large onion, chopped	Chopped parsley to garnish
250 g mushrooms, sliced	Buttered noodles (optional)
1 tablespoon plain flour	

1. Preheat browning dish according to the manufacturer's instructions. Coat surface of dish with half the oil. Place half the steak strips on dish; quickly press with a spatula and stir to brown meat.

2. Cook steak on High (100% power) for 30–50 seconds, until sealed, turning once; transfer to a bowl. Repeat with remaining oil and steak strips. Loosely cover bowl; put aside.

3. Heat butter in a 20-cm x 20-cm baking dish on High for 1 minute, or until melted. Stir in onion and mushrooms. Cook on High for 3–4 minutes, until softened, stirring once. Stir in flour. Cook on High for 2 minutes, stirring once.

4. Gradually add Worcestershire sauce, sour cream, salt and pepper, and any juices from meat. Cook on High for 2–3 minutes, stirring often; do not boil. Add meat and cook on High for 2 minutes, or until fork-tender.

5. Season mixture with salt and pepper; garnish with parsley. Serve, if you like, with buttered noodles.

BEEF GOULASH

Colour Index page 67. 6 servings. 1239 kJ per serving. Good source of vitamin A, vitamin C, iron.
Begin 1½ hours ahead.

1½ tablespoons olive or vegetable oil	440 g can tomato purée
2 large onions, sliced	½ cup beef stock
2 green capsicums, cut into thin strips	Salt and pepper to taste
4 cloves garlic, crushed	Buttered noodles (optional)
1½ tablespoons paprika	
750 g blade or chuck steak, cut into thin strips	

1. Place oil, onions, capsicum, garlic and paprika in a 33-cm x 23-cm baking dish. Cook, covered with paper towel, on High (100% power) for 5–6 minutes, stirring twice.

2. Add beef strips, tomato purée and stock; stir. Cook, covered, on Medium (50% power) for 45–60 minutes, until meat is fork-tender, stirring occasionally. Allow to stand, loosely covered, for 5 minutes.

3. Season goulash with salt and pepper. Serve, if you like, with buttered noodles.

BEEF BOURGUIGNON

Colour Index page 66. 1880 kJ per serving. Good source of vitamin A, riboflavin, niacin, iron.
Begin 1½ hours ahead.

Ingredients for 4 servings		Microwave cookware
4 rashers rindless bacon, chopped	1 bay leaf	33-cm x 23-cm baking dish
250 g mushrooms, cut into quarters	2 teaspoons chopped fresh thyme or ½ teaspoon dried thyme	
2 carrots, diced	250 g frozen pearl onions, thawed, or tiny white pickling onions, peeled and trimmed	
2 celery stalks, diced		
500 g chuck steak, cut into 4-cm cubes	30 g butter or margarine, softened	
1 cup dry red wine	2 tablespoons plain flour	
1 cup beef stock	Salt and pepper to taste	
1 tablespoon tomato paste	Parsley sprigs to garnish	
1 teaspoon sugar		

1 Cook bacon in baking dish, covered with paper towel, on High (100% power) for 4–5 minutes, until browned, stirring twice. Transfer to paper towel to drain.

2 Stir mushrooms, carrots and celery into bacon drippings. Cook on High for 4–6 minutes, until vegetables are softened, stirring twice.

3 Add chuck steak; stir to coat with bacon drippings. Add red wine, stock, tomato paste, sugar, bay leaf and thyme. Cook, covered, on Medium (50% power) for 45–60 minutes, until meat is fork-tender, stirring occasionally.

4 Add onions to baking dish. Cook, covered, on Medium for 5 minutes. Skim fat from surface; discard bay leaf.

5 Combine butter and flour in a bowl to form a soft paste. Stir small pieces into baking dish, a little at a time, until blended. Cook on High for 3–4 minutes, until thickened and piping hot, stirring twice. Allow to stand, loosely covered, for 5 minutes.

6 Season with salt and pepper. If you like, transfer to warmed serving dish; garnish with reserved bacon and parsley.

STEAK AND KIDNEY PUDDING

Colour Index page 66. 2746 kJ per serving. Good source of vitamin A, vitamin B$_{12}$, riboflavin, niacin, calcium, iron, zinc.
Begin 1½ hours ahead.

Ingredients for 4 servings		Microwave cookware
1 tablespoon vegetable oil	¼ teaspoon pepper	Large bowl
1 onion, chopped	1 bay leaf	1-litre pudding
250 g mushrooms, cut in half	2 tablespoons chopped fresh parsley	basin
500 g rump steak, cut into thin strips	1 cup self-raising flour	
4 lamb kidneys, skinned, cored and cut into 12-mm pieces	½ cup wholemeal flour	
	1 teaspoon baking powder	
¼ cup plain flour	¼ teaspoon ground allspice	
1 cup red wine or beef stock	Salt to taste	
2 teaspoons chopped fresh thyme or ½ teaspoon dried thyme	90 g shredded beef suet	
	1 egg, beaten	
	3–4 tablespoons water	
	3 teaspoons milk	

1 Place oil, onion and mushrooms in large bowl. Cook on High (100% power) for 4–5 minutes, until vegetables are softened.

2 Toss steak and kidneys in plain flour on a plate; stir into vegetables. Cook on High for 3–4 minutes. Stir in wine, thyme, pepper and bay leaf. Cook, loosely covered, on High for 10 minutes, stirring occasionally; discard bay leaf. Stir in parsley; allow mixture to cool.

3 Meanwhile, combine self-raising flour, wholemeal flour, baking powder, allspice and salt in a bowl; stir in suet. Make well in centre; stir in egg and enough cold water to mix to soft dough. Knead dough lightly until smooth; form into a ball.

4 Cut off one-quarter of pastry. Roll out on a lightly floured surface to fit top of pudding basin; put aside. Roll out remaining pastry and use to line basin.

5 Spoon mixture into lined basin. Fold over excess pastry and dampen edges. Place reserved pastry round on top; crimp to seal. If you like, reroll trimmings and cut out shapes; place on top of pudding. Brush with milk to glaze.

6 Cover basin loosely with plastic wrap, allowing for pastry to rise. Cook on High for 8–10 minutes, until pastry is done. Allow to stand, covered, for 5 minutes. Serve hot, from basin wrapped in table napkin.

STEAK AND MUSHROOM PIE

Colour Index page 66. 8 servings. 1327 kJ per serving. Good source of iron.
Begin 1½ hours ahead or early in day.

30 g butter or margarine
4 small onions, sliced
250 g mushrooms, cut into quarters
750 g chuck steak, cut into 2.5-cm cubes
½ cup dry red wine
½ cup beef stock
2 tablespoons bottled steak sauce
1 tablespoon tomato paste

2 tablespoons cornflour dissolved in ¼ cup cold water
Salt and pepper to taste
1 sheet frozen puff pastry or shortcrust pastry, thawed
1 egg yolk
Water

1. Heat butter in a 23-cm pie plate, covered with paper towel, on High (100% power) for 45 seconds, or until melted.
2. Add onions and mushrooms. Cook on High for 5–6 minutes, until onions are tender, stirring twice.
3. Add chuck steak, red wine, stock, steak sauce and tomato paste. Stir until blended. Cook, covered, on Medium (50% power) for 40–60 minutes, until meat is fork-tender, stirring occasionally.
4. Stir in dissolved cornflour. Cook on High for 2–3 minutes, until sauce has thickened, stirring halfway through cooking. Season with salt and pepper. Allow to cool completely.
5. Preheat conventional oven to 200°C.
6. Gently roll pastry sheet on to rolling pin; place loosely over cooled meat mixture. Trim edge of pastry with kitchen scissors, leaving 2.5-cm overhang. Fold overhang under; then bring up over plate rim; pinch to form high edge on pie, then make decorative edge of your choice (page 336).
7. Cut several slits in pastry top. Beat egg yolk with 1 teaspoon water; brush over pastry. If you like, reroll pastry scraps and, with decorative cutter, cut out shapes; place on top of pie. Brush cut-outs with egg-yolk mixture. Bake pie conventionally for 20 minutes, or until crust is golden and filling is hot.

Decorating the top of the pie

With the tip of a small sharp knife, slash pastry top to allow steam to escape.

Cut out leaves or other shapes and decorate top of glazed pie; glaze again.

TRADITIONAL BEEF STEW

Colour Index page 67. 6 servings. 1574 kJ per serving. Good source of vitamin A, niacin, vitamin C, iron, fibre.
Begin 1¾ hours ahead.

30 g butter or margarine	3 small turnips, cut into
2 large onions, cut into	5-cm chunks
wedges	750 g chuck steak, cut
4 carrots, cut into	into 4-cm cubes
7.5-cm pieces, then into	1½ cups beef stock
quarters lengthways	½ teaspoon dried thyme
3 celery stalks, cut into	1 bay leaf
7.5-cm pieces, then	2 tablespoons tomato
in half lengthways	paste
6 small potatoes, cut in	Salt and pepper to taste
half	

1. Heat butter in a 33-cm x 23-cm baking dish, covered with paper towel, on High (100% power) for 45 seconds, or until melted.
2. Add onions, carrots, celery, potatoes and turnips. Cook on High for 5–6 minutes, until softened, stirring twice.
3. Add beef cubes, stock, thyme, bay leaf and tomato paste. Cook, covered, on Medium (50% power) for 45–60 minutes, until meat is fork-tender, stirring occasionally. Allow to stand, loosely covered, for 10–15 minutes.
4. Discard bay leaf; season stew with salt and pepper. Serve hot.

BEEF CARBONNADE

Colour Index page 67. 8 servings. 1122 kJ per serving. Good source of iron.
Begin 1½ hours ahead.

4 rashers rindless	3 teaspoons browning
bacon, chopped	sauce
3 large onions, thinly	1 tablespoon cornflour
sliced	dissolved in
1 kg chuck steak, cut	2 tablespoons cold
into 4-cm cubes	water
375 ml can beer	1 tablespoon red wine
1 cup beef stock	vinegar
1 bay leaf	Salt and pepper to taste

1. Cook bacon in a 33-cm x 23-cm baking dish, covered with paper towel, on High (100% power) for 4–5 minutes, until browned, stirring twice. Transfer to paper towel to drain.
2. Stir onions into bacon drippings. Cook on High for 7–10 minutes, until onions are softened, stirring occasionally.
3. Add beef cubes, beer, stock, bay leaf and browning sauce to onions. Cook, covered, on Medium (50% power) for 45–60 minutes, until meat is fork-tender, stirring occasionally.
4. Skim fat. Stir in dissolved cornflour. Cook on High for 3–4 minutes, until thickened slightly, stirring twice. Allow to stand, loosely covered, for 10–15 minutes.
5. Discard bay leaf; stir vinegar, salt and pepper into carbonnade just before serving.

Meal in Minutes *for 8 people*

Superfast Barbecue

Mexican Dip (page 112)
with crudités and potato crisps
Barbecued Chicken (page 188)
Barbecued Beef with Vegetables (page 206)
Corn-on-the-Cob with Flavoured Butters (page 263)
Hot French bread
Vanilla Ice Cream (page 332)
and chocolate ice cream (bought)
Strawberries and melon slices
Lemonade

PREPARATION TIMETABLE

1 day ahead:	*Make Vanilla Ice Cream; store in freezer. Make double quantity of Mexican Dip; cover and refrigerate.*
2 hours ahead:	*Prepare vegetables for crudités; store in plastic bags in refrigerator. Prepare strawberries and melon, arrange on attractive serving platter and cover; if you like, store in refrigerator.*
1 hour ahead:	*Prepare Barbecued Chicken up to the end of step 2, to be finished later on barbecue. Assemble Mexican Dip, crudités and crisps on a plate. Preheat barbecue and cook Barbecued Beef with Vegetables.*
15 minutes before serving:	*Brush chicken with barbecue sauce and complete cooking on barbecue. Cook Corn-on-the-Cob and melt Flavoured Butters as in recipe instructions. Heat French bread in microwave on High (100% power) for 1 minute.*

INDIVIDUAL MEAT LOAVES

Colour Index page 61. 1967 kJ per serving. Good source of riboflavin, niacin, calcium, iron.
Begin 25 minutes ahead.

Ingredients	For 4	For 2	For 1
Cucumber (about 250 g), peeled	1	½	¼
Beef mince	500 g	250 g	125 g
Fresh breadcrumbs	¾ cup	⅓ cup	2 tablespoons
Grated onion	1 tablespoon	2 teaspoons	1 teaspoon
Salt	½ teaspoon	¼ teaspoon	⅛ teaspoon
Pepper	¼ teaspoon	⅛ teaspoon	to taste
Eggs/Water	1 egg	2 tablespoons	1 tablespoon
Processed cheese slices	8 slices	4 slices	2 slices
Salad and parsley sprigs	garnish	garnish	garnish
Microwave cookware	30-cm x 20-cm baking dish	20-cm x 20-cm baking dish	20-cm x 20-cm baking dish
Time on Medium-High (70% power)			
Meat loaves	9 minutes	4 minutes	2 minutes
With cheese topping	2 minutes	1 minute	30 seconds
Standing time	3 minutes	2 minutes	2 minutes

1 Cut cucumber in half lengthways. Remove seeds. Cut a few slices for garnish; reserve. Coarsely shred remaining cucumber.

2 Combine shredded cucumber, beef mince, breadcrumbs, onion, salt, pepper, egg or water (see Chart) in a bowl. Divide mixture into the required number of servings.

3 Reserve half the cheese slices; fold each remaining slice into a 4-cm x 2-cm x 1-cm chunk.

4 Shape each portion of meat around a chunk of cheese to make a 10-cm x 5-cm loaf. Arrange loaves in baking dish (see Chart). Cook, covered loosely with greaseproof paper, on Medium-High for time in Chart.

5 Remove greaseproof paper; rotate dish. Top each loaf with 1 slice remaining cheese. Cook on Medium-High for time in Chart.

6 Allow meat loaves to stand, covered, for time in Chart. Arrange on a warmed serving platter; garnish with salad, parsley and reserved cucumber slices.

MEAT LOAF MILANESE

Colour Index page 63. 6 servings. 1465 kJ per serving. Good source of niacin, vitamin C, iron, fibre.
Begin 45 minutes ahead.

500 g small new potatoes, cut in half
250 g green beans, topped, tailed and cut in half
¼ cup water
1 small onion, chopped
1 celery stalk, chopped
3 teaspoons lemon juice
750 g beef mince
½ cup dried breadcrumbs
1 teaspoon browning sauce
1 egg, lightly beaten
⅔ cup dry red wine
1 tablespoon shredded fresh basil or
1 teaspoon dried basil
425 g can tomatoes, chopped
1 teaspoon sugar

1. Place potatoes, beans and water in a 1-litre casserole. Cook, covered, on High (100% power) for 12 minutes, or until potatoes are tender, stirring twice. Drain; allow to stand, covered.
2. Place onion, celery and lemon juice in a 2.5-litre bowl. Cook, covered, on High for 3 minutes. Add beef mince, breadcrumbs, browning sauce, egg, ½ cup wine and half the basil; mix well. Shape mixture into a 20-cm x 10-cm loaf in a 30-cm x 20-cm baking dish.
3. Cook meat, covered loosely with greaseproof paper, on Medium-High (70% power) for 15 minutes, rotating dish halfway through cooking. Allow to stand, covered, while preparing sauce.
4. Place tomatoes with their liquid, sugar, remaining wine and remaining basil in a medium bowl. Cook, covered, on High for 5 minutes, or until bubbling, stirring twice.
5. Arrange meat loaf with vegetables on a warmed serving platter. Serve tomato and basil sauce separately.

MEAT LOAF VARIATIONS

Cheesy Meat Loaf: Combine *500 g beef mince, ¾ cup fresh breadcrumbs (1½ slices), 1 egg, 1 tablespoon grated onion, 1 teaspoon chopped fresh oregano or ¼ teaspoon dried oregano* and *¼ teaspoon pepper.* Pat meat into a loaf shape in a 30-cm x 20-cm baking dish. Cook, covered loosely with greaseproof paper, on Medium-High (70% power) for 10–12 minutes, rotating dish once. Remove greaseproof paper and rotate dish. Top with *4 slices processed cheese* and *1 peeled and sliced tomato.* Cook on Medium-High for 2 minutes. Allow to stand for 3 minutes.

Pineapple Meat Loaf: Prepare as for Cheesy Meat Loaf (above), omitting oregano, cheese and tomato. Top with slices from *225 g can pineapple slices.* Cook on Medium-High for 2 minutes. Allow to stand for 3 minutes.

CHEESEBURGERS

Colour Index page 60. 4 servings. 1700 kJ per serving. Good source of riboflavin, niacin, calcium, iron.
Begin 25 minutes ahead.

1 onion, sliced	*2 tablespoons iced water*
125 g champignons, sliced	*2 teaspoons cornflour*
30 g butter or margarine	*½ teaspoon ground black pepper*
1¼ teaspoons paprika	*1 teaspoon browning sauce*
500 g beef mince	
90 g Cheddar, Fontina or Gruyère cheese, grated (¾ cup) or 60 g blue vein cheese, crumbled (½ cup)	*Parsley sprigs to garnish*
	4 slices white bread, toasted (optional)

1. Place onion, champignons, half the butter and ¼ teaspoon paprika in a 30-cm round baking dish. Cook, covered, on High (100% power) for 5–6 minutes, until vegetables are tender, stirring twice. Spoon mixture into a bowl; put aside.
2. Combine beef mince, cheese and iced water in a large bowl. Shape into 4 patties. Mix cornflour, pepper and remaining paprika on a sheet of greaseproof paper. Place remaining butter in a 1-cup glass jug. Heat on High for 30 seconds, or until melted; stir in browning sauce. Brush on patties; coat with seasoned cornflour.
3. Place patties in same baking dish used to cook vegetables. Cook, covered loosely with grease-proof paper, on Medium-High (70% power) for 5 minutes, rotating dish halfway through cooking. Spoon vegetables over burgers. Cook on Medium-High for 1 minute longer, or until hot.
4. Garnish cheeseburgers with parsley. Serve, if you like, on toast.

HEATING HAMBURGER BUNS
Heating hamburger buns in the microwave is fast and easy; the same technique can be used for heating pita bread. Use paper towel when heating bread, rolls and other baked goods as it absorbs moisture and prevents sogginess.

Wrap 2 hamburger buns in paper towel. Place on a paper plate or directly on oven floor. Cook on High (100% power) for 12–17 seconds, until buns are warm. For 1 bun, heat on High for 10–15 seconds.

Minced meat of all kinds works well for burgers cooked in the microwave, although lean meat is best if you are counting kilojoules. When making Surprise Burgers (below), take care not to overhandle the meat, or the end result will be rubbery and tough.

SURPRISE BURGERS

Colour Index page 60. 1591 kJ per serving. Good source of niacin, iron.
Begin 20 minutes ahead.

Ingredients	For 4	For 2	For 1
Beef mince	*500 g*	*250 g*	*125 g*
Water	*3 teaspoons*	*1½ teaspoons*	*¾ teaspoon*
Salt	*½ teaspoon*	*¼ teaspoon*	*⅛ teaspoon*
Pepper	*½ teaspoon*	*¼ teaspoon*	*⅛ teaspoon*
Canned pimientos, diced	*¼ cup*	*2 tablespoons*	*1 tablespoon*
Stoned black olives, thinly sliced	*4 large*	*2 large*	*1 large*
Bottled chilli sauce	*¼ cup*	*2 tablespoons*	*1 tablespoon*
Hamburger buns	*4*	*2*	*1*
Microwave cookware	30-cm x 20-cm baking dish with rack	23-cm x 23-cm baking dish with rack	23-cm pie plate with rack
Time on High (100% power)			
Burgers	3 minutes	2 minutes	1 minute
After rotating	1½ (1:30)–3 minutes	1½ (1:30)–2 minutes	1½ (1:30) minutes

1 Mix beef mince, water, salt and pepper in a bowl; divide meat into 2 portions per serving.

2 Shape each portion into an 8.5-cm patty; flatten on a sheet of greaseproof paper. Combine pimientos, olives and chilli sauce in a bowl.

3 Top half the patties with an equal amount of pimiento mixture, to within 6 mm of edges.

4 Place a plain patty on top of each patty with filling. With fingers, gently press edges together to seal.

5 Place burgers on rack in baking dish or pie plate (see Chart). Cook on High for time in Chart.

6 Turn burgers over with a spatula; rotate dish. Cook on High for time in Chart, until burgers are done to your liking. Serve in hamburger buns.

PARTY BURGERS

Colour Index page 67. 444 kJ per serving. Low in cholesterol.
Begin early in day.

For easy entertaining, dishes such as Party Burgers can be prepared
and frozen, then removed from the freezer and cooked in the
microwave just before serving.

Ingredients for 12 servings		Microwave cookware
250 g sirloin steak, minced	2 teaspoons shredded fresh basil or ½ teaspoon dried basil	Platter 30-cm x 20-cm baking dish with rack
30 g Cheddar cheese, grated, or blue vein cheese, crumbled (¼ cup)	6 slices white bread 45 g butter or margarine, melted	
½ teaspoon browning sauce	Garnishes: lettuce and cherry tomato slices;	
½ teaspoon Worcestershire sauce	small white onion slices; canned sliced champignons and	
2 tablespoons chopped fresh parsley	chopped pimiento; grated cheese and	
2 teaspoons crushed black peppercorns	chopped cooked bacon	

1 Combine sirloin
mince, cheese,
browning sauce and
Worcestershire sauce
in a bowl. Shape into a
15-cm x 4-cm log; wrap in
greaseproof paper.
Freeze for 1 hour, or
until firm.

2 Combine parsley,
pepper and basil in a
bowl; put aside. Using a
5-cm round biscuit
cutter, cut 2 rounds from
each slice of bread; toast.
Dip edges of toast in
melted butter, then coat
in parsley mixture. Place
in a freezer container;
cover and freeze.

3 When meat is firm,
cut crossways into
twelve 12-mm slices.
Freeze patties until firm
on a tray lined with
greaseproof paper. Place
in a freezer container;
cover and freeze.

4 About 15 minutes
before serving,
arrange toast rounds in a
single layer on platter.
Heat on High (100%
power) for 20 seconds, or
until thawed; put aside.

5 Place burgers on
rack in baking dish.
Cook on Medium (50%
power) for 5–5½ (5:30)
minutes for medium-
rare, rotating dish
halfway through cooking.

6 Arrange each burger
on a toast round.
Garnish with lettuce,
tomato slices, onion
slices, sliced
champignons and
chopped pimiento, or
cheese and bacon. Heat
cheese-topped burgers
just until cheese melts.

DINNER BURGERS

Colour Index page 60. 2 servings. 1440 kJ per
serving. Good source of vitamin A, niacin, calcium,
iron.
Begin 25 minutes ahead.

1 large carrot	¼ teaspoon black pepper
1 small zucchini	½ teaspoon browning
45 g butter or margarine	sauce
250 g beef mince	2 small onions, sliced
1 teaspoon cornflour	2 tablespoons dry red
½ teaspoon paprika	wine

1. With vegetable peeler, shred carrot and zucchini. Place in a 1-litre casserole. Add 1 tablespoon butter; cover and put aside.
2. Shape beef mince into two 2-cm-thick oval
patties. Mix cornflour, paprika and pepper on a
sheet of greaseproof paper. Heat 2 teaspoons
butter in a 1-cup glass jug on High (100% power)
for 30 seconds, or until melted; stir in browning
sauce. Brush on patties; coat with seasoned
cornflour.
3. Place burgers, onions and remaining butter
in a 20-cm x 20-cm baking dish. Cook, covered
loosely with greaseproof paper, on Medium-High
(70% power) for 4–5 minutes for medium-rare,
rotating dish halfway through cooking. Transfer
burgers to a serving platter; keep warm.
4. Stir wine into baking dish. Cook, covered, on
High for 4 minutes; keep warm.
5. Cook shredded vegetables, covered, on High
for 2–3 minutes, until tender-crisp, stirring
halfway through cooking. Spoon onion mixture
over burgers and accompany with vegetables.

KEEMA CURRY

Colour Index page 61. 4 servings. 1457 kJ per
serving. Low in salt. Good source of vitamin A,
riboflavin, thiamine, niacin, calcium, iron, fibre.
Begin 25 minutes ahead.

3 teaspoons vegetable oil	3 teaspoons ground
1 large onion, sliced	coriander
2 cloves garlic, chopped	½ teaspoon chilli
1 green capsicum, chopped	powder
2-cm piece green ginger, finely chopped	500 g beef mince
1 teaspoon garam masala	4 tomatoes, peeled, seeded and chopped
1 teaspoon turmeric	250 g frozen peas, thawed

1. Place oil, onion, garlic, capsicum and ginger
in a large bowl. Cook on High (100% power) for
3–4 minutes, until softened, stirring once.
2. Stir in garam masala, turmeric, coriander
and chilli powder. Cook on High for 2 minutes.
3. Add beef mince to vegetable mixture. Cook on
High for 5 minutes, or until beef is no longer
pink, stirring twice.
4. Stir in tomatoes. Cook on High for 10 minutes. Stir in peas. Cook on High for 5 minutes, or
until peas are hot.

CHILLI CON CARNE

Colour Index page 61. 6 servings. 1047 kJ per serving. Good source of vitamin A, iron, fibre. Begin 25 minutes ahead.

500 g beef mince	425 g can tomatoes,
1 onion, chopped	chopped with their
3 cloves garlic, crushed	juice
1 green capsicum,	2 teaspoons tomato
chopped	paste
2 tablespoons chilli	½ cup water
powder	440 g can red kidney
1 tablespoon chopped	beans
fresh oregano or	Sour cream, grated
1 teaspoon dried	Cheddar cheese and
oregano	chopped fresh
1 bay leaf	coriander to garnish
2 teaspoons ground	Corn chips (optional)
cumin (optional)	

1. Place beef mince in a colander set over a large bowl. Cook on High (100% power) for 4 minutes, or until beef is no longer pink, stirring twice. Discard all but 3 tablespoons drippings from bowl.
2. Combine drippings, beef, onion, garlic, capsicum, chilli powder, oregano and bay leaf in a 2-litre casserole. Add cumin, if you like. Cook on High for 3 minutes, stirring twice.
3. Add chopped tomatoes, tomato paste and water; stir well to combine. Cook, covered with paper towel, on High for 5 minutes, stirring twice; discard bay leaf.
4. Drain and rinse kidney beans; stir into meat. Cook, covered with paper towel, on High for 3 minutes, stirring halfway through cooking.
5. Ladle chilli into individual bowls; garnish with sour cream, cheese and chopped coriander. Serve, if you like, with corn chips.

MEXICAN BEEF CASSEROLE

Colour Index page 61. 6 servings. 2600 kJ per serving. Good source of riboflavin, niacin, iron. Begin 25 minutes ahead.

750 g beef mince	1 cup bottled taco sauce
1 onion, chopped	1 cup canned tomatoes,
1 clove garlic, crushed	chopped
185 g stoned black	2 x 50 g packets corn
olives, drained and	chips
sliced	125 g tasty cheese,
1 cup frozen	grated (1 cup)
whole-kernel corn,	Coriander sprigs to
thawed	garnish

1. Place beef mince, onion and garlic in a colander set over a large bowl. Cook on High (100% power) for 5–6 minutes, until beef is no longer pink, stirring twice. Discard drippings. Add ¾ cup olives, corn and taco sauce to meat.
2. Place alternate layers of chopped tomatoes, corn chips, meat mixture and cheese in a 33-cm x 23-cm baking dish. Cook, covered, on High (100% power) for 10–12 minutes.
3. Garnish with remaining olives and coriander. Serve hot.

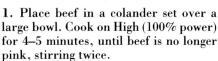

Taste-tempting light meals can be made in just a matter of minutes with a microwave oven. Use leftovers from Chilli Beef Dinner (below) or Chilli con Carne (left) to make the tacos or the pie.

CHILLI BEEF DINNER

4 servings.
Begin 20 minutes ahead.

500 g beef mince
3 tablespoons tomato sauce
2 teaspoons chilli powder
3 teaspoons dried onion flakes
½ teaspoon garlic salt
250 g can refried beans
Assorted accompaniments:
  sour cream, radishes, fresh
  coriander, corn chips, taco sauce

1. Place beef in a colander set over a large bowl. Cook on High (100% power) for 4–5 minutes, until beef is no longer pink, stirring twice.
2. Discard drippings. Place meat in bowl. Stir in tomato sauce, chilli powder, onion flakes, garlic salt and refried beans. Cook on High for 4–6 minutes, until hot, stirring twice. Serve with accompaniments.

CHILLI TACO

2 servings.
Begin 5 minutes ahead.

2 taco shells
3 tablespoons cooked chilli
½ cup grated Cheddar cheese
Lettuce, tomato slices and parsley
  sprigs to garnish

1. Heat taco shells on a plate on High (100% power) for 1 minute. Spoon equal amounts of chilli into each shell. Heat on High for 1 minute, or until hot.
2. Sprinkle cheese over chilli; arrange on individual plates with lettuce leaf and tomato slice. Garnish with parsley. Serve immediately.

CHILLI PIE

2 servings.
Begin 5 minutes ahead.

1 cup cooked chilli
½ cup drained canned corn kernels
3 tablespoons grated Cheddar cheese
3 tablespoons crumbled corn chips
Parsley sprig to garnish

1. Place chilli in individual soup plates. Top with corn, cheese and corn chips. Cook on High (100% power) for 3½ (3:30)–4 minutes, until hot.
2. Garnish with parsley. Serve hot.

The microwave oven can really come into its own
when you want to, or need to, serve a nutritious snack in a hurry.
And these recipes are so simple to prepare, even a child can try them
(for safety tips when children are using the microwave, see
Children in the Kitchen, page 372).

SUPERQUICK BURGERS

2 servings.
Begin 10 minutes
ahead.

250 g beef mince
2 hamburger buns
2 lettuce leaves
2 slices tomato
Potato crisps

1 Shape beef into 2 patties, about 2.5-cm thick. Line a 23-cm pie plate with paper towel; place patties on top.

2 Cook, covered with paper towel, on High (100% power) for 2–3 minutes, turning over halfway through cooking. Allow to stand for 2 minutes. Place burgers in buns with lettuce and tomato. Serve with crisps.

EASY PIZZAS

4 servings.
Begin 10 minutes
ahead.

1 cup bottled Italian
tomato sauce
4 muffins, split and
toasted
8 slices mozzarella
cheese
Assorted pizza
toppings: peperoni,
olives, grated
Parmesan or other
cheese, sliced
champignons, red or
green capsicum strips

1 Spread 1 tablespoon tomato sauce over each muffin half. Add 1 slice mozzarella cheese and toppings of your choice.

2 Place 4 pizza halves on a paper plate. Cook on High (100% power) for 1–2 minutes, until cheese melts. Repeat with remaining 4 halves.

EASY SLOPPY JOES

4 servings.
Begin 15 minutes
ahead.

500 g beef mince
1 tablespoon dried
onion flakes
½ teaspoon garlic salt
¼ teaspoon pepper
½ cup bottled barbecue
sauce
2 tablespoons dried
parsley
4 hamburger buns
Lettuce leaves and
cherry tomatoes

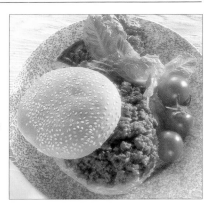

1 Combine beef mince and onion in a colander set over a large bowl. Cook on High (100% power) for 4–5 minutes, until beef is no longer pink, stirring twice.

2 Discard drippings. Place meat in bowl with garlic salt, pepper, barbecue sauce and parsley. Cook on Medium (50% power) for 4–5 minutes. Spoon on to buns and serve with lettuce and tomatoes.

HAM AND CHEESE MELTS

2 servings.
Begin 5 minutes ahead.

4 slices white bread,
toasted
2 teaspoons mild
mustard
2 slices ham
2 slices Swiss cheese
2 gherkins
2 cherry tomatoes

1 Spread 2 slices toast with an equal amount of mustard. Place 1 slice ham on each. Cover with 1 slice cheese and remaining toast slice.

2 Place sandwiches on paper plates. Cook on High (100% power) for 20–30 seconds, just until cheese melts. Cut in half and serve with gherkins and cherry tomatoes.

PASTA BOLOGNESE

Colour Index page 66. 6 servings. 1750 kJ per serving. Good source of vitamin A, thiamine, niacin, vitamin C, iron, fibre.
Begin 55 minutes ahead.

500 g beef mince	825 g can tomatoes,
3 teaspoons olive or	chopped with their
vegetable oil	juice
2 onions, chopped	90 g tomato paste
1 large carrot, chopped	½ cup water
2 celery stalks, chopped	2 cloves garlic, crushed
1 tablespoon shredded	250 g large pasta shells
fresh basil or	Grated Parmesan cheese
1 teaspoon dried basil	(optional)
1 tablespoon chopped	Parsley sprigs to garnish
fresh oregano or	
1 teaspoon dried	
oregano	

1. Place beef mince in a colander set over a large bowl. Cook on High (100% power) for 5–6 minutes, until beef is no longer pink, stirring twice; discard drippings from bowl.
2. Combine oil, onions, carrot, celery, basil and oregano in a 30-cm x 20-cm baking dish. Cook on High for 6 minutes, stirring twice.
3. Add beef, tomatoes, tomato paste and water to vegetables; stir well. Cook on High for 10 minutes, or until slightly thickened, turning twice. Stir in garlic. Cook on High for 5 minutes.
4. Meanwhile, cook pasta shells conventionally; drain.
5. Stir pasta into beef mixture; mix well. Sprinkle, if you like, with Parmesan cheese. Cook, covered loosely with greaseproof paper, on High for 7–10 minutes, until hot. Allow to stand, loosely covered, for 10 minutes.
6. Sprinkle, if you like, with Parmesan cheese; garnish with parsley. Serve immediately.

PREPARING MINCED MEAT

Precooking is an ideal way to prepare minced meat for use in casseroles and stews because it reduces the kilojoule count by getting rid of excess fat, making the meat healthier for you.

Place raw minced meat in a plastic or other microwave-safe colander set over a bowl.

Cook mince on High (100% power) until no longer pink, stirring twice to break up pieces. Discard drippings from bowl.

The microwave oven can produce traditional slow-cooking dishes, like Stuffed Cabbage (below), in a fraction of the usual time and without losing that authentic taste. The combination of minced meat, rice, raisins and seasonings makes for a flavoursome stuffing that can be varied by adding different herbs.

STUFFED CABBAGE

Colour Index page 65. 2399 kJ per serving. Good source of vitamin A, thiamine, niacin, vitamin C, calcium, iron, fibre.
Begin 55 minutes ahead.

Ingredients for 4 servings		Microwave cookware
1 cabbage (about 1 kg)	Pepper to taste	33-cm x 23-cm
1 large onion, finely	825 g can tomatoes,	baking dish
chopped	chopped with their	
1 large carrot, finely	juice	
chopped	2 beef stock cubes,	
½ cup long-grain rice	crumbled	
½ cup seedless raisins	⅛ teaspoon ground	
500 g beef mince	cloves	
1 tablespoon bottled	3 teaspoons brown sugar	
steak sauce	½ teaspoon cider vinegar	
¼ teaspoon ground	⅓ cup tomato paste	
allspice	Parsley sprigs to garnish	

1 Discard tough outer leaves from cabbage. Remove 8 large leaves for cabbage rolls (reserve remaining cabbage to use another day).

2 Place cabbage leaves in baking dish. Cook, covered, on High (100% power) for 3–4 minutes, until leaves wilt. Transfer to paper towel to cool while preparing stuffing.

3 Combine onion, carrot, rice, raisins, beef mince, steak sauce, allspice and pepper in a bowl.

4 With a small, sharp knife, remove rib from each cooled cabbage leaf. Place an equal amount of beef mixture on the centre of each leaf.

5 Fold 2 sides of leaf towards centre over meat, overlapping edges. Starting at a narrow edge, roll up to completely enclose filling. Arrange rolls, seam side down, in baking dish.

6 Combine tomatoes, stock cubes, cloves, brown sugar, vinegar and tomato paste in a jug. Pour over cabbage rolls. Cook, covered, on Medium (50% power) for 30–40 minutes, until fork-tender, spooning sauce over and rotating dish halfway through cooking. Arrange cabbage rolls on a warmed serving platter. Spoon sauce around rolls; garnish with parsley. Serve immediately.

Meal in Minutes *for 8 people*

Mexican Buffet

Margaritas
Guacamole (below) with fresh vegetables and fruit, olives and corn chips
Chilli con Carne (page 215)
Spicy Pork Turnovers (page 230)
Mexican Pancakes (page 195)
Lime or lemon sorbet (bought)
Mexican Wedding Biscuits (page 365)

PREPARATION TIMETABLE	
1 day ahead:	*Make double quantity of Mexican Wedding Biscuits; store in an airtight container. Cook Chilli con Carne; cover and refrigerate. Check bar supplies and ice for Margaritas.*
Early in day:	*Make double quantity of Spicy Pork Turnovers up to the end of step 5; do not bake. Prepare Mexican Pancakes up to the end of step 4 and prepare sauce as in step 5. Cover pancakes and sauce and refrigerate. Prepare fresh vegetables; store in plastic bags in refrigerator.*
2 hours ahead:	*Prepare glasses for Margaritas by dipping rims in lime juice and salt. Make Guacamole; cover and refrigerate.*
15 minutes before serving:	*Complete Spicy Pork Turnovers. Reheat Chilli con Carne on High (100% power), until bubbling. Pour sauce over pancakes and finish in microwave as in recipe. Assemble Guacamole, vegetables, fruit, olives and corn chips. Make the Margaritas as the guests arrive.*

GUACAMOLE

Set the Mexican mood when your guests arrive by serving spicy hot Guacamole as a first course.

Peel *2 tomatoes* (page 30), then dice. Chop *1 onion*. Crush *2 cloves garlic*. Cut *4 avocados* in half lengthways; remove seeds and peel. In bowl, mash avocado flesh with *¼ cup lemon juice*. Add tomatoes, onion, garlic, *3–4 drops Tabasco sauce* and *salt* to taste; stir well to combine. Spoon into a serving bowl; garnish with *sliced fresh green chillies* and *coriander sprigs* if you like.

Lamb

ZESTY LEG OF LAMB

Colour Index page 64. 8 servings. 925 kJ per serving.
Good source of niacin, iron.
Begin 55 minutes ahead.

1.75 kg–2 kg leg of lamb	1 tablespoon red wine
¼ cup mango chutney	vinegar
2 tablespoons French	1 tablespoon
mustard	Worcestershire sauce
2 cloves garlic, crushed	Mint sprig to garnish

1. Trim large pieces of fat from lamb. Place leg on a rack set in a 33-cm x 23-cm baking dish.
2. Combine chutney, mustard, garlic, vinegar and Worcestershire sauce in a 2-cup glass jug. Cook on High (100% power) for 3–4 minutes, until bubbling, stirring halfway through cooking. With brush, coat lamb with half the mixture.
3. Shield thin (shank) end of leg with smooth strips of foil. Cook on High for 5 minutes. Reduce power level to Medium (50% power) and cook for 15–20 minutes, until a thermometer inserted in centre reaches 57°C for medium-rare, removing foil, turning meat over and brushing with remaining mixture halfway through cooking.
4. Transfer lamb to a platter. Allow to stand, tented with foil, for 10–15 minutes; temperature will reach 65°C–68°C.
5. Garnish with mint. Serve with vegetables of your choice.

LAMB PILAF

Colour Index page 69. 8 servings. 1197 kJ per serving. Good source of calcium, iron.
Begin 1 hour ahead.

30 g butter or margarine	155 g frozen peas,
1 large onion, chopped	thawed
1 green capsicum,	Salt and pepper to taste
chopped	1 cup natural yoghurt
1½ cups long-grain rice	2 spring onions, thinly
1½ tablespoons curry	sliced
powder	½ small cucumber, diced
3 cups chicken stock	Mint sprigs to garnish
2 cups cooked roast	
lamb, cut into 4-cm	
cubes	

1. Heat butter in a 33-cm x 23-cm baking dish, covered with paper towel, on High (100% power) for 45 seconds, or until melted.
2. Stir in onion, capsicum, rice and curry powder. Cook on High for 3–4 minutes, until softened, stirring halfway through cooking.
3. Add stock and lamb. Cook on Medium (50% power) for 20–30 minutes, until rice is tender and liquid is absorbed, stirring occasionally.
4. Stir in peas. Season with salt and pepper. Cook, covered, on Medium for 5 minutes. Allow to stand, covered, for 10 minutes.
5. Meanwhile, combine yoghurt, spring onions and cucumber in a bowl. Season.
6. Top each portion of pilaf with yoghurt sauce; garnish with mint.

For roast lamb that is medium-rare, remove the meat from the microwave when its temperature registers 57°C. Left to stand, tented with foil, the internal temperature will rise to 65°C–68°C. For a well-done roast, remove the lamb from the microwave when the temperature registers 65°C–71°C. Left to stand, the temperature will rise to 79°C.

APRICOT-GLAZED RACK OF LAMB

Colour Index page 65. 3470 kJ per serving. Good source of vitamin A, niacin, iron, fibre.
Begin 45 minutes ahead.

Ingredients for 4 servings		Microwave cookware
½ teaspoon browning sauce	3 teaspoons lemon juice	30-cm x 20-cm baking dish with rack
1 teaspoon water	3 teaspoons French mustard	Large bowl
1.25 kg lamb rack (ask butcher to cut through backbone for easier carving)	¼ teaspoon salt	
	2 x 425 g cans small whole carrots, drained	
½ cup apricot jam	Watercress sprigs to garnish	

1 Combine browning sauce and water in a bowl. Brush on lamb rack. Shield bone ends of cutlets with smooth strips of foil.

2 Place lamb, fat side up, on rack in baking dish. Cook, covered loosely with greaseproof paper, on Medium-High (70% power) for 8 minutes.

3 Meanwhile, combine apricot jam, lemon juice, mustard and salt in a bowl. Spoon ¼ cup apricot mixture into large bowl; put aside.

4 Discard foil from bone ends. Cook on Medium-High for 7–8 minutes longer for medium-rare, until a meat thermometer inserted in centre reaches 57°C. Brush meat with apricot mixture.

5 Allow lamb to stand, tented with foil, on a heatproof surface for 5–10 minutes; temperature will reach 65°C–68°C. Meanwhile, stir carrots into reserved apricot mixture in large bowl. Cook, covered, on High (100% power) for 3–5 minutes, until hot, stirring twice.

6 Place lamb rack on a warmed serving platter. Spoon carrots around roast; garnish with watercress sprigs. Decorate bone ends, if you like, with paper cutlet frills.

MARINATED CUTLETS WITH MINTED PEAS

Colour Index page 69. 908 kJ per serving. Good source of niacin, zinc, fibre. Begin early in day or 1 day ahead.

Ingredients	For 4	For 2	For 1
Apple jelly	*2 tablespoons*	*1 tablespoon*	*2 teaspoons*
French mustard	*2 tablespoons*	*1 tablespoon*	*2 teaspoons*
Garlic, crushed	*2 cloves*	*1 clove*	*½ clove*
Mint leaves, chopped	*2 tablespoons*	*1 tablespoon*	*2 teaspoons*
Lamb cutlets (2.5 cm thick)	*8*	*4*	*2*
Frozen peas	*250 g*	*125 g*	*60 g*
Water	*2 tablespoons*	*1 tablespoon*	*2 teaspoons*
Butter or margarine	*15 g*	*1½ teaspoons*	*¾ teaspoon*
Mint sprigs	*garnish*	*garnish*	*garnish*
Microwave cookware	Browning dish 6-cup soufflé dish	Browning dish 6-cup soufflé dish	Browning dish 23-cm pie plate
Time on High (100% power)			
Cutlets	3–4½ (4:30) minutes each batch	3–4½ (4:30) minutes	2–2½ (2:30) minutes
Peas	4–5 minutes	2½ (2:30)–3½ (3:30) minutes	1½ (1:30)–2 minutes

1 Combine apple jelly, mustard, garlic and half the mint in a dish large enough to hold cutlets in a single layer.

2 Add lamb cutlets, turning to coat. Cover dish and refrigerate for 2 hours or overnight, turning cutlets occasionally.

3 Preheat browning dish according to the manufacturer's instructions. Arrange cutlets on dish with bones towards centre.

4 Cook cutlets on High for time in Chart, turning halfway through cooking. If cooking for 4, cook in 2 batches, reheating browning dish between batches. Transfer cutlets to a platter; keep warm.

5 Place peas and water in soufflé dish or pie plate (see Chart). Cook, covered, on High for time in Chart, until peas are tender; drain. Toss with butter and remaining mint.

6 Place 2 cutlets and a serving of peas on each warmed plate; garnish with mint sprigs.

BACON-WRAPPED LAMB CHOPS

Colour Index page 62. 4 servings. 2076 kJ per serving. Good source of niacin, iron, fibre. Begin 25 minutes ahead.

Redcurrant and Orange Sauce (below)
4 rashers bacon
15 g butter or margarine
8 pitted prunes
8 dried apricot halves
2 slices white bread, cubed
1 teaspoon chopped fresh thyme or ¼ teaspoon dried thyme
1 teaspoon shredded fresh basil or ¼ teaspoon dried basil
4 lamb loin chops (4 cm thick)

1. Prepare Redcurrant and Orange Sauce.
2. Cook bacon in a 23-cm pie plate, covered with paper towel, on High (100% power) for 1½ (1:30)–2 minutes, just until bacon begins to curl. Transfer to paper towel to drain.
3. Add butter to bacon drippings in pie plate. Heat, covered with paper towel, on High for 30–45 seconds, until melted. Add prunes, apricots, bread cubes, thyme and basil. Stir to coat; put aside.
4. Starting at one side of backbone of each lamb chop, cut through meat along bone, keeping knife blade against bone. Cut down both sides of bone to separate bone from meat, making sure that meat remains in one piece. Trim off any excess fat from chops.
5. Fill each chop where the bone has been removed with an equal amount of filling. To keep filling in place, wrap 1 bacon rasher tightly around each chop; secure with toothpicks.
6. Place chops on a rack set in a 30-cm x 20-cm baking dish. Cook on High for 3–5 minutes, until chops are done to your liking, rotating dish halfway through cooking.
7. Reheat Redcurrant and Orange Sauce on High for 1 minute. Place lamb chops on a warmed serving platter. Serve sauce separately.

REDCURRANT AND ORANGE SAUCE:

Combine *2 teaspoons grated orange rind, ½ cup orange juice, ¼ cup redcurrant jelly* and *1 teaspoon honey* in a 2-cup glass jug; stir until smooth. Cook on High (100% power) for 4–5 minutes, until boiling and thickened slightly, stirring occasionally. Serve warm. Makes ½ cup. 151 kJ per tablespoon.

LAMB NOISETTES WITH ORANGE

Colour Index page 62. 8 servings. 2110 kJ per serving. Good source of niacin, iron, zinc. Begin 45 minutes ahead.

½ cup Béarnaise Sauce (page 381)	8 x 7.5-cm bread rounds, toasted
½ teaspoon grated orange rind	¼ cup chopped fresh parsley
75 g butter or margarine	8 orange slices
1 teaspoon browning sauce	Rosemary sprigs to garnish
8 lamb noisettes (rolled boneless loin chops about 2.5 cm thick)	

1. Make Béarnaise Sauce; stir in orange rind. Keep warm.
2. Heat 45 g butter in a small bowl, covered with paper towel, on High (100% power) for 45 seconds–1 minute, until melted. Add browning sauce; brush on lamb noisettes.
3. Arrange noisettes in a 33-cm x 23-cm baking dish. Cook, covered loosely with greaseproof paper, on Medium-High (70% power) for 9–12 minutes, turning meat over occasionally.
4. Heat remaining butter in a small bowl, covered with paper towel, on High for 45 seconds, or until melted. Dip edges of toast in melted butter and roll in parsley to coat.
5. Arrange toast on a warmed serving platter; top each round with an orange slice and a noisette. Spoon over Béarnaise Sauce; garnish with rosemary.

CITRUS THAI KEBABS

Colour Index page 69. 4 servings. 1540 kJ per serving. Good source of vitamin A, niacin, vitamin C. Begin early in day or 1 day ahead.

2 tablespoons lemon juice	1½ tablespoons olive or vegetable oil
1½ tablespoons lime juice	1 clove garlic, crushed
2 tablespoons chopped fresh mint	500 g boneless lamb, cut into 4-cm cubes
½ teaspoon ground coriander	1 pawpaw, peeled and cut into 5-cm chunks
½ teaspoon ground cumin	1 green capsicum, cut into 4-cm chunks
3 teaspoons Worcestershire sauce	2 cups Hot Cooked Rice (page 295)

1. Combine lemon juice, lime juice, mint, coriander, cumin, Worcestershire sauce, oil, garlic and lamb cubes in a large bowl; cover and refrigerate for 2 hours or overnight.
2. Thread lamb alternately with pawpaw and capsicum on eight 20-cm–25-cm wooden skewers. Arrange on a 25-cm x 30-cm platter. Cook on High (100% power) for 5–7 minutes, until lamb is fork-tender, turning over once.
3. Spoon rice on to a warmed serving platter. Place kebabs on top. Serve immediately.

Meal in Minutes *for 4 people*
Mother's Day Lunch

Cheesy Stuffed Prawns (page 121)
Apricot-glazed Rack of Lamb (page 219)
Wild Rice and Mushroom Pilaf (page 294)
Mint Jelly (page 378)
Bread rolls
Orange Chiffon Pie (page 340)

PREPARATION TIMETABLE

Up to 1 week ahead:	*Make Mint Jelly. Prepare Cheesy Stuffed Prawns up to the end of step 4.*
1 day ahead:	*Make Orange Chiffon Pie but do not decorate; store in an airtight container.*
Early in day:	*Cook Wild Rice and Mushroom Pilaf; cover and put aside.*
45 minutes ahead:	*Cook Apricot-glazed Rack of Lamb; allow to stand as in recipe. Decorate pie.*
About 15 minutes before serving:	*Reheat pilaf on High (100% power) until hot. If you like, heat dinner rolls on High. Complete Cheesy Stuffed Prawns.*

Lamb, like any meat that has been cut into uniform cubes, cooks quickly and evenly in the microwave. For the almond garnish in the Lamb Curry (below), place ½ cup blanched flaked almonds in a shallow pie plate and heat on High (100% power) for 1–1½ (1:30) minutes, until lightly browned, stirring twice.

LAMB CURRY

Colour Index page 69. 1683 kJ per serving. Good source of vitamin A, thiamine, niacin, vitamin C, calcium, iron, fibre.
Begin 1½ hours ahead.

Ingredients for 4 servings		Microwave cookware
1 lemon wedge 2 cooking apples 30 g butter or margarine 2 tablespoons curry powder 1 large onion, cut into 5-cm chunks 1 green capsicum, cut into 5-cm chunks 500 g boneless lamb, cut into 4-cm cubes ½ cup dried apricots, finely chopped	1 cup chicken stock 1 tablespoon tomato paste 250 g frozen peas, thawed ½ cup natural yoghurt Hot Cooked Rice (page 295, optional) Toasted flaked almonds and coriander leaves to garnish	33-cm x 23-cm baking dish

1 Place lemon wedge in a medium bowl; fill bowl with cold water. Peel, core and cut apples into 4-cm chunks; place in lemon water to prevent discoloration.

2 Heat butter in baking dish, covered with paper towel, on High (100% power) for 45 seconds, or until melted.

3 Stir in curry powder, onion, capsicum and drained apple chunks. Cook on High for 3–4 minutes, until vegetables are warm, stirring halfway through cooking.

4 Add lamb cubes, apricots, stock and tomato paste. Cook, covered, on Medium (50% power) for 45–60 minutes, until lamb is fork-tender, stirring occasionally.

5 Stir peas into lamb mixture. Cook on High for 3–4 minutes, until hot, stirring halfway through cooking.

6 Gradually stir in yoghurt until blended. Spoon curry, if you like, alongside hot rice; garnish with toasted almonds and coriander leaves. Serve immediately.

MOROCCAN LAMB WITH COUSCOUS

Colour Index page 69. 6 servings. 1411 kJ per serving. Good source of vitamin A, niacin, iron, potassium, fibre.
Begin 2 hours ahead.

2 tablespoons olive or vegetable oil
2 carrots, cut into 7.5-cm chunks, then into quarters lengthways
2 large onions, sliced
500 g boneless lamb, cut into 4-cm cubes
1½ cups tomato juice
2 tablespoons red wine vinegar
1 cinnamon stick
1 bay leaf
2 teaspoons chopped fresh thyme or ½ teaspoon dried thyme

1 teaspoon ground cumin
1 teaspoon ground coriander
⅛ teaspoon cayenne pepper
185 g okra, stalks removed
2 cups cooked chick peas
1½ cups chicken stock
¼ teaspoon turmeric
1 cup couscous

1. Heat oil in a 33-cm x 23-cm baking dish, covered with paper towel, on High (100% power) for 45 seconds–1 minute, until hot.
2. Stir in carrots, onions and lamb cubes. Cook on High for 5–6 minutes, until onions are softened, stirring twice.
3. Meanwhile, combine tomato juice, vinegar, cinnamon stick, bay leaf, thyme, cumin, coriander and cayenne pepper in a 4-cup glass jug. Stir into lamb mixture. Cook, covered, on Medium (50% power) for 30–40 minutes, until carrots are tender, stirring occasionally.
4. Add okra and chick peas. Cook, covered, on Medium for 15–20 minutes, until lamb is fork-tender, stirring occasionally; discard bay leaf. Allow lamb to stand, covered, on a heatproof surface while preparing couscous.
5. Combine stock and turmeric in jug. Cook on High for 4–6 minutes, until boiling. Add couscous. Allow to stand, covered, on a heatproof surface for 5 minutes.
6. Fluff couscous with a fork; spoon on to a warmed serving platter. Top with lamb stew. Serve immediately.

COUSCOUS Couscous is precooked semolina derived from durum wheat, forming fine, yellow, rice-like pellets. The traditional way to cook couscous involves steaming it over a highly spiced stew. A quick, modern alternative, using the microwave, is to place couscous in boiling stock or water, with spices such as turmeric added to taste, then to leave it to absorb the liquid; it is fluffed up with a fork before serving. Couscous is an attractive alternative to rice in many lamb or chicken dishes.

LAMB STEW WITH FETA

Colour Index page 69. 6 servings. 1808 kJ per serving. Good source of thiamine, niacin, calcium. Begin 2 hours ahead.

2 tablespoons olive oil	*2 tablespoons stoned*
2 large onions, chopped	*black olives*
2 cloves garlic, crushed	*500 g tomatoes, chopped*
500 g boneless lamb, cut	*½ cup dry white wine*
into 4-cm cubes	*2 zucchini, cut into 4-cm*
1 bay leaf	*chunks*
1 tablespoon finely	*250 g macaroni, cooked*
chopped fresh	*250 g feta cheese,*
rosemary	*crumbled*
1 tablespoon chopped	*2 tablespoons chopped*
fresh oregano	*fresh dill*

1. Combine oil, onions, garlic, lamb cubes, bay leaf, rosemary, oregano and olives in a 33-cm x 23-cm baking dish. Cook on High (100% power) for 5–6 minutes, until lamb is no longer pink, stirring halfway through cooking.
2. Stir in tomatoes and wine. Cook, covered, on Medium (50% power) for 45 minutes, stirring occasionally. Add zucchini. Cook, covered, on Medium for 15–20 minutes longer, until meat is fork-tender, stirring occasionally.
3. Combine macaroni, feta and dill. Spoon on to a serving platter; top with stew. Cook, covered, on High for 4–5 minutes, until hot.
4. Discard bay leaf. Serve immediately.

SHEPHERD'S PIE

Colour Index page 64. 6 servings. 1762 kJ per serving. Good source of vitamin B$_{12}$, riboflavin, thiamine, niacin, iron, zinc, fibre. Begin 45 minutes ahead.

3 teaspoons vegetable oil	*2 teaspoons*
1 large onion, chopped	*Worcestershire sauce*
6 mushrooms, chopped	*½ teaspoon dried thyme*
750 g lamb mince	*½ teaspoon pepper*
1½ tablespoons plain	*¼ cup chopped fresh*
flour	*parsley*
215 g can tomatoes	*2 cups mashed potato*
2 tablespoons tomato	
paste	

1. Place oil, onion and mushrooms in a large bowl. Cook on High (100% power) for 4 minutes, stirring halfway through cooking.
2. Add lamb mince; stir to combine. Cook on High for 7–8 minutes, until meat is no longer pink, stirring twice. Skim off any excess fat. Stir in flour. Cook on High for 1 minute; stir.
3. Add tomatoes, tomato paste, Worcestershire sauce, thyme and pepper; stir to mix and break up tomatoes. Cook on High for 10–12 minutes, until mixture thickens, stirring often. Stir in parsley. Transfer to a 33-cm oval baking dish.
4. Spread potato over meat mixture; rough up surface with a fork. Cook on High for 10–12 minutes, until bubbling, turning dish every 4 minutes. Serve immediately.

MOUSSAKA

Colour Index page 69. 1570 kJ per serving. Good source of vitamin A, vitamin B$_{12}$, niacin, iron, zinc, fibre. Begin 1¼ hours ahead.

Ingredients for 6 servings		Microwave cookware
500 g eggplant	*2 teaspoons chopped*	30-cm x 20-cm
2 tablespoons water	*fresh thyme or*	baking dish
3 teaspoons olive or	*½ teaspoon dried*	Large bowl
vegetable oil	*thyme*	2-cup glass jug
1 large onion, chopped	*¼ cup chopped fresh*	
2 cloves garlic, crushed	*coriander or parsley*	
500 g lamb mince	*¼ teaspoon pepper*	
215 g can tomatoes,	*185 g feta cheese,*	
drained	*crumbled*	
2 tablespoons tomato	*30 g butter or margarine*	
paste	*¼ cup plain flour*	
1 tablespoon chopped	*1 cup milk*	
fresh oregano or	*¼ teaspoon paprika*	
1 teaspoon dried	*Coriander leaves to*	
oregano	*garnish*	

1 Cut eggplant into 6-mm slices. Place half the slices in baking dish; sprinkle with 1 tablespoon water. Cook, covered, on High (100% power) for 4–5 minutes, until tender, turning dish once. Transfer to paper towel to drain. Repeat with remaining eggplant slices and water.

2 Place oil, onion and garlic in bowl. Cook on High for 2–3 minutes, until onion softens. Stir in lamb, breaking up any lumps with a fork. Cook on High for 5–6 minutes, until meat is no longer pink, stirring twice.

3 Add tomatoes; stir to break up large pieces. Stir in tomato paste, oregano and thyme. Cook on High for 8–10 minutes, until tomato liquid is absorbed. Add chopped coriander, pepper and half the feta cheese.

4 Line base and sides of cleaned baking dish with eggplant slices. Spoon in meat mixture, layering in any remaining eggplant; put aside.

5 Heat butter in jug on High for 45 seconds–1 minute, until melted. Stir in flour until smooth and blended. Cook on High for 1 minute. Gradually stir in milk. Cook on High for 4–5 minutes, until thickened, stirring often. Stir in remaining cheese.

6 Pour sauce over meat mixture in dish. Cook on High for 10–12 minutes, until hot, turning dish a half turn every 4 minutes. Allow to stand on a heatproof surface for 5 minutes. Sprinkle top with paprika; garnish with coriander. Serve hot.

Veal

PARTY VEAL ROAST

Colour Index page 68. 1813 kJ per serving. Good source of vitamin A, niacin, calcium, iron.
Begin 2 hours ahead.

Ingredients for 12 servings		Microwave cookware
2 kg boneless veal breast, trimmed of fat	30 g butter or margarine, melted	33-cm x 23-cm baking dish
375 g packet frozen chopped spinach, thawed	½ teaspoon browning sauce	2-cup glass jug
125 g Cheddar cheese, grated (1 cup)	1 onion, chopped	
¼ cup grated Parmesan cheese	¼ cup plus 2 tablespoons water	
½ teaspoon salt	Capsicum Medley (right, optional)	
1 egg	3 teaspoons plain flour	
198 g can pimientos, drained		

CAPSICUM MEDLEY
Cut *10 large capsicums (red, green and yellow)* into 2.5-cm strips. Thinly slice *1 large onion*. Place capsicum, onion, *2 tablespoons vegetable oil, 1 tablespoon chopped fresh oregano or 1 teaspoon dried oregano* and *½ teaspoon salt* in a 4-litre casserole. Cook, covered, on High (100% power) for 10–12 minutes, until vegetables are tender-crisp, stirring occasionally. Serve hot as an accompaniment to roast meats. 12 servings. 297 kJ per serving.

1 Spread veal breast flat. With rolling pin or meat mallet, pound meat to a 45-cm x 25-cm rectangle, about 2.5 cm thick.

2 Drain spinach well. Mix with cheese, salt and egg in a bowl; spread evenly over surface of meat.

3 If pimientos are thick, cut each horizontally in half, then into 4-cm pieces. Arrange randomly over spinach mixture.

4 Starting from a narrow end, roll up meat tightly; tie with string at 2.5-cm intervals.

5 Mix melted butter and browning sauce in a bowl; brush over meat. Combine onion and ¼ cup water in baking dish; add meat, seam side up.

6 Cook, covered, on Medium (50% power) for 30 minutes. With fork, turn meat seam side down; rotate dish.

7 Cook meat, covered, on Medium for 25–30 minutes longer, until a meat thermometer inserted in centre reaches 71°C. Allow meat to stand, tented with foil, on a heatproof surface for 15 minutes; temperature will reach 77°C.

8 If you like, during standing time, prepare Capsicum Medley. When meat has reached desired temperature, strain meat juices from baking dish into jug. With spoon, skim fat from surface.

9 Combine flour and remaining water in a bowl until smooth; stir into meat juices. Cook on High (100% power) for 4–6 minutes, until thickened slightly, stirring halfway through cooking.

10 Cut veal into slices, removing and discarding string as you carve. Arrange on a warmed serving platter. Accompany, if you like, with Capsicum Medley. Serve gravy separately.

STUFFED SHOULDER OF VEAL

Colour Index page 68. 10 servings. 1854 kJ per serving. Good source of riboflavin, thiamine, niacin, calcium, iron.
Begin 2 hours ahead.

250 g fresh spinach-filled ravioli (2.5-cm–4-cm squares)	2 tablespoons olive oil
	2 kg boned veal shoulder
	1 cup dry white wine
60 g thinly sliced prosciutto, diced	1 cup beef stock
	1 tablespoon cornflour dissolved in 2 tablespoons cold water
60 g Provolone cheese, diced	
3 spring onions, sliced	Salt and pepper to taste
2 teaspoons shredded fresh basil or ½ teaspoon dried basil	Parsley sprigs to garnish

1. Combine ravioli, prosciutto, Provolone, spring onions, basil and half the oil; put aside.
2. Place veal shoulder, fat side down, on a flat surface. Even out the thickness of the meat by cutting horizontal slices from the thicker parts of veal and placing where needed along edges of roast. Then, if necessary, pound veal to an even thickness of about 2.5 cm with the dull edge of a heavy knife or the smooth edge of a meat mallet.
3. Spoon ravioli mixture along centre of meat; pull meat up and over stuffing. With heavy string, tie roast at 5-cm intervals.
4. Heat remaining oil in a 30-cm frying pan over medium-high heat. Add meat and quickly brown on all sides. Place meat, seam side up, on a rack set in a 33-cm x 23-cm baking dish.
5. Pour wine and stock into pan; stir to loosen any browned bits. Bring to the boil over high heat; pour over meat in baking dish.
6. Cook meat, covered, on Medium (50% power) for 20 minutes. Turn meat seam side down. Cook, covered, on Medium for 20–30 minutes longer, until a meat thermometer inserted in centre reaches 71°C. Transfer meat to a warmed serving platter and tent with foil. Allow to stand for 10–15 minutes; temperature will reach 77°C.
7. Meanwhile, strain meat juices from baking dish into a 2-cup glass jug. With spoon, skim off excess fat. Add dissolved cornflour and cook on High (100% power) for 5–6 minutes, until gravy is thickened, stirring twice. Season with salt and pepper.
8. Cut veal into slices, removing and discarding string as you carve. Arrange slices on a warmed serving platter; garnish with parsley. Serve hot with gravy.

To hold in heat and reduce spatter when cooking a roast, meat can be tented loosely with greaseproof paper. To prevent paper sticking to the fat or skin, brush the 'food side' of paper with a little vegetable oil or a nonstick cooking spray. Remove greaseproof paper and tent with foil during standing time, according to instructions in recipe.

ROAST LOIN OF VEAL WITH PURÉE OF SWEDE

Colour Index page 68. 984 kJ per serving. Low in fat. Good source of iron, fibre. Begin 1½ hours ahead.

Ingredients for 8 servings		Microwave cookware
500 g swede or turnip 1 small onion, chopped 2 cloves garlic, crushed 2 tomatoes, chopped ½ teaspoon ground cumin 30 g butter or margarine	1.5 kg boned and rolled loin of veal ¼ cup chicken stock Salt and pepper to taste Watercress sprigs to garnish	33-cm x 23-cm baking dish

1 Peel swede with a sharp knife; cut into 2.5-cm chunks.

2 Combine swede, onion, garlic, tomatoes, cumin and butter in baking dish. Cook, covered with paper towel, on High for 45 seconds–1 minute, until butter has melted, stirring halfway through cooking.

3 Push vegetables to sides of dish. Place veal roast in centre of dish; add stock. Cook, covered, on Medium (50% power) for 20 minutes.

4 Turn meat over. Cook, covered, on Medium for 20–30 minutes longer, until a thermometer inserted in centre reaches 71°C. Transfer roast to a warmed serving platter. Allow to stand, tented with foil, for 10–15 minutes; temperature will reach 74°C–77°C.

5 Meanwhile, prepare purée. In food processor with knife blade attached or in blender, process vegetables and cooking juices until smooth. Season with salt and pepper.

6 Cut veal into thin slices, removing and discarding string as you carve. Spoon a small amount of purée on to each of 8 warmed plates. Arrange slices of veal on purée; garnish with watercress sprigs. Serve immediately.

VEAL MARSALA

Colour Index page 62. 1574 kJ per serving. Good source of niacin, iron. Begin 25 minutes ahead.

Ingredients	For 4	For 2	For 1
Veal steaks, 12 mm thick (about 125 g each)	4	2	1
Butter or margarine	60 g	30 g	15 g
Paprika	½ teaspoon	¼ teaspoon	⅛ teaspoon
Marsala	½ cup	¼ cup	2 tablespoons
Dried breadcrumbs	¾ cup	½ cup	¼ cup
Chopped fresh parsley	garnish	garnish	garnish
Microwave cookware	23-cm pie plate 33-cm x 23-cm baking dish	23-cm pie plate 30-cm x 20-cm baking dish	23-cm pie plate 20-cm x 20-cm baking dish
Time on High (100% power)			
Marsala mixture	3–4 minutes	2–3 minutes	1½ (1:30)–2 minutes
Veal	5–8 minutes	3–5 minutes	2–3 minutes
Reheating Marsala mixture	1–2 minutes	1 minute	30 seconds

1 Pound veal to 3 mm thickness with the dull edge of a heavy knife or the smooth edge of a meat mallet.

2 Place butter, paprika and Marsala in pie plate (see Chart). Cook, covered with paper towel, on High for time in Chart, until butter is melted, stirring once.

3 Spread breadcrumbs on a sheet of greaseproof paper. Dip veal in Marsala mixture, then in crumbs, coating on both sides. Reserve remaining Marsala mixture.

4 Place veal steaks, 6 mm apart, in baking dish (see Chart). Cook, covered loosely with greaseproof paper, on High for time in Chart, until juices run clear.

5 Place veal on a warmed platter; keep warm. Reheat reserved Marsala mixture on High for time in Chart.

6 Drizzle Marsala mixture over veal; garnish with parsley. Serve immediately.

VEAL WITH SPINACH

Colour Index page 62. 4 servings. 1800 kJ per serving. Good source of vitamin A, riboflavin, niacin. Begin 25 minutes ahead.

90 g butter or margarine	¾ cup dried breadcrumbs
¼ cup chicken stock	
2 tablespoons lemon juice	500 g veal steak, about 6 mm thick
1 clove garlic, crushed	
½ teaspoon paprika	250 g spinach
¼ teaspoon salt	1 punnet cherry tomatoes

1. Place butter, chicken stock, lemon juice and garlic in a 3-litre casserole. Cook, covered, on High (100% power) for 4 minutes.
2. Mix paprika, salt and breadcrumbs on a sheet of greaseproof paper. Pound veal to 3 mm thickness. Dip in butter, then in seasoned crumbs.
3. Toss spinach and tomatoes in remaining butter mixture; put aside.
4. Place veal in a 33-cm x 23-cm baking dish. Cook, covered, on High for 8 minutes, rearranging veal once. Transfer to a warmed platter.
5. Place spinach and tomato mixture in baking dish. Cook, covered, on High for 3–4 minutes, until spinach wilts. Serve immediately with veal.

HERBED VEAL AND RICE

Colour Index page 68. 4 servings. 2072 kJ per serving. Good source of riboflavin, thiamine, iron. Begin 2 hours ahead.

2 onions, chopped	1 tablespoon chopped fresh oregano or
2 celery stalks, chopped	
2 cloves garlic, crushed	1 teaspoon dried oregano
2 tablespoons olive oil	
1.5 kg shin of veal, cut into 5-cm pieces	2 teaspoons finely chopped fresh rosemary or
1 cup dry white wine	
215 g can tomatoes, chopped	½ teaspoon dried rosemary
½ cup beef stock	1 bay leaf
1 tablespoon shredded fresh basil or	½ cup long-grain rice
	Salt and pepper to taste
1 teaspoon dried basil	Parsley sprigs to garnish

1. Combine onions, celery, garlic and half the oil in a 33-cm x 23-cm baking dish. Cook on High (100% power) for 5 minutes, stirring twice.
2. Heat remaining oil in a 30-cm frying pan over high heat. Add veal pieces and brown on all sides. Arrange meat on vegetables in baking dish, keeping pieces at least 2.5 cm apart.
3. Pour wine into frying pan; stir to loosen brown bits. Bring to the boil over high heat; pour over meat in baking dish. Add tomatoes, stock, basil, oregano, rosemary and bay leaf.
4. Cook, covered, on High for 5 minutes. Reduce power level to Medium (50% power) and cook, covered, for 45 minutes, or until meat is fork-tender, turning meat over every 10 minutes.
5. Stir in rice. Cook on High for 12–15 minutes, until cooked, stirring twice. Season with salt and pepper; garnish with parsley.

VEAL PROVENÇALE

Colour Index page 68. 4 servings. 1578 kJ per serving. Good source of vitamin A, niacin, vitamin C, iron.
Begin 1½ hours ahead.

500 g boneless veal, cut into 4-cm cubes	1 tablespoon chopped fresh thyme or
½ cup plain flour	1 teaspoon dried thyme
¼ teaspoon salt	1 tablespoon finely
¼ teaspoon pepper	chopped fresh
2 tablespoons olive oil	rosemary or
3 small onions, chopped	1 teaspoon dried
1 green capsicum,	rosemary
chopped	1 tablespoon chopped
1 red capsicum, chopped	oregano or 1 teaspoon
1 cup dry white wine	dried oregano
1 tablespoon tomato	2 cloves garlic, crushed
paste	10 stoned black olives
1 beef stock cube,	Hot cooked pasta
crumbled	(optional)

1. Trim fat from veal. Combine flour, salt and pepper on a sheet of greaseproof paper. Lightly coat veal cubes in seasoned flour.
2. Heat oil in a 30-cm frying pan over high heat. Add meat and brown on all sides. With slotted spoon, transfer meat to a 2-litre casserole.
3. Cook onions and capsicums in same pan, over medium-high heat, until softened. Add to veal.
4. Combine wine, tomato paste, stock cube, thyme, rosemary and oregano. Pour over veal. Cook, covered, on Medium (50% power) for 30 minutes, stirring occasionally.
5. Add garlic and olives; stir. Cook, covered, on Medium (50% power) for 15–20 minutes longer, until veal is fork-tender.
6. Spoon on to individual warmed plates. Serve, if you like, with pasta tossed with parsley.

MEAT GLAZES

These glazes are ideal for dressing up plain cooked lamb, pork, veal and ham.

Fruity Glaze: In blender at low speed, blend ½ cup drained bottled fruit mince and ¼ cup orange marmalade until smooth. Makes about ¾ cup.

Syrup Glaze: Combine ⅔ cup maple syrup, 3 teaspoons curry powder and 3 teaspoons grated orange rind in a small bowl until well blended. Makes about ⅔ cup.

Tomato Glaze: Place 15 g butter or margarine and 2 tablespoons finely chopped onion in a 4-cup glass jug. Cook on High (100% power) for 1 minute, or until onion softens. Stir in 215 g can tomatoes, chopped, 1 tablespoon brown sugar and 1 teaspoon Worcestershire sauce. Cook, covered, on High for 3–5 minutes, until glaze thickens slightly. Makes about 1 cup.

VEAL RAGOÛT

Colour Index page 68. 2750 kJ per serving. Good source of vitamin A, riboflavin, niacin, calcium, iron, fibre.
Begin 1½ hours ahead.

Ingredients for 4 servings		Microwave cookware
500 g boneless veal, cut into 4-cm cubes	250 g frozen pearl onions, thawed, or tiny white pickling onions, peeled and trimmed	8-cup soufflé dish or 2-litre casserole
2 cups water		
30 g butter or margarine	8 large button mushrooms	
1 large carrot, diced	3 teaspoons plain flour	
1 large celery stalk, diced	1 cup cream	
1 clove garlic, crushed	2 egg yolks	
1 tablespoon chopped fresh thyme or	Salt and pepper to taste	
1 teaspoon dried thyme	2 cups Hot Cooked Rice (page 295, optional)	
1 bay leaf	2 teaspoons chopped fresh parsley (optional)	
1 cup chicken stock		

1 Place veal in soufflé dish or casserole; add water. Cook, covered, on High (100% power) for 8–10 minutes, until water boils. With slotted spoon, transfer veal to paper towel to drain. Pour cooking liquid through a muslin-lined strainer into a bowl; put aside.

2 Heat butter in dish used for veal, covered with paper towel, on High for 45 seconds, or until melted. Add carrot, celery, garlic, thyme and bay leaf. Cook on High for 5–7 minutes, until vegetables are softened, stirring twice. Add veal and stock; stir. Cook, covered, on Medium (50% power) for 20 minutes, stirring occasionally.

3 Add onions and mushrooms to mixture; stir. Cook, covered, on Medium for 15–25 minutes longer, until meat is fork-tender.

4 Place flour in a bowl. Gradually add ½ cup reserved cooking liquid, stirring until smooth. Add flour mixture to ragoût. Cook on High for 3–5 minutes, until sauce has thickened slightly, stirring twice.

5 Meanwhile, combine cream and egg yolks in same bowl. Stir small amount of hot cooking liquid from ragoût into cream mixture; slowly pour cream mixture back into ragoût, stirring to prevent lumping.

6 Cook ragoût on Medium-Low (30% power) for 2–3 minutes, until mixture has thickened, stirring twice; discard bay leaf. Season with salt and pepper. Serve, if you like, with Hot Cooked Rice tossed with chopped parsley.

Pork

Choose pork roasts which are uniform in diameter. Allow about 22 minutes per 500 g for a boneless joint and 20 minutes per 500 g for meat on the bone. Turn the meat over and rotate the dish halfway through cooking; meat is done when a thermometer inserted in several places reaches 77°C.

PORK LOIN WITH APRICOT STUFFING

Colour Index page 67. 682 kJ per serving. Good source of vitamin A, riboflavin, thiamine, niacin, iron.
Begin 1½ hours ahead.

Ingredients for 12 servings		Microwave cookware
15 g butter or margarine 1 onion, chopped 1 large celery stalk, chopped 1 medium cooking apple, cored and chopped 125 g dried apricots, chopped ½ teaspoon poultry seasoning	1½ cups fresh bread cubes (about 5 slices) 1 kg boneless loin of pork, tail removed Pepper to taste 3 teaspoons vegetable oil Parsley sprigs to garnish	30-cm x 20-cm baking dish

1 Place butter, onion, celery, apple and apricots in baking dish. Cook on High (100% power) for 3 minutes, or until onion is softened, stirring twice. Stir in poultry seasoning and bread cubes; mix well. Push towards sides of dish.

2 Season pork loin with pepper. Heat oil in a 30-cm frying pan over high heat; add meat and quickly brown on all sides.

3 Place meat in centre of baking dish, surrounded by stuffing. Cook, covered, on Medium (50% power) for 15 minutes.

4 Turn meat over and rotate dish. Cook, covered, on Medium for 20–30 minutes longer, until a meat thermometer inserted in several places reaches 74°C.

5 Allow meat to stand in dish, tented with foil, on a heatproof surface for 10–15 minutes; temperature will reach 77°C.

6 Thinly slice pork; arrange on a warmed serving platter with apricot stuffing. Garnish with parsley sprigs. Serve hot.

PORK LOIN WITH GARLIC SAUCE

Colour Index page 64. 10 servings. 820 kJ per serving. Low in sodium. Good source of thiamine, niacin.
Begin 55 minutes ahead.

20 garlic cloves
1½ cups chicken stock
1.25 kg boneless loin of pork, rolled

Salt and pepper to taste
Lemon juice to taste
Watercress to garnish

1. Place garlic cloves and stock in a 30-cm x 20-cm baking dish. Cook, covered, on High (100% power) for 10 minutes.
2. Season pork loin with salt and pepper. Quickly brown meat on all sides in a 30-cm frying pan over high heat.
3. Place meat in centre of baking dish with garlic and stock. Cook, covered, on Medium (50% power) for 30–35 minutes, until a meat thermometer inserted in several places reaches 74°C, turning meat over and rotating dish after 15 minutes. Transfer roast to a warmed serving platter. Allow to stand, tented with foil, on a heatproof surface for 10–15 minutes; temperature will reach 77°C.
4. Meanwhile, in food processor with knife blade attached or in blender, process garlic and stock until smooth. Add salt, pepper and lemon juice.
5. Thinly slice pork and arrange on warmed plates; garnish with watercress. Serve garlic sauce separately.

HASH BROWN PORK AND POTATOES

Colour Index page 62. 4 servings. 1532 kJ per serving. Good source of thiamine.
Begin 20 minutes ahead.

2 cups cubed cooked roast pork
2 cups cubed boiled potatoes
1 large onion, chopped
¼ teaspoon dried thyme

Salt and pepper to taste
2 eggs
2 tablespoons cream
30 g butter or margarine
Paprika to taste
Parsley sprig to garnish

1. Preheat browning dish according to the manufacturer's instructions. Meanwhile, combine pork, potatoes and onion in a bowl. Add thyme, salt and pepper; stir.
2. Lightly beat eggs and cream in a small bowl. Add to pork mixture; stir.
3. Place butter on browning dish. Add pork mixture, pressing lightly with a spatula. Cook on High for 7–10 minutes, until mixture is set, rotating dish halfway through cooking.
4. Slide hash on to a serving platter; if dish is suitable, brown under a pre-heated griller. Sprinkle with paprika; garnish with parsley. Serve immediately.

PORK WITH VEGETABLES

Colour Index page 62. 4 servings. 1842 kJ per serving. Good source of vitamin A, thiamine, niacin, vitamin C, iron, fibre.
Begin 25 minutes ahead.

500 g pork schnitzels, cut 6 mm thick	2 heads chicory, cut in half lengthways
15 g butter or margarine	1/3 cup cream
1 spring onion, finely chopped	3 teaspoons plain flour
1/2 cup chicken stock	2 tablespoons French mustard
375 g baby carrots	1 tablespoon brandy (optional)
500 g asparagus, cut into 5-cm pieces	

1. Pound pork to 3-mm thickness with the dull edge of a heavy knife or the smooth edge of a meat mallet. Place pork, butter, spring onion and 1/4 cup stock in a 30-cm x 20-cm baking dish. Cook, covered, on High (100% power) for 8–10 minutes, until pork is tender and juices run clear, rearranging meat once. Cover and put aside on a heatproof surface.
2. Pour remaining stock into a shallow 2-litre casserole; add carrots. Cook, covered, on High for 4 minutes. Stir in asparagus. Cook, covered, on High for 4–5 minutes longer, until tender. Add chicory; put aside.
3. Transfer pork to a serving platter. Stir cream and flour into baking dish until blended. Cook on High for 2–3 minutes, until thickened, stirring halfway through cooking. Stir in mustard and, if you like, brandy.
4. Spoon vegetables around pork; pour sauce over meat and vegetables. Cook on High for 1–2 minutes, until hot.

COOKING PORK CHOPS
Choose chops (with or without bone) cut 2.5-cm thick.

4 x 185 g chops	2 x 185 g chops	185 g chop
Microwave cookware		
30-cm x 20-cm baking dish with rack	25-cm x 15-cm baking dish with rack	23-cm pie plate with rack
Time on Medium-Low (30% power)		
20–30 minutes	11–14 minutes	7–9 minutes

Place chops on rack in baking dish or pie plate. Cook, covered, for time in Chart, until juices run clear, turning the meat over and rotating dish halfway through cooking.

Stir-frying is a traditional method of quickly cooking slivers of meat and vegetables in very little oil. Even less oil is necessary when you use a browning dish in the microwave oven, as in Stir-Fried Pork Fillet (below), so microwave 'stir-frying' is delicious and nutritious!

STIR-FRIED PORK FILLET

Colour Index page 61. 1465 kJ per serving. Good source of vitamin A, riboflavin, thiamine, niacin, vitamin C, iron, fibre.
Begin 25 minutes ahead.

Ingredients for 4 servings		Microwave cookware
2 tablespoons dry sherry	250 g golden zucchini	Browning dish
2 tablespoons soy sauce	250 g mushrooms	1-cup glass jug
1 teaspoon cornflour	2 tablespoons vegetable oil	2-litre casserole
1/4 teaspoon ground ginger	30 g butter or margarine	
500 g pork fillet	1 tablespoon lemon juice	
3 spring onions, cut into thin strips	125 g snow peas	
3 large carrots	2 tablespoons water	
	Spinach leaves to garnish	

1 Combine sherry, soy sauce, cornflour and ginger in a bowl. With knife held at a slant, cut pork into thin slices crossways. Add to mixture in bowl; stir in spring onions. Preheat browning dish according to the manufacturer's instructions.

2 Cut carrots and zucchini into matchstick-thin strips. Trim and slice mushrooms. Put vegetables aside.

3 Coat surface of browning dish with oil. Add pork and onion mixture; stir quickly to brown. Cook, covered, on High (100% power) for 1½ (1:30)–2 minutes. Transfer to a dish; put aside.

4 Place butter and lemon juice in jug. Heat, covered with paper towel, on High for 45 seconds, or until melted.

5 Place carrots, snow peas and water in casserole. Cook, covered, on High for 5–5½ (5:30) minutes, stirring halfway through cooking. Drain. Add zucchini, mushrooms and melted butter mixture to casserole. Cook, covered, on High for 3–4 minutes, until vegetables are tender-crisp, stirring halfway through cooking. Place pork mixture on top of vegetables. Cook, covered, on High for 1 minute longer, or until pork is hot.

6 Arrange pork and vegetables on warmed plates; garnish with spinach leaves. Serve immediately.

LIVER PROVENCAL

4 servings. 999 kJ per serving. Good source of riboflavin, niacin, iron.
Begin 15 minutes ahead.

1 tablespoon olive oil
1 clove garlic, crushed
1 onion, sliced
1 tablespoon tomato paste
60 g mushrooms, sliced
1 tablespoon chopped fresh parsley
¼ teaspoon dried oregano
500 g calves liver or lamb's fry
2 teaspoons cornflour
½ cup beef stock

1. Place oil, garlic and onion in a 2-litre casserole. Cook on High (100% power) for 2 minutes, stirring once. Add tomato paste, mushrooms, parsley and oregano; stir well. Cook, covered, on High for 2 minutes. Add liver. Cook, covered, on High for 5 minutes, stirring halfway through cooking.
2. Blend cornflour and stock; stir into casserole. Cook on High for 2 minutes, stirring once. Allow to stand, covered, for 2 minutes. Serve hot.

BRAISED OXTAIL

4 servings. 1525 kJ per serving. Good source of iron.
Begin 1 day ahead.

2 teaspoons vegetable oil
2 onions, sliced
2 carrots, sliced
½ parsnip, diced
2 stalks celery, sliced
1 large oxtail, jointed
1 tablespoon tomato paste
2 cups beef stock
1 tablespoon plain flour
½ cup water

1. Place oil, onions, carrots, parsnip and celery in a 3-litre casserole. Cook, covered, on High (100% power) for 4 minutes, stirring once.
2. Add oxtail to casserole. Dissolve tomato paste in stock and pour over the meat. Cook, covered, on High for 5 minutes. Reduce power level to Medium (50% power) and cook for 60 minutes, or until meat is tender, stirring once. Allow to cool (overnight if possible) then remove fat from surface.
3. Heat on High for 2 minutes. Mix flour with water; stir into casserole. Cook on High for 10 minutes, stirring once. Serve hot.

TRIPE AND ONIONS WITH PARSLEY SAUCE

4 servings. 1508 kJ per serving. Low in sodium.
Begin 1 hour ahead.

750 g tripe, cut into 2.5-cm squares
3 cups water
2 onions, sliced
60 g butter
2 tablespoons plain flour
1 cup milk
Salt and pepper
1 tablespoon chopped fresh parsley

1. Place tripe in a 2-litre casserole. Pour over 2 cups cold water. Cook, covered, on High (100% power) for 10 minutes. Drain.
2. Return tripe to casserole with onions and 1 cup water. Cook, covered, on High for 10 minutes. Reduce power level to Medium (50% power) and cook for 30 minutes, or until tender, stirring once. Drain and reserve 1 cup of liquid for sauce.
3. Heat butter, covered with paper towel, in a 1.5-litre glass jug on high for 45 seconds, or until melted. Stir in flour. Cook on High for 1 minute, stirring once. Gradually stir in reserved liquid. Cook on High for 1 minute; stir in milk. Cook on High for 3 minutes, or until thick and smooth, stirring twice.
4. Season sauce with salt and pepper; stir in parsley. Pour sauce over tripe and mix well. Return to oven; cook on High for 2 minutes longer, stirring once. Serve hot.

SPICY PORK TURNOVERS

Colour Index page 68. 4 servings. 2637 kJ per serving. Good source of riboflavin, thiamine, niacin, iron, fibre.
Begin 2 hours ahead.

500 g boneless pork loin, trimmed of fat and minced
1 onion, finely chopped
2½ teaspoons chilli powder
¼ cup raisins
¼ cup slivered almonds
2 tablespoons tomato paste
5 pimiento-stuffed olives, chopped
1 cup plain flour
½ cup yellow cornmeal
60 g tasty cheese, grated (½ cup)
60 g firm cooking margarine
4–5 tablespoons water
Coriander leaves to garnish
Creamy Avocado Sauce (below) or bottled taco sauce and sour cream (optional)

1. Place pork mince and onion in a 30-cm x 20-cm baking dish. Cook, covered with paper towel, on High (100% power) for 5–7 minutes, until pork is no longer pink, stirring twice.
2. Add chilli powder, raisins, almonds, tomato paste and chopped olives; stir well. Cook, covered with paper towel, on High for 8–10 minutes, until raisins are plumped and sauce thickened slightly, stirring occasionally. Put aside to cool while preparing pastry.
3. Combine flour and cornmeal in a bowl; add cheese and margarine. With fingers or 2 knives used scissors-fashion, cut and rub in cheese and margarine until mixture resembles crumbs. Sprinkle water, 1 tablespoon at a time, into mixture, mixing lightly with fork, until pastry just holds together. Shape into a ball; flatten slightly. Wrap in greaseproof paper and refrigerate for about 1 hour, until well chilled.
4. On lightly floured surface, with floured rolling pin, roll half the pastry into a round about 3 mm thick. Using a 12.5-cm plate as a guide, cut out 4 rounds from pastry. Repeat with remaining pastry to make 8 rounds in all.
5. Preheat conventional oven to 200°C. On to half of 1 pastry round, spoon one-eighth of pork filling. Brush pastry edge lightly with water; fold pastry over filling. With fork, firmly press edges together to seal. Place turnover on an ungreased large baking tray. Repeat with remaining pastry.
6. Bake turnovers conventionally for 15 minutes, or until golden brown.
7. Transfer turnovers to a warmed serving platter; garnish with coriander. Serve, if you like, with Creamy Avocado Sauce, or with taco sauce and sour cream.

CREAMY AVOCADO SAUCE:
In food processor with knife blade attached or in blender, process *1 ripe avocado* until smooth with *¾ cup natural yoghurt*, *2 sliced spring onions*, *1 tablespoon lime juice* and *1 teaspoon ground cumin*. Season with *Tabasco sauce to taste*. Cover and store in refrigerator.
Makes 1½ cups. 104 kJ per tablespoon.

PORK JAMBALAYA

Colour Index page 67. 6 servings. 1222 kJ per serving. Good source of vitamin A, thiamine, vitamin C, iron.
Begin 1½ hours ahead.

45 g butter or margarine	⅛ teaspoon cayenne
2 tablespoons plain flour	pepper
2 large onions, chopped	1 tablespoon tomato
2 cloves garlic, crushed	paste
3 medium celery stalks,	1 medium green
chopped	capsicum, chopped
500 g boneless pork loin,	1 medium red capsicum,
cut into 4-cm cubes	chopped
2 cups chicken stock	4 spring onions, sliced
½ teaspoon poultry	½ cup long-grain rice
seasoning	Salt and pepper to taste
½ teaspoon filé powder	
(see below)	

1. Heat butter in a deep 1.5-litre casserole, covered with paper towel, on High (100% power) for 45 seconds–1 minute, until melted.

2. Stir in flour until blended. Cook on High for 5–7 minutes, until golden brown, stirring frequently.

3. Add onions, garlic, celery and pork cubes; stir until coated with flour mixture. Stir in stock, poultry seasoning, filé powder, cayenne pepper and tomato paste. Cook, covered, on Medium (50% power) for 30 minutes, or until pork is cooked, stirring occasionally.

4. Add capsicums, spring onions and rice. Cook, covered, on Medium for 15–20 minutes, until rice is tender but still firm; season with salt and pepper. Allow to stand, covered, on a heatproof surface for 10 minutes.

5. Transfer to a warmed serving dish. Serve immediately.

FILÉ Filé powder is derived from ground sassafras leaves. It is used as a thickener and a flavouring in traditional Creole and Cajun dishes, such as gumbo. It can be added straight to cooking juices or dissolved in water first. If not available, you can substitute ground sage for an alternative flavouring.

PAPER TOWELS
Plain white absorbent paper towels and paper napkins can safely be used in the microwave; patterned and coloured paper and napkins should not be used as dyes can transfer to foods or to the oven floor during the heating process.

If paper towel sticks slightly to bacon after cooking – or brown spots occur on the paper – it is caused by the sugar content in the bacon; it is not a problem.

SWEDISH MEATBALLS

Colour Index page 64. 1679 kJ per serving. Low in salt. Good source of vitamin A, vitamin B₁₂, niacin, iron.
Begin 45 minutes ahead.

Ingredients for 6 servings		Microwave cookware
45 g butter or margarine, softened	½ teaspoon pepper	Small bowl
1 onion, chopped	½ teaspoon ground nutmeg	23-cm flan dish
250 g boneless pork loin, trimmed of fat and minced	¼ teaspoon salt	Large bowl
125 g beef mince	3 tablespoons chopped fresh dill	
125 g veal mince	2 tablespoons plain flour	
½ cup dried breadcrumbs	1 cup beef stock	
1 egg, beaten	½ cup sour cream	
¼ cup cream	1 teaspoon gravy browning (optional)	
¼ cup soda water or light beer		

1 Place 15 g butter and chopped onion in small bowl. Cook on High (100% power) for 3–4 minutes, until onion is softened, stirring halfway through cooking.

2 Combine minced pork, beef and veal in a bowl. Add softened onion, breadcrumbs, egg, cream, soda water, pepper, nutmeg, salt and half the dill. Stir well to mix; mixture will be soft.

3 With wet hands, form mixture into 2-cm balls. Brush flan dish with 15 g butter. Arrange half the meatballs in 2 circles in dish.

4 Cook meatballs on High for 6–8 minutes, turning over and rearranging after 3 minutes; transfer to large bowl and keep warm. Repeat with remaining butter and meatballs.

5 Add flour to drippings in flan dish; stir to combine. Cook on High for 1 minute. Stir in stock and sour cream. Cook on High for 3–4 minutes, until thickened, stirring often. Add, if you like, gravy browning.

6 Pour sauce over meatballs. Cook on High, covered, for 2–3 minutes, until heated through. Garnish with remaining chopped dill. Serve hot.

Bacon is best cooked in the microwave; it does not curl or shrink as it does when cooked conventionally, and cleaning up is easier. Bacon rashers vary in thickness, as well as in sugar and fat content; to ensure that bacon cooks evenly, choose rashers of an equal thickness and with a similar fat-to-lean ratio. Do not let bacon rashers overlap or they will not cook properly. When done, bacon will be evenly browned. It should be left to stand for about 5 minutes, after which time it will be crisp.

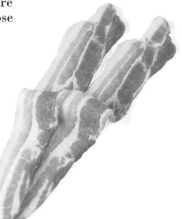

Cooking for one

Place 2 sheets of paper towel, one on top of the other, on a plate or paper plate; place 2 bacon rashers on paper. Cover with 1 more sheet of paper towel. Cook on High for 1½ (1:30)–2 minutes, until bacon is browned; or cook on microwave bacon rack. Allow to stand for 5 minutes.

Cooking bacon in batches

Place 2 sheets of paper towel in a 30-cm x 20-cm baking dish. Arrange 5 bacon rashers on paper; cover with 2 sheets of paper towel. Add 5 more bacon rashers, then 1 more sheet of paper. Cook on High for 7½ (7:30)–9 minutes, until browned, rotating dish once. Allow to stand for 5 minutes.

BACON WITH KIDNEYS AND MUSHROOMS
This popular breakfast and brunch dish is quicker and easier to make in a microwave than ever before; it can be on the table in less than 5 minutes.

For 2 servings, split *2 lamb's kidneys* in half; remove membranes and core. Remove stalks from *4 flat mushrooms.* Arrange *2 rashers rindless bacon* in a single layer in a 23-cm pie plate. Cook, covered with paper towel, on High (100% power) for 1 minute. Transfer to a warmed serving plate.

Place the mushrooms in the centre of the pie plate. Cook on High for 1 minute. Arrange the kidneys around the outside edge of the plate; cook, covered, on High for 1 minute. Turn kidneys over and rearrange mushrooms. Cook, covered, on High for 1½–2 minutes longer.

If very crisp bacon is preferred, return rashers to microwave and cook on High for 60 seconds.

PORK STEW WITH LEEKS
Colour Index page 67. 6 servings. 1507 kJ per serving. Good source of vitamin A, niacin, iron. Begin 1¼ hours ahead.

2 leeks (about 375 g)	½ teaspoon salt
1½ tablespoons vegetable oil	½ teaspoon pepper Water
750 g boneless pork, cut into 4-cm cubes	4 carrots, cut into 5-cm pieces
500 g small new potatoes	2 tablespoons plain flour

1. Trim root and leaf ends of leeks. Cut each leek in half lengthways; separate into leaves. Carefully wash under cold running water until all grit is removed. Cut leaves crossways into 5-cm pieces.
2. Place leeks and oil in a 4-litre casserole. Cook, covered, on High (100% power) for 8 minutes, or until softened, stirring twice.
3. Add pork cubes, potatoes, salt, pepper and ¾ cup water. Cook, covered, on High for 30 minutes, stirring mixture after 10 minutes.
4. Stir in carrots. Reduce power level to Medium (50% power) and cook, covered, for 20 minutes, or until meat and vegetables are fork-tender, stirring occasionally.
5. Combine flour and 2 tablespoons water in a bowl, stirring until smooth. Stir flour mixture into casserole. Cook, covered, on High for 2–3 minutes, until liquid has thickened slightly, stirring halfway through cooking.

SAVOURY RIBS
Colour Index page 64. 4 servings. 1980 kJ per serving. Good source of vitamin A, thiamine, vitamin C, iron.
Begin 55 minutes ahead.

1 large onion, chopped	2 tablespoons brown sugar
1 large green capsicum, cut into thin strips	1 chicken stock cube, crumbled
2 tablespoons vegetable oil	½ teaspoon caraway seeds, crushed
1 tablespoon paprika	1 kg pork spareribs
425 g can sauerkraut	Sour cream (optional)
1 cup bottled Italian tomato sauce	

1. Place onion, capsicum and oil in a 3-litre casserole. Cook, covered, on High (100% power) for 6 minutes, or until vegetables are softened, stirring twice. Add paprika; stir. Cook on High for 1 minute.
2. Stir in undrained sauerkraut, tomato sauce, brown sugar, stock cube and caraway seeds. Place ribs in casserole; coat with sauce. Cook, covered, on High for 35–40 minutes, until meat is fork-tender, turning ribs over and rotating casserole after 15 minutes.
3. Transfer ribs to a warmed serving platter. Spoon sauce over. Serve, if you like, with sour cream.

Ham

GLAZED HAM

Colour Index page 67. 8 servings. 1356 kJ per serving. Good source of thiamine, niacin, iron, zinc. Begin 1½ hours ahead.

¼ cup brown sugar	1.5 kg fully cooked
¼ cup Apple Purée	boneless ham
(page 354)	Whole cloves (optional)
2 tablespoons prepared	2 tablespoons water
mustard	Watercress to garnish

1. Combine brown sugar, apple purée and mustard in a 2-cup glass jug. Cook on High (100% power) for 3–4 minutes, until glaze is syrupy, stirring twice.
2. With sharp knife, remove excess fat from ham, leaving a 5-mm layer; score top of ham in a decorative diamond pattern. If you like, insert whole cloves in centre of each diamond.
3. Place ham in a 3-litre casserole, fat side uppermost. Spoon water into base of casserole. Cook, covered, on Medium-Low (30% power) for 1 hour, turning ham over every 20 minutes.
4. Uncover ham; brush with prepared glaze. Cook, uncovered, on Medium-Low for 20 minutes, or until a thermometer inserted in several places reaches 54°C, brushing with glaze every 5 minutes.
5. Allow ham to stand, tented with foil, on a heatproof surface for 10–15 minutes; temperature will reach 60°C.
6. Transfer to a warmed serving platter; garnish with watercress.

HAM AND BEAN CASSEROLE

Colour Index page 62. 6 servings. 1239 kJ per serving. Good source of vitamin A, thiamine, niacin, calcium, iron, fibre. Begin 25 minutes ahead.

1 onion, chopped	½ cup chicken stock
1 clove garlic, crushed	1 teaspoon finely
3 teaspoons vegetable	chopped fresh
oil	rosemary or
4 cups cooked haricot	¼ teaspoon dried
beans	rosemary
2 celery stalks, thinly	¼ teaspoon pepper
sliced	500 g fully cooked
2 carrots, coarsely	boneless smoked ham
grated	½ bunch curly endive

1. Place onion, garlic and oil in a 3-litre casserole. Cook, covered, on High (100% power) for 5 minutes, or until onion has softened, stirring twice.
2. Add beans, celery, carrots, stock, rosemary and pepper; stir. Cook, covered, on High for 12–15 minutes, until hot, stirring twice.
3. Meanwhile, cut ham into 2-cm cubes. Tear endive into bite-sized pieces.
4. Stir ham and endive into bean mixture. Cook, covered, on High for 2–3 minutes, until endive wilts, stirring halfway through cooking. Serve immediately.

HAM STEAKS WITH ORANGE AND HONEY GLAZE

Colour Index page 64. 1691 kJ per serving. Good source of thiamine, iron, zinc. Begin 35 minutes ahead.

Mustard and spices give a piquant flavour to Ham Steaks with Orange and Honey Glaze, and the decorative orange garnish adds a touch of sweetness which helps offset the salty taste of the ham. If you like, you can use canned pineapple slices in natural juice instead of the oranges used here.

Ingredients for 2 servings		Microwave cookware
2 large oranges	¼ teaspoon ground	2-cup glass jug
1 tablespoon coarse-grained mustard	ginger	23-cm flan dish
2 tablespoons clear honey	2 ham steaks (185 g each)	
¼ teaspoon ground cinnamon	Parsley sprigs to garnish	

1 With vegetable peeler, remove strips of rind from 1 orange, taking care to remove as little of the bitter white pith as possible. Cut rind into julienne strips.

2 Squeeze juice from orange; pour into jug. Add mustard, honey, cinnamon, ginger and prepared orange rind. Cook, loosely covered, on High (100% power) for 3–4 minutes, until sauce is bubbling and syrupy.

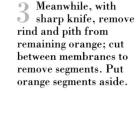

3 Meanwhile, with sharp knife, remove rind and pith from remaining orange; cut between membranes to remove segments. Put orange segments aside.

4 Trim fat from ham steaks; with kitchen shears, snip around edges of each steak at 12-mm intervals (this helps prevent steaks from curling during cooking).

5 Place steaks in flan dish. Cook, covered with greaseproof paper, on High for 2 minutes. Brush with orange glaze. Cook, covered with greaseproof paper, on High for 2 minutes longer. Allow to stand for 1–2 minutes.

6 Place ham steaks on warmed plates with glaze poured over; garnish with reserved orange segments and parsley. Serve hot.

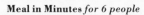

Celebration Lunch

Tartlets with Asparagus and Brie Filling (page 119)
Glazed Ham (page 233)
Capsicum Jelly (page 378) and Corn Relish (page 376)
Combination Vegetables (page 276)
Light Lemon and Almond Tart (page 344)

PREPARATION TIMETABLE

Up to 1 week ahead:	*Make Capsicum Jelly and Corn Relish.*
1 day ahead:	*Make Light Lemon and Almond Tart but do not decorate; store in an airtight container.*
Early in day:	*Make Tartlets with Asparagus and Brie Filling; cover loosely. Prepare and cook Combination Vegetables: cover.*
1½ hours ahead:	*Cook Glazed Ham as recipe; allow to stand. Decorate lemon tart.*
Just before serving:	*Reheat vegetables on High (100% power). If you like, reheat Tartlets with Asparagus and Brie Filling on High.*

DECORATING A HAM

Scoring the fat on top of a ham gives it an attractive finish for a festive occasion or special celebration.

Score fat on top of ham in a decorative, diamond-shaped pattern. Insert 1 whole clove into each diamond shape; glaze and cook according to recipe instructions.

Sausages

SAVOURY SAUSAGES

Colour Index page 65. 6 servings. 1863 kJ per serving. Good source of thiamine, vitamin C, iron. Begin 45 minutes ahead.

750 g spicy-hot fresh sausages	425 g can tomatoes, chopped
½ teaspoon browning sauce	2 tablespoons tomato paste
1 teaspoon water	¼ teaspoon salt
3 large green, yellow or red capsicums, each cut into 2-cm strips	¼ teaspoon pepper
2 onions, each cut into 6 wedges	¼ teaspoon fennel seeds, crushed

1. Pierce each sausage in several places. Place on a rack in a 33-cm x 23-cm baking dish. Mix browning sauce with water; brush on sausages. Cook, covered, on High (100% power) for 9–10 minutes, until meat is no longer pink, turning sausages over and rotating dish halfway through cooking. Remove sausages and rack; keep meat warm.

2. Add capsicum and onion to drippings in baking dish. Cook, covered, on High for 12–13 minutes, until softened, stirring twice.

3. Cut sausages into 2.5-cm pieces. Stir sausages, tomatoes, tomato paste, salt, pepper and fennel seeds into vegetable mixture. Cook, covered, on High for 5 minutes, stirring halfway through cooking. Serve immediately.

SAUSAGES WITH GLAZED ONIONS

Colour Index page 63. 4 servings. 2185 kJ per serving. Good source of vitamin B$_{12}$, iron. Begin 35 minutes ahead.

30 g butter or margarine	2 tablespoons chopped fresh parsley
2 large onions, sliced	8 thick pork or beef sausages
½ cup beef stock	
3 teaspoons soy sauce	3 teaspoons vegetable oil
3 teaspoons brown sugar	
¼ teaspoon dried thyme	

1. Combine butter, onions, stock, soy sauce, brown sugar and thyme in a large bowl. Cook, covered, on High (100% power) for 5 minutes, stirring once.

2. Uncover bowl. Cook on High for 15–20 minutes longer, until onions are tender and liquid has evaporated, stirring occasionally. Stir in chopped parsley; cover and put aside.

3. Preheat browning dish according to manufacturer's instructions. Pierce each sausage in several places. Coat browning dish with oil. Add sausages and press to brown on underside; turn sausages over. Cook on High for 4–6 minutes, turning over and rearranging twice.

4. Push sausages under onion mixture in bowl. Cook on High for 2 minutes, or until onions are heated through, stirring once. Serve hot.

KNACKWURST AND POTATOES

Colour Index page 65. 2834 kJ per serving. Good source of thiamine, niacin, vitamin C, iron, fibre. Begin 40 minutes ahead.

Knackwurst and Potatoes adapts easily to many variations. For example, instead of knackwurst use frankfurters, chunks of salami or ham, or even shelled hard-boiled eggs for a different flavour.

Ingredients for 4 servings		Microwave cookware
1 kg potatoes, well scrubbed and cut into 4-cm chunks	2 teaspoons mild mustard	2-litre casserole
2 rashers bacon, diced	¼ teaspoon salt	3-litre casserole
1 onion, chopped	¼ teaspoon pepper	
1½ tablespoons brown sugar	500 g knackwurst	
3 teaspoons plain flour	Curly endive leaves	
2 tablespoons cider vinegar	Sliced baby beetroot or sweet dill pickles to garnish	

1 Place potatoes and ½ cup water in 2-litre casserole. Cook, covered, on High (100% power) for 10 minutes, stirring once; drain. Cover and put aside.

2 Cook bacon in 3-litre casserole, covered with paper towel, on High for 2–3 minutes, until browned. Transfer bacon to paper towel to drain.

3 Add onion to bacon drippings in casserole. Cook on High for 3–4 minutes, until softened, stirring halfway through cooking.

4 Stir in brown sugar, flour, vinegar, mustard, salt, pepper and ⅔ cup water, until mixture is well blended. Cook on High for 3 minutes, or until flavours blend, stirring halfway through cooking.

5 Cut several diagonal slashes in each knackwurst. Add knackwurst and potatoes to onion mixture. Cook, covered, on High for 6–8 minutes, until potatoes are tender, stirring twice.

6 Line a serving platter with endive leaves; spoon knackwurst and potato mixture on to leaves. Sprinkle with bacon; garnish with sliced beetroot. Serve hot.

Hearty Hot Dogs

Frankfurters heat through in seconds in the microwave, and if you cook them in their buns there's no need for washing up. Just remember to slash or pierce the casings with a knife before putting them in the oven.

Hot Dogs in Buns
Place *slashed frankfurter* in *bun* and wrap in paper towel; place on paper plate. Heat on High (100% power) for 30–40 seconds, until hot. For 2 frankfurters in buns, heat on High for 1 minute.

Hot Dog Melt
Make slit lengthways in *frankfurter* and fill with *1 slice processed cheese*. Place on paper plate. Heat on High (100% power) for 30–40 seconds, until hot. Serve with *potato crisps*.

Mini-franks and Beans
Place contents of *440 g can baked beans* in a soup bowl. Place in centre of a dinner plate. Cook, covered loosely with greaseproof paper, on High (100% power) for 2–3 minutes, until bubbling. Meanwhile, push wooden toothpicks into *8 cocktail frankfurters*. Arrange in a circle around bean-filled bowl. Heat on High for 45 seconds–1 minute, until hot. Serve with *mustard*. 2 servings.

Chilli Dogs
Place *2 cups leftover Chilli con Carne* (page 215) in a medium bowl. Cook, covered, on High (100% power) for 4–5 minutes, until bubbling, stirring twice; put aside. Wrap *4 hot dogs* in *buns* in paper towels; place in a circle on oven floor. Heat on High for 2–3 minutes, until hot. Unwrap; place on platter. Top hot dogs with *chilli, sour cream, bottled taco sauce* and *coriander leaves*. 4 servings.

FRANKFURTERS AND RED CABBAGE

Colour Index page 63. 4 servings. 1892 kJ per serving. Good source of thiamine, niacin, vitamin C, calcium, iron, zinc, folic acid, fibre.
Begin 35 minutes ahead.

30 g butter or margarine	3 teaspoons sugar
2 red-skinned apples	2 tablespoons red wine
2 onions, thinly sliced	vinegar
1 small red cabbage (about 750 g), thinly shredded	500 g frankfurters, cut into 5-cm pieces
⅓ cup apple juice	Watercress sprigs to garnish

1. Heat butter in a 33-cm x 23-cm baking dish, covered with paper towel, on High (100% power) for 45 seconds, or until melted.
2. Core and dice 1 apple. Stir onions and diced apple into melted butter. Cook on High for 5 minutes, or until softened, stirring twice.
3. Add cabbage, apple juice, sugar and vinegar; mix well. Cook, covered, on High for 7–10 minutes, until cabbage is tender, stirring halfway through cooking.
4. Cut remaining apple into wedges; add to mixture with frankfurters. Cook, covered, on High for 5–7 minutes, until frankfurters are hot, stirring twice.
5. Garnish with watercress. Serve hot.

FRANKFURTER CASSEROLE

Colour Index page 63. 6 servings. 1432 kJ per serving. Good source of thiamine, vitamin C, potassium, iron, fibre.
Begin 25 minutes ahead.

2 onions, each cut into 8 wedges	1 tablespoon chopped fresh oregano or 1 teaspoon dried oregano
1 yellow or green capsicum, chopped	
2 cloves garlic, crushed	500 g frankfurters, cut into 2.5-cm pieces
2 tablespoons olive or vegetable oil	425 g can tomatoes
1 small eggplant (about 500 g), cut into 5-cm x 2.5-cm pieces	1 cup cooked chick peas
	¼ teaspoon salt
	¼ teaspoon pepper
1 zucchini, cut into 2.5-cm pieces	

1. Place onions, capsicum, garlic and oil in a 3-litre casserole. Cook, covered, on High (100% power) for 2–3 minutes, until vegetables are just slightly softened, stirring halfway through cooking.
2. Stir in eggplant, zucchini and oregano. Cook, covered, on High for 10–12 minutes, until tender-crisp, stirring twice.
3. Add frankfurters, tomatoes with their liquid, chick peas, salt and pepper. Cook, covered, on High for 2–3 minutes, until hot, stirring halfway through cooking. Serve immediately.

Vegetables and Salads

INDIVIDUAL VEGETABLES · MIXED VEGETABLES
WARM SALADS · VEGETABLE SALADS
CHICKEN SALADS · MEAT SALADS · PRAWN SALADS

Vegetables and Salads

Cooking vegetables is one of the things the microwave oven does best; most vegetables cook quickly with a minimum amount of water, so they retain nutrients and have the taste, colour and texture of fresh-from-the-garden produce. Small portions can be cooked with a minimum of trouble and a microwave is also ideal for peeling vegetables such as garlic, onions and tomatoes (see Cook's Tips, page 30), and for precooking vegetables for the barbecue in order to save time and prevent them from charring (see page 267).

Charts for cooking vegetables in the microwave (pages 239–253) give cooking instructions for a wide variety of fresh vegetables and several frozen ones. For best results, remember the following tips: pierce skins of whole vegetables; make sure vegetables are uniform in size – small pieces and quantities cook more quickly as do freshly picked young vegetables; slice dense vegetables, such as potatoes and turnips; arrange vegetables with tender tops, like asparagus and broccoli, with tops towards the centre of the dish,

less tender stems or stalks towards the edges. If using salt, add it after cooking or dissolve it in the cooking liquid – it can cause dark spots if sprinkled on to food. Covering is important for most vegetables; plastic wrap is recommended because it holds in heat and steam. To prevent it from splitting, 'vent' it by turning back a small corner or by puncturing the plastic. And remember that round shallow cookware produces the best results.

Frozen vegetables are tastier when cooked in the microwave and they keep more of their nutrients. Some are used straight from the freezer in recipes, but cooking charts are included for portions of some of the most popular frozen vegetables. Many fresh vegetables require blanching before freezing; instructions are given on page 259. After patting dry, pack in freezer containers, leaving head space, or pack into plastic bags, pressing out all air. Seal, label and freeze. Smaller vegetables, such as shelled peas, can be open-frozen; freeze on a tray until firm, then pack in a bag or container.

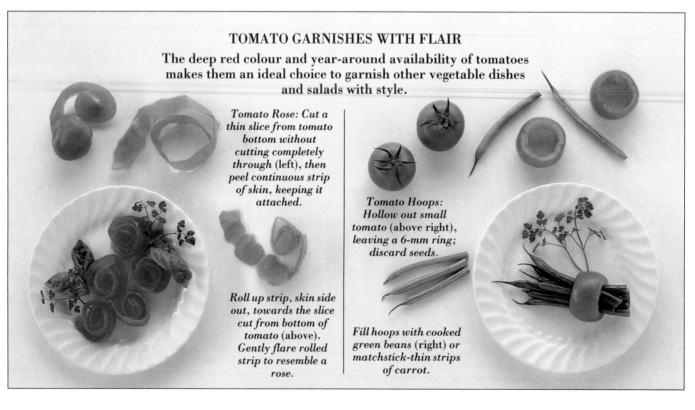

TOMATO GARNISHES WITH FLAIR
The deep red colour and year-around availability of tomatoes makes them an ideal choice to garnish other vegetable dishes and salads with style.

Tomato Rose: Cut a thin slice from tomato bottom without cutting completely through (left), *then peel continuous strip of skin, keeping it attached.*

Roll up strip, skin side out, towards the slice cut from bottom of tomato (above). *Gently flare rolled strip to resemble a rose.*

Tomato Hoops: Hollow out small tomato (above right), *leaving a 6-mm ring; discard seeds.*

Fill hoops with cooked green beans (right) *or matchstick-thin strips of carrot.*

Cooking vegetables in the microwave

These charts will be an invaluable help as a reference for the basic preparation and cooking of a wide variety of vegetables. You will be able to use your favourite vegetables in other microwave recipes or on their own with a little lemon juice, butter or margarine, salt, pepper, or a sauce.

Because vegetables vary in size, texture and density, it is important to follow the instructions carefully. Remember to rotate the dish a half turn or stir the vegetables during cooking, rearranging the larger pieces if necessary. Cover tightly to keep in heat; this helps vegetables cook more quickly and evenly.

Key			
Microwave cookware	Water	Cooking time	Standing time

ARTICHOKES, GLOBE

Rinse artichokes under cold running water. Cut off stalks and 2.5 cm of tops. Trim thorny tips of leaves with kitchen shears. Brush cut edges with lemon juice to prevent discoloration. Pull off loose leaves from around bottoms.

About 105 kJ per serving		
For 4	**For 2**	**For 1**
4 artichokes (about 375 g each)	2 artichokes (about 375 g each)	1 artichoke (about 375 g)
Wrap each individually in plastic wrap; *arrange on oven floor in a circle*	Wrap each individually in plastic wrap; *arrange on oven floor*	Wrap in plastic wrap; *place on oven floor*
Whatever clings after rinsing	Whatever clings after rinsing	Whatever clings after rinsing
16 minutes; *rotate each artichoke halfway through cooking*	10 minutes; *rotate each artichoke halfway through cooking*	7 minutes; *rotate halfway through cooking*
5 minutes	5 minutes	5 minutes

Cook artichokes, wrapped, on High (100% power) for time in Chart. Allow to stand, still wrapped, for time in Chart. Globe artichokes are done when an outer leaf as well as one close to the centre core can be pulled out without resistance.

ARTICHOKES, JERUSALEM

Scrub under cold running water. Separate larger knobs and tubers for easier peeling; peel. Cut knobs and tubers into 12-mm pieces.

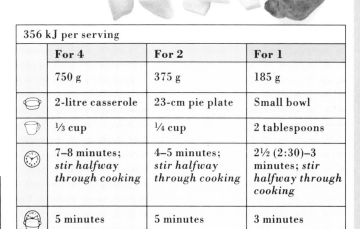

356 kJ per serving		
For 4	**For 2**	**For 1**
750 g	375 g	185 g
2-litre casserole	23-cm pie plate	Small bowl
⅓ cup	¼ cup	2 tablespoons
7–8 minutes; *stir halfway through cooking*	4–5 minutes; *stir halfway through cooking*	2½ (2:30)–3 minutes; *stir halfway through cooking*
5 minutes	5 minutes	3 minutes

Cook artichokes and water, covered, on High (100% power) for time in Chart. Allow to stand, covered, for time in Chart. Jerusalem artichoke pieces are done when centres are tender-crisp if pierced with a sharp knife. Drain.

ASPARAGUS

Select asparagus with 12-mm-thick stalks. Hold base of stalk firmly and bend stalk; the end will break off at the spot where it becomes too tough to eat. Discard ends; trim scales if stalks are gritty.

About 87 kJ per serving		
For 4	**For 2**	**For 1**
500 g (15–16 spears)	250 g (7–8 spears)	125 g (3–4 spears)
30-cm x 20-cm baking dish; *arrange tips overlapping in centre*	20-cm x 20-cm baking dish; *arrange tips facing in same direction*	20-cm plate; *arrange tips facing in same direction*
2 tablespoons	1 tablespoon	2 teaspoons
4½ (4:30)–6 minutes; *rotate dish halfway through cooking*	2½ (2:30)–3 minutes; *rotate dish halfway through cooking*	1½ (1:30)–2 minutes
3–5 minutes	3–5 minutes	3–5 minutes

Cook asparagus and water, covered, on High (100% power) for time in Chart. Allow to stand, covered, for time in Chart. Asparagus spears are done when tender-crisp. Drain.

BEANS, BROAD (FROZEN)

544 kJ per serving		
For 4	**For 2**	**For 1**
625 g	310 g	155 g
2-litre casserole	1-litre casserole	1-cup glass jug
½ cup	¼ cup	1 tablespoon
10–12 minutes; *stir every 3 minutes*	7–8 minutes; *stir twice during cooking*	2–3 minutes; *stir halfway through cooking*
5 minutes	5 minutes	5 minutes
Cook broad beans and water, covered, on High (100% power) for time in Chart. Allow to stand, covered, for time in Chart. Frozen broad beans are done when tender. Drain.		

BEANS, BUTTER

(ALSO CALLED YELLOW WAX BEANS)
Rinse under cold
running water.
Top and tail.

88 kJ per serving		
For 4	**For 2**	**For 1**
500 g	250 g	125 g
20-cm x 20-cm baking dish	23-cm pie plate	Small bowl
1 cup	½ cup	⅓ cup
12–14 minutes; *stir every 4 minutes*	6–7 minutes; *stir halfway through cooking*	3½ (3:30)– 4½ (4:30) minutes; *stir halfway through cooking*
5 minutes	5 minutes	5 minutes
Cook beans and water, covered, on High (100% power) for time in Chart. Allow to stand, covered, for time in Chart. Butter beans are done when tender-crisp. Drain.		

BEANS, GREEN
Rinse under cold running
water. Top and tail.

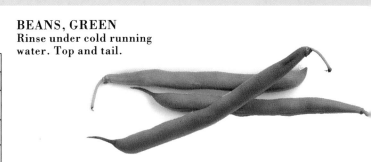

112 kJ per serving		
For 4	**For 2**	**For 1**
500 g	250 g	125 g
20-cm x 20-cm baking dish	23-cm pie plate	Small bowl
1 cup	½ cup	⅓ cup
12–14 minutes; *stir every 4 minutes*	6–7 minutes; *stir halfway through cooking*	3½ (3:30)– 4½ (4:30) minutes; *stir halfway through cooking*
5 minutes	5 minutes	5 minutes
Cook beans and water, covered, on High (100% power) for time in Chart. Allow to stand, covered, for time in Chart. Green beans are done when tender-crisp. Drain.		

BEANS, GREEN (FROZEN)

About 100 kJ per serving		
For 4	**For 2**	**For 1**
500 g	250 g	125 g
2-litre casserole	1-litre casserole	Small bowl
None	None	None
8–10 minutes; *stir halfway through cooking*	6–7 minutes; *stir halfway through cooking*	2–3 minutes; *stir halfway through cooking*
4 minutes	3 minutes	1–2 minutes
Cook beans, covered, on High (100% power) for time in Chart. Allow to stand, covered, for time in Chart. Frozen beans are done when tender-crisp.		

BEANS, RUNNER
Rinse under cold running water. Top and tail, then cut into 2.5-cm pieces.

92 kJ per serving			
	For 4	**For 2**	**For 1**
	500 g	250 g	125 g
🍲	2-litre casserole	1-litre casserole	1-litre casserole
☕	3 tablespoons	1½ tablespoons	3 teaspoons
⏰	10–14 minutes; *stir 3 times during cooking*	4–6 minutes; *stir halfway through cooking*	3–4 minutes; *stir halfway through cooking*
⏲	2 minutes	2 minutes	1 minute

Cook beans and water, covered, on High (100% power) for time in Chart. Allow to stand, covered, for time in Chart. Runner beans are done when tender-crisp. Drain.

BEETROOT

Cut off tops; leave part of stalks and roots on beetroot. Wash; take care not to damage skins as this will cause 'bleeding' during cooking. Cut off stalks and roots and peel after standing. Skin will slip off easily if it is peeled from bottom to top. If you like, wear rubber gloves when handling beetroot to prevent staining hands.

250 kJ per serving			
	For 4	**For 2**	**For 1**
	8 beetroot (about 125 g each)	4 beetroot (about 125 g each)	2 beetroot (about 125 g each)
🍲	30-cm x 20-cm baking dish; *arrange along long edges with root ends overlapping in centre*	1-litre casserole; *arrange around edge with root ends overlapping in centre*	1-litre casserole; *arrange with root ends overlapping in centre*
☕	None	None	None
⏰	20 minutes; *turn beetroot over and rotate dish halfway through cooking*	12 minutes; *turn beetroot over and rotate dish halfway through cooking*	8 minutes; *turn beetroot over and rotate dish halfway through cooking*
⏲	5 minutes	5 minutes	5 minutes

Cook beetroot, covered, on High (100% power) for time in Chart. Allow to stand, covered, for time in Chart. Beetroot are done when centres are tender if pierced with a sharp knife.

BROCCOLI (SPEARS)
Remove large leaves and trim woody ends of stalks. Cut through stalks lengthways 2–3 times. Rinse under cold running water.

About 125 kJ per serving			
	For 4	**For 2**	**For 1**
	500 g	250 g	125 g
🍲	30-cm x 20-cm baking dish; *arrange with flowerets overlapping in centre*	23-cm pie plate; *arrange spears facing in same direction*	20-cm plate; *arrange spears facing in same direction*
☕	¼ cup	¼ cup	Whatever clings after rinsing
⏰	5–6 minutes; *rotate dish halfway through cooking*	3½ (3:30)–4 minutes; *rotate dish halfway through cooking*	1½ (1:30)–1¾ (1:45) minutes
⏲	5 minutes	3–4 minutes	3–4 minutes

Cook broccoli and water, covered, on High (100% power) for time in Chart. Allow to stand, covered, for time in Chart. Broccoli spears are done when tender-crisp. Drain.

BROCCOLI (PIECES)
Remove leaves and trim woody ends of stalks. Cut stalks and flowerets into bite-sized pieces. Rinse under cold running water.

About 125 kJ per serving			
	For 4	**For 2**	**For 1**
	500 g	250 g	125 g
🍲	2-litre casserole	1-litre casserole	Small bowl
☕	¼ cup	2 tablespoons	1 tablespoon
⏰	6–7 minutes; *stir halfway through cooking*	3½ (3:30)–4 minutes; *stir halfway through cooking*	1½ (1:30)–2 minutes; *stir halfway through cooking*
⏲	5 minutes	5 minutes	5 minutes

Cook broccoli and water, covered, on High (100% power) for time in Chart. Allow to stand, covered, for time in Chart. Broccoli pieces are done when tender-crisp. Drain.

BRUSSELS SPROUTS

Look for firm, bright green sprouts with tight-fitting outer leaves free from black spots. Puffy or soft sprouts are usually poor in quality. Remove any yellow leaves and trim stems; rinse under cold running water.

About 170 kJ per serving		
For 4	**For 2**	**For 1**
625 g	310 g	155 g
2-litre casserole	23-cm pie plate	Small bowl
¼ cup	¼ cup	2 tablespoons
8–9 minutes; *stir halfway though cooking*	6–7 minutes; *stir halfway through cooking*	3–3½ (3:30) minutes; *stir halfway through cooking*
5 minutes	5 minutes	5 minutes

Cook Brussels sprouts and water, covered, on High (100% power) for time in Chart. Allow to stand, covered, for time in Chart. Brussels sprouts are done when centres are tender-crisp if pierced with a sharp knife. Drain.

CABBAGE, CHINESE

Trim stalk end. Rinse leaves under cold running water. Cut crossways into 4-cm slices.

About 55 kJ per serving		
For 4	**For 2**	**For 1**
625 g	310 g	155 g
3-litre casserole	2-litre casserole	1-litre casserole
¼ cup	2 tablespoons	Whatever clings after rinsing
4–5 minutes; *stir halfway through cooking*	3–4 minutes; *stir halfway through cooking*	2–3 minutes; *stir halfway through cooking*
3–4 minutes	3 minutes	2–3 minutes

Cook cabbage and water, covered, on High (100% power) for time in Chart. Allow to stand, covered, for time in Chart. Chinese cabbage slices are done when tender-crisp; the volume will be reduced by about half. Drain.

CABBAGE, GREEN
(WEDGES)

Discard any tough outer leaves. Cut cabbage in half, then into quarters; cut cores from wedges, leaving just enough to hold leaves together.

About 87 kJ per serving		
For 4	**For 2**	**For 1**
1 small head (about 500 g)	½ small head (about 250 g)	¼ small head (about 125 g)
20-cm x 20-cm baking dish; *arrange wedges spoke fashion*	20-cm x 20-cm baking dish; *arrange wedges 2.5 cm apart*	23-cm pie plate
¼ cup	¼ cup	2 tablespoons
12 minutes; *rotate dish halfway through cooking*	6–7 minutes; *rotate dish halfway through cooking*	3½ (3:30)–4 minutes
5 minutes	3 minutes	3 minutes

Cook cabbage and water, covered, on High (100% power) for time in Chart. Allow to stand, covered, for time in Chart. Green cabbage wedges are done when tender-crisp. Drain.

CABBAGE, GREEN
(SHREDS)

Discard any tough outer leaves. Cut cabbage in half, then into quarters; cut cores from wedges. Shred cabbage with a knife or in a food processor.

About 87 kJ per serving		
For 4	**For 2**	**For 1**
1 medium head (about 750 g)	½ medium head (about 375 g)	¼ medium head (about 185 g)
2-litre casserole	1-litre casserole	Small bowl
¼ cup	2 tablespoons	1 tablespoon
6–7 minutes; *stir every 3 minutes*	4–5 minutes; *stir halfway through cooking*	2–3 minutes; *stir halfway through cooking*
5 minutes	5 minutes	3 minutes

Cook cabbage and water, covered, on High (100% power) for time in Chart. Allow to stand, covered, for time in Chart. Green cabbage shreds are done when tender-crisp. Drain.

CABBAGE, RED

Prepare as for green cabbage shreds (left). The vinegar is added to the cooking liquid to prevent cabbage from turning an unappetising blue colour.

About 89 kJ per serving		
	For 4	**For 2**	**For 1**
	1 small head (about 375 g)	½ small head (about 185 g)	¼ small head (about 90 g)
	1-litre casserole	Small bowl	Small bowl
	¼ cup water *plus ¼ cup white vinegar; toss well*	2 tablespoons water *plus 2 tablespoons white vinegar; toss well*	1 tablespoon water *plus 1 tablespoon white vinegar; toss well*
	14–16 minutes; *stir halfway through cooking*	10–12 minutes; *stir halfway through cooking*	5–6 minutes; *stir halfway through cooking*
	5 minutes	5 minutes	5 minutes

Cook cabbage, water and vinegar, covered, on High (100% power) for time in Chart. Allow to stand, covered, for time in Chart. Red cabbage shreds are done when tender-crisp. Drain.

CARROTS

Scrape or peel; rinse under cold running water. Cut off both ends.

About 137 kJ per serving		
	For 4	**For 2**	**For 1**
	500 g	250 g	125 g
	20-cm x 20-cm baking dish; *alternate narrow ends*	23-cm pie plate; *alternate narrow ends*	20-cm plate; *alternate narrow ends*
	¼ cup	¼ cup	2 tablespoons
	7–9 minutes; *rearrange carrots halfway through cooking*	5–6½ (6:30) minutes; *rearrange carrots halfway through cooking*	2½ (2:30)–3 minutes; *rotate plate halfway through cooking*
	5 minutes	5 minutes	5 minutes

Cook carrots and water, covered, on High (100% power) for time in Chart. Allow to stand, covered, for time in Chart. Carrots are done when thickest sections are tender-crisp if pierced with a sharp knife. Drain.

CAPSICUM

Rinse under cold running water. Cut a slice from stalk end; remove core, seeds and white membranes. Cut capsicums in half lengthways; cut each half lengthways into 12-mm strips.

About 131 kJ per serving		
	For 4	**For 2**	**For 1**
	4 capsicums (125 g–155 g each)	2 capsicums (125 g–155 g each)	1 capsicum (125 g–155 g)
	2-litre casserole	1-litre casserole	Small bowl
	2 tablespoons	1½ tablespoons	3 teaspoons
	5½ (5:30)–7 minutes; *stir after 3 minutes*	4–5 minutes; *stir after 3 minutes*	2–3 minutes; *stir halfway through cooking*
	5 minutes	5 minutes	5 minutes

Cook capsicums and water, covered, on High (100% power) for time in Chart; after stirring, check texture and stop cooking when slightly less done than desired. Allow to stand, covered, for time in Chart. Capsicum strips are done when tender-crisp. Drain.

CARROTS (SLICES)

Scrape or peel; rinse under cold running water. Cut off both ends. Cut crossways into 6-mm slices.

About 137 kJ per serving		
	For 4	**For 2**	**For 1**
	500 g	250 g	125 g
	1-litre casserole; *arrange larger slices around edge*	23-cm pie plate; *arrange larger slices around edge*	Small bowl
	½ cup	¼ cup	2 tablespoons
	7–9 minutes; *stir twice during cooking*	5–6½ (6:30) minutes; *stir halfway through cooking*	2½ (2:30)–3½ (3:30) minutes; *stir halfway through cooking*
	5 minutes	5 minutes	5 minutes

Cook carrots and water, covered, on High (100% power) for time in Chart. Allow to stand, covered, for time in Chart. Carrot slices are done when larger and smaller pieces are equally tender-crisp. Drain.

CARROTS, BABY
(FROZEN)

206 kJ per serving			
	For 4	**For 2**	**For 1**
	625 g	310 g	155 g
⊝	20-cm x 20-cm baking dish	23-cm pie plate	Small bowl
🝐	None	None	None
🕐	5–7 minutes; *stir halfway through cooking*	4 minutes; *stir halfway through cooking*	3 minutes; *stir halfway through cooking*
⌛	4 minutes	3 minutes	2 minutes

Cook carrots, covered, on High (100% power) for time in Chart. Allow to stand, covered, for time in Chart. Frozen baby carrots are done when tender.

CAULIFLOWER
Keeping cauliflower whole, remove leaves and cut out core. Rinse under cold running water.

About 200 kJ per serving			
	For 4	**For 2**	**For 1**
	1 medium head (about 1 kg)	1 small head (about 500 g)	½ small head (about 250 g)
⊝	23-cm pie plate	23-cm pie plate	23-cm pie plate
🝐	¼ cup	2 tablespoons	1 tablespoon
🕐	12–14 minutes; *rotate plate halfway through cooking*	8–9 minutes; *rotate plate halfway through cooking*	5–6 minutes; *rotate plate halfway through cooking*
⌛	5 minutes	5 minutes	5 minutes

Cook cauliflower and water, covered, on High (100% power) for time in Chart. Allow to stand, covered, for time in Chart. Cauliflower is done when stalk end is fork-tender. Drain.

CAULIFLOWER
(FLOWERETS)
Remove outer green leaves and core. Separate into flowerets; large flowerets can be cut in half for more even cooking. Rinse under cold running water.

About 200 kJ per serving			
	For 4	**For 2**	**For 1**
	1 medium head (about 1 kg)	1 small head (about 500 g)	½ small head (about 250 g)
⊝	2-litre casserole; *arrange larger pieces around edge*	1-litre casserole; *arrange larger pieces around edge*	Small bowl
🝐	¼ cup	¼ cup	2 tablespoons
🕐	8–9 minutes; *stir every 3 minutes*	5–6 minutes; *stir halfway through cooking*	3–4 minutes; *stir halfway through cooking*
⌛	5 minutes	5 minutes	3–4 minutes

Cook cauliflower and water, covered, on High (100% power) for time in Chart. Allow to stand, covered, for time in Chart. Cauliflower flowerets are done when tender-crisp. Drain.

CELERIAC
Cut off roots; peel and cut out any pitted areas. Rinse celeriac under cold running water. Cut into 12-mm-thick pieces.

About 225 kJ per serving			
	For 4	**For 2**	**For 1**
	1 large celeriac (about 750 kg)	½ large celeriac (about 375 g)	1 small celeriac (about 185 g)
⊝	2-litre casserole	1-litre casserole	Small bowl
🝐	½ cup	¼ cup	2 tablespoons
🕐	9–10 minutes; *stir every 3 minutes*	4–5 minutes; *stir halfway through cooking*	2½ (2:30)–3 minutes
⌛	5 minutes	5 minutes	3 minutes

Cook celeriac and water, covered, on High (100% power) for time in Chart. Allow to stand, covered, for time in Chart. Celeriac pieces are done when tender-crisp. Drain.

CELERY

Remove leaves; trim root end. Scrub stalks under cold running water. Peel off any coarse strings. Cut stalks crossways into 6-mm slices

About 62 kJ per serving			
	For 4	**For 2**	**For 1**
	1 medium bunch (about 500 g)	½ bunch (about 250 g)	¼ bunch (about 125 g)
🍲	1-litre casserole	Small bowl	Small bowl
🥤	¼ cup	2 tablespoons	1 tablespoon
🕐	6–7 minutes; *stir halfway through cooking*	4–5 minutes; *stir halfway through cooking*	2–3 minutes; *stir halfway though cooking*
⏲	5 minutes	5 minutes	5 minutes

Cook celery and water, covered, on High (100% power) for time in Chart. Allow to stand, covered, for time in Chart. Celery slices are done when tender-crisp. Drain.

CHICORY

Rinse under cold running water. Remove any bruised leaves. Trim root ends without disconnecting leaves; remove bitter cone-shaped core by inserting the point of a sharp knife about 2.5 cm into base, cutting around the circular outline.

About 160 kJ per serving			
	For 4	**For 2**	**For 1**
	8 heads (about 125 g each)	4 heads (about 125 g each)	2 heads (about 125 g each)
🍲	30-cm x 20-cm baking dish; *arrange along narrow ends with tips pointing towards centre*	20-cm x 20-cm baking dish; *alternate tips*	23-cm pie plate; *alternate tips*
🥤	1 cup	⅔ cup	⅔ cup
🕐	16–18 minutes; *turn each head over and rotate dish halfway through cooking*	12–14 minutes; *turn each head over and rotate dish halfway through cooking*	8–10 minutes; *turn each head over and rotate dish halfway through cooking*
⏲	5 minutes	5 minutes	5 minutes

Cook chicory and water, covered, on High (100% power) for time in Chart. Allow to stand, covered, for time in Chart. Chicory is done when tender. Drain.

CHOKOS

Select firm, very young chokos. Rinse under cold running water; pat dry. With fork, pierce skin.

About 139 kJ per serving			
	For 4	**For 2**	**For 1**
	4 chokos (about 185 g each)	2 chokos (about 185 g each)	1 choko (about 185 g)
🍲	Wrap individually in plastic wrap; *arrange on oven floor in a circle*	Wrap individually in plastic wrap; *arrange on oven floor in a circle*	Wrap in plastic wrap; *place in centre of oven floor*
🥤	None	None	None
🕐	10–12 minutes; *turn and rearrange halfway through cooking*	7–8 minutes; *turn and rearrange halfway through cooking*	5–6 minutes; *turn choko over halfway through cooking*
⏲	5 minutes	5 minutes	5 minutes

Cook chokos, wrapped, on High (100% power) for time in Chart. Allow to stand, still wrapped, for time in Chart. Chokos are done when thickest area of flesh can be pierced easily down to the seed with a sharp knife.

CORN-ON-THE-COB (see page 263)
CORN COBS (FROZEN)

About 475 kJ per serving			
	For 4	**For 2**	**For 1**
	4 cobs	2 cobs	1 cob
🍲	Wrap individually in plastic wrap; *arrange on oven floor in a circle*	Wrap individually in plastic wrap; *arrange on oven floor*	Wrap in plastic wrap; *place in centre of oven floor*
🥤	None	None	None
🕐	8–10 minutes; *turn and rearrange halfway through cooking*	6–7 minutes; *turn and rearrange halfway through cooking*	3–4 minutes; *turn cob over halfway through cooking*
⏲	5 minutes	5 minutes	5 minutes

Cook corn, wrapped, on High (100% power) for time in Chart. Allow to stand, wrapped, for time in Chart. Frozen corn cobs are done when tender.

CORN KERNELS (FROZEN)

About 335 kJ per serving		
	For 4	**For 2**	**For 1**
	625 g	310 g	155 g
🍲	1-litre casserole	Small bowl	Small bowl
🥛	2 tablespoons	1 tablespoon	2 teaspoons
🕐	8–9 minutes; *stir halfway through cooking*	5–7 minutes; *stir halfway through cooking*	1½ (1:30)–2½ (2:30) minutes; *stir halfway through cooking*
⏲	5 minutes	3–5 minutes	1–2 minutes

Cook corn and water, covered, on High (100% power) for time in Chart. Allow to stand, covered, for time in Chart. Frozen corn kernels are done when hot. Drain.

EGGPLANT

Prepare just before cooking because flesh turns brown if exposed to air. Rinse under cold running water and pat dry. Trim off stalk end. Cut eggplant into 12-mm pieces.

131 kJ per serving		
	For 4	**For 2**	**For 1**
	1 large eggplant (about 750 g)	1 medium eggplant (about 375 g)	½ medium eggplant (about 185 g)
🍲	3-litre casserole	1.5-litre casserole	1-litre casserole
🥛	¼ cup	2 tablespoons	1 tablespoon
🕐	8–9 minutes; *stir halfway through cooking*	6–7 minutes; *stir halfway through cooking*	3–4 minutes; *stir halfway through cooking*
⏲	5 minutes	5 minutes	5 minutes

Cook eggplant and water, covered, on High (100% power) for time in Chart. Allow to stand, covered, for time in Chart. Eggplant pieces are done when tender. Drain.

FENNEL

Rinse under cold running water. Cut off root ends and leaves from bulbs. Cut bulbs in half lengthways, then slice crossways into 6-mm slices.

100 kJ per serving		
	For 4	**For 2**	**For 1**
	2 bulbs (about 250 g each)	1 bulb (about 250 g)	½ bulb (about 125 g)
🍲	20-cm x 20-cm baking dish	20-cm pie plate	Small bowl
🥛	1 cup	½ cup	¼ cup
🕐	10–12 minutes; *stir every 3–4 minutes*	7–8 minutes; *stir halfway through cooking*	4–4½ (4:30) minutes; *stir halfway through cooking*
⏲	5 minutes	5 minutes	5 minutes

Cook fennel and water, covered, on High (100% power) for time in Chart. Allow to stand, covered, for time in Chart. Fennel slices are done when tender-crisp. Drain.

KOHLRABI

Cut off tops and discard. Rinse under cold running water. Peel thinly and cut into 6-mm slices.

About 175 kJ per serving		
	For 4	**For 2**	**For 1**
	500 g	250 g	125 g
🍲	1-litre casserole; *arrange larger slices around edge*	23-cm pie plate; *arrange larger slices around edge*	Small bowl
🥛	¼ cup	2 tablespoons	1 tablespoon
🕐	13–14 minutes; *stir halfway through cooking*	9–10 minutes; *stir halfway through cooking*	5–6 minutes; *stir halfway through cooking*
⏲	5 minutes	5 minutes	5 minutes

Cook kohlrabi and water, covered, on High (100% power) for time in Chart. Allow to stand, covered, for time in Chart. Kohlrabi slices are done when tender. Drain.

LEEKS

Trim off roots and leaf ends, leaving 2.5 cm–5 cm above white parts. Cut each leek in half lengthways. Carefully wash under cold running water to remove all grit. Divide leeks into number of servings. Tie loosely into bundles with string.

MUSHROOMS

Do not peel or soak; soaking will make mushrooms soggy. Instead, wipe with a damp cloth if necessary. Cut off thin slice from base of each stalk.

About 275 kJ per serving		
For 4	**For 2**	**For 1**
8 leeks (about 1 kg)	4 leeks (about 500 g)	2 leeks (about 250 g)
30-cm x 20-cm baking dish; *arrange bundles along edges with centre empty*	20-cm x 20-cm baking dish	Small bowl
1½ cups	1 cup	½ cup
18–20 minutes; *turn leeks over halfway through cooking*	15–18 minutes; *turn leeks over halfway through cooking*	10–12 minutes; *turn leeks over halfway through cooking*
5 minutes	5 minutes	5 minutes

Cook leeks and water, covered, on High (100% power) for time in Chart. Allow to stand, covered, for time in Chart. Leek halves are done when tender. Drain and untie.

119 kJ per serving (without butter or margarine)		
For 4	**For 2**	**For 1**
500 g	250 g	125 g
2-litre casserole	1-litre casserole	Small bowl
3 teaspoons water; *or 30 g melted butter or margarine*	1½ teaspoons water; *or 15 g melted butter or margarine*	¾ teaspoon water; *or 1½ teaspoons melted butter or margarine*
5–7 minutes; *stir twice during cooking*	4–6 minutes; *stir twice during cooking*	1½ (1:30)–2 minutes; *stir halfway through cooking*
3–4 minutes	3–4 minutes	1–2 minutes

Cook mushrooms and water or melted butter, covered, on High (100% power) for time in Chart. Allow to stand, covered, for time in Chart. Mushrooms are done when tender. Drain if cooked with water.

MARROW

Select marrows that are firm and not too large. Peel and cut in half; scoop out seeds. Cut flesh into 2.5-cm slices or into chunks.

MUSHROOMS (SLICES)

Prepare as for mushrooms (above). With sharp knife, cut vertically into slices.

75 kJ per serving		
For 4	**For 2**	**For 1**
500 g	250 g	125 g
2-litre casserole	1-litre casserole	1-litre casserole
2 tablespoons	1 tablespoon	2 teaspoons
8–10 minutes; *stir halfway through cooking*	5–6 minutes; *stir halfway through cooking*	3–4 minutes; *stir halfway through cooking*
3 minutes	2 minutes	1 minute

Cook marrow and water, covered, on High (100% power) for time in Chart. Allow to stand, covered, for time in Chart. Marrow pieces are done when tender. Drain.

119 kJ per serving (without butter or margarine)		
For 4	**For 2**	**For 1**
500 g	250 g	125 g
2-litre casserole	1-litre casserole	Small bowl
3 teaspoons water; *or 30 g melted butter or margarine; stir well to coat*	1½ teaspoons water; *or 15 g melted butter or margarine; stir well to coat*	¾ teaspoon water; *or 1½ teaspoons melted butter or margarine; stir well to coat*
5–7 minutes; *stir halfway through cooking*	4–6 minutes; *stir halfway through cooking*	1½ (1:30)–2 minutes; *stir halfway through cooking*
3–4 minutes	3–4 minutes	1–2 minutes

Cook mushrooms and water or melted butter, covered, on High (100% power) for time in Chart. Allow to stand, covered, for time in Chart. Mushroom slices are done when tender. Drain if cooked with water.

OKRA

Select pods 6 cm–10 cm long. Wash under cold running water. Cut off stalks without cutting into pods.

84 kJ per serving		
For 4	**For 2**	**For 1**
500 g	250 g	125 g
30-cm x 20-cm baking dish; *arrange larger pods along edges*	23-cm pie plate; *arrange larger pods around edges*	Small bowl; *place smaller pods on bottom*
1 cup *plus 1 teaspoon white vinegar*	½ cup *plus ½ teaspoon white vinegar*	¼ cup *plus ¼ teaspoon white vinegar*
7–8 minutes; *stir halfway through cooking; check if done after 3 further minutes*	5–6 minutes; *stir halfway through cooking; check if done after 2 further minutes*	2½–3 minutes; *stir halfway through cooking; check if done after 1 further minute*
5 minutes	5 minutes	5 minutes

Cook okra, water and vinegar, covered, on High (100% power) for time in Chart. Allow to stand, covered, for time in Chart. Okra are done when pods are tender-crisp. Drain.

ONIONS

Select onions of uniform size, about 7.5 cm in diameter. Cut off tops. Trim root ends just enough to allow onions to stand upright; peel.

About 187 kJ per serving		
For 4	**For 2**	**For 1**
4 large onions (about 750 g)	2 large onions (about 375 g)	1 large onion (about 185 g)
20-cm x 20-cm baking dish; *arrange in circle*	23-cm pie plate; *arrange in centre of plate*	Small bowl
None	None	None
9–10 minutes; *rotate dish halfway through cooking*	6–7 minutes; *rotate plate halfway through cooking*	3½ (3:30)–4 minutes; *rotate bowl halfway through cooking*
5 minutes	5 minutes	5 minutes

Cook onions, covered, on High (100% power) for time in Chart. Allow to stand, covered, for time in Chart. Whole onions are done when tender-crisp if pierced with a sharp knife.

ONIONS, SMALL PICKLING

For even cooking, select onions of uniform size. Peel onions, leaving a little of the root ends to help them hold shape during cooking.

187 kJ per serving		
For 4	**For 2**	**For 1**
750 g	375 g	185 g
2-litre casserole	1-litre casserole	Small bowl
3 teaspoons	2 teaspoons	1 teaspoon
7–8 minutes; *stir halfway through cooking*	4–6 minutes; *stir halfway through cooking*	2½ (2:30)–3 minutes; *stir once*
5 minutes	5 minutes	5 minutes

Cook onions and water, covered, on High (100% power) for time in Chart. Allow to stand, covered, for time in Chart. Small pickling onions are done when centres are tender and outsides are slightly resistant if pierced with a sharp knife. Drain.

PARSNIPS

Scrub under cold running water. Cut off tops and root ends.

About 262 kJ per serving		
For 4	**For 2**	**For 1**
500 g	250 g	125 g
20-cm x 20-cm baking dish; *arrange with narrow ends alternating*	20-cm x 20-cm baking dish; *arrange with narrow ends alternating*	20-cm x 20-cm baking dish; *arrange with narrow ends alternating*
½ cup	½ cup	½ cup
7–9 minutes; *turn parsnips and rearrange halfway through cooking; do not rearrange if centre ones are smaller than those at edges*	5–7 minutes; *turn parsnips and rearrange halfway though cooking; do not rearrange if centre ones are smaller than those at edges*	3–4 minutes; *turn parsnips and rearrange halfway though cooking*
5 minutes	5 minutes	5 minutes

Cook parsnips and water, covered, on High (100% power) for time in Chart. Allow to stand, covered, for time in Chart. Parsnips are done when tender if pierced with a sharp knife. Drain.

PARSNIPS (PIECES)
Prepare as for parsnips (below left). Cut into 4-cm-long pieces. If mature parsnips are used, remove woody cores.

About 262 kJ per serving		
For 4	**For 2**	**For 1**
500 g	250 g	125 g
1-litre casserole; *arrange larger pieces around edge*	23-cm pie plate; *arrange larger pieces around edge*	Small bowl
½ cup	¼ cup	2 tablespoons
7–9 minutes; *stir every 3 minutes*	5–7 minutes; *stir halfway through cooking*	3–4 minutes; *stir halfway through cooking*
5 minutes	5 minutes	5 minutes

Cook parsnips and water, covered, on High (100% power) for time in Chart. Allow to stand, covered, for time in Chart. Parsnip pieces are done when tender. Drain.

PEAS
Shell peas by pressing pods between thumb and forefinger to open them.

About 251 kJ per serving		
For 4	**For 2**	**For 1**
1 kg (about 2 cups shelled)	500 g (about 1 cup shelled)	250 g (about ½ cup shelled)
1-litre casserole	Small bowl	Small bowl
¼ cup	2 tablespoons	1 tablespoon
6–7 minutes; *stir halfway through cooking*	4–5 minutes; *stir halfway through cooking*	2–2½ (2:30) minutes; *stir halfway through cooking*
3–5 minutes	3–5 minutes	3–5 minutes

Cook peas and water, covered, on High (100% power) for time in Chart. Allow to stand, covered, for time in Chart. Shelled peas are done when tender. Drain.

PEAS (FROZEN)

About 312 kJ per serving		
For 4	**For 2**	**For 1**
500 g	250 g	125 g
1-litre casserole	Small bowl	Small bowl
None	None	None
8–9 minutes; *stir halfway through cooking*	5–6 minutes; *stir halfway through cooking*	1½ (1:30)–2½ (2:30) minutes; *stir halfway through cooking*
5 minutes	3–4 minutes	1–2 minutes

Cook peas, covered, on High (100% power) for time in Chart. Allow to stand, covered, for time in Chart. Frozen peas are done when hot.

PEAS, SNOW
Rinse under cold running water. Remove stalks ends; remove strings along both sides of pods if necessary; do not shell.

88 kJ per serving		
For 4	**For 2**	**For 1**
250 g	125 g	60 g
20-cm x 20-cm baking dish	23-cm pie plate	Small bowl
2 tablespoons	1 tablespoon	2 teaspoons
4–5 minutes; *stir halfway through cooking; test after 4 minutes*	2–3 minutes; *stir halfway through cooking; test after 2½ (2:30) minutes*	1–1½ (1:30) minutes; *stir halfway through cooking; test after 1 minute*
30 seconds– 1 minute	30 seconds– 1 minute	30 seconds– 1 minute

Cook peas and water on High (100% power) for time in Chart. Allow to stand, covered, for time in Chart. Snow peas are done when tender. Drain.

VEGETABLES

POTATOES
Buy oval-shaped potatoes of uniform size. Scrub under cold running water. Pierce skin several times.

About 690 kJ per serving

	For 4	For 2	For 1
	4 large potatoes (about 250 g each)	2 large potatoes (about 250 g each)	1 large potato (about 250 g)
(pot)	Arrange in circle on paper towel on oven floor	Arrange on paper towel on oven floor	Place in centre of paper towel on oven floor
(jug)	None	None	None
(clock)	14–16 minutes; *turn potatoes over and rearrange halfway through cooking*	7–8 minutes; *turn potatoes over and rearrange halfway through cooking*	4–6 minutes; *turn potato over halfway through cooking*
(stand)	5 minutes; *wrap in foil or clean tea towel before standing*	5 minutes; *wrap in foil or clean tea towel before standing*	5 minutes; *wrap in foil or clean tea towel before standing*

Cook potatoes on High (100% power) for time in Chart. Allow to stand, wrapped, for time in Chart. Whole potatoes are done when tender if squeezed.

POTATOES (SLICES)
Scrub under cold running water. Peel old potatoes; new potatoes can be cooked with their skins on. Cut into 6-mm slices.

About 345 kJ per serving

	For 4	For 2	For 1
	500 g	250 g	125 g
(pot)	20-cm x 20-cm baking dish; *arrange larger slices around edges*	23-cm pie plate; *arrange larger slices around edge*	23-cm pie plate; *arrange larger slices around edge*
(jug)	½ cup	⅓ cup	2 tablespoons
(clock)	7–9 minutes; *stir halfway through cooking*	4½ (4:30)–5 minutes; *stir halfway through cooking*	3–3½ (3:30) minutes; *stir halfway through cooking*
(stand)	5 minutes	5 minutes	5 minutes

Cook potatoes and water, covered, on High (100% power) for time in Chart. Allow to stand, covered, for time in Chart. Potato slices are done when tender. Drain.

POTATOES (CHUNKS)
Scrub potatoes under cold running water. Peel and remove any blemishes or sprouts. Cut into 2.5-cm chunks.

About 517 kJ per serving

	For 4	For 2	For 1
	750 g	375 g	185 g
(pot)	20-cm x 20-cm baking dish	23-cm pie plate	4-cup glass jug
(jug)	¾ cup	½ cup	¼ cup
(clock)	10–12 minutes; *stir halfway through cooking*	6–8 minutes; *stir halfway through cooking*	5–6 minutes; *stir halfway through cooking*
(stand)	5 minutes	5 minutes	5 minutes

Cook potatoes and water, covered, on High (100% power) for time in Chart. Allow to stand, covered, for time in Chart. Potato chunks are done when tender. Drain.

POTATOES, NEW
Scrub potatoes under cold running water. Pierce each potato once with a fork or peel strip around centre of each with a vegetable peeler.

345 kJ per serving

	For 4	For 2	For 1
	500 g	250 g	125 g
(pot)	23-cm pie plate; *arrange larger potatoes around edge*	Small bowl	Small bowl
(jug)	¼ cup	2 tablespoons	1 tablespoon
(clock)	6–7 minutes; *turn potatoes over halfway through cooking*	3½ (3:30)–4 minutes; *turn potatoes over halfway through cooking*	2–2½ (2:30) minutes; *turn potatoes over halfway through cooking*
(stand)	5 minutes	5 minutes	3–5 minutes

Cook potatoes and water, covered, on High (100% power) for time in Chart. Allow to stand, covered, for time in Chart. New potatoes are done when tender if pierced with a sharp knife. Drain.

POTATOES, SWEET

Buy oval-shaped sweet potatoes of uniform size.
Scrub under cold running water; pierce skin several times.
If potatoes have tapered ends, arrange ends pointing
towards centre as these parts will cook more rapidly than
the rest of the vegetable. If ends seem tender halfway
through cooking, shield them with thin strips of foil.

About 674 kJ per serving		
For 4	**For 2**	**For 1**
4 sweet potatoes (about 250 g each)	2 sweet potatoes (about 250 g each)	1 sweet potato (about 250 g)
Arrange on paper towel on oven floor	Arrange on paper towel on oven floor	Place on paper towel on oven floor
None	None	None
10–11 minutes; *turn potatoes over and rearrange halfway through cooking*	7–8 minutes; *turn potatoes over halfway through cooking*	4–5 minutes; *turn potato over halfway through cooking*
5 minutes; *wrap in foil or clean tea towel before standing*	5 minutes; *wrap in foil or clean tea towel before standing*	5 minutes; *wrap in foil or clean tea towel before standing*

Cook potatoes on High (100% power) for time in Chart.
Allow to stand, covered, for time in Chart. Sweet potatoes
are done when tender.

PUMPKIN

Choose firm pumpkin with bright, well-coloured flesh.
Wipe over and cut into 2.5-cm chunks or slices;
peel or leave skin on.

About 285 kJ per serving		
For 4	**For 2**	**For 1**
750 g	375 g	185 g
2-litre casserole; *arrange thicker parts around edge*	1-litre casserole; *arrange thicker parts around edge*	23-cm pie plate; *arrange thicker parts around edge*
None	None	None
12–16 minutes; *rearrange halfway through cooking*	8–10 minutes; *rearrange halfway through cooking*	5–6 minutes; *rearrange halfway through cooking*
5 minutes	5 minutes	4 minutes

Cook pumpkin, covered, on High (100% power) for time
in Chart. Allow to stand, covered, for time in Chart.
Pumpkin pieces are done when tender if pierced with a
sharp knife.

PUMPKIN, BUTTERNUT

Rinse under cold running water and pat dry.
Cut in half lengthways; if pumpkin is heavier than 1 kg,
cut into quarters. Scoop out seeds.

About 502 kJ per serving		
For 4	**For 2**	**For 1**
1 large butternut pumpkin (about 1.5 kg)	1 medium butternut pumpkin (about 1 kg)	1 small butternut pumpkin (about 625 g)
Wrap quarters individually in plastic wrap; *arrange on oven floor, alternating narrow ends*	Wrap halves individually in plastic wrap; *arrange on oven floor, alternating narrow ends*	Wrap halves individually in plastic wrap; *arrange on oven floor, alternating narrow ends*
None	None	None
20–24 minutes; *rearrange halfway through cooking*	10–12 minutes; *rearrange halfway through cooking*	7–8 minutes; *rearrange halfway through cooking*
5 minutes	5 minutes	5 minutes

Cook pumpkin on High (100% power) for time in Chart.
Allow to stand, still wrapped, for time in Chart. Butternut
pumpkin is done when flesh is tender and can be scooped
easily from the shell; any pale yellow areas will continue
to cook during standing. If any area remains pale yellow
after standing, cook, rewrapped, for 30 seconds at a time
until rich yellow-orange.

SILVERBEET

Use only tender, green leaves.
Discard any damaged, dry or
yellow leaves and coarse
stalks. Wash under cold
running water; drain.

About 137 kJ per serving		
For 4	**For 2**	**For 1**
1 kg	500 g	250 g
4-litre casserole	3-litre casserole	1-litre casserole
Whatever clings after washing	Whatever clings after washing	Whatever clings after washing
12–14 minutes; *stir every 3 minutes*	8–9 minutes; *stir halfway through cooking and after completion*	5–6 minutes; *stir halfway through cooking and after completion*
5 minutes	5 minutes	5 minutes

Cook silverbeet, covered, on High (100% power) for time
in Chart. Allow to stand, covered, for time in Chart.
Silverbeet is done when tender. Drain.

SPINACH

Discard any yellowish and
wilted leaves. Remove stems
from spinach. Wash leaves
under cold running water;
chop roughly.

About 122 kJ per serving		
For 4	**For 2**	**For 1**
750 g	375 g	185 g
3-litre casserole	3-litre casserole	2-litre casserole
Whatever clings after washing	Whatever clings after washing	Whatever clings after washing
6–7 minutes; *stir halfway through cooking*	5½ (5:30)–6½ (6:30) minutes; *stir halfway through cooking*	3–3½ (3:30) minutes; *stir halfway through cooking*
4 minutes	3 minutes	3 minutes

Cook spinach, covered, on High (100% power) for time in
Chart. Allow to stand, covered, for time in Chart.
Spinach is done when leaves are wilted. Drain.

SQUASH, BUTTON
(ALSO CALLED PATTYPAN SQUASH)
Select squash which are uniform in size; halve any
large ones. Rinse under cold running water; drain.
Trim off stem, if necessary; do not peel.

About 88 kJ per serving		
For 4	**For 2**	**For 1**
500 g	250 g	125 g
1-litre casserole	1-litre casserole	Small bowl
1 tablespoon	2 teaspoons	1 teaspoon
6–8 minutes; *rearrange halfway through cooking*	4–5 minutes; *rearrange halfway through cooking*	2–3 minutes; *rearrange halfway through cooking*
5 minutes	5 minutes	3 minutes

Cook squash and water, covered, on High (100% power)
for time in Chart. Allow to stand, covered, for time in
Chart. Button squash are done when tender-crisp. Drain.

SQUASH, SPAGHETTI

Rinse under cold running water.
Cut squash in half lengthways.
Scrape out seeds and
membranes; discard.

About 285 kJ per serving		
For 4	**For 2**	**For 1**
1 large squash (about 2 kg)	1 medium squash (about 1 kg)	1 small squash (about 625 g)
Wrap each half individually in plastic wrap; *arrange on oven floor*	Wrap each half individually in plastic wrap; *arrange on oven floor*	Wrap each half individually in plastic wrap; *arrange on oven floor*
None	None	None
22–24 minutes; *rearrange halves halfway through cooking*	12–14 minutes; *rearrange halves halfway through cooking*	9–10 minutes; *rearrange halves halfway through cooking*
5 minutes	5 minutes	5 minutes

Cook squash, wrapped, on High (100% power) for time in
Chart. Allow to stand, still wrapped, for time in Chart.
Spaghetti squash halves are done when fork can easily pull
and separate squash strands. The texture is crisp compared
with other squash.

SWEDES
Cut into quarters.
Peel and cut into
2-cm chunks.

About 117 kJ per serving		
For 4	**For 2**	**For 1**
625 g	310 g	155 g
1-litre casserole	1-litre casserole	1-litre casserole
½ cup	¼ cup	¼ cup
17–19 minutes; *stir twice during cooking*	12–14 minutes; *stir twice during cooking*	7–9 minutes; *stir halfway through cooking*
5 minutes	5 minutes	5 minutes

Cook swede and water, covered, on High (100% power)
for time in Chart. Allow to stand, covered, for time in
Chart. Swede chunks are done when tender. Drain.

SWEETCORN
See corn (page 245)

TURNIPS
Peel. Cut into 2-cm chunks.

200 kJ per serving			
	For 4	**For 2**	**For 1**
	1 kg	500 g	250 g
⊖	2-litre casserole	1-litre casserole	Small bowl
⊔	½ cup	¼ cup	2 tablespoons
🕐	8–9½ (9:30) minutes; *stir halfway through cooking*	5–7 minutes; *stir halfway through cooking*	3½ (3:30)–4 minutes; *stir halfway through cooking*
🍲	5 minutes	5 minutes	5 minutes

Cook turnips and water, covered, on High (100% power) for time in Chart. Allow to stand, covered, for time in Chart. Turnip chunks are cooked when tender. Drain.

YAMS
Cook as for sweet potatoes (page 251)

ZUCCHINI
Choose zucchini which are uniform in size with same diameter top to bottom for even cooking. Rinse under cold running water. Trim ends; do not peel. Cut crossways into 6-mm slices.

About 87 kJ per serving			
	For 4	**For 2**	**For 1**
	500 g	250 g	125 g
⊖	1-litre casserole; *arrange larger slices around edge*	1-litre casserole; *arrange larger slices around edge*	Small bowl
⊔	2 tablespoons	1 tablespoon	1 teaspoon
🕐	6–7 minutes; *stir halfway through cooking*	4–5 minutes; *stir halfway through cooking*	2–2½ (2:30) minutes; *stir halfway through cooking*
🍲	5 minutes	5 minutes	3 minutes

Cook zucchini and water, covered, on High (100% power) for time in Chart. Allow to stand, covered, for time in Chart. Zucchini slices are done when tender-crisp. Drain.

SPECIAL TECHNIQUES FOR VEGETABLES
Use the microwave to help make a simple vegetable look really special, and dress up a dinner party meal by serving a colourful selection of puréed vegetables, or delicate vegetable ribbons or rings. Use your imagination to create different combinations of colours, flavours and shapes.

Vegetable purées are particularly good to serve when entertaining because they can be made in advance and reheated in the microwave; they go well with roast meats and grilled chicken. The ribbons and rings can also be served uncooked as a salad with a favourite dressing.

Vegetable purées Root vegetables such as potatoes, carrots and parsnips cook quickly in the microwave; leafy green vegetables such as spinach and broccoli remain bright and green.

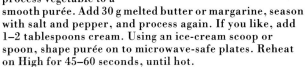

Cook vegetables, covered, on High (100% power) for 2 minutes longer than time in Charts; drain well. In processor with knife blade attached, process vegetable to a smooth purée. Add 30 g melted butter or margarine, season with salt and pepper, and process again. If you like, add 1–2 tablespoons cream. Using an ice-cream scoop or spoon, shape purée on to microwave-safe plates. Reheat on High for 45–60 seconds, until hot.

Ribbon vegetables With vegetable peeler, shred 1 large carrot, 1 medium zucchini and 1 white radish (mooli) into long ribbons, about 2.5-cm wide, pressing lightly with peeler. Toss vegetables in a large bowl with 15 g melted butter or margarine. Cook, covered, on High (100% power) for 30 seconds–1 minute, until tender-crisp.

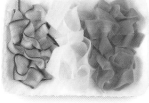

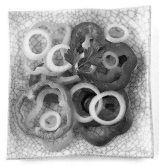

Vegetable rings Cut 3 capsicums (green, yellow and red) and 1 small onion into rings; remove cores, seeds and membranes from capsicums. Toss vegetables in a 33-cm x 23-cm baking dish with 15 g melted butter or margarine, 3 teaspoons vegetable oil or 1 tablespoon water. Cook, covered, on High (100% power) for 1–2 minutes, until tender-crisp. Serve hot, or refrigerate to serve chilled later with dressing.

Individual vegetables

ASPARAGUS BUNDLES

Colour Index page 70. 285 kJ per serving. Low in cholesterol, sodium. Good source of vitamin A.
Begin 25 minutes ahead.

Ingredients	For 4	For 2	For 1
Asparagus spears	500 g	250 g	125 g
Spring onions	2	1	1
Water	2 tablespoons	1 tablespoon	2 teaspoons
Butter or margarine	30 g	15 g	1½ teaspoons
Canned pimiento, diced	2 tablespoons	1 tablespoon	2 teaspoons
Lemon juice	1 tablespoon	2 teaspoons	1 teaspoon
Microwave cookware	30-cm x 20-cm baking dish Small bowl	30-cm x 20-cm baking dish Small bowl	30-cm x 20-cm baking dish Small bowl
Time on High (100% power) Asparagus	5–7 minutes	3–5 minutes	1½ (1:30)–2½ (2:30) minutes
Butter mixture	45 seconds	30 seconds	15 seconds

1 Hold base of each asparagus spear firmly and bend; the end will break off where the spear becomes too tough to eat. Discard tough ends; trim scales if stalks are gritty.

2 Cut spring onions where white ends and green starts. Cut green ends in half lengthways. Thinly slice white ends and reserve.

3 Divide asparagus into bundles, with tips pointing in same direction. Use green ends of spring onions to tie up asparagus bundles.

4 Arrange asparagus bundles in baking dish (see Chart) with tips overlapping in centre of dish and tougher, thicker ends pointing towards edges of dish.

5 Sprinkle bundles with water. Cook, covered, on High for time in Chart, until asparagus is tender-crisp, rotating dish halfway through cooking. Drain; cover loosely and put aside while preparing sauce.

6 In small bowl (see Chart), place reserved sliced spring onions, butter and pimiento. Cook, covered with paper towel, on High for time in Chart, or until butter has melted. Stir in lemon juice. Spoon sauce over asparagus. Serve immediately.

ASPARAGUS WITH CELERY AND WALNUTS

Colour Index page 70. 4 servings. 243 kJ per serving. Low in cholesterol, sodium.
Begin 25 minutes ahead.

2 teaspoons olive or vegetable oil
2 tablespoons chopped walnuts
3 celery stalks
375 g asparagus spears
1 clove garlic, crushed
Salt to taste

1. Combine oil and walnuts in a 23-cm pie plate. Heat on High (100% power) for 1–3 minutes, until walnuts are lightly toasted, stirring once. With slotted spoon, transfer walnuts to paper towel to drain.
2. Meanwhile, cut celery stalks diagonally into 5-cm pieces. Discard tough ends and trim scales from asparagus; cut asparagus diagonally into 5-cm pieces.
3. Stir celery, asparagus and garlic into oil remaining in pie plate. Cook on High for 6–8 minutes, until asparagus is tender-crisp, stirring twice. Season with salt. Add walnuts and toss lightly.
4. Arrange vegetables on a warmed serving dish. Serve immediately.

BRAISED BEANS WITH TOMATOES AND ONIONS

Colour Index page 76. 4 servings. 519 kJ per serving. Low in cholesterol. Good source of vitamin C, iron.
Begin 35 minutes ahead.

2 tablespoons olive or vegetable oil
2 red onions, sliced
2 teaspoons chopped fresh oregano or ½ teaspoon dried oregano
215 g can tomatoes, chopped
500 g green beans
½ cup beef stock
Salt to taste
¼ cup grated Parmesan cheese

1. Place oil, onions and oregano in a 2-litre casserole. Cook on High (100% power) for 5–6 minutes, until softened, stirring twice.
2. Add tomatoes, beans and stock; mix well. Cook, covered, on High for 20 minutes, or until beans are tender and flavours blend, stirring occasionally. Season with salt.
3. Spoon beans on to a warmed serving dish; sprinkle with grated Parmesan cheese.

BROAD BEANS WITH BUTTERED BREADCRUMBS

Colour Index page 70. 643 kJ per serving. Low in cholesterol.
Begin 20 minutes ahead.

Ingredients	For 4	For 2	For 1
Butter or margarine	30 g	15 g	1½ teaspoons
Fresh breadcrumbs	½ cup	¼ cup	2 tablespoons
Frozen broad beans, thawed	375 g	185 g	90 g
Water	2 tablespoons	1 tablespoon	2 teaspoons
Grated Parmesan cheese	2 tablespoons	1 tablespoon	2 teaspoons
Microwave cookware	23-cm pie plate Medium bowl	23-cm pie plate Small bowl	23-cm pie plate Soup bowl
Time on High (100% power) Butter	45 seconds	30–45 seconds	15 seconds
Breadcrumbs	2–2½ (2:30) minutes	1½ (1:30)–1¾ (1:45) minutes	1–1¼ (1:15) minutes
Broad beans	6–8 minutes	4–5 minutes	2–3 minutes

1 Heat butter in pie plate (see Chart), covered with paper towel, on High for time in Chart, or until melted.

2 Stir in breadcrumbs. Cook on High for time in Chart, until crumbs are dried and golden, stirring twice; put aside.

3 Place broad beans and water in bowl (see Chart). Cook, covered, on High for time in Chart, until tender, stirring once; drain. Stir in Parmesan cheese. Transfer to a warmed serving dish; sprinkle with buttered breadcrumbs. Serve immediately.

GREEN BEANS WITH PEANUT SAUCE

Colour Index page 71. 1017 kJ per serving. Low in cholesterol. Good source of vitamin A, niacin, vitamin C, iron, fibre.
Begin 25 minutes ahead.

Ingredients	For 4	For 2	For 1
Garlic	2 cloves	1 clove	½ clove
Red capsicum	1	½	¼
Crunchy peanut butter	½ cup	¼ cup	2 tablespoons
Vegetable or chicken stock	½ cup	¼ cup	2 tablespoons
Soy sauce	3 teaspoons	1½ teaspoons	¾ teaspoon
Cider vinegar	3 teaspoons	1½ teaspoons	¾ teaspoon
Sesame oil	¼ teaspoon	⅛ teaspoon	to taste
Grated green ginger or ground ginger	1 tablespoon or 1 teaspoon	2 teaspoons or ½ teaspoon	1 teaspoon or ¼ teaspoon
Tabasco sauce	to taste	to taste	to taste
Green beans	500 g	250 g	125 g
Water	¼ cup	2 tablespoons	1 tablespoon
Coriander sprigs and capsicum strips	garnish	garnish	garnish
Microwave cookware	2-cup glass jug 30-cm x 20-cm baking dish	1-cup glass jug 20-cm x 20-cm baking dish	1-cup glass jug 20-cm x 20-cm baking dish
Time on High (100% power) Sauce	1–1½ (1:30) minutes	45 seconds–1 minute	30–45 seconds
Beans	7–10 minutes	4–5 minutes	3–4 minutes

1 Finely chop garlic and capsicum; place in jug (see Chart). Add peanut butter, stock, soy sauce, vinegar, sesame oil, ginger and Tabasco sauce. Cook on High for time in Chart, just until sauce is warm, stirring once. Stir and put aside.

2 Place beans and water in baking dish (see Chart). Cook, covered, on High for time in Chart, until tender-crisp, stirring once. Drain.

3 Add peanut sauce; toss to coat beans.

4 Transfer to a serving dish; garnish with coriander and capsicum strips. Serve hot or cover and refrigerate to serve chilled later.

Cooking fresh beetroot in the microwave is quick and easy. Simply cut off the leafy tops, leaving on part of the stalks and roots, then wash beetroot under cold running water; take care not to damage the skins as this will cause 'bleeding'. Cook in the microwave as in step 1 of Fresh Beetroot with Endive (below) and allow to cool, covered. Cut off the stalks and roots, then peel or rub off skins. Very large beetroot cook better if individually wrapped in plastic wrap and arranged in a circle on the oven floor.

FRESH BEETROOT WITH ENDIVE

Colour Index page 74. 599 kJ per serving. Low in cholesterol. Good source of fibre.
Begin 45 minutes ahead.

Ingredients for 6 servings		Microwave cookware
8 fresh beetroot (about 1 kg without tops)	3 teaspoons French mustard	33-cm x 23-cm baking dish
1/2 cup water	1 teaspoon chopped fresh oregano or 1/4 teaspoon dried oregano	
1/4 cup olive or vegetable oil	1/4 teaspoon salt	
2 tablespoons red wine vinegar	1/2 small head curly endive	
3 teaspoons sugar		

1 Place beetroot and water in baking dish. Cook, covered, on High (100% power) for 14–15 minutes, until tender, rotating dish twice.

2 Allow beetroot to stand, covered, on a heatproof surface until cool. Meanwhile, beat oil, vinegar, sugar, mustard, oregano and salt in a bowl; put aside.

3 Peel or rub off skins from beetroot and cut into 6-mm slices; cut slices into 6-mm strips. Toss in bowl of dressing.

4 Tear endive into bite-sized pieces; add to beetroot. Arrange on a serving plate.

PICKLED BEETROOT

Colour Index page 70. 260 kJ per serving. Low in cholesterol, fat. Good source of fibre.
Begin 15 minutes ahead.

Ingredients	For 4	For 2	For 1
425 g can sliced beetroot	1 can	1/2 can	1/4 can
Liquid from can	1/2 cup	1/4 cup	2 tablespoons
Cider vinegar	2 tablespoons	1 tablespoon	2 teaspoons
Caster sugar	1 1/2 tablespoons	3 teaspoons	1 1/2 teaspoons
Salt	1/4 teaspoon	1/8 teaspoon	to taste
Cornflour	1 1/2 teaspoons	1 teaspoon	1/2 teaspoon
Orange julienne (page 316)	garnish	garnish	garnish
Microwave cookware	2-litre casserole or bowl	1-litre casserole or bowl	Soup bowl
Time on High (100% power)			
Sauce	2–3 minutes	1 1/2 (1:30)–2 minutes	1–1 1/4 (1:15) minutes
Beetroot	3–4 minutes	2–2 1/2 (2:30) minutes	45 seconds–1 minute

1 Drain beetroot, reserving liquid (see Chart). Combine liquid, vinegar, sugar, salt and cornflour in casserole or bowl (see Chart) until blended.

2 Cook mixture on High for time in Chart, until sauce thickens, stirring twice.

3 Add sliced beetroot; stir to coat. Cook on High for time in Chart, until hot, stirring once.

4 Spoon beetroot and sauce into a warmed serving dish; garnish with orange julienne. Serve hot.

NEAPOLITAN BROCCOLI

Colour Index page 70. 4 servings. 473 kJ per serving. Low in cholesterol. Good source of vitamin A, vitamin C, fibre.
Begin 25 minutes ahead.

2 tablespoons olive or vegetable oil	*2 tablespoons capers*
1 red or green capsicum, thinly sliced	*5 stoned black olives*
1 clove garlic, finely chopped	*750 g broccoli*
2 spring onions, sliced	*1½ teaspoons red wine vinegar*
	Flaked blanched almonds to garnish

1. Place oil, capsicum, garlic, spring onions, capers and olives in a 2-litre casserole. Cook on High (100% power) for 5–6 minutes, until capsicum is softened, stirring twice.
2. Meanwhile, remove large leaves from broccoli and trim woody stalk ends; separate flowerets from stalks.
3. Add broccoli flowerets to casserole (refrigerate stalks to use another day); stir to coat. Cook, covered, on High for 7–10 minutes, until broccoli is tender, stirring twice. Add vinegar; toss.
4. Garnish with almonds. Serve hot or cover and refrigerate to served chilled later.

BROCCOLI WITH SESAME SAUCE

Colour Index page 73. 4 servings. 414 kJ per serving. Low in cholesterol. Good source of vitamin A, vitamin C, calcium, iron, fibre.
Begin 25 minutes ahead.

1 tablespoon sesame seeds	*2 tablespoons soy sauce*
1 tablespoon sesame oil	*2 spring onions, finely sliced*
1 tablespoon vegetable oil	*500 g broccoli*
1 clove garlic, chopped	*3 tablespoons water*

1. Make sesame sauce: Spread sesame seeds on a flat plate. Cook on High (100% power) for 2–3 minutes, until golden, stirring often. Combine sesame seeds, sesame oil, vegetable oil, garlic, soy sauce and spring onions in a bowl; put aside.
2. Remove large leaves from broccoli and trim woody stalk ends. Separate stalks from heads. Peel stalks and cut into 2-cm pieces; break heads into small flowerets.
3. Arrange broccoli in a 23-cm round baking dish with flowerets in centre and stalks around edge; sprinkle over water. Cook on High (100% power) for 5 minutes, or until tender-crisp, rearranging or stirring twice.
4. Plunge broccoli into a large bowl of iced water. Drain in a colander, then drain on paper towel.
5. Arrange in a serving dish; pour over sesame sauce. Serve cold.

BROCCOLI MORNAY

Colour Index page 74. 883 kJ per serving. Good source of vitamin A, vitamin C, calcium, fibre.
Begin 40 minutes ahead.

Ingredients for 4 servings		Microwave cookware
500 g broccoli	*Salt and pepper to taste*	4-cup glass jug
45 g butter or margarine	*2 tablespoons water*	20-cm x 20-cm baking dish
2 tablespoons plain flour	*¼ cup fresh breadcrumbs*	Small bowl
1 cup milk	*1 small onion, finely chopped*	
⅛ teaspoon mustard powder		
60 g Cheddar cheese, grated (½ cup)		

1 Remove large leaves from broccoli and trim woody stalk ends. Cut through stalks lengthways 2–3 times. Rinse well and put aside.

2 Heat 30 g butter in jug, covered with paper towel, on High (100% power) for 45 seconds, or until melted. Stir in flour until smooth and blended. Gradually beat in milk and mustard powder. Cook on High for 3–4 minutes, until sauce thickens and is smooth, beating twice.

3 Gradually add cheese, beating until cheese has melted. Season with salt and pepper; cover and keep warm.

4 Arrange broccoli in baking dish with flowerets pointing towards centre of dish and stalks towards edges. Sprinkle with water. Cook, covered, on High for 6–8 minutes, until tender-crisp, rotating dish halfway through cooking; drain.

5 Rearrange broccoli in attractive pattern in same baking dish or in a warmed serving dish. Top with cheese sauce; cover and keep warm. Heat remaining butter in a small bowl, covered with paper towel, on High for 30–45 seconds, until melted.

6 Stir in breadcrumbs and onion. Cook on High for 2–3 minutes, until crumbs are dried and golden, stirring twice. Sprinkle evenly over broccoli and sauce. Serve immediately.

BRUSSELS SPROUTS WITH CHESTNUTS

Colour Index page 75. 331 kJ per serving. Low in cholesterol, sodium. Good source of vitamin C, fibre.
Begin 35 minutes ahead.

Ingredients	For 4	For 2	For 1
Brussels sprouts	*375 g*	*185 g*	*90 g*
Vegetable or chicken stock	*½ cup*	*¼ cup*	*2 tablespoons*
Butter or margarine	*15 g*	*1½ teaspoons*	*1 teaspoon*
Peeled cooked chestnuts (below)	*8*	*6*	*4*
Salt and pepper	*to taste*	*to taste*	*to taste*
Lemon juice (optional)	*½ teaspoon*	*¼ teaspoon*	*⅛ teaspoon*
Microwave cookware	30-cm x 20-cm baking dish	20-cm x 20-cm baking dish	Soup bowl
Time on High (100% power)			
Brussels sprouts	7–9 minutes	5–6 minutes	3½ (3:30)–4½ (4:30) minutes
With chestnuts	5–6 minutes	3–3½ (3:30) minutes	1½ (1:30)–2½ (2:30) minutes

1 Place Brussels sprouts and stock in baking dish or bowl (see Chart). Cook, covered tightly with plastic wrap, on High for time in Chart, until tender-crisp, stirring twice.

2 Add butter and chestnuts. Cook on High for time in Chart, until flavours blend. Season with salt and pepper.

3 If you like, just before serving sprinkle lemon juice over Brussels sprouts. Serve hot.

PEELING AND COOKING CHESTNUTS

Make horizontal cut through shells of 125 g chestnuts, cutting across rounded side. Do not cut through meat.

Place chestnuts and 1 cup water in a 4-cup glass jug. Heat, covered, on High (100% power) for 2½ (2:30)–4 minutes, until boiling; boil for 1 minute longer.

Allow to stand for 7 minutes. Peel off shells and skins; reboil any that are unopen. Cook shelled nuts in a shallow dish, in single layer, on High for 1½ (1:30) minutes, or until tender.

BRUSSELS SPROUTS WITH ONIONS

Colour Index page 71. 6 servings. 452 kJ per serving. Good source of vitamin C, fibre.
Begin 25 minutes ahead.

2 rashers rindless bacon, chopped
500 g white pickling onions, peeled and trimmed
¼ cup chicken stock or water
500 g Brussels sprouts

1. Cook bacon in a 3-litre casserole on High (100% power) for 2–3 minutes, until browned. With slotted spoon, transfer bacon to paper towel to drain.
2. Stir onions and stock into bacon drippings in casserole. Cook, covered, on High for 4 minutes, stirring halfway through cooking.
3. Add Brussels sprouts. Cook, covered, on High for 10–12 minutes, until sprouts are tender-crisp, stirring halfway through cooking.
4. Sprinkle bacon over vegetables; toss to mix. Serve immediately.

SCALLOPED CABBAGE

Colour Index page 74. 8 servings. 519 kJ per serving. Low in sodium. Good source of vitamin C, fibre.
Begin 45 minutes ahead.

45 g butter or margarine
½ cup fresh breadcrumbs
2 onions, thinly sliced
1 small green cabbage (about 750 g), shredded
½ cup cream
Salt and pepper to taste

1. Heat 30 g butter in a 3-litre casserole, covered with paper towel, on High (100% power) for 45 seconds, or until melted.
2. Stir in breadcrumbs. Cook on High for 3–4 minutes, until crumbs are dried and golden, stirring twice. Transfer to a small bowl; put aside.
3. Place remaining butter and onions in same casserole. Cook, covered with paper towel, on High for 5–6 minutes, until softened, stirring twice.
4. Add cabbage; stir to coat. Cook, covered, on High for 10–12 minutes, until cabbage is tender, stirring occasionally. Stir in cream; season with salt and pepper.
5. Sprinkle cabbage with breadcrumbs. Cook on High for 3–4 minutes, until cabbage is hot and cream bubbles. If dish is suitable, brown top lightly under a preheated griller.

PIQUANT RED CABBAGE

Colour Index page 74. 8 servings. 155 kJ per serving.
Low in cholesterol, fat, sodium. Good source of
vitamin C, fibre.
Begin 35 minutes ahead.

1 small red cabbage	*1 bay leaf*
(about 750 g), shredded	*Salt and pepper to taste*
1½ tablespoons brown	*Apple slices and parsley*
sugar	*sprig to garnish*
¼ cup red wine vinegar	

1. Combine cabbage, sugar, vinegar and bay
leaf in a 3-litre casserole. Cook, covered, on High
(100% power) for 15 minutes, stirring twice.
2. Uncover; stir. Cook on High for 5–10 minutes
longer, until cabbage is done to your liking. Discard bay leaf; season with salt and pepper.
3. Spoon cabbage on to a serving platter; garnish with apple and parsley. Serve immediately.

GINGERED CARROTS

Colour Index page 71. 4 servings. 243 kJ per serving.
Low in cholesterol, fat. Good source of vitamin A.
Begin 25 minutes ahead.

500 g carrots, peeled and	*2 teaspoons soy sauce*
cut into matchstick-	*1 teaspoon ground ginger*
thin strips	*2 spring onions, thinly*
3 teaspoons orange juice	*sliced*
2 teaspoons finely grated	*Orange julienne (page*
orange rind	*316) to garnish*

1. Place carrots and orange juice in a 23-cm pie
plate. Cook, covered, on High (100% power) for
7–9 minutes, until carrots are tender-crisp, stirring occasionally.
2. Add orange rind, soy sauce, ginger and spring
onions; stir to combine well. Cook on High for
1–2 minutes, until carrot mixture is hot.
3. Spoon on to a serving platter; garnish with
orange julienne. Serve hot or cover and refrigerate to serve chilled later.

MAKING 'BABY' CARROTS

For dinner parties or as a special garnish,
fresh carrots can be carved before cooking to
resemble whole baby carrots.

Cut medium carrots in 7.5-cm pieces. Shape each
piece with a vegetable peeler until about 12 mm in
diameter, tapering to a point at one end. Use
trimmings in salads or stocks.

Blanching Vegetables

Blanching vegetables for the freezer helps preserve their
flavours. Prepare each according to the charts on
pages 239–253, then blanch in the microwave for the minimum
time below: the vegetable should be bright in colour and
evenly heated through. Chill in iced water for as long as
blanching time. Drain, pat dry and freeze.

Method	High (100% power)

ASPARAGUS
Amount to buy: 500 g
Blanching quantity: about 440 g

Blanch, covered, in a 2-litre casserole with ¼ cup water, stirring halfway through cooking.	2½ (2:30)–3½ (3:30) minutes

BEANS, GREEN AND BUTTER
Amount to buy: 500 g
Blanching quantity: about 375 g

Blanch, covered, in a 1.5-litre casserole with ½ cup water, stirring halfway through cooking.	2½ (2:30)–3½ (3:30) minutes

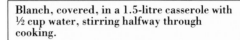

BROCCOLI AND CAULIFLOWER (FLOWERETS)
Broccoli – Amount to buy: 750 g
  Blanching quantity: about 500 g
Cauliflower – Amount to buy: 500 g
  Blanching quantity: about 375 g

Blanch, covered, in a 2-litre casserole with ¼ cup water, rearranging halfway through cooking.	Broccoli: 4–6 minutes Cauliflower: 4–5 minutes

CARROTS (SLICES)
Amount to buy: 500 g
Blanching quantity: about 375 g

Blanch, covered, in a 1.5-litre casserole with ¼ cup water, stirring halfway through cooking.	4½ (4:30)–5½ (5:30) minutes

PEAS (SHELLED)
Amount to buy: 1 kg
Blanching quantity: about 250 g

Blanch, covered, in a 1-litre casserole with ¼ cup water, stirring halfway through cooking.	3–4½ (4:30) minutes

Carrots may be prepared in a variety of ways. Baby carrots are best microwaved whole if they are a similar size, but large carrots can be cut into matchstick-thin strips or into slices. For a quick lunchtime snack or vegetable accompaniment, try grating carrots and combining them with another vegetable, as in Carrot and Potato Pancakes (below).

CARROT AND POTATO PANCAKES

Colour Index page 74. 469 kJ per serving. Good source of vitamin A, fibre.
Begin 35 minutes ahead.

Ingredients for 4 servings		Microwave cookware

2 medium carrots
1 large potato
  (about 250 g), peeled
1½ tablespoons plain
  flour
¼ teaspoon salt
¼ teaspoon baking
  powder
	1 egg
	1 small onion, finely
	  chopped
	Pepper to taste
	15 g butter or margarine
	Dill sprigs to garnish
	Sour cream (optional)
		23-cm pie plate
		Browning dish

1 Pour 1 cup cold water into a medium bowl. Coarsely grate carrots and potato into the bowl (the water prevents the potato discolouring).

2 Drain carrots and potato; place in pie plate. Cook, covered, on High (100% power) for 5 minutes, or until tender-crisp; drain again and put aside.

3 Meanwhile, combine flour, salt and baking powder in a bowl until blended. Add egg and onion; stir until mixed.

4 Stir vegetables into egg mixture; season with pepper. Meanwhile, preheat browning dish according to the manufacturer's instructions. Add butter; stir to coat dish.

5 Drop mounds of batter on to browning dish; flatten slightly. Cook on High for 2½ (2:30) minutes, or until set, turning pancakes halfway through cooking. (If necessary, cook in batches, reheating browning dish between batches.)

6 Arrange hot pancakes on a warmed serving platter; garnish with dill sprigs. Serve, if you like, with sour cream.

GLAZED CARROTS

Colour Index page 71. 4 servings. 368 kJ per serving.
Low in cholesterol, sodium. Good source of vitamin A, fibre.
Begin 25 minutes ahead.

500 g carrots, cut into 6-mm slices ¼ cup chicken stock 2 teaspoons sugar	15 g butter or margarine Salt and pepper to taste Parsley sprig to garnish

1. Combine carrots, stock and sugar in a 23-cm pie plate. Cook, covered, on High (100% power) for 5–7 minutes, until carrots are tender-crisp, stirring twice.
2. Uncover; cook on High for 3–5 minutes longer, until carrots are tender and liquid has almost evaporated, stirring twice.
3. Add butter; stir until carrots are glazed. Season with salt and pepper.
4. Transfer carrots to a warmed serving dish; garnish with parsley. Serve immediately.

CAULIFLOWER WITH LEMON AND DILL SAUCE

Colour Index page 72. 8 servings. 373 kJ per serving.
Good source of vitamin C, fibre.
Begin 25 minutes ahead.

1 large cauliflower
  (about 1.5 kg)
¼ cup water
45 g butter or margarine
1 clove garlic, crushed
3 teaspoons plain flour
	¾ cup cream
	2 tablespoons lemon juice
	1 tablespoon chopped
	  fresh dill
	Lemon slices and dill
	  sprigs to garnish

1. Keeping cauliflower whole, remove large leaves and cut out core. Place cauliflower, cored side up, in a 3-litre casserole; add water. Cook, covered, on High (100% power) for 9–10 minutes, until cauliflower is tender-crisp, rotating casserole halfway through cooking. Allow to stand, covered, on a heatproof surface while preparing sauce.
2. Place butter and garlic in a 4-cup glass jug. Heat, covered with paper towel, on High for 45 seconds–1 minute, until melted. Stir in flour until blended. Cook on High for 1 minute, stirring halfway through cooking.
3. Gradually stir in cream. Cook on High for 2–3 minutes, until sauce thickens slightly, stirring twice. Stir in lemon juice and dill.
4. Drain cauliflower; place on warmed serving platter. Spoon sauce over; garnish with lemon and dill. Serve immediately.

CAULIFLOWER WITH MINTED SPINACH

Colour Index page 72. 6 servings. 176 kJ per serving.
Good source of vitamin A, vitamin C, calcium, iron, fibre.
Begin 25 minutes ahead.

*250 g packet frozen
    spinach, thawed*
¼ cup fresh mint leaves
*½ teaspoon crushed
    dried chillies*
1 clove garlic
*1 medium cauliflower
    (about 1 kg), trimmed,
    rinsed and cut into
    flowerets*

¼ cup water
½ cup natural yoghurt
Salt to taste
Mint sprig to garnish

1. Squeeze and drain spinach. In food processor with knife blade attached or in blender, process spinach, mint, chillies and garlic in batches until smooth.
2. Place cauliflower and water in a 2-litre casserole. Cook, covered, on High (100% power) for 5 minutes, stirring halfway through cooking. Drain.
3. Add spinach mixture to cauliflower; stir well. Cook, covered, on High for 5–7 minutes, until cauliflower is tender, stirring occasionally.
4. Add yoghurt; season with salt. Garnish with mint. Serve hot or cover and refrigerate to serve chilled later.

CELERIAC PURÉE

Colour Index page 75. 6 servings. 594 kJ per serving.
Good source of fibre.
Begin 35 minutes ahead.

*500 g celeriac, peeled
    and diced*
*250 g potatoes, peeled
    and diced*
*1 cup vegetable or
    chicken stock*

45 g butter or margarine
¼ cup cream
Salt and pepper to taste
Parsley sprig to garnish

1. Place celeriac and potatoes in a 2-litre casserole; add stock. Cook, covered, on High (100% power) for 10–15 minutes, until vegetables are fork-tender, stirring occasionally.
2. In food processor with knife blade attached or in blender, process vegetables until smooth. Add butter and cream; process until blended. Season with salt and pepper.
3. Return purée to casserole. Cook on High for 3–4 minutes, until hot, stirring twice.
4. Transfer to a warmed serving dish; garnish with parsley. Serve immediately.

Meal in Minutes *for 8 people*

Chinese New Year Party

Dim sum (bought)
Szechuan Lobster (page 169)
Stir-fried Prawns and Broccoli (page 168)
Stir-fried Pork Fillet (page 229)
Szechuan Eggplant (page 264)
Hot Cooked Rice (page 295)
Fortune cookies and Jasmine tea

PREPARATION TIMETABLE	
Early in day:	*Prepare all vegetables and store in plastic bags in refrigerator. Slice pork for Stir-fried Pork Fillet; cover and refrigerate. Prepare Szechuan Lobster up to the end of step 1; cover and refrigerate. Prepare Szechuan Eggplant up to the end of step 4; place on a serving platter, cover and refrigerate.*
1 hour ahead:	*Prepare Stir-fried Prawns and Broccoli up to the end of step 2. Complete Szechuan Lobster; arrange in a warmed serving dish, cover and keep warm. Cook rice; keep warm. Place fortune cookies in a serving bowl.*
30 minutes ahead:	*Complete Stir-fried Prawns and Broccoli; keep warm. Cook Stir-fried Pork Fillet; keep warm. Prepare bought dim sum and arrange in bamboo steamers or bowls. Make jasmine tea.*

Chicory is normally used as a salad vegetable, but it is equally delicious cooked. Remember to arrange the heads with the delicate, leafy tips pointing towards the centre of the dish and the denser stalk ends towards edges to ensure even cooking.

BRAISED CHICORY

Colour Index page 74. 327 kJ per serving. Low in sodium.
Begin 35 minutes ahead.

Ingredients	For 4	For 2	For 1
Chicory	*4 heads*	*2 heads*	*1 head*
Vegetable or chicken stock	*1 cup*	*½ cup*	*¼ cup*
Spring onions, sliced	*2*	*1*	*½*
Fresh thyme, chopped, or dried thyme	*2 teaspoons or ½ teaspoon*	*1 teaspoon or ¼ teaspoon*	*½ teaspoon or ⅛ teaspoon*
Fresh basil, shredded, or dried basil	*2 teaspoons or ½ teaspoon*	*1 teaspoon or ¼ teaspoon*	*½ teaspoon or ⅛ teaspoon*
Butter or margarine	*30 g*	*15 g*	*1½ teaspoons*
Caster sugar	*1 teaspoon*	*½ teaspoon*	*¼ teaspoon*
Lemon juice	*1 teaspoon*	*½ teaspoon*	*¼ teaspoon*
Salt and pepper	*to taste*	*to taste*	*to taste*
Microwave cookware	33-cm x 23-cm baking dish	20-cm x 20-cm baking dish	20-cm x 20-cm baking dish
Time on High (100% power)			
Chicory	12–15 minutes	8–10 minutes	4–6 minutes
Stock mixture	5 minutes	3–3½ (3:30) minutes	1½ (1:30)–2 minutes

1 Trim root ends from heads of chicory; cut each head in half lengthways. Arrange, cut side down, in baking dish (see Chart), with stalk ends towards edges and leafy tips towards the centre.

2 Pour stock over chicory; add spring onions, thyme and basil. Cook, covered, on High for time in Chart, until chicory is tender, rearranging heads and rotating dish halfway through cooking.

3 Transfer chicory to a warmed serving platter, arranging cut side up. Cover and keep warm.

4 Add butter, sugar, lemon juice, salt and pepper to baking dish.

5 Cook on High for time in Chart, until bubbling, stirring once.

6 Spoon cooking liquid over chicory. Serve immediately.

CHICORY WITH CHEESE SAUCE

Colour Index page 74. 4 servings. 900 kJ per serving.
Good source of calcium.
Begin 45 minutes ahead.

4 heads chicory
½ cup vegetable or chicken stock
3 teaspoons lemon juice
½ teaspoon sugar
30 g butter or margarine
2 tablespoons plain flour
¾ cup cream
1 clove garlic, crushed (optional)

125 g Swiss or Gruyère cheese, grated (1 cup)
1 egg yolk
Salt and pepper to taste
2 tablespoons grated Parmesan cheese (optional)

1. Trim root ends from heads of chicory. Cut each head in half lengthways. Arrange, cut side down, in a 33-cm x 23-cm baking dish, with stalk ends towards edges and leafy tips towards the centre.
2. Add stock, lemon juice and sugar. Cook, covered, on High (100% power) for 7–10 minutes, until chicory is tender-crisp, rearranging heads and rotating dish halfway through cooking. Drain liquid from dish and reserve. Turn chicory cut side up in dish; cover and put aside.
3. Heat butter in a large bowl, covered with paper towel, on High for 45 seconds, or until melted. Stir in flour until smooth and blended. Cook on High for 1 minute, stirring once.
4. Gradually add cream, reserved cooking liquid and, if you like, garlic; mix well. Cook on High for 3–4 minutes, until thickened, stirring twice. Add Swiss cheese; stir until cheese melts.
5. Lightly beat egg yolk in a small bowl; stir in ¼ cup hot cheese sauce, taking care that yolk does not curdle. Slowly pour egg mixture back into remaining sauce, beating rapidly to prevent lumping. Season with salt and pepper.
6. Pour sauce over chicory. Cook on Medium (50% power) for 3–5 minutes, until hot. If dish is suitable, sprinkle Parmesan cheese over chicory and sauce and brown lightly under a preheated griller. Serve immediately.

> **BABY VEGETABLES**
> Miniature vegetables are fun to serve whole: their bright colours dress up dinner plates and party platters. Place 250 g baby carrots, zucchini or button squash in a 30-cm x 20-cm baking dish; add ¼ cup water. Cook on High (100% power) for 4–6 minutes, until tender-crisp, stirring halfway through cooking. Drain and serve.

CREAMED CORN
WITH CAPSICUM

Colour Index page 70. 4 servings. 636 kJ per serving.
Good source of fibre.
Begin 25 minutes ahead.

30 g butter or margarine	1 teaspoon chopped fresh
2 small onions, thinly	oregano or ¼ teaspoon
sliced	dried oregano
1 small green capsicum,	¼ cup cream
cut into strips	1 small tomato, cut into
4 cobs corn, husked, or	thin wedges
440 g can corn kernels,	Salt and pepper to taste
drained	

1. Heat butter in a 30-cm x 20-cm baking dish, covered with paper towel, on High (100% power) for 45 seconds–1 minute, until melted.
2. Add onions and capsicum; stir to coat. Cook on High for 4–5 minutes, until onions are softened, stirring once.
3. Meanwhile, if using fresh corn, cut kernels from cobs.
4. Stir corn, oregano and cream into onion mixture. Cook, covered, on High for 5–7 minutes (3–5 minutes for canned corn), until corn is tender, stirring twice.
5. Add tomato. Cook on High for 1–2 minutes, until tomato is hot but still firm. Season with salt and pepper. Serve immediately.

SUCCOTASH

Colour Index page 71. 4 servings. 1553 kJ per serving. Low in cholesterol. Good source of vitamin C, iron.
Begin 25 minutes ahead.

4 rashers rindless	1 tomato, chopped
bacon, diced	250 g frozen corn
500 g potatoes, peeled	kernels, thawed
and diced	1 green capsicum, diced
1 onion, finely chopped	1 teaspoon sugar
250 g frozen broad	Salt to taste
beans, thawed	¼ teaspoon pepper

1. Cook bacon in a 2-litre casserole, covered with paper towel, on High (100% power) for 4–5 minutes, until browned, stirring once. With slotted spoon, transfer bacon to paper towel to drain.
2. Add potatoes and onion to bacon drippings; stir to coat. Cook on High for 5–7 minutes, until potatoes are almost cooked, stirring halfway through cooking.
3. Stir in beans, tomato, corn, capsicum and sugar. Cook, covered, on High for 5–7 minutes, until vegetables are tender, stirring once.
4. Season with salt and pepper; sprinkle bacon over succotash. Serve hot.

Corn-on-the-Cob

Whole corn cooks perfectly in the microwave. Simply remove the husks and silks, then rinse and tightly wrap each corn cob in plastic wrap. Cook 1 cob on High (100% power) for 3–4 minutes; 2 cobs for 5–6 minutes; 3 cobs for 7–8 minutes; 4 cobs for 9–11 minutes. Halfway through cooking, turn the corn over and rearrange, moving the front cobs to the back and vice versa for even, thorough cooking. Serve corn whole with one of the Flavoured Butters (below) or, using a sharp knife, cut cooked kernels from each cob and serve as a side vegetable, or add to salads or hot dishes.

Preparing whole corn

Just before cooking, remove outer husks and silks from cobs.

Rinse under cold running water; remove any remaining silk with a vegetable brush.

After cooking, hold each cob at an angle. With a sharp knife, cut down the cob to remove the kernels.

FLAVOURED BUTTERS
Colour Index page 71. Each butter makes enough for 4 cobs of corn. 435 kJ per tablespoon. Begin 15 minutes ahead.

Golden Spiced Butter: Place *45 g butter or margarine, 3 teaspoons lemon juice, ½ teaspoon curry powder and ½ teaspoon French mustard* in a 2-cup glass jug. Stir until well mixed. Heat, covered, on High (100% power) for 45 seconds–1 minute, until butter is melted, stirring once.

Capsicum Butter: Place *45 g butter or margarine, 2 tablespoons very finely chopped green capsicum, ¼ teaspoon crushed black peppercorns and ¼ teaspoon cayenne pepper* in a 2-cup glass jug. Stir until well mixed. Cook, covered, on High (100% power) for 45 seconds–1 minute, until butter is melted, stirring once.

Fresh Herb Butter: Place *45 g butter or margarine* and *2 teaspoons lemon juice* in a 2-cup glass jug. Stir until well mixed. Heat, covered, on High (100% power) for 45 seconds–1 minute, until butter is melted, stirring once. Add *1 teaspoon chopped fresh herbs* of your choice; stir well to combine.

EGGPLANT WITH TABOULEH

Colour Index page 77. 1269 kJ per serving. Low in cholesterol. Good source of vitamin C, calcium, iron, fibre.
Begin 1¼ hours ahead.

This nutritious main course has a Middle Eastern flavour, with its use of burghul, vegetables, garlic, raisins and mint. Burghul, also known as cracked wheat, is available from health food shops, specialty food halls and larger supermarkets.

Ingredients for 4 main-course servings		Microwave cookware
2 small eggplants (about 375 g each)	½ cup burghul, soaked	30-cm x 20-cm baking dish
Salt	1 tablespoon finely chopped fresh mint	30-cm x 20-cm platter
2 onions, chopped	2 teaspoons chopped fresh thyme or ½ teaspoon dried thyme	
3 celery stalks, chopped		
2 tablespoons olive or vegetable oil		
3 cloves garlic, crushed	⅓ cup tomato juice	
1 small green capsicum, chopped	3 teaspoons lemon juice	
	Pepper to taste	
½ cup seedless raisins	Lemon wedges and mint leaves to garnish	
½ cup vegetable or chicken stock		
2 tablespoons capers, drained		

1 Cut each eggplant in half lengthways. Scoop out flesh from each half, leaving a 12-mm shell. Finely chop eggplant flesh; put aside.

2 Sprinkle hollowed-out halves with salt. Place eggplant, cut side down, on a double thickness of paper towel; allow to stand for 20 minutes.

3 Place onions, celery and 1½ tablespoons oil in baking dish. Cook on High (100% power) for 3–4 minutes, until softened slightly, stirring halfway through cooking.

4 Add garlic, capsicum, raisins, stock and chopped eggplant. Cook on High for 10–12 minutes, until eggplant is fork-tender, stirring occasionally. Stir in capers, burghul, mint, thyme, tomato juice and lemon juice. Season with pepper; put aside.

5 Rinse salt from eggplant shells; pat dry. Lightly brush with remaining oil. Arrange on platter. Cook on High for 5 minutes, or until fork-tender (do not cook longer or shells will collapse when filled).

6 Spoon an equal amount of tabouleh into each eggplant shell. Cook on High for 4–6 minutes, just until filling is hot. Garnish with lemon wedges and mint. Serve immediately.

SZECHUAN EGGPLANT

Colour Index page 72. 4 servings. 306 kJ per serving. Low in cholesterol. Good source of fibre.
Begin 25 minutes ahead.

1 small eggplant (about 500 g)	½ teaspoon Tabasco sauce
1 teaspoon sugar	3 teaspoons peanut or vegetable oil
1 teaspoon cornflour	
1 tablespoon grated green ginger	1 spring onion, thinly sliced
¾ cup chicken stock	Spring onion curls (page 134) to garnish
3 teaspoons soy sauce	

1. Preheat browning dish according to the manufacturer's instructions. Meanwhile, cut eggplant into 10-cm x 1-cm x 1-cm strips.
2. Combine sugar, cornflour and ginger in a bowl. Gradually stir in stock, soy sauce and Tabasco sauce until blended.
3. Coat browning dish with half the oil. Arrange half the eggplant strips on dish. Cook on High (100% power) for 3–4 minutes, until eggplant softens, stirring once. Transfer to paper towel to drain. Repeat with remaining oil and eggplant.
4. Return all eggplant strips to browning dish; stir in sauce. Cook on High for 3–4 minutes, until slightly thickened, stirring halfway through cooking. Stir in spring onion.
5. Transfer eggplant to a serving platter; garnish with spring onion curls. Serve hot or cover and refrigerate to serve chilled later.

VEGETABLE PRESENTATION
Simply cooked vegetables make an elegant presentation for a special occasion.

Matchstick carrots and parsnips: Cooked matchstick-thin strips of carrot and parsnip in a lattice pattern accentuate the colour of a pretty plate.

Asparagus parcels: Asparagus spears tied with a strip of cooked leek echo the shape of a long plate. Lemon twists (page 134) give the finishing touch.

EGGPLANT BROCHETTES WITH SATAY SAUCE

Colour Index page 74. 4 servings. 800 kJ per serving. Low in cholesterol. Good source of vitamin C, fibre. Begin 35 minutes ahead.

3 tablespoons peanut butter	Water
1 teaspoon tomato paste	2 tablespoons olive oil
3 teaspoons soy sauce	2 teaspoons chopped
1½ tablespoons lime or lemon juice	fresh oregano or ½ teaspoon dried
1 green chilli, deseeded and thinly sliced	oregano
2-cm green ginger, peeled and finely chopped	12 baby eggplant (total weight about 500 g)
2 cloves garlic, chopped	Yellow tomato halves and fresh coriander leaves to garnish

1. Prepare sauce: Combine peanut butter, tomato paste, soy sauce, lime juice, chilli, ginger, half the garlic and 3 tablespoons water in a 2-cup glass jug. Cook, covered, on High (100% power) for 2–3 minutes, until boiling, stirring twice; put aside.
2. Combine olive oil, oregano and remaining garlic in a small bowl. Cook on High for 25 seconds. Allow to stand while preparing eggplants.
3. Cut slits in one side of 1 eggplant at 12-mm intervals; turn eggplant over and cut slits in other side, in between first slits. Do not remove stalk end. Repeat with each eggplant.
4. Beginning at bottom end, push eggplants on to short wooden skewers. Gently pull out each eggplant to create a concertina effect.
5. Brush brochettes with oil and garlic mixture; arrange half, spoke-fashion, on a 30-cm platter. Cook on High for 3–4 minutes, until tender, turning brochettes over and rearranging halfway through cooking. Keep warm while cooking remaining brochettes.
6. Reheat sauce on High for 45 seconds. Pour sauce over brochettes; garnish with tomatoes and coriander. Serve immediately.

Preparing the eggplants for cooking

Cut slits down one side of eggplant at 12-mm intervals, without cutting right through. Repeat on other side.

Push each eggplant on to a wooden skewer. Gently pull out eggplant to create a concertina effect.

LEEKS WITH HAM IN CHEESE SAUCE

Colour Index page 75. 1536 kJ per serving. Good source of calcium, iron, fibre. Begin 50 minutes ahead.

Ingredients	For 4	For 2	For 1
Leeks (about 250 g each)	4	2	1
Chicken stock	½ cup	¼ cup	2 tablespoons
Butter or margarine	30 g	15 g	1½ teaspoons
Plain flour	2 tablespoons	1 tablespoon	2 teaspoons
Cream	1 cup	½ cup	¼ cup
Swiss or Gruyère cheese, grated	125 g (1 cup)	60 g (½ cup)	30 g (¼ cup)
Salt and pepper	to taste	to taste	to taste
Cooked ham slices (about 15 g each)	8	4	2
Parsley	garnish	garnish	garnish
Microwave cookware	30-cm x 20-cm baking dish	20-cm x 20-cm baking dish	20-cm x 20-cm baking dish
Time on High (100% power)			
Leeks	5–7 minutes	3–4 minutes	2–2½ (2:30) minutes
Sauce	3–3½ (3:30) minutes	2–2½ (2:30) minutes	1–1½ (1:30) minutes
Leeks with sauce	5–6 minutes	3–3½ (3:30) minutes	1½ (1:30)–2 minutes

1 Cut roots from leeks; trim tops. Cut leeks in half lengthways; carefully rinse under cold running water to remove any grit.

2 Arrange leeks, cut side down, in baking dish (see Chart).

3 Add stock and butter to dish. Cook, covered, on High for time in Chart, until leeks are tender, rearranging once. Transfer to a platter.

4 Stir flour into dish until blended. Gradually stir in cream. Cook on High for time in Chart, until smooth, stirring twice. Add cheese; stir until melted. Season with salt and pepper.

5 Wrap each leek half with 1 slice of ham. Place wrapped leeks in cheese sauce.

6 Cook, covered, on High for time in Chart, until leeks are hot and cheese sauce is bubbling. Garnish with parsley. Serve immediately.

Middle Eastern Dinner

Fresh Tomato Soup (page 129)
Eggplant with Tabouleh (page 264)
Hot pita bread
Tossed green salad
Goat cheese with dried fruit and nuts

PREPARATION TIMETABLE

Early in day:	*Prepare Fresh Tomato Soup; cover and refrigerate. Prepare salad ingredients; store in plastic bags in refrigerator. Prepare salad dressing of your choice; refrigerate.*
1 hour ahead:	*Cook Eggplant with Tabouleh; cover and put aside. Arrange an assortment of cheese, dried fruit and nuts on a serving platter; cover and put aside.*
Just before serving:	*Ladle soup into individual bowls and garnish. Reheat stuffed eggplant on High (100% power) until hot; garnish. Lightly toast pitas under a preheated griller; arrange on a warmed platter. Place salad ingredients in a bowl and toss with dressing.*

MUSHROOMS À LA GRECQUE

Colour Index page 72. 6 servings. 833 kJ per serving.
Low in cholesterol, sodium.
Begin 25 minutes ahead.

½ cup olive or vegetable oil	*2 bay leaves*
½ cup chicken stock	*1 tablespoon chopped fresh thyme or*
3 cloves garlic, thinly sliced	*1 teaspoon dried thyme*
2 small onions, cut into 6-mm wedges	*12 black peppercorns*
2 small tomatoes, cut into chunks	*12 whole coriander seeds (optional)*
½ cup dry white wine	*500 g button mushrooms, trimmed*
¼ cup tarragon vinegar or white wine vinegar	*Chopped parsley to garnish*

1. Place all ingredients except mushrooms and parsley in a 2-litre casserole. Cook on High (100% power) for 5–7 minutes, until bubbling, stirring halfway through cooking.
2. Add mushrooms. Cook, covered, on High for 10 minutes, or until tender, stirring occasionally.
3. Discard bay leaves; garnish with parsley. Serve hot or cover and refrigerate to serve chilled later.

ORIENTAL MUSHROOMS

Colour Index page 75. 4 main-course servings. 515 kJ per serving. Low in cholesterol. Good source of thiamine, iron.
Begin 45 minutes ahead.

125 g boneless pork	*2 cloves garlic, crushed*
1 teaspoon cornflour	*250 g mushrooms, sliced*
½ cup chicken stock	*125 g snow peas, cut in half*
2 teaspoons grated green ginger or 1 teaspoon ground ginger	*1 small tomato, cut into matchstick-thin strips*
3 teaspoons soy sauce	*Parsley sprig to garnish*
1 teaspoon rice wine or cider vinegar	

1. Thinly slice pork; cut slices into slivers. Combine cornflour, stock, ginger, soy sauce, vinegar and garlic in a bowl. Add pork; stir to coat. Cover and marinate for 10 minutes.
2. Preheat browning dish according to the manufacturer's instructions. Arrange pork in a single layer on browning dish; reserve marinade. Cook on High (100% power) for 3–4 minutes, until cooked, stirring halfway through cooking. Transfer pork to a warmed serving platter; cover and keep warm.
3. Reheat browning dish. Add mushrooms. Cook on High for 3–4 minutes, until softened, stirring halfway through cooking.
4. Add snow peas, tomato, reserved marinade and cooked pork. Cook on High for 3–4 minutes, until sauce bubbles and has thickened, stirring twice.
5. Arrange vegetables on a warmed platter with pork; garnish with parsley. Serve immediately.

OKRA, HAM AND TOMATOES

Colour Index page 72. 4 main-course servings. 264 kJ per serving. Low in cholesterol. Good source of vitamin C, fibre.
Begin 25 minutes ahead.

1 onion, chopped	¼ teaspoon Tabasco
⅓ cup diced cooked ham (about 45 g)	sauce
425 g can tomatoes, chopped	3 teaspoons lemon juice
310 g okra, stalks removed	Lemon slices to garnish
	Hot Cooked Rice (page 295, optional)

1. Combine onion and ham in a 33-cm x 23-cm baking dish. Cook on High (100% power) for 3 minutes, or until onion has softened, stirring halfway through cooking.
2. Stir in tomatoes, okra and Tabasco sauce. Cook on High for 6–9 minutes, until okra is crisptender and tomatoes are bubbling, stirring twice.
3. Stir in lemon juice until blended. Garnish with lemon slices. Serve, if you like, with Hot Cooked Rice.

MARINATED OKRA

Colour Index page 77. 4 servings. 607 kJ per serving. Low in cholesterol, sodium.
Begin 1 day ahead.

½ cup olive or vegetable oil	½ teaspoon mustard powder
⅓ cup tarragon vinegar or white wine vinegar	½ teaspoon sugar
2 teaspoons chopped fresh thyme or ½ teaspoon dried thyme	¼ teaspoon crushed dried chillies
	310 g okra, stalks removed
	Parsley to garnish

1. Combine oil, vinegar, thyme, mustard, sugar and chillies in a 1.5-litre casserole. Cook on High (100% power) for 3 minutes, or until flavours blend, stirring halfway through cooking.
2. Add okra; stir to coat. Cook on High for 5–6 minutes, until okra is crisp-tender, stirring twice.
3. Cover casserole and refrigerate for 4 hours or overnight, stirring occasionally.
4. Drain off marinade. Arrange okra on a serving platter; garnish with parsley. Serve chilled.

Barbecuing Vegetables

Use the microwave to precook vegetables for the barbecue, thus saving on time and reducing the risk of overcooking or charring. The vegetables will have that delicious outdoor flavour, yet stay tender-crisp. Cook vegetables in ¼ cup water, covered, on High (100% power) for time in Chart, or until almost tender; drain. Cook on the barbecue over high heat, brushing with vegetable oil and turning until brown.

Vegetable	Amount	In Microwave	On Barbecue
Asparagus spears	500 g	4–6 minutes	2 minutes
Capsicums	4 medium, seeds removed	8–10 minutes	5 minutes
Carrots	500 g	6–8 minutes	5 minutes
Cauliflower	500 g, cut into flowerets	6–8 minutes	5 minutes
Chicory	4 heads, about 125 g each	4–5 minutes	2 minutes
Eggplant	1 medium, about 375 g, cut into 8 wedges	4–6 minutes	3–5 minutes
Fennel	2 bulbs, about 1 kg, cut in half lengthways	9–11 minutes	5 minutes
Leeks	4 medium, cut in half lengthways	4–5 minutes	5 minutes
Mushrooms	500 g	4–6 minutes	5 minutes
Onions	12 white pickling onions, peeled	6–8 minutes	5 minutes
Potatoes	4 medium, about 500 g, cut into 6-mm slices	7–9 minutes	5 minutes
Pumpkin	2 golden nuggets, about 1 kg, cut in half and seeds removed	12–14 minutes	5 minutes
Zucchini	2 medium, cut in half lengthways	3–5 minutes	5 minutes

When preparing a mixture of vegetables for kebabs, prevent the outsides of onion, zucchini or capsicum chunks from charring before the insides are tender by precooking them in the microwave. Place vegetables in a baking dish with ¼ cup water; cook, covered, on High (100% power) for 3–4 minutes, until tender-crisp, stirring twice.

Preparing vegetables for kebabs

Place 2 large onions, cut into 4-cm wedges, 2 medium zucchini, cut into 2.5-cm chunks, and 1 large red capsicum, seeded and cut into 2.5-cm chunks, in baking dish; add ¼ cup water. Cook, covered, on High for 3–4 minutes. Drain; put aside.

When vegetables are cool enough to handle, thread carefully on to skewers. Finish cooking on barbecue over high heat, brushing lightly with vegetable oil and turning frequently until evenly browned, about 5 minutes.

STUFFED ONIONS

Colour Index page 75. 473 kJ per serving. Good source of fibre.
Begin 45 minutes ahead.

Ingredients	For 4	For 2	For 1
Large onions	4	2	1
Vegetable or chicken stock	½ cup	¼ cup	2 tablespoons
Butter or margarine	30 g	15 g	1½ teaspoons
Celery	1 stalk	½ stalk	¼ stalk
Small red capsicum	1	½	¼
Dried mixed herbs	1 teaspoon	½ teaspoon	¼ teaspoon
Fresh wholemeal breadcrumbs	1 cup (2 slices)	½ cup (1 slice)	¼ cup (½ slice)
Salt	¼ teaspoon	⅛ teaspoon	to taste
Parsley sprigs	garnish	garnish	garnish
Microwave cookware	8-cup soufflé dish	4-cup soufflé dish	Small bowl
Time on High (100% power)			
Onions	5–7 minutes	4–6 minutes	2½ (2:30)–3 minutes
Butter	45 seconds	30–45 seconds	30 seconds
Vegetable mixture	3–5 minutes	2–3 minutes	1½ (1:30)–2 minutes
Stuffed onions	4–6 minutes	2–3 minutes	1½ (1:30)–2 minutes
Standing time	5 minutes	3 minutes	2 minutes

1 Cut a small slice from the bottom of each onion so they stand upright. Hollow out centres, leaving 2-cm shells. Reserve centres.

2 Place onion shells in dish or bowl (see Chart); add stock. Cook, covered, on High for time in Chart, rotating dish once. Remove onions; put aside.

3 Add butter to stock. Cook on High for time in Chart. Finely chop onion centres, celery and capsicum. Add to stock with mixed herbs. Cook on High for time in Chart.

4 Add breadcrumbs and salt; stir until stuffing is well mixed.

5 Fill onion shells with equal amounts of stuffing.

6 Place onions in same dish or bowl. Cook on High for time in Chart, until hot, rotating dish or bowl halfway through cooking. Allow to stand, loosely covered, on a heatproof surface for time in Chart. Transfer to a warmed serving plate; garnish with parsley. Serve hot.

CREAMED ONIONS

Colour Index page 72. 8 servings. 343 kJ per serving.
Low in sodium.
Begin 25 minutes ahead.

30 g butter or margarine
1 small onion, finely chopped
1½ tablespoons plain flour
1½ cups milk
¼ teaspoon salt
¼ teaspoon pepper
Ground nutmeg to taste
500 g frozen pearl onions, thawed, or tiny white pickling onions, peeled and trimmed
Paprika (optional)

1. Heat butter in a 4-cup glass jug, covered with paper towel, on High (100% power) for 45 seconds, or until melted.
2. Add onion. Cook on High for 2–3 minutes, until softened, stirring once. Stir in flour until blended. Cook on High for 1 minute, stirring halfway through cooking.
3. Gradually stir in milk. Cook on High for 3–4 minutes, until sauce has thickened and is smooth, stirring twice. Season with salt, pepper and nutmeg.
4. Combine onions and sauce in a 23-cm round baking dish. Cook on High for 3–5 minutes, until sauce bubbles, stirring halfway through cooking.
5. Sprinkle, if you like, with paprika. Serve immediately.

SWEET AND SOUR ONIONS

Colour Index page 75. 8 servings. 289 kJ per serving.
Low in sodium.
Begin 40 minutes ahead.

500 g onions, sliced
45 g butter or margarine
3 teaspoons sugar
½ cup beef stock
¼ cup dry red wine
3 teaspoons red wine vinegar
Salt and pepper to taste

1. Combine onions, butter, sugar, stock and wine in a 23-cm pie plate. Cook, covered, on High (100% power) for 5 minutes, stirring halfway through cooking.
2. Uncover; stir. Cook on High for 15–20 minutes longer, until onions brown and cooking liquid has evaporated, stirring occasionally.
3. Stir in vinegar. Cook on High for 5 minutes, or until vinegar has evaporated, stirring halfway through cooking.
4. Season with salt and pepper. Transfer to a warmed serving dish. Serve hot.

PETITS POIS À LA FRANÇAISE

Colour Index page 70. 6 servings. 674 kJ per serving.
Good source of thiamine, iron, fibre.
Begin 20 minutes ahead.

1 small head crisp lettuce	*500 g frozen peas, thawed*
6 rashers rindless bacon, diced	*Pepper to taste*
1 onion, chopped	*Chopped parsley*

1. Cut lettuce in half lengthways. With cut side down, slice lettuce crossways into 12-mm shreds; put aside.
2. Cook bacon in a 3-litre casserole on High (100% power) for 3–4 minutes, until browned, stirring halfway through cooking.
3. Add onion; stir to mix with bacon. Cook on High for 2 minutes, or until onion has softened, stirring halfway through cooking.
4. Add peas to casserole. Cook for 2 minutes, or until peas are hot; stir in shredded lettuce. Cook, covered, on High for 3–4 minutes, until lettuce is wilted, stirring twice.
5. Add pepper; stir in chopped parsley. Serve immediately.

PEAS WITH ONIONS AND BACON

Colour Index page 72. 4 servings. 440 kJ per serving.
Good source of fibre.
Begin 15 minutes ahead.

2 rashers bacon, diced	*Salt and pepper to taste*
310 g frozen peas, thawed	
250 g frozen pearl onions, thawed, or tiny white pickling onions, peeled and trimmed	

1. Cook bacon in a 23-cm pie plate, covered with paper towel, on High (100% power) for 2–3 minutes, until browned, stirring occasionally. With slotted spoon, transfer bacon to paper towel to drain. Discard all but 1 tablespoon bacon drippings.
2. Stir peas and onions into bacon drippings. Cook, covered, on High for 3–5 minutes, until peas and onions are hot, stirring halfway through cooking.
3. Season with salt and pepper. Spoon mixture into a warmed serving dish; garnish with reserved bacon.

LEMON PEAS

Colour Index page 73. 339 kJ per serving. Good source of fibre.
Begin 15 minutes ahead.

Ingredients	For 4	For 2	For 1
Butter or margarine	*15 g*	*1½ teaspoons*	*¾ teaspoon*
Frozen peas, thawed	*310 g*	*155 g*	*75 g*
Lemon rind, finely grated	*2 teaspoons*	*1 teaspoon*	*½ teaspoon*
Water	*3 teaspoons*	*1½ teaspoons*	*1 teaspoon*
Salt	*¼ teaspoon*	*⅛ teaspoon*	*to taste*
Pepper	*to taste*	*to taste*	*to taste*
Lemon slices and mint sprigs	*garnish*	*garnish*	*garnish*
Microwave cookware	2-litre casserole	1-litre casserole	2-cup glass jug
Time on High (100% power)			
Butter	30–45 seconds	30 seconds	15–30 seconds
Peas	4–5 minutes	2–3 minutes	1½ (1:30)–2½ (2:30) minutes

1 Heat butter in casserole or jug (see Chart), covered with paper towel, on High for time in Chart, until melted.

2 Stir in peas, lemon rind, water, salt and pepper. Cook, covered, on High for time in Chart, until peas are tender, stirring occasionally.

3 Transfer peas to a warmed serving dish; garnish with lemon slices and mint sprigs. Serve immediately.

SNOW PEAS AND SUGAR PEAS
Both these edible pea pods are delicious cooked in the microwave. Snow peas, also known as mange-touts, have thin, delicate skins and the pods contain peas that are not fully formed. Sugar peas, a newer variety, are shorter and rounder than snow peas and have thicker pods containing fully formed peas. Both can be eaten raw or cooked as a vegetable using any recipe for shelled peas. See page 249 for preparation tips and cooking times. Both varieties are quick-cooking, although sugar peas require slightly longer cooking than snow peas.

NEW POTATOES with BUTTER and CHIVES

Colour Index page 73. 900 kJ per serving. Good source of vitamin C, fibre.
Begin 25 minutes ahead.

Ingredients	For 4	For 2	For 1
New potatoes, well scrubbed	750 g	375 g	185 g
Butter or margarine	45 g	25 g	2 teaspoons
Chopped fresh chives	¼ cup	2 tablespoons	1 tablespoon
Salt and pepper	to taste	to taste	to taste
Microwave cookware	30-cm x 20-cm baking dish	20-cm x 20-cm baking dish	20-cm x 20-cm baking dish
Time on High (100% power)	8–10 minutes	5–7 minutes	3–4 minutes

1 With a vegetable peeler, remove a strip of skin from around the centre of each potato; discard.

2 Place potatoes and butter in baking dish (see Chart). Cook, covered, on High for time in Chart, until tender, stirring halfway through cooking.

3 Stir in chives. Season with salt and pepper. Serve immediately, spooning butter over potatoes.

QUICK POTATO SNACKS
Use the microwave to cook tasty snacks in next-to-no-time.

Cheesy Potato Slices: Arrange *12 unpeeled potato slices, each 5 cm in diameter and 6-mm thick,* in a 33-cm x 23-cm baking dish. Sprinkle lightly with *dried oregano.* Cook, covered, on High (100% power) for 3½ (3:30)–4 minutes. Top each slice with about *2 teaspoons grated tasty cheese.* Cook on High for 30 seconds, or just until cheese melts. 2 servings. 643 kJ per serving.

Pizza Potatoes: Wash *1 potato (about 185 g)* under cold running water; do not peel. Pierce potato in several places; place on paper towel on oven floor. Cook on High (100% power) for 5 minutes, or until potato feels soft when pierced with the tip of a sharp knife. Cut potato in half lengthways. Place halves on a paper plate. Top each half with *1 tablespoon Italian-style tomato sauce, 1 tablespoon grated mozzarella cheese* and *2 slices pepperoni sausage.* Cook on High for 1–1½ (1:30) minutes, until cheese melts. 2 servings. 984 kJ per serving.

POTATOES au GRATIN

Colour Index page 75. 984 kJ per serving. Good source of vitamin C, iron, fibre.
Begin 35 minutes ahead.

One of the best ways to cook potatoes is in the microwave, since this retains their full flavour, texture and nutritional value. When preparing potatoes, cut slices the same thickness to ensure even cooking.

Ingredients for 8 servings		Microwave cookware
60 g butter or margarine	¼ teaspoon paprika	25-cm round baking dish
1 small onion, finely chopped	1.5 kg potatoes, peeled or unpeeled	
¼ cup dried breadcrumbs	¼ cup water	
¼ teaspoon salt	60 g Cheddar cheese, grated (½ cup)	
¼ teaspoon pepper		

1 Place butter and onion in baking dish. Cook, covered, on High (100% power) for 2–3 minutes, stirring once; put aside.

2 Combine breadcrumbs, salt, pepper and paprika in a small bowl. Stir in cooked onion.

3 Cut potatoes into 3-mm slices. Arrange in overlapping circles in dish used for onion; add water.

4 Cook, covered, on High for 13–15 minutes, until tender, rotating dish once. Drain off water, pressing with a spatula.

5 Sprinkle cheese, then seasoned crumbs, over potatoes. Cook on High for 1½ (1:30) minutes, or until cheese melts.

MASHED POTATOES

Colour Index page 73. 4 servings. 975 kJ per serving.
Good source of vitamin C, fibre.
Begin 25 minutes ahead.

750 g potatoes, peeled and diced	1/4 teaspoon pepper
1 cup water	1/4–1/2 cup cream
60 g butter or margarine	Chopped fresh chives to garnish
1/4 teaspoon salt	

1. Place potatoes and water in a 2-litre casserole. Cook, covered, on High (100% power) for 10–15 minutes, until potatoes are very tender, stirring occasionally. Drain.
2. Add butter, salt and pepper. Beat until potato mixture is fluffy. Gradually add cream as needed, beating until smooth. Cook, covered, on High for 3–5 minutes, until hot, stirring halfway through cooking.
3. Transfer to a warmed serving dish; garnish with chives. Serve immediately.

COUNTRY-STYLE POTATOES

Colour Index page 73. 4 servings. 787 kJ per serving.
Good source of vitamin C, fibre.
Begin 25 minutes ahead.

3 rashers rindless bacon, diced	Salt and pepper to taste
1 large onion, sliced	Chopped fresh parsley to garnish
750 g potatoes, peeled and diced	

1. Cook bacon in a 30-cm x 20-cm baking dish, covered with paper towel, on High (100% power) for 3–4 minutes, until browned, stirring halfway through cooking. With slotted spoon, transfer bacon to paper towel to drain. Discard all but 2 tablespoons bacon drippings.
2. Stir onion and potatoes into bacon drippings. Cook on High for 12–15 minutes, until potatoes are tender, stirring occasionally. Season with salt and pepper; stir in reserved bacon.
3. Arrange potato mixture on a warmed serving platter; garnish with chopped parsley. Serve hot.

SERVING WHOLE POTATOES
Small new potatoes become dinner party fare when served in crisp leaves of colourful radicchio and garnished with fresh dill.

STUFFED POTATOES ORIENTALE

Colour Index page 75. 1896 kJ per main-course serving. Good source of niacin, vitamin C, iron.
Begin 45 minutes ahead.

Ingredients	For 4	For 2	For 1
Large potatoes (about 250 g each), well scrubbed	4	2	1
Chicken breasts, skinned, boned and cut into 6-mm strips	500 g	250 g	125 g
Peanut oil	3 teaspoons	1 1/2 teaspoons	3/4 teaspoon
Cornflour	2 teaspoons	1 teaspoon	1/2 teaspoon
Garlic, crushed	1 clove	1/2 clove	1/4 clove
Ground ginger	1/2 teaspoon	1/4 teaspoon	1/8 teaspoon
Frozen stir-fry vegetables	375 g	185 g	90 g
Soy sauce	2 tablespoons	1 tablespoon	2 teaspoons
Sweet chilli sauce	1 teaspoon	1/2 teaspoon	1/4 teaspoon
Butter or margarine	60 g	30 g	15 g
Microwave cookware	1-litre baking dish	1-litre baking dish	23-cm pie plate
Time on High (100% power)			
Potatoes	14–16 minutes	7–8 minutes	4–6 minutes
Chicken	4–5 minutes	2–3 minutes	1–2 minutes
With vegetables	4–6 minutes	2–4 minutes	1–2 minutes

1 Pierce potatoes with a fork several times. Place in a circle on paper towel on oven floor.

2 Cook on High for time in Chart, turning and rearranging halfway through cooking. Wrap in foil; allow to stand while preparing filling.

3 Combine chicken, oil, cornflour, garlic and ginger in baking dish or pie plate (see Chart).

4 Cook, covered, on High for time in Chart, until chicken is no longer pink, stirring halfway through cooking.

5 Stir in frozen vegetables, soy sauce and chilli sauce.

6 Cook on High for time in Chart, until vegetables are tender, stirring once. Stir until sauce is smooth. Remove potatoes from foil. Cut a slit lengthways in each potato; place an equal amount of butter in each slit. Fluff potatoes with a fork, then top each with chicken and vegetable mixture. Place on a warmed serving platter. Serve immediately.

Potatoes can be baked in the microwave in a matter of minutes – see the charts on page 250 for exact cooking times. Sweet potatoes make an appetising change from plain baked potatoes; Twice-Baked Sweet Potatoes (below) are especially delicious.

TWICE-BAKED SWEET POTATOES

Colour Index page 77. 615 kJ per serving. Low in cholesterol, sodium. Good source of vitamin A, fibre.
Begin 40 minutes ahead.

Ingredients	For 4	For 2	For 1
Sweet potatoes, well scrubbed	2 large	1 large	1 small
Natural low-fat yoghurt	¼ cup	2 tablespoons	1 tablespoon
Chilli powder	¼ teaspoon	⅛ teaspoon	to taste
Butter or margarine	30 g	15 g	1½ teaspoons
Salt	to taste	to taste	to taste
Microwave cookware	Baking tray Dinner plate	Baking tray Dinner plate	Baking tray Dinner plate
Time on High (100% power)			
Sweet potatoes	8–10 minutes	5–7 minutes	3–5 minutes
With filling	4–5 minutes	2½ (2:30)–3 minutes	1–2 minutes

1 Pierce skin of each sweet potato with a fork several times. Place on paper towel on baking tray (see Chart) with narrow ends pointing towards the centre.

2 Cook sweet potatoes on High for time in Chart, until tender, turning over and rearranging halfway through cooking.

3 Wrap sweet potatoes in foil; allow to stand for 5 minutes. Remove foil; cut each sweet potato in half lengthways.

4 Scoop flesh from sweet potatoes into a bowl, leaving 6-mm shells; reserve flesh. Arrange shells on dinner plate (see Chart).

5 In bowl with mixer at low speed, beat sweet-potato flesh, yoghurt, chilli powder and butter until well mixed and fluffy. Season with salt.

6 Spoon mashed sweet potato mixture into reserved shells. Reheat on High for time in Chart, until hot. Serve immediately.

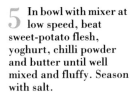

CURRIED POTATOES WITH PEAS

Colour Index page 73. 6 servings. 624 kJ per serving. Low in cholesterol, fat, sodium. Good source of iron, fibre.
Begin 25 minutes ahead.

2 tablespoons peanut oil	1 teaspoon lemon juice
1 onion, chopped	1 teaspoon garam masala
1 clove garlic, chopped	1 teaspoon turmeric
2.5-cm green ginger, peeled and chopped	½ teaspoon chilli powder
500 g potatoes, peeled and cut into 2.5-cm pieces	250 g frozen peas, thawed
215 g can tomatoes, drained	1 tablespoon chopped fresh coriander
2 teaspoons ground coriander	Chilli flower (page 115) to garnish

1. Place oil, onion, garlic and ginger in a 3-litre bowl. Cook on High (100% power) for 3–4 minutes, stirring once.
2. Add potatoes, tomatoes, coriander, lemon juice, garam masala, turmeric and chilli powder. Cook, covered, on High for 5 minutes, or until liquid boils, stirring once. Uncover and cook for 7–8 minutes, until liquid has almost evaporated, stirring twice.
3. Stir in peas and fresh coriander. Cook on High for 5 minutes.
4. Transfer to a warmed serving dish; garnish with chilli flower. Serve immediately.

PUMPKIN BAKE

Colour Index page 77. 10 servings. 1168 kJ per serving. Good source of vitamin A, fibre.
Begin 1½ hours ahead.

1 large butternut pumpkin (about 1.5 kg), cut in half and seeds removed	1 teaspoon ground mixed spice
90 g butter or margarine	½ cup fresh wholemeal breadcrumbs
1 cup cream	½ cup chopped walnuts

1. Wrap each pumpkin half in plastic wrap; arrange on oven floor, alternating narrow ends. Cook on High (100% power) for 20–25 minutes, until tender, turning over and rearranging halfway through cooking. Allow to stand, wrapped, for 5 minutes. Scoop flesh into a large bowl.
2. Heat butter in a 23-cm pie plate, covered with paper towel, on High for 1–1½ (1:30) minutes, until melted.
3. Add 3 tablespoons melted butter to pumpkin in bowl; beat in cream and mixed spice. Spoon mixture into a deep 23-cm pie plate.
4. Stir breadcrumbs and walnuts into remaining melted butter. Cook on High for 5–6 minutes, until crisp, stirring every minute.
5. Sprinkle crumb mixture over pumpkin. Cook on High for 8 minutes, or until hot. Allow to stand, loosely covered, for 5 minutes. Serve hot.

CREAMED SPINACH

Colour Index page 75. 6 servings. 389 kJ per serving.
Good source of vitamin A, riboflavin, vitamin C,
calcium, iron, fibre.
Begin 40 minutes ahead.

750 g spinach or	*1½ cups milk*
silverbeet	*½ teaspoon salt*
30 g butter or margarine	*¼ teaspoon pepper*
1½ tablespoons plain	*Ground nutmeg to taste*
flour	*Lemon slices to garnish*

1. Remove stems from spinach. Rinse leaves
under cold running water; drain lightly. Place
spinach with water remaining on leaves in a
3-litre casserole. Cook, covered, on High (100%
power) for 5–7 minutes, until leaves are wilted,
stirring twice. Drain; put aside.
2. Heat butter in a 4-cup glass jug, covered with
paper towel, on High for 45 seconds, or until
melted. Stir in flour until smooth and blended.
Cook on High for 1 minute, stirring once.
3. Gradually add milk, stirring well. Cook on
High for 4–6 minutes, until thickened and
smooth, stirring occasionally. Season with salt,
pepper and nutmeg.
4. Stir spinach into sauce. Cook on High for
3–5 minutes, until hot.
5. Spoon into a warmed serving dish; garnish
with lemon slices. Serve immediately.

ALTERNATIVE SERVING IDEAS
For a special occasion, Creamed Spinach
can be served in a vegetable shell such as an
artichoke bottom or hollowed-out tomato (as
on page 274), or in an individual serving dish
(below) with Buttered Crumb Topping and a
dill sprig garnish.

Buttered Crumb Topping: Heat *30 g butter
or margarine* in a 2-cup glass jug on High
(100% power) for 45 seconds, or until
melted. Stir in *½ cup fresh breadcrumbs*
and *¼ teaspoon dried thyme or basil*. Cook,
covered, on High for 2–2½ (2:30) minutes,
until crumbs are dried and golden.

SPINACH GNOCCHI WITH BUTTER AND PARMESAN

Colour Index page 77. 975 kJ per serving. Good source of vitamin A, calcium,
fibre.
Begin 2 hours ahead.

Spinach gnocchi – Italian-style 'dumplings' made with spinach and
ricotta and spiced with Parmesan cheese for extra flavour – make a
light meal when served with salad and crusty bread, but are equally
delicious as an accompaniment to roast veal.

Ingredients for 8 servings		Microwave cookware
125 g butter or margarine	*2 eggs*	*30-cm x 20-cm baking dish*
375 g packet frozen chopped spinach, thawed and well drained	*1 cup plain flour*	*2-cup glass jug*
	½ cup grated Parmesan cheese	
	¼ teaspoon salt	
125 g ricotta cheese	*¼ teaspoon pepper*	
1 small onion, finely chopped	*Ground nutmeg to taste*	

1 Heat 2 tablespoons
butter in baking dish,
covered with paper
towel, on High (100%
power) for 45 seconds, or
until melted. Stir in
spinach, ricotta and
onion. Cook on High for
5 minutes.

2 Add eggs, half the
flour and half the
Parmesan cheese; season
with salt, pepper and
nutmeg. Stir until
blended. Refrigerate,
loosely covered, until
cool enough to handle.

3 Half fill a 5-litre
saucepan with water.
Bring to the boil over
high heat. Meanwhile,
roll 1 tablespoon spinach
mixture in remaining
flour and form into an
oval shape with floured
hands. Repeat with
remaining mixture.

4 Carefully add half
the gnocchi to the
boiling water. Cook for
about 7 minutes, or until
slightly puffed and set.

5 With slotted spoon,
transfer gnocchi to
paper towel to drain.
Repeat with remaining
gnocchi. Meanwhile, heat
remaining butter in glass
jug, covered with paper
towel, on High for
1–1½ (1:30) minutes,
until melted.

6 Arrange gnocchi in a
warmed serving dish.
Pour melted butter over
gnocchi; sprinkle with
remaining Parmesan
cheese. Serve hot.

SPAGHETTI SQUASH WITH MEAT SAUCE

Colour Index page 76. 2361 kJ per serving. Good source of thiamine, niacin, vitamin C, iron.
Begin 55 minutes ahead.

Ingredients for 4 main-course servings		Microwave cookware
1 spaghetti squash (about 1 kg) 500 g pork sausage meat 1 small onion, finely chopped 1 green capsicum, finely chopped 425 g can tomatoes, chopped	2 tablespoons tomato paste 1 tablespoon shredded fresh basil or 1 teaspoon dried basil Salt to taste Basil leaves to garnish	33-cm x 23-cm baking dish

1 Pierce squash with a fork several times. Place on a double thickness of paper towel on oven floor.

2 Cook squash on High (100% power) for 12–15 minutes, until flesh is tender when pierced with a sharp knife, turning over halfway through cooking. Wrap in foil; allow to stand while preparing sauce.

3 Place sausage meat and onion in baking dish. Cook, covered with paper towel, on High for 5–7 minutes, until meat is no longer pink, stirring often to break up lumps.

4 Add capsicum, tomatoes, tomato paste and basil to meat; stir to mix. Cook on High for 15–18 minutes, until vegetables are tender and sauce has thickened slightly, stirring occasionally. Season with salt.

5 Split squash in half lengthways; discard seeds. With 2 forks, lift up flesh of squash to form spaghetti-like strands; transfer to a warmed large serving platter.

6 Spoon meat sauce over spaghetti squash; garnish with shredded basil leaves. Serve immediately.

STEWED FRESH TOMATOES

Colour Index page 72. 6 servings. 285 kJ per serving. Good source of vitamin A.
Begin 25 minutes ahead.

30 g butter or margarine	1½ teaspoons sugar
4 spring onions, sliced	½ teaspoon garlic salt
1 kg tomatoes, peeled and each cut into 8 wedges	¼ teaspoon pepper Spring onion curls (page 134, optional)

1. Place butter and sliced spring onions in a 33-cm x 23-cm baking dish. Cook, covered with paper towel, on High (100% power) for 45 seconds–1 minute, until butter is melted.
2. Stir in tomato wedges, sugar, garlic salt and pepper. Cook, covered, on High for 5 minutes, stirring halfway through cooking. Uncover; stir again. Cook on High, covered loosely with paper towel, for 10–15 minutes longer, until tomatoes are soft, stirring twice.
3. Spoon into a warmed serving dish; garnish, if you like, with spring onion curls. Serve hot.

GREEN TOMATO CURRY

Colour Index page 72. 4 servings. 507 kJ per serving. Good source of vitamin A, vitamin C.
Begin 25 minutes ahead.

30 g butter or margarine	1 teaspoon curry powder
1 small onion, chopped	¼ teaspoon chilli powder
1 large cooking apple, peeled and sliced	¼ teaspoon salt 4 green tomatoes, cut into wedges
2 teaspoons sugar	

1. Heat butter in a 30-cm x 20-cm baking dish, covered with paper towel, on High (100% power) for 45 seconds, or until melted.
2. Add onion. Cook on High for 2–3 minutes, until softened, stirring twice.
3. Stir in apple, sugar, curry powder, chilli powder and salt. Cook on High for 3–4 minutes, until apple has softened, stirring twice.
4. Stir in green tomatoes. Cook on High for 5–7 minutes, until tender, stirring occasionally.
5. Transfer to a warmed serving dish. Serve hot.

STUFFED TOMATOES
Hollowed out tomato shells filled with a cooked vegetable of a contrasting colour, such as Creamed Spinach (page 273), create a stunning effect presented on a white plate.

ZUCCHINI WITH SUN-DRIED TOMATOES AND PINE NUTS

Colour Index page 77. 4 servings. 816 kJ per serving. Low in cholesterol. Good source of iron, fibre. Begin 35 minutes ahead.

4 medium zucchini
2 tablespoons olive or
  vegetable oil
1 clove garlic, crushed
¼ cup pine nuts
⅓ cup chopped sun-dried
  tomatoes, drained if
  packed in oil

1 tablespoon shredded
  fresh basil or
  1 teaspoon dried basil
Salt and pepper to taste
Basil leaves to garnish

1. Cut each zucchini into 6 slices lengthways; cut each slice lengthways into 6-mm strips. Put aside.
2. Place oil, garlic and pine nuts in a 33-cm x 23-cm baking dish. Cook on High (100% power) for 2–3 minutes, until pine nuts are lightly toasted, stirring twice.
3. Add zucchini strips, sun-dried tomatoes and basil; stir well. Cook, covered, on High for 5–7 minutes, until zucchini is tender-crisp, stirring halfway through cooking. Season with salt and pepper.
4. Transfer mixture to a warmed serving platter; garnish with basil leaves. Serve immediately.

Making the zucchini strips

Cut each zucchini into 6 slices lengthways. Cut each slice lengthways into 6-mm strips. When cooked, zucchini will resemble very thin pasta.

STEAMING VEGETABLES
To ensure even cooking, use vegetables of similar size and density (such as broccoli and cauliflower flowerets) or cut vegetables into pieces of uniform size (such as sticks of carrot and zucchini). Lightly moisten 1 sheet of paper towel; place vegetables on top. Twist corners of paper towel together. Place on oven floor. Cook 250 g of vegetables on High (100% power) for 4–5 minutes, until tender-crisp.

Zucchini of any size make ideal containers for savoury vegetable fillings. If you have extra large zucchini, they can be served as a main-course dish; with nutty brown rice and a crisp side salad they make a well-balanced and filling vegetarian meal. The Stuffed Zucchini (below) are delicious as an accompaniment to lamb or fish; they are also very good served cold as a first course. To save time, they can be prepared ahead up to the end of step 4, then cooked at the last minute.

STUFFED ZUCCHINI

Colour Index page 77. 364 kJ per serving. Low in cholesterol, sodium. Begin 35 minutes ahead.

Ingredients for 2 servings		Microwave cookware

2 medium zucchini
1½ teaspoons olive or
  vegetable oil
½ red capsicum, finely
  chopped
½ tomato, finely chopped
1 clove garlic, crushed
⅛ teaspoon dried thyme
	2 tablespoons dried
	  breadcrumbs
	1 tablespoon grated
	  Parmesan cheese
	Salt to taste
	Lemon twists (page 134)
	  and basil leaves to
	  garnish
		30-cm x 20-cm
		baking dish

1 Cut zucchini in half lengthways. Scoop out flesh leaving a 6-mm shell. Reserve flesh.

2 Arrange zucchini shells, cut side down, in baking dish. Cook, covered, on High (100% power) for 2–3 minutes, until tender but not soft. Transfer shells to a platter; put aside.

3 Dice reserved zucchini flesh. Place in baking dish with oil, capsicum, tomato, garlic and thyme; stir well. Cook on High for 2–3 minutes, until tender, stirring halfway through cooking.

4 Stir in breadcrumbs and Parmesan cheese; season with salt. Mound equal amounts of vegetable mixture in each zucchini shell.

5 Arrange zucchini in cleaned baking dish with stem ends towards edges. Cook on High for 2–3 minutes, until hot. Allow to stand, loosely covered, on a heatproof surface for 2 minutes.

6 Arrange stuffed zucchini on a warmed serving platter; garnish with lemon twists and basil. Serve immediately.

Mixed vegetables

The microwave brings out the best in different vegetables cooked together in the same dish. In the selection in Combination Vegetables (below), all the vegetables have different densities and water content, so they each cook at different speeds. To prevent the vegetables from cooking unevenly, they are added to the microwave in stages.

COMBINATION VEGETABLES

Colour Index page 76. 448 kJ per serving. Low in cholesterol. Good source of vitamin A, vitamin C, fibre.
Begin 45 minutes ahead.

Ingredients for 8 servings		Microwave cookware
4 spring onions 500 g carrots 2 tablespoons peanut oil 1/4 teaspoon crushed dried chillies	2 tablespoons soy sauce 1/4 cup water 500 g broccoli 1 medium red capsicum 250 g button mushrooms	Medium bowl 4-litre casserole

1 Cut spring onions diagonally into 2.5-cm pieces; cut carrots into 6-mm slices.

2 Place spring onions, oil and chillies in bowl. Cook on High (100% power) for 3 minutes, or until tender-crisp, stirring once. Stir in soy sauce; cover and put aside.

3 Place carrots and water in casserole. Cook, covered, on High for 8–10 minutes, until carrots are tender-crisp, stirring halfway through cooking.

4 Meanwhile, cut broccoli into 5-cm x 2.5-cm pieces. Cut capsicum into matchstick-thin strips; put aside.

5 Add broccoli to carrots. Cook, covered, on High for 5 minutes, stirring halfway through cooking. Add mushrooms. Cook, covered, on High for 5 minutes longer, or until vegetables are tender, stirring halfway through cooking. Drain liquid from vegetables.

6 Add capsicums and spring-onion mixture to vegetables. Toss to coat well. Arrange on a warmed serving platter. Serve immediately.

GOLDEN MASHED VEGETABLES

Colour Index page 76. 8 servings. 565 kJ per serving. Good source of vitamin C, fibre.
Begin 45 minutes ahead.

750 g pumpkin
750 g swede
1/2 cup water
60 g butter or margarine
2 teaspoons brown sugar
1/2 teaspoon salt
1 tablespoon orange-flavoured liqueur

1 teaspoon finely grated orange rind
1/8 teaspoon ground cinnamon
Orange julienne (page 316) and parsley sprig to garnish

1. Peel pumpkin and swede. Cut each into 2-cm pieces.
2. Place pumpkin, swede and water in a 4-litre casserole. Cook, covered, on High (100% power) for 18 minutes, or until vegetables are very tender, stirring occasionally.
3. Add butter, sugar, salt, liqueur, orange rind and cinnamon; mash thoroughly.
4. Spoon mixture into a serving dish. Reheat on High for 2 minutes, or until hot; garnish with orange julienne and parsley. Serve immediately.

GARDEN MEDLEY

Colour Index page 76. 6 servings. 762 kJ per serving. Low in cholesterol, sodium. Good source of vitamin A, vitamin C, iron, fibre.
Begin 45 minutes ahead.

500 g potatoes, peeled
2 small eggplants (about 250 g each)
2 onions
4 red or yellow capsicums
2 large zucchini (about 250 g each)
1/4 cup water
1 clove garlic, crushed

1/4 cup vegetable oil
2 tablespoons cider vinegar
1 teaspoon chopped fresh oregano or 1/4 teaspoon dried oregano
1 medium tomato, cut into 8 wedges
Basil leaves to garnish

1. Cut potatoes into 4-cm chunks. Cut each eggplant into quarters lengthways. Cut each onion into 6 wedges. Cut capsicums into 2.5-cm strips. Cut zucchini diagonally into 2.5-cm slices.
2. Place potatoes and water in a 33-cm x 23-cm baking dish. Cook, covered, on High (100% power) for 5 minutes, stirring halfway through cooking. Drain.
3. Add eggplant, onions, capsicum, zucchini, garlic, oil, vinegar and oregano; stir. Cook, covered, on High for 15 minutes, stirring twice.
4. Add tomato to vegetable mixture. Cook, covered, on High for 4–5 minutes, until vegetables are tender, stirring halfway through cooking.
5. Spoon vegetables on to a serving platter; garnish with basil leaves. Serve hot or cover and refrigerate to serve chilled later.

RATATOUILLE

Colour Index page 76. 8 servings. 481 kJ per serving. Low in cholesterol. Good source of vitamin C, fibre. Begin 45 minutes ahead.

¼ cup olive or vegetable oil	1 tablespoon chopped fresh oregano or 1 teaspoon dried oregano
1 large onion, chopped	
2 cloves garlic, crushed	
1 red or green capsicum, cut into 2.5-cm pieces	1 teaspoon sugar
	1 teaspoon salt
1 medium eggplant (about 750 g), cut into 2.5-cm chunks	2 large tomatoes, each cut into 8 wedges
	2 tablespoons tomato paste
3 medium zucchini, cut into 2.5-cm chunks	Basil leaves to garnish

1. Place oil, onion and garlic in a 33-cm x 23-cm baking dish. Cook on High (100% power) for 3–4 minutes, until onion has softened, stirring halfway through cooking.

2. Stir in capsicum, eggplant and zucchini. Cook, covered, on High for 10–12 minutes, until vegetables are slightly softened, stirring twice during cooking.

3. Add oregano, sugar, salt, tomatoes and tomato paste; mix well. Cook on High for 15–18 minutes, until vegetables are tender and juices thicken slightly, stirring occasionally.

4. Spoon ratatouille on to a serving platter; garnish with basil leaves. Serve hot or cover and refrigerate to serve chilled later.

RATATOUILLE-FILLED CAPSICUMS: Prepare Ratatouille (above) up to the end of step 3. Cut *4 medium capsicums (red, green and/or yellow)* in half lengthways; remove seeds and stems. Brush capsicums on all sides with *1 tablespoon vegetable oil.* Arrange, cut side down, in a single layer in a 30-cm x 20-cm baking dish. Cook, covered, on High (100% power) for 3–4 minutes, just until softened; cool slightly. Spoon equal amounts of Ratatouille into capsicum halves and arrange on a serving platter. If you like, reheat filled capsicums on Medium-High (70% power) for 3–4 minutes before serving.

Oiling and arranging the capsicums

Lightly and evenly brush oil over capsicums.

Place capsicums, cut side down, in a single layer in a baking dish. Cook, covered, as above.

When cooking a variety of fresh seasonal vegetables in the microwave, be sure to arrange them so that the thicker parts are pointing towards the edges of the dish, where they will receive most microwave energy. If necessary, overlap the pieces slightly, as in the recipe for Spring Vegetables with Lemon and Chive Butter (below).

SPRING VEGETABLES WITH LEMON AND CHIVE BUTTER

Colour Index page 73. 590 kJ per serving. Low in cholesterol. Good source of vitamin A, vitamin C, fibre. Begin 25 minutes ahead.

Ingredients for 6 servings		Microwave cookware
750 g asparagus spears	2 teaspoons French or mild mustard	30-cm x 20-cm baking dish
3 small golden zucchini		Small bowl
6 medium carrots	1½ tablespoons lemon juice	
2 bunches radishes		
½ cup water	1 tablespoon lemon julienne (page 316)	
60 g butter or margarine		
2 tablespoons finely chopped fresh chives	¼ teaspoon salt	

1 Trim tough ends from asparagus. Cut zucchini into quarters lengthways; cut carrots in half lengthways. Trim radishes.

2 Arrange carrots in baking dish so that tips are overlapping in centre; add water. Cook, covered, on High (100% power) for 4 minutes.

3 Arrange asparagus on top of carrots in baking dish so that tips are overlapping in centre.

4 Arrange zucchini and radishes in layers on top of carrots and asparagus. Cook, covered, on High for 8–10 minutes, until vegetables are tender-crisp, rotating dish halfway through cooking.

5 Combine butter, chives, mustard, lemon juice, lemon julienne and salt in bowl. Cook on High for 2½ (2:30)–3 minutes, until butter has melted.

6 Arrange vegetables on a warmed serving platter. Top with lemon and chive butter.

Warm salads

Various salad greens such as cos, watercress and radicchio are delicious served wilted with a warm dressing. Curly endive, with its pungent flavour, is a particularly good choice.

SPINACH SALAD WITH HOT BACON DRESSING

Colour Index page 78. 643 kJ per serving. Low in cholesterol. Good source of vitamin A.
Begin 20 minutes ahead.

Ingredients	For 4	For 2	For 1
Fresh young spinach or silverbeet leaves	375 g	185 g	90 g
Rindless bacon, diced	4 rashers	2 rashers	1 rasher
Cider vinegar	3 teaspoons	1½ teaspoons	¾ teaspoon
Dijon mustard	3 teaspoons	1½ teaspoons	¾ teaspoon
Caster sugar	1 teaspoon	½ teaspoon	¼ teaspoon
Red onion, sliced	1 medium	1 small	½ small
Microwave cookware	Large bowl 23-cm pie plate	Medium bowl 23-cm pie plate	Small bowl 23-cm pie plate
Time on High (100% power)			
Bacon	4–5 minutes	2–3 minutes	1–1½ (1:30) minutes
Dressing	1–2 minutes	30 seconds–1 minute	15–30 seconds
Salad	2–3 minutes	1–1½ (1:30) minutes	45 seconds–1 minute

1 Wash spinach well; tear into bite-sized pieces in bowl (see Chart).

2 Cook bacon in pie plate (see Chart), covered with paper towel, on High for time in Chart, until browned, stirring twice. Transfer to paper towel to drain.

3 Stir vinegar, mustard and sugar into bacon drippings in pie plate. Cook, covered with paper towel, on High for time in Chart, until hot.

4 Add onion and hot dressing to spinach; toss to coat well. Sprinkle reserved bacon over spinach. Cook salad on High for time in Chart, just until spinach wilts.

LEAVES FOR SALAD

While roundhead lettuce remains the favourite salad green, there is a wide variety of other leaves available to add interest to salads, including rocket, lamb's lettuce, mignonette, silverbeet, spinach, chicory, endive, radicchio and cos. Try varying different colours and shapes in the salad bowl, tossing them together with a favourite dressing.

Radicchio: Bitter-flavoured, ruby-red leaves, used frequently in Italian salads.

Lamb's lettuce (mâche): A spring and summer salad green with spoon-shaped leaves; tangy and good with other leaves.

Curly endive: Somewhat bitter tasting; outer leaves are darker and stronger in flavour than inner ones.

Mignonette: Curly red-tinged leaves.

Cos (romaine): Wide flat leaves, curled at the edges.

WARM SALAD OF ROCKET AND CORN

Colour Index page 78. 8 servings. 586 kJ per serving.
Low in cholesterol. Good source of fibre.
Begin 20 minutes ahead.

4 rashers rindless bacon, diced	4 cups shredded rocket or watercress
1 large onion, sliced	2 tablespoons red wine vinegar
2 cloves garlic, crushed	Salt and pepper to taste
375 g frozen corn kernels, thawed	Avocado slices to garnish

1. Cook bacon in a 33-cm x 23-cm baking dish, covered with paper towel, on High (100% power) for 3–4 minutes, until browned, stirring twice. Transfer to paper towel to drain.
2. Stir onion, garlic and corn into bacon drippings in dish. Cook on High for 4–5 minutes, until onion has softened, stirring halfway through cooking.
3. Stir in rocket and vinegar. Cook on High for 2–4 minutes, until rocket has wilted, stirring halfway through cooking. Season with salt and pepper.
4. Spoon salad on to warmed plates; garnish with avocado slices and sprinkle with diced bacon. Serve immediately.

CAPSICUM SALAD

Colour Index page 78. 6 servings. 695 kJ per serving.
Low in cholesterol. Good source of vitamin A, vitamin C, calcium.
Begin 25 minutes ahead.

1 large red onion	1 teaspoon sugar
2 red capsicums	½ teaspoon fennel seeds, crushed
2 green capsicums	¼ teaspoon salt
2 yellow capsicums	90 g stoned black olives, drained and cut in half
2 tablespoons olive or vegetable oil	125 g feta cheese, crumbled
2 tablespoons white wine vinegar	

1. Cut onion into 8 wedges. Separate each wedge to loosen layers. Cut capsicums into 12-mm strips.
2. Place oil and onion in a 33-cm x 23-cm baking dish. Cook, covered, on High (100% power) for 3–4 minutes, until softened slightly, stirring halfway through cooking.
3. Add capsicums. Cook, covered, on High for 7–10 minutes, until tender, stirring occasionally.
4. Combine vinegar, sugar, fennel seeds and salt in a bowl. Add capsicum mixture, olives and feta cheese. Toss gently to mix well. Serve warm or cover and refrigerate to serve chilled later.

Warm salads make a welcome alternative to plainly cooked green vegetables. They are also delicious served as a first course. An entrée salad should be light and tangy – to whet the appetite for heartier dishes to come.

WARM SALAD OF ARTICHOKE HEARTS AND CHERRY TOMATOES

Colour Index page 79. 779 kJ per serving. Good source of vitamin C, fibre.
Begin 55 minutes ahead.

Ingredients for 6 servings		Microwave cookware
125 g butter or margarine	1 teaspoon finely chopped fresh tarragon or ¼ teaspoon dried tarragon	33-cm x 23-cm baking dish
400 g can artichoke hearts, drained	1 egg yolk	2-cup glass jug
1 punnet cherry tomatoes	Salt and pepper to taste	Medium bowl
1 teaspoon grated onion	Dill sprigs to garnish (optional)	
3 teaspoons tarragon vinegar		
3 teaspoons dry white wine		

1 Heat 15 g butter in baking dish, covered with paper towel, on High (100% power) for 30 seconds, or until melted.

2 Add artichoke hearts. Cook on High for 1–2 minutes, until hot, stirring twice. Add cherry tomatoes. Cook on High for 2–3 minutes, until hot, stirring halfway through cooking. Keep warm.

3 Place onion, vinegar, wine and tarragon in jug. Cook on High for 2–3 minutes, until liquid evaporates. Spoon into bowl.

4 Stir egg yolk into onion mixture. Place remaining butter in jug used for onion. Heat, covered with paper towel, on High for 1–1½ (1:30) minutes, until melted.

5 Beating constantly, pour hot butter in a thin steam into onion mixture until butter is incorporated and mixture thickens. Season with salt and pepper. Cook on Medium (50% power) for 30 seconds–1 minute, until hot and slightly thickened, stirring every 15 seconds.

6 Arrange artichoke hearts in a circle on a warmed serving platter. Arrange cherry tomatoes in centre; spoon warm sauce over vegetables. Garnish, if you like, with dill sprigs. Serve immediately.

Vegetable salads

Pasta shapes combine beautifully with a variety of vegetables; prepare them in advance and, if you like, reheat them in the microwave. Use the smaller shells, bow ties and spirals to turn any salad from a light and tasty side dish into a satisfying main course everyone will enjoy.

VEGETABLE AND PASTA SALAD

Colour Index page 79. 1833 kJ per serving. Good source of vitamin A, thiamine, riboflavin, vitamin C, calcium, iron, fibre.
Begin 55 minutes ahead.

Ingredients for 6 main-course servings		Microwave cookware
1/3 cup cider vinegar 1/4 cup olive or vegetable oil 1 tablespoon chopped fresh oregano or 1 teaspoon dried oregano 1/2 teaspoon salt 1/4 teaspoon crushed dried chillies 6 spring onions, chopped 125 g green beans 3 carrots, sliced	1/4 cup water 500 g broccoli, cut into bite-sized pieces 2 zucchini, cut into 12-mm slices 250 g farfelle (bow tie pasta) 125 g Cheddar cheese, cubed 125 g Swiss cheese, cubed 1/2 punnet cherry tomatoes	30-cm x 20-cm baking dish

1 Mix vinegar, oil, oregano, salt, chillies and spring onions in a large bowl. Place beans, carrots and water in baking dish. Cook on High (100% power) for 6–8 minutes, until tender-crisp, stirring once.

2 With a slotted spoon, transfer beans and carrots to dressing in bowl; toss to coat. Cover and put aside.

3 Add broccoli to baking dish. Cook, covered, on High for 6–7 minutes, until tender-crisp, stirring halfway through cooking. Transfer to bowl with vegetables and dressing; toss to mix.

4 Place zucchini in baking dish. Cook, covered, on High for 3–4 minutes, until tender-crisp, stirring halfway through cooking. Transfer to bowl with vegetables and dressing. Toss all vegetables together to mix thoroughly.

5 Cook pasta conventionally; drain and put aside.

6 Add pasta, cheese and cherry tomatoes to vegetables. Toss gently and transfer to a serving dish. Serve warm or cover and refrigerate to serve chilled later.

LENTILS VINAIGRETTE

Colour Index page 79. 8 servings. 766 kJ per serving. Low in cholesterol. Good source of iron, fibre.
Begin 2½ hours ahead or early in day.

1/3 cup olive or vegetable oil 1 onion, chopped 1 tablespoon chopped fresh thyme or 1 teaspoon dried thyme 1 bay leaf 1 cup dry lentils 3 cups water	2 tablespoons red wine vinegar 2 tablespoons chopped fresh mint or parsley 3 spring onions, sliced 1 green capsicum, diced 1 large tomato, diced Salt and pepper to taste

1. Place 2 tablespoons oil, onion, thyme and bay leaf in a 30-cm x 20-cm baking dish. Cook on High (100% power) for 3–5 minutes, until onion has softened, stirring twice.
2. Add lentils and water. Cook, covered, on High for 15–20 minutes, until lentils are tender but not mushy, stirring occasionally. Drain; discard bay leaf.
3. Combine remaining oil, vinegar, mint, spring onions, capsicum and tomato in a bowl; add to lentil mixture in baking dish. Toss well; season with salt and pepper.
4. Cover salad and refrigerate for at least 2 hours to blend flavours before serving.

HIGH-FIBRE SALAD

Colour Index page 79. 8 servings. 1034 kJ per serving. Low in cholesterol. Good source of potassium, fibre.
Begin 2¼ hours ahead or early in day.

2 tablespoons sugar 1/2 cup olive or vegetable oil 1/2 cup cider vinegar 1/4 teaspoon salt 500 g sliced green beans, cooked 500 g cooked chick peas	440 g can kidney beans, drained and rinsed 1 onion, chopped 1/4 cup chopped sweet dill pickle 1/2 small green capsicum, chopped

1. Combine sugar, oil, vinegar and salt in a 4-cup glass jug. Heat on High (100% power) for 3–5 minutes, until mixture boils and sugar has dissolved.
2. Place green beans, chick peas, kidney beans, onion, dill pickle and capsicum in a large serving bowl. Pour dressing over salad; mix well.
3. Cover salad and refrigerate for at least 2 hours to blend flavours before serving.

WILD RICE SALAD

Colour Index page 79. 8 servings. 783 kJ per serving.
Low in cholesterol, sodium.
Begin 1½ hours ahead.

3 cups water
½ cup wild rice
½ cup long-grain rice
¼ cup olive or vegetable
  oil
3 teaspoons cider vinegar
3 teaspoons lemon juice
¼ teaspoon ground
  coriander (optional)

4 spring onions, sliced
1 cooking apple, peeled,
  cored and diced
2 celery stalks, sliced
¼ cup pine nuts
¼ cup seedless raisins
Salt to taste

1. Heat water in a 2-litre bowl on High (100%
power) for 5–7 minutes, until boiling.
2. Stir in wild rice. Cook, covered tightly with
plastic wrap, on High for 20 minutes. Uncover;
stir in long-grain rice. Cover again and cook on
High for 15–20 minutes longer, until rice is tender. Drain in colander and rinse under cold running water until cooled.
3. Meanwhile, combine oil, vinegar, lemon juice
and, if you like, coriander in a bowl. Add spring
onions, apple, celery, pine nuts and raisins. Stir
in rice; season with salt.
4. Cover salad and allow to stand for 30 minutes
to blend flavours. Serve at room temperature or
cover and refrigerate to serve chilled later.

CLASSIC POTATO SALAD

Colour Index page 78. 6 servings. 712 kJ per serving.
Good source of fibre.
Begin 25 minutes ahead.

750 g potatoes,
  cut into 2-cm chunks
¼ cup water
⅓ cup mayonnaise
3 teaspoons milk
1 teaspoon vinegar

¼ teaspoon salt
¼ teaspoon pepper
1 celery stalk, thinly
  sliced
1 hard-boiled egg
  (below), finely chopped

1. Place potatoes and water in a 2-litre casserole. Cook, covered, on High (100% power) for
7–9 minutes, until tender, stirring twice. Drain;
allow potatoes to cool slightly.
2. Combine mayonnaise, milk, vinegar, salt and
pepper. Add potatoes, celery and egg; toss to coat
well.
3. Serve immediately or cover and refrigerate to
serve chilled later.

HARD-BOILED EGGS: Break 1 egg into a small
ramekin; prick yolk in several places. Cook,
covered, on Medium (50% power) for 1½ (1:30)–
2½ (2:30) minutes. Allow to stand on a heatproof
surface for 2 minutes, or until yolk and white are
firmly set. Cook 2 eggs for 2½ (2:30)–3½ (3:30)
minutes; 3 eggs for 3–4 minutes.

TOMATO ASPIC

Colour Index page 79. 159 kJ per serving. Low in cholesterol, fat.
Begin early in day.

Ingredients	For 4	For 2	For 1
Tomato juice	2 cups	1 cup	½ cup
Water	¾ cup	⅓ cup	2 tablespoons
Celery, sliced	1 stalk	½ stalk	¼ stalk
Lemon	2 slices	1 slice	½ slice
Tabasco sauce	to taste	to taste	to taste
Powdered gelatine	1 envelope (3 teaspoons)	1½ teaspoons	¾ teaspoon
Cider vinegar	1½ teaspoons	¾ teaspoon	⅓ teaspoon
Caster sugar	½ teaspoon	¼ teaspoon	⅛ teaspoon
Salt	¼ teaspoon	⅛ teaspoon	to taste
Natural low-fat yoghurt and chives	garnish	garnish	garnish
Microwave cookware	8-cup glass jug	4-cup glass jug	2-cup glass jug
Time on High (100% power) Tomato mixture	5–7 minutes	3–5 minutes	2–2½ (2:30) minutes
With gelatine	3–4 minutes	2–3 minutes	1–1½ (1:30) minutes

1 Pour tomato juice
and water into glass
jug (see Chart). Add
celery, lemon and
Tabasco sauce. Cook,
covered, on High for time
in Chart, stirring once.

2 Pour mixture
through a strainer
into a bowl. Discard
vegetables and return
tomato mixture to
original glass jug.

3 Sprinkle gelatine
evenly over tomato
mixture; allow to stand
for 1 minute to soften
slightly.

4 Cook mixture,
covered, on High for
time in Chart, until
gelatine completely
dissolves, stirring twice.
Stir in vinegar, sugar and
salt. Taste and adjust
seasoning.

5 Ladle mixture into
½-cup ramekins or
individual moulds. Cover
and refrigerate until
firmly set.

6 Dip ramekins in
warm water. With
knife, loosen aspic from
sides. Place a small plate
upside down over each
and invert. Shake gently
and remove ramekin;
garnish aspic with
yoghurt and chives.

Chicken salads

OLD-FASHIONED CHICKEN SALAD

Colour Index page 78. 1670 kJ per serving. Good source of niacin. Begin 55 minutes ahead.

Ingredients	For 4	For 2	For 1
Chicken breasts, skinned and boned	4	2	1
Chicken stock	2 tablespoons	1 tablespoon	2 teaspoons
Celery, diced	1 stalk	½ stalk	¼ stalk
Onion, finely chopped	1 small	½ small	¼ small
Canned pimiento, diced	1 tablespoon	2 teaspoons	1 teaspoon
Mayonnaise	⅔ cup	⅓ cup	2 tablespoons
Lemon juice	3 teaspoons	1½ teaspoons	¾ teaspoon
Poultry seasoning	½ teaspoon	¼ teaspoon	⅛ teaspoon
Salt	to taste	to taste	to taste
Microwave cookware	23-cm pie plate	23-cm pie plate	23-cm pie plate
Time on High (100% power)	5–7 minutes	3½ (3:30)–5 minutes	2½ (2:30)–3½ (3:30) minutes

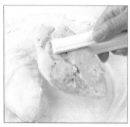  

1 Place chicken breasts and stock in pie plate (see Chart). Cook, covered, on High for time in Chart, until chicken juices run clear, turning pieces over and rotating plate halfway through cooking. Allow to stand, loosely covered, on a heatproof surface while preparing dressing.

2 Combine celery, onion, pimiento, mayonnaise, lemon juice and poultry seasoning in a bowl; mix until well blended.

3 Drain chicken; cut into chunks. Stir into dressing; mix well. Season with salt. For best flavour, cover and refrigerate for 30 minutes before serving.

SALAD DRESSINGS

Vinaigrette: Whisk *1 finely chopped small onion, ¼ cup olive oil, ¼ cup red wine vinegar, 1 teaspoon finely chopped fresh herbs* and *¼ teaspoon salt* in a small bowl until blended.

Zesty Mayonnaise: Whisk *½ cup mayonnaise, 2 tablespoons milk, 1½ tablespoons lemon juice, ½ teaspoon mustard powder, ¼ teaspoon salt, ¼ teaspoon pepper* and *¼ teaspoon dried basil* in a small bowl until blended.

CHICKEN CLUB SALAD

Colour Index page 78. 2 main-course servings. 1415 kJ per serving. Good source of niacin, iron. Begin 40 minutes ahead.

2 chicken breasts (about 185 g each), skinned and boned
⅛ teaspoon dried thyme
4 rashers rindless bacon
2 slices bread
Lettuce leaves
1 tomato, sliced
Vinaigrette (below left)

1. Place chicken breasts in a 23-cm pie plate; sprinkle with thyme. Cook, covered with greaseproof paper, on High (100% power) for 5–6 minutes, until chicken juices run clear, turning pieces over and rotating dish halfway through cooking. Discard cooking juices. Cover and refrigerate chicken.
2. Meanwhile, place bacon on a double thickness of paper towel. Cook, covered with paper towel, on High for 3½ (3:30) minutes, or until browned; put aside.
3. Cut chicken crossways into 6-mm slices. Toast bread; cut into quarters. Chop bacon.
4. Arrange lettuce leaves, tomato, chicken and toast on individual plates; sprinkle bacon over salad. Serve with Vinaigrette.

CHICKEN AND POTATO SALAD

Colour Index page 79. 6 main-course servings. 1733 kJ per serving. Good source of niacin, vitamin C, iron, fibre. Begin 1¼ hours ahead.

1.75 kg chicken, jointed and skinned
750 g small new potatoes, cut into 12-mm slices
¼ cup water
1 yellow capsicum, sliced
1 small red onion, sliced
10 stoned black olives, cut in half
¼ cup milk
⅓ cup mayonnaise
¼ cup sour cream
2 tablespoons prepared horseradish
2 tablespoons lemon juice
¼ teaspoon salt

1. Place chicken legs, thighs and wings at the edges of a 33-cm x 23-cm baking dish; arrange breasts in the centre. Cook, covered, on High (100% power) for 22–24 minutes, until chicken juices run clear, turning over and rearranging pieces halfway through cooking. Put aside to cool.
2. Place potatoes and water in a 2-litre casserole. Cook on High for 8–9 minutes, stirring once. Drain; put aside to cool.
3. Cut reserved chicken into bite-sized pieces; discard bones. Place chicken meat, potatoes, capsicum, onion and olives in a large bowl; toss.
4. Combine milk, mayonnaise, sour cream, horseradish, lemon juice and salt in a bowl. Pour dressing over salad, or serve separately.

Meat salads

ANTIPASTO SALAD

Colour Index page 78. 6 main-course servings.
1804 kJ per serving. Good source of vitamin A,
vitamin C, calcium.
Begin 25 minutes ahead.

1 small cauliflower, trimmed and cut into flowerets	3 medium carrots, cut into matchstick-thin strips
2 tablespoons water	250 g smoked Gouda, mozzarella or other cheese, sliced
3 small zucchini, cut into 12-mm slices	
Vinaigrette (page 282)	250 g salami, cut into chunks
400 g can artichoke hearts, drained	2 tomatoes, cut into wedges
Salad greens	

1. Place cauliflower and water in a 25-cm round
dish. Cook, covered, on High (100% power) for
5 minutes, stirring halfway through cooking.
Add zucchini. Cook on High for 3–5 minutes,
until vegetables are tender-crisp. With slotted
spoon, transfer vegetables to a small bowl. Pour
over half the Vinaigrette; toss.
2. Arrange artichoke hearts, salad greens,
cooked vegetables, carrots, cheese, salami and
tomatoes on a platter. Serve remaining dressing
separately.

DELICATESSEN SALAD

Colour Index page 78. 6 main-course servings.
1528 kJ per serving. Good source of niacin, calcium,
iron, fibre.
Begin 50 minutes ahead.

1 kg small new potatoes, peeled and diced	1 onion, chopped
¾ cup chicken stock	3 teaspoons plain flour
¼ teaspoon caraway seeds	½ cup cider vinegar
¼ teaspoon pepper	2 tablespoons brown sugar
4 rashers rindless bacon, diced	Salad greens
2 celery stalks, sliced	250 g sliced cold meats
	125 g Cheddar cheese, cut into strips

1. Combine potatoes, stock, caraway seeds and
pepper in a 3-litre casserole. Cook, covered, on
High (100% power) for 11–13 minutes, until
potatoes are tender, stirring halfway through
cooking. Drain cooking liquid, reserving ¼ cup.
Cover potatoes; put aside.
2. Cook bacon in a medium bowl, covered with
paper towel, on High for 4–5 minutes, until
browned. Transfer to paper towel to drain.
3. Stir celery and onion into bacon drippings in
bowl. Cook on High for 3 minutes.
4. Add flour, reserved cooking liquid, vinegar
and sugar; stir. Cook on High for 3–5 minutes,
until mixture has thickened, stirring once. Pour
over potatoes; add bacon. Allow to stand for
10 minutes.
5. Arrange salad greens on a platter; spoon
potatoes into the centre and surround with sliced
meats and cheese.

Both hot and cold pasta can be combined with a selection of crisply
cooked vegetables and thin slivers of meat to make a hearty salad.
In Thai-style Beef and Noodle Salad (below), crushed dried chillies,
spring onions, mint and cashews create an authentic Thai flavour.
This dish can be served hot, or prepared well in advance to serve
chilled later.

THAI-STYLE BEEF AND NOODLE SALAD

Colour Index page 79. 3788 kJ per serving. Good source of vitamin A, riboflavin,
thiamine, vitamin C, iron.
Begin 1½ hours ahead or early in day.

Ingredients for 4 main-course servings		Microwave cookware
500 g beef fillet	250 g egg noodles	Large bowl
½ cup peanut or vegetable oil	2 tablespoons chopped fresh mint	Browning dish
2 tablespoons lime or lemon juice	1 small red capsicum, diced	
2 tablespoons soy sauce	4 spring onions, thinly sliced	
2 tablespoons cider vinegar	¼ cup dry-roasted unsalted cashews	
2 tablespoons caster sugar		
¼ teaspoon crushed dried chillies		

1 Cut beef fillet crossways into 3-mm slices. Cut each slice into thin strips.

2 Combine oil, lime juice, soy sauce, vinegar, sugar and chillies in a bowl. Add beef; stir to coat. Cover and marinate for 30 minutes.

3 Drain beef over large bowl; reserve marinade. Preheat browning dish according to the manufacturer's instructions.

4 Spread half the beef on browning dish. Cook on High (100% power) for 1–2 minutes, just until beef is done to your liking, stirring halfway through cooking. Remove beef; put aside and keep warm. Reheat browning dish and cook remaining beef slices.

5 Meanwhile, cook egg noodles conventionally. Drain; add to reserved marinade in bowl and toss well to mix. Heat noodles on High for 2–3 minutes, until hot.

6 Toss noodles with mint, capsicum, spring onions and cashews. Place on a serving platter; arrange beef over noodles. Serve hot or cover and refrigerate to serve chilled later.

Summer Salad Bar

Delicatessen Salad (page 283)
Prawn and Snow Pea Salad (right)
Warm Salad of Rocket and Corn (page 279)
Tossed green salad and hot bread rolls
Fresh fruit platter
Banana Coconut Tart (page 340)

PREPARATION TIMETABLE

Early in day:	*Prepare Prawn and Snow Pea Salad. Prepare green salad ingredients; store in plastic bags in refrigerator. Prepare salad dressing of your choice. Arrange fresh fruit assortment on platter; loosely cover. Prepare Banana Coconut Tart up to the end of step 5.*
1¼ hours ahead:	*Make Delicatessen Salad and arrange on a serving platter. Make Warm Salad of Rocket and Corn; spoon into a warmed serving dish.*
Just before serving:	*Complete Banana Coconut Tart. Toss green salad ingredients with dressing. Wrap bread rolls in paper towel and heat on High (100% power).*

Prawn salads

PRAWN AND SNOW PEA SALAD

Colour Index page 79. 4 servings. 1122 kJ per serving. Good source of vitamin A, vitamin C, iron. Begin 2 hours ahead.

500 g medium green prawns, shelled and deveined (page 166)
155 g snow peas, cut in half crossways
1 small red capsicum, thinly sliced
425 g can whole baby corn, drained
4 spring onions, sliced
¼ cup olive or vegetable oil
1½ tablespoons dry white wine
1½ tablespoons lemon juice
1 tablespoon chopped fresh dill
Salt and pepper to taste

1. Place prawns, snow peas, capsicum, corn, spring onions, oil and wine in a 33-cm x 23-cm baking dish. Cook, covered, on High (100% power) for 5–7 minutes, just until prawns turn pink, stirring halfway through cooking.
2. Stir in lemon juice and dill; season with salt and pepper. Transfer to a serving dish; cover and refrigerate for 1–2 hours. Serve chilled.

PRAWN SALAD SUPREME

Colour Index page 79. 6 servings. 1578 kJ per serving. Good source of vitamin C, iron, potassium, fibre.
Begin 45 minutes ahead.

500 g medium green prawns, shelled and deveined (page 166)
3 teaspoons lemon juice
3 teaspoons dry sherry
500 g small new potatoes, cut into quarters
2 tablespoons water
250 g green beans
1 cup cooked chick peas
1 small red capsicum, thinly sliced
½ cup stoned black olives, cut in half
Zesty Mayonnaise (page 282)

1. Arrange prawns in a circle in a 25-cm round baking dish with tails pointing towards centre. Sprinkle with lemon juice and sherry. Cook, covered, on High (100% power) for 3–4 minutes, just until prawns turn pink, turning prawns over and rotating dish halfway through cooking. Drain; cover and refrigerate.
2. Meanwhile, place potatoes and water in a 1-litre casserole. Cook on High for 7–9 minutes, until tender, stirring halfway through cooking. With slotted spoon, transfer potatoes to a colander. Cool potatoes under cold running water; transfer to a large bowl.
3. Add beans to water remaining in casserole. Cook, covered, on High for 4–5 minutes, until tender-crisp, stirring once. Transfer beans to colander; cool under cold running water.
4. Add beans, chick peas, capsicum, olives and reserved prawns to potatoes. Pour dressing over and toss gently. Serve immediately or cover and refrigerate to serve chilled later.

Pasta, Grains and Nuts

**PASTA · RICE · WILD RICE · BARLEY · BURGHUL
CORNMEAL · NUTS**

Pasta, Grains and Nuts

Cooking pasta in a microwave is usually no faster than cooking it conventionally; the microwave is best used to cook the delicious sauces that accompany the pasta – they are so quick and easy to prepare and cook that many can be ready in the same time it takes to boil the pasta. Although specific types of pasta are given in the recipes, as in Penne with Double-Cheese Sauce (page 288), other forms of pasta – such as spaghetti, fettuccine, farfalle or tagliatelle – can usually be substituted.

Layered and filled pasta dishes do cook more quickly in the microwave, however, and the recipes usually call for a single piece of cookware which saves on the washing up. The microwave is perfect, too, for reheating pasta dishes because tenderness and flavour are retained. Place a single serving on a microwave-safe dinner plate. Cook, covered, on Medium-High (70% power) for 2 minutes, or until the plate is warm underneath and the food is hot.

Cooking in the microwave is the preferred method for rice because there is no need to heat the cooking liquid before adding the rice to it. For other grains, such as barley, burghul and couscous – where it is advised that the cooking liquid be boiled first – the liquid can be heated in the microwave before it is combined with the grain.

Nourishing breakfasts can be made instantly in the microwave with quick-cooking grains. Try Snappy Breakfast Porridge: For each serving, pour ⅔ cup water into a 4-cup glass jug or individual cereal bowl; heat on High (100% power) for 1½ (1:30)–2 minutes, until boiling. Stir. Add ⅓ cup quick-cooking oats and a pinch of salt. Cook on High for 1–2 minutes longer, until mixture thickens; stir well. If you like, add 2 tablespoons strawberry or apricot jam, or 1 tablespoon brown sugar; stir well and serve immediately, with or without milk.

Nuts can be blanched, peeled and toasted in the microwave. On page 296 there are easy-to-follow instructions for these techniques, plus quick-cooking ideas for a delicious variety of nuts flavoured with spices, herbs and other seasonings.

ATTRACTIVELY MOULDED RICE

Moulded rice always looks special yet is so easy to prepare. Use large moulds or rings for parties, small moulds for individual servings. Lightly oil the moulds and fill with Hot Cooked Rice (page 295), gently pressing down. Turn out on to an attractive plate or platter. Serve hot or chilled.

Saffron-flavoured rice ring (left) filled with chopped cooked ham and cherry tomatoes; garnished with mixed salad greens.

White and wild rice moulded together in a ramekin (right). Here with poached salmon garnished with mayonnaise and dill, lemon slices and mixed salad greens.

Pasta Shapes

Pasta is available in a wide variety of shapes, sizes and colours. Italian delicatessens often have a large selection of the more unusual and hard-to-find types. Teamed with a quick microwave sauce, pasta makes a fast and nutritious meal for any occasion.

Fusilli: *Long spirals or corkscrew coils of various lengths*

Spaghetti: *Long, thin 'strings';* **spaghettini** *is thinner*

Wholemeal spaghetti: *Made from wholemeal flour*

Linguine: *Thin, flat ribbon noodles*

Lasagna: *Extra wide noodles, sometimes with ruffled edges*

Cappelletti: *Small hat-shaped pasta*

Tagliatelle/ Fettuccine: *Flat ribbon noodles, about 6 mm wide*

Pastini: *Small pasta shapes – letters, shells, animals; for soups and children's dishes*

Egg Noodles: *Flat noodles wider than tagliatelle; available in white or green*

Conchiglie rigate: *Ridged shell shapes in various sizes; large shells can be stuffed*

Cannelloni: *Large smooth tubes for stuffing; sometimes available ridged*

Rotelle/Spirale: *Short spiral, coil or spring shapes*

Ruoti: *Cartwheel or wagon-wheel shapes*

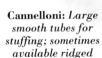

Penne: *Short, tubular pasta with angled ends; available small or large*

Farfalle: *Bow tie or butterfly shapes*

Rigatoni: *Short-cut, ridged rubes*

Pasta

SPAGHETTI WITH SPICY MEAT SAUCE

Colour Index page 80. 2344 kJ per serving. Good source of vitamin A, riboflavin, thiamine, niacin, vitamin C, iron.
Begin 25 minutes ahead.

Ingredients	For 4	For 2	For 1
Carrot, chopped	*1*	*½*	*¼*
Water	*2 tablespoons*	*1 tablespoon*	*2 teaspoons*
Beef mince	*375 g*	*185 g*	*90 g*
Mushrooms, cut into quarters	*125 g*	*60 g*	*30 g*
Onion, chopped	*1 small*	*½ small*	*¼ small*
Zucchini, chopped	*1 small*	*½ small*	*¼ small*
Garlic, crushed	*1 clove*	*½ clove*	*¼ clove*
Canned tomatoes	*425 g can*	*215 g can*	*½ cup*
Tomato paste	*2 tablespoons*	*1 tablespoon*	*2 teaspoons*
Fresh basil, shredded, or dried basil	*2 teaspoons or ½ teaspoon*	*1 teaspoon or ¼ teaspoon*	*½ teaspoon or ⅛ teaspoon*
Dry red wine (optional)	*2 tablespoons*	*1 tablespoon*	*2 teaspoons*
Salt and pepper	*to taste*	*to taste*	*to taste*
Spaghetti or other pasta	*250 g*	*125 g*	*60 g*
Parsley	*garnish*	*garnish*	*garnish*
Microwave cookware	8-cup soufflé dish	4-cup soufflé dish	4-cup soufflé dish
Time on High (100% power)			
Carrot	3–5 minutes	2–3 minutes	1–2 minutes
With beef	4–6 minutes	3–4 minutes	2–3 minutes
With tomatoes	8–10 minutes	6–7 minutes	4–5 minutes

1 Place carrot and water in soufflé dish (see Chart). Cook, covered, on High for time in Chart, until carrot is tender. Drain.

2 Add beef mince, mushrooms, onion, zucchini and garlic; stir. Cook, covered, on High for time in Chart, until meat just loses its pink colour, stirring twice.

3 Add tomatoes with their liquid, tomato paste and basil. If you like, add wine. Season with salt and pepper; stir well.

4 Cook sauce, covered, on High for time in Chart, until sauce bubbles, stirring often.

5 Meanwhile, cook pasta conventionally; drain.

6 Place pasta on warmed plates; ladle sauce over. Garnish with parsley. Serve immediately.

PENNE WITH DOUBLE-CHEESE SAUCE

Colour Index page 80. 4 servings. 2466 kJ per serving. Good source of vitamin A, thiamine, vitamin C, calcium, iron.
Begin 20 minutes ahead.

2 onions, thinly sliced
2 large red capsicums, very thinly sliced
¼ cup olive or vegetable oil
250 g penne or other pasta
125 g mozzarella cheese, cut into 6-mm cubes
125 g Cheddar or Fontina cheese, grated (1 cup)
90 g stoned black olives, cut in half
½ cup loosely packed shredded fresh parsley or basil
Salt and pepper to taste

1. Combine onion, capsicum and oil in a 30-cm x 20-cm baking dish. Cook, covered, on High (100% power) for 10–12 minutes, until vegetables are tender, stirring twice.
2. Meanwhile, cook pasta conventionally; drain.
3. Toss pasta and vegetable mixture together with cheeses, olives, parsley, salt and pepper. Serve immediately.

TAGLIATELLE WITH BACON, MUSHROOMS AND PEAS

Colour Index page 80. 4 servings. 2432 kJ per serving. Good source of vitamin A, riboflavin, thiamine, niacin, calcium, iron, fibre.
Begin 25 minutes ahead.

4 rashers rindless bacon, diced
250 g mushrooms, cut in half
2 spring onions, sliced
1½ tablespoons plain flour
1 cup cream
1 cup milk
¼ teaspoon salt
¼ teaspoon pepper
250 g tagliatelle or other pasta
250 g frozen peas, thawed
½ cup grated Parmesan cheese

1. Cook bacon in a 3-litre casserole, covered with paper towel, on High (100% power) for 4–5 minutes, until browned, stirring halfway through cooking. With slotted spoon, transfer to paper towel to drain.
2. Add mushrooms and spring onions to bacon drippings. Cook on High for 2 minutes. Stir in flour until smooth and blended. Gradually stir in cream and milk; season with salt and pepper. Cook, covered, on High for 8–10 minutes, until sauce thickens, stirring often.
3. Meanwhile, cook pasta conventionally; drain.
4. Stir peas into sauce. Cook, covered, on High for 1–2 minutes, until hot.
5. Toss pasta and sauce together. Transfer to a warmed serving dish; sprinkle with Parmesan cheese and diced bacon. Serve immediately.

FETTUCINE PRIMAVERA

Colour Index page 81. 4 servings. 3039 kJ per serving. Good source of vitamin A, riboflavin, thiamine, niacin, vitamin C, calcium, iron, fibre. Begin 40 minutes ahead.

3 small leeks, trimmed	250 g fettucine or other
30 g butter or margarine	pasta
500 g broccoli	1½ tablespoons plain
8 mushrooms, sliced	flour
2 zucchini, cut into 6-mm	2 cups cream
slices	2 tomatoes, diced
2 medium capsicums	185 g Cheddar cheese,
(green and red), cut	grated (1½ cups)
into 12-mm chunks	Salt and pepper to taste
2 carrots, cut into 6-mm	
slices	

1. Cut leeks in half lengthways; wash under cold running water. Cut into 2.5-cm pieces.
2. Place butter and leeks in a 3-litre casserole. Cook, covered, on High (100% power) for 3–4 minutes, until softened, stirring twice.
3. Trim woody stalk ends from broccoli. Separate flowerets from stalks; peel stalks and slice. Stir broccoli, mushrooms, zucchini, capsicums and carrots into leeks. Cook, covered, on High (100% power) for 8–10 minutes, until vegetables are tender-crisp, stirring twice.
4. Meanwhile, cook pasta conventionally; drain.
5. Place flour in a medium bowl; gradually stir in cream until smooth. Cook on High for 5–7 minutes, until sauce bubbles and thickens, stirring occasionally.
6. Add pasta, tomatoes, cheese and sauce to vegetables; toss. Cook on High for 3–5 minutes, until hot, stirring twice.
7. Season with salt and pepper. Serve hot.

CHEESE TORTELLINI WITH BROCCOLI AND PINE NUTS

Colour Index page 80. 8 servings. 1285 kJ per serving. Good source of vitamin A, riboflavin, thiamine, niacin, vitamin C, calcium, iron, fibre. Begin 25 minutes ahead.

750 g broccoli	500 g fresh or frozen
⅓ cup olive oil	cheese-filled
¼ cup pine nuts	tortellini
2 cloves garlic, crushed	¼ cup grated Parmesan
¼ teaspoon crushed	cheese
dried chillies (optional)	Salt to taste

1. Trim woody stalk ends from broccoli. Separate flowerets from stalks; peel stalks and slice.
2. Combine broccoli, oil, pine nuts, garlic and chillies in a 30-cm x 20-cm baking dish. Cook, covered, on High (100% power) for 6–9 minutes, until broccoli is tender-crisp, stirring twice.
3. Meanwhile, cook pasta conventionally; drain.
4. Lightly toss pasta, broccoli, Parmesan cheese and salt in a warmed serving bowl. Serve hot.

You can cook colourful and delicious combinations of your favourite fresh vegetables and pasta shapes in the microwave. In the recipe for Chicken and Vegetable Pasta (below), pasta spirals or shells can be used instead of the farfelle.

CHICKEN AND VEGETABLE PASTA

Colour Index page 81. 2089 kJ per serving. Good source of vitamin A, riboflavin, thiamine, niacin, vitamin C, calcium, iron, fibre. Begin 35 minutes ahead.

Ingredients for 4 servings		Microwave cookware
500 g chicken breasts, skinned and boned	½ teaspoon ground ginger	3-litre casserole
500 g broccoli	¾ cup water	
⅓ cup soy sauce	250 g mushrooms, cut in half	
2 tablespoons sesame or peanut oil	4 spring onions, cut into 2.5-cm pieces	
2 tablespoons cornflour dissolved in 2 tablespoons sherry	185 g radishes, sliced	
1 clove garlic, crushed	250 g farfelle (bow tie pasta) or other pasta	

1 Cut chicken crossways into thin strips; put aside. Trim woody stalk ends from broccoli. Separate flowerets from stalks; peel stalks and slice. Put aside.

2 Combine soy sauce, oil, dissolved cornflour, garlic, ginger and water in casserole. Cook on High (100% power) for 5 minutes, or until sauce thickens, stirring halfway through cooking.

3 Add broccoli, mushrooms and spring onions; stir to coat. Cook, covered, on High for 5–7 minutes, until vegetables are tender-crisp, stirring halfway through cooking.

4 Stir in chicken and radishes. Cook, covered, on High for 3–4 minutes, until chicken is fork-tender, stirring halfway through cooking.

5 Meanwhile, cook pasta conventionally; drain and transfer to a warmed serving bowl.

6 Add chicken and vegetables to pasta; toss to mix well. Serve immediately.

Save time on preparation, cooking and washing up by using the microwave for cooking the sauce and the top of the stove for cooking the pasta. The Lasagna (below) is a classic Italian-style dish: a rich, meat-based sauce layered with ricotta and mozzarella cheeses and pasta.

LASAGNA

Colour Index page 83. 1176 kJ per serving. Good source of vitamin A, riboflavin, thiamine, niacin, calcium, iron.
Begin 1¾ hours ahead.

Ingredients for 10 servings		Microwave cookware

500 g beef mince
4 cups bottled Italian
   tomato sauce
2 tablespoons tomato
   paste
500 g ricotta cheese
2 eggs
	310 g lasagna (about
	   14 sheets)
	500 g mozzarella cheese,
	   thinly sliced
	½ cup grated Parmesan
	   cheese
		8-cup soufflé dish
		33-cm x 23-cm
		   baking dish

1 Cook beef mince in soufflé dish on High (100% power) for 5–7 minutes, until meat just loses its pink colour, stirring occasionally.

2 Stir in tomato sauce and tomato paste until blended. Cook, covered, on High for 5–7 minutes, until boiling, stirring occasionally. Uncover and cook on High for 5–7 minutes longer.

3 Beat ricotta and eggs in a medium bowl until smooth. Meanwhile, cook pasta conventionally; drain.

4 Cover bottom of baking dish with one-third of meat sauce. Arrange one-third of pasta over sauce, overlapping if necessary; top with one-third of ricotta mixture, then one-third of mozzarella. Repeat layers twice, finishing with mozzarella.

5 Cook lasagna, covered, on Medium (50% power) for 25–35 minutes, until cheese melts and meat sauce bubbles, rotating dish halfway through cooking. Allow lasagna to stand, covered loosely with foil, on a heatproof surface for 15–20 minutes.

6 Uncover lasagna. Sprinkle top of pasta evenly with Parmesan cheese. Serve hot on warmed plates.

CHEESE-FILLED SHELLS

Colour Index page 81. 4 servings. 1323 kJ per serving. Good source of vitamin A, calcium.
Begin 55 minutes ahead.

500 g large pasta shells
   (about 20 shells)
500 g ricotta cheese
125 g mozzarella cheese,
   grated (1 cup)
¼ cup grated Parmesan
   cheese
1 egg
	¼ cup chopped fresh
	   parsley
	Salt and pepper to taste
	2 cups bottled Italian
	   tomato sauce
	Chopped parsley and
	   grated Parmesan
	   cheese to garnish

1. Cook pasta conventionally. Drain immediately under warm running water to stop the cooking (cold water causes shells to break); drain again.
2. Combine ricotta, mozzarella, Parmesan cheese, egg and parsley in a bowl; season with salt and pepper. Fill each shell with an equal amount of cheese mixture.
3. Pour half the tomato sauce into a 33-cm x 23-cm baking dish. Arrange shells, filled side up, in a single layer in dish. Pour remaining sauce over shells. Cook, covered, on High (100% power) for 5 minutes. Reduce power level to Medium (50% power) and cook for 10–15 minutes longer, until sauce bubbles, rotating dish halfway through cooking. Allow to stand, covered loosely, on a heatproof surface for 10 minutes.
4. Arrange filled shells on a warmed serving platter; spoon sauce over. Garnish with chopped parsley and grated Parmesan cheese. Serve immediately.

MADE-IN-MINUTES SPAGHETTI SAUCE

Colour Index page 80. Makes 6 cups. 1716 kJ per cup. Good source of vitamin A, riboflavin, thiamine, niacin, vitamin C, iron.
Begin 25 minutes ahead.

500 g beef mince
125 g mushrooms, sliced
1 onion, chopped
1 clove garlic, crushed
810 g can tomatoes
1 teaspoon sugar
3 tablespoons tomato
   paste
	2 teaspoons shredded
	   fresh basil or
	½ teaspoon dried basil
	2 teaspoons chopped
	   fresh thyme or
	½ teaspoon dried
	   thyme
	¼ teaspoon salt

1. Place beef mince, mushrooms, onion and garlic in a large bowl. Cook on High (100% power) for 5 minutes, or just until meat loses its pink colour, stirring occasionally.
2. Add tomatoes with their liquid, sugar, tomato paste, basil, thyme and salt. Cook, covered, on High (100% power) for 8 minutes, stirring occasionally. Reduce power level to Medium (50% power) and cook for 10 minutes longer, stirring occasionally.
3. Serve hot over pasta of your choice.

CANNELLONI WITH SPINACH AND MUSHROOMS

Colour Index page 83. 4 servings. 2637 kJ per serving. Good source of vitamin A, riboflavin, thiamine, niacin, calcium, iron, fibre. Begin 1¼ hours ahead.

1½ tablespoons vegetable oil	16 small cannelloni tubes, cooked, or
2 cloves garlic, crushed	8 sheets lasagne,
155 g mushrooms, sliced	cooked and cut in half
500 g frozen chopped spinach, thawed	2 cups Creamy Tomato Sauce (below) or Basic
250 g cream cheese	White Sauce (page 381)
Salt, ground nutmeg and cayenne pepper to taste	Parsley sprigs to garnish

1. Place oil, garlic and mushrooms in a 33-cm x 23-cm baking dish. Cook, covered, on High (100% power) for 2–3 minutes, until mushrooms are tender, stirring twice.
2. Squeeze spinach to remove excess moisture; stir into mushroom mixture. Cook on High for 5–7 minutes, stirring twice. Stir in cream cheese until well blended. Season with salt, nutmeg and cayenne pepper. Transfer spinach mixture to a bowl.
3. Fill each cannelloni tube with 2 tablespoons of spinach mixture (if using lasagne sheets, roll up around filling).
4. Arrange tubes (or rolls, seam side down) in a single layer in baking dish. Pour sauce over rolls. Cook, covered, on High for 5 minutes. Reduce power level to Medium (50% power) and cook for 10–15 minutes longer, until sauce bubbles, rotating dish halfway through cooking. Allow to stand, covered loosely, on a heatproof surface for 10 minutes.
5. Garnish cannelloni with parsley sprigs. Serve immediately.

CREAMY TOMATO SAUCE

Colour Index page 80. Makes 2 cups. 1030 kJ per serving. Good source of vitamin C. Begin 20 minutes ahead.

425 g can tomatoes, drained and chopped	1 tablespoon shredded fresh basil or
½ cup cream	1 teaspoon dried basil
2 teaspoons chopped fresh oregano or	2 cloves garlic, crushed
½ teaspoon dried oregano	Salt and pepper to taste

1. Combine tomatoes, cream, oregano, basil and garlic in a 2-litre bowl or jug. Cook on High (100% power) for 10–15 minutes, until sauce thickens slightly and flavours blend, stirring occasionally. Season with salt and pepper.
2. Serve hot over pasta of your choice.

Instead of the usual cheese- or tomato-based fillings for large pasta shells or tubes, try a mixture of minced beef or veal, as in the recipe for Cannelloni Milanese (below). This can make a substantial meal when served with a crunchy mixed salad.

CANNELLONI MILANESE

Colour Index page 83. 3512 kJ per serving. Good source of riboflavin, thiamine, niacin, calcium, iron. Begin 1½ hours ahead.

Ingredients for 4 servings		Microwave cookware
3 teaspoons olive oil	1 tablespoon tomato paste	33-cm x 23-cm baking dish
1 onion, chopped	½ cup currants	
2 celery stalks, chopped	⅓ cup pine nuts	
250 g beef mince	250 g cannelloni tubes	
250 g veal mince	2 cups Basic White Sauce (page 381) or Creamy Tomato Sauce (below left)	
1 tablespoon chopped fresh oregano or 1 teaspoon dried oregano	½ cup grated Parmesan cheese	
1 tablespoon shredded fresh basil or 1 teaspoon dried basil	Basil leaves to garnish	
1 bay leaf		
215 g can tomatoes, chopped		

1 Combine oil, onion and celery in baking dish. Cook, covered, on High (100% power) for 3–4 minutes, until vegetables are soft, stirring halfway through cooking.

2 Add beef and veal; mix well. Cook on High for 10 minutes, stirring occasionally. Add oregano, basil, bay leaf, tomatoes, tomato paste, currants and pine nuts. Cook on High for 10–15 minutes, stirring occasionally.

3 Meanwhile, cook pasta conventionally. Drain immediately under warm running water to stop cooking (cold water causes tubes to break); drain again. Prepare sauce. Cover and keep warm.

4 Discard cooking juices from meat mixture. Fill each cannelloni tube with an equal amount of meat mixture. Arrange tubes in a single layer in baking dish.

5 Pour sauce over pasta. Cook, covered, on High for 5 minutes. Reduce power level to Medium (50% power) and cook for 10–15 minutes longer, until sauce bubbles.

6 Allow cannelloni to stand, covered loosely, on a heatproof surface for 5–10 minutes. Just before serving, sprinkle with Parmesan cheese; garnish with basil leaves.

Rice

ARROZ CON POLLO

Colour Index page 82. 2696 kJ per serving. Good source of thiamine, niacin. Begin 55 minutes ahead.

Ingredients	For 4	For 2	For 1
Onion, chopped	1 large	2 small	1 small
Celery, chopped	2 stalks	1 stalk	½ stalk
Green capsicum, chopped	1 large	1 small	½ small
Smoked ham, chopped	125 g	60 g	30 g
Turmeric	½ teaspoon	¼ teaspoon	⅛ teaspoon
Olive or vegetable oil	3 tablespoons	1½ tablespoons	3 teaspoons
Long-grain rice	1 cup	½ cup	¼ cup
Chicken stock	2 cups	1 cup	½ cup
Bay leaf	1	½	to taste
Chicken pieces	750 g	375 g	185 g
Plain flour	½ cup	½ cup	⅓ cup
Pimiento and parsley	garnish	garnish	garnish
Microwave cookware	33-cm x 23-cm baking dish	23-cm x 23-cm baking dish	20-cm x 20-cm baking dish
Time on High (100% power) Chicken and rice	5 minutes	4 minutes	2½ (2:30) minutes
Time on Medium (50% power) Chicken and rice	25–30 minutes	10–15 minutes	7–10 minutes
Standing time	5 minutes	5 minutes	3 minutes

1 Combine onion, celery, capsicum, ham, turmeric and half the oil in a frying pan over medium heat. Stir for 2 minutes.

2 Place mixture in baking dish. Add rice, stock and bay leaf; stir well.

3 Pat chicken pieces dry with paper towel. Place flour on a sheet of greaseproof paper; coat chicken in flour.

4 Heat remaining oil in same frying pan over medium heat. Add chicken and cook for 5 minutes, or until browned. Transfer to baking dish.

5 Cook, covered tightly with plastic wrap, on High for time in Chart, or until stock boils. Reduce power to Medium and cook for time in Chart, turning chicken once.

6 Allow to stand, covered, on a heatproof surface for time in Chart, or until liquid is absorbed. Garnish with pimiento and parsley.

SAUSAGE, RICE AND BEANS

Colour Index page 83. 4 servings. 2353 kJ per serving. Good source of thiamine, niacin, calcium, iron, fibre.
Begin 35 minutes ahead.

250 g fresh pork sausages
2 onions, sliced
2 cloves garlic, crushed
440 g can red kidney beans, drained and rinsed
425 g can tomatoes, chopped

1 tablespoon chopped fresh oregano or
1 teaspoon dried oregano
4 cups Hot Cooked Rice (page 295)
¼ cup grated Parmesan cheese
Basil leaves to garnish

1. Cut sausages into 4-cm pieces. Cook in a 30-cm x 20-cm baking dish, covered with paper towel, on High (100% power) for 5 minutes, or until meat is no longer pink, stirring occasionally.
2. Add onion and garlic. Cook on High for 2–3 minutes, until onion is hot, stirring halfway through cooking.
3. Add kidney beans, tomatoes and oregano; stir. Cook, covered, on Medium (50% power) for 10–15 minutes, until mixture bubbles, stirring occasionally.
4. Stir in rice. Cook on High for 3–5 minutes, until hot.
5. Stir in Parmesan cheese; garnish with basil. Serve immediately.

ORIENTAL RICE WITH PORK

Colour Index page 82. 4 servings. 1645 kJ per serving. Good source of thiamine, iron.
Begin 35 minutes ahead.

250 g boneless pork loin, cut into 2.5-cm cubes
1 onion, chopped
1 celery stalk, sliced
1 medium red capsicum, chopped
3 teaspoons peanut or vegetable oil
1 cup long-grain rice

2 cups beef stock
2 tablespoons soy sauce
2 cloves garlic, crushed
1 tablespoon grated green ginger
Dash Tabasco sauce
¼ cup chopped fresh coriander or parsley

1. Combine pork, onion, celery, capsicum and oil in a 30-cm x 20-cm baking dish. Cook on High (100% power) for 3–5 minutes, until meat is no longer pink, stirring twice.
2. Stir rice and stock into mixture. Cook, covered tightly with plastic wrap, on High for 5 minutes. Reduce power level to Medium (50% power) and cook for 20–25 minutes longer, until liquid is absorbed and rice is tender.
3. Meanwhile, combine soy sauce, garlic, ginger, Tabasco sauce and coriander in a bowl. Pour over hot rice; mix well. Serve immediately.

MILANESE-STYLE RISOTTO

Colour Index page 81. 4 servings. 1394 kJ per serving. Low in cholesterol. Good source of calcium, iron.
Begin 40 minutes ahead.

30 g butter or margarine	Pinch powdered saffron
1 onion, finely chopped	155 g frozen peas, thawed
2 cloves garlic, crushed	
1 cup arborio rice or short-grain rice	½ cup grated Parmesan cheese
2 cups chicken stock	Salt and pepper to taste
1 tablespoon lemon juice	Basil leaves to garnish

1. Place butter, onion and garlic in a 30-cm x 20-cm baking dish. Cook on High (100% power) for 2–3 minutes, until onion has softened, stirring twice.
2. Add rice; stir to coat. Cook on High for 3 minutes, stirring twice.
3. Stir in stock, lemon juice and saffron. Cook, covered, on High (100% power) for 15–20 minutes, until most of liquid is absorbed and rice is tender, stirring halfway through cooking.
4. Stir peas into risotto. Cook on High for 2–3 minutes. Stir in Parmesan cheese; season with salt and pepper. Allow to stand, covered, on a heatproof surface for 5 minutes.
5. Garnish with basil. Serve hot.

RED BEANS AND RICE

Colour Index page 82. 4 servings. 2235 kJ per serving. Low in cholesterol. Good source of thiamine, calcium, iron, fibre.
Begin 40 minutes ahead.

3 rashers rindless bacon, diced	¼ teaspoon cayenne pepper
1 onion, diced	2 tablespoons tomato paste
1 celery stalk, diced	
1 bay leaf	730 g can red kidney beans, drained
1 tablespoon chopped fresh oregano or 1 teaspoon dried oregano	Tabasco sauce to taste
	4 cups Hot Cooked Rice (page 295)
1 teaspoon ground cumin	Parsley sprigs to garnish

1. Cook bacon in a 30-cm x 20-cm baking dish, covered with paper towel, on High (100% power) for 3–4 minutes, until browned, stirring twice. With a slotted spoon, transfer bacon to paper towel to drain.
2. Stir onion, celery, bay leaf, oregano, cumin and cayenne pepper into bacon drippings. Cook on High for 3–4 minutes, until vegetables soften, stirring twice.
3. Add tomato paste and kidney beans. Cook on Medium (50% power) for 10–15 minutes, until mixture thickens slightly, stirring occasionally. Season with Tabasco sauce.
4. Spoon hot rice on to warmed plates; ladle bean mixure over rice. Sprinkle with diced bacon; garnish with parsley. Serve hot.

SAVOURY RICE

Colour Index page 81. 1666 kJ per serving. Good source of vitamin A, calcium, iron.
Begin 45 minutes ahead.

Ingredients	For 4	For 2	For 1
Butter or margarine	30 g	15 g	1½ teaspoons
Onion, chopped	1 medium	1 small	½ small
Green capsicum, chopped	1 medium	1 small	½ small
Long-grain rice	1 cup	½ cup	¼ cup
Chicken stock	2 cups	1 cup	½ cup
Cheddar or Fontina cheese, grated	125 g (1 cup)	60 g (½ cup)	30 g (¼ cup)
Sour cream	½ cup	¼ cup	2 tablespoons
Salt and pepper	to taste	to taste	to taste
Parsley or coriander sprigs	garnish	garnish	garnish
Microwave cookware	30-cm x 20-cm baking dish	20-cm x 20-cm baking dish	20-cm x 20-cm baking dish
Time on High (100% power) Butter	45 seconds	30–45 seconds	30 seconds
With vegetables and rice	3–4 minutes	2–3 minutes	1–2 minutes
With stock	5 minutes	4 minutes	2 minutes
Time on Medium (50% power) Vegetables, rice and stock	15–20 minutes	10–12 minutes	7–10 minutes
With cheese	2–3 minutes	2 minutes	1½ (1:30) minutes

1 Heat butter in baking dish (see Chart), covered, on High for time in Chart, until melted.

2 Add onion, capsicum and rice; stir to coat.

3 Cook, covered tightly with plastic wrap, on High for time in Chart, until vegetables soften, stirring once.

4 Pour stock into vegetables and rice; stir. Cook, covered tightly with plastic wrap, on High for time in Chart, or until boiled.

5 Reduce power level to Medium and cook for time in Chart, until liquid is absorbed and rice is tender.

6 Stir in cheese and sour cream; season. Cook, covered, on Medium for time in Chart. Garnish with parsley.

Simple Spaghetti Lunch

Salami and capsicum platter with grissini
Spaghetti with Spicy Meat Sauce (page 288)
Tossed green salad
Garlic Bread (page 306)
Blue vein cheese and biscuits
Neapolitan ice cream and wafers (bought)

PREPARATION TIMETABLE

Early in day:	*Prepare double quantity of Spaghetti with Spicy Meat Sauce, in 2 batches, up to the end of step 4. Cover sauce and refrigerate. Prepare salad ingredients: store in plastic bags in refrigerator. Prepare salad dressing of your choice.*
45 minutes ahead:	*Prepare double quantity of Garlic Bread but do not cook; wrap in paper towels and put aside. Arrange a selection of sliced salami and fresh capsicums on a serving platter with grissini (breadsticks). Place cheese on a serving platter with biscuits and cover until required.*
Just before serving:	*Cook spaghetti conventionally. Meanwhile, reheat sauce on High (100% power) until bubbling. Drain spaghetti: place on warmed dinner plates and ladle sauce over; garnish. Heat Garlic Bread in microwave. Place salad ingredients in a serving bowl and toss with dressing.*

INDIAN PILAF

Colour Index page 82. 4 servings. 1603 kJ per serving. Good source of iron.
Begin 45 minutes ahead.

30 g butter or margarine	¼ cup seedless raisins
1 onion, finely chopped	2 cups chicken stock
2 cloves garlic, crushed	¼ cup chopped fresh
1 teaspoon ground cumin	coriander or parsley
1 teaspoon ground coriander	⅓ cup slivered almonds
1 cup long-grain rice	Coriander sprigs to garnish

1. Heat butter in a 30-cm x 20-cm baking dish, covered with paper towel, on High (100% power) for 45 seconds, or until melted.
2. Add onion, garlic, cumin and coriander; stir. Cook, covered, on High for 3–4 minutes, until onion softens, stirring twice. Stir in rice. Cook, covered, on High for 2 minutes.
3. Add raisins and stock. Cook, covered tightly with plastic wrap, on High for 5 minutes. Reduce power level to Medium (50% power) and cook for 20 minutes longer, or until liquid is absorbed. Stir in coriander. Allow to stand, covered loosely, on a heatproof surface for 5 minutes.
4. Meanwhile, place almonds in a shallow dish. Heat on High for 2–2½ (2:30) minutes, until browned, stirring twice.
5. Transfer pilaf to a warmed serving platter. Top with almonds; garnish with coriander. Serve immediately.

WILD RICE AND MUSHROOM PILAF

Colour Index page 83. 4 servings. 988 kJ per serving. Good source of iron.
Begin 1¼ hours ahead.

3 cups water	125 g mushrooms, sliced
1 chicken stock cube, crumbled	¼ teaspoon poultry seasoning
1 cup wild rice	Salt to taste
45 g butter or margarine	Coriander sprigs to garnish
1 onion, chopped	

1. Heat water in a 2-litre casserole on High (100% power) for 6–8 minutes, until boiling. Stir in stock cube and wild rice. Cook, covered tightly with plastic wrap, on High for 30–40 minutes, until wild rice is tender. Allow to stand, covered loosely, on a heatproof surface while preparing mushrooms.
2. Heat butter in a 30-cm x 20-cm baking dish, covered with paper towel, on High for 45 seconds, or until melted.
3. Stir in onion, mushrooms, poultry seasoning and salt. Cook, covered, on High for 5–7 minutes, until vegetables soften, stirring twice.
4. Stir vegetables into rice. Cook, covered, on High for 3–5 minutes, until hot, stirring twice.
5. Spoon on to a warmed serving plate; garnish with coriander. Serve hot.

Barley, burghul and cornmeal

BARLEY WITH DRIED MUSHROOMS

Colour Index page 83. 4 servings. 1088 kJ per serving. Low in cholesterol, sodium. Good source of fibre.
Begin 40 minutes ahead.

2 tablespoons vegetable oil	7 g dried mushrooms, broken into 12-mm pieces
1 cup pearl barley	
3 cups beef stock	Parsley sprigs to garnish
Salt to taste	

1. Place oil and barley in a 2-litre casserole. Cook, covered, on High (100% power) for 5 minutes, stirring twice.
2. Add stock, salt and mushrooms; stir to mix well. Cook, covered, on High for 20–30 minutes, until liquid is absorbed and barley is tender, stirring occasionally.
3. Garnish with parsley. Serve immediately.

BURGHUL PILAF

Colour Index page 82. 8 servings. 582 kJ per serving. Low in cholesterol, sodium. Good source of vitamin C, iron.
Begin 45 minutes ahead.

3 cups chicken stock	3 medium capsicums (green, yellow, red), cut into 12-mm chunks
1 cup burghul (cracked wheat)	
2 tablespoons olive oil	Salt to taste
2 cloves garlic, crushed	2 tablespoons shredded fresh basil
8 mushrooms, sliced	

1. Heat stock in a 4-cup glass jug on High (100% power) for 5–7 minutes, until boiling. Place burghul in a bowl; pour in boiling stock. Allow to stand, covered, on a heatproof surface for 30 minutes.
2. Meanwhile, combine oil, garlic, mushrooms and capsicums in a 30-cm x 20-cm baking dish. Cook on High for 8–10 minutes, until vegetables are tender, stirring occasionally.
3. Drain burghul well, squeezing out excess moisture. Stir into vegetable mixture; season with salt. Cook, covered, on High for 4–5 minutes, until hot. Stir in basil.
4. Serve hot or cover and refrigerate to served chilled later.

HOT COOKED RICE
To cook rice in the microwave: Combine **1 cup long-grain rice**, **2 cups water** and **½ teaspoon salt** in a large bowl. Cook, covered, on High (100% power) for 5 minutes. Reduce power level to Medium (50% power) and cook for 15–20 minutes longer, until liquid is absorbed and the rice is tender.

Cornmeal is a nice change from pasta or rice; also known as polenta and maize meal, it is finely ground corn that can be white or yellow. Yellow cornmeal is used in the recipe for Polenta with Meat Sauce (below). After cooking, cut it with crescent-shaped, star-shaped or heart-shaped biscuit cutters, before topping it with Made-in-Minutes Spaghetti Sauce (page 290).

POLENTA WITH MEAT SAUCE

Colour Index page 83. 2562 kJ per serving. Good source of vitamin A, niacin, calcium, iron.
Begin 50 minutes ahead.

Ingredients for 4 servings		Microwave cookware
4 cups chicken stock 1½ cups yellow cornmeal 60 g butter or margarine 125 g mozzarella cheese, grated (1 cup) Salt and pepper to taste 2 cups Made-in-Minutes Spaghetti Sauce (page 290) or 425 g can spaghetti sauce with meat	¼ cup grated Parmesan cheese Basil leaves to garnish	2-litre bowl 30-cm serving platter

1 Combine stock and cornmeal in bowl. Cook on High (100% power) for 12–15 minutes, until very thick, stirring occasionally.

2 Add butter, mozzarella, salt and pepper; stir.

3 Line a 33-cm x 23-cm baking tray with oiled greaseproof paper. Spread polenta mixture in an even layer on tray. Allow to cool while preparing sauce.

4 With biscuit cutter or a knife, cut shapes from cooled polenta. Arrange on serving platter.

5 Spoon sauce over polenta. Cook on High for 7–10 minutes, until both polenta and sauce are hot.

6 Sprinkle polenta and sauce with Parmesan cheese; garnish with basil leaves. Serve hot.

Spiced nuts are always a popular appetiser to serve with drinks. They are so quick and easy to make in the microwave that you can always have some on hand for unexpected guests. Using the recipe for Bombay Mixed Nuts (below) as a guide, you can vary the flavours depending on what nuts and spices you have.

BOMBAY MIXED NUTS

Colour Index page 38. Makes 2 cups. 293 kJ per tablespoon. Low in cholesterol.
Begin 25 minutes ahead.

375 g unsalted mixed nuts	*1½ teaspoons ground cumin*
3 teaspoons vegetable oil	*½ teaspoon ground coriander*
3 teaspoons chilli powder	*1 teaspoon rock salt*

1. Place nuts and oil in a 23-cm x 23-cm baking dish; stir to coat. Cook on High (100% power) for 2 minutes.
2. Combine chilli powder, cumin, coriander and salt; add to nuts and toss well to combine. Cook on High for 3 minutes, stirring twice. With a slotted spoon, transfer nuts to sheets of paper towel to drain and cool completely. Store nuts in an airtight container; use within 2 weeks.

Peppery Pecans: Prepare as for Bombay Mixed Nuts (left), using *375 g shelled pecan halves* instead of mixed nuts. In step 2, use *1 tablespoon soy sauce* and *¼ teaspoon Tabasco sauce.*
419 kJ per tablespoon.

Curried Almonds: Prepare as for Bombay Mixed Nuts (left), using *500 g blanched whole almonds* instead of mixed nuts. In step 2, use *2 tablespoons curry powder* and *½ teaspoon salt.* Makes 3 cups. 368 kJ per tablespoon.

Herbed Pistachios: Prepare as for Bombay Mixed Nuts (left), using *375 g shelled pistachios* instead of mixed nuts. In step 2, use *¼ teaspoon dried thyme* and *¼ teaspoon paprika.* 364 kJ per tablespoon.

Chilli Cashews: Prepare as for Bombay Mixed Nuts (left), using *375 g roasted unsalted cashews* instead of mixed nuts. In step 2, use *3 teaspoons chilli powder* and *½ teaspoon salt.* 368 kJ per tablespoon.

Toasting coconut

Spread *250 g shredded or desiccated coconut* in a 23-cm pie plate. Heat on High (100% power) for 5–6 minutes, until toasted, stirring twice.

Blanching almonds

Heat *1 cup water* in a 1-litre bowl on High (100% power) for 3–4 minutes, until boiling. Add *1 cup shelled whole almonds.* Heat on High for 1 minute; drain. When cool, rub off skins between sheets of paper towel; dry on paper towels.

Peeling chestnuts

Slit the shells of *125 g chestnuts* with a sharp knife. Place in a 4-cup glass jug with *1 cup water.* Heat, covered, on High (100% power) for 2½ (2:30)–4 minutes, until boiling; boil 1 minute longer. Allow to stand for 5–10 minutes. Peel shells and inner skins. Reboil any not open.

Toasting nuts

Heat *½ cup shelled nuts* in a 20-cm pie plate on High (100% power) for 2½ (2:30)–4 minutes, until lightly browned, stirring occasionally.

Snacks and Sandwiches

HOT POULTRY, FISH, VEGETABLE, MEAT AND
CHEESE SANDWICHES · SAVOURY BREADS · PIZZAS

Snacks and Sandwiches

Traditional, hard-crusted breads and rolls cannot be cooked successfully in the microwave because of its moist heat, but sandwiches and other snacks using commercially available bread are quick and easy to prepare, with excellent results. Day-old bread, buns and rolls are perfect to use; because they are slightly dry, they absorb enough moisture from the fillings during the heating period to refresh them but not make them soggy.

Sandwiches, always popular, can be made special enough for almost any meal, from a quick snack to a hearty one-dish dinner. The recipes in this chapter use a wide range of bases – including sliced white bread, wholemeal bread, French bread sticks, crusty Italian bread, rye bread, pita bread, croissants and bagels – with an equally wide assortment of both classic and innovative fillings, guaranteed to suit all tastes. On page 299 there is a selection of unusual and interesting breads to experiment with, all of which – plus many more – are widely available in supermarkets and hot bread shops.

If you are making bread at home, speed up the rising process by proofing dough in the microwave. Place in a large bowl, cover with plastic wrap and heat on High for 15 seconds; allow to stand for 5 minutes. Repeat the heating and standing process until the dough has doubled in size.

Commercially frozen bread dough can also be defrosted in the microwave. Heat in a freezer bag on Medium-Low (30% power) for 2–4 minutes; allow to stand for 10 minutes.

Most cooked breads reheat successfully in the microwave if they are wrapped in sheets of paper towel to absorb moisture. Breads and rolls can also be reheated in a straw basket, provided it has no metal parts. A roll or hamburger bun can be reheated in 10–15 seconds on High (100% power). Baked goods should be just warmed through or they will become tough.

Use the microwave, too, for defrosting and warming frozen breads and rolls, taking individual slices or single items from the freezer as needed.

SANDWICHES WITH A DIFFERENCE

Use the microwave to soften the Simple Cheese Spreads (page 113) and any other firm fillings to create sandwiches with a difference for a light meal. Make pretty open-faced sandwiches with a variety of thinly sliced meats, fish, shellfish or vegetables.

Wholemeal toast triangles (below) topped with Smoked Salmon and Chive Spread and latticed smoked salmon; fresh herbs are used as a garnish.

Wholemeal bread rounds (below) spread with cream cheese and topped with hard-boiled egg slices and tiny prawns; garnished with chervil.

Corn chips (above) topped with refried beans, sour cream and taco sauce; garnished with coriander and lime twists (page 134).

Rye bread sandwiches (above) filled with cooked ham and Cheddar Cheese Spread; garnished with salad greens.

Poultry

OPEN TURKEY SANDWICHES WITH GRAVY

Colour Index page 85. 2 servings. 1340 kJ per serving. Good source of niacin, iron, fibre. Begin 15 minutes ahead.

15 g butter or margarine	*Salt and pepper to taste*
3 teaspoons plain flour	*2 slices wholemeal bread, toasted*
1 cup chicken stock	
4 drops Parisian essence or other browning sauce	*250 g cooked turkey or chicken breast, thinly sliced*

1. Heat butter in a 4-cup glass jug on High (100% power) for 30–45 seconds, until melted.
2. Add flour; stir until blended. Gradually stir in stock until smooth. Cook on High for 4–6 minutes, until gravy boils and thickens, stirring occasionally. Stir in Parisian essence. Season gravy with salt and pepper.
3. Arrange toast on 2 serving plates. Top with equal amounts of turkey; pour over gravy. Cook on High for 2–3 minutes, until turkey is warm.

SMOKED CHICKEN AND CHEESE ON CROISSANTS

Colour Index page 84. 4 servings. 1708 kJ per serving. Good source of niacin, calcium. Begin 10 minutes ahead.

4 croissants	*250 g Swiss or Gruyère cheese, thinly sliced*
250 g smoked chicken, thinly sliced	*1 tablespoon Dijon mustard*
1 large tomato, thinly sliced	

1. If you like, preheat conventional oven to 200°C. Heat croissants for 5 minutes while preparing filling.
2. Arrange smoked chicken in 4 portions on a large platter, leaving at least 2.5 cm between each portion. Top each with sliced tomato and cheese, cutting cheese to fit. Cook on High (100% power) for 2–4 minutes, until cheese melts and chicken is warm.
3. Slice each croissant horizontally in half; spread bottom halves with mustard.
4. Arrange each portion of chicken on the bottom half of each croissant; replace top halves of croissants. Serve immediately.

Special Breads

There is such a variety of different breads available in the shops that it is difficult to know which to choose. Here is a selection of some of the most attractive, to add interest to your sandwiches and snacks. They can all be heated in the microwave, wrapped in sheets of paper towel, for a few seconds on High (100% power).

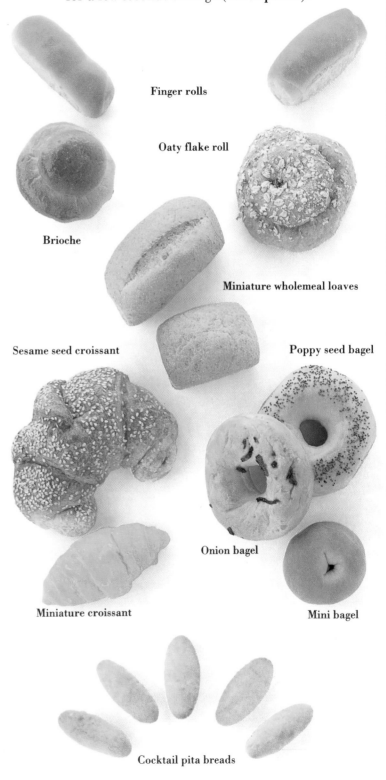

Finger rolls

Oaty flake roll

Brioche

Miniature wholemeal loaves

Sesame seed croissant

Poppy seed bagel

Onion bagel

Miniature croissant

Mini bagel

Cocktail pita breads

Remember that several thin slices of meat or poultry microwave more efficiently than 1 thick slice, so slice meat thinly across the grain, or use pounded schnitzels or minced meat, as in the hearty sandwiches on these pages. Cook the sandwiches only for the time given – they're best served warm, not hot. Overcooking can also dry out the fillings.

CHICKEN CLUB SANDWICHES

Colour Index page 85. 1775 kJ per serving. Good source of niacin, iron, fibre. Begin 55 minutes ahead.

Ingredients for 4 servings		Microwave cookware

8 rashers rindless bacon
1 egg, beaten
1 cup packaged
  seasoning mix
4 chicken breasts,
  skinned and boned
	4 large lettuce leaves
	2 tomatoes, sliced
	8 slices wholemeal bread,
	  toasted
	Mayonnaise (optional)
		33-cm x 23-cm
		baking dish

1 Cook bacon in baking dish, covered with a double thickness of paper towel, on High (100% power) for 8–9 minutes. Transfer to paper towel to drain.

2 Discard all but 2 teaspoons bacon drippings; allow dish to cool slightly. Pour beaten egg into drippings; stir until well mixed. Put aside.

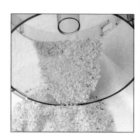

3 In food processor with knife blade attached or in blender, process seasoning mix until fine crumbs form. Place crumbs on a sheet of greaseproof paper; put aside.

4 Cut each chicken breast in half crossways; pound to 6-mm thickness with the dull edge of a heavy knife or the smooth edge of a meat mallet.

5 Dip chicken pieces into egg mixture, then coat in crumbs; place in cleaned baking dish. Cook, covered loosely with greaseproof paper, on High for 6–8 minutes, until juices run clear, rearranging pieces halfway through cooking. Allow to stand on a heatproof surface for 5 minutes.

6 Arrange lettuce leaves and tomato slices on 4 slices wholemeal toast. Top each slice with 2 pieces of chicken and 2 rashers of bacon. If you like, top with mayonnaise. Cover with remaining slices of toast. Cut each sandwich diagonally into quarters.

CHICKEN FAJITAS

Colour Index page 86. 4 servings. 1578 kJ per serving. Good source of thiamine, niacin, calcium, iron.
Begin 55 minutes ahead.

4 chicken breasts,
  skinned and boned
1 onion, sliced
1 green capsicum, sliced
2 tablespoons lime juice
½ teaspoon ground
  cumin
1 teaspoon caster sugar
	1 teaspoon vegetable oil
	4 pita bread, pulled
	  apart to make 8 layers
	Guacamole (page 218),
	  sour cream and grated
	  Cheddar cheese to
	  garnish
	Pico de Gallo (below)

1. Cut chicken breasts into 7.5-cm x 2.5-cm pieces. Combine with onion, capsicum, lime juice, cumin and sugar in a bowl. Cover and refrigerate for 15 minutes, stirring twice.
2. Preheat a browning dish according to the manufacturer's instructions; brush with oil. Arrange chicken, onion and capsicum in a single layer on dish. Cook on High (100% power) for 7–10 minutes, until chicken juices run clear, stirring twice. Transfer to a plate and allow to stand on a heatproof surface for 5 minutes.
3. Place 1 layer of pita bread between sheets of lightly moistened paper towel; repeat with remaining bread. Stack on oven floor. Heat on High for 1–3 minutes, until hot.
4. Place pita bread on warmed plates. Spoon an equal amount of chicken mixture on to centre of each. Top with Guacamole, sour cream and grated cheese. Fold 1 side of each pita bread over filling, turn bottom up and fold other side over to seal in filling. Serve with Pico de Gallo.

PICO DE GALLO Place *2 finely chopped large tomatoes, 1 finely chopped medium red onion, 1 chopped small green chilli, ⅓ cup chopped fresh coriander, 2 tablespoons lime juice* and *salt to taste* in a bowl. Stir well to mix, then cover and allow to stand at room temperature for 10 minutes, to let flavours blend. Makes 2 cups. 22 kJ per tablespoon.

TOASTED SANDWICHES
With the aid of a browning dish, the microwave oven will make toasted sandwiches as good as those from conventional sandwich makers.

Preheat the dish according to the manufacturer's instructions. Butter *4 slices bread* on 1 side only; place, buttered side down, on a sheet of greaseproof paper. Add *filling of your choice* to 2 slices of bread, then top with other 2 slices, buttered side up. Press sandwiches on to browning dish, turn to brown other side, then cook on High (100% power) for 45–60 seconds each side.

Fish

HOT TUNA MUFFINS

Colour Index page 85. 4 servings. 1808 kJ per serving. Good source of calcium, iron.
Begin 15 minutes ahead.

90 g cream cheese	*2 tablespoons*
1 small onion, chopped	*mayonnaise*
1 celery stalk, chopped	*Tabasco sauce (optional)*
¼ cup sweet pickled	*185 g can tuna in water,*
gherkins, chopped	*drained*
¼ cup pimiento-stuffed	*4 muffins, split*
green olives, chopped	*4 slices processed cheese*

1. Heat cheese in a small bowl on Medium-Low (30% power) for 1½ (1:30)–2 minutes, until softened.
2. Stir in chopped onion, celery, gherkins, olives and mayonnaise until blended. If you like, season with Tabasco sauce. Fold in tuna, stirring to break up fish.
3. Lightly toast bottom halves of muffins under a preheated griller; arrange on a platter. Spoon an equal amount of tuna mixture on to each toasted half and top with 1 slice cheese. Cook on High (100% power) for 2–3 minutes, until cheese melts and tuna mixture is warm.
4. Meanwhile, toast top halves of muffins. When cheese is melted, replace tops of muffins. Serve immediately.

DESIGNER BAGELS

Colour Index page 85. Makes 12 bagel halves. 272 kJ each. Good source of calcium.
Begin 25 minutes ahead.

6 bagels	*Sliced stoned black*
60 g ricotta cheese,	*olives; chopped*
crumbled	*sun-dried tomatoes;*
¼ cup Smoked Salmon	*shredded basil leaves;*
and Chive Spread	*capsicum strips;*
(page 113)	*orange julienne (page*
4 tablespoons Orange	*316) to garnish*
Butter (page 322)	

1. Split bagels with a serrated knife. Place halves, cut side up, on a board. Spread 4 bagel halves with ricotta cheese, 4 halves with Smoked Salmon and Chive Spread, and 4 halves with Orange Butter.
2. Place 6 bagel halves on a serving platter lined with paper towel. Heat on Medium-Low (30% power) for 1½ (1:30) minutes, or just until topping is softened. Repeat with remaining 6 bagel halves.
3. Garnish ricotta-topped bagels with olives, sun-dried tomatoes and basil; garnish salmon-topped bagels with capsicum strips; garnish butter-topped bagels with orange julienne. Serve warm.

Vegetables

WARM VEGETABLE SALAD IN PITA

Colour Index page 84. 2386 kJ per serving. Good source of vitamin A, riboflavin, thiamine, niacin, vitamin C, calcium, iron, fibre.
Begin 20 minutes ahead.

Ingredients	For 4	For 2	For 1
Carrot, thinly sliced	*1*	*½*	*¼*
Water	*2 tablespoons*	*1 tablespoon*	*2 teaspoons*
Red onion, sliced	*1 large*	*1 small*	*½ small*
Red or green capsicum, sliced	*1*	*½*	*¼*
Celery, sliced	*1 stalk*	*½ stalk*	*¼ stalk*
Broccoli, cut into flowerets	*500 g*	*250 g*	*125 g*
Mushrooms, sliced	*125 g*	*60 g*	*30 g*
Vinaigrette dressing	*3 tablespoons*	*1½ tablespoons*	*3 teaspoons*
Tomatoes, diced	*2 medium*	*1 medium*	*1 small*
Cheddar cheese, diced	*250 g*	*125 g*	*60 g*
Pita bread	*4*	*2*	*1*
Microwave cookware	8-cup soufflé dish	4-cup soufflé dish	23-cm pie plate
Time on High (100% power) Carrot	2–3 minutes	1½ (1:30)–2 minutes	1–1½ (1:30) minutes
With other vegetables	5–7 minutes	4–5 minutes	2–3 minutes

1 Place carrot and water in soufflé dish or pie plate (see Chart). Cook, covered, on High for time in Chart, until carrot is lightly cooked; drain.

2 Stir in onion, capsicum, celery, broccoli and mushrooms.

3 Add vinaigrette to vegetables; stir to coat. Cook, covered, on High for time in Chart, until vegetables are tender-crisp, stirring twice.

4 While vegetables are hot, add tomatoes and cheese; stir gently until cheese begins to melt.

5 Lightly toast pita bread under a preheated griller until hot and softened. Cut each in half crossways and separate to form 2 pockets.

6 Spoon an equal amount of vegetable and cheese mixture into each pocket. Spoon any remaining dressing over filling. Serve immediately.

Meat

REUBEN SANDWICHES

Colour Index page 85. 2202 kJ per serving. Good source of calcium, iron, fibre. Begin 20 minutes ahead.

Ingredients	For 4	For 2	For 1
Corned beef, thinly sliced	*250 g*	*125 g*	*60 g*
Sauerkraut, drained	*¾ cup*	*⅓ cup*	*¼ cup*
Swiss cheese	*4 slices*	*2 slices*	*1 slice*
Rye bread	*8 slices*	*4 slices*	*2 slices*
Thousand Island dressing	*¼ cup*	*2 tablespoons*	*1 tablespoon*
Dill pickles	*4*	*2*	*1*
Microwave cookware	33-cm x 23-cm baking dish	30-cm x 20-cm baking dish	20-cm x 20-cm baking dish
Time on High (100% power)	5–6 minutes	3–4 minutes	2–3 minutes

1 Arrange corned beef slices in 60 g portions in baking dish (see Chart), leaving at least 2.5 cm between each portion and shaping them to fit bread slices.

2 Spoon sauerkraut over corned beef; cover with cheese slices.

3 Cook fillings on High for time in Chart, until cheese melts and corned beef is warm, rotating dish halfway through cooking.

4 Meanwhile, lightly toast rye bread conventionally. Spread 1 side of each slice with Thousand Island dressing.

5 Arrange half the toast slices on a warmed serving platter. Transfer fillings on to toast. Top with remaining toast slices.

6 Cut each sandwich in half; secure with toothpicks. Serve immediately with dill pickles.

PITA POCKETS WITH SOUVLAKI

Colour Index page 84. 4 servings. 2034 kJ per serving. Good source of riboflavin, thiamine, niacin, calcium, iron.
Begin 25 minutes ahead.

1 tablespoon olive or vegetable oil
500 g lamb fillets
1 small red onion, sliced
½ small cucumber, peeled, cut in half lengthways, seeded and sliced
8 large stoned black olives, sliced
2 tablespoons chopped fresh dill or
¾ teaspoon dried dill

2 small tomatoes, each cut into 8 wedges
90 g feta cheese, diced
Salt and pepper to taste
4 pita breads
Natural yoghurt, lemon wedges and mint sprigs to garnish

1. Preheat browning dish according to the manufacturer's instructions. Lightly brush dish with 1 teaspoon oil. Place meat on browning dish, pressing firmly with spatula. Cook on High (100% power) for 4–7 minutes, until done to your liking, turning meat over and pressing with a spatula after 3–4 minutes. Allow meat to stand, covered, on a heatproof surface for 5 minutes.
2. Meanwhile, place remaining oil, onion, cucumber, olives, dill, tomatoes and feta cheese in a bowl; stir gently to mix. Season with salt and pepper.
3. Thinly slice meat across the grain. Add meat and cooking juices to vegetable mixture; toss lightly.
4. Toast pitas under a preheated griller until hot and softened. Cut each in half crossways and separate to form 2 pockets.
5. Spoon an equal amount of meat and vegetable mixture into each pocket; garnish with yoghurt, lemon wedges and mint sprigs. Serve warm.

Making the pita pockets

Lightly toast pita bread under a preheated griller until hot and softened. Cut each pita bread in half crossways with a serrated knife and separate to form 2 pockets. Spoon an equal amount of meat and vegetable filling into each pita pocket.

PORK SCHNITZEL ROLLS

Colour Index page 84. 4 servings. 2683 kJ per serving. Good source of riboflavin, thiamine, niacin. Begin 25 minutes ahead.

4 slices pork schnitzel, cut 6 mm thick (about 500 g)	*4 hamburger buns or large soft bread rolls, split*
2 egg yolks	*¼ cup bottled barbecue sauce*
¾ cup dried breadcrumbs	*sauce*
Salt and pepper to taste	*1 cup coleslaw*

1. Pound pork to 3-mm thickness with the dull edge of a heavy knife or the smooth edge of a meat mallet. Beat egg yolks in a pie plate. Spread breadcrumbs on a sheet of greaseproof paper.
2. Dip each pork schnitzel into egg mixture, then coat with crumbs.
3. Cook pork in a 33-cm x 23-cm baking dish, covered loosely with greaseproof paper, on High (100% power) for 8–9 minutes, until tender, rearranging halfway through cooking. Season with salt and pepper.
4. Meanwhile, lightly toast buns under a preheated griller. Place 1 pork schnitzel on the bottom half of each bun. Spoon on barbecue sauce, then coleslaw. Replace top halves of buns. Serve immediately.

BEEF AND BRIE SIZZLER

Colour Index page 84. 4 servings. 2461 kJ per serving. Good source of riboflavin, thiamine, niacin, calcium, iron.
Begin 25 minutes ahead.

1 French bread stick, about 30 cm long	*250 g roast beef, thinly sliced*
30 g butter or margarine	*250 g Brie cheese, thinly sliced*
1 teaspoon chopped fresh tarragon or ¼ teaspoon dried tarragon	*Cherry tomatoes and tarragon sprigs to garnish*
1 teaspoon French mustard	

1. Cut French bread diagonally into 8 thin slices; put aside.
2. Heat butter in a small bowl, covered with paper towel, on Medium (50% power) for 15–30 seconds, until softened. Stir in tarragon and mustard.
3. Spread 1 side of each bread slice with butter mixture.
4. Preheat a browning dish according to the manufacturer's instructions. Place half the bread slices, buttered side down, on greaseproof paper. Arrange beef and Brie on bread. Cover with remaining bread, buttered side up.
5. Arrange sandwiches on browning dish, pressing lightly with a spatula. Cook on High (100% power) for 3–4½ (4:30) minutes, until golden, turning over and pressing lightly with a spatula after 2–2½ (2:30) minutes.
6. Transfer to serving plates; garnish with tomatoes and tarragon. Serve immediately.

SLICED STEAK SANDWICHES

Colour Index page 86. 2897 kJ per serving. Good source of riboflavin, thiamine, niacin, calcium, iron.
Begin 35 minutes ahead.

Ingredients	For 4	For 2	For 1
Rump steak, 2 cm thick, trimmed of all fat	*500 g*	*250 g*	*125 g*
Green capsicum, sliced	*1*	*½*	*¼*
Red onion, sliced	*1 small*	*½*	*¼*
French bread stick, about 60 cm long	*1 loaf*	*½ loaf*	*¼ loaf*
French mustard	*1 tablespoon*	*2 teaspoons*	*1 teaspoon*
Cheddar or Swiss cheese, grated	*125 g (1 cup)*	*60 g (½ cup)*	*30 g (¼ cup)*
Microwave cookware	Browning dish 30-cm platter	Browning dish 23-cm plate	Browning dish 18-cm plate
Time on High (100% power)			
Steak	5–7 minutes	3–4 minutes	2–3 minutes
Vegetable mixture	5–6 minutes	3–4 minutes	2–3 minutes
Sandwiches	2–2½ (2:30) minutes	1–2 minutes	45 seconds–1½ (1:30) minutes

1 Preheat browning dish according to the manufacturer's instructions. Place steak on browning dish, pressing firmly with a spatula.

2 Cook steak on High for time in Chart, until almost done to your liking, turning over halfway through cooking. Remove from dish; put aside and keep warm.

3 Reheat browning dish. Stir capsicum and onion slices into drippings in dish. Cook vegetables on High for time in Chart, until tender, stirring twice.

4 Meanwhile, cut bread crossways into 15-cm sections. Split each section horizontally in half; toast lightly. Arrange bottom halves on platter or plate (see Chart); thinly spread with mustard.

5 Thinly slice steak across the grain. Arrange on bottom halves of bread; top with vegetable mixture. Sprinkle with cheese. Cook on High for time in Chart, just until cheese melts. Cover with top halves of bread. Serve immediately.

Breakfast in a Hurry

Fresh fruit juice
Chilled grapefruit and orange segments
Scrambled Eggs and Bacon Breakfast (page 141)
Toast with jam, marmalade or honey
Café au Lait (below)

PREPARATION TIMETABLE

15 minutes ahead:	*Make Scrambled Eggs and Bacon Breakfast.*
10 minutes ahead:	*Spoon jam, marmalade or honey into a small bowl. Mix fruit segments in individual bowls.*
Just before serving:	*Make coffee and heat milk for Café au Lait. Toast bread conventionally. Pour fruit juice into glasses. Complete Café au Lait.*

CAFÉ AU LAIT

This French-style coffee can be made in minutes in the microwave; you can use any blend of coffee, prepared in your usual way.

Heat **2 cups milk** in a 4-cup glass jug, covered, on High (100% power) for 2–3 minutes, until almost boiling. Remove from oven; stir in **2 cups hot black coffee**. Pour into 4 large cups. Top with **whipped cream**; sprinkle each with **¼ teaspoon cocoa.**

EASY BEEF TORTILLAS

Colour Index page 84. 4 servings. 1352 kJ per serving. Good source of niacin, iron.
Begin 10 minutes ahead.

500 g beef mince
1 onion, chopped
1 clove garlic, crushed
1 cup tomato purée
1 teaspoon Mexican-style chilli powder

4 corn or flour tortillas (bought)
4 lettuce leaves
Grated cheese, sour cream and bottled taco sauce (optional)

1. Place beef mince, onion and garlic in a plastic colander set over a large bowl. Cook on High (100% power) for 5–6 minutes, until meat is no longer pink, stirring twice. Discard drippings.
2. In same bowl, combine meat mixture, tomato purée and chilli powder. Cook, covered, on High for 3 minutes, or until hot, stirring once.
3. Place 1 tortilla between sheets of lightly moistened paper towel; repeat with remainder. Stack on oven floor. Heat on High for 30 seconds, or until hot.
4. Place tortillas on warmed plates. Arrange 1 lettuce leaf and one-quarter of meat mixture on each tortilla. Serve, if you like, with grated cheese, sour cream and taco sauce.

TACO BAR
Easy Beef Tortillas (above) are tasty on their own; they can be made even better by setting out a 'taco bar' offering a choice of accompaniments: chopped fresh coriander, chopped jalapeño chillies, corn relish and grated Cheddar cheese.

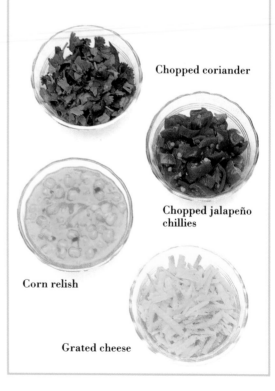

Chopped coriander

Chopped jalapeño chillies

Corn relish

Grated cheese

Cheese

CHILLI BUNS

Colour Index page 84. 4 servings. 2214 kJ per serving. Good source of niacin, vitamin C, iron. Begin 20 minutes ahead.

1 onion, chopped	2 tablespoons chilli
1 green capsicum,	sauce
chopped	2 tablespoons water
1 celery stalk, chopped	Salt and pepper to taste
500 g beef mince	4 hamburger buns, split
½ cup tomato sauce	and toasted

1. Place chopped onion, capsicum, celery and beef mince in a 30-cm x 20-cm baking dish. Cook on High (100% power) for 5–6 minutes, until meat is no longer pink, stirring often. Drain off fat.
2. Add tomato sauce, chilli sauce and water to meat mixture; stir. Cook on High for 5–7 minutes, until flavours blend, stirring occasionally. Season with salt and pepper.
3. Arrange bottom halves of toasted buns on warmed dinner plates and spoon one-quarter of meat mixture over each. Replace tops of buns. Serve immediately.

MEATBALL ROLLS

Colour Index page 86. 4 servings. 2520 kJ per serving. Good source of vitamin A, thiamine, riboflavin, niacin, iron. Begin 35 minutes ahead.

1 small onion, diced	Salt and pepper to taste
1 clove garlic, crushed	500 g bottled Italian
60 g mushrooms, finely	tomato sauce
chopped	4 long crusty rolls or
500 g beef mince	hot-dog buns, split and
½ cup fresh breadcrumbs	toasted
(1 slice)	Parsley sprigs to garnish
½ teaspoon dried basil	

1. Mix onion, garlic, mushrooms, beef mince, breadcrumbs and basil in a large bowl until well combined; season with salt and pepper.
2. Shape mixture into 12 meatballs; arrange, 2.5 cm apart, in a 30-cm x 20-cm baking dish. Cook, covered with paper towel, on High (100% power) for 4–5 minutes, until meatballs are no longer pink, rearranging halfway through cooking.
3. Pour sauce over meatballs; stir gently to coat. Cook on High for 5–7 minutes, until sauce bubbles and flavours blend, stirring occasionally.
4. Arrange bottom halves of rolls on warmed plates. Place 3 meatballs on each half and top with any remaining sauce. Replace top halves of rolls; garnish with parsley. Serve immediately.

CROQUE MONSIEUR

Colour Index page 86. 1423 kJ per serving. Good source of thiamine, calcium, iron.
Begin 35 minutes ahead.

Ingredients	For 4	For 2	For 1
Eggs	2	1	1
Milk	½ cup	¼ cup	¼ cup
White bread	8 slices	4 slices	2 slices
Cooked ham	4 slices	2 slices	1 slice
Swiss cheese	4 slices	2 slices	1 slice
Butter or margarine	30 g	15 g	2 teaspoons
Microwave cookware	Browning dish	Browning dish	Browning dish
Time on High (100% power)	3–4 minutes each batch	3–4 minutes	1½ (1:30)–2½ (2:30) minutes
Standing time	2 minutes	1 minute	1 minute

1 Beat eggs and milk in a pie plate until blended.

2 Arrange half the bread slices on a board; top each with 1 slice ham and 1 slice cheese, trimming to fit if necessary. Top with remaining bread. Put aside.

3 Preheat browning dish according to the manufacturer's instructions; add butter.

4 Dip each sandwich into egg mixture to coat both sides of bread.

5 Place sandwiches on browning dish, pressing lightly with a spatula. Cook on High for time in Chart, until golden, turning sandwiches over halfway through cooking. (If cooking for 4, cook sandwiches in 2 batches, reheating browning dish between batches.)

6 Allow sandwiches to stand for time in Chart. Cut each diagonally in half. Serve immediately.

Savoury breads

Cheese is one of the most versatile of foods, and the microwave will help transform simple cheese sandwiches into tasty snacks or original main courses. For a change, try using Brie instead of Camembert in the toasted sandwiches below, but be careful in all cheese-sandwich recipes to cook only for the time given; if you overcook cheese even slightly in the microwave, it will become rubbery and stringy.

TOASTED SANDWICHES WITH CAMEMBERT AND PEARS

Colour Index page 86. 1172 kJ each. Good source of fibre.
Begin 35 minutes ahead.

Ingredients for 4 servings		Microwave cookware

8 thin slices white bread
30 g butter or margarine
125 g Camembert cheese,
   chilled
	1 ripe pear
	8 mint leaves
	Pear slices and mint
	   leaves to garnish
		Small bowl
		Browning dish

1 Remove crusts from bread. Heat butter in bowl, covered with paper towel, on Medium (50% power) for 15–30 seconds, until softened but not melted.

2 Spread 1 side of each slice of bread with softened butter. Cut chilled Camembert into thin slices; arrange on unbuttered sides of 4 bread slices, cutting cheese to fit.

3 Cut pear into quarters lengthways; remove core but do not peel. Cut each quarter into 4 slices lengthways.

4 Arrange pear slices on top of Camembert. Place 2 mint leaves in centre of each sandwich. Top with remaining slices of bread, buttered side up.

5 Preheat browning dish according to the manufacturer's instructions. Place 2 sandwiches on dish, pressing lightly with a spatula. Cook on High (100% power) for 3–5 minutes, until golden, turning sandwiches and pressing after 2–3 minutes. Put aside; keep warm. Reheat browning dish and repeat with remaining sandwiches.

6 Cut each sandwich diagonally into quarters; garnish with pear slices and mint leaves. Serve warm.

CHEESY GARLIC BREAD

Colour Index page 85. Makes 6 pieces. 984 kJ each.
Good source of calcium.
Begin 10 minutes ahead.

45 g butter or
   margarine, softened
1 clove garlic, crushed
¾ teaspoon dried
   oregano

1 loaf Italian bread,
   about 45 cm long
60 g mozzarella cheese,
   grated (½ cup)

1. Combine softened butter, garlic and oregano in a small bowl. Cut bread crossways into three 15-cm sections. Split each section horizontally in half to make 6 pieces of bread.
2. Spread cut side of each piece of bread with garlic butter. Sprinkle mozzarella evenly over buttered sides. Arrange bread in a circle on sheets of paper towel on oven floor. Cook on High (100% power) for 45 seconds, or just until cheese begins to melt. Do not overcook or bread will become too chewy. Serve immediately.

GARLIC BREAD: Prepare Cheesy Garlic Bread (above), omitting mozzarella cheese. Cook on High (100% power) for 30 seconds, or just until garlic butter melts.

MOZZARELLA BREAD

Colour Index page 85. 8 servings. 1239 kJ per serving. Good source of calcium.
Begin 40 minutes ahead.

250 g mozzarella cheese,
   diced
⅓ cup pimiento-stuffed
   green olives, chopped
4 spring onions, sliced
2 slices prosciutto,
   finely chopped

1½ tablespoons olive or
   vegetable oil
Salt to taste
1 French bread stick,
   about 60 cm long

1. Combine mozzarella, olives, spring onions, prosciutto and oil in a bowl. Season with salt; put aside.
2. Cut French bread crossways into four 15-cm sections. Scoop out bread leaving a 6-mm crust. (Reserve scooped-out bread for use as bread-crumbs another day.)
3. Fill each hollowed-out section of bread with cheese mixture.
4. Wrap each piece loosely in paper towel; place on oven floor. Heat on Medium (50% power) for 45 seconds–1½ (1:30) minutes, just until cheese begins to soften. Do not overcook or bread will become too chewy.
5. Cut each piece into 12 slices. Serve immediately.

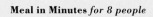

School Holiday Party

Meatball Rolls (page 305)
Pizza of your choice (page 308)
Ice-cream Pie (bought)
Butterscotch Squares (page 362)
Toffee apples
Butter Caramels (page 370)
Popcorn, peanuts, potato crisps and potato straws
Fresh fruit juice

PREPARATION TIMETABLE

1 day ahead:	Early in day:	2 hours ahead:	15 minutes ahead:	Just before serving:
Make Butterscotch Squares and Butter Caramels; store in airtight containers. Buy ice-cream pie; keep frozen.	Prepare double quantity of Meatball Rolls up to the end of step 2; cover and refrigerate. Chill fruit juice.	Prepare and cook double quantity of pizza.	Put out popcorn, peanuts, potato crisps and potato straws. Arrange toffee apples, Butterscotch Squares and Butter Caramels on plates.	Complete Meatball Rolls. Reheat pizza in microwave.

Pizza

The finished appearance of pizzas cooked in the microwave can more closely resemble those cooked conventionally if, just before serving, the pizza is transferred to a suitable platter and the top browned lightly under a preheated griller.

CALZONE

Colour Index page 85. 2110 kJ per serving (without extra fillings). Good source of iron.
Begin 35 minutes ahead.

Ingredients for 2 servings		Microwave cookware
1½ cups pizza base mix ⅓ cup water 500 g Italian-style tomato or other pasta sauce (without meat) 30 g mozzarella cheese, grated (¼ cup) 1 teaspoon vegetable oil Basil leaves to garnish	Fillings: Chopped green or red capsicum; shredded prosciutto; thinly sliced pepperoni; thinly sliced mushrooms; drained canned anchovy fillets	Browning dish 4-cup glass jug

1 Combine pizza base mix and water to form a soft dough. Knead well on a lightly floured surface for 5 minutes; divide dough in half. Roll out each half, then shape into a 15-cm circle.

2 Spoon ¼ cup sauce on to half of each circle; reserve remaining sauce. Sprinkle with mozzarella. Top with fillings of your choice (above).

3 With a pastry brush, moisten edge of each circle with water. Fold each circle in half; press edges together to seal, crimping to decorate.

4 Preheat browning dish according to the manufacturer's instructions; lightly brush with oil. Place calzone on browning dish.

5 Cook calzone on High (100% power) for 2–3 minutes, until lightly browned on underside. Turn over with a spatula; cook on High for 3–4 minutes longer. Transfer to a warmed serving platter; allow to stand, covered, for 3–5 minutes.

6 Meanwhile, pour reserved sauce into jug. Heat, covered, on High for 2–3 minutes, until hot, stirring twice. Spoon sauce over calzone; garnish with basil. Serve immediately.

FOUR SEASONS PIZZA

Colour Index page 86. 4 servings. 1536 kJ per serving. Good source of vitamin A, thiamine, vitamin C, calcium, iron, fibre.
Begin 35 minutes ahead.

1½ cups pizza base mix
⅓ cup water
1 teaspoon vegetable oil
2 tablespoons prepared pesto or 1 tablespoon dried basil
140 g jar artichoke hearts, drained and sliced

185 g canned pimientos, drained and sliced
60 g prosciutto, thinly sliced
2 tomatoes, sliced
¼ cup grated Parmesan cheese

1. Combine pizza base mix and water to form a soft dough. Knead well on a lightly floured surface for 5 minutes; roll out to a 25-cm circle. Make a 6-mm rim around edge; crimp rim with fingers.
2. Preheat a 23-cm round browning dish according to the manufacturer's instructions; lightly brush with oil. Carefully transfer dough to dish; prick with a fork to prevent puffing. Spread with pesto or sprinkle with dried basil.
3. Lightly mark pizza dough into quarters with a knife. Arrange artichoke hearts, pimiento strips, prosciutto and tomato slices separately on each quarter. Sprinkle Parmesan evenly over pizza. Cook on High (100% power) for 10 minutes, or until crust is firm and vegetables are tender, piercing crust with a fork occasionally.

MEDITERRANEAN PIZZA

Colour Index page 86. 4 servings. 2177 kJ per serving. Good source of calcium, iron.
Begin 35 minutes ahead.

1½ cups pizza base mix
⅓ cup water
2 tablespoons olive or vegetable oil
1 large onion, thinly sliced
½ teaspoon dried rosemary

¼ teaspoon dried basil
¼ teaspoon dried thyme
Salt and pepper to taste
250 g soft goat or feta cheese, crumbled

1. Combine pizza base mix and water to form a soft dough. Knead well on a lightly floured surface for 5 minutes; roll out to a 25-cm circle. Make a 12-mm rim around edge; press with fork to make decorative edge.
2. Preheat a 23-cm round browning dish according to the manufacturer's instructions; lightly brush with 1 teaspoon oil. Carefully transfer dough to browning dish; prick with a fork to prevent puffing.
3. Combine onion slices, rosemary, basil, thyme and remaining oil in a small bowl. Season with salt and pepper.
4. Spread onion mixture over pizza dough; top with cheese. Cook on High (100% power) for 10 minutes, or until crust is firm, piercing crust with a fork occasionally.

Fruit and Desserts

**COOKING FRUIT · FRUIT DESSERTS
CHOCOLATE DESSERTS · PUDDINGS · CUSTARDS
ICE CREAM AND SORBETS**

Fruit and Desserts

Fruit cooked in the microwave keeps its shape better and looks more attractive than conventionally cooked fruit. Using the charts on pages 311–313, a wide range of fresh and dried fruits, some with added sugar for extra sweetness, can be quickly prepared. Plainly cooked apples, peaches, pears and plums can be served hot or cold as accompaniments to roast meats and poultry, or served chilled with their cooking juices as delicious and nutritious desserts. More elaborate fruit dishes are given among the dessert recipes, such as poached peaches and pears in sweet sauces, apples caramelised with sugar and spices, cherries in a red wine sauce, creamy soufflés and sorbets.

The microwave also comes in handy when preparing fruit juices, not only making the task easier but increasing the quantity extracted. Warm the fruit on High (100% power) for 30 seconds a piece; allow to stand for 3 minutes before squeezing.

Many dessert recipes contain delicate ingredients that benefit particularly from being cooked in a microwave. Egg-based creams and mousses that can curdle will be smooth and creamy with only occasional stirring when cooked on Medium (50% power). Delicate mixtures should be elevated on a trivet, rack or ramekin, then cooked on Medium, rotating them for even cooking.

The delicious milk-based puddings in this chapter – many, like Old-Fashioned Bread and Butter Pudding, are family favourites – are a particular treat when made in the microwave. They cook quickly and do not stick or scorch. These, too, are usually elevated and cooked on Medium power.

Chocolate will melt perfectly in the microwave without special equipment such as a double boiler. Do not cover it, however, as the moisture that builds up inside a cover or lid can drop on to the chocolate as it melts and make it stiff. Remove chocolate from the oven when it changes from dull to shiny, bearing in mind that pieces and squares will retain their shapes until the chocolate is removed from the microwave and stirred.

INSTANT DESSERTS

Create an easy, last-minute dessert by combining ice cream or sorbet with canned fruit or fresh baked pastries, then topping with a sweet sauce. Use one of the quick sauces on pages 382–383.

Peach Melba (left): A canned peach half filled with vanilla ice cream, set on Melba Sauce and decorated with a sprig of mint.

Apple Tart à La Mode (right): A small apple tart and scoop of vanilla ice cream, topped with Butterscotch Sauce and decorated with mint leaves.

Cooking fruit in the microwave

Fruit cooked in the microwave keeps its fresh flavour and retains its shape because it doesn't need constant stirring. Plastic wrap is the best choice for covering a dish of fruit during cooking. 'Vent' the plastic a little, turning back a small corner or puncturing it to allow steam to escape.

Key				
Microwave cookware	Sugar	Water	Cooking time	Standing time

APPLES

Wash under cold running water and pat dry, then core and peel one-third of the way down from the top.

About 553 kJ per serving		
For 4	**For 2**	**For 1**
4 cooking apples (about 250 g each)	2 cooking apples (about 250 g each)	1 cooking apple (about 250 g)
20-cm x 20-cm baking dish	20-cm x 20-cm baking dish	Small bowl
None	None	None
7–9 minutes; *rotate apples and dish halfway through cooking*	4–5 minutes; *rotate apples and dish halfway through cooking*	2–3 minutes
5 minutes	5 minutes	5 minutes

Cook apples, standing upright and covered, on High (100% power) for time in Chart. Allow to stand, covered, for time in Chart. Whole apples are done when tender yet retaining their shape.

APPLES (SLICES)

Wash under cold running water, then core and, if you like, peel. Cut each apple in half lengthways; cut each half lengthways into eighths.

About 452 kJ per serving		
For 4	**For 2**	**For 1**
4 cooking apples (about 185 g each)	2 cooking apples (about 185 g each)	1 cooking apple (about 185 g)
2-litre casserole	1-litre casserole	Small bowl
2 teaspoons	1 teaspoon	½ teaspoon
¼ cup water *plus ½ teaspoon lemon juice*	2 tablespoons water *plus ¼ teaspoon lemon juice*	1 tablespoon water *plus ¼ teaspoon lemon juice*
9–11 minutes; *stir 3 times during cooking*	5–6 minutes; *stir halfway through cooking*	2–3 minutes; *stir halfway through cooking*
5 minutes	5 minutes	5 minutes

Stir sugar, water and lemon juice together. Add apples and stir to coat. Cook, covered, on High (100% power) for time in Chart. Allow to stand, covered, for time in Chart. Apple slices are done when tender yet retaining their shape.

CHERRIES

Wash under cold running water and drain. Remove stalks and stones. Cherries boil vigorously and foam towards the end of cooking; do not allow to boil over.

335 kJ per serving		
For 4	**For 2**	**For 1**
500 g (about 3 cups)	250 g (about 1½ cups)	125 g (about ¾ cup)
2-litre casserole	1-litre casserole	Small bowl
1 tablespoon	2 teaspoons	1 teaspoon
4–5 minutes; *stir halfway through cooking*	3–4 minutes; *stir halfway through cooking*	1½ (1:30)–2 minutes; *stir halfway through cooking*
2–3 minutes	2–3 minutes	2–3 minutes

Cook cherries and water, covered, on High (100% power) for time in Chart. Allow to stand, covered, for time in Chart. Cherries are done when tender.

FRUIT

PEACHES

Rinse under cold running water. To peel, dip whole peaches in rapidly boiling water for 15–20 seconds, then plunge them into a bowl of cold water; pull off skins.

About 167 kJ per serving		
For 4	**For 2**	**For 1**
4 peaches (about 125 g each)	2 peaches (about 125 g each)	1 peach (about 125 g)
20-cm x 20-cm baking dish	23-cm pie plate	Small bowl
None	None	None
3–6 minutes; *rotate dish halfway through cooking*	2–3½ (3:30) minutes; *rotate plate halfway through cooking*	45 seconds–2 minutes
2 minutes	2 minutes	2 minutes

Cook peaches, standing upright and covered, on High (100% power) for time in Chart. Allow to stand, covered, for time in Chart. Peaches are done when tender yet retaining their shapes.

PEARS (SLICES)

Prepare as whole pears (left). Cut in half and, if you like, peel. Cut halves lengthways into eighths.

About 469 kJ per serving		
For 4	**For 2**	**For 1**
4 pears (about 185 g each)	2 pears (about 185 g each)	1 pear (about 185 g)
2-litre casserole	1-litre casserole	Small bowl
2 teaspoons	1 teaspoon	½ teaspoon
¼ cup water *plus ½ teaspoon lemon juice*	2 tablespoons water *plus ¼ teaspoon lemon juice*	2 tablespoons water *plus ⅛ teaspoon lemon juice*
10–12 minutes; *stir 3 times during cooking*	7–9 minutes; *stir halfway through cooking*	3–5 minutes; *stir halfway through cooking*
5 minutes	3–5 minutes	2–3 minutes

Stir sugar, water and lemon juice together. Add pears and stir to coat. Cook, covered, on High (100% power) for time in Chart. Allow to stand, covered, for time in Chart. Pear slices are done when tender yet retaining their shapes.

PEARS

Rinse under cold running water. With apple corer, remove cores from base of pears but do not remove stalks. Peel pears. To prevent browning, brush the exposed flesh with lemon juice.

About 582 kJ per serving		
For 4	**For 2**	**For 1**
4 large pears (about 250 g each)	2 large pears (about 250 g each)	1 large pear (about 250 g)
20-cm x 20-cm baking dish	23-cm pie plate	Small bowl
None	None	None
5–7 minutes; *rotate pears and dish halfway through cooking*	4–6 minutes; *rotate pears and plate halfway through cooking*	2–3 minutes
5 minutes	5 minutes	5 minutes

Cook pears, standing upright and covered, on High (100% power) for time in Chart. Allow to stand, covered, for time in Chart. Pears are done when tender yet retaining their shapes.

PINEAPPLES (PIECES)

Cut off about 2.5 cm from top and base of fruit. Cut pineapple in half lengthways, then into quarters. Cut away fibrous woody cores. Cut off skin, cutting close to fruit. Cut pineapple quarters in half lengthways, then cut crossways into 1-cm–2-cm pieces.

About 209 kJ per serving		
For 4	**For 2**	**For 1**
1 pineapple (1.75 kg–2 kg)	1 pineapple (1.75 kg–2 kg; use half and refrigerate remainder)	1 pineapple (1.75 kg–2 kg; use one-quarter and refrigerate remainder)
2-litre casserole	1-litre casserole	Small bowl
None	None	None
8–9 minutes; *stir halfway through cooking*	4–5 minutes; *stir halfway through cooking*	2½ (2:30)–3 minutes; *stir halfway through cooking*
5 minutes	5 minutes	5 minutes

Cook pineapple, covered, on High (100% power) for time in Chart. Allow to stand, covered, for time in Chart. Pineapple pieces are done when tender.

PLUMS (HALVES)

Wash plums under cold running water. Pat dry. Cut each plum in half and remove stone

About 335 kJ per serving		
For 4	**For 2**	**For 1**
8 plums (about 60 g each)	4 plums (about 60 g each)	2 plums (about 60 g each)
30-cm x 20-cm baking dish; *arrange around edges*	23-cm pie plate; *arrange around edge*	23-cm pie plate; *arrange around edge*
None	None	None
3–4 minutes; *rotate dish halfway through cooking*	2–3 minutes; *rotate plate halfway through cooking*	1–2 minutes; *rotate plate halfway through cooking*
3–4 minutes	3–4 minutes	2–3 minutes

Cook plums, covered, on High (100% power) for time in Chart. Allow to stand, covered, for time in Chart. Plum halves are done when tender.

DRIED FRUIT (APRICOTS, PEACHES AND PRUNES)

About 787 kJ per serving for each fruit		
For 4	**For 2**	**For 1**
250 g	125 g	60 g
1.5-litre casserole	1-litre casserole	2-cup glass jug
¼ cup	2 tablespoons	1 tablespoon
2 cups	1 cup	½ cup
10–12 minutes; *stir in sugar halfway through cooking*	6–7 minutes; *stir in sugar halfway through cooking*	3–4 minutes; *stir in sugar at start of cooking*
30 minutes	30 minutes	30 minutes

Cook dried fruit and water, covered, on High (100% power) for time in Chart, stirring in sugar when indicated. Allow to stand, covered, for time in Chart. Dried apricots, peaches and prunes are done when tender; prunes should remain whole.

RHUBARB (PIECES)

Wash rhubarb and trim any discoloured ends; cut off any leaves and discard. Cut rhubarb crossways into 2.5-cm pieces.

Rhubarb boils vigorously towards the end of cooking; do not allow to boil over.

About 586 kJ per serving		
For 4	**For 2**	**For 1**
750 g	375 g	185 g
4-litre casserole	2-litre casserole	1-litre casserole
⅔ cup	⅓ cup	2½ tablespoons
¼ cup	2 tablespoons	1 tablespoon
7–8 minutes; *stir halfway through cooking, then stir in sugar before final minute*	4–6 minutes; *stir halfway through cooking, then stir in sugar before final minute*	2½ (2:30)–3 minutes; *stir halfway through cooking, then stir in sugar*
10 minutes	10 minutes	10 minutes

Cook rhubarb and water, covered, on High (100% power) for time in Chart. Allow to stand, covered, for time in Chart. Rhubarb pieces are done when tender.

DRIED FRUIT (FIGS)

879 kJ per serving		
For 4	**For 2**	**For 1**
375 g	185 g	90 g
1.5-litre casserole	1-litre casserole	2-cup glass jug
2 cups water *plus 2 teaspoons lemon juice*	1 cup water *plus 1 teaspoon lemon juice*	½ cup water *plus ½ teaspoon lemon juice*
12–15 minutes; *stir halfway through cooking*	7–8 minutes; *stir halfway through cooking*	3–5 minutes; *stir halfway through cooking*
30 minutes	30 minutes	30 minutes

Cook dried figs, water and lemon juice, covered, on High (100% power) for time in Chart. Allow to stand, covered, for time in Chart. Dried figs are done when plump and soft.

Decorating with Fruit

Many exciting tropical fruits are now widely available. They make ideal additions to simple dishes by providing extra colour, flavour and texture, as well as interesting shapes.

Date: Use whole or chopped as a topping for cakes, biscuits, desserts and salads.

Lychee: Peel off skin, remove stone and use halves or quarters in fruit salads and stir-fried dishes.

Pomegranate: The juicy seeds make an unusual topping for cheesecakes, ice creams and sorbets.

Kumquat: Cut into slices to garnish fruit salads, stir-fried dishes and desserts.

Mango: Peel and remove large stone, then slice the sweet, juicy flesh. Use to garnish fish and rice dishes, or fruit salads, mousses, soufflés and other desserts.

Prickly pear: Peel thorny skin as you would peel an apple. Use on salads.

Pawpaw: Halve and remove seeds; peel and slice. Serve on rice dishes, desserts and salads.

Fig: Cut in half lengthways and serve with cold cooked meats or with cheese.

Kiwifruit: Peel and slice. Use with fish or poultry, and desserts.

Passionfruit: Cut in half crossways, then spoon out seeds and juice to use as a topping for sorbets and other desserts.

Carambola: Use this citrus-flavoured fruit to garnish fish, vegetables and desserts.

Fruit desserts

GLAZED APPLE RINGS

Colour Index page 87. 4 servings. 657 kJ per serving. Low in fat, sodium. Good source of vitamin C, fibre. Begin 25 minutes ahead.

1½ cups apple juice	2 cinnamon sticks
¼ cup packed brown sugar	3 whole cloves
2 teaspoons grated lemon rind	3 whole allspice
	4 small apples
	2 tablespoons lemon juice

1. Combine apple juice, brown sugar, lemon rind, cinnamon sticks, cloves and allspice in a 30-cm x 20-cm baking dish. Cook on High (100% power) for 7–9 minutes, until sugar has dissolved and liquid boiled, stirring occasionally.
2. Meanwhile, peel and core apples. Slice crossways into 6-mm rings. If you like, cut edges with fluted biscuit cutter for a more decorative look. Sprinkle apple rings with lemon juice.
3. Add half the apple rings to the spiced liquid in baking dish. Cook on High for 3–5 minutes, until tender, turning over halfway through cooking. Transfer rings with a slotted spoon to a warmed serving dish; keep warm. Cook remaining apple rings; transfer to serving dish. Strain liquid over apples in dish.
4. Serve apple rings warm or cover and refrigerate to serve chilled later.

SPICED APPLE BETTY

Colour Index page 88. 6 servings. 892 kJ per serving. Good source of fibre. Begin 35 minutes ahead.

30 g butter or margarine	¼ cup cream
¾ cup unsweetened apple sauce	1 teaspoon vanilla essence
1 cup wholemeal breadcrumbs	½ teaspoon ground cinnamon
¼ cup plain flour	¼ teaspoon ground ginger
¼ cup brown sugar	⅛ teaspoon ground allspice
3 eggs	
½ teaspoon baking powder	

1. Lightly grease a 1-litre bowl. Line bottom of bowl with greaseproof paper; lightly grease paper. Put aside.
2. In food processor with knife blade attached or in blender, process butter, apple sauce, breadcrumbs, flour, brown sugar, eggs, baking powder, cream, vanilla essence, cinnamon, ginger and allspice until smooth and well blended.
3. Pour batter into lined bowl. Cook, covered, on Medium (50% power) for 12 minutes, or until a knife inserted in the centre comes out clean. Allow to stand, covered, on a heatproof surface for 10 minutes.
4. Invert bowl on to a platter. Carefully unmould dessert. Serve warm or cover and refrigerate to serve chilled later.

DELUXE BAKED APPLES

Colour Index page 88. 1507 kJ per serving. Low in sodium. Begin 40 minutes ahead.

Ingredients	For 4	For 2	For 1
Large cooking apples	4	2	1
Butter or margarine, softened	30 g	15 g	2 teaspoons
Seedless raisins or currants	¼ cup	2 tablespoons	1 tablespoon
Finely chopped walnuts	2 tablespoons	1 tablespoon	2 teaspoons
Ground cinnamon	½ teaspoon	¼ teaspoon	⅛ teaspoon
Apple juice	¼ cup	2 tablespoons	1 tablespoon
Golden syrup or maple syrup	¾ cup	½ cup	¼ cup
Microwave cookware	20-cm x 20-cm baking dish	23-cm x 13-cm loaf dish	Small bowl
Time on High (100% power) Filled apples	7–9 minutes	4–6 minutes	2–2½ (2:30) minutes
Syrup	3–5 minutes	2–3 minutes	1–1½ (1:30) minutes

1 Wash apples well; starting from stalk end, core apples, making an opening about 4 cm in diameter and taking care not to cut through to the base. Peel apples one-third of the way down.

2 Arrange apples, peeled end up, in baking dish, loaf dish or bowl (see Chart).

3 Combine butter, raisins, walnuts and cinnamon in a bowl. Spoon an equal amount of spiced mixture into hollow centre of each apple.

4 Combine apple juice and golden syrup in a jug; pour over and around filled apples. Cook, covered, on High for time in Chart, until fork-tender, basting with syrup and rearranging apples twice during cooking.

5 Transfer apples to a warmed serving platter. Put aside and keep warm.

6 Cook syrup remaining in dish on High for time in Chart, until slightly thickened. Spoon over apples. Serve hot or cover and refrigerate to serve chilled later.

APPLE CARAMEL DESSERT

Colour Index page 88. 1314 kJ per serving. Low in sodium. Good source of fibre. Begin 40 minutes ahead.

Ingredients for 6 servings		Microwave cookware
¾ cup plain flour 2 tablespoons brown sugar ¾ teaspoon ground cinnamon 30 g vegetable shortening (Copha) 75 g butter or margarine, chilled	2–3 tablespoons iced water 3 tablespoons sugar 2 tablespoons cold water 8 small apples, peeled, cored and thickly sliced Ice cream or cream	23-cm flameproof pie plate

1 In food processor with knife blade attached, process flour, brown sugar and cinnamon until blended. Add shortening and 45 g butter; process until mixture resembles coarse crumbs. (Or use fingertips.)

2 Sprinkle 2 tablespoons iced water into mixture. With pulsing motion, process just until mixture begins to hold together. If necessary, add more iced water. Do not overprocess or mixture will be tough. Shape into ball; flatten slightly. Wrap in greaseproof paper and refrigerate for 30 minutes.

3 Prepare caramel: Heat remaining butter in pie plate, covered with paper towel, on High (100% power) for 45 seconds, or until melted. Stir in sugar and cold water. Cook on High for 6–9 minutes, without stirring, just until mixture turns golden, watching carefully since caramel burns easily and continues to cook and darken when removed from the microwave.

4 Stir caramel once to distribute colour evenly; carefully arrange apple slices in concentric circles in the caramel (there will be enough for 2–3 layers); cool slightly.

5 Using a floured rolling pin, roll dough into a 23-cm round, 6 mm thick, on a lightly floured surface. Place on top of apples. Cook on High for 7–10 minutes, until surface looks dry. Lightly brown under a preheated griller. Allow to stand for 5 minutes.

6 Loosen dessert from side of pie plate with a knife. Invert on to a serving platter. Carefully unmould dessert. Serve warm or cover and refrigerate to serve chilled later. Accompany with ice cream or cream.

APPLE AND WALNUT CRUMBLE

Colour Index page 87. 8 servings. 1030 kJ per serving. Low in sodium. Good source of fibre. Begin 35 minutes ahead.

½ cup walnuts, chopped
½ cup plain flour
⅓ cup brown sugar
1 teaspoon ground cinnamon
½ teaspoon ground nutmeg
½ teaspoon ground ginger
60 g chilled butter or margarine, cubed
5 large cooking apples
3 teaspoons lemon juice

1. In food processor with knife blade attached, process walnuts, flour, brown sugar, cinnamon, nutmeg and ginger until blended. Add butter; process until mixture resembles coarse crumbs. (Or use fingertips.) Put aside.
2. Peel, core and slice apples. Place in a round 1.5-litre casserole; sprinkle with lemon juice.
3. Sprinkle crumb mixture over apple slices. Cook on High (100% power) for 14–16 minutes, until apple is tender. If dish is suitable, brown top lightly under a preheated griller. Serve warm or cover and refrigerate to serve chilled later.

ORANGE, LEMON AND LIME JULIENNE

Julienne garnish can intensify the flavours of a dish, as in Glazed Bananas (opposite) or provide a zesty contrast, as in Pickled Beetroot (page 256).

With a vegetable peeler, remove rind from orange, lemon or lime, leaving bitter white pith behind. Stack rind and cut into fine strips.

Or use a zester to remove fine strips of rind as shown. A zester is best for the thinner skin of limes.

GLAZED BANANAS

Colour Index page 87. 4 servings. 1080 kJ per serving. Low in sodium. Good source of vitamin C, fibre.
Begin 15 minutes ahead.

4 medium bananas	⅓ cup pecan or walnut
2 medium oranges	halves
45 g butter or margarine	Orange julienne (page
2 tablespoons brown	316) to decorate
sugar	
¼ teaspoon ground	
cinnamon	

1. Peel bananas and cut into 5-cm pieces. Peel oranges; separate into segments, removing membranes and any pith. Place fruit in a bowl and put aside.
2. Heat butter in a 4-cup glass jug, covered with paper towel, on High (100% power) for 45 seconds–1 minute, until melted. Add brown sugar and cinnamon. Cook on High for 2–4 minutes, until sugar has dissolved and mixture boiled, stirring twice.
3. Add bananas, orange segments and pecans; stir. Cook on High for 2–3 minutes, until hot, stirring twice.
4. Spoon glazed fruit and nuts into a warmed serving dish; decorate with orange julienne. Serve warm.

TO FLAMBÉ: Place Glazed Bananas (above) in a heatproof serving dish. Heat ¼ **cup dark rum** in a 1-cup glass jug on High (100% power) for 30–45 seconds, until hot. Pour over fruit; ignite with a long match. Allow flames to subside before serving.

CHERRIES IN RED WINE

Colour Index page 87. 6 servings. 460 kJ per serving. Low in cholesterol, fat, sodium.
Begin 15 minutes ahead.

2 cups red wine	2 teaspoons cornflour
⅓ cup redcurrant jelly	dissolved in
1 cinnamon stick	2 tablespoons cold
500 g fresh cherries,	water
stoned, or 425 g can	Ice cream (optional)
stoneless dark	
cherries, drained	

1. Pour red wine into a 2-litre bowl; add redcurrant jelly and cinnamon stick. Cook on High (100% power) for 3–4 minutes, until mixture has boiled; remove cinnamon stick.
2. Stir cherries into wine mixture. Cook on High for 3–4 minutes, stirring halfway through cooking. Stir in dissolved cornflour. Cook on High for 2–3 minutes, until mixture has thickened, stirring twice.
3. Spoon cherries into dessert dishes. Serve warm or cover and refrigerate to serve chilled later. Accompany, if you like, with ice cream.

ZABAGLIONE WITH CHERRIES

Colour Index page 89. 913 kJ per serving. Low in sodium.
Begin 45 minutes ahead.

Zabaglione is a rich and versatile dessert. It can be served by itself, or with a variety of fruit: strawberries, raspberries and peaches work well. As an alternative serving idea, arrange fruit in a single layer in a flameproof gratin dish, spoon zabaglione over fruit and brown lightly under a preheated griller; dust with icing sugar immediately before serving.

Ingredients for 4 servings		Microwave cookware
500 g fresh cherries, stoned, or 425 g can stoneless dark cherries, drained	¼ cup caster sugar	4-cup glass jug
5 egg yolks	3–4 tablespoons kirsch or sweet Marsala	
	Orange julienne (page 316) to decorate	

1. Spoon cherries into goblets or dessert dishes; put aside.

2. With mixer at high speed, beat egg yolks and sugar in glass jug until thick and lemon coloured. Cook on Medium (50% power) for 1½ (1:30)–2 minutes, until mixture is thick and fluffy, beating halfway through cooking.

3. Add kirsch to egg mixture; beat well.

4. Cook on Medium for 30 seconds–1½ (1:30) minutes, until thickened and hot, beating every 30 seconds. Do not boil or mixture will curdle. With mixer at high speed, beat zabaglione for 10–15 minutes, until it is fluffy and mounds slightly when dropped from a spoon.

5. Spoon zabaglione over cherries in dishes.

6. Decorate each serving with orange julienne. Serve immediately.

All these attractive fruit dishes make delicious desserts and the fruits used are naturally sweet, so only a minimal amount of sugar is needed. If you like, you can substitute strawberries for the raspberries in the sauce used in Elegant Poached Peaches (below); or try using different fruits suitable for poaching, such as ripe nectarines instead of peaches.

ELEGANT POACHED PEACHES

Colour Index page 91. 1155 kJ per serving. Good source of vitamin A, vitamin C, fibre.
Begin 4 hours ahead or early in day.

Ingredients for 4 servings		Microwave cookware
3 cups water ½ cup sugar 1 tablespoon grenadine syrup 4 large ripe slipstone peaches 310 g raspberries, fresh or frozen	½ teaspoon almond essence 6 amaretti biscuits or crisp macaroons Raspberries and mint leaves to decorate	2-litre glass jug or bowl

1 Combine water, sugar and grenadine syrup in glass jug. Cook, covered, on High (100% power) for 5–6 minutes, until mixture has boiled, stirring once. Uncover and cook on High for 5 minutes longer, stirring twice.

2 Cut each peach in half and twist apart; remove stones. Place peach halves in hot syrup. Cook on High for 4–6 minutes, until tender. Cool slightly; remove skins. Refrigerate peach halves in syrup until cold.

3 Meanwhile, in food processor with knife blade attached or in blender, process raspberries until puréed. Sieve purée to remove seeds. Stir in almond essence and 2 tablespoons syrup from peaches. Cover and refrigerate.

4 When peach halves are cold, remove from jug, reserving syrup. Arrange, cut side down, in a dish to drain.

5 Coarsely crumble amaretti biscuits in a small bowl. Add 1–2 tablespoons reserved peach syrup; stir to moisten. Fill peach halves with mixture.

6 Pour one-quarter of raspberry sauce on to each of 4 dessert dishes. Place 2 peach halves on top, filled sides up; decorate with raspberries and mint. Serve chilled.

PEARS WITH CHOCOLATE AND RASPBERRY SAUCE

Colour Index page 90. 6 servings. 1323 kJ per serving. Low in sodium. Good source of fibre.
Begin 4 hours ahead or early in day.

310 g raspberries, fresh or frozen
⅓ cup caster sugar
3 teaspoons lemon juice
6 large pears
1 tablespoon cornflour dissolved in 2 tablespoons water

30 g cooking chocolate, chopped
½ cup cream
1 tablespoon icing sugar
Mint leaves to decorate

1. In food processor with knife blade attached or in blender, process raspberries until puréed. Sieve purée to remove seeds. Stir in sugar and lemon juice; put aside.
2. Peel pears. Starting from base, core pears, taking care not to cut through the tops; do not remove stalks.
3. Arrange pears, spoke-fashion, in raspberry purée in casserole, with wide ends towards the edge and stalk ends towards the centre; overlap stalk ends if necessary. Spoon purée over pears. Cook on High (100% power) for 15–20 minutes, until nearly tender, turning halfway through cooking.
4. Stir in dissolved cornflour until blended. Cook, covered, on High for 2–5 minutes, until purée has thickened slightly and pears are tender. Cover and refrigerate for about 3 hours, or until flavours blend, spooning raspberry purée over pears occasionally.
5. Just before serving, place 1 cup purée from casserole in a 2-cup glass jug. Cook on High for 2–3 minutes, until very hot. Remove from oven. Add chopped chocolate; stir until chocolate has melted.
6. With mixer at medium speed, beat cream and icing sugar in a small bowl until soft peaks form.
7. Pour sauce on to 6 dessert plates, reserving some for glaze; place pears on top. Spoon some of the reserved sauce over each pear; decorate with mint. Serve with whipped cream.

POACHED PEARS WITH CHOCOLATE SAUCE

Colour Index page 87. 4 servings. 703 kJ per serving. Low in sodium.
Begin 40 minutes ahead.

2 medium pears	1 tablespoon cocoa
⅓ cup water	¼ cup thickened cream
4 tablespoons caster sugar	Mint leaves to decorate
½ teaspoon vanilla essence	

1. Peel pears; cut in half lengthways and remove cores. Place pear halves, cut side down, on a board. Starting 12 mm from stalk end, slice each pear half lengthways several times, leaving pear connected at stalk end. Press down on each pear half to fan slices slightly; put aside.
2. Combine water and sugar in a 23-cm pie plate; add vanilla essence. Cook on High (100% power) for 5–7 minutes, until sugar has dissolved and syrup boiled, stirring occasionally.
3. Transfer pear fans to pie plate; arrange spoke-fashion, with wide ends towards the edge and stalk ends towards the centre. Spoon syrup over each fan. Cook, covered, on High for 3–5 minutes, until tender; reserve syrup.
4. Spoon cocoa into a 2-cup glass jug. Slowly beat in cream until blended but not whipped. Stir in ⅓ cup reserved syrup. Cook on High for 3–5 minutes, until sauce has thickened slightly, stirring frequently. (If sauce is too thick, stir in more syrup.)
5. Pour one-quarter of sauce on to each of 4 dessert plates. Arrange pear fans on top; decorate with mint. Serve warm.

CANELLE KNIFE
Use this special tool to cut thin strips from peeled or unpeeled fruits such as pears, apples, lemons or oranges.

CARAMEL PEARS IN STRAWBERRY SAUCE

Colour Index page 88. 1047 kJ per serving. Low in sodium. Good source of vitamin C, fibre.
Begin 45 minutes ahead.

Ingredients	For 4	For 2	For 1
Large pears	4	2	1
Lemon juice	1 tablespoon	2 teaspoons	1 teaspoon
Water	4 tablespoons	3 tablespoons	2 tablespoons
Fresh or frozen strawberries	310 g	155 g	75 g
Sugar	½ cup	⅓ cup	⅓ cup
Thickened cream	2 tablespoons	1½ tablespoons	1½ tablespoons
Microwave cookware	20-cm x 20-cm baking dish 4-cup glass jug	23-cm x 13-cm loaf dish 2-cup glass jug	Small bowl 1-cup glass jug
Time on High (100% power) Pears Caramel With cream	10–12 minutes 2–4 minutes 1 minute	5–6 minutes 2–4 minutes 1 minute	2–3 minutes 2–4 minutes 1 minute
Standing time	2 minutes	2 minutes	2 minutes

1. Peel pears. Starting from base, core pears, taking care not to cut through the tops; do not remove stalks. Cut spirals into pears with a canelle knife (left) or the tines of a fork. Brush pears with lemon juice.

2. Place pears in baking dish, loaf dish or small bowl (see Chart); add water, reserving 1 tablespoon. Cook, covered, on High for time in Chart, until tender, rotating dish halfway through cooking. Put aside.

3. Meanwhile, in food processor with knife blade attached or in blender, process strawberries until puréed. Sieve purée to remove seeds; put aside.

4. Prepare caramel: Place sugar in glass jug (see Chart); add reserved water. Cook on High for time in Chart, without stirring, just until mixture turns golden, watching carefully since caramel burns easily and continues to cook and darken when removed from the oven.

5. Gradually add cream to caramel, stirring constantly. Cook on High for time in Chart; stir. Allow to stand for time in Chart; stir until blended.

6. Pour strawberry purée on to a serving dish or dessert dishes; place pears on top. Spoon caramel over pears. Serve immediately.

Chilled Champagne
Chilli Prawn Cocktail (below)
Steak au Poivre (page 207)
Asparagus Bundles (page 254)
Sautéed potatoes
Crème Brûlée (page 331)

PREPARATION TIMETABLE

Early in day:	*Make Crème Brûlée; cover and refrigerate. Chill Champagne.*
2 hours ahead:	*Prepare Chilli Prawn Cocktail without dressing and Asparagus Bundles up to the end of step 4; cover and refrigerate.*
45 minutes ahead:	*Make sautéed potatoes conventionally; keep warm. Prepare Steak au Poivre up to the end of step 4. Complete Asparagus Bundles; keep warm.*
Just before serving:	*Complete Steak au Poivre. Complete Chilli Prawn Cocktail.*

CHILLI PRAWN COCKTAIL

King prawns are the best choice for this good-looking starter.

Line 2 serving bowls with *salad leaves*. Arrange *125 g shelled and deveined cooked king prawns* in each bowl.

Spoon over *bottled chilli sauce* to taste. Garnish with *lemon twists* (page 134) just before serving.

SPICED PINEAPPLE

Colour Index page 87. 4 servings. 314 kJ per serving.
Low in fat, sodium. Good source of fibre.
Begin 25 minutes ahead.

1 small pineapple
2 tablespoons brown sugar
⅛ teaspoon ground ginger or cinnamon

Lime julienne (page 316) and mint leaves to decorate

1. Remove leaves and stalk end from pineapple; remove skin and eyes. Cut pineapple in half lengthways; remove core. Cut each half crossways into 12-mm slices.
2. Cook pineapple slices in a shallow round baking dish, covered, on High (100% power) for 3–4 minutes.
3. Meanwhile, combine brown sugar and ginger in a small bowl; sprinkle evenly over pineapple. Cook on High for 1–2 minutes, just until sugar melts.
4. Transfer pineapple slices to a warmed serving dish; garnish with lime julienne and mint leaves. Serve immediately.

PLUM KUCHEN

Colour Index page 89. 6 servings. 1938 kJ per serving. Good source of fibre.
Begin 50 minutes ahead.

30 g butter or margarine, softened
Brown sugar
3 cups pizza base mix
1 cup warm water
10 plums

½ cup melba-toast crumbs (page 193)
125 g butter or margarine, chilled and cubed

1. Lightly grease a 23-cm x 23-cm baking dish. Sprinkle with 1 tablespoon brown sugar.
2. Combine pizza base mix and water to form a dough. Knead well on a lightly floured surface for 5 minutes. Press dough evenly into baking dish. Spread with remaining softened butter.
3. Cut plums in half; remove stones. Cut plums into quarters. Press, skin side down, into dough, overlapping if necessary.
4. In food processor with knife blade attached, process melba-toast crumbs, ½ cup brown sugar and chilled butter until mixture resembles coarse crumbs. (Or use fingertips.)
5. Sprinkle crumbs evenly over plums; press lightly. Cook on High (100% power) for 12–14 minutes, shielding corners with foil for first 5 minutes and piercing dough with a fork halfway through cooking.
6. If dish is suitable, brown kuchen under a preheated griller. Allow to stand on a heatproof surface for 5 minutes before serving.

RASPBERRY PARFAITS

Colour Index page 91. 6 servings. 1369 kJ per serving. Low in sodium.
Begin 3½ hours ahead or early in day.

310 g raspberries, fresh or frozen	½ teaspoon lemon juice
2 tablespoons water	½ cup sugar
1 envelope (3 teaspoons) gelatine	1½ cups thickened cream
	2 egg whites

1. In food processor with knife blade attached or in blender, process raspberries until puréed. Sieve purée to remove seeds; put aside.
2. Pour water into a small bowl. Sprinkle gelatine evenly over water; allow to soften for 1 minute. Heat on High (100% power) for 1–2 minutes, until gelatine has dissolved, stirring twice. Do not boil. Stir into raspberry purée.
3. Stir lemon juice and half the sugar into purée. Cover and refrigerate for 15–20 minutes, stirring often, until mixture mounds slightly when dropped from a spoon.
4. With mixer at medium speed, beat cream in a bowl until soft peaks form. Fold half the cream into raspberry mixture; reserve remainder.
5. With mixer at high speed, beat egg whites in a bowl until soft peaks form. Gradually sprinkle in remaining sugar, 1 tablespoon at a time, beating well after each addition, until sugar has dissolved and whites stand in stiff, glossy peaks. Fold into raspberry mixture.
6. Place a spoonful of raspberry mixture in each parfait glass. Top with a spoonful of reserved whipped cream. Repeat layering once more. Cover and refrigerate until set. Served chilled.

RED FRUIT COMPOTE

Colour Index page 87. 8 servings. 473 kJ per serving. Low in fat, sodium. Good source of vitamin C, fibre.
Begin 20 minutes ahead.

425 g can stoneless dark cherries	2 tablespoons orange-flavoured liqueur
1 punnet strawberries	1 kiwifruit, peeled and thinly sliced, to decorate
1 punnet raspberries	
1 tablespoon cornflour	
¼ cup redcurrant jelly	

1. Drain cherries, reserving ½ cup syrup; put aside. If strawberries are large, cut in half lengthways or into quarters.
2. Combine cherries, strawberries and raspberries in a 30-cm x 20-cm baking dish. Cook, covered, on High (100% power) for 2½ (2:30)–3 minutes, until just warm. Spoon into a warmed serving dish; cover and keep warm.
3. Dissolve cornflour in reserved syrup in a 2-cup glass jug. Stir in redcurrant jelly. Cook on High for 2½ (2:30)–4 minutes, until thickened. Stir in liqueur.
4. Pour sauce over fruit. Serve compote warm or cover and refrigerate to serve chilled later. Decorate with kiwifruit just before serving.

For many desserts, such as the lighter-than-traditional Individual Raspberry Cheesecakes (below), attractive microwave-safe cookware can double as serving dishes. This easy way to cook and serve in individual ramekins makes a nice presentation and eliminates having to unmould the desserts. It also saves on the washing up!

INDIVIDUAL RASPBERRY CHEESECAKES

Colour Index page 91. 1829 kJ per serving. Good source of calcium.
Begin 3½ hours ahead or early in day.

Ingredients for 8 servings		Microwave cookware
60 g butter or margarine	¾ cup sugar	4-cup glass jug
1 cup plain sweet biscuit crumbs	2 eggs	Large bowl
310 g raspberries, fresh or frozen	1 teaspoon vanilla essence	8 x ½-cup ramekins
500 g cream cheese	Icing sugar to taste	

1. Heat butter in glass jug, covered with paper towel, on High (100% power) for 45 seconds–1 minute, until melted. Stir in biscuit crumbs; put aside.

2. In food processor with knife blade attached or in blender, process raspberries until puréed. Sieve purée to remove seeds; put aside.

3. Heat cream cheese in large bowl on Medium (50% power) for 2–3 minutes, until softened. With mixer at low speed, beat cream cheese, sugar, eggs, vanilla essence and ½ cup raspberry purée until smooth and well blended, occasionally scraping bowl. Cook on High for 4–6 minutes, until very hot, beating 3 times during cooking. Remove from oven; beat until smooth.

4. Spoon crumb mixture into ramekins; lightly press on to bottom to form a crust. Spoon cream-cheese mixture on top of crust, smoothing surface. Arrange ramekins in a circle on oven floor, at least 2.5 cm apart. Cook on Medium for 3–4 minutes, until almost set, rearranging ramekins twice.

5. Allow ramekins to stand on a heatproof surface for 15 minutes, or until cheesecakes are set. Sweeten remaining raspberry purée with icing sugar. Refrigerate cheesecakes and purée until well chilled.

6. Decorate each cheesecake with a swirl of raspberry purée. Place ramekins on dessert dishes. Serve chilled. Serve remaining purée separately.

These easy-to-make spreads, flavoured with a variety of fruits, can be used to turn plain cakes and simple loaves into something really special for a quick dessert. They can be prepared in a matter of seconds, will keep well if covered and stored in the refrigerator – and taste equally good on breakfast toast, too!

To soften butter for fruit-flavoured butters:
Heat **125 g butter** in a small bowl, covered with paper towel, on Medium-Low (30% power) for 30–40 seconds, until just softened.

Orange Butter:
Into softened butter (above), stir *grated rind of 1 orange* and *2 tablespoons orange juice*.
Makes 8 servings.
452 kJ per serving.

Strawberry or Raspberry Butter:
Into softened butter (above), stir *2 tablespoons strawberry or raspberry jam*.
Makes 8 servings.
486 kJ per serving.

Cinnamon and Apple Butter:
Into softened butter (above), stir *2 tablespoons apple sauce* and *½ teaspoon ground cinnamon*.
Makes 8 servings.
456 kJ per serving.

RHUBARB RICE CREAM

Colour Index page 92. 8 servings. 758 kJ per serving.
Low in sodium. Good source of vitamin A, vitamin C, calcium, fibre.
Begin 3½ hours ahead or early in day.

1 cup milk	½ cup cream
1 cup water	1 tablespoon icing sugar
¾ cup sugar	¼ teaspoon vanilla
2 tablespoons	essence
short-grain rice	
750 g fresh rhubarb,	
sliced	

1. Combine milk, water, sugar and rice in a 4-litre casserole; allow to stand for 5 minutes. Stir in rhubarb. Cook, covered, on High (100% power) for 20–25 minutes, stirring every 5 minutes. Spoon mixture into dessert dishes; cover and refrigerate for 2½ hours, or until well chilled.
2. With mixer at medium speed, beat cream, icing sugar and vanilla essence in a bowl until soft peaks form. Pipe or spoon on top of each dessert. Serve chilled.

STRAWBERRIES 'NOUVELLES'

Colour Index page 90. 6 servings. 590 kJ per serving.
Good source of vitamin C, fibre.
Begin 2½ hours ahead or early in day.

1 cup cream	½ teaspoon vanilla
2 tablespoons caster	essence
sugar	15 g cooking chocolate,
⅛ teaspoon salt	chopped
2 egg yolks	18 large strawberries,
1 tablespoon orange-	cut in half
flavoured liqueur	Mint leaves to decorate

1. Pour cream into a medium bowl; add sugar and salt. Cook on High (100% power) for 3 minutes, or until mixture is almost boiled, stirring halfway through cooking.
2. Beat egg yolks in a 2-cup glass jug. Stir a small amount of hot cream mixture into egg yolks. Slowly pour egg mixture back into remaining cream mixture, beating rapidly to prevent lumping. Cook on Medium (50% power) for 3 minutes, or until thickened slightly, beating twice. Stir in liqueur and vanilla essence.
3. Reserve half the sauce. Add chocolate to remaining sauce, stirring until melted. Refrigerate both sauces until well chilled.
4. Spoon equal amounts of each sauce on to dessert plates. Place strawberries on top; decorate with mint. Serve chilled.

STRAWBERRY CHARLOTTE

Colour Index page 90. 12 servings. 1310 kJ per serving. Low in sodium.
Begin early in day or 1 day ahead.

12–16 savoiardi (sponge fingers)	4 eggs, separated
625 g strawberries, fresh or frozen	½ cup caster sugar
2 cups milk	½ teaspoon almond essence
2 envelopes (1½ tablespoons) gelatine	2 cups thickened cream
	Strawberries to decorate

1. Line the bottom of an 8-cup soufflé dish with greaseproof paper. Trim 1 end of each savoiardi to fit dish. Line side of dish with savoiardi, cut side up; put aside.
2. In food processor with knife blade attached or in blender, process strawberries until puréed; put aside.
3. Pour milk into a 2-litre glass bowl. Sprinkle gelatine evenly over milk; allow to soften for 1 minute. Heat on High (100% power) for 4–6 minutes, until small bubbles form around edge, stirring twice.
4. With mixer at high speed, beat egg yolks and half the sugar in a medium bowl until thick and lemon coloured. Stir a small amount of hot milk into egg-yolk mixture. Slowly pour egg mixture back into remaining hot milk, beating rapidly to prevent lumping.
5. Cook on Medium (50% power) for 5–6 minutes, until thickened slightly, stirring twice. Do not boil or mixture will curdle.
6. Pour into a large bowl. Stir in strawberry purée and almond essence. Cover and refrigerate for about 45 minutes, stirring occasionally, until mixture mounds slightly when dropped from a spoon.
7. With mixer at high speed, beat egg whites in a medium bowl until soft peaks form. Gradually sprinkle in remaining sugar, 1 tablespoon at a time, beating well after each addition, until sugar has completely dissolved and whites stand in stiff, glossy peaks. Spoon on top of strawberry mixture.
8. In same bowl, with same beaters, and with mixer at medium speed, beat cream until soft peaks form. Spoon over strawberry mixture, reserving ½ cup.
9. Gently fold whipped cream and beaten egg whites into strawberry mixture. Carefully spoon into prepared soufflé dish. Cover and refrigerate for about 4 hours, or until set.
10. Loosen charlotte from side of dish with a thin-bladed knife. Invert dish on to a chilled serving platter. Carefully unmould charlotte; remove paper. Decorate with reserved cream and strawberries. Serve chilled.

ICED LEMON SOUFFLÉS

Colour Index page 91. 904 kJ per serving. Low in sodium.
Begin early in day or 1 day ahead.

Ingredients for 8 servings		Microwave cookware
2 teaspoons plain flour	4 medium lemons	4-cup glass jug
¾ cup caster sugar	1 cup thickened cream	
¾ cup milk	Lemon slices and mint leaves to decorate	
2 eggs, separated		

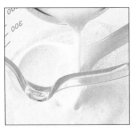

1 Combine flour and ½ cup sugar in glass jug until blended. Gradually pour in milk, stirring until smooth. Cook on High (100% power) for 4–6 minutes, until mixture has thickened and boiled, stirring occasionally.

2 Beat egg yolks in a small bowl. Stir a small amount of hot milk into egg yolks. Slowly pour egg-yolk mixture back into remaining hot milk, beating rapidly to prevent lumping. Cook on Medium (50% power) for 2–3 minutes, until mixture has thickened, stirring often. Do not boil. Pour into a large bowl. Lightly press plastic wrap on to surface. Refrigerate for 1 hour, or until chilled.

3 Grate 1 tablespoon rind from lemons and squeeze ⅔ cup juice. Stir rind and juice into chilled mixture.

4 With mixer at high speed, beat egg whites in a medium bowl until soft peaks form. Gradually sprinkle in remaining sugar, 1 tablespoon at a time, beating well after each addition, until sugar has completely dissolved and whites stand in stiff, glossy peaks. Spoon on top of lemon mixture. In same bowl, with same beaters, and with mixer at medium speed, beat cream until soft peaks form.

5 Gently fold whipped cream and beaten egg whites into lemon base. Spoon soufflé mixture into 8 freezerproof glasses or dishes; freeze for about 4 hours, or overnight.

6 Allow soufflés to stand at room temperature for about 10 minutes, to soften slightly. Decorate with lemon slices and mint leaves. Serve immediately.

For the busy working person, the microwave is a great help in preparing delicious desserts ahead of time. The Light Cheese Ring with Fruit (below) is ideal for a buffet table since it can be made the day before and refrigerated, then simply unmoulded when ready to serve. Try a combination of any of your favourite fruits for the centre.

LIGHT CHEESE RING WITH FRUIT

Colour Index page 90. 1197 kJ per serving. Good source of calcium.
Begin 4½ hours ahead or early in day.

Ingredients for 8 servings		Microwave cookware

500 g cottage cheese
500 g low-fat cream
  cheese
½ cup caster sugar
2 tablespoons plain flour
3 eggs
1 tablespoon grated
  orange rind
	Sliced strawberries,
	  sliced kiwifruit, sliced
	  nectarines and
	  pineapple chunks
	Mint sprigs to decorate
		2-litre glass jug or
		  bowl
		Medium bowl
		6-cup ring mould

1 Position a sieve over glass jug. Press cottage cheese through sieve until smooth.

2 Place cream cheese in medium bowl. Heat on Medium (50% power) for 2–3 minutes, until softened.

3 Add cream cheese, sugar, flour, eggs and orange rind to cottage cheese in jug. Beat with a fork until smooth. Cook on High (100% power) for 5–8 minutes, until very hot, beating 3 times during cooking.

4 Lightly oil ring mould with a pastry brush. Pour cheese mixture into mould. Cook on Medium for 6–8 minutes, until almost set. Allow to stand on a heatproof surface for 30 minutes. Cover and refrigerate for 2–3 hours, until well chilled and firm.

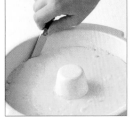

5 Loosen cheese ring from side of ring mould with a knife. Invert mould on to a serving platter; carefully remove mould.

6 Spoon prepared fruit into the centre of cheese ring; decorate with mint sprigs. Serve chilled.

DRIED FRUIT COMPOTE

Colour Index page 87. 8 servings. 716 kJ per serving.
Low in fat, sodium. Good source of vitamin A, fibre.
Begin 40 minutes ahead.

1½ cups water	4 whole cloves
¼ cup cider vinegar	Orange julienne from
½ cup sugar	1 orange (page 316)
1 cinnamon stick	½ cup dried apricots
1 vanilla pod, split	½ cup stoned prunes
lengthways, or	½ cup dried figs
1 teaspoon vanilla	½ cup glacé cherries
essence	(optional)
6 whole allspice	

1. Pour water and vinegar into a 2-litre casserole; add sugar, cinnamon stick, vanilla pod, allspice, cloves and orange julienne, reserving some for decoration. Cook on High (100% power) for 5–7 minutes, until mixture has boiled and sugar dissolved, stirring occasionally.
2. Add apricots, prunes, figs and cherries, if using, to spiced syrup. Cook on High for 8–10 minutes, until fruit plumps, stirring occasionally. Transfer fruit with a slotted spoon to a serving dish.
3. Cook syrup in casserole on High for 10–15 minutes, until slightly thickened. Pour over fruit through a sieve; discard spices.
4. Serve compote warm or cover and refrigerate to serve chilled later. Decorate with reserved orange julienne before serving.

CHOCOLATE-DIPPED FRUIT

Colour Index page 89. Makes 14–30 pieces. About 130 kJ per piece. Low in sodium.
Begin 35 minutes ahead.

90 g dark or white	14 large strawberries; or
chocolate	24 grapes; or segments
1 teaspoon vegetable	from 2 oranges
shortening (Copha)	

1. Line a baking tray with greaseproof paper. Place chocolate and shortening in a 2-cup glass jug. Heat on High (100% power) for 1½ (1:30)– 2 minutes, until melted, stirring once. Remove from oven; stir until smooth.
2. Dip fruit halfway into melted chocolate. Gently shake off excess; place dipped fruit on lined baking tray.
3. Allow chocolate-dipped fruit to stand for about 10 minutes, or until chocolate sets; do not refrigerate. Serve same day.

Chocolate desserts

TINY CHOCOLATE CONES

Colour Index page 92. Makes 25 cones. 226 kJ each.
Low in sodium.
Begin early in day.

125 g dark cooking chocolate, chopped	*½ teaspoon vanilla essence*
30 g butter or margarine	*½ cup shelled macadamia nuts, finely chopped*
2 tablespoons thickened cream	

1. To form cones: Cut twenty-five 9-cm foil squares. Fold each square diagonally in half to make a triangle. Hold each triangle with long side towards you. Bring lower right point over to meet top point. Roll left side of foil around right side to form a cone with a tight point at the bottom; secure with tape. Repeat with remaining foil squares.

2. Place chocolate and butter in a medium bowl. Heat, covered with paper towel, on High (100% power) for 2–2½ (2:30) minutes, until melted. Remove from oven; stir until smooth. Stir in cream and vanilla essence. Set bowl over iced water; beat mixture until fluffy. Fold in nuts, reserving 1 tablespoon.

3. Spoon chocolate mixture into piping bag fitted with a medium star tube; pipe into foil cones. Sprinkle with reserved nuts. Refrigerate for about 1 hour, or until set.

WHITE CHOCOLATE MOUSSE

Colour Index page 89. 8 servings. 1013 kJ per serving. Low in sodium.
Begin 55 minutes ahead.

185 g white chocolate, chopped	*1 cup thickened cream*
2 tablespoons milk	*Raspberries and mint leaves to decorate*
2 eggs	
½ teaspoon vanilla essence	

1. Heat chocolate in a medium bowl on High (100% power) for 2–3 minutes, until melted, stirring twice. Remove from oven; stir until smooth.

2. Beat milk and eggs in a small bowl. Gradually beat egg mixture into melted chocolate until blended. Cook chocolate mixture on Medium (50% power) for 2½ (2:30)–3 minutes, until thickened slightly, stirring halfway through cooking; do not boil. Stir in vanilla essence. Cover and refrigerate for about 30 minutes, or until well chilled, stirring occasionally.

3. With mixer at medium speed, beat chilled chocolate mixture for 1 minute. With same beaters, and with mixer at medium speed, beat cream in a bowl until soft peaks form. Gently fold whipped cream into chocolate mixture.

4. Spoon mousse into a serving dish or dessert dishes. Serve immediately or cover and refrigerate to serve chilled later. Decorate with raspberries and mint before serving.

CHOCOLATE ALMOND DESSERT

Colour Index page 92. 2579 kJ per serving. Good source of iron.
Begin 3½ hours ahead or early in day.

Ingredients for 8 servings		Microwave cookware
⅓ cup seedless raisins, chopped	*⅓ cup dried breadcrumbs*	8-cup soufflé dish
2 tablespoons almond-flavoured liqueur	*6 amaretti biscuits or crisp macaroons, crushed*	2-cup glass jug
250 g dark cooking chocolate	*3 teaspoons sugar*	Trivet, rack or ramekin
60 g butter or margarine, softened	*Chocolate Cream (page 357)*	
½ cup brown sugar	*Toasted flaked almonds to decorate*	
3 eggs, separated		
½ teaspoon baking powder		

1 Line bottom of soufflé dish with a double thickness of greaseproof paper. Combine raisins and liqueur in a small bowl; put aside.

2 Heat chocolate in glass jug on High (100% power) for 2½ (2:30)–3 minutes, until melted, stirring once. Remove from oven; stir until smooth. Put aside.

3 With mixer at low speed, beat butter and brown sugar in a medium bowl until blended. Increase speed to high; beat until light and fluffy. Reduce speed to medium; add egg yolks, one at a time, beating well after each addition. Fold in melted chocolate, baking powder, breadcrumbs and crushed biscuits. Add plumped raisins and liqueur.

4 With mixer at high speed, beat egg whites in another bowl until soft peaks form. Add sugar, beating well until sugar has completely dissolved and whites stand in stiff, glossy peaks. Gently fold beaten egg whites into chocolate mixture until blended. Spoon evenly into prepared soufflé dish.

5 Elevate soufflé dish on trivet, rack or ramekin turned upside down. Cook on High (100% power) for 6–8 minutes, just until set, rotating dish every 2 minutes. Allow to stand, covered, on a heatproof surface for 10 minutes. Loosen dessert from dish with a knife. Invert on to a serving platter; remove paper. Allow to cool completely.

6 Cover top and sides of cake with Chocolate Cream, making decorative swirls with a metal spatula. Decorate with flaked almonds.

CHOCOLATE MOUSSE TORTE

Colour Index page 90. 1243 kJ per serving. Low in sodium.
Begin 4½ hours ahead or early in day.

Ingredients for 16 servings		Microwave cookware

1½ cups milk
¼ teaspoon salt
Sugar
1 envelope (3 teaspoons)
  gelatine
4 eggs, separated
250 g cooking chocolate,
  chopped
	30 g butter or margarine
	1 cup shelled nuts,
	  chopped
	2 cups thickened cream
	Chocolate Rounds (page
	  358, optional)
		Large bowl
		Small bowl

1 Combine milk, salt and ⅓ cup sugar in large bowl. Evenly sprinkle gelatine over mixture; allow to soften for 1 minute. Stir. Cook on High (100% power) for 3 minutes, or until gelatine has completely dissolved, stirring halfway through cooking. Do not boil.

2 Beat egg yolks in small bowl. Stir a small amount of hot milk mixture into egg yolks. Slowly pour egg mixture back into remaining hot milk mixture, beating rapidly to prevent lumping. Cook on Medium (50% power) for 4 minutes, or until thickened slightly, stirring occasionally. Add 185 g chocolate; stir until melted. Cover and chill for 20 minutes. Meanwhile, lightly oil a 23-cm x 23-cm springform tin.

3 Place remaining chocolate and butter in small bowl. Heat, covered with paper towel, on High for 1½ (1:30) minutes, or until melted. Stir in nuts, reserving 1 tablespoon for garnish. Spread chocolate mixture over bottom of springform tin. Place tin in freezer for about 15 minutes, or until mixture sets into a crust.

4 With mixer at high speed, beat egg whites in a medium bowl until soft peaks form. Gradually sprinkle in ¼ cup sugar, beating well after each addition, until sugar is completely dissolved and whites stand in stiff, glossy peaks. Spoon on top of chocolate mixture. In same bowl, with same beaters, and with mixer at medium speed, beat 1¼ cups cream until soft peaks form.

5 Gently fold whipped cream and egg whites into chocolate mixture. Spoon mousse over crust in tin. Cover and refrigerate for about 3 hours, or until set.

6 Loosen mousse from side of springform tin with a knife. Remove side of tin. With mixer at medium speed, beat remaining cream in a small bowl until soft peaks form; spoon into piping bag fitted with a star tube. Pipe top of torte with whipped cream and sprinkle with reserved nuts. Decorate, if you like, with chocolate rounds. Serve chilled.

COCONUT CHOCOLATE CUPS

Colour Index page 89. 6 servings. 975 kJ per serving. Low in sodium.
Begin 40 minutes ahead.

90 g cooking chocolate,
  chopped
2 teaspoons vegetable
  shortening (Copha)
	1 cup desiccated coconut
	600 ml ice cream
	Chocolate-dipped Fruit
	  (page 324)

1. Place six 6-cm paper cake cases on a baking tray; place another case inside each to make a double thickness.

2. Place chocolate and shortening in a small bowl. Heat on High (100% power) for 1½ (1:30)– 2 minutes, until melted and smooth, stirring occasionally.

3. Stir in coconut. Place 1 rounded tablespoon of mixture into each paper case. Press mixture on to bottom and up sides of each case. Place in freezer for about 10 minutes, or until firm.

4. Lift out chilled chocolate cups; carefully remove paper cases and discard. Spoon an equal amount of ice cream into each cup. Top with Chocolate-dipped Fruit. Serve immediately.

RICH CHOCOLATE MOUSSE

Colour Index page 92. 4 servings. 716 kJ per serving. Low in sodium.
Begin early in day.

90 g dark cooking
  chocolate, chopped
3 eggs, separated
	1 teaspoon vanilla
	  essence

1. Heat chocolate in a medium bowl on High (100% power) for 1–1½ (1:30) minutes, until melted. Remove from oven; stir until smooth.

2. Beat egg yolks and vanilla essence in a small bowl. Slowly pour mixture into melted chocolate, beating until blended. Cook on Medium (50% power) for 30 seconds, stirring twice.

3. With mixer at high speed, beat egg whites in a bowl until stiff peaks form. Gently fold into chocolate mixture until blended.

4. Spoon one-quarter of chocolate mixture into each of 4 pot de crème cups or small dessert dishes. Cover and refrigerate mousse for at least 4 hours, or until firm. Serve chilled.

CHOCOLATE CREAM LOAF

Colour Index page 92. 16 servings. 1252 kJ per serving. Low in sodium.
Begin early in day.

375 g raspberries, fresh or frozen	*375 g cooking chocolate, chopped*
2 tablespoons sugar	*125 g butter or margarine*
6 egg yolks	
1½ cups thickened cream	
2 tablespoons finely chopped pistachio nuts	

1. In food processor with knife blade attached or in blender, process raspberries and sugar until puréed. Sieve purée to remove seeds; cover and refrigerate.
2. Beat egg yolks and ½ cup cream in a medium bowl. Cook on Medium (50% power) for 3½ (3:30)–4 minutes, stirring occasionally, until mixture coats the back of a spoon; do not boil. Cover and refrigerate for 10 minutes, stirring once.
3. Line a 23-cm x 13-cm loaf dish with foil. Evenly sprinkle bottom with nuts; put aside.
4. Place chocolate and butter in a large bowl. Heat, covered with paper towel, on High for 2–3 minutes, until melted. Remove from oven; stir until smooth.
5. With mixer at medium speed, beat remaining cream in a small bowl until soft peaks form. Beat egg-yolk mixture into melted chocolate mixture. Fold in whipped cream.
6. Spoon mixture into prepared loaf dish. Refrigerate for about 3 hours, or until firm. Loosen loaf from sides of pan with a knife. Invert loaf on to a serving platter; cut into slices. Serve chilled, with reserved raspberry purée.

GRATING CHOCOLATE
Grated chocolate sprinkled over desserts, pies and tarts gives a special effect for very little effort. It can also be used to cover uneven surfaces on the sides of iced cakes.

Coarsely grate cooking chocolate (or process in food processor with grating disc attached). Keep any leftover grated chocolate in an airtight container in the refrigerator.

All milk-based chocolate desserts, or those with a high milk content, turn out particularly well when cooked in the microwave – because they do not stick or scorch as they tend to do when cooked conventionally. Nutty Chocolate Delight (below) is especially popular with children. Easy to make in the microwave, it is irresistible when topped with whipped cream.

NUTTY CHOCOLATE DELIGHT

Colour Index page 92. 1833 kJ per serving. Good source of calcium.
Begin 2½ hours ahead or early in day.

Ingredients for 6 servings		Microwave cookware
⅔ cup sugar	*1 egg*	2-litre glass jug or bowl
¼ cup plain flour	*1 teaspoon vanilla essence*	
¼ teaspoon salt	*½ cup shelled nuts, chopped*	
¼ teaspoon ground cinnamon	*½ cup cream*	
2 cups milk	*Ground cinnamon to decorate*	
60 g butter or margarine		
90 g cooking chocolate, chopped		

1 Combine sugar, flour, salt and cinnamon in glass jug. Stir in milk until blended. Add butter and chocolate. Cook on High (100% power) for 5–7 minutes, until mixture bubbles and has thickened slightly, stirring occasionally.

2 Meanwhile, beat egg in a small bowl. Stir a small amount of hot chocolate mixture into beaten egg. Slowly pour egg mixture back into chocolate mixture, beating rapidly to prevent lumping. Cook on Medium (50% power) for 2–3 minutes, until thickened, stirring frequently. Do not boil or mixture will curdle. Stir in vanilla essence and chopped nuts.

3 Pour an equal amount of mixture into each of 6 glasses or dessert bowls.

4 Lightly press plastic wrap or dampened greaseproof paper on to surface of hot mixture to prevent a skin forming. Refrigerate for about 2 hours, or until set.

5 With mixer at medium speed, beat cream in a small bowl until soft peaks form.

6 Remove plastic wrap from desserts. Top each with whipped cream; lightly sprinkle with cinnamon. Serve chilled.

Puddings

CHOCOLATE CHESTNUT CREAM

Colour Index page 92. 1800 kJ per serving. Low in sodium. Good source of calcium, iron, fibre.
Begin 4½ hours ahead or early in day.

Ingredients for 12 servings		Microwave cookware

2 cups milk
440 g can sweetened
  chestnut purée
60 g cooking chocolate,
  chopped
4 eggs, separated
2 envelopes
  (1½ tablespoons)
  gelatine
	¼ cup caster sugar
	2½ cups thickened cream
	Chocolate Curls (page
	  358) to decorate
		2-litre glass jug or
		bowl

1 Prepare collar for 6-cup soufflé dish: Fold a 60-cm strip of greaseproof paper lengthways to make a 60-cm x 15-cm strip. Wrap strip around outside of dish so collar stands 7.5 cm above rim. Secure with tape and put aside.

2 Combine milk and chestnut purée in glass jug. Heat on High (100% power) for 6–8 minutes, until bubbles form around edge. Stir chestnut mixture until smooth and well blended. Add chopped chocolate and stir until melted.

3 Beat egg yolks in a large bowl. Stir a small amount of hot chestnut mixture into beaten egg yolks. Slowly pour egg mixture back into remaining hot mixture, beating rapidly to prevent lumping. Sprinkle gelatine evenly over mixture; allow to soften for 1 minute. Cook on Medium (50% power) for 4–6 minutes, until mixture has thickened, stirring twice. Cover and refrigerate for about 45 minutes, stirring occasionally, until mixture mounds when dropped from a spoon.

4 With mixer at high speed, beat egg whites in a medium bowl until soft peaks form. Gradually beat in sugar until completely dissolved and whites stand in stiff, glossy peaks. Spoon on top of chestnut mixture. In same bowl, with same beaters, and with mixer at medium speed, beat 2 cups cream until soft peaks form. Fold cream and beaten egg whites into chestnut mixture.

5 Spoon mixture into prepared soufflé dish; cover and refrigerate for about 2½ hours, or until set.

6 Remove collar from soufflé dish. With mixer at medium speed, beat remaining cream in a small bowl until soft peaks form; spoon into piping bag fitted with a star tube. Pipe top of dessert with whipped cream; decorate with Chocolate Curls. Serve chilled.

CHOCOLATE AND WALNUT PUDDING

Colour Index page 88. 8 servings. 1147 kJ per serving. Good source of vitamin B.
Begin 45 minutes ahead.

60 g butter or margarine
1 cup plain flour
½ teaspoon instant coffee
  powder (optional)
2 teaspoons baking
  powder
¾ cup sugar
⅓ cup cocoa
	½ cup cream
	1 teaspoon vanilla
	  essence
	⅓ cup brown sugar
	¼ cup shelled walnuts,
	  chopped
	1 cup water
	Icing sugar

1. Heat butter in a 2-cup glass jug, covered with paper towel, on High (100% power) for 45 seconds–1 minute, until melted; put aside.
2. Combine flour, instant coffee, if using, baking powder, ½ cup sugar and half the cocoa in a medium bowl. Stir cream and vanilla essence into melted butter. Stir cream mixture into flour mixture until smooth. Pour into a 23-cm deep pie plate.
3. Combine brown sugar, walnuts and remaining sugar and cocoa in a small bowl. Sprinkle evenly over batter. Carefully pour water over top. Elevate pie plate on a trivet, rack or ramekin turned upside down. Cook on Medium (50% power) for 12–15 minutes, until pudding rises and is almost set, rotating every 3 minutes.
4. Allow pudding to stand on a heatproof surface for 15 minutes. Dust top with icing sugar. Serve warm.

RICH NOODLE PUDDING

Colour Index page 88. 8 servings. 1335 kJ per serving. Good source of calcium.
Begin 45 minutes ahead.

250 g thin noodles
  (such as tagliatelle)
90 g butter or margarine,
  melted
1 cup fresh breadcrumbs
250 g cottage cheese
¾ cup sour cream
	1 egg, beaten
	2 tablespoons sugar
	¼ cup sultanas
	¼ cup dried apricots,
	  chopped
	1 teaspoon ground
	  cinnamon

1. Lightly grease a 30-cm x 20-cm flameproof and microwave-safe baking dish. Cook noodles conventionally; drain and keep warm.
2. Mix half the melted butter with breadcrumbs in a small bowl; put aside.
3. Combine cottage cheese, sour cream, beaten egg and sugar in a large bowl until blended. Stir in noodles, sultanas, apricots and cinnamon. Add remaining melted butter; stir. Pour mixture into baking dish. Cook, covered, on Medium (50% power) for 10–12 minutes, until set.
4. Sprinkle pudding with crumb mixture; brown under a preheated griller. Allow to stand on a heatproof surface for 5 minutes. Serve hot.

CREAMY RICE PUDDING

Colour Index page 89. 6 servings. 1185 kJ per serving. Low in sodium. Good source of calcium. Begin 50 minutes ahead.

3 cups milk	*½ cup thickened cream*
½ cup short-grain rice	*¼ teaspoon ground*
1 teaspoon vanilla	*cinnamon*
essence	*¼ teaspoon ground*
2 egg yolks	*allspice*
2 tablespoons sugar	*½ cup seedless raisins*

1. Combine milk, rice and vanilla essence in a 2-litre casserole. Cook on High (100% power) for 5 minutes, or until boiling. Reduce power level to Medium-High (70% power) and cook for 20–30 minutes longer, until rice is tender, stirring often.
2. Beat egg yolks, sugar, cream, cinnamon and allspice in a small bowl until blended. Stir a small amount of rice mixture into egg mixture. Pour egg mixture back into remaining rice mixture, stirring rapidly to prevent lumping. Stir in raisins. Cook on Medium (50% power) for 3–4 minutes, until slightly thickened, stirring every minute.
3. Allow pudding to stand, covered, on a heat-proof surface for 5 minutes. Serve warm or cover and refrigerate to serve chilled later.

ORANGE BREAD PUDDING

Colour Index page 89. 10 servings. 1130 kJ per serving. Good source of vitamin C. Begin 45 minutes ahead.

1 loaf French bread	*¼ teaspoon ground*
1½ cups cream	*nutmeg*
1½ cups orange juice	*Icing sugar*
4 eggs	*Orange julienne (page*
½ cup sugar	*316) to decorate*
1 teaspoon vanilla	
essence	

1. Lightly grease a 2-litre baking dish. Cut bread into 2.5-cm slices; arrange in baking dish.
2. Heat cream in a 4-cup glass jug on High (100% power) for 3–4 minutes, until small bubbles form around edge.
3. Beat orange juice, eggs, sugar, vanilla essence and nutmeg in a 2-cup glass jug. Stir a small amount of hot cream into egg mixture. Slowly pour egg mixture back into remaining hot cream, beating rapidly to prevent lumping. Carefully ladle over bread in baking dish.
4. Elevate baking dish on a trivet, rack or ramekins turned upside down. Cook on Medium (50% power) for 14–16 minutes, until a knife inserted 2.5 cm from the edge comes out clean, rotating dish twice. If dish is suitable, brown top under a preheated griller.
5. Dust pudding with icing sugar; decorate with orange julienne. Serve warm.

Use the microwave to make traditional bread-based desserts. These puddings are a delicious and economical way to use up day-old bread you may have left over, as in Old-Fashioned Bread and Butter Pudding (below), in which the crusts are removed for a more attractive presentation. For a nutritious change, substitute wholemeal bread for the white bread.

OLD-FASHIONED BREAD AND BUTTER PUDDING

Colour Index page 89. 1214 kJ per serving. Good source of calcium. Begin 45 minutes ahead.

Ingredients for 10 servings		Microwave cookware
12 slices day-old white bread	*⅛ teaspoon ground nutmeg*	Shallow 2-litre baking dish
60 g butter or margarine, softened	*⅛ teaspoon ground cloves*	4-cup glass jug
2 cups cream	*1 teaspoon vanilla essence*	Trivet, rack or ramekins
1 cup milk	*Icing sugar*	
4 eggs		
¾ cup sugar		
½ teaspoon ground cinnamon		

1 Remove crusts from bread. Cut slices diagonally in half to form triangles. Arrange slices on a baking tray; toast lightly. Spread each with softened butter.

2 Working from outer edge towards the centre, arrange toast triangles in overlapping circles in baking dish.

3 Pour cream and milk into glass jug. Heat on High (100% power) for 4–6 minutes, until small bubbles form around edge.

4 With mixer at medium speed, beat eggs, sugar, cinnamon, nutmeg, cloves and vanilla essence in a medium bowl until blended. Stir a small amount of hot milk mixture into egg mixture. Slowly pour egg mixture back into remaining hot milk, beating rapidly to prevent lumping.

5 Carefully ladle mixture over toast in baking dish.

6 Elevate baking dish on a trivet, rack or ramekins turned upside down. Cook on Medium (50% power) for 14–16 minutes, until a knife inserted 2.5 cm from edge comes out clean, rotating dish twice. Allow to stand on a heatproof surface until slightly cooled. Dust with icing sugar. Serve warm.

Shower Tea

Strawberry Charlotte (page 323)
Tartlets filled with Crème Pâtissière (page 337) and fruit
Caramel Pears in Strawberry Sauce (page 319)
Black Forest Cake (page 356)
Pink Champagne

PREPARATION TIMETABLE

Early in day:	*Chill Champagne. Prepare Strawberry Charlotte up to the end of step 5. Prepare fruit for tartlets; cover and refrigerate.*
4 hours ahead:	*Prepare double quantity of Caramel Pears in Strawberry Sauce in 2 batches, up to the end of step 5. Make Black Forest Cake; cover loosely and refrigerate. Make Crème Pâtissière in flavours of your choice; cover with plastic wrap and refrigerate. Complete Strawberry Charlotte.*
30 minutes ahead:	*If you like, reheat tartlet shells to crisp; put aside to cool. Fill tartlet shells with Crème Pâtissière and decorate with fruit; arrange on a serving platter.*
Just before serving:	*Complete Caramel Pears in Strawberry Sauce.*

SYRUP SPONGE PUDDING

Colour Index page 88. 4 servings. 1164 kJ per serving. Good source of calcium.
Begin 35 minutes ahead.

60 g butter or margarine, softened	*½ teaspoon vanilla essence*
¼ cup caster sugar	*1 cup self-raising flour*
1 egg, beaten	*¼ cup milk*
1 teaspoon grated lemon rind	*2 tablespoons golden syrup*

1. Cream butter and sugar in a bowl until light and fluffy. Slowly beat in egg, lemon rind and vanilla essence. Lightly fold in flour alternately with milk.
2. Grease the inside of a 3-cup pudding basin. Place golden syrup in the bottom of the basin; spoon pudding mixture on top.
3. Cook, covered tightly with plastic wrap, on High (100% power) for 3–4 minutes, until well risen and a toothpick inserted in centre comes out clean, turning basin every minute.
4. Allow pudding to stand on a heatproof surface for 2 minutes. Loosen edges of pudding with a knife; unmould on to a serving plate. Allow to stand, loosely covered, for 2 minutes. Serve hot.

TIRAMISÚ

Colour Index page 92. 16 servings. 1239 kJ per serving. Good source of vitamin A, calcium.
Begin 4 hours ahead or early in day.

280 g packet sponge cake mix	*½ cup icing sugar*
2 eggs	*2 tablespoons strong coffee*
½ cup water	*2 tablespoons Kahlúa or other coffee liqueur*
½ teaspoon almond essence	*1 teaspoon vanilla essence*
500 g mascarpone	
1½ cups thickened cream	*Cocoa*

1. Line bottom of an 18-cm round baking dish with a double thickness of greaseproof paper.
2. With mixer at low speed, beat cake mix, eggs, water and almond essence in a small bowl until blended. Increase speed to high; beat for 5 minutes. Spoon mixture into prepared dish.
3. Elevate dish on a trivet, rack or ramekins turned upside down. Cook on High (100% power) for 10–12 minutes, until cake springs back when lightly touched, rotating dish twice. Allow to stand for 5 minutes. Loosen cake from sides of dish with a knife. Invert on to a rack; remove paper. Allow to cool.
4. Heat mascarpone in a 4-cup glass jug on High for 1–2 minutes, until softened. With mixer at low speed, beat in cream, icing sugar, coffee, liqueur and vanilla essence until well blended.
5. Cut cooled cake into 5-cm pieces. Place one-third in a 2.5-litre serving bowl. Pour in one-third of cheese mixture. Repeat layers twice. Cover and refrigerate until well chilled. Dust surface with cocoa before serving.

Custards

CRÈME BRÛLÉE

Colour Index page 90. 4 servings. 1754 kJ per serving. Low in sodium. Good source of vitamin A. Begin early in day or 1 day ahead.

1½ cups thickened cream	2 tablespoons brown
3 egg yolks	sugar
2 tablespoons caster	4 large strawberries to
sugar	decorate
½ teaspoon vanilla	
essence	

1. Heat cream in a 4-cup glass jug on High (100% power) for 3–5 minutes, until small bubbles form around edge.
2. Beat egg yolks and sugar in a small bowl. Stir a small amount of hot cream into egg mixture. Slowly pour egg mixture back into remaining hot cream, beating rapidly to prevent lumping. Cook on Medium (50% power) for 4–6 minutes, until mixture has thickened, stirring frequently. Do not boil. Stir in vanilla essence.
3. Pour hot mixture into 4 x ½-cup flameproof ramekins. Cover and refrigerate for about 6 hours, or until well chilled.
4. About 1 hour before serving, preheat griller. Sprinkle brown sugar evenly over each ramekin so that custard is completely covered; arrange in a baking dish with ice cubes between ramekins to prevent custard from curdling. Place under griller for 3–4 minutes, until sugar melts and forms a shiny crust; refrigerate for about 30 minutes, or until crust hardens.
5. Place ramekins on small plates; decorate with strawberries. Serve chilled.

Sprinkling the sugar and adding the ice cubes

Sprinkle brown sugar evenly over the surface of the custard mixture to cover completely.

To prevent custard from curdling, place ice cubes between ramekins in the baking dish.

MAKING CARAMEL

Caramel is easy and quick to prepare in the microwave, but it is essential to watch the mixture carefully, without stirring, and to remove it from the microwave as soon as it starts to turn golden, since it continues to cook and darken (even burn) afterwards.
To clean glass jug after making caramel: Fill with warm water and heat on High (100% power) until water boils.

CRÈME CARAMEL

Colour Index page 90. 946 kJ per serving. Low in sodium. Good source of calcium. Begin 2½ hours ahead or early in day.

Ingredients for 4 servings		Microwave cookware
½ cup caster sugar	4 eggs	4-cup glass jug
2 tablespoons water	1 teaspoon vanilla	4 x ¾-cup ramekins
1¼ cups milk	essence	30-cm x 20-cm baking dish

1 Place half the sugar in glass jug; add water. Cook on High (100% power) for 4–6 minutes, without stirring, just until mixture turns light golden, watching carefully since caramel burns easily and continues to cook and darken when removed from the oven. Allow to cool for 30 seconds.

2 Pour caramel into ramekins, swirling to coat bottoms of dishes; put aside to harden. Pour milk into same cleaned jug (see Making Caramel, below left). Heat on High for 4–6 minutes, until small bubbles form around edge.

3 Beat eggs and remaining sugar in a bowl until blended. Stir a small amount of hot milk into egg mixture. Slowly pour egg mixture into remaining hot milk, beating rapidly to prevent lumping. Stir in vanilla essence. Strain custard through a sieve into a large jug.

4 Place ramekins in baking dish; pour in custard. Fill baking dish with water to within 2.5 cm of top of ramekins. Cook on Medium-High (70% power) for 10–14 minutes, until custards are set but centres are still soft, carefully rotating baking dish 3 times during cooking.

5 Remove ramekins from baking dish. Allow custards to stand, covered, on a heatproof surface for 5 minutes, or until firmly set. Cover and refrigerate until ready to serve.

6 Loosen custards from sides of ramekins with a thin-bladed knife. Invert each custard on to a chilled dessert plate. Carefully remove ramekin, allowing caramel to drip on to custard. Serve chilled.

Ice cream and sorbets

The custard and syrup bases for ice cream and sorbets are quick to make in the microwave and the resulting desserts are delicious on their own – or served with fruit and toppings. Be sure to cool custards and syrups completely before freezing so that they freeze quickly and the consistency remains smooth.

VANILLA ICE CREAM

Colour Index page 91. 745 kJ per serving. Low in sodium.
Begin early in day.

Ingredients for 8 servings		Microwave cookware
½ cup caster sugar 1 tablespoon plain flour ¼ teaspoon salt 1½ cups milk 1 egg	1 egg yolk ¾ cup thickened cream 1 teaspoon vanilla essence	2-litre glass jug or bowl

1. Combine sugar, flour and salt in glass jug. Pour in milk and stir until smooth. Cook on High (100% power) for 4–6 minutes, until mixture has boiled and thickened slightly, stirring occasionally.

2. Beat egg and egg yolk in a small bowl. Stir a small amount of hot milk mixture into beaten eggs.

3. Slowly pour egg mixture back into remaining hot milk mixture, beating rapidly to prevent lumping. Cook custard on Medium (50% power) for 2–3 minutes, until thickened, beating frequently. Do not boil or custard will curdle.

4. Lightly press plastic wrap or dampened greaseproof paper on to surface of custard to prevent a skin forming. Refrigerate for 2 hours, or until completely chilled, stirring occasionally.

5. Pour chilled custard, cream and vanilla essence into a 1.5-litre–2-litre container of electric ice-cream maker. Freeze mixture according to the manufacturer's instructions. When freezing is finished, ice cream will be soft. Scoop ice cream into a freezerproof serving dish. Pack down; smooth surface and, if you like, make decorative pattern on top. Cover with plastic wrap. Place dish in freezer for at least 2 hours, until ice cream is firm.

6. Soften ice cream slightly before serving by heating on Medium-Low (30% power) for 30 seconds–1 minute. Remove from serving dish with ice-cream scoop. Serve immediately.

MANGO SORBET

Colour Index page 91. 4 servings. 687 kJ per serving.
Low in fat. Good source of vitamin A, vitamin C.
Begin early in day.

1 cup water	1 tablespoon lime juice
½ cup caster sugar	2 tablespoons dark rum

1 large ripe mango
  (about 500 g), peeled
  and cut into 12-mm
  chunks
	Lime julienne (page 316)
	  to decorate

1. Pour water into a 4-cup glass jug; add sugar. Cook on High (100% power) for 3–4 minutes, until mixture begins to boil, stirring halfway through cooking. Cook on High for 5 minutes longer, stirring occasionally. Cover and refrigerate for about 45 minutes, or until chilled.
2. In food processor with knife blade attached or in blender, process mango, lime juice and rum until puréed.
3. Stir purée into cooled syrup. Pour into a 23-cm x 23-cm baking dish; press plastic wrap on to surface. Freeze for about 3 hours, until sorbet is partially frozen, stirring occasionally.
4. Spoon into a chilled large bowl. With mixer at medium speed, beat sorbet until smooth but still frozen. Transfer to a freezerproof dish; smooth surface. Cover and freeze again until firm.
5. Allow sorbet to stand at room temperature for 5–10 minutes to soften. Decorate with lime julienne. Serve immediately.

KIWIFRUIT SORBET

Colour Index page 91. 4 servings. 599 kJ per serving.
Low in fat, sodium. Good source of vitamin C.
Begin early in day.

1 cup water	1 tablespoon lemon juice
½ cup caster sugar	Mint leaves to decorate
4 ripe kiwifruit, peeled and cut into quarters	

1. Pour water into a 4-cup glass jug; add sugar. Cook on High (100% power) for 3–4 minutes, until mixture begins to boil, stirring halfway through cooking. Cook on High for 5 minutes longer, stirring occasionally. Cover and refrigerate for about 45 minutes, or until chilled.
2. In food processor with knife blade attached or in blender, process kiwifruit and lemon juice until puréed.
3. Stir purée into cooled syrup. Pour into a 23-cm x 23-cm baking dish; press plastic wrap on to surface. Freeze for about 3 hours, or until sorbet is partially frozen, stirring occasionally.
4. Spoon into a chilled large bowl. With mixer at medium speed, beat until smooth but still frozen. Transfer to a freezerproof dish; smooth surface. Cover and freeze again until firm.
5. Allow sorbet to stand at room temperature for 5–10 minutes to soften. Decorate with mint leaves. Serve immediately.

Pies and Tarts

**PASTRY SHELLS AND CRUSTS · CRUMB CRUSTS
DECORATIVE PASTRY EDGES · FRUIT PIES AND TARTS
CREAM PIES AND TARTS · NUT PIES AND TARTS**

Pies and Tarts

A combination of both microwave and conventional cooking is ideal for producing quick-to-prepare, mouth-watering pies and tarts. Although shortcrust pastry cooked in a microwave turns out crisp and flaky, it looks better when cooked in a conventional oven; while the pastry shell is baking, the microwave can be used to prepare a delicious fruit, custard, cream, chiffon or nutty filling.

To create a shiny top on a two-crust pie, brush it with slightly beaten egg white before baking; for a golden-brown glaze, use beaten whole egg; for an even richer colour, apply beaten egg yolk. To add a little sparkle to a pastry crust, sprinkle it lightly with sugar.

As an alternative to conventional pastry crusts and shells, crumb crusts made with plain sweet biscuits or wafers can be cooked in the microwave. When making a biscuit crumb crust, press the crumbs firmly and evenly on to the bottom and up the sides of the pie plate; after cooking in the microwave, allow the crust to cool on a rack before filling.

When filled with ice cream, commercially prepared pudding or mousse, or a canned pie filling, crumb crusts can make almost instant desserts.

The egg-enriched fillings of custard and cream pies work particularly well in the microwave. Cooked on Medium (50% power), these fillings are creamy and smooth. If you press plastic wrap or dampened greaseproof paper directly on to the surface of the warm custard it will prevent a skin from forming while the custard chills. Some fillings depend upon both gelatine and beaten egg whites for their lightness and height; some also have whipped cream folded into their base mixture. Cooking the filling on Medium results in a smooth mixture that blends well with the additions.

The microwave can also help provide the finishing touches to a cooked pie or tart. Use it to toast almonds or coconut (see page 296), to soften chocolate for making Chocolate Curls (see page 358), or make a delicious glaze from jam or jelly to set off a fruit filling (see page 336).

PRETTY PIES AND TARTLETS

Conventionally baked pie shells or bought tartlet shells make ideal bases for last-minute pastry treats. You can create desserts fit for any occasion by using a variety of fillings such as jam, ice cream, custard or mousse, topped with berries or tropical fruit.

Bought tartlets shells filled with Mocha Crème Pâtissière (page 337) and topped with piped whipped cream (left). Sugared cake decorations add a decorative touch.

Bought tartlet shells filled with mango, nectarine and kumquat slices (right) decorated with whipped cream and sprigs of mint.

Shells and crusts

PASTRY FLAN SHELL

Colour Index page 93. Makes one 23-cm–25-cm flan shell. 6790 kJ. Good source of vitamin A, riboflavin, thiamine, niacin, iron.
Begin 2½ hours ahead.

1¼ cups plain flour	60 g butter or margarine,
2 teaspoons sugar	chilled
¼ teaspoon salt	2–3 tablespoons water
¼ cup vegetable	
shortening (Copha)	

1. Combine flour, sugar and salt in a mixing bowl. With 2 knives or with fingertips, cut or rub in shortening and butter until mixture resembles crumbs.
2. Sprinkle water into mixture, 1 tablespoon at a time, mixing lightly with a fork until pastry just holds together. Shape into a ball; flatten slightly. Wrap in greaseproof paper or foil; refrigerate for about 1 hour, or until firm and well chilled.
3. Preheat conventional oven to 220°C. On a lightly floured surface, with a floured rolling pin, roll pastry into a round about 2.5 cm larger than a 23-cm or 25-cm flan tin with removable base. Roll pastry on to rolling pin; transfer to flan tin and unroll, pressing pastry on to bottom and up sides of tin.
4. Trim edge of pastry even with the top of the tin. Prick bottom and sides several times with a fork; line with foil; add beans, lentils or rice (see Baking pastry blind, page 339) and bake for 10 minutes. Remove beans, lentils or rice and foil; prick pastry again. Bake for 15 minutes longer, or until golden. Allow to cool on a rack.

BISCUIT CRUMB CRUST

Colour Index page 93. Makes one 23-cm crumb crust. About 5260 kJ. Good source of vitamin A, riboflavin. Begin 1¼ hours ahead.

90 g butter or margarine	½ teaspoon ground
185 g plain sweet biscuits,	cinnamon
finely crushed	
(1½ cups)	

1. Heat butter in a 23-cm pie plate, covered with paper towel, on High (100% power) for 1–1½ (1:30) minutes, until melted. Stir in biscuit crumbs and cinnamon. Press mixture on to bottom and up sides of plate.
2. Elevate pie plate on a trivet, rack or ramekin turned upside down. Cook on High for 1–2 minutes, until warm. Allow to cool on a rack.

GINGER CRUMB CRUST: Prepare as for Biscuit Crumb Crust (above), using **gingernut** or **gingersnap biscuits** to make crumbs and omitting the cinnamon. About 5170 kJ.

VANILLA OR CHOCOLATE CRUMB CRUST: Prepare as for Biscuit Crumb Crust (above), using **vanilla** or **chocolate wafers** to make crumbs. About 5587 kJ.

When making pastry, handle it as little as possible. If it becomes too soft to handle, shape it into a ball then flatten it slightly with a floured rolling pin and wrap in greaseproof paper or foil; refrigerate for 30 minutes, or until firm. When rolling pastry into a round, flour the rolling pin and roll from centre to edge. Add more flour if pastry begins to stick.

SHORTCRUST PASTRY BASE

Colour Index page 93. 4755 kJ. Good source of riboflavin, thiamine, niacin. Begin 2½ hours ahead.

When making Shortcrust Pastry Base in a conventional oven, check the recipe first to see if the filling is to be later cooked in the base. If so, bake the pastry in a pie plate that can be used in both a conventional and a microwave oven.

Ingredients for 23-cm base

1 cup plain flour	2 tablespoons iced water
¼ teaspoon salt	
90 g vegetable shortening	
(Copha)	

1 Combine flour and salt in a mixing bowl. With 2 knives or with fingertips, cut or rub in shortening until mixture resembles crumbs.

2 Sprinkle water into mixture, 1 tablespoon at a time, mixing lightly with a fork until pastry just holds together. Shape into a ball, flatten slightly. Wrap in greaseproof paper or foil; refrigerate for about 1 hour, or until firm and well chilled.

3 On a lightly floured surface, with a floured rolling pin, roll pastry into a round about 5 cm larger than pie plate.

4 Gently roll pastry on to rolling pin; transfer to pie plate and unroll, pressing pastry on to bottom and up sides of plate.

5 Trim edge of pastry, leaving 2.5 cm overhang. Fold overhang under, then bring up over rim; make a decorative Pastry Edge (page 336) of your choice. Preheat conventional oven to 220°C.

6 Prick pastry several times with a fork. Bake for 15 minutes, or until golden. (If pastry puffs up, gently press into pie plate with a spoon.) Allow to cool on a rack.

Pastry Edges

Fluted Edge: Pinch to form stand-up edge. Place 1 index finger on inside edge of pastry; with index finger and thumb of other hand, pinch pastry to make a flute. Repeat around edge, leaving 6 mm between each flute.

Sharp Fluted Edge: Pinch to form stand-up edge. Use the pointed edge of a biscuit cutter or the back of a knife to make deeper indentations in the pastry.

Leaf Edge: With a sharp knife or leaf-shaped cutter, cut leaves from rolled-out pastry trimmings. Press each leaf on to lightly moistened pastry rim, overlapping leaves slightly to cover edge.

Pinched Edge: Pinch to form stand-up edge. Pinch pastry edge at an angle between thumb and knuckle of index finger. Repeat around edge, rotating pie plate clockwise.

Scalloped Edge: Pinch to form stand-up edge. Place thumb against outside pastry edge and press towards centre while pressing down next to it with a 4-tined fork. Repeat around edge, alternating fork marks and ruffles.

Plaited Edge: Prepare double quantity of pastry for Shortcrust Pastry Base (page 335), using half to line pie plate. Roll out remaining pastry 6 mm thick and cut into 6-mm-wide strips. Gently plait 3 strips together and press on to lightly moistened pastry rim. Join ends of plait together to cover edge completely.

TWO-CRUST PIE PASTRY

Makes double crust for one 23-cm pie. 9502 kJ. Good source of riboflavin, thiamine, niacin, iron. Begin 2½ hours ahead.

2 cups plain flour
1 teaspoon salt
¾ cup vegetable
  shortening (Copha)

4 tablespoons water

1. Combine flour and salt in a mixing bowl. With 2 knives or with fingertips, cut or rub in shortening until mixture resembles crumbs.
2. Sprinkle water into mixture, 1 tablespoon at a time, mixing lightly with a fork until pastry just holds together. Shape into 2 balls, 1 slightly larger; flatten slightly. Wrap both in greaseproof paper or foil; refrigerate for about 1 hour, or until firm and well chilled.
3. On a lightly floured surface, with a floured rolling pin, roll larger ball into a round about 5 cm larger than a 23-cm pie plate. Gently roll pastry on to rolling pin; transfer to pie plate and unroll, pressing pastry on to bottom and up sides of plate.
4. Fill pie according to recipe instructions. For top crust, roll out smaller ball of pastry. Moisten edge of bottom crust with water; centre top crust over filling. Trim pastry edges, leaving 2.5 cm overhang. Fold overhang under, then bring up over rim; make Sharp Fluted Edge (left). Cut slashes or design in centre. Brush with Milk or Egg Glaze (below). If you like, decorate top of pie with shapes cut from pastry trimmings (see page 210); brush with glaze. Bake conventionally, according to recipe instructions.

GLAZES FOR PIES AND TARTS

Milk or Egg Glaze: Before baking a two-crust pie conventionally, brush top lightly with milk, cream or undiluted evaporated milk to enhance browning. For a shiny top, brush with beaten egg white; for a richer, golden-brown colour, brush with beaten egg yolk.

Fruit glazes are the ideal way to enhance the colours of fresh fruit tarts. Use apricot jam to complement pale or yellow fruit, and redcurrant jelly or strawberry jam for berries or plums.

Fruit Glaze: Combine *¼ cup jam or jelly* and *1 tablespoon water* in a 1-cup glass jug. Heat on High (100% power) for 1½ (1:30)–2 minutes, until glaze coats the back of a spoon, stirring often. If using jam, strain glaze through a fine sieve until smooth. Lightly brush over fruit.

Fruit pies

CRÈME PÂTISSIÈRE

Colour Index page 93. Makes 3 cups. 1252 kJ per serving. Low in sodium.
Begin 25 minutes ahead.

2 cups milk	5 egg yolks
¼ cup caster sugar	½ teaspoon vanilla
2 tablespoons plain flour	essence

1. Heat milk in a 2-litre glass jug on High (100% power) for 4–6 minutes, until small bubbles form around edge.
2. Combine sugar and flour in a medium bowl. Add egg yolks, one at a time, beating well after each addition.
3. Stir a small amount of hot milk into egg mixture. Slowly pour egg mixture back into remaining hot milk, beating rapidly to prevent lumping. Cook on High for 2–3 minutes, until mixture has thickened, beating every minute; do not boil. Stir in vanilla essence.
4. Press plastic wrap or dampened greaseproof paper on to surface to prevent a skin from forming. Refrigerate until chilled.
5. Press cream through a fine sieve to remove any lumps. Use chilled Crème Pâtissière plain, or with flavourings (below), in tartlets, pies and flans, and decorate with fresh fruit or other toppings. Crème Pâtissière can also be used as a filling in cakes, profiteroles and éclairs.

FLAVOURED FILLINGS
The plain Crème Pâtissière (above) can be varied with different flavours and used to fill decoratively shaped pastry cases.

Almond Filling:
Prepare Crème Pâtissière, substituting *½ teaspoon almond essence* for the vanilla essence.

Orange Filling:
Prepare Crème Pâtissière, substituting *1 tablespoon orange-flavoured liqueur* and *1 teaspoon grated orange rind* for the vanilla essence.

Mocha Filling:
Prepare Crème Pâtissière. At the end of step 3, stir in *¼ cup dark chocolate bits* and *½ teaspoon instant coffee powder* until chocolate is melted.

DELUXE APPLE PIE

Colour Index page 94. 1214 kJ per serving. Good source of fibre.
Begin 3½ hours ahead.

Unlike traditional apple pie, which has a top pastry crust, this Deluxe Apple Pie has an unusual oat-based crumble topping that is both quick and nourishing.

Ingredients for 10 servings		Microwave cookware
6 medium cooking apples, peeled, cored and cut into 4-cm chunks Plain flour ⅓ cup caster sugar 2 teaspoons lemon juice ½ teaspoon grated lemon rind ½ teaspoon ground cinnamon	¼ teaspoon ground nutmeg Shortcrust Pastry Base (page 335) ½ cup brown sugar ¼ cup rolled oats 60 g butter or margarine, chilled Ice cream or whipped cream (optional)	Large bowl Trivet, rack or ramekin

1 Combine apple, 2 tablespoons flour, caster sugar, lemon juice, lemon rind, cinnamon and nutmeg in bowl. Cook, covered, on High (100% power) for 5 minutes. Uncover; stir. Cook on High for 5–7 minutes longer, until apples are tender, stirring twice.

2 Spoon apple mixture into cooled pastry base; put aside.

3 Combine brown sugar, rolled oats, butter and ¼ cup flour in a small bowl. With 2 knives or with fingertips, cut or rub in butter until mixture resembles coarse crumbs.

4 Sprinkle crumb mixture over apple filling. Elevate pie plate on trivet, rack or ramekin turned upside down.

5 Cook pie on High for 7–10 minutes, until topping is crisp, rotating plate halfway through cooking.

6 Serve pie warm or cover and refrigerate to serve chilled later. Serve, if you like, with ice cream or whipped cream.

SUMMER FRUIT TART

Colour Index page 94. 1298 kJ per serving. Good source of vitamin A, vitamin C, calcium, iron, fibre.
Begin 2½ hours ahead.

For a seasonal treat, try this Summer Fruit Tart – a crumb crust filled with vanilla custard and topped with a mixture of juicy strawberries, raspberries, blueberries and sliced kiwifruit.

Ingredients for 10 servings		Microwave cookware
90 g butter or margarine	1½ teaspoons vanilla essence	23-cm pie plate
1 tablespoon brown sugar	¼ cup apple or redcurrant jelly	Trivet, rack or ramekin
185 g plain sweet biscuits, finely crushed (about 1½ cups)	1 tablespoon water	Medium bowl
½ cup caster sugar	1 punnet strawberries	Small bowl
1½ tablespoons cornflour	½ punnet raspberries	
2 cups cream	½ punnet blueberries	
3 egg yolks	1 kiwifruit, peeled and sliced	

1 Place butter and brown sugar in pie plate. Heat, covered with paper towel, on High (100% power) for 1–1½ (1:30) minutes, until butter has melted and sugar dissolved, stirring halfway through cooking. Stir in biscuit crumbs until blended.

2 Press crumb mixture on to bottom and up sides of pie plate. Elevate on trivet, rack or ramekin turned upside down. Cook on High for 1 minute. Allow to cool on a rack.

3 Combine caster sugar and cornflour in medium bowl. Beat in cream and egg yolks until well blended. Cook on High for 5–6 minutes, until custard has thickened slightly and coats the back of a spoon, stirring often. Stir in vanilla essence.

4 Pour custard into cooled crumb crust. Lightly press plastic wrap or dampened greaseproof paper on to surface to prevent a skin from forming. Refrigerate for about 2 hours, or until custard is set.

5 Combine apple jelly and water in small bowl. Heat on High for 1½ (1:30)–2 minutes, until jelly is melted and smooth, stirring often. Hull strawberries and cut in half. If you like, reserve 1 whole berry for decoration.

6 When custard is set, remove plastic wrap. Carefully arrange strawberries, raspberries, blueberries and sliced kiwifruit on top of custard. Decorate, if you like, with whole strawberry. Brush glaze over fruit. Refrigerate tart for 15 minutes, or until glaze is set.

QUICK APRICOT FLAN

Colour Index page 96. 10 servings. 1088 kJ per serving. Good source of vitamin A, thiamine, fibre.
Begin 1¼ hours ahead.

½ cup cream	Pastry Flan Shell (page 335) or bought shell
2 egg yolks	
2 tablespoons sugar	825 g can apricot halves, drained
3 teaspoons plain flour	
½ teaspoon almond essence	¼ cup flaked almonds, toasted

1. Heat cream in a 4-cup glass jug on High (100% power) for 2–3 minutes, until bubbles form around edge.
2. Beat egg yolks, sugar, flour and almond essence in a small bowl. Stir a small amount of hot cream into egg mixture. Slowly pour egg mixture back into remaining hot cream, beating rapidly to prevent lumping. Cook on Medium (50% power) for 3–5 minutes, until custard has thickened slightly and coats the back of a spoon, stirring often.
3. Place cooled flan shell on a serving platter. Arrange apricots in shell; pour custard over apricots. Cook on Medium for 7–10 minutes, until custard is softly set, rotating platter halfway through cooking.
4. Sprinkle almonds over top of flan. Allow to stand on a heatproof surface for 10 minutes. Serve at room temperature or cover and refrigerate to serve chilled later.

RASPBERRY CUSTARD TART

Colour Index page 96. 10 servings. 1331 kJ per serving. Good source of vitamin A, thiamine, riboflavin, calcium, iron, fibre.
Begin 1¼ hours ahead.

3 tablespoons raspberry jam	Crème Pâtissière (page 337)
Shortcrust Pastry Base (page 335)	1 punnet raspberries

1. Heat raspberry jam in a small bowl on High (100% power) for 1–1½ (1:30) minutes, until spreadable, stirring once.
2. Evenly spread jam over pastry base. Spoon Crème Pâtissière over jam. Lightly press plastic wrap or dampened greaseproof paper on to surface to prevent a skin from forming. Refrigerate for about 40 minutes, or until cold.
3. Remove plastic wrap and arrange raspberries neatly on top of tart. Serve immediately or cover and refrigerate to serve chilled later.

PEACHES AND CREAM PIE

Colour Index page 94. 10 servings. 1185 kJ per serving. Good source of vitamin A, riboflavin, calcium, iron.
Begin 2 hours ahead.

6 peaches, peeled, stoned and sliced	1 tablespoon peach jam
½ cup sugar	Crème Pâtissière (page 337)
1 tablespoon plain flour	Biscuit Crumb Crust (page 335)
½ teaspoon vanilla essence	

1. Place peach slices, sugar, flour and vanilla essence in a large bowl; toss to coat. Cook, covered, on High (100% power) for 8–10 minutes, until peaches are tender and juices thicken, stirring twice. Put aside.
2. Stir peach jam into Crème Pâtissière. Pour mixture into crumb crust; arrange peach slices on top. Cover and refrigerate for about 30 minutes, or until well chilled.

BAKING PASTRY BLIND

Many pastry cases and flan shells are baked first, then filled when cool. This is known as 'baking blind'. To prevent the pastry from puffing, or browning too much, larger cases and shells must be protected during cooking.

Line pastry with a piece of foil slightly larger than flan tin or pie plate. Press foil on to bottom and up sides of pastry shell.

Fill foil lining with dried beans, lentils or rice to prevent shell from puffing during baking. After baking, remove beans, lentils or rice and foil; prick pastry again and return to oven until golden.

A creamy custard base such as Crème Pâtissière is perfect for fruit such as the peaches in Peaches and Cream Pie (left). In Lemon Meringue Pie (below), the texture of custard contrasts delightfully with the fluffy meringue and the crunchy, crisp pastry.

LEMON MERINGUE PIE

Colour Index page 94. 1218 kJ per serving. Good source of vitamin C, riboflavin, thiamine, niacin, iron.
Begin 3½ hours ahead.

Ingredients for 10 servings		Microwave cookware
⅓ cup cornflour 1¼ cups sugar 1½ cups water 4 eggs, separated ½ cup lemon juice 15 g butter or margarine	1 teaspoon grated lemon rind Shortcrust Pastry Base (page 335) ¼ teaspoon cream of tartar	4-cup glass jug

1 Combine cornflour and ¾ cup sugar in glass jug. Gradually add water, stirring until smooth. Cook on High (100% power) for 3–5 minutes, until mixture has thickened, stirring often.

2 Beat egg yolks in a small bowl. Stir a small amount of hot cornflour mixture into egg yolks. Slowly pour egg-yolk mixture back into remaining hot mixture, beating rapidly to prevent lumping.

3 Cook custard on Medium (50% power) for 2–3 minutes, until custard has thickened slightly and coats the back of a spoon, stirring often. Do not boil or custard will curdle.

4 Add lemon juice, butter and lemon rind, stirring until butter has melted. Pour into pastry base. Lightly press plastic wrap or dampened greaseproof paper on to surface to prevent a skin from forming. Refrigerate for about 30 minutes, or until set.

5 Preheat conventional oven to 200°C. With mixer at high speed, beat egg whites and cream of tartar in a large bowl until soft peaks form. Gradually sprinkle in remaining sugar, beating until sugar has completely dissolved and whites stand in stiff, glossy peaks.

6 When custard is set, remove plastic wrap. Spread beaten egg whites over custard to edge of pastry. Swirl to make an attractive design. Bake conventionally for 10 minutes, or until golden. Serve warm or refrigerate to cool slightly.

Cream pies

BANANA COCONUT TART

Colour Index page 93. 1817 kJ per serving. Good source of vitamin A, riboflavin, thiamin, niacin, iron.
Begin early in day.

Use the microwave to make the lusciously creamy filling in this Banana Coconut Tart. When the tart is assembled, refrigerate until ready to serve, sprinkling the toasted coconut over the top at the last minute.

Ingredients for 10 servings		Microwave cookware

1⅓ cups milk
4 eggs, separated
¼ teaspoon salt
¾ cup sugar
2 envelopes
  (1½ tablespoons)
  gelatine
1 cup cream
	1½ teaspoons vanilla
	  essence
	Shortcrust Pastry Base
	  (page 335) made in a
	  23-cm flan tin
	1 large banana, sliced
	½ cup shredded coconut
		4-cup glass jug
		Shallow pie plate

1 Pour milk into glass jug. Add egg yolks, salt and ½ cup sugar; beat until blended. Evenly sprinkle gelatine over mixture; allow to stand for 1 minute to soften slightly. Cook on High (100% power) for 4–6 minutes, until custard has thickened slightly, stirring often. Do not boil or custard will curdle.

2 Pour custard into large bowl. Cover and refrigerate for 30–40 minutes, until custard mounds slightly when dropped from a spoon, stirring often.

3 Meanwhile, with mixer at high speed, beat egg whites in a large bowl until soft peaks form. Gradually sprinkle in remaining sugar, beating until sugar has completely dissolved and whites stand in stiff, glossy peaks. Spoon on top of chilled custard.

4 In same bowl, with same beaters and mixer at medium speed, beat cream and vanilla essence until soft peaks form. Spoon over custard. Gently fold whipped cream and beaten egg whites into custard.

5 Cover bottom of cooled pastry base with banana slices. Carefully spoon custard mixture over banana. Cover and refrigerate for about 3 hours, or until set.

6 Spread coconut in pie plate. Heat on High for 3–4 minutes, until toasted, stirring often. Just before serving, sprinkle toasted coconut over tart.

ORANGE CHIFFON PIE

Colour Index page 93. 10 servings. 1595 kJ per serving. Good source of vitamin C.
Begin 3 hours ahead.

¾ cup sugar
1 envelope (3 teaspoons) gelatine
1 teaspoon grated orange rind
1 cup orange juice
2 tablespoons lemon juice

3 eggs, separated
1½ cups thickened cream
Biscuit Crumb Crust (page 335)
Orange julienne (page 316) to decorate

1. Combine ½ cup sugar, gelatine, orange rind, orange juice and lemon juice in a 4-cup glass jug. Cook on High (100% power) for 3–4 minutes, until small bubbles form, stirring twice.
2. Beat egg yolks in a small bowl. Stir a small amount of hot juice into beaten egg yolks. Slowly pour egg-yolk mixture back into remaining hot juice, beating rapidly to prevent lumping. Cook on Medium (50% power) for 3–5 minutes, until custard has thickened slightly, stirring often. Pour into a large bowl. Cover and refrigerate for 45 minutes, or until custard mounds slightly when dropped from a spoon, stirring often.
3. With mixer at high speed, beat egg whites in another large bowl until soft peaks form. Gradually sprinkle in remaining sugar, beating until sugar completely dissolves and whites stand in stiff, glossy peaks. Spoon over chilled custard. In same bowl, with same beaters and mixer at medium speed, beat ½ cup cream until soft peaks form. Spoon over custard.
4. Gently fold whipped cream and beaten egg whites into custard. Spoon into cooled crumb crust. Cover and refrigerate for about 30 minutes, or until set.
5. Beat remaining cream until peaks form. Spoon into a piping bag fitted with a medium star tube. Pipe cream around edge of pie; decorate with orange julienne.

MAKING CRUMB CRUSTS
Crushed biscuits, mixed with butter or margarine, and sometimes sugar and spices, make a quick and easy alternative to baked pastry cases.

Combine finely crushed biscuits, melted butter and flavourings according to recipe in a pie plate. Using the back of a metal spoon, firmly press mixture on to bottom and up sides of pie plate.

HIGHLAND CREAM PIE

Colour Index page 96. 10 servings. 1473 kJ per serving. Good source of vitamin A, riboflavin. Begin 4 hours ahead.

1¼ cups milk	*Shortcrust Pastry Base*
1 envelope (3 teaspoons)	*(page 335)*
gelatine	¼ *teaspoon ground*
½ cup sugar	*nutmeg*
3 eggs, separated	*Chocolate Curls (page*
2 tablespoons whisky	*358) to decorate*
1 cup thickened cream	

1. Heat milk in a 4-cup glass jug on High (100% power) for 3–4 minutes, until small bubbles form.
2. Combine gelatine and ¼ cup sugar in a small bowl. Beat in egg yolks and whisky. Stir a small amount of hot milk into egg-yolk mixture. Slowly pour egg-yolk mixture back into remaining hot milk, beating rapidly to prevent lumping. Cook on Medium (50% power) for 2–3 minutes, until custard has thickened slightly and coats the back of a spoon, stirring often. Pour into a large bowl. Cover and refrigerate for about 45 minutes, or until custard mounds slightly when dropped from a spoon, stirring often.
3. With mixer at high speed, beat egg whites in another large bowl until soft peaks form. Gradually sprinkle in remaining sugar, beating until sugar has completely dissolved and whites stand in stiff, glossy peaks. Spoon over chilled custard.
4. In same bowl, with same beaters and mixer at medium speed, beat cream until soft peaks form.
5. Gently fold whipped cream and beaten egg whites into custard. Spoon into pastry base; sprinkle top with ground nutmeg. Refrigerate pie for about 3 hours, or until set. Decorate with Chocolate Curls before serving.

DECORATING WITH CREAM

Whipped cream complements a custard or chiffon filling or it can be used as a contrast on rich or nutty tarts. Take care not to overwhip cream for piping; it should just hold its shape. Spoon whipped cream into a piping bag fitted with a medium star tube.

Zig-Zag Edge:
Pipe a border around edge of tart where filling meets crust. As you pipe, move tube to left and right.

Lattice Design:
Pipe 4 lines of cream, 5 cm apart, over tart. Pipe 4 more lines diagonally across first lines to create a lattice.

STRAWBERRY CHIFFON PIE

Colour Index page 96. 1247 kJ per serving. Good source of vitamin C. Begin 3 hours ahead.

Ingredients for 10 servings		Microwave cookware
2 punnets strawberries	1 cup water	4-cup glass jug
¾ cup sugar	2 eggs, separated	Small bowl
3 teaspoons lemon juice	⅓ cup thickened cream	
1 teaspoon cornflour	Biscuit Crumb Crust	
1 envelope (3 teaspoons)	(page 335)	
gelatine	Fruit Glaze (page 336)	

1 Hull and slice strawberries, reserving 1 whole strawberry. Cover and refrigerate half the sliced berries. Combine the remaining sliced berries with ¼ cup sugar and lemon juice in a small bowl; toss lightly. Crush berries slightly with a fork; put aside.

2 Combine ¼ cup sugar, cornflour and gelatine in glass jug; stir in 1 cup water. Cook on High (100% power) for 3–4 minutes, until mixture has thickened slightly and coats the back of a spoon, stirring often. Beat egg yolks in a small bowl. Stir a small amount of hot gelatine mixture into egg yolks. Slowly pour egg-yolk mixture back into remaining hot gelatine mixture, beating rapidly.

3 Cook custard on Medium (50% power) for 2–3 minutes, until custard has thickened slightly and coats the back of a spoon, stirring often. Stir in crushed strawberry mixture. Cover and refrigerate for about 45 minutes, or until custard mounds slightly when dropped from a spoon, stirring often.

4 With mixer at high speed, beat egg whites in a large bowl until soft peaks form. Gradually sprinkle in remaining sugar, beating until sugar has completely dissolved and whites stand in stiff, glossy peaks. Spoon over chilled custard.

5 In same bowl, with same beaters and mixer at medium speed, beat cream until soft peaks form. Spoon over custard. Gently fold whipped cream and beaten egg whites into custard. Spoon into cooled crumb crust. Cover and refrigerate for about 30 minutes, or until set.

6 Cover top of pie with reserved sliced berries. Place the whole strawberry in the centre. Brush glaze over top of pie. Refrigerate for about 15 minutes, or until glaze is set.

BLACK BOTTOM PIE

Colour Index page 94. 1252 kJ per serving. Good source of vitamin A, riboflavin, calcium.
Begin 3½ hours ahead.

Ingredients for 10 servings		Microwave cookware
1¼ cups milk 3 eggs, separated 2¼ teaspoons cornflour ¾ cup sugar 1 envelope (3 teaspoons) gelatine 1 teaspoon vanilla essence	1 tablespoon dark rum 60 g cooking chocolate, chopped Ginger Crumb Crust (page 335) ½ cup thickened cream	4-cup glass jug

1 Heat milk in glass jug on High (100% power) for 3–4 minutes, until small bubbles form around edge. Beat egg yolks, cornflour and ½ cup sugar in a medium bowl. Whisk a small amount of hot milk into egg-yolk mixture. Slowly pour egg-yolk mixture back into remaining hot milk, beating rapidly to prevent lumping.

2 Evenly sprinkle gelatine over custard mixture; allow to stand for 1 minute to soften slightly. Cook on Medium (50% power) for 2–3 minutes, until custard has thickened slightly and coats the back of a spoon, stirring often. Stir in vanilla essence.

3 Pour half the custard into a small bowl; stir in rum. Cover and refrigerate for about 30 minutes, or until custard mounds slightly when dropped from a spoon, stirring often. Meanwhile, stir chocolate into remaining custard until melted. Spread chocolate custard evenly in cooled crumb crust; cover and refrigerate.

4 With mixer at high speed, beat egg whites in a medium bowl until soft peaks form. Gradually sprinkle in remaining sugar, beating until sugar has completely dissolved and whites stand in stiff, glossy peaks. Spoon on top of chilled rum custard.

5 Gently fold beaten egg whites into rum custard. Spoon on to chocolate custard in crumb crust, taking care not to overfill. Cover and refrigerate for 10 minutes. Spoon any remaining rum custard on top. Cover and refrigerate for about 20 minutes, or until set.

6 With mixer at medium speed, beat cream in a small bowl until soft peaks form. Spoon whipped cream into a piping bag fitted with a medium star tube; pipe cream around edge of pie. Serve at room temperature.

MINTY CHOCOLATE TART

Colour Index page 95. 10 servings. 1344 kJ per serving. Good source of vitamin A, riboflavin.
Begin 4½ hours ahead or early in day.

1 envelope (3 teaspoons) gelatine ½ cup sugar ½ cup water 3 eggs, separated ¼ cup crème de menthe	½ cup cold black coffee 1 cup thickened cream Chocolate Crumb Crust (page 335) Chocolate Curls to decorate (page 358)

1. Combine gelatine and ¼ cup sugar in a 4-cup glass jug. Beat water and egg yolks in a small bowl. Gradually stir egg-yolk mixture into gelatine mixture until blended. Cook on Medium (50% power) for 1–2 minutes, until mixture has thickened slightly and coats the back of a spoon, stirring often. Do not boil.

2. Pour into a large bowl and stir in crème de menthe and coffee. Cover and refrigerate for about 20 minutes, or until custard mounds slightly when dropped from a spoon, stirring often.

3. With mixer at high speed, beat egg whites in a medium bowl until soft peaks form. Gradually sprinkle in remaining sugar, beating until sugar has completely dissolved and whites stand in stiff, glossy peaks. Spoon on top of chilled custard.

4. In same bowl, with same beaters and mixer at medium speed, beat cream until soft peaks form. Spoon over custard. Gently fold beaten egg whites and whipped cream into custard. Spoon into cooled crumb crust.

5. Cover and refrigerate for about 3 hours, or until set. Decorate with Chocolate Curls.

FLAVOURED WHIPPED CREAM
Whipped cream is an ideal finish for pies, as well as for cakes and desserts.

Basic Whipped Cream: With mixer at medium speed, beat *1½ cups cream* and *¼ cup icing sugar* in a mixing bowl until peaks form. Fold in *½ teaspoon vanilla essence*. Makes 3 cups. 312 kJ per tablespoon.

Chocolate Cream: Prepare Basic Whipped Cream. Fold in *250 g dark chocolate bits,* melted and cooled. 580 kJ per tablespoon.

Coffee Cream: Prepare Basic Whipped Cream, folding in *1 teaspoon instant coffee powder* with the icing sugar. 319 kJ per tablespoon.

Orange Cream: Prepare Basic Whipped Cream, folding in *1 teaspoon grated orange rind* and *⅛ teaspoon orange flower water* with vanilla essence. 319 kJ per tablespoon.

CHOCOLATE CREAM PIE

Colour Index page 96. 10 servings. 1645 kJ per serving. Good source of vitamin A, riboflavin, calcium.
Begin early in day.

2 cups milk	1 teaspoon vanilla
½ cup sugar	essence
⅓ cup plain flour	Vanilla or Chocolate
3 egg yolks	Crumb Crust (page
45 g butter or margarine	335)
60 g cooking chocolate,	1 cup thickened cream
chopped	

1. Heat milk in a 2-litre bowl on High (100% power) for 3–5 minutes, until small bubbles form around edge.
2. Combine sugar and flour in a 4-cup glass jug. Gradually pour in hot milk, stirring until smooth. Pour milk mixture back into 2-litre bowl. Cook on High for 6–8 minutes, until thick and smooth, stirring occasionally.
3. Beat egg yolks in same 4-cup jug. Stir a small amount of hot milk mixture into egg yolks. Slowly pour egg mixture back into remaining hot milk mixture, beating rapidly to prevent lumping. Cook on Medium (50% power) for 2–3 minutes, until custard is very thick, stirring often. Do not boil or custard will curdle.
4. Stir butter and chocolate into custard until melted and smooth. Stir in vanilla essence. Pour custard into cooled crumb crust. Lightly press plastic wrap or dampened greaseproof paper on to surface to prevent a skin from forming. Refrigerate pie for about 3 hours, or until set.
5. Just before serving, remove plastic wrap from top of pie. With mixer at medium speed, beat cream in a small bowl until soft peaks form. Swirl cream over filling to edge of crumb crust. Spoon remaining cream into a piping bag fitted with a star tube; pipe cream around edge of pie.

Preventing a skin from forming on filling

Light press plastic wrap or dampened greaseproof paper on to surface of hot filling to prevent a skin from forming during cooling and setting.

When filling is set, carefully remove the plastic or greaseproof paper from surface.

Light and creamy chiffon fillings are ideal for use in a variety of crusts – pastry, biscuit crumb or coconut are all subtly different.

COCONUT CREAM PIE

Colour Index page 96. 1448 kJ per serving. Low in sodium. Good source of vitamin A, riboflavin, fibre.
Begin 4 hours ahead.

Ingredients for 10 servings		Microwave cookware
1¾ cups shredded coconut	3 eggs, separated	30-cm x 20-cm baking dish
¼ cup icing sugar	¼ teaspoon almond essence	4-cup glass jug
45 g butter or margarine, softened	1 cup thickened cream	
1¼ cups milk	Whipped cream and toasted coconut to decorate	
½ cup sugar		
1 envelope (3 teaspoons) gelatine		

1 Heat coconut in baking dish on High (100% power) for 5–6 minutes, until toasted, stirring often. Reserve ½ cup toasted coconut.

2 Combine remaining toasted coconut, icing sugar and butter in a bowl. Press mixture on to bottom and up sides of a 23-cm pie plate. Refrigerate.

3 Heat milk in glass jug on High (100% power) for 3–4 minutes, until small bubbles form around edge.

4 Combine sugar and gelatine in a small bowl. Beat in egg yolks and almond essence. Stir a small amount of hot milk into egg-yolk mixture. Slowly pour egg-yolk mixture back into remaining hot milk, beating rapidly to prevent lumping. Cook on Medium (50% power) for 2–3 minutes, until custard has thickened slightly and coats the back of a spoon, stirring often. Pour into a large bowl. Cover and refrigerate for about 45 minutes, or until custard mounds slightly when dropped from a spoon, stirring often.

5 With mixer at high speed, beat egg whites in another large bowl until soft peaks form. Gradually sprinkle in remaining sugar, beating until sugar has completely dissolved and whites stand in stiff, glossy peaks. Spoon over chilled custard. In same bowl, with same beaters and mixer at medium speed, beat cream until soft peaks form. Spoon over custard.

6 Gently fold reserved toasted coconut, cream and beaten egg whites into custard. Spoon into chilled coconut crust. Cover and refrigerate pie for about 3 hours, or until set. Decorate pie with whipped cream and toasted coconut just before serving.

Nut pies

AMARETTO PIE

Colour Index page 95. 1113 kJ per serving. Good source of calcium, fibre. Begin early in day.

This light Amaretto Pie has the delicate flavour of almonds in both the amaretti crumb crust and the custard filling. Create a special look by piping cream in a Lattice Design (page 341), then decorate the pie with toasted flaked almonds.

Ingredients for 10 servings		Microwave cookware
90 g butter or margarine 30 amaretti biscuits or crisp macaroons, crushed (about 1¼ cups) ¼ cup sugar 1 envelope (3 teaspoons) gelatine 3 eggs, separated	Water ⅓ cup amaretto (almond-flavoured liqueur) 1 cup thickened cream Whipped cream and toasted flaked almonds to decorate	23-cm pie plate Trivet, rack or ramekin 4-cup glass jug

1 Heat butter in pie plate, covered with paper towel, on High (100% power) for 1–1½ (1:30) minutes, until melted. Stir in amaretti crumbs. Press mixture firmly on to bottom and up sides of pie plate. Elevate plate on trivet, rack or ramekin turned upside down. Cook on High for 1 minute. Allow to cool on rack.

2 Combine sugar and gelatine in glass jug. Beat egg yolks and ½ cup water in a small bowl. Gradually stir egg-yolk mixture into gelatine mixture until blended. Cook on Medium (50% power) for 1–2 minutes, until custard has thickened slightly and coats the back of a spoon, stirring often. Do not boil or custard will curdle. Stir in liqueur.

3 Pour custard into a large bowl. Cover and refrigerate for about 4 minutes, or until custard mounds slightly when dropped from a spoon, stirring often.

4 With mixer at high speed, beat egg whites in another large bowl until soft peaks form. Spoon over custard. In same bowl, with same beaters and mixer at medium speed, beat cream until soft peaks form. Spoon over custard.

5 Gently fold whipped cream and beaten egg whites into custard. Spoon into cooled amaretti crust. Cover and refrigerate for about 3 hours, or until set.

6 Spoon whipped cream into a piping bag fitted with a medium star tube. Pipe cream in Lattice Design (page 341) on top of pie; decorate with toasted flaked almonds.

LIGHT LEMON AND ALMOND TART

Colour Index page 94. 10 servings. 2445 kJ per serving. Good source of vitamin A, thiamine, riboflavin, calcium, fibre. Begin 3½ hours ahead.

2 cups thickened cream 1½ cups sugar 1 teaspoon vanilla essence ¼ teaspoon almond essence 1 tablespoon grated lemon rind	1 tablespoon lemon juice 1 cup slivered almonds Shortcrust Pastry Base (page 335) ¼ cup flaked almonds Lemon julienne (page 316) to decorate

1. Preheat conventional oven to 180°C. Pour 1½ cups cream into a 2-litre bowl; add sugar. Cook on High (100% power) for 10 minutes, or until sugar has dissolved, stirring occasionally. Stir in vanilla essence, almond essence, lemon rind, lemon juice and slivered almonds.
2. Pour mixture into cooled pastry base. Bake for 10–15 minutes, until golden; cool on a rack.
3. Heat flaked almonds in a 23-cm pie plate on High for 3½ (3:30)–4½ (4:30) minutes, until toasted, stirring occasionally. Put aside.
4. With mixer at medium speed, whip remaining cream in a medium bowl until peaks form. Spoon whipped cream into a piping bag fitted with a medium star tube; pipe cream around edge of pie. Sprinkle toasted flaked almonds over top; decorate with lemon julienne.

CHOCOLATE WALNUT PIE

Colour Index page 95. 10 servings. 1515 kJ per serving. Good source of thiamine, riboflavin, iron. Begin early in day.

60 g butter or margarine 60 g dark cooking chocolate, chopped ½ cup sugar ½ cup milk ¼ cup plain flour 2 tablespoons golden syrup	1 teaspoon vanilla essence 3 eggs 1 cup chopped walnuts Shortcrust Pastry Base (page 335) Whipped cream and walnuts to decorate

1. Place butter and chocolate in a 2-litre bowl. Heat, covered with paper towel, on High (100% power) for 45 seconds–1 minute, until melted, stirring twice.
2. Beat in sugar, milk, flour, golden syrup, vanilla essence and eggs until blended. Stir in walnuts. Cook on Medium (50% power) for 5–6 minutes, until mixture has thickened slightly and coats the back of a spoon, stirring often.
3. Spoon chocolate mixture into cooled pastry base. Elevate pie plate on a trivet, rack or ramekin turned upside down. Cook on Medium for 10–12 minutes, until mixture is puffed and set, rotating plate halfway through cooking.
4. Allow pie to cool completely on a rack. Decorate with cream and walnut halves before serving.

STICKY WALNUT TART

Colour Index page 94. 10 servings. 1562 kJ per serving. Good source of thiamine, calcium.
Begin 1½ hours ahead.

60 g butter or margarine	1 teaspoon vanilla
3 eggs	essence
1 cup brown sugar	1½ cups shelled walnuts,
⅓ cup golden syrup	chopped
1 teaspoon ground	Shortcrust Pastry Base
cinnamon	(page 335)

1. Heat butter in a small bowl, covered loosely with paper towel, on High (100% power) for 30 seconds–1 minute, until melted. Cool slightly.
2. Beat eggs in a large bowl. Add melted butter, sugar, golden syrup, cinnamon and vanilla essence; beat until smooth. Stir in walnuts.
3. Pour walnut filling into cooled pastry base. Elevate pie plate on a trivet, rack or ramekin turned upside down. Cook on Medium (50% power) for 16–19 minutes, until set, rotating plate a half turn 3 times during cooking.
4. Allow to stand on a heatproof surface for 10 minutes; continue cooling on a rack. Serve at room temperature.

PECAN PIE

Colour Index page 95. 10 servings. 1553 kJ per serving. Good source of vitamin A, iron.
Begin 3½ hours ahead.

60 g butter or margarine	Shortcrust Pastry Base
1 cup golden syrup	(page 335) made in a
¼ cup brown sugar	shallow 25-cm pie plate
1 teaspoon vanilla	1 cup shelled pecan
essence	halves
3 eggs	

1. Preheat conventional oven to 180°C. Heat butter in a 2-litre bowl, covered with paper towel, on High (100% power) for 45 seconds–1 minute, until melted.
2. Beat in golden syrup, sugar, vanilla essence and eggs until blended. Cook on Medium (50% power) for 6–8 minutes, until mixture has thickened slightly and coats the back of a spoon, stirring often.
3. Pour into cooled pastry base; sprinkle with pecan halves. Bake conventionally for 10–15 minutes, until a knife inserted 2.5 cm from the edge comes out clean. Allow pie to cool on a rack.

Nuts can be used as a main ingredient, as in Pecan Pie (below left), or to add texture and flavour to other ingredients such as the fruit mince filling in the Fruit and Nut Tartlets (below).

FRUIT AND NUT TARTLETS

Colour Index page 95. 2863 kJ each. Low in cholesterol. Good source of thiamine, calcium, iron, fibre.
Begin 2½ hours ahead.

Ingredients for 10 tartlets		Microwave cookware
Double quantity of uncooked pastry for Flan Shell (page 335) Milk 750 g prepared fruit mince 1 large cooking apple, peeled, cored and diced	1 cup shelled walnuts, coarsely chopped ½ cup brown sugar 1 tablespoon lemon juice ¼ cup brandy or rum (optional)	2-litre glass jug or bowl

1 Preheat conventional oven to 220°C. On a lightly floured surface, with floured rolling pin, roll pastry 3 mm thick. Cut out 10 rounds with a floured 10-cm-round biscuit cutter. Reserve pastry trimmings.

2 Gently press each round into 7.5-cm fluted tartlet tins. Prick pastry several times with a fork. Arrange tins in 2 baking dishes for ease of handling.

3 Bake conventionally for 20–25 minutes, until pastry is golden. Leave oven on 220°C. Allow tartlet shells to cool on a rack for 10 minutes. Loosen tartlet shells from tins with a knife. Carefully remove pastry and place on rack. Allow to cool completely.

4 Meanwhile, reroll pastry trimmings. Cut out decorative shapes and place on a baking tray; brush with milk. Bake conventionally for 15–20 minutes, until golden. Allow to cool on a rack.

5 Combine fruit mince, apple, walnuts, brown sugar and lemon juice in glass jug. Stir in brandy or rum, if using. Cook, covered, on High (100% power) for 5 minutes, stirring twice. Uncover; stir. Cook on High for 5–7 minutes longer, until apple is tender and flavours are blended, stirring halfway through cooking.

6 Spoon warm fruit mixture into tartlet shells, mounding it slightly in centre; decorate with cooked pastry cut-outs. Serve warm.

Summer Pie Party

Iced fruit cup
Minty Chocolate Tart (page 342)
Strawberry Chiffon Pie (page 341)
Lemon Meringue Pie (page 339)
Summer Fruit Tart (page 338)
Peaches and Cream Pie (page 339)
Raspberry Custard Tart (page 338)
Summer berry selection

PREPARATION TIMETABLE

1 day ahead:	**Early in day:**	**About 2 hours ahead:**	**Just before serving:**
Make Minty Chocolate Tart but do not decorate; cover and refrigerate. Prepare Strawberry Chiffon Pie up to the end of step 5; cover and refrigerate. Prepare pastry bases and crumb crusts for remaining pies and tarts; cover and refrigerate. Prepare fruit cup; cover and refrigerate.	*Make custard and cream fillings for Lemon Meringue Pie, Summer Fruit Tart and Peaches and Cream Pie; fill, cover and refrigerate.*	*Make custard filling for Raspberry Custard Tart; fill, cover and refrigerate. Complete Strawberry Chiffon Pie, Lemon Meringue Pie, Summer Fruit Tart and Peaches and Cream Pie. Arrange a selection of summer berries in a bowl; cover and refrigerate.*	*Garnish Minty Chocolate Tart. Top Raspberry Custard Tart with raspberries. Remove summer berries from refrigerator. Place ice cubes, citrus fruit slices and mint sprigs in glasses for fruit cup.*

Cakes, Biscuits and Sweets

**MUFFINS · FRUIT LOAVES
SIMPLE CAKES · SPECIAL CAKES · CHEESECAKES
SLICES · BISCUITS · CAKE DECORATIONS
HARD SWEETS · SOFT SWEETS · POPCORN**

Cakes, Biscuits and Sweets

Cakes cooked in the microwave are light textured, moist and delicious. In keeping with the time-saving qualities of microwave cooking, this chapter includes a range of cakes based on packet mixes as well as on a simple sponge. You can produce family-pleasing cakes each time you bake in the microwave by following a few simple tips: elevate the cake dishes on a trivet or rack, or on ramekins turned upside down, and rotate dishes halfway through cooking so that cakes will be cooked evenly throughout. Cakes should be removed from the microwave when they spring back if lightly touched with a finger. Any moist spots on the top of the cake will dry during the standing time in the dish, and the cake will begin to pull away from the sides of the dish by the end of the standing time. The cake is completely cooked when a toothpick inserted in the centre comes out clean.

To cool a cake after standing time, invert it on to a wire rack and remove the lining paper. To keep moist, wrap cakes when completely cool.

In addition to large family-sized cakes and gâteaux for special occasions, a wide range of fruit loaves, slices and biscuits can be made very quickly. These delicious snacks will keep for days in an airtight container; fruit loaves wrapped in plastic wrap will stay fresh for up to 1 week if refrigerated. When removed from the oven, biscuits will be soft; allow them to stand as instructed, then place them carefully on a wire rack to cool completely and become crisp and firm. Plain biscuits and cakes can be made to look more appealing or tailored to specific occasions with the decorations featured on pages 366–367.

Confectionery mixtures cook quickly and cleanly in the microwave, and washing up afterwards is much easier than it is when making sweets by the conventional methods. When boiling sugar mixtures for fudge or other sweets in the microwave, it is important to use a large container – the mixture tends to boil up – and to cook them to exactly the right stage. The Cold Water Test (page 369) provides an accurate and simple way to judge when the correct temperature has been reached, and it requires no special equipment.

PRETTY GIFTS

Use the microwave oven to make Christmas baking easier than ever.
Make any of the delicious biscuits and sweets from this chapter,
then pack them in pretty tins and boxes lined with colourful paper.
These gifts will be as much fun to give as receive.

Pistachio Bites (page 372), Chocolate Marshmallow Fudge (page 371) and Mint Imperials (page 369) arranged in a heart-shaped tin (left).

Mint Imperials (page 369) and Tiny Chocolate Cones (page 325) are packed together to make an attractive gift (right).

Muffins

BANANA MUFFINS

Colour Index page 97. Makes 12. 343 kJ each. Low in cholesterol, sodium.
Begin 25 minutes ahead.

⅔ cup plain flour	1½ tablespoons milk
1 teaspoon baking powder	1 cup mashed banana (about 2 very ripe medium bananas)
2 tablespoons sugar	
¼ teaspoon salt	¼ teaspoon ground cinnamon
½ teaspoon grated orange rind	
1 egg yolk	⅛ teaspoon ground nutmeg
1½ tablespoons butter, melted	

1. Combine flour, baking powder, 1½ tablespoons sugar, salt and orange rind in a large bowl.
2. Combine egg yolk, butter, milk and mashed banana in a 4-cup glass jug until blended. Add banana mixture all at once to flour mixture. Stir just until flour is moistened.
3. Line 6 muffin-pan cups with a double thickness of paper patty cases. Spoon half the batter into muffin-pan cups, filling only half full.
4. Combine remaining sugar, cinnamon and nutmeg in a bowl. Sprinkle muffins with half the topping mixture. Cook on High (100% power) for time in Chart (right), rotating pan halfway through cooking. Lift muffins from muffin-pan cups; remove paper cases. Place muffins on a rack to cool. Repeat with remaining mixture.

GINGER MUFFINS

Colour Index page 97. Makes 12. 954 kJ each. Low in sodium.
Begin 20 minutes ahead.

1½ cups plain flour	¼ teaspoon ground nutmeg
½ cup brown sugar	
1 teaspoon bicarbonate of soda	125 g butter or margarine
¼ teaspoon salt	2 eggs
1 teaspoon ground ginger	½ cup sour cream
½ teaspoon ground cinnamon	½ cup golden syrup or treacle
¼ teaspoon ground cloves	

1. Combine flour, brown sugar, bicarbonate of soda, salt, ginger, cinnamon, cloves and nutmeg in a large bowl; put aside.
2. Heat butter in a 4-cup glass jug, covered with paper towel, on High (100% power) for 2 minutes, or until melted. Allow to cool slightly. Beat in eggs, sour cream and golden syrup until blended. Pour egg mixture all at once into flour mixture. Stir just until flour is moistened.
3. Line 6 muffin-pan cups with a double thickness of paper patty cases. Spoon half the batter into muffin-pan cups, filling only half full. Cook on High for time in Chart (right), rotating pan halfway through cooking. Lift muffins from muffin-pan cups; remove outer cases. Place muffins on a rack to cool. Repeat with remaining mixture.

Quick and Easy Muffins

Use the microwave to make quick and easy American-style muffins, either from a muffin mix (below) or from one of the original recipes (left). Line each muffin-pan cup with a double thickness of paper patty cases and fill only half full. If you do not have a muffin pan, use ¾-cup ramekins lined with a double thickness of paper cases. For even cooking, arrange in a circle, 12 mm apart; rearrange halfway through cooking. Muffins made in the microwave are best eaten fresh, but they can be frozen and then reheated (see Chart, below).

MUFFINS FROM A MIX

Makes 14 muffins. 787 kJ each. Low in cholesterol.
Begin 25 minutes ahead.

500 g packet muffin mix
1 egg
¼ cup cold water
½ cup natural low-fat yoghurt

1. Pour muffin mix into a large bowl.
2. Beat egg, water and yoghurt in a 4-cup glass jug. Pour into muffin mix. Stir just until mix is moistened.
3. Line 6 muffin-pan cups with a double thickness of paper patty cases. Spoon half the batter into muffin-pan cups, filling only half full. Cook on High (100% power) according to Chart (below).
4. Lift muffins from muffin-pan cups; remove outer papers. Place muffins on a rack to cool.
5. Reline muffin-pan cups and repeat with remaining batter.

COOKING AND REHEATING MUFFINS IN THE MICROWAVE

You can use your own recipe for muffins, following this Chart for timing. Or, for 'just-baked' freshness, wrap frozen muffins in paper towel and reheat in the microwave for time in Chart. If you are cooking or reheating only 1 muffin, be sure to place it in the centre of the oven floor.

Muffins	Cooking from a mix and homemade on High (100% power)	Defrosting and reheating on High (100% power)
1 muffin	30–45 seconds	10–15 seconds
2 muffins	45 seconds–1¼ (1:15) minutes	20–30 seconds
4 muffins	1½ (1:30)–2 minutes	45 seconds–1 minute
6 muffins	2½ (2:30)–3 minutes	1–1½ (1:30) minutes

Fruit loaves

Fruit loaves are traditionally served sliced, with pats of butter or margarine. They are always popular as a snack with tea or coffee, or as an after-school treat. For a nice change, try them with one of the Fruit-Flavoured Butters on page 322. Zucchini Loaf (below) is especially nice when served with Orange Butter.

ZUCCHINI LOAF

Colour Index page 97. 661 kJ per serving. Good source of fibre.
Begin 35 minutes ahead.

Ingredients for 12 servings		Microwave cookware
1 cup plain flour 1/3 cup cornflake crumbs 3/4 cup sugar 1 1/2 teaspoons baking powder 1/2 teaspoon salt 1/2 cup chopped walnuts 2 tablespoons poppy seeds	2 eggs 1/3 cup vegetable oil 125 g zucchini, shredded (1 cup) 1 teaspoon grated lemon rind	23-cm x 12.5-cm glass loaf dish Trivet, rack or ramekins

1 Line bottom of loaf dish with paper towel. Put aside.

2 Combine flour, cornflake crumbs, sugar, baking powder, salt, walnuts and poppy seeds in a large bowl.

3 Beat eggs in a 4-cup glass jug. Stir in oil, zucchini and lemon rind.

4 Pour zucchini mixture all at once into flour mixture. Stir just until flour is moistened.

5 Spoon mixture into prepared loaf dish. Elevate on a trivet, rack or ramekins turned upside down. Cook, covered loosely with greaseproof paper, on Medium (50% power) for 7–10 minutes, until loaf springs back when lightly touched with a finger, rotating pan a quarter turn every 2 minutes.

6 Allow loaf to stand in dish on a heatproof surface for 10 minutes. Invert on to a rack; carefully remove paper; turn loaf right way up. Allow to cool.

BERRY AND WALNUT LOAF

Colour Index page 97. 12 servings. 762 kJ per serving. Low in cholesterol, sodium.
Begin 40 minutes ahead.

1/2 cup plain flour 90 g plain sweet biscuits (about 3/4 cup crumbs) 1/2 teaspoon bicarbonate of soda 1/2 teaspoon baking powder 1/2 cup packed brown sugar	1/2 cup chopped walnuts 1 cup fresh blueberries, coarsely chopped 1 tablespoon grated orange rind 1 egg 1/2 cup milk 1/3 cup vegetable oil 1/4 cup orange juice

1. Line bottom of a 23-cm x 12.5-cm glass loaf dish with paper towel; put aside.
2. Combine flour, biscuit crumbs, bicarbonate of soda, baking powder and sugar in a large bowl. Add walnuts, blueberries and orange rind.
3. Beat egg, milk, oil and orange juice in a 4-cup glass jug until blended. Pour egg mixture into flour mixture. Stir just until flour is moistened.
4. Spoon mixture into prepared dish. Elevate on a trivet, rack or ramekins turned upside down. Cook, covered loosely with greaseproof paper, on Medium (50% power) for 7–10 minutes, until loaf springs back when lightly touched with a finger, rotating dish a quarter turn every 2 minutes.
5. Allow loaf to stand in dish for 10 minutes. Invert on to a rack; carefully remove paper. Turn right way up; allow to cool.

DATE AND NUT LOAF

Colour Index page 97. 12 servings. 766 kJ per serving. Good source of thiamine, calcium.
Begin 45 minutes ahead.

90 g butter 1/2 cup brown sugar 2/3 cup milk 1 egg, beaten 1 cup plain flour 1 cup self-raising flour	1 teaspoon baking powder 1 teaspoon mixed spice 1/2 teaspoon salt 3/4 cup chopped dates 1/2 cup chopped walnuts

1. Line bottom of a 23-cm x 12.5-cm glass loaf dish with paper towel; put aside.
2. Cream butter and sugar in a large bowl until light and fluffy. Gradually beat in milk and egg.
3. Combine plain flour, self-raising flour, baking powder, mixed spice and salt in a medium bowl; fold into butter. Stir in dates and walnuts.
4. Spoon mixture into prepared loaf dish. Elevate on a trivet, rack or ramekins turned upside down. Cook, covered loosely with greaseproof paper, on Medium (50% power) for 15–20 minutes, until loaf springs back when lightly touched with a finger, rotating dish a quarter turn every 2 minutes.
5. Allow loaf to stand in dish for 10 minutes. Invert on to a rack; carefully remove paper. Turn right way up; allow to cool.

Simple cakes

CARROT AND PINEAPPLE LOAF

Colour Index page 97. 12 servings. 649 kJ per serving. Good source of vitamin A, vitamin C. Begin 25 minutes ahead.

125 g butter	1 teaspoon ground ginger
½ cup brown sugar	2 teaspoons treacle
2 eggs, beaten	1 cup crushed
1 cup plain flour	pineapple, drained
2 teaspoons baking powder	1 carrot, finely grated

1. Lightly grease a 23-cm x 12.5-cm glass loaf dish; put aside.
2. Cream butter and sugar in a large bowl until light and fluffy. Gradually beat in eggs.
3. Combine flour, baking powder and ginger in a medium bowl; fold into creamed mixture. Stir in treacle, pineapple and carrot.
4. Spoon mixture into prepared dish; smooth top. Elevate on a trivet, rack or ramekins turned upside down. Cook, loosely covered with greaseproof paper, on Medium (50% power) for 6 minutes. Increase power level to High (100% power) and cook for 6–7 minutes longer, until loaf springs back when lightly touched with a finger, rotating dish 3–4 times.
5. Allow loaf to stand in dish for 10 minutes. Invert on to a rack; turn right way up. Cool.

GINGERBREAD

Colour Index page 97. 12 servings. 787 kJ per serving. Good source of calcium, iron. Begin 55 minutes ahead.

1 cup plain flour	1 teaspoon mixed spice
½ cup self-raising flour	125 g butter
½ cup brown sugar	2 eggs
1 teaspoon bicarbonate of soda	⅓ cup sour cream
1 teaspoon ground ginger	3 tablespoons treacle

1. Lightly grease a 23-cm x 12.5-cm glass loaf dish; put aside.
2. Combine plain flour, self-raising flour, sugar, bicarbonate of soda, ginger and mixed spice in a mixing bowl.
3. Heat butter in a 1-cup glass jug, covered with paper towel, on High (100% power) for 2–3 minutes, just until melted. Cool slightly; beat in eggs, sour cream and treacle.
4. Make a well in the centre of flour. Pour in egg mixture; stir until blended. Pour into prepared dish; smooth top. Elevate dish on a trivet, rack or ramekins turned upside down; shield corners with smooth pieces of foil.
5. Cook gingerbread on Medium-High (70% power) for 12–15 minutes, until top springs back when lightly touched with a finger, rotating dish a quarter turn every 2 minutes and removing foil halfway through cooking.
6. Allow loaf to stand in dish for 7 minutes. Invert on to a rack; turn right way up. Cool.

PINEAPPLE UPSIDE-DOWN CAKE

Colour Index page 98. 1787 kJ per serving. Good source of iron. Begin 1¼ hours ahead.

Pineapple Upside-Down Cake is an old-time favourite as well as one of the most popular choices for novice cooks. It is quick and easy to make in the microwave oven, and it rises just as well as when conventionally baked. Whipped cream or vanilla ice cream is the perfect accompaniment.

Ingredients for 8 servings		Microwave cookware
1¼ cups packed brown sugar	2 eggs	33-cm x 23-cm baking dish
250 g butter or margarine	1 teaspoon vanilla essence	Trivet, rack or ramekins
450 g can pineapple slices, drained	Yellow food colouring	
Maraschino cherries	1½ cups self-raising flour	
½ cup caster sugar	2 tablespoons milk	

1 Place brown sugar and 125 g butter in baking dish. Cook on High (100% power) for 3–5 minutes, until butter has melted, stirring twice.

2 Arrange pineapple slices in sugar mixture. Place 1 maraschino cherry in centre of each slice and, if you like, place extra cherries between slices. Put aside.

3 With mixer at low speed, beat caster sugar and remaining butter in a large bowl until light and fluffy, occasionally scraping bowl. Gradually beat in eggs, vanilla essence and 1–2 drops food colouring. Gently fold in flour alternately with milk, until blended. Carefully pour over fruit in baking dish; smooth surface.

4 Elevate baking dish on a trivet, rack or ramekins turned upside down. Cook on High for 10–12 minutes, until cake springs back when lightly touched with a finger, rotating dish halfway through cooking.

5 Allow cake to stand in dish on a heatproof surface for 10 minutes. Loosen cake from sides of dish with a knife. Invert dish on to a serving platter; carefully unmould cake.

6 Cut cake into 8 portions. Serve warm or cover and refrigerate to serve chilled later.

CARROT CAKE

Colour Index page 100. 2543 kJ per serving (1955 kJ without frosting). Good source of vitamin A, calcium, iron.
Begin 3 hours ahead or early in day.

Ingredients for 10 servings		Microwave cookware
1½ cups self-raising flour	2 eggs	21-cm round cake dish
¾ cup caster sugar	½ cup vegetable oil	Medium bowl
1 teaspoon bicarbonate of soda	3 medium carrots, peeled and grated (1½ cups)	Trivet, rack or ramekin
1 teaspoon baking powder	¼ cup sultanas	
1 teaspoon ground cinnamon	¼ cup chopped walnuts	
½ teaspoon ground allspice	125 g cream cheese	
½ teaspoon ground nutmeg	1 tablespoon milk	
½ teaspoon ground ginger	1½ cups icing sugar	
	1 teaspoon vanilla essence	
	Walnut halves to decorate	

1 Grease bottom and sides of cake dish; line bottom with nonstick baking paper or greaseproof paper. Combine flour, sugar, bicarbonate of soda, baking powder, cinnamon, allspice, nutmeg and ginger in a large mixing bowl.

2 Beat eggs with oil in a smaller bowl. Add egg mixture to flour mixture and, with mixer at low speed, beat for 30 seconds, or until well blended, constantly scraping bowl. Stir in carrots, sultanas and walnuts.

3 Spoon half the mixture into prepared dish; smooth surface. Elevate on a trivet, rack or ramekin turned upside down. Cook on High (100% power) for 4–6 minutes, until cake springs back when lightly touched with a finger, rotating dish halfway through cooking.

4 Allow cake to stand in dish for 5 minutes. Invert cake on to a rack; remove lining paper. Allow cake to cool completely. Meanwhile, grease and line dish again. Spoon in remaining mixture; smooth surface. Cook and cool as for first cake layer.

5 Prepare Cream Cheese Frosting: Heat cream cheese in bowl on Medium (50% power) for 1–2 minutes, until softened. With mixer on low speed, beat in milk until smooth. Gradually add icing sugar and vanilla essence; beat until smooth.

6 Place 1 cake layer, rounded side down, on a serving platter; spread with frosting. Top with second layer, rounded side up. Cover top and sides of cake with remaining frosting. Decorate with walnut halves.

VICTORIA SPONGE

Colour Index page 98. 12 servings. 1494 kJ per serving. Good source of vitamin A, calcium.
Begin 3 hours ahead or early in day.

185 g butter or margarine, softened
¾ cup caster sugar
3 eggs, beaten
½ teaspoon vanilla essence
Yellow food colouring (optional)

1½ cups self-raising flour
½ teaspoon baking powder
3 tablespoons milk
¾ cup cream
¾ cup strawberry jam
Icing sugar for dusting

1. Grease bottom and sides of a 23-cm round cake dish; line the bottom with paper towel or greaseproof paper.
2. With mixer at low speed, beat butter and sugar until light and fluffy, occasionally scraping bowl.
3. Gradually beat eggs, vanilla essence and, if you like, 1–2 drops yellow food colouring, into butter mixture. Gently fold in flour and baking powder alternately with milk; mixture should have soft, dropping consistency.
4. Spoon half the mixture into prepared dish; smooth surface. Elevate dish on a trivet, rack or ramekin turned upside down. Cook on High (100% power) for 2½ (2:30)–3½ (3:30) minutes, until cake springs back when lightly touched with a finger, rotating dish halfway through cooking.
5. Allow cake to stand in dish on a heatproof surface for 5 minutes. Invert cake on to a rack, remove lining paper; leave cake to cool completely.
6. Grease and line dish again. Spoon in remaining mixture; smooth surface. Cook and cool as for first cake layer.
7. With mixer at medium speed, whip cream in a small bowl until soft peaks form.
8. Place 1 cake layer, rounded side down, on a serving plate; spread with strawberry jam. Spread cream on top of jam; top with second cake layer, rounded side up. Dust top of cake with icing sugar. Refrigerate until ready to serve.

MAKING SPONGE CAKES
Both homemade and packet sponge mixtures cook beautifully in the microwave, but while they rise well they will not brown. If you do not intend to ice or otherwise decorate the sponge, grease the cake dish then coat with dried breadcrumbs or toasted desiccated coconut before adding the cake mixture. This will give a more appetising appearance to plain sponges.

SUNNY ORANGE LAYER CAKE

Colour Index page 100. 10 servings. 1633 kJ per serving. Good source of vitamin C, calcium. Begin early in day.

½ quantity Lemon Butter (below)	1 egg
370 g packet yellow cake mix	1 teaspoon grated orange rind
⅓ cup frozen orange juice concentrate, thawed	Orange Whipped Cream (page 342)
⅓ cup plus 1 tablespoon water	Mandarin segments to decorate

1. Prepare Lemon Butter. Line the bottom of a 23-cm x 5-cm round cake dish with greaseproof paper.
2. Combine cake mix, orange juice, water, egg and orange rind in a large bowl. With mixer at low speed, beat for 2 minutes.
3. Spoon mixture into prepared dish; smooth surface. Elevate on a trivet, rack or ramekin turned upside down. Cook on High (100% power) for 5–5½ (5:30) minutes, until cake springs back when lightly touched with a finger, rotating dish halfway through cooking.
4. Allow cake to stand in dish on a heatproof surface for 5 minutes. Invert cake on to a rack and remove lining paper; allow to cool completely.
5. Using a serrated knife, slice cake in half horizontally. Prepare Orange Whipped Cream.
6. Place 1 cake layer, cut side up, on a serving plate; spread with Lemon Butter. Top with remaining cake layer, rounded side up. Spread Orange Whipped Cream over top and sides of cake; chill for 15 minutes. Decorate with mandarin segments just before serving.

LEMON BUTTER: Combine *1 tablespoon grated lemon rind, 2 tablespoons lemon juice, 185 g butter or margarine* and *1 cup sugar* in a 4-cup glass jug. Cook on High (100% power) for 1–2 minutes, until butter has melted, stirring once. Beat *3 eggs* in a small bowl. Stir a small amount of hot butter mixture into beaten eggs. Slowly pour egg mixture back into remaining hot butter mixture, beating rapidly to prevent lumping. Cook on Medium (50% power) for 2–3 minutes, until mixture is very thick, stirring occasionally. Do not boil or mixture will curdle. Lightly press plastic wrap or dampened greaseproof paper on to surface to prevent a skin from forming. Refrigerate for about 3 hours, until well chilled. Makes enough to fill two 2-layer cakes. 9397 kJ.

TWO-TONED LAYER CAKE

Colour Index page 98. 1984 kJ per serving. Good source of calcium, iron. Begin 3 hours ahead or early in day.

Ingredients for 12 servings		Microwave cookware
370 g packet yellow cake mix	1 quantity Rich Chocolate Mousse (page 326)	23-cm x 5-cm round cake dish
1½ cups water	Chocolate Cream (page 357)	Trivet, rack or ramekin
2 eggs		
370 g packet chocolate cake mix		

1 Line bottom of cake dish with greaseproof paper. With mixer at low speed, beat yellow cake mix, half the water and 1 egg until blended. Increase speed to high; beat for 2 minutes. Spoon mixture into prepared dish; smooth surface.

2 Elevate cake dish on a trivet, rack or ramekin turned upside down. Cook on High (100% power) for 5–5½ (5:30) minutes, until cake springs back when lightly touched with a finger, rotating dish halfway through cooking.

3 Allow cake to stand in dish on a heatproof surface for 5 minutes. Invert cake on to a rack; remove lining paper. Allow to cool completely.

4 Meanwhile, line cake dish again. Prepare chocolate mixture, using mix, remaining water and egg. Spoon into dish; smooth surface. Cook and cool as for first cake layer. Meanwhile, prepare Rich Chocolate Mousse; cover and refrigerate until chilled.

5 Prepare Chocolate Cream. Using a serrated knife, slice each cake layer in half horizontally.

6 Place 1 yellow cake layer, cut side up, on a serving platter. Spread with one-third of Rich Chocolate Mousse. Top with 1 chocolate cake layer, cut side down; spread with half the remaining Rich Chocolate Mousse. Repeat layering, ending with chocolate cake layer. Cover top and sides of cake with Chocolate Cream. Cover loosely with greaseproof paper and refrigerate to serve chilled.

STRAWBERRY CREAM LAYER CAKE

Colour Index page 99. 2499 kJ per serving. Good source of vitamin A, riboflavin, thiamine, vitamin C, calcium, iron, fibre.
Begin 3 hours ahead.

Ingredients for 8 servings		Microwave cookware
Ingredients for Victoria Sponge (page 352) *2 punnets strawberries, hulled and cut into quarters lengthways* *2 tablespoons sugar*	*1½ cups thickened cream* *2 tablespoons icing sugar* *1 teaspoon vanilla essence* *10 whole strawberries to decorate*	23-cm x 5-cm round cake dish Trivet, rack or ramekin

1 Grease bottom and sides of cake dish; line bottom with nonstick baking paper or greaseproof paper. Prepare mixture for Victoria Sponge.

2 Spoon one-third of cake mixture into prepared dish; smooth surface. Elevate on a trivet, rack or ramekin turned upside down. Cook on High (100% power) for 1½ (1:30)–2½ (2:30) minutes, until cake springs back when lightly touched with a finger, rotating dish halfway through cooking. Allow cake to stand in dish on a heatproof surface for 5 minutes.

3 Invert cake on to a rack; remove lining paper. Allow cake to cool completely. Meanwhile, grease and line dish again. Spoon in half the remaining cake mixture; smooth surface. Cook and cool as for first cake layer. Repeat with remaining mixture to make 3 cake layers altogether.

4 Place quartered strawberries and sugar in a small bowl. Stir gently until sugar dissolves; put aside. In another small bowl, with mixer at medium speed, beat cream, icing sugar and vanilla essence until soft peaks form.

5 Place 1 cake layer, rounded side down, on a serving platter. Spread with one-third of whipped cream; top with half the strawberry mixture. Place second cake layer on top of strawberries. Spread with half the whipped cream and top with remaining strawberries. Cover with remaining cake; spread with remaining whipped cream.

6 Arrange largest whole strawberry in centre of cake. Hull remaining strawberries, cut in half lengthways and place around edge of cake. Refrigerate if not serving immediately.

APPLE SPICE CAKE

Colour Index page 100. 6 servings. 1775 kJ per serving. Good source of iron.
Begin 1¼ hours ahead.

370 g packet yellow cake mix
1 teaspoon ground cinnamon
⅛ teaspoon ground cloves
⅛ teaspoon ground nutmeg
½ cup Apple Purée (below)
2 tablespoons butter, melted

1 egg
1 apple, peeled, cored and sliced
¼ cup plain flour
¼ cup packed brown sugar
30 g butter or margarine, cubed
½ cup chopped walnuts
Glacé Icing (below)

1. Lightly grease the bottom of a 23-cm x 5-cm round cake dish.
2. With mixer at low speed, beat cake mix, ½ teaspoon cinnamon, cloves, nutmeg, Apple Purée, melted butter and egg in a large bowl until blended, constantly scraping bowl. Increase speed to high; beat 2 minutes, occasionally scraping bowl.
3. Pour batter into prepared cake dish; smooth surface. Arrange apple slices on top of mixture.
4. In food processor with knife blade attached or in blender, process flour, brown sugar and remaining cinnamon. Add butter; process until mixture resembles coarse crumbs. (Or use fingertips.) Stir in walnuts. Sprinkle topping over apples in dish. Elevate on a trivet, rack or ramekin turned upside down.
5. Cook on High (100% power) for 6–8 minutes, until cake springs back when lightly touched with a finger, rotating the dish halfway through cooking. Allow cake to stand in dish on a heatproof surface for 5 minutes.
6. Prepare Glacé Icing. Drizzle over top of cake. Serve warm or cover loosely and refrigerate to serve chilled later.

GLACÉ ICING: Combine *¾ cup icing sugar* and *3 teaspoons milk* in a small bowl. Use immediately. Makes ¾ cup. 138 kJ per tablespoon.

APPLE PURÉE: Cut *6 medium cooking apples* into quarters; do not peel or core. Place in a 2-litre casserole with *¼ cup water*. Cook, covered, on High (100% power) for 10–15 minutes, until tender. Press apples through a strainer; discard skin and seeds. Add *⅓ cup sugar* and *1 teaspoon lemon juice* to purée; stir to dissolve sugar. Cover and refrigerate. Makes 4 cups. 753 kJ per cup.

CHOCOLATE CREAM SPONGE

Colour Index page 99. 12 servings. 1478 kJ per serving. Good source of vitamin A, riboflavin, calcium.
Begin 2 hours ahead or early in day.

Ingredients for Victoria Sponge (page 352)
Chocolate Glaze (below)
Glacé Icing (page 354)
½ quantity of Crème Pâtissière (page 337)

1. Grease bottom and sides of a 23-cm x 5-cm round cake dish; line bottom with nonstick baking paper or greaseproof paper.
2. Prepare mixture for Victoria Sponge. Spoon half of cake mixture into prepared dish; smooth surface. Elevate dish on a trivet, rack or ramekin turned upside down. Cook on High (100% power) for 2½ (2:30)–3½ (3:30) minutes, until cake springs back when lightly touched with a finger, rotating dish halfway through cooking.
3. Allow cake to stand in dish on a heatproof surface for 5 minutes. Invert cake on to a rack; remove lining paper. Allow cake to cool completely.
4. Meanwhile, grease and line dish again. Spoon in remaining cake mixture; smooth surface. Cook and cool as for first cake layer.
5. Make Chocolate Glaze and Glacé Icing. Place 1 cake layer, rounded side down, on a serving platter. Spread with Crème Pâtissière. Top with second cake layer, rounded side up. Cover top of cake with Chocolate Glaze; feather with Glacé Icing. Refrigerate for at least 15 minutes before serving.

CHOCOLATE GLAZE: Place **90 g dark chocolate bits (½ cup), 15 g butter, 1½ teaspoons milk** and **1½ teaspoons golden syrup** in a 4-cup glass jug. Cook on High for 2–3 minutes, until chocolate melts, stirring once. Remove from oven; stir until smooth.

Feathering with the Glacé Icing

Spoon Glacé Icing in a piping bag fitted with a small round tube and pipe parallel lines at regular intervals over top of cake.

Hold a skewer or the tip of a knife at right angles to piped lines. Starting at edge, draw lines at same regular intervals over top of cake, alternating direction of lines.

Meal in Minutes *for 6 people*

Afternoon Tea Party

Strawberry Cream Layer Cake (page 354)
Lemon Tuiles (page 364)
Assorted sandwiches of your choice
Tea with milk or lemon

PREPARATION TIMETABLE

Early in day:	*Make Lemon Tuiles; store in an airtight container. Make cake for Strawberry Cream Layer Cake; cool and wrap in plastic wrap.*
2 hours ahead:	*Prepare a selection of sandwiches with white and wholemeal bread and fillings of your choice, such as smoked salmon, thinly sliced cucumber, egg mayonnaise and thinly sliced ham. Cut off crusts, then cut diagonally into quarters to make triangles; wrap in plastic wrap and refrigerate.*
30 minutes ahead:	*Fill small jugs with milk and cut lemon slices for tea; cover and refrigerate. Complete Strawberry Cream Layer Cake.*
Just before serving:	*Arrange Lemon Tuiles and sandwiches on attractive serving plates. Make tea.*

Special cakes

BLACK FOREST CAKE

Colour Index page 99. 1846 kJ per serving. Good source of vitamin A.
Begin early in day.

Ingredients for 12 servings		Microwave cookware
510 g packet devil's food cake mix	*125 g dark cooking chocolate*	23-cm x 5-cm round cake dish
1⅓ cups water	*1½ cups thickened cream*	Trivet, rack or ramekin
⅓ cup vegetable oil	*1 tablespoon caster sugar*	
3 eggs	*Maraschino cherries and*	
425 g can pitted black cherries	*Chocolate Curls (page 358) to decorate*	
3 tablespoons kirsch		

1 Grease bottom and sides of cake dish; line bottom with nonstick baking paper or greaseproof paper. With mixer at low speed, beat cake mix, water, oil and eggs in a large bowl until blended, constantly scraping bowl. Increase speed to medium; beat for 2 minutes, occasionally scraping bowl.

2 Spoon half the mixture into prepared dish; smooth surface. Elevate dish on a trivet, rack or ramekin turned upside down. Cook on High (100% power) for 6–8 minutes, until cake springs back when lightly touched with a finger, rotating dish halfway through cooking.

3 Allow cake to stand in dish on a heatproof surface for 5 minutes. Invert cake on to a rack; remove lining paper. Allow cake to cool completely. Meanwhile, grease and line baking dish again. Spoon in remaining cake mixture; smooth surface. Cook and cool as for first cake layer.

DECORATING THE CAKE
A simple packet cake mix can be turned into something that looks really special with a decoration of cream, chocolate and maraschino cherries.

Using a spoon, gently press grated chocolate on to the sides of the cream-covered cake until evenly coated.

Spoon remaining whipped cream into a piping bag fitted with a medium star tube.

Pipe a decorative border around the top edge of the cake.

Decorate the top of the cake with maraschino cherries and Chocolate Curls.

4 Drain cherries, reserving 2 tablespoons syrup. Cut each cherry in half; put aside. Combine reserved syrup and 2 tablespoons kirsch in a small bowl; put aside.

5 With hand grater or in food processor with grating disc attached, coarsely grate chocolate; put aside.

6 Place 1 cake layer, rounded side down, on a serving platter. Prick with a fork. Evenly spoon over half the syrup mixture. With mixer at medium speed, beat cream, sugar and remaining kirsch in a small bowl until soft peaks form.

7 Evenly spread one-quarter of whipped cream over cake layer. Spoon cherries on to cream. Top with remaining cake layer, rounded side up. Prick top with a fork; spoon over remaining syrup.

8 Cover top and sides of cake with two-thirds of remaining whipped cream. Decorate with grated chocolate, remaining whipped cream, maraschino cherries and Chocolate Curls (see Box, above). Cover loosely and keep refrigerated until ready to serve.

Use the microwave to make the different stages of cake-making quick and easy, as in this version of the classic French Christmas cake, Bûche de Noël (below).

BÛCHE DE NOËL

Colour Index page 99. 1716 kJ per serving. Good source of iron.
Begin 3½ hours ahead or early in day.

Ingredients for 14 servings		Microwave cookware
125 g butter, softened ½ cup caster sugar 3 eggs, separated 1 cup self-raising flour 2 tablespoons ground almonds	1 cup cocoa ½ cup milk Ingredients for Rich Chocolate Mousse (page 326) Chocolate Cream (right)	35-cm x 28-cm shallow baking dish or tray Trivet, rack or ramekins

CHOCOLATE CREAM
Using this frosting or its variations is an easy way to dress up a plain cake.

Heat ¾ *cup cream* in a medium bowl on High (100% power) for 2–4 minutes, until small bubbles form around edge. Add *375 g chopped dark cooking chocolate*; stir until melted; add *1 teaspoon vanilla essence*. Cover and refrigerate.

With mixer at medium speed, beat chocolate mixture until fluffy and thick enough to spread. Makes enough to cover one 2-layer cake. 9435 kJ.

Orange Chocolate Cream: Prepare frosting (above), adding *1 tablespoon grated orange rind* with the vanilla essence.

Almond Chocolate Cream: Prepare frosting (above), substituting *1 teaspoon almond essence* for the vanilla essence.

Rum Chocolate Cream: Prepare frosting (above), substituting *1 teaspoon rum or rum essence* for the vanilla essence.

1 Line bottom of baking dish or tray with nonstick baking paper or greaseproof paper. With mixer at low speed, beat butter and all but 1 tablespoon sugar until light and fluffy. Beat in egg yolks. Mix flour, almonds and ¾ cup cocoa together in another bowl; stir into butter mixture alternately with milk.

2 With mixer at high speed, beat egg whites until soft peaks form. Gradually sprinkle in remaining sugar, beating well, until sugar has completely dissolved and whites stand in stiff, glossy peaks.

3 Gently fold beaten egg whites into cake mixture until evenly blended. Spoon mixture into prepared dish or tray.

4 Evenly spread mixture in dish or tray; smooth surface. Elevate on a trivet, rack or ramekins turned upside down. Cook on High (100% power) for 6–9 minutes, until cake springs back when lightly touched with a finger, rotating dish or tray halfway through cooking.

5 Meanwhile, evenly sift remaining cocoa on to a clean tea towel. When cake is done, immediately invert on to towel; remove lining paper. Starting from a long end, roll cake with towel, Swiss-roll fashion. Cool completely, seam side down, on a rack. Meanwhile, prepare Rich Chocolate Mousse; cover and refrigerate until chilled.

6 Carefully unroll cooled cake; spread evenly with Rich Chocolate Mousse. Starting at same long end, roll up cake without towel. Place cake, seam side down, on a serving platter. Prepare Chocolate Cream.

7 Using a serrated knife, diagonally cut an 8-cm slice from end of cake. Spread a small amount of Chocolate Cream on to diagonal side of slice. Firmly press frosted side of slice to cake about halfway down side, to form a 'branch'.

8 Cover cake with remaining Chocolate Cream. Mark frosting with a small knife to resemble bark. Keep cake refrigerated until ready to serve.

CHOCOLATE LEAVES

Makes about 20 leaves. 1804 kJ. Low in sodium.
Begin 40 minutes ahead.

90 g dark chocolate bits (½ cup)

1. You will need about 20 nontoxic leaves (rose, lemon, ivy or geranium) to use as forms. Rinse leaves and pat dry.
2. Heat chocolate in a 2-cup glass jug on High (100% power) for 1½ (1:30)–2 minutes, until melted, stirring once. Remove from oven; stir until smooth. Using a small pastry brush, brush melted chocolate on to underside of leaves. Refrigerate for about 15 minutes, or until set. With cool hands, carefully peel leaves from set chocolate.

CHOCOLATE ROUNDS

Makes about 12 x 5-cm rounds. 138 kJ each. Low in sodium.
Begin 25 minutes ahead.

60 g dark or milk cooking chocolate
1 tablespoon white vegetable shortening (Copha)

1. Line a baking tray with greaseproof paper or nonstick baking paper.
2. Place chocolate and shortening in a 2-cup glass jug. Heat on High (100% power) for 1½ (1:30) minutes, or until melted, stirring once. Remove from oven; stir until smooth.
3. Drop teaspoonfuls of hot chocolate mixture on to prepared tray. Spread out slightly with the back of a spoon. Refrigerate for about 15 minutes, or until set. Lift off with a metal spatula.

CHOCOLATE CURLS

Makes enough curls to decorate the top of a 23-cm cake. 603 kJ. Low in sodium.
Begin 15 minutes ahead.

30 g dark chocolate, in a block

1. Heat chocolate in a small bowl on High (100% power) for 15 seconds at a time, just until beginning to soften.
2. Using a vegetable peeler, draw along wide surface of chocolate to form large curls. For short curls, draw along sides of block. To avoid breaking, use a toothpick to pick up and place curls on cakes and desserts.

WHITE CHOCOLATE AND STRAWBERRY GÂTEAU

Colour Index page 100. 12 servings. 2579 kJ per serving. Good source of vitamin A, thiamine, vitamin C, calcium.
Begin early in day.

Ingredients for double quantity of White Chocolate Mousse (page 325)
Ingredients for Victoria Sponge (page 352)

3 punnets strawberries
Strawberry fans (below) to decorate

1. Prepare White Chocolate Mousse; cover with plastic wrap and refrigerate until well chilled.
2. Grease bottom and sides of a 23-cm x 5-cm round cake dish; line bottom with nonstick baking paper or greaseproof paper.
3. Prepare mixture for Victoria Sponge. Spoon half the mixture into prepared dish; smooth surface. Elevate dish on a trivet, rack or ramekin turned upside down. Cook on High (100% power) for 2½ (2:30)–3½ (3:30) minutes, until cake springs back when lightly touched with a finger, rotating dish halfway through cooking.
4. Allow cake to stand in dish on a heatproof surface for 5 minutes. Invert cake on to a rack; carefully remove lining paper. Allow cake to cool completely.
5. Meanwhile, grease and line cake dish again. Spoon in remaining cake mixture; smooth surface. Cook and cool as for first cake layer.
6. Hull and slice strawberries.
7. Place 1 cake layer, rounded side down, on a serving platter. Spread with one-third of White Chocolate Mousse. Cover with sliced strawberries. Top with remaining cake layer, rounded side up. Cover top and sides of cake with remaining White Chocolate Mousse.
8. Decoratively top with strawberry fans. Keep gâteau refrigerated until ready to serve.

Making the strawberry fans

Select firm whole strawberries with stalks. Starting just below stalk end, thinly slice each strawberry lengthways several times, leaving strawberry connected at stalk end.

With fingertips, gently press down on each strawberry to fan the slices slightly.

APRICOT CREAM ROULADE

Colour Index page 99. 14 servings. 1792 kJ per serving. Good source of iron.
Begin 3 hours ahead or early in day.

185 g butter or margarine, softened	*½ teaspoon baking powder*
¾ cup caster sugar	*3 tablespoons milk*
3 eggs, separated	*½ cup icing sugar*
1 teaspoon almond essence	*1 cup apricot jam*
1½ cups self-raising flour	*2 cups thickened cream*

1. Line bottom of a 30-cm x 23-cm baking dish or tray with nonstick baking paper or greaseproof paper.

2. With mixer at low speed, beat butter and ⅔ cup sugar until light and fluffy, occasionally scraping bowl. Beat in egg yolks and ½ teaspoon almond essence. Stir in flour and baking powder alternately with milk.

3. With mixer at high speed, beat egg whites in a medium bowl until soft peaks form. Gradually sprinkle in remaining sugar, 1 tablespoon at a time, beating well after each addition, until sugar has completely dissolved and whites stand in stiff, glossy peaks.

4. Gently fold beaten egg whites into cake mixture until blended.

5. Spoon mixture into prepared dish or tray; smooth surface. Elevate on a trivet, rack or ramekins turned upside down. Cook on High (100% power) for 6–8 minutes, until cake springs back when lightly touched with a finger, rotating dish or tray halfway through cooking.

6. Meanwhile, evenly sift ¼ cup icing sugar on to clean tea towel. When cake is done, immediately invert on to towel; remove lining paper. Starting at a short end, roll cake with towel, Swiss-roll fashion. Cool completely, seam side down, on a rack.

7. Heat apricot jam in a medium bowl on High for 2–3 minutes, until warm, stirring twice. Press through a fine sieve to make a smooth purée.

8. Carefully unroll cooled cake; spread evenly with purée. Starting at same short end, roll up cake without towel. Place cake, seam side down, on a serving platter.

9. With mixer at medium speed, beat cream, remaining icing sugar and almond essence in a large bowl until soft peaks form.

10. Spoon whipped cream into a piping bag fitted with a medium star tube. Pipe cream decoratively on to cake. Cover loosely and keep refrigerated until ready to serve.

MARBLED CHOCOLATE RING

Colour Index page 100. 16 servings. 1231 kJ per serving. Good source of calcium. Begin early in day.

This rich cake has a delicious cream-cheese filling. For a special decorative effect, dust finished cake with icing sugar and pipe whipped cream around the bottom.

Ingredients for 16 servings		Microwave cookware
250 g cream cheese, softened *⅓ cup sugar* *4 eggs* *½ teaspoon vanilla essence* *510 g packet devil's food cake mix*	*1⅓ cups water* *⅓ cup vegetable oil* *Chocolate Glaze (page 355)* *Whipped cream (optional)*	12-cup deep fluted ring mould Trivet, rack or ramekin

1 Grease ring mould. With mixer at low speed, beat cream cheese in a small bowl until smooth. Add sugar, 1 egg and vanilla essence; beat until well blended.

2 With mixer at low speed, beat cake mix, water, oil and remaining eggs in a large bowl until blended, constantly scraping bowl. Increase speed to medium; beat 2 minutes, occasionally scraping bowl.

3 Spoon one-third of mixture into prepared mould. Drop tablespoonsful of cream-cheese mixture in a ring on to cake mixture, being careful not to let cream-cheese mixture touch the side of the mould. Carefully cover cream-cheese mixture with remaining cake mixture.

4 Elevate mould on a trivet, rack or ramekin turned upside down. Cook on High (100% power) for 10–15 minutes, until cake springs back when lightly touched with a finger, rotating pan halfway through cooking.

5 Allow cake to stand in mould on a heatproof surface for 15 minutes, or until bottom of mould is almost cool. Loosen cake from side of mould with a knife. Invert mould on to a serving platter; carefully unmould cake. Allow cake to cool completely.

6 Meanwhile, make Chocolate Glaze. Drizzle glaze over cooled cake. Decorate, if you like, with cream.

CHOCOLATE PROFITEROLES

Colour Index page 98. 749 kJ each. Low in sodium.
Begin 1½ hours ahead.

Ingredients for 12 profiteroles		Microwave cookware

1 cup water
140 g butter or
  margarine
1 cup plain flour
4 eggs
90 g dark chocolate bits
1½ teaspoons milk
	1½ teaspoons corn syrup
	  or golden syrup
	Crème Pâtissière (page
	  337), chilled, or
	Vanilla Ice Cream
	  (page 332)
		2-litre glass jug or
		  bowl
		4-cup glass jug

1 Lightly brush 1 large baking tray with oil. Preheat conventional oven to 200°C.

2 Pour water into glass jug; add all but 15 g butter. Heat on High (100% power) for 5–7 minutes, until water has boiled.

3 Add flour all at once. Vigorously beat with a wooden spoon until mixture forms a ball and leaves side of jug.

4 Add eggs, one at a time, to flour mixture, beating well after each addition, until mixture is smooth and satiny. Allow to stand until slightly cooled.

5 Spoon mixture on to greased baking tray in 12 mounds, about 5 cm apart. Bake for 40 minutes, or until golden.

6 Turn off oven; allow puffs to remain in oven for 10 minutes to dry, then remove from oven and place on racks to cool.

7 Make glaze: Place chocolate bits, reserved butter, milk and corn syrup in 4-cup jug.

8 Cook chocolate mixture on High for 2–3 minutes, until chocolate has melted, stirring halfway through cooking. Remove from oven. Stir until smooth.

9 When puffs are cool, cut off tops. Fill shells with chilled Crème Pâtissière or Vanilla Ice Cream. Replace tops and drizzle with warm glaze. Serve immediately.

CHOCOLATE MOUSSE BOMBE

Colour Index page 101. 10 servings. 2516 kJ per serving. Good source of calcium, iron.
Begin early in day.

510 g packet chocolate
  fudge cake mix
1⅓ cups water
⅓ cup vegetable oil
3 eggs
Ingredients for Rich
  Chocolate Mousse
  (page 326)

2 cups thickened cream
¼ cup icing sugar
Cocoa

1. Grease a 2-litre bowl. Line bottom of bowl with a 7.5-cm circle of nonstick baking paper or greaseproof paper.
2. With mixer at low speed, beat cake mix, water, oil and eggs in a large bowl until blended, constantly scraping bowl. Increase speed to medium; beat for 2 minutes, occasionally scraping bowl. Spoon into prepared bowl; smooth surface.
3. Elevate bowl on a trivet, rack or ramekin turned upside down. Cook on High (100% power) for 9–12 minutes, until cake springs back when lightly touched with a finger, rotating bowl halfway through cooking.
4. Allow cake to stand in bowl on a heatproof surface for 10 minutes. Cover and allow to cool completely on a rack.
5. Meanwhile, prepare Rich Chocolate Mousse; cover and refrigerate.
6. Using a serrated knife, cut out centre of cake, leaving a 4-cm shell; reserve removed cake centre. Spoon chocolate mousse into centre of shell. Cut reserved cake into small chunks and press on to surface of mousse. Invert on to a serving platter. Carefully unmould cake. Cover and refrigerate until chilled.
7. With mixer at medium speed, beat cream and icing sugar in a medium bowl until soft peaks form. Spoon cream into a piping bag fitted with a medium star tube. Pipe rosettes over surface of cake. Dust with cocoa. Keep refrigerated until ready to serve.

Decorating the bombe

Pipe rows of cream rosettes to cover surface of cake.

Using a fine sieve, lightly dust cocoa over cream rosettes.

Cheesecakes

CHOCOLATE AND AMARETTI CHEESECAKE

Colour Index page 98. 12 servings. 2269 kJ per serving. Good source of vitamin A, calcium. Begin early in day or 1 day ahead.

125 g amaretti biscuits or crisp macaroons, crushed (about 1½ cups crumbs)	750 g cream cheese 1 cup sugar 3 eggs ¼ cup milk
90 g butter or margarine, melted	¼ teaspoon almond essence
90 g dark cooking chocolate, chopped	1 cup thickened cream, whipped

1. Line a 23-cm x 5-cm round cake dish with a double thickness of greaseproof paper.
2. Combine biscuit crumbs and melted butter in a mixing bowl until well blended. Press one-third of crumb mixture on to sides of prepared dish to form a crust. Put aside with remaining crumb mixture.
3. Place chocolate and cream cheese in a large bowl. Heat on Medium (50% power) for 2–3 minutes, until cream cheese has softened and chocolate melted, stirring halfway through cooking. With mixer at medium speed, beat until smooth. Add sugar, eggs, milk and almond essence; beat until blended, occasionally scraping bowl. Cook on High (100% power) for 5–8 minutes, until very hot, beating 3 times.
4. Pour cheesecake mixture into prepared dish. Lightly press remaining crumbs evenly on to surface to form a crust. Elevate the dish on a trivet, rack or ramekin turned upside down. Cook on Medium (50% power) for 6–8 minutes, until softly set. Allow to stand in dish on a heatproof surface for 30 minutes, until set. Cover and refrigerate for 4–5 hours, or overnight.
5. Loosen cheesecake from side of dish with a thin-bladed knife. Invert dish on to a serving platter. Carefully unmould cheesecake; remove lining paper.
6. Decorate cheesecake with whipped cream. Serve remaining whipped cream separately.

CHEESECAKE TOPPINGS

Dress up a basic cheesecake with a mouth-watering topping. Spread with sour cream and top with fresh fruit, such as hulled and sliced strawberries, whole blueberries or kiwifruit slices. Or brush with melted redcurrant jelly or sieved strawberry jam for an elegant glazed finish. Or use a canned fruit filling with *1 tablespoon grated lemon rind* and *½ teaspoon lemon juice* added for extra zest. Or pipe whipped cream in decorative rosettes and garnish with Chocolate Curls (page 358) or whole berries.

CREAMY CHEESECAKE

Colour Index page 98. 1758 kJ per serving. Good source of calcium. Begin early in day or 1 day ahead.

Ingredients for 12 servings		Microwave cookware
90 g butter or margarine, melted 155 g plain sweet biscuits, crushed (about 1½ cups crumbs) 1¼ cups sugar 750 g cream cheese 2 tablespoons plain flour 3 eggs	¼ cup milk 2 tablespoons grated lemon rind 1 teaspoon vanilla essence Fresh berries, or sour cream and canned pie filling for topping (optional)	1-cup glass jug 23-cm x 5-cm round cake dish Large bowl Trivet, rack or ramekin

1 Heat butter in glass jug, covered with paper towel, on High (100% power) for 1–1½ (1:30) minutes, until melted. Combine biscuit crumbs and ¼ cup sugar in a mixing bowl. Pour in melted butter; stir with a fork until well blended.

2 Lightly oil bottom and sides of cake dish with a pastry brush. Line the bottom with nonstick baking paper or a double thickness of greaseproof paper. Press one-third of crumb mixture on to sides of dish to form a crust. Put aside with remaining crumb mixture.

3 Heat cream cheese in a large bowl on Medium (50% power) for 2–3 minutes, until softened. With mixer at medium speed, beat cheese until smooth. Gradually beat in remaining sugar. With mixer at low speed, add flour, eggs, milk, lemon rind and vanilla essence; beat for 5 minutes, occasionally scraping bowl.

4 Cook cream-cheese mixture on High for 5–8 minutes, until hot, beating 3 times. Spoon into prepared cake dish, smoothing surface. Lightly press remaining crumb mixture evenly on to surface to form a crust. Elevate dish on a trivet, rack or ramekin turned upside down.

5 Cook cheesecake on Medium for 6–10 minutes, until softly set, rotating dish twice. Do not overcook or cheesecake will not be creamy. Allow to stand in dish on a heatproof surface for about 30 minutes, until set. Cover and refrigerate for at least 4 hours, until well chilled.

6 Loosen cheesecake from sides of dish with a thin-bladed knife. Invert dish on to a serving platter. Carefully unmould cheesecake; remove lining paper. If you like, spread top with fresh berries, or with sour cream and canned fruit pie filling.

Slices

It's easy to see why brownies – which take their name from the dark-brown chocolate traditionally used in making them – are one of America's favourite sweet snacks. They adapt beautifully to cooking in the microwave, turning out moist, chewy and tempting.

FUDGE BROWNIES

Colour Index page 101. 800 kJ each. Low in sodium.
Begin early in day.

Ingredients for 24 brownies		Microwave cookware
125 g butter or margarine 125 g dark cooking chocolate 2 cups sugar 4 eggs	⅔ cup plain flour 1 teaspoon vanilla essence 125 g dark chocolate bits ½ cup shelled walnuts, chopped	30-cm x 20-cm baking dish 2-litre glass jug or bowl Trivet, rack or ramekins

1 Grease baking dish; line bottom with nonstick baking paper or greaseproof paper.

2 Place butter and cooking chocolate in glass jug. Heat on High (100% power) for 1½ (1:30)–2 minutes, until melted, stirring once. Remove from oven; stir until smooth.

3 Add sugar and eggs to chocolate mixture. Beat until well blended. Stir in flour and vanilla essence until smooth. Spoon mixture evenly into prepared dish.

4 Sprinkle chocolate bits and walnuts over mixture.

5 Elevate baking dish on a trivet, rack or ramekins turned upside down. Cook on High for 5–6 minutes, just until beginning to set (do not overbake), rotating dish halfway through cooking.

6 Allow brownie mixture to stand in dish on a heatproof surface for 5 minutes. Cover and refrigerate until well chilled. Cut into 24 squares; store in an airtight container.

CREAM CHEESE BROWNIES

Colour Index page 101. Makes 16. 1329 kJ each.
Begin 2½ hours ahead.

250 g cream cheese 3 tablespoons caster sugar ½ teaspoon almond essence 3 eggs	125 g butter 1 cup brown sugar 90 g dark chocolate bits 1 cup plain flour 1 teaspoon baking powder

1. Grease two 23-cm pie plates; line bottom of each with greaseproof paper.
2. Heat cream cheese in a small bowl on Medium (50% power) for 1–2 minutes, until softened. Add caster sugar, almond essence and 1 egg; stir until smooth. Put aside.
3. Heat butter in a medium bowl on High (100% power) for 1–1½ (1:30) minutes, until melted. Stir in brown sugar and chocolate bits. Cook for 1 minute on Medium; stir well and put aside.
4. Sift flour and baking powder into a large bowl. Add cooled chocolate mixture and remaining eggs. Beat until well blended.
5. Spoon batter evenly into prepared pie plates. Drop cream-cheese mixture by spoonfuls on top of brownie mixture. With a knife, cut through mixtures to obtain a marbled effect.
6. Elevate 1 pie plate on a trivet, rack or ramekin turned upside down. Cook on High (100% power) for 5–7 minutes, until top puffs slightly, rotating pie plate halfway through cooking. Allow to cool completely in plate on a rack. Meanwhile, cook remaining mixture.
7. When cool, cut each round into 8 wedges; store in an airtight container.

MINT CHOCOLATE SQUARES

Colour Index page 101. Makes 24. 975 kJ each. Low in sodium.
Begin 2½ hours ahead.

185 g mint-flavoured chocolates (not filled) 185 g dark chocolate bits 60 g butter or margarine 250 g plain sweet biscuits, crushed (about 2½ cups crumbs)	1½ cups shelled walnuts, chopped 400 g can sweetened condensed milk 1 teaspoon vanilla essence

1. Grease a 30-cm x 20-cm baking dish; flour.
2. Place mint chocolates, chocolate bits and butter in a 4-cup glass jug. Heat on High (100% power) for 2–3 minutes, until melted, stirring once. Stir until smooth.
3. Combine biscuit crumbs and walnuts in a large bowl. Stir in condensed milk, vanilla essence and chocolate mixture until blended. Spoon mixture evenly into prepared dish; smooth surface. Leave at room temperature for about 2 hours, or until firm.
4. Cut mixture into 24 squares; store in an airtight container.

ROCKY ROAD BROWNIES

Colour Index page 101. Makes 8. 1440 kJ each. Good source of iron.
Begin 2½ hours ahead.

60 g butter or margarine	½ teaspoon vanilla
60 g dark cooking	essence
chocolate	½ cup chopped walnuts
1 cup sugar	30 g miniature
2 eggs, lightly beaten	marshmallows
½ cup plain flour	90 g dark chocolate bits

1. Grease a 23-cm pie plate; line bottom with greaseproof paper.
2. Place butter and cooking chocolate in a 4-cup glass jug. Heat on High (100% power) for 1 minute, or until melted, stirring once. Remove from oven; stir until smooth.
3. Add sugar and eggs. Beat until well blended. Stir in flour and vanilla essence. Spoon evenly into prepared pie plate; smooth surface.
4. Combine walnuts, marshmallows and chocolate bits in a bowl. Sprinkle over mixture.
5. Elevate pie plate on a trivet, rack or ramekin turned upside down. Cook on High (100% power) for 5–7 minutes, until top puffs lightly, rotating plate halfway through cooking. Allow to cool completely in pie plate on a rack.
6. When cool, cut round into 8 wedges; store in an airtight container.

BUTTERSCOTCH SQUARES

Colour Index page 101. Makes 24. 561 kJ each. Low in sodium.
Begin early in day.

125 g butter or	1 teaspoon vanilla
margarine, softened	essence
¾ cup packed brown	1 egg
sugar	¾ cup desiccated
1 cup plain flour	coconut
1 teaspoon baking	¾ cup shelled walnuts
powder	or pecans, chopped
¼ teaspoon salt	90 g dark chocolate bits

1. Grease a 30-cm x 20-cm baking dish; line bottom with greaseproof paper.
2. With mixer at low speed, beat butter and sugar in a large bowl until blended. Add flour, baking powder, salt, vanilla essence, egg, ½ cup coconut and ¼ cup walnuts; beat until well blended, constantly scraping bowl. Spoon mixture evenly into prepared dish; smooth surface. Sprinkle remaining coconut, walnuts and chocolate bits over the mixture.
3. Elevate baking dish on a trivet, rack or ramekins turned upside down. Cook on High (100% power) for 5–6 minutes, just until beginning to set (do not overbake), rotating dish halfway through cooking. Allow mixture to stand in dish on a heatproof surface for 5 minutes.
4. Cover and refrigerate until well chilled. Cut into 24 squares; store in an airtight container.

ALMOND SHORTBREAD

Colour Index page 102. 741 kJ each. Good source of vitamin A.
Begin 1½ hours ahead or early in day.

Almond Shortbread is a classic made special by the addition of toasted flaked almonds. Shortbread dough can be very delicate and somewhat difficult to handle, but cooking it in the microwave makes the finished biscuit beautifully light. As an alternative to the almond flavouring, substitute ¼ teaspoon ground ginger for the ½ teaspoon almond essence, and decorate the top of the shortbread with thin slivers of crystallised ginger to emphasise the flavour.

Ingredients for 8 wedges		Microwave cookware
125 g butter or	½ teaspoon vanilla	23-cm pie plate
margarine, softened	essence	Trivet, rack or
⅓ cup icing sugar,	½ teaspoon almond	ramekin
sifted	essence	
1 cup plain flour	¼ teaspoon salt	
½ teaspoon baking	Flaked almonds,	
powder	toasted, to decorate	

1 Grease pie plate; line bottom with greaseproof paper.

2 With mixer at low speed, beat butter and sugar in a large bowl until blended. Add flour, baking powder, vanilla essence, almond essence and salt; beat until blended, constantly scraping bowl.

3 Pat dough evenly into prepared pie plate. Prick dough all over with a fork. Mark dough into 8 wedges.

4 Press toasted flaked almonds into dough in a decorative pattern.

5 Elevate pie plate on a trivet, rack or ramekin turned upside down. Cook on Medium (50% power) for 7–8 minutes, until puffed and set, rotating pie plate halfway through cooking.

6 Allow shortbread to stand in pie plate on a heatproof surface for 5 minutes. Cut into wedges along knife marks; allow to cool completely in pie plate. Remove and store in an airtight container.

Biscuits

Delicate biscuits are perfect with after-dinner coffee. For a change, substitute the same quantity of grated lemon rind for the orange rind in the recipe for Coconut Rounds (below). Store soft and crisp biscuits in separate containers with tight-fitting covers for maximum freshness.

COCONUT ROUNDS

Colour Index page 102. 184 kJ each. Low in sodium.
Begin 1½ hours ahead.

Ingredients for 30 biscuits		Microwave cookware
½ cup shredded coconut 1½ tablespoons plain flour ¼ cup sugar 3 teaspoons grated orange rind	¼ teaspoon vanilla essence 2 egg whites 60 g butter or margarine 90 g dark cooking chocolate	23-cm pie plate 2-cup glass jug 30-cm flat round platter Trivet, rack or ramekins Small bowl

1 Heat coconut in pie plate on High (100% power) for 3–4 minutes, until lightly toasted, stirring occasionally.

2 In food processor with knife blade attached or in blender, process toasted coconut until finely ground. Add flour, sugar, orange rind, vanilla essence and egg whites. Process until blended.

3 Heat butter in glass jug, covered with paper towel, on High for 45 seconds–1 minute, until melted. With motor running in food processor or blender, pour hot butter in a thin, steady stream into coconut mixture. Process until blended.

4 Lightly grease platter. Drop 6 teaspoonsful mixture on to platter in a ring, at least 5 cm apart. Elevate on trivet, rack or ramekins turned upside down. Cook on Medium-High (70% power) for 3–4 minutes, until biscuits begin to brown lightly, rotating platter halfway through cooking. Allow to stand for 1–2 minutes.

5 Transfer biscuits to a rack. Allow to cool completely. Meanwhile, cook and cool remaining mixture. (If you like, only use some of the mixture, then cover and refrigerate the rest for up to 5 days.)

6 Heat chocolate in a small bowl on High for 2–3 minutes, until melted, stirring once. Remove from oven; stir until smooth. Drizzle melted chocolate over each cooled biscuit. Allow to cool completely. Store in an airtight container.

LEMON TUILES

Colour Index page 102. Makes 30. 180 kJ each. Low in sodium.
Begin 1½ hours ahead.

½ cup sugar
¼ cup plain flour
1½ tablespoons cornflour
½ teaspoon grated lemon rind
½ teaspoon almond essence
2 egg whites
60 g butter or margarine
½ cup flaked almonds

1. Grease a 30-cm flat round platter.
2. In food processor with knife blade attached or in blender, process sugar, flour, cornflour, lemon rind, almond essence and egg whites until blended.
3. Heat butter in a 2-cup glass jug, covered with paper towel, on High (100% power) for 45 seconds–1 minute, until melted. With motor running in food processor or blender, pour hot butter in a thin, steady stream into mixture. Process until blended.
4. Drop 6 teaspoonsful mixture on to prepared platter in a ring, at least 5 cm apart. Sprinkle with almonds. Elevate on a trivet, rack or ramekins turned upside down. Cook on Medium-High (70% power) for 3–4 minutes, until biscuits begin to brown lightly, rotating platter halfway through cooking. Allow to stand for 2 minutes.
5. Transfer biscuits to a rack. Or, if you like, quickly remove each biscuit and roll around a rolling pin for characteristic shape. Allow to cool completely. Meanwhile, repeat with remaining mixture. Allow to cool completely; store in an airtight container.

VIENNESE MELTAWAYS

Colour Index page 103. Makes 36. 213 kJ each. Low in sodium.
Begin 1½ hours ahead.

125 g butter or margarine
Icing sugar
1 cup plain flour
½ cup slivered blanched almonds, ground
1 teaspoon almond essence

1. Grease a 30-cm round platter; line with greaseproof paper.
2. Heat butter in a medium bowl, covered with paper towel, on Medium (50% power) for 45 seconds, or just until softened; do not melt.
3. Add ¼ cup icing sugar, flour, ground almonds and almond essence; stir until blended.
4. Shape dough, 1 teaspoon at a time, into 2.5-cm balls. Place on prepared platter in a ring, 2.5 cm apart. Elevate on a trivet, rack or ramekins turned upside down. Cook on Medium for 4–5 minutes, until dry, rotating platter halfway through cooking. Allow to stand for 2 minutes.
5. Transfer biscuits to a rack. Allow to cool completely. Meanwhile, cook and cool remaining mixture. Store in an airtight container. Just before serving, dust with icing sugar.

FLORENTINES

Colour Index page 102. Makes 24. 465 kJ each. Low in sodium.
Begin 2½ hours ahead.

60 g butter or margarine	*¼ cup flaked almonds*
½ cup sugar	*125 g dark cooking*
½ cup thickened cream	*chocolate*
1½ tablespoons honey	
⅓ cup plain flour	
½ cup glacé fruit or	
mixed peel, finely	
chopped	

1. Grease a 30-cm flat round platter.
2. Place butter, sugar, cream and honey in a 4-cup glass jug. Heat on High (100% power) for 4 minutes, or until butter has melted, stirring once. Stir in flour until blended. Fold in glacé fruit and almonds.
3. Drop 6 teaspoonsful mixture on to prepared platter in a ring, at least 5 cm apart. Elevate on a trivet, rack or ramekins turned upside down. Cook on Medium-High (70% power) for 2–4 minutes, until biscuits begin to brown lightly, rotating platter halfway through cooking.
4. Trim uneven edges off biscuits with a 6-cm round biscuit cutter. Allow to stand for 1–2 minutes, until slightly firm. Transfer biscuits to a rack. Allow to cool completely. Meanwhile, cook and cool remaining mixture.
5. Heat chocolate in a small bowl on High for 2–3 minutes, until melted, stirring once. Remove from oven; stir until smooth. Spread smooth side of cooled biscuits with melted chocolate. If you like, make a design in the chocolate with a fork. Allow to cool completely; store in an airtight container.

MAPLE SNAPS

Colour Index page 103. Makes 24. 205 kJ each. Low in sodium.
Begin 1½ hours ahead.

60 g butter or margarine	*⅓ cup plain flour*
¼ cup maple syrup	*¼ cup shelled walnuts,*
¼ cup golden syrup	*finely chopped*

1. Grease a 30-cm round platter.
2. Place butter, maple syrup and golden syrup in a 4-cup glass jug. Heat on High (100% power) for 4 minutes, or until butter has melted, stirring once. Fold in flour and walnuts.
3. Drop 6 teaspoonsful mixture on to prepared platter in a ring, at least 5 cm apart. Elevate on a trivet, rack or ramekins turned upside down. Cook on Medium-High (70% power) for 2–4 minutes, until biscuits begin to brown lightly, rotating platter halfway through cooking.
4. Allow biscuits to stand for 1–2 minutes, until slightly firm. Transfer to a rack. Allow to cool completely. Meanwhile, cook and cool remaining mixture. Store in an airtight container.

MEXICAN WEDDING BISCUITS

Colour Index page 102. 335 kJ each. Low in sodium.
Begin early in day.

Make an unusual and attractive addition to your baking repertoire with these Mexican Wedding Biscuits, made light and delicate in the microwave. Chilling helps make dough easier to handle. For an alternative, striking effect, decorate half the biscuits with icing sugar and half with cocoa.

Ingredients for 24 biscuits		Microwave cookware
125 g butter or margarine	*½ teaspoon vanilla essence*	30-cm flat round platter
1¼ cups plain flour	*⅓ cup shelled walnuts, finely chopped*	Medium bowl
¾ cup icing sugar		Trivet, rack or ramekins

1. Grease platter; line with nonstick baking paper or greaseproof paper. Heat butter in bowl on Medium (50% power) for 45 seconds, or until softened; do not melt.

2. Add flour, ¼ cup icing sugar, vanilla essence and chopped walnuts to butter; stir until blended. Shape dough into a ball; flatten slightly. Wrap in plastic wrap and refigerate for about 1 hour, or until dough is firm.

3. With floured rolling pin, roll out chilled dough 6 mm thick on a lightly floured surface. Using a crescent-shaped cutter, cut out as many biscuits as possible. Reroll trimmings and cut again. Place biscuits on prepared platter in a ring and in centre, at least 6 mm apart.

4. Elevate platter on a trivet, rack or ramekins turned upside down. Cook on Medium (50% power) for 4–5 minutes, until biscuits are firm and look dry, rotating platter halfway through cooking. Allow to stand for 2 minutes.

5. Transfer biscuits to a rack. Allow to cool completely. Meanwhile, repeat with remaining cut-out biscuits; cool completely.

6. Sift remaining icing sugar over cooled biscuits to coat completely. Store in an airtight container.

Cake Decorations

There are many decorations, confections and colourings available to make cakes, biscuits, pies and desserts look even prettier. Choose from hard and soft sweets, as well as glacé and crystallised fruits and chocolate decorations.

These confections (above) are commercial products made from boiled hard sugar tinted with food colourings. They range from pretty little flowers to larger shapes such as teddy bears and clowns; all can be used as instant decorations.

Diamond Jellies: Soft and chewy sugar decorations

Marzipan Fruits: Tinted almond paste shaped to resemble fruits

Cachous: Shiny, smooth-coated, hard sugar balls

Glacé Cherries: Cherries coated with sugar glaze

Glacé fruits and other sugar-based decorations make ideal finishing touches for cakes and biscuits. Glacé fruits can also be used as ingredients in cakes and sweets

Orange and Lemon Jellies: 'Fruit slices' made of sugar and gelatine

Angelica: Stalk of the herb coated in sugar

Rainbow Sugar Crystals: Small refined sugar crystals coloured with vegetable dyes

Candles: Small decorative candles with a variety of patterns; used for celebration cakes

Chocolate Milk Flake: Can be used in pieces or crumbled

Chocolate Vermicelli: Tiny tube-shaped decorations

Chocolate Flakes: Dark chocolate and milk chocolate pieces

Chocolate Leaves: Small, commercially made chocolate decorations

Chocolate is one of the most versatile forms of decoration for cakes, biscuits and all kinds of desserts, as the taste goes well with most other flavours. Chocolate can be bought in a variety of shapes such as these above, or made into Chocolate Rounds and Chocolate Leaves (page 358)

Chocolate Curls: Homemade Chocolate Curls (page 358)

CARAMEL PECAN BARS

Colour Index page 103. 703 kJ per bar. Low in sodium.
Begin 2 hours ahead.

Ingredients for 24 bars		Microwave cookware
125 g butter or margarine 1 cup packed brown sugar ¾ cup plain flour ¼ teaspoon salt 1 teaspoon vanilla essence	1 cup shelled pecan halves ⅓ cup thickened cream ⅓ cup golden syrup ¾ cup dark chocolate bits	4-cup glass jug 1-cup glass jug

1 Preheat conventional oven to 180°C. Grease bottom and sides of a 20-cm x 20-cm baking dish.

2 With mixer at medium speed, beat 4 tablespoons butter in a large bowl until creamy. Add ⅓ cup brown sugar, flour, salt and ½ teaspoon vanilla essence; beat until smooth, constantly scraping bowl.

3 Pat dough evenly into prepared baking dish. Evenly arrange pecans on top. Bake conventionally for 20–25 minutes, until pecans are toasted and dough is golden.

4 Meanwhile, in 4-cup glass jug, combine remaining brown sugar, butter and vanilla essence. Stir in cream and golden syrup. Cook on High (100% power) for 6–8 minutes, until Soft Ball Stage (see Cold Water Test, page 369), stirring twice.

5 Pour caramel mixture over baked layer in baking dish. Allow caramel to cool completely in dish on a rack.

6 Heat chocolate bits in 1-cup glass jug on High for 2–3 minutes, until melted, stirring once. Remove from oven; stir until smooth. Drizzle melted chocolate over cooled caramel layer. When set, cut into 24 bars; store in an airtight container.

FRUIT AND NUT BARS

Colour Index page 102. Makes 16. 946 kJ each. Low in sodium.
Begin 1¼ hours ahead.

1 cup blanched almonds 1 cup walnuts 1 cup dried apricots 1 cup seedless raisins	1 cup pitted prunes 185 g dark chocolate bits (1 cup)

1. Line bottom of a 20-cm x 20-cm baking dish with foil.
2. In food processor with knife blade attached or in blender, process almonds and walnuts until finely chopped; spoon into a medium bowl. Process apricots, raisins and prunes into very small pieces (do not purée); add to chopped nuts. Press evenly into prepared baking dish.
3. Heat chocolate bits in a small bowl on High (100% power) for 2–3 minutes, until melted, stirring once. Remove from oven; stir until smooth. Spread melted chocolate over fruit and nut mixture. Cover and refrigerate until firm.
4. Cut mixture into 16 bars; store in an airtight container.

CHOCOLATE NUT CRISPS

Colour Index page 103. Makes 30. 289 kJ each. Low in sodium.
Begin 1½ hours ahead.

1 cup shelled walnuts ½ cup packed brown sugar ⅛ teaspoon ground cinnamon 2 egg whites	½ teaspoon vanilla essence 60 g butter or margarine ½ cup dark chocolate bits

1. Grease a 30-cm round platter.
2. In food processor with knife blade attached or in blender, process ½ cup walnuts until coarsely chopped; remove. Process remaining walnuts until ground. Add brown sugar, cinnamon, egg whites and vanilla essence; process until smooth.
3. Heat butter in a 2-cup glass jug, covered with paper towel, on High (100% power) for 45 seconds–1 minute, until melted. With motor running in food processor or blender, pour hot butter in a thin, steady stream into walnut mixture. Process until blended.
4. Drop 6 teaspoonsful mixture on to prepared platter in a ring, at least 5 cm apart. Sprinkle each biscuit with chocolate bits and chopped walnuts. Elevate on a trivet, rack or ramekins turned upside down. Cook on Medium-High (70% power) for 3–4 minutes, until biscuits begin to brown lightly, rotating platter halfway through cooking. Allow to stand for 1–2 minutes.
5. Transfer biscuits to a rack. Allow to cool completely. Meanwhile, cook and cool remaining mixture. Store in an airtight container.

Hard sweets

GOLDEN WALNUT DROPS

Colour Index page 104. Makes 42. 268 kJ each. Low in sodium.
Begin 1½ hours ahead.

1 cup packed brown sugar	*1 cup shelled walnuts, chopped*
1 cup sugar	*15 g butter or margarine*
¼ cup golden syrup	*1 teaspoon vanilla essence*
¼ cup water	

1. Lightly grease baking trays; line with grease-proof paper.
2. Combine brown sugar, sugar, golden syrup and water in a large bowl. Cook on High (100% power) for 7½ (7:30)–8 minutes without stirring, until Soft Ball Stage (see Cold Water Test, below).
3. Add chopped walnuts, butter and vanilla essence to syrup mixture; stir until well combined. Allow to stand for 2 minutes.
4. Drop teaspoonsful mixture on to prepared trays. Allow to cool on a rack for about 1 hour, or until set. Store in an airtight container.

COLD WATER TEST
This Cold Water Test is a simple way to measure the temperature of a sugar mixture. Fill a glass jug with very cold water. With a clean spoon, drop ½ teaspoon hot mixture into water. Allow to stand for 1 minute, then test firmness with your fingers.

Soft Ball Stage

A small amount of syrup dropped into cold water forms a soft ball that flattens between forefinger and thumb when removed.

Hard Crack Stage

A small amount of syrup dropped into cold water separates into hard, brittle threads.

MINT IMPERIALS

Colour Index page 103. 293 kJ each. Low in sodium.
Begin early in day.

Washing up is so much easier when you cook the sugar syrup for Mint Imperials in the microwave. Use different food colours for a pretty effect.

Ingredients for 36 mints		Microwave cookware
3 cups caster sugar *2 tablespoons golden syrup* *Water* *1 teaspoon peppermint essence*	*Food colouring (optional)* *Melted chocolate (optional)*	Large bowl

1 Place sugar, golden syrup and ¾ cup water in large bowl. Cook on High (100% power) for 7–8 minutes, until sugar has completely dissolved, stirring twice.

2 Cook fondant on High for 5–6 minutes, until Soft Ball Stage (see Cold Water Test, left). Do not stir.

3 Without scraping side of bowl, pour fondant into 38-cm x 26-cm Swiss-roll tin. Place tin on a rack and allow fondant to cool until mixture is cool to touch.

4 With a wide, stiff metal spatula or clean, wide putty knife, push mixture to one end of tin, fold over, then spread out to 6-mm thickness. Repeat pushing, folding and spreading until fondant turns white and clay-like. Knead mixture to form a ball. Store in an airtight container for up to 1 week.

5 When ready to use, lightly grease baking trays; line with greaseproof paper. Crumble fondant into a large bowl; add peppermint essence, 2 drops food colouring, if using, and 2 teaspoons water. Heat on High for 1½ (1:30) minutes, until softened, stirring once. Remove from oven; stir until smooth.

6 Working quickly, drop teaspoonsful of mixture on to prepared baking trays. (If fondant becomes too hard and thick, add a few drops of water and heat on High for 20–30 seconds.) If you like, dip into melted chocolate when mints are firm. Store in an airtight container.

Soft sweets

PEANUT BRITTLE

Colour Index page 103. 594 kJ per 30 g serving. Low in sodium.
Begin 1¼ hours ahead.

Peanut Brittle is one of the simplest and most delicious sweets to make conventionally because of the all-in-one preparation and cooking process. Using the microwave oven makes it even quicker! Be sure to grease the baking tray well before pouring the peanut mixture on to it; this will help make it easier to lift and break the brittle into pieces for serving.

Ingredients for 500 g brittle		Microwave cookware

1 cup sugar
½ cup golden syrup
¼ cup water
¼ teaspoon salt
1 cup shelled roasted
  peanuts
	30 g butter or margarine
	1 teaspoon bicarbonate
	  of soda
		2-litre glass jug
		or bowl

1 Generously oil a large baking tray.

2 Place sugar, golden syrup, water and salt in glass jug; stir until well blended.

3 Cook syrup mixture on High (100% power) for 12–15 minutes, without stirring, until Hard Crack Stage (see Cold Water Test, page 369), just until caramel begins to turn light golden. Watch carefully as caramel burns easily and continues to cook and darken when removed from the oven.

4 Add peanuts, butter and bicarbonate of soda. Stir well until peanuts are evenly coated. Immediately pour peanut mixture on to prepared baking tray.

5 With 2 forks, quickly lift and stretch peanut mixture into a 35-cm x 30-cm rectangle. Allow to cool on a rack until firm.

6 Break cold brittle into small pieces. Store in an airtight container.

BUTTER CARAMELS

Colour Index page 104. Makes 64. 188 kJ each. Low in sodium.
Begin 1½ hours ahead.

1½ cups thickened cream 1 cup sugar ½ cup golden syrup	60 g butter 1 teaspoon vanilla essence

1. Lightly grease a 20-cm x 20-cm baking dish.
2. Combine cream, sugar and golden syrup in a 2-litre glass bowl. Cook on High (100% power) for 15–20 minutes, without stirring, until Soft Ball Stage (see Cold Water Test, page 369).
3. Stir butter and vanilla essence into mixture. Pour caramel immediately into prepared dish; smooth surface. Allow to cool completely in baking dish on a rack until firm.
4. Invert baking dish on to a board; remove dish to unmould. Cut caramel with a sharp knife into 2.5-cm squares. Wrap each square in cellophane or plastic wrap; store in an airtight container.

CHOCOLATE CHERRY CUPS

Colour Index page 104. Makes 36. 285 kJ each. Low in sodium.
Begin 1½ hours ahead.

185 g dark cooking
  chocolate, chopped
30 g white vegetable
  shortening (Copha)
1¼ cups icing sugar
2 tablespoons orange-
  flavoured liqueur
	2 teaspoons cream
	2 x 275 g jars maraschino
	  cherries with stalks,
	  well drained

1. Arrange 36 fluted paper petit four cases on a baking tray.
2. Place chocolate and shortening in a medium bowl. Heat on High (100% power) for 1½ (1:30) minutes, or until melted, stirring once. Remove from oven; stir until smooth.
3. Using a small pastry brush, coat the inside of each paper case with chocolate mixture. Refrigerate for about 30 minutes, or until set.
4. When chocolate is set, carefully remove paper cases, handling cups as little as possible so that chocolate keeps its shape.
5. Combine icing sugar, liqueur and cream in a small bowl until smooth. Spoon 1 teaspoon filling into each chocolate cup; top with a cherry. Cover and refrigerate until ready to serve.

CHOCOLATE TRUFFLES

Colour Index page 104. Makes 30. 247 kJ each. Low in sodium.
Begin 1½ hours ahead.

250 g dark cooking chocolate	*¼ cup thickened cream*
60 g butter or margarine	*¼ teaspoon almond essence*

1. Arrange 30 foil cases on a baking tray.
2. Place chocolate and butter in a medium bowl. Heat on High (100% power) for 1½ (1:30)–2 minutes, until melted, stirring once. Remove from oven; stir until smooth.
3. Stir in cream and almond essence until evenly blended. Set bowl over a dish of iced water. Beat mixture with a whisk until soft peaks form.
4. Spoon truffle mixture into a piping bag fitted with a medium star tube; pipe into foil cups. Refrigerate for about 1 hour, or until truffles are set.

CHOCOLATE MARSHMALLOW FUDGE

Colour Index page 103. Makes 36. 465 kJ each. Low in sodium.
Begin 1¼ hours ahead.

1½ cups sugar	*1 cup shelled walnuts, chopped*
½ cup evaporated milk	
60 g butter or margarine	*185 g milk chocolate bits*
125 g marshmallows, chopped	*60 g dark cooking chocolate, chopped*

1. Lightly grease a 20-cm x 20-cm baking dish.
2. Combine sugar, evaporated milk and butter in a 2-litre glass jug or bowl. Cook on High (100% power) for 8–9 minutes, stirring after 3 minutes, until Soft Ball Stage (see Cold Water Test, page 369).
3. Add marshmallows, walnuts, chocolate bits and chopped dark chocolate. Stir until marshmallows and chocolate melt. Spread fudge into prepared baking dish; smooth surface.
4. Allow fudge to cool completely in dish on a rack until firm. Cut into 36 pieces; store in an airtight container.

MELTING CHOCOLATE
Using the microwave is the quick, no-fuss way to melt chocolate, but at first its appearance can be deceptive. Always remember that chocolate does not lose its shape during the cooking time; it will not melt until stirred. If, after stirring, extra time is necessary, add only 1–2 seconds at a time.

Chocolate-based sweets cook easily in the microwave and can be stored in the refrigerator as long as you like. Adding water to the caramel in the fudge slices (below) makes it much easier to handle and spread, while the sweetened condensed milk added to the chocolate makes the fudge rich and creamy.

CHOCOLATE AND CHERRY FUDGE SLICES

Colour Index page 104. 406 kJ each. Low in sodium.
Begin 3 hours ahead or early in day.

Ingredients for 36 slices		Microwave cookware
185 g dark chocolate bits	*275 g jar maraschino cherries, drained*	Medium bowl
½ cup sweetened condensed milk	*220 g caramels*	23-cm pie plate
½ cup icing sugar	*3 teaspoons water*	
1½ teaspoons vanilla essence	*1 cup shelled walnuts, chopped*	

1 Combine chocolate bits and condensed milk in bowl. Heat on High (100% power) for 1½ (1:30) minutes, or until chocolate has melted, stirring halfway through cooking. Add icing sugar and vanilla essence; stir until smooth and well blended.

2 Spread half the fudge mixture on to a square piece of foil to make a 15-cm square. Repeat with remaining mixture on another piece of foil. Freeze fudge about for 5 minutes, or until easy to handle.

3 Pat cherries dry with paper towel. Arrange in a single line on each fudge square, about 12 mm from one edge.

4 Starting at edge with cherries, loosen fudge from foil and roll up like a Swiss roll. Press to seal seam. Wrap roll in greaseproof paper; refrigerate for 1 hour, or until well chilled and set.

5 Place caramels and water in pie plate. Heat on High (100% power) for 1½ (1:30)–2 minutes, stirring halfway through cooking. Remove from oven; stir until smooth. Working quickly, spread half the caramel mixture over 1 fudge roll, then coat with half the chopped walnuts.

6 Reheat caramel mixture remaining in pie plate on High for 30 seconds. Spread remaining fudge roll with caramel mixture and coat with remaining walnuts. Refrigerate both rolls for about 1 hour, or until set. Cut each roll into 8 slices.

It's so quick and easy to make popcorn in the microwave now that microwave popcorn is readily available. Always follow the manufacturer's instructions on the packet; never pop corn in your microwave using any bag other than the one provided with the packet – it could catch fire.

POPCORN BALLS

6 servings. 1038 kJ per serving. Low in sodium. Good source of iron.
Begin 25 minutes ahead.

6 cups popped corn 125 g glacé cherries, cut in half 1 cup golden syrup 1½ teaspoons white vinegar 1 teaspoon vanilla essence Salt (optional)	1. Using a pastry brush, oil a large bowl. Mix popped corn with cherries. 2. Heat golden syrup and vinegar in a 2-litre glass bowl on High (100% power) for 10–12 minutes, without stirring, until a small amount of syrup dropped into cold water forms a hard but pliable ball. Stir in vanilla essence. Season, if you like, with salt. 3. Quickly pour hot syrup over popcorn, tossing well. With greased hands, shape into 7.5-cm balls, using as little pressure as possible, so balls will not be too compact.

Making the Popcorn Balls

Lightly brush the inside of a large bowl with oil.

Pour hot syrup over popcorn mixture, tossing to coat well.

With greased hands, scoop up handfuls of popcorn mixture; shape into balls.

CHILDREN IN THE KITCHEN
The microwave oven is not only one of the safest cooking appliances in the home, it is simple enough for children to use. But to keep the cooking fun, they should read these guidelines before using it:

1. Always read the recipe through completely to make certain you understand it and have the necessary ingredients and cookware.
2. Use only the amounts given in the recipe and cook for the recommended times on the given power.
3. Always use potholders. While the oven may feel cool, the dishes will be hot from the heat of the food.
4. Be sure cookware is microwave-safe. Ask an adult to mark microwave-safe items with an 'M', using an indelible marker.
5. When using plastic wrap or covers, carefully lift off the food so that steam escapes away from your face and fingers.

DO NOT
* Turn on the microwave with nothing in it.
* Put any metal or foil in the microwave.
* Cook an egg in its shell.
* Cook a hot dog without pricking or cutting the outside of the frankfurter.
* Make microwave popcorn in anything other than the manufacturer's container or bag.

COCONUT HAYSTACKS

Colour Index page 104. Makes 20. 301 kJ each. Low in sodium.
Begin 1¼ hours ahead.

1 cup desiccated coconut	250 g dark cooking chocolate

1. Line baking trays with greaseproof paper.
2. Heat coconut in a 23-cm pie plate on High (100% power) for 3–4 minutes, until lightly toasted, stirring occasionally.
3. Heat chocolate in a medium bowl on High (100% power) for 2–4 minutes, until chocolate melts, stirring once. Add toasted coconut; stir until smooth.
4. Drop teaspoonsful of coconut mixture on to prepared trays, mounding the mixture slightly to resemble haystacks.
5. Allow to cool completely until firm; store in an airtight container.

PISTACHIO BITES

Colour Index page 104. Makes 32. 306 kJ each. Low in sodium.
Begin 3 hours ahead.

375 g white chocolate, chopped ⅓ cup thickened cream 15 g butter or margarine ¾ teaspoon vanilla essence	Green food colouring 2 tablespoons finely chopped pistachios

1. Line bottom and sides of a 23-cm x 12.5-cm loaf tin with foil.
2. Heat chocolate in a medium bowl on High (100% power) for 3–4 minutes, until melted, stirring once. Remove from oven; stir until smooth.
3. Add cream and butter; stir until smooth. Transfer half the mixture to another medium bowl; put aside.
4. Add vanilla essence and a few drops of green food colouring to mixture remaining in bowl. Evenly spread green mixture in prepared loaf tin. Refrigerate.
5. Add chopped pistachios to reserved white mixture; stir until blended. Evenly spread pistachio mixture over green layer in loaf tin. Refrigerate for about 2 hours, or until set.
6. Invert pan on to a board; remove tin to unmould; remove foil. Cut layered chocolate mixture in half lengthways, then cut each strip into 16 pieces. Cover and refrigerate until ready to serve.

Preserves
and Sauces

JAMS · SPREADS · RELISHES · CHUTNEYS
SAVOURY JELLIES · SAVOURY SAUCES
SWEET SAUCES

Preserves and Sauces

When favourite fruits are in season, the microwave is ideal for making small amounts of jams and spreads; as long as you are not preparing any more than 1.5 kg of fruit, it is much quicker and easier than the bulk jam-making sessions of days gone by. Other preserves, such as savoury jellies, relishes and chutneys, are also worthwhile preparing in small quantities. They require little stirring and there is no danger of scorching. It is important, however, to stir according to the instructions given in the recipe in order to redistribute the sugar in the mixture so that it cooks evenly.

Jars and lids must be sterilised first, but this cannot be done in the microwave; simply boil them in water on top of the stove for at least 10 minutes, then keep hot. Add the hot preserve directly to the hot jars and remember to leave 6 mm space between the preserve and the top of the jar. Cover with lids while still hot.

Apart from the obvious benefits of having easily prepared preserves on hand at home, attractively bottled and decorated they make a delightful present.

This chapter also contains a wide variety of savoury and sweet sauces, all based on traditional recipes but much quicker to prepare. It is important to always use a large enough container to prevent sauces from boiling over; ideally, the cookware should hold twice the volume of the sauce. For safe and easy pouring, a glass jug is the best choice, but remember to use oven gloves as the handle may get hot. Also, be certain to stir the mixture when indicated to prevent lumping, especially if sauces are flour-based.

Most sauces cook well on High (100% power) but delicate egg-based sauces – such as Hollandaise, Béarnaise and custard – are smoother when cooked on Medium (50% power); the lower temperature prevents boiling, which would result in curdling.

Sweet sauces are especially quick and easy to make in the microwave and are delicious toppings for ice cream, puddings and other desserts. As well as recipes for traditional chocolate, fudge, Melba and butterscotch sauces, there are also simple fruit-based sauces, such as orange, mulberry and peach.

FRESH FRUIT FLAVOURS

Jams and spreads are quick and easy to make in the microwave so, if you prepare a few jars as fruits ripen, you will always have a selection of favourite flavours on hand.

Accompany a croissant or breakfast roll with a fruit preserve, such as (left to right) Strawberry Jam (page 375), Blackberry Spread (page 375) and Apricot and Pineapple Spread (page 375).

Jams and spreads

STRAWBERRY JAM

Colour Index page 108. Makes about 4 cups. 251 kJ per tablespoon. Low in cholesterol, fat, sodium. Begin 1 day ahead.

750 g strawberries   ¼ cup lemon juice
3 cups sugar

1. Sterilise four 250-ml jars and lids conventionally by placing in enough water to cover and boiling for 10 minutes; keep hot.
2. Using a potato masher or slotted spoon, thoroughly crush strawberries in an 8-cup glass jug.
3. Stir in sugar and lemon juice. Cook, covered, on High (100% power) for 10–15 minutes, until mixture has boiled and thickened slightly, stirring occasionally. Skim foam from surface of hot strawberry mixture.
4. Immediately ladle mixture into hot jars, to within 6 mm of tops. Cover with lids. Keep jam in the refrigerator for up to 3 weeks.

RASPBERRY JAM: Prepare Strawberry Jam (above), substituting 3 punnets (750 g) raspberries for the strawberries.
Makes about 4 cups. 291 kJ per tablespoon.

APRICOT AND PINEAPPLE SPREAD

Colour Index page 107. Makes about 2 cups. 201 kJ per tablespoon. Low in cholesterol, fat, sodium. Begin 55 minutes ahead.

1½ cups water   ¼ cup sugar
250 g dried apricot   1 cup canned crushed
    halves   unsweetened pineapple

1. Sterilise two 250-ml jars and lids conventionally by placing in enough water to cover and boiling for 10 minutes; keep hot.
2. Pour water into an 8-cup glass jug; add apricots, sugar and crushed pineapple with juice. Cook on High (100% power) for 15–20 minutes, until apricots are very tender, stirring occasionally.
3. Press hot fruit mixture through a strainer into a large bowl.
4. Immediately ladle mixture into hot jars, to within 6 mm of tops. Cover with lids. Keep spread in the refrigerator for up to 3 weeks.

PEACH SPREAD: Prepare Apricot and Pineapple Spread (above), substituting 250 g dried peach halves for the dried apricots and ¾ cup orange juice for the crushed pineapple and its juice.
Makes about 2 cups. 168 kJ per tablespoon.

When making jams, spreads and other preserves, choose fruit that is just ripe. If necessary, use fruit that is slightly underripe, rather than overripe, because the early fruit contains more of the natural pectin necessary for the jam or preserve to set.

BLACKBERRY SPREAD

Colour Index page 108. 212 kJ per tablespoon. Low in cholesterol, fat, sodium. Begin 1 day ahead.

Ingredients for 4 cups		Microwave cookware
750 g blackberries 2 cooking apples	2½ cups sugar ¼ cup lemon juice	Large bowl

1 Sterilise four 250-ml jars and lids conventionally by placing in enough water to cover and boiling for 10 minutes; keep hot.

2 Pick over blackberries, removing any stalks. Peel and core apples, then cut into quarters.

3 Combine blackberries, apples and sugar in bowl. Cook on High (100% power) for 10–12 minutes, until apples soften and sugar has dissolved, stirring twice.

4 Press fruit mixture through a strainer into another bowl. Return puréed mixture to cooking bowl. Cook on High for 8–10 minutes, until mixture has thickened slightly, stirring occasionally.

5 Skim foam from surface of hot blackberry mixture; stir in lemon juice.

6 Immediately ladle mixture into hot jars, to within 6 mm of tops. Cover with lids. Keep spread in the refrigerator for up to 3 weeks.

Relishes

PEACH PRESERVES

Colour Index page 108. 207 kJ per tablespoon. Low in cholesterol, fat, sodium.
Begin 1 day ahead.

Ingredients for 4 cups		Microwave cookware
6 large slipstone peaches (about 1.5 kg)	2½ cups sugar ¼ cup lemon juice	8-cup glass jug

1 Sterilise four 250-ml jars and lids conventionally by placing in enough water to cover and boiling for 10 minutes; keep hot. Meanwhile, peel peaches. Cut each peach in half lengthways and twist apart. Remove stones; discard.

2 Thinly slice peaches; combine with sugar and lemon juice in glass jug.

3 Cook peach mixture, covered, on High (100% power) for 5 minutes, or until boiled. Uncover; stir. Cook on High for 20–30 minutes longer, stirring occasionally, until syrup has thickened and fruit is translucent.

4 Remove jug from oven; place on a heatproof surface. Skim foam from surface of hot peach mixture.

5 Immediately ladle mixture into hot jars, to within 6 mm of tops.

6 Cover with lids. Keep preserves in the refrigerator for up to 3 weeks.

TESTING FOR SETTING POINT OF JAMS
Because the fruit juices do not evaporate as much during the shorter cooking time, jams made in the microwave usually have lemon juice, citric acid or commercial pectin added to aid setting.

To test if the jam will set, at the end of the recommended cooking time pour a little on to a saucer and leave to cool for several minutes; if the skin on top of the jam wrinkles when touched, setting point has been reached. Alternatively, leave the saucer in the refrigerator for 30 minutes; if the jam on the saucer has set, the rest of the mixture is ready. If not, extend the cooking time as needed.

CRANBERRY RELISH

Colour Index page 108. Makes 4 cups. 268 kJ per tablespoon. Low in cholesterol, sodium.
Begin 1 day ahead.

3 cups frozen cranberries, thawed, or canned cranberries, drained
375 g tiny white pickling onions, peeled and trimmed
½ cup sultanas
2 cups packed brown sugar

½ cup water
⅓ cup cider vinegar
1 teaspoon mustard powder
¼ teaspoon ground cinnamon
310 g marrons (chestnuts) in syrup, drained

1. Sterilise four 250-ml jars and lids conventionally by placing in enough water to cover and boiling for 10 minutes; keep hot.
2. Combine cranberries, onions, sultanas, sugar, water, vinegar, mustard and cinnamon in a 3-litre casserole. Cook, covered, on High (100% power) for 10 minutes. Uncover; stir. Cook on High for 15 minutes longer, or until mixture has thickened, stirring occasionally. Stir in marrons.
3. Immediately ladle mixture into hot jars, to within 6 mm of tops. Cover with lids. Keep relish in the refrigerator for up to 3 weeks.

CORN RELISH

Colour Index page 107. Makes about 4 cups. 72 kJ per tablespoon. Low in cholesterol, fat, sodium.
Begin 1 day ahead.

4 cobs corn, husked, or 440 g can whole-kernel corn, drained
1 small green capsicum, diced
1 small red capsicum, diced
1 small tomato, diced

1 small onion, diced
1 cup cider vinegar
½ cup sugar
¼ teaspoon celery seeds
¼ teaspoon mustard powder
¼ teaspoon turmeric

1. Sterilise four 250-ml jars and lids conventionally by placing in enough water to cover and boiling for 10 minutes; keep hot.
2. If using fresh corn, cut kernels from cobs with a sharp knife to make about 2½ cups.
3. Combine corn, capsicums, tomato, onion, vinegar, sugar, celery seeds, mustard and turmeric in a 2-litre casserole. Cook, covered, on High (100% power) for 5–7 minutes, until mixture has boiled. Uncover; stir. Cook on High for 10–15 minutes longer, until vegetables are tender-crisp, stirring occasionally.
4. Immediately ladle mixture into hot jars, to within 6 mm of tops. Cover with lids. Keep relish in the refrigerator for up to 3 weeks.

Chutneys

APPLE AND ONION CHUTNEY

Colour Index page 108. Makes about 4 cups. 151 kJ per tablespoon. Low in cholesterol, fat, sodium. Begin 1 day ahead.

2 large cooking apples, peeled, cored and diced	*375 g pitted prunes, cut into quarters*
2 onions, diced	*1 tablespoon grated green ginger*
1 green or red capsicum, diced	*2 tablespoons mustard seeds*
1 clove garlic, crushed	*½ teaspoon dried crushed chilli*
¾ cup sugar	
¾ cup white vinegar	
½ cup water	

1. Sterilise four 250-ml jars and lids conventionally by placing in enough water to cover and boiling for 10 minutes; keep hot.
2. Place apples, onions, capsicum, garlic, sugar, vinegar and water in a large bowl. Cook, covered, on High (100% power) for 10 minutes, or until mixture has boiled. Uncover; stir. Cook on High for 10 minutes longer, or until vegetables are tender, stirring occasionally.
3. Stir in prunes, ginger, mustard seeds and chilli. Cook on High for 10–15 minutes, until mixture has thickened and become slightly syrupy, stirring often.
4. Immediately ladle mixture into hot jars, to within 6 mm of tops. Cover with lids. Keep chutney in the refrigerator for up to 3 weeks.

ROCKMELON CHUTNEY

Colour Index page 108. Makes about 4 cups. 168 kJ per tablespoon. Low in cholesterol, fat. Begin 1 day ahead.

4 cloves garlic, crushed	*¾ cup cider vinegar*
3 onions, cut into 2.5-cm chunks	*½ cup sultanas*
2 tomatoes, cut into 2.5-cm chunks	*3 teaspoons curry powder*
1 rockmelon, peeled, seeded and cut into 2.5-cm chunks	*3 teaspoons mustard seeds*
1½ cups packed brown sugar	*2 tablespoons cornflour dissolved in 2 tablespoons cold water*

1. Sterilise four 250-ml jars and lids conventionally by placing in enough water to cover and boiling for 10 minutes; keep hot.
2. Combine garlic, onions, tomatoes, rockmelon, sugar, vinegar, sultanas, curry powder and mustard seeds in a large bowl. Cook, covered, on High (100% power) for 10 minutes, stirring twice. Uncover; stir. Cook on High for 10–15 minutes longer, until vegetables are tender, stirring occasionally.
3. Stir in dissolved cornflour until blended. Cook on High for 3–5 minutes, until mixture has thickened, stirring twice.
4. Immediately spoon mixture into hot jars, to within 6 mm of tops. Cover with lids. Keep chutney in the refrigerator for up to 3 weeks.

Cooking chutneys in the microwave makes quick work of a job that used to take hours – and it won't leave strong smells in your kitchen! Try a delicious, traditional chutney such as Apple and Onion Chutney (left), or an unusual combination of fruit as in Rockmelon Chutney (below left). Both add contrast and texture to cold meats, cheese, curries and savoury rice dishes.

GREEN TOMATO CHUTNEY

Colour Index page 108. 117 kJ per tablespoon. Low in cholesterol, fat. Good source of vitamin C. Begin 1 day ahead.

Ingredients for 4 cups		Microwave cookware
500 g green tomatoes, cut into quarters	*1¼ cups sugar*	Large bowl
2 cups cider vinegar	*3 teaspoons mustard seeds*	
2 green capsicums, cut into quarters	*3 teaspoons celery seeds*	
2 red capsicums, cut into quarters	*¾ teaspoon ground allspice*	
1 large onion	*¼ teaspoon ground cinnamon*	

1 Sterilise four 250-ml jars and lids conventionally by placing in enough water to cover and boiling for 10 minutes; keep hot.

2 In food processor with knife blade attached or in blender, process tomatoes and 1 cup vinegar until tomatoes are roughly chopped. Transfer tomato mixture to bowl.

3 In food processor with knife blade attached or in blender, process capsicums and onion until roughly chopped. Stir into tomato mixture in bowl. Cook, covered, on High (100% power) for 10 minutes, or until softened; stir once. Uncover; drain liquid and discard.

4 To vegetable mixture, add sugar, mustard seeds, celery seeds, allspice and cinnamon. Stir to combine.

5 Cook vegetables, covered, on High for 10–15 minutes, until sugar has dissolved and vegetables are tender, stirring twice.

6 Immediately ladle mixture into hot jars, to within 6 mm of tops. Cover with lids. Keep chutney in the refrigerator for up to 3 weeks.

Savoury jellies

CAPSICUM JELLY

Colour Index page 108. 262 kJ per tablespoon. Low in cholesterol, fat, sodium. Begin 1 day ahead.

Capsicum Jelly makes a great accompaniment to a ham or any cold roast meat. In this recipe, sweet red capsicums are used, with the added zest of a fresh red chilli, to create a clear jelly with a jewel-like colour. If you like, use green capsicums and flavour them with a fresh green chilli.

Ingredients for 2 cups		Microwave cookware
2 large red capsicums 1 large hot red chilli ½ cup apple juice ⅓ cup white vinegar	1½ cups sugar 1–2 drops red food colouring (optional)	8-cup glass jug

1 Sterilise two 250-ml jars and lids conventionally by placing in enough water to cover and boiling for 10 minutes; keep hot.

2 Finely chop capsicums and chilli. Place a fine sieve over glass jug; transfer capsicum mixture to sieve.

3 Using the back of a spoon, press mixture in sieve until liquid drains into jug, making about ½ cup juice. Discard chopped capsicum mixture.

4 Add apple juice, vinegar and sugar to juice in bowl; stir. Cook, covered, on High (100% power) for 8–10 minutes, until mixture has boiled, stirring twice.

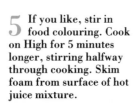

5 If you like, stir in food colouring. Cook on High for 5 minutes longer, stirring halfway through cooking. Skim foam from surface of hot juice mixture.

6 Immediately ladle mixture into hot jars, to within 6 mm of tops. Cover with lids. Keep jelly in the refrigerator for up to 3 weeks.

MINT JELLY

Colour Index page 107. Makes 4 cups. 251 kJ per tablespoon. Low in cholesterol, fat, sodium. Begin 1 day ahead.

2 cups apple juice	Water
½ cup cider vinegar	2 cups sugar

1 cup packed mint
    leaves, chopped
	1–2 drops green food
	    colouring (optional)

1. Sterilise four 250-ml jars and lids conventionally by placing in enough water to cover and boiling for 10 minutes; keep hot.
2. Pour apple juice and vinegar into an 8-cup glass jug; add chopped mint. Cook, covered, on High (100% power) for 8–10 minutes, until mixture has boiled, stirring twice.
3. Place a strainer over a medium bowl. Pour mint mixture through strainer; discard chopped mint. Pour liquid back into jug. If necessary, add enough water to make 2 cups liquid. Stir in sugar. Cook, covered, on High for 8–10 minutes, until mixture has boiled, stirring twice.
4. If you like, add green food colouring. Cook on High for 4 minutes longer, stirring halfway through cooking. Skim foam from surface of hot mint mixture.
5. Immediately ladle mixture into hot jars, to within 6 mm of tops. Cover with lids. Keep jelly in the refrigerator for up to 3 weeks.

SAUCES FOR VEGETABLES
Use a sauce to add zest to plain cooked fresh or frozen vegetables.

Lemon Butter Sauce: Heat *60 g butter or margarine* in a 2-cup glass jug, covered with paper towel, on High (100% power) for 45 seconds–1 minute, until melted. Stir in *1 tablespoon lemon juice, 1 tablespoon chopped fresh parsley* and a *pinch of cayenne pepper*. Makes about ⅓ cup. 502 kJ per tablespoon.

Fines Herbs Sauce: Prepare Lemon Butter Sauce (above), substituting *2 tablespoons dry white wine* for the lemon juice; add *2 tablespoons chopped fresh chives* and *1 teaspoon chopped fresh dill*. Makes about ⅓ cup. 532 kJ per tablespoon.

Mustard and Chive Sauce: Heat *60 g butter or margarine* in a large bowl, covered with paper towel, on High (100% power) for 45 seconds–1 minute, until melted. Stir in *3 tablespoons plain flour*. Cook on High for 1 minute, stirring once. Gradually stir in *2 cups milk*. Cook on High for 3–5 minutes, until sauce thickens, stirring twice. Stir in *1 tablespoon French mustard* and *1 tablespoon chopped fresh chives*. Makes about 2 cups. 147 kJ per tablespoon.

Savoury sauces

BARBECUE SAUCE

Colour Index page 106. Makes about 1 cup. 179 kJ per tablespoon. Low in cholesterol, fat.
Begin 25 minutes ahead.

1 onion, diced
1 clove garlic, crushed
2 tablespoons olive or vegetable oil
1 fresh green chilli, seeded and finely chopped
⅔ cup bottled tomato sauce
2 tablespoons cider vinegar
¼ teaspoon mustard powder

1. Combine onion, garlic and oil in a 4-cup glass jug. Cook, covered with paper towel, on High (100% power) for 2–3 minutes, until onion has softened slightly, stirring twice.
2. Stir in chopped chilli, tomato sauce, vinegar and mustard until well blended. Cook, covered, on High for 3–5 minutes, until sauce has thickened, stirring occasionally. Allow to stand, covered, on a heatproof surface for 10 minutes, or until flavours blend. Spoon sauce into a bowl. Serve hot.

HOT CHILLI SAUCE: Prepare Barbecue Sauce (above) adding *1 tablespoon Mexican-style chilli powder* and *1 tablespoon Worcestershire sauce* in step 2.

SATAY SAUCE

Colour Index page 106. Makes about 1⅓ cups. 223 kJ per tablespoon. Low in cholesterol.
Begin 10 minutes ahead.

2 cloves garlic, crushed
1 red capsicum, diced
½ cup crunchy peanut butter
Chicken stock
1 tablespoon grated green ginger
3 teaspoons cider vinegar
3 teaspoons soy sauce
¼ teaspoon sesame oil (optional)
Coriander sprigs to garnish

1. Combine garlic, capsicum, peanut butter, ½ cup stock, ginger, vinegar and soy sauce in a 2-cup glass jug. If you like, stir in sesame oil. Cook on High (100% power) for 1–2 minutes, until hot, stirring halfway through cooking.
2. If necessary, add a few additional drops of stock to thin sauce to the desired consistency. Spoon sauce into a serving bowl; garnish with coriander sprigs. Serve warm.

The microwave is so good for making small, easily stored quantities of preserves that it is possible to have a far wider range than usual on hand at any one time. Try the spicy Tomato Sauce (below) – it's easier to make than you think!

TOMATO SAUCE

Colour Index page 107. 161 kJ per tablespoon. Low in cholesterol, fat, sodium.
Begin 1 day ahead.

Ingredients for 3 cups		Microwave cookware
1 kg ripe tomatoes, cut into quarters	*¼ teaspoon ground cloves*	2 large bowls
1½ cups sugar	*⅛ teaspoon cayenne pepper*	
1 cup cider vinegar	*1 tablespoon cornflour dissolved in*	
1 teaspoon mustard powder	*2 tablespoons cold water*	
½ teaspoon ground cinnamon		
¼ teaspoon celery seeds		

1 Sterilise three 250-ml jars and lids conventionally by placing in enough water to cover and boiling for 10 minutes; keep hot.

2 Place tomato quarters, sugar, cider vinegar, mustard, cinnamon, celery seeds, cloves and cayenne pepper in large bowl. Stir to combine.

3 Cook tomato mixture, covered, on High (100% power) for 20 minutes, or until thickened slightly, stirring occasionally.

4 In food processor with knife blade attached or in blender, process tomato mixture until smooth, in batches if necessary. Place a fine sieve over another large bowl. Press tomato mixture through sieve to remove seeds; discard seeds.

5 Stir dissolved cornflour into tomato mixture until blended. Cook on High for 8–10 minutes, until sauce has boiled and thickened, stirring occasionally.

6 Immediately ladle sauce into hot jars, to within 6 mm of tops. Cover with lids. Keep sauce in the refrigerator for up to 3 weeks.

Making gravy sometimes creates a last-minute rush in the kitchen, but with the microwave you can prepare perfect Giblet Gravy (below) hours ahead. Cook, cover and refrigerate it, then reheat to serve with roast chicken or turkey. Brown Gravy (right) goes beautifully with beef or veal roasts, or juicy steaks.

GIBLET GRAVY

Colour Index page 107. 12 kJ per tablespoon. Good source of vitamin A, riboflavin, niacin, iron.
Begin 40 minutes ahead.

Ingredients for 4 cups		Microwave cookware
2 cups chicken stock	½ bay leaf	8-cup glass jug
Giblets and neck of	30g butter or margarine	Medium bowl
1 chicken or turkey	2 tablespoons plain flour	
2 cloves garlic	1 teaspoon browning	
1 small onion, sliced	sauce	
1 carrot, sliced	Salt and pepper to taste	
1 celery stalk, sliced		

1 Pour stock into glass jug; add giblets and neck, garlic, onion, carrot, celery and bay leaf. Cook, covered, on High (100% power) for 15–20 minutes, until giblets are tender, stirring occasionally.

2 Remove giblets and neck from stock with a slotted spoon. Transfer to a board.

3 Place a strainer over a bowl. Pour stock through strainer to remove vegetables and seasonings; discard. Put stock aside.

4 Finely chop giblets. Cut off meat from neck. Put giblets and meat aside.

5 Heat butter in bowl, covered with paper towel, on High for 45 seconds, or until melted. Stir in flour until smooth and well blended. Cook on High for 45 seconds, stirring once.

6 Gradually stir in strained stock. Cook on High for 3–5 minutes, until gravy has thickened and is smooth, stirring twice. Stir in browning sauce and reserved giblets and meat. Cook on High for 1 minute, or until giblets and meat are hot. Season with salt and pepper. Serve hot.

BROWN GRAVY

Colour Index page 106. Makes about 2 cups. 72 kJ per tablespoon. Low in cholesterol, fat, sodium.
Begin 20 minutes ahead.

2 tablespoons meat drippings, or 30 g butter or margarine, melted
½ small carrot, diced
½ celery stalk, minced
½ small onion, diced
2 tablespoons plain flour
2 cups beef stock
½ bay leaf
Salt and pepper to taste
½ teaspoon browning sauce (optional)

1. Place meat drippings in an 8-cup glass jug. Stir in carrot, celery and onion. Cook on High (100% power) for 2½ (2:30)–3 minutes, until vegetables are tender-crisp, stirring twice.
2. Stir in flour until blended. Gradually stir in stock; add bay leaf. Cook on High for 6–8 minutes, until gravy has boiled and thickened, stirring occasionally.
3. Place a strainer over a medium bowl. Pour gravy through strainer to remove vegetables and bay leaf; discard. Season gravy with salt and pepper. If you like, add browning sauce. Heat on High for 2 minutes, or until gravy is hot. Serve immediately.

TOMATO AND BASIL SAUCE

Colour Index page 107. Makes about 2½ cups. 61 kJ per tablespoon. Low in cholesterol.
Begin 45 minutes ahead.

2 cloves garlic, crushed
1 spring onion, sliced
1 tablespoon olive or vegetable oil
6 ripe tomatoes, cut into quarters
¼ cup chopped fresh parsley
1 teaspoon red wine vinegar
¾ teaspoon sugar
1 tablespoon shredded fresh basil
⅛ teaspoon pepper
2 tablespoons tomato paste

1. Combine garlic, spring onion and oil in an 8-cup glass jug. Cook on High (100% power) for 1–2 minutes, until softened. Stir in tomatoes, parsley, vinegar, sugar, basil and pepper. Cook, covered, on High for 10–12 minutes, until mixture has thickened, stirring occasionally.
2. In food processor with knife blade attached or in blender, process tomato mixture until smooth. Place a strainer over a large bowl. Press tomato mixture through strainer to remove seeds and skins; discard.
3. Return tomato mixture to glass jug. Stir in tomato paste. Cook on High for 10–12 minutes, until flavours are blended and sauce is thickened slightly, stirring occasionally. Serve warm or cover and refrigerate to serve chilled later.

HOLLANDAISE SAUCE

Colour Index page 106. Makes about 1 cup. 329 kJ per tablespoon. Low in sodium.
Begin 20 minutes ahead.

125 g butter or margarine	*Salt and cayenne pepper to taste*
2 egg yolks	
3 teaspoons lemon or lime juice	

1. Heat butter in a 2-cup glass jug, covered with paper towel, on High (100% power) for 1½ (1:30) –2 minutes, until melted.
2. Beat egg yolks, lemon juice, salt and cayenne pepper in a small bowl until smooth.
3. Gradually pour hot butter in a thin, steady stream into egg-yolk mixture, beating constantly, until butter is completely incorporated.
4. Cook sauce on Medium (50% power) for 30 seconds–1 minute, until slightly thickened, beating every 15 seconds. Do not boil or sauce will curdle. Keep warm over hot, not boiling, water or in a vacuum flask until ready to serve.

BÉARNAISE SAUCE

Colour Index page 106. Makes about 1 cup. 475 kJ per tablespoon. Low in sodium.
Begin 20 minutes ahead.

¼ cup white wine vinegar	*185 g butter or margarine*
1 tablespoon finely chopped spring onion	*2 egg yolks*
1½ teaspoons dried tarragon	*1 tablespoon chopped fresh parsley*
¼ teaspoon pepper	

1. Pour vinegar into a small bowl; add spring onion, tarragon and pepper. Cook on High (100% power) for 2–4 minutes, until vinegar is reduced to about 1 tablespoon. Put aside.
2. Heat butter in a 2-cup glass jug, covered with paper towel, on High for 2¼ (2:15) minutes, or until melted.
3. Beat egg yolks in a medium bowl until smooth. Gradually pour in hot butter in a thin, steady stream, beating constantly, until butter is completely incorporated.
4. Cook sauce on Medium (50% power) for 30 seconds–1 minute, until slightly thickened, beating every 15 seconds. Do not boil or sauce will curdle. Stir in spring-onion mixture and chopped parsley. Keep warm over hot, not boiling, water or in a vacuum flask until ready to serve.

BASIC WHITE SAUCE

Makes 2 cups. 95 kJ per tablespoon. Low in sodium.
Begin 15 minutes ahead.

60 g butter or margarine	
3 tablespoons plain flour	
2 cups milk	
Salt, pepper and ground nutmeg to taste	

1. Heat butter in an 8-cup glass jug, covered with paper towel, on High (100% power) for 45 seconds–1 minute, until melted.
2. Stir in flour until smooth and blended. Cook on High for 45 seconds–1 minute, stirring once. Gradually stir in milk. Cook on High for 3–5 minutes, until sauce has thickened and is smooth, stirring twice.
3. Season sauce with salt, pepper and nutmeg. Serve immediately.

PARSLEY AND LEMON SAUCE: Prepare Basic White Sauce (above). Stir in *1 teaspoon grated lemon rind, 1½ tablespoons lemon juice* and *1 tablespoon chopped fresh parsley.*
99 kJ per tablespoon.

CHEESE SAUCE: Prepare Basic White Sauce (above). Stir in *30 g grated cheese (¼ cup)* until melted.
296 kJ per tablespoon.

MUSHROOM SAUCE

In this variation of a white sauce, the sliced mushrooms are lightly sautéed in butter or margarine before the sauce is thickened and enriched with cream and sherry. It is delicious with grilled steaks and veal chops.

Makes 2 cups. 128 kJ per tablespoon. Low in sodium.
Begin 25 minutes ahead.

30 g butter or margarine	
250 g mushrooms, thinly sliced	
3 teaspoons plain flour	
1¼ cups cream	
3 teaspoons dry sherry	
2 tablespoons sour cream	
Salt and pepper to taste	
2 tablespoons chopped fresh parsley	

1. Heat butter in an 8-cup glass jug, covered with paper towel, on High (100% power) for 45 seconds, or until melted.
2. Add sliced mushrooms; stir to coat. Cook on High for 5–6 minutes, until mushrooms soften, stirring occasionally. Stir in flour until blended.
3. Gradually stir in cream and dry sherry until blended. Cook on High for 5–7 minutes, until mixture has thickened, stirring occasionally.
4. Stir in sour cream until well blended; season with salt and pepper. Stir in chopped parsley. Serve immediately.

Brandied Strawberry Sauce

Custard Sauce

Orange Sauce

Hot Fruit Sauce

Chocolate Sauce

Butterscotch Sauce

HOT FRUIT SAUCE

Colour Index page 105. Makes 4 cups. 72 kJ per tablespoon. Low in cholesterol, sodium. Good source of vitamin A, vitamin C, iron.
Begin 10 minutes ahead.

3 large nectarines, stoned and chopped
3 large plums, stoned and chopped
½ cup sugar
½ cup orange juice
1 tablespoon brandy (optional)

1. Combine nectarines, plums, sugar and orange juice in an 8-cup glass jug.
2. Cook on High (100% power) for 3–5 minutes, until fruit is tender, stirring twice. If you like, stir in brandy. Serve warm, with ice cream.

BRANDIED STRAWBERRY SAUCE

Colour Index page 105. Makes 2½ cups. 196 kJ per tablespoon. Low in cholesterol, fat, sodium. Good source of riboflavin, vitamin C, iron.
Begin 10 minutes ahead.

1 kg frozen strawberries, thawed and sliced
1 tablespoon cornflour dissolved in 1 tablespoon cold water
½ cup redcurrant jelly
¼ cup brandy

1. Drain strawberries; put aside, reserving ½ cup juice. Stir dissolved cornflour into juice.
2. Heat redcurrant jelly on High (100% power) for 30 seconds–1 minute, until melted; stir once. Stir in dissolved cornflour; cook on High for 1–2 minutes, until slightly thickened.
3. Stir in reserved strawberries and brandy. Serve warm, with pancakes, ice cream or rice pudding.

CHOCOLATE SAUCE

Colour Index page 105. Makes about 3 cups. 301 kJ per tablespoon. Good source of vitamin A, riboflavin, calcium.
Begin 10 minutes ahead.

1 cup thickened cream
1¼ cups caster sugar
125 g cooking chocolate, chopped
30 g butter or margarine
1 teaspoon vanilla essence

1. Pour cream into an 8-cup glass jug; add sugar, chocolate and butter. Cook on High (100% power) for 8–9 minutes, until chocolate has melted and mixture boils, stirring occasionally.
2. Stir in vanilla essence. Serve warm, with banana splits or ice cream.

BUTTERSCOTCH SAUCE

Colour Index page 106. Makes 1 cup. 424 kJ per tablespoon. Low in sodium.
Begin 10 minutes ahead.

1 cup packed brown sugar
¼ cup cream
2 tablespoons golden syrup
30 g butter or margarine

1. Combine sugar, cream, syrup and butter in an 8-cup glass jug. Cook on High (100% power) for 5 minutes, or until sugar has dissolved and sauce boils, stirring twice.
2. Serve warm, with waffles or ice cream.

CUSTARD SAUCE

Colour Index page 105. Makes about 1¼ cups. 151 kJ per tablespoon. Low in sodium.
Begin 15 minutes ahead.

½ cup cream
½ cup milk
2 tablespoons caster sugar
2 egg yolks
½ teaspoon vanilla essence

1. Pour cream and milk into a 4-cup glass jug; add sugar. Cook on High (100% power) for 3 minutes, or until mixture has boiled, stirring twice.
2. Lightly beat egg yolks in a small bowl. Stir a small amount of cream mixture into beaten egg yolks. Slowly pour egg mixture back into cream mixture, beating rapidly to prevent lumping.
3. Cook mixture on Medium (50% power) for 3–4 minutes, until sauce has thickened slightly, beating twice. Do not boil or sauce will curdle. Stir in vanilla essence. Serve warm, with apple pie.

ORANGE SAUCE

Colour Index page 105. Makes 2½ cups. 56 kJ per tablespoon. Low in cholesterol, fat, sodium.
Begin 10 minutes ahead.

2 cups water
⅓ cup sugar
1 tablespoon grated orange rind
½ cup orange-flavoured liqueur

1. Pour water into a 4-cup glass jug; add sugar and orange rind. Cook on High (100% power) for 4–5 minutes, until sugar has dissolved and mixture boils; stir twice.
2. Stir in liqueur until blended. Serve warm, with fruit or ice cream.

Cherry Sauce

Hard Sauce

Peach Sauce

Mulberry Sauce

Fudge Sauce

Melba Sauce

PEACH SAUCE

Colour Index page 105. Makes 1 cup. 95 kJ per tablespoon. Low in cholesterol, fat, sodium.
Begin 10 minutes ahead.

310 g canned peaches in natural juice
¼ teaspoon almond essence
¼ teaspoon ground nutmeg

1. In food processor with knife blade attached, process peaches, almond essence and nutmeg until smooth.
2. Transfer peach mixture to a 4-cup glass jug. Heat on High (100% power) for 1–2 minutes, until hot, stirring twice. Serve warm, with ice cream or fruit.

CHERRY SAUCE

Colour Index page 106. Makes 2 cups. 84 kJ per tablespoon. Low in cholesterol, sodium.
Begin 5 minutes ahead.

500 g cherries, stoned
¼ cup sugar
1 tablespoon water
¼ teaspoon almond essence

1. Combine cherries, sugar and water in an 8-cup glass jug. Cook on High (100% power) for 2–3 minutes, until sugar has dissolved and mixture boils, stirring twice.
2. Stir in almond essence. Serve warm, with waffles or pancakes.

MULBERRY SAUCE

Colour Index page 105. Makes about 1 cup. 145 kJ per tablespoon. Low in cholesterol, fat, sodium.
Begin 20 minutes ahead.

310 g mulberries, stalks removed
½ cup sugar
¼ teaspoon ground cinnamon
⅛ teaspoon ground nutmeg
⅛ teaspoon grated lemon rind
1 teaspoon lemon juice

1. Combine mulberries, sugar, cinnamon, nutmeg and lemon rind in an 8-cup glass jug. Cook, covered, on High (100% power) for 5 minutes, or until sugar has dissolved. Uncover; stir. Cook on High for 3–4 minutes longer, until sauce has thickened slightly.
2. Stir in lemon juice. Serve warm, with poached or fresh fruit, or ice cream.

FUDGE SAUCE

Colour Index page 105. Makes 1¼ cups. 424 kJ per tablespoon. Low in sodium.
Begin 10 minutes ahead.

¾ cup sugar
½ cup cocoa
½ cup thickened cream
60 g butter or margarine
1 teaspoon vanilla essence

1. Combine sugar, cocoa and cream in an 8-cup glass jug. Cook on High (100% power) for 2–3 minutes, until sugar has dissolved and mixture boils, stirring twice.
2. Add butter. Cook on High for 2–4 minutes, until butter has melted and mixture thickens slightly, stirring occasionally. Stir in vanilla essence. Serve warm, with ice cream or waffles.

HARD SAUCE

Colour Index page 106. Makes about ⅔ cup. 408 kJ per tablespoon. Low in sodium.
Begin 5 minutes ahead.

45 g butter or margarine
1 cup icing sugar
½ teaspoon vanilla essence

1. Heat butter in a 1-cup glass jug on High (100% power) for 5–10 seconds, until softened.
2. Gradually beat in sugar until creamy. Stir in vanilla essence. Serve with Christmas pudding.

MELBA SAUCE

Colour Index page 105. Makes 1 cup. 184 kJ per tablespoon. Low in cholesterol, fat, sodium.
Begin 15 minutes ahead.

310 g frozen raspberries
¼ cup redcurrant jelly
1 tablespoon cornflour dissolved in 1 tablespoon cold water

1. Place raspberries and redcurrant jelly in an 8-cup glass jug. Heat on High (100% power) for 5–6 minutes, until jelly has melted and raspberries are thawed.
2. Stir in dissolved cornflour. Cook on High for 3–4 minutes, until mixture has boiled and thickened; stir twice. Press mixture through a fine sieve to remove seeds; discard. Serve warm, with poached pears or ice cream.

COOKWARE

What can I use to keep butter or margarine and bacon from spattering when I cook them in my microwave?

Foods that tend to spatter should be covered with absorbent paper towels, which soak up any fat but also allow microwaves to penetrate and cook the food. Lightly moisten paper towels to cook food such as poultry, fish and vegetables; wrap in the towel and then 'steam' in the microwave.

I have been told that some paper towels are unsafe for microwave use. Is this true and, if so, which ones are they?

It is true that towels made of recycled paper are unsuitable for use in the microwave because they contain impurities, such as small amounts of metal, that may cause blue sparks (arcing).

Look for plain white paper towels that contain all-natural fibres and no artificial colours; some manufacturers state on the packaging whether their paper is safe for microwave use or not.

How can I be sure that my china bowl will not break during cooking before I actually use it in the microwave?

Place the bowl in the microwave beside a glass measuring jug containing 1 cup cold water. Heat on High (100% power) for 1 minute. If the bowl remains cool and the water in the jug is warm, the bowl is microwave-safe. If the bowl is hot, it has absorbed too much microwave energy for efficient cooking and should not be used.

Can I use plastic containers, measuring jugs and bowls in the microwave?

Avoid using plastic containers, jugs and bowls to cook anything with a high fat or sugar content. For other foods, the safest plastic cookware to use is the specially formulated type labelled 'microwave-safe'.

Dishwasher-safe plastic containers can be used for brief reheating in the microwave. Plastic containers that hold shop-bought takeaway food are generally considered to be unsafe because they may break or melt.

Which cookware is best used for making desserts in the microwave?

Desserts that have a high sugar or fat content reach very high temperatures during the cooking process; therefore, they should always be cooked in microwave-safe glass measuring jugs or bowls, not plastic cookware.

Which cookware is recommended for making sauces and gravies?

A microwave-safe glass measuring jug is convenient and saves on washing up. Always use a jug that holds twice the volume of the sauce or gravy to be cooked in it.

TECHNIQUES

How can I prevent chocolate from overcooking when I melt it in the microwave?

Melting chocolate in the microwave is almost risk-free. However, when chocolate is melted in the microwave it retains its shape; you may not realise it is ready. When the chocolate loses its dull look and becomes shiny, that's your clue it is done; remove from oven and stir until smooth.

Why do my cakes overcook when done in the microwave?

If you remove cakes from the microwave when they *look* done, they will be overcooked and will become hard on standing. Cakes should look moist when removed from the microwave; they will spring back when lightly touched with a finger.

Standing time is necessary to complete the cooking process; after standing time, the cake will pull away from the sides of the dish and a toothpick inserted into the centre will come out clean.

Why do my vegetables sometimes have dark spots on them when cooked in the microwave?

Salt may be the culprit. If you use salt, add it to vegetables after cooking, or dissolve it in the cooking liquid or sauce.

Q How can I keep foods cooked in the microwave warm without retaining steam? I find breadcrumbed chicken dishes get soggy if I use a cover.

 A Casserole lids and plastic wraps hold in steam, which may make certain foods limp, such as breads, cakes, or anything with a crumb coating. To prevent this, cover these foods with greaseproof paper or paper towel, which holds in heat but not steam.

 Q When I scramble eggs in the microwave, I find the edges too set and hard while the centre is still liquid. Why does this happen and how can I prevent it?

 A Microwaves penetrate food to a depth of about 4 cm, thereby cooking the food nearest the edge of the dish first. To prevent this, push the cooked part at the edges towards the centre of the dish before it is set completely, allowing the uncooked eggs to flow to the edges. Remove from oven while still moist. Eggs will complete cooking during the standing time.

 Q I find that after heating water in the microwave, it boils over when I add instant coffee, tea or packet soup mix. How can I prevent this?

 A Be sure to stir the water *before* heating it. This incorporates air into the liquid, which will prevent boiling over once cooking has started.

 Q How can I keep gravy from becoming lumpy and the edge of the gravy from becoming too thick?

 A Stir gravies and sauces frequently with a whisk or fork to obtain a smooth consistency throughout.

Q Why am I advised not to deep-fry food in the microwave?

A This potentially hazardous procedure is not recommended because the temperature of the cooking oil can climb rapidly in the microwave and the oil can suddenly burst into flames. In addition, microwave-safe cookware may not be able to withstand the intense heat and has been known to crack or explode.

 Q My food seems to cool more quickly when it has been cooked in the microwave. Why?

 A In the microwave, only the food gets hot from the cooking process – any warmth you feel in the dish has been transferred from the food. This is the opposite of what happens in a conventional oven, where the cooking heats up the dish first, then the food, and the hot dish keeps food warmer longer after it is removed from the oven.

To help keep foods warm, heat food that has been stored in the refrigerator an extra minute or so to give the cooking vessel time to warm. Cover foods while reheating or cooking to hold in warmth. At the table, wrap a covered dish in a pretty towel or quilted casserole holder, or keep warm on a warming tray.

 Q When I cook eggs in the microwave, I find the yolks are always tougher than they should be. How can I prevent this?

 A Egg yolks contain more fat than egg whites, therefore they attract more microwave energy and cook faster. To avoid overcooking the yolk while waiting for the white to be done, you must remove the eggs before the whites are completely set and allow to stand for the time recommended in the recipe; this allows the white to finish cooking outside the microwave. Don't forget to gently prick yolks with a toothpick before cooking. This permits the steam to escape and prevents the egg from exploding during cooking.

 Q How can I make poultry, meat and fish look as if it has been conventionally cooked?

 A Make a sauce to rub on food before the start of cooking: Place enough butter or margarine to coat the food in a glass jug. Heat, covered with paper towel, on High (100% power) until butter or margarine melts. Stir in gravy browning, teriyaki sauce, soy sauce or Worcestershire sauce. For a zestier flavour, mix in mustard or tomato sauce.

To glaze poultry and give it a lovely golden colour, brush with marmalade, honey or apricot jam during cooking.

You can also brush meat, poultry or fish with butter or margarine, beaten egg, milk or water, then coat with breadcrumbs, crushed cornflakes, herbs, grated cheese or onion soup mix. There are also specially formulated coating mixes with seasonings to complement the taste of meat, poultry or fish.

How can I make breads, cakes, biscuits and pastry cooked in the microwave look as if they have been conventionally baked?

 For a baked appearance, choose recipes that call for brown sugar or treacle; alternatively, you can add ground allspice, cinnamon or nutmeg to cake mixtures, or add a few drops of yellow food colouring. Try substituting wholemeal flour for part of the white flour in fruit loaves, muffins and scones. For an attractive coating to conceal an underdone appearance, evenly sprinkle finely chopped nuts or wheat germ into greased cake or loaf dishes before adding mixture.

Toppings that add texture and flavour include sugar, chopped nuts, ground cinnamon and toasted coconut.

 When I make caramel in the microwave, I frequently find it burns. How can I prevent this?

 Cook the mixture just until the sugar is golden; it will continue to cook during its standing time outside the oven, and a deeper colour will develop. A microwave-safe glass measuring jug should always be used. Its handle makes pouring easier, and the special glass can withstand the high cooking temperature of sugar.

 How can I convert conventional recipes for use in the microwave?

 Not all recipes can be converted for microwave cooking, but in general the following rules should be applied: Keep serving numbers small – up to eight at the most; reduce liquids, fat and seasonings; use microwave-safe cookware; cut cooking time down to a quarter or a half of the conventional recipe time.

 What foods should be pierced before being cooked in the microwave, and why?

 Any food enclosed in a skin or membrane should be pierced to release steam and prevent the food from bursting during cooking. Whole vegetables with skins, such as potatoes, chokos, tomatoes and capsicums, should be pierced with a fork. Use a toothpick for anything with a delicate membrane, such as egg yolks or liver. Sausage casings should also be pierced with a fork or slashed diagonally with a sharp knife.

 Why do some microwave cookbooks give a range of timings for recipes?

 This is because of the variations in microwave wattage and differences in cookware and density of food. It is advisable to cook for the shorter time, check to see if food is done, then cook for the longer time if necessary.

My microwave has a different wattage from those used in most microwave recipes. How do I adjust the timing to give good results?

If a recipe has been developed in a 600-watt oven, reduce the timing by 10 seconds per minute if you have a 700-watt oven and increase it by 15 seconds per minute if you have a 500-watt oven. This is a very general guide, so check the food frequently to prevent it from overcooking.

I am instructed to rotate certain foods in the microwave. Why is this?

In general, foods that cannot be stirred – such as lasagna, meat loaf and bread pudding – must be rotated to ensure even cooking throughout. If your microwave does not have a carousel/automatic turntable, this rotation must be done by hand. Get to know your oven's personality (cooking pattern) by observing how food cooks – for example, food may cook more quickly on one side than the other; if that happens, rotate the dish for more even cooking. Other foods that must be rotated in their dishes include fish that may be too delicate to move and cake mixtures that have to set. Make certain you rotate the dish in one direction only.

How can I be sure that the microwave has heated shop-bought microwave dinners thoroughly?

To ensure that food is piping hot and thoroughly heated through, it is important to follow packet instructions to the letter. Most important is to know the wattage output of the oven and to realise that if your oven has a low wattage, the food will take longer to reach its required temperature. It is also very important to stir, rotate (either manually or on a carousel), turn or rearrange food during heating, if this is instructed, so that the food is heated properly throughout. Microwave ovens have 'cold' spots, so it is important that food is not left to stay in the same position for the total cooking time.

My microwave retains the smell of any strongly spiced dishes I cook, such as curry or chilli con carne. How can I prevent this?

 Be certain to wipe the oven clean with a damp cloth after each use. Use a mild detergent when needed. For a quick oven refresher, pour ½ cup water into a 4-cup microwave-safe glass measuring jug or bowl. Add one of the following fresheners: 2 slices lemon, orange or lime; 1 tablespoon lemon juice; ¼ teaspoon ground cinnamon; 8 whole cloves with 8 whole allspice; 1 teaspoon bicarbonate of soda. Heat on High (100% power) for 1–2 minutes, or until water boils. Your oven will smell fresh and clean.

To make the whole kitchen smell wonderfully fresh, try this oven potpourri: Pour 1 cup warm water into a 1-litre jug; add 2 teaspoons mixed spice or a few thyme sprigs. Heat on High (100% power) for 3 minutes.

DEFROSTING AND REHEATING

 Since the microwave is so useful for reheating food, why am I advised not to reheat egg dishes?

 Most leftovers, such as meat and pasta dishes, reheat very well in the microwave, but delicate egg dishes will overcook if reheated. The same principle applies when trying to reheat cheese dishes in the microwave; the cheese toughens and becomes stringy.

 Is it a good idea to use the microwave for defrosting food from my freezer?

 Yes. Follow the instructions that come with your oven. In general, most small items can be defrosted by placing them in the microwave for a few seconds on High (100% power). Larger items are best defrosted, covered, on Medium-Low (30% power) or Defrost power level for several minutes at a time, then allowed to stand. They are briefly microwaved again, allowed to stand, and so on until defrosted. This standing time is very important when defrosting larger items because it allows the temperature to equalise throughout the food. Do not microwave until the centre defrosts because the outer edges will start to cook; delicate parts of chicken and fish may have to be shielded with smooth strips of foil. Melted ice should be drained off at intervals. Food should be cooked immediately after defrosting in the microwave.

 How can I tell when an individual dinner reheated in the microwave is ready to serve?

 Allow about 2 minutes for 1 dinner plate of food. Heat, covered, on Medium-High (70% power). Remove from the microwave and feel the centre bottom of plate. If it is warm, the food is ready to serve; if cool, cook, covered, for 1 minute longer.

 When I reheat dinners, the centre sometimes stays cold. How can I ensure even reheating?

 If food at edge of plate is hot while food at the centre is not, cut out a doughnut-shaped piece of foil to place over the food, making sure that the foil is smooth and at least 2.5 cm away from the oven walls. The centre will then become hot while the edges will be shielded from microwaves. (See also Arranging Food for Reheating, page 19.)

 What size container should I use for defrosting and cooking frozen food?

 Always use a dish that fits the food as closely as possible so that the edges of the food do not melt, spread out over the bottom of a large dish and burn before the centre of the food is hot. Cover while defrosting to retain heat.

 My family loves hamburgers, so I often make them up in bulk and freeze them. How can I use my microwave for speedier defrosting?

 Freeze the hamburgers with sheets of greaseproof paper between them. Defrost on Medium-Low (30% power) or Defrost; discard the paper as soon as possible, separate the still partially frozen hamburgers, and place in a single layer on a microwave-safe rack set in a baking dish. Using a rack prevents the hamburgers from stewing in their own juices, which could cause the surfaces to start cooking.

 When I reheat breads such as rolls or hamburger buns, they become dry. Am I doing something wrong?

 You are overcooking them. Baked goods should be *just* warmed through, otherwise they become dry and tough. Most breads reheat successfully in the microwave if they are wrapped in paper towels to absorb moisture. Heat rolls and hamburger buns on High (100% power) for 10–15 seconds.

The Index

394